THE EPISTLES OF ST JOHN

THE EPISTLES OF ST JOHN

THE GREEK TEXT WITH NOTES

BY THE LATE

BROOKE FOSS WESTCOTT, D.D., D.C.L.

LORD BISHOP OF DURHAM

SOMETIME REGIUS PROFESSOR OF DIVINITY
IN THE UNIVERSITY OF CAMBRIDGE

NEW INTRODUCTION

JOHANNINE STUDIES SINCE WESTCOTT'S DAY

BY

F. F. BRUCE, D.D.

RYLANDS PROFESSOR OF BIBLICAL CRITICISM AND EXEGESIS
IN THE UNIVERSITY OF MANCHESTER

WM. B. EERDMANS PUBLISHING COMPANY
GRAND RAPIDS   MICHIGAN

First Edition printed 1883, *Second* 1885, *Third* 1892.

This edition 1966

New material © F. F. Bruce and Marcham Manor Press

Reprinted, August 1971

καὶ τὸ Πνεῦμα καὶ ἡ Νύμφη λέγογcιν Ἔρχογ.
καὶ ὁ ἀκογων εἰπάτω Ἔρχογ.
καὶ ὁ Διψῶν ἐρχέcθω,
ὁ θέλων λαβέτω ῢδωρ ζωῆc Δωρεάν.

Apoc. xxii. 17.

PHOTOLITHOPRINTED BY GRAND RAPIDS BOOK MANUFACTURERS, INC.
GRAND RAPIDS, MICHIGAN
1971

IN the present Commentary I have endeavoured to follow the plan which I sketched in the notes on the Gospel of St John in *The Speaker's Commentary*. It formed no part of my design to collect and discuss the conflicting opinions which have been held on the structure of the writings or on the interpretation of separate passages. Such a labour is indeed of the deepest interest and utility; but it appeared to me that I might help the student more by giving the results at which I have arrived, and by indicating the lines of inquiry by which they have been reached. In pursuing this end it has been my main desire to call attention to the minutest points of language, construction, order, as serving to illustrate the meaning of St John. I do not venture to pronounce that any variation is trivial or unimportant. The exact words are for us the decisive expression of the Apostle's thought. I have therefore, if I may borrow words which have been applied in a somewhat different sense, begun by interpreting the Epistles as I should 'interpret any other book', neglecting nothing which might contribute to a right apprehension of its full meaning. I do not feel at liberty to set aside the letter of a document till it has been found to be untenable.

Many writings, it is true, will not bear the consistent application of such a method of interpretation; but each day's study brings home to me more forcibly the conviction that in no other way can we hope to gain the living truth of apostolic teaching. The verification of the method lies in the result. If it discloses to patient investigation unsuspected harmonies and correspondences of thought: if it suggests good reasons for holding that views of faith which seem to be conflicting are really complementary: if it inspires with a vital power dogmatic statements which grow rigid by the necessities of controversy: if it opens on this side and that subjects of study which await fuller investigation: if it enables us to feel that the difficulties of our own time were not unnoticed by those who, under the guidance of the Holy Spirit, saw the Eternal: if it brings a sense of rest and confidence which grows firmer with increasing knowledge: then it seems to me that it needs no further justification.

It cannot but be that I have often erred in the application of the principles which I hold; but no one, I trust, will condemn the method till he has tested it by personal labour. A few hours spent in tracing out the use of a word or a form, in comparing phrases often held to be synonymous, in estimating the force of different tenses of the same verb in regard to the contexts in which they are found, will bring assurance which no acceptance of another's work can give. Several notes in which I have sought to bring together materials serviceable for such inquiries will at least, I hope, encourage some to make the trial for themselves.

The study of Scripture is, I believe, for us the way by which God will enable us to understand His present revelation through history and nature. When once we can feel the divine power of human words, which gather in themselves the results of cycles of intellectual discipline, we shall be prepared to pass from the study of one book to the study of 'the Divine Library'. And the inquiries which thus come

before us are not mere literary speculations. The fulness of
the Bible, apprehended in its historical development, answers
to the fulness of life. If we can come to see in it the variety,
the breadth, the patience of the past dealings of God with
humanity, we shall gain that courageous faith from a view
of the whole world which is commonly sought by confining
our attention to a little fragment of it.

The Bible is indeed the symbol and the pledge of the
Catholicity of our Faith; and the real understanding of the
Bible rests upon the acknowledgment of its Catholicity, of the
universal range in which it includes in its records typical
examples of the dealings of God with men under every variety
of circumstance and being, social and personal. We are all so
familiar with certain lessons which the Bible contains that we
come to regard them, perhaps unconsciously, as the complete
sum of its teaching. Special words, phrases, incidents, inspire
our own souls and mould our own faith, and we forget that
we are not the measure of the wants and powers of man. So
it is that we pass over large sections of Scripture unstudied,
or force them into unison with what we hear most easily.
We neglect to take account of periods of silence in revelation
scarcely less eloquent with instruction than the messages of
prophets. We lose just those helps to knowing how God
disciplines races, classes, individuals, who are most unlike
ourselves, which we need sorest when we look on the sad
spectacle of a disordered and divided world.

This Catholicity of the Bible is made more impressive by the
fact that the Bible is in a large degree historical. It has pleased
God to reveal Himself in and through life; and the record of
the revelation is literary and not dogmatic. From first to last
God is seen in the Bible conversing with man. He speaks to
man as man can hear, and man replies as he can use the gift of
the Spirit. But word and answer alike are according to the

truth of life. All that has been written for us has been part of real human experience, and therefore it has an unending value. Thus in the main the Bible is the continuous unfolding in many parts and many ways of the spiritual progress of mankind. It may be a law, a narrative, a prophecy, a psalm, a proverb, but in each case it comes from life and enters into life ; it belongs to a distinct epoch ; it is only in its vital context, so to speak, that it can be perfectly understood.

In this long series of spiritual records the first Epistle of St John probably holds the last place. It is probably the final interpretation of the whole series of the divine revelations; and under this aspect it proclaims and satisfies the highest hope of man. It declares that in the Presence of Christ there has been given and there will be given that knowledge of God for which man was made, issuing in fellowship which is realised here in the Christian Society, and which reaches to the Source of all life. In this consummation the past finds accomplishment, and the sufferings and riddles of the present are shewn to be part of a sovereign counsel which passes beyond our sight. As we look back and look forward in the light thus thrown over the world we can work and wait.

The Son of God is come and hath given us an understanding that we may know Him that is true, and we are in Him that is true, even in His Son Jesus Christ.

That which we have seen and heard declare we unto you also, that ye also may have fellowship with us: yea, and our fellowship is with the Father and with His Son Jesus Christ.

Though I am quite unable to acknowledge or even to distinguish in detail my obligations to earlier writers in the course of a work which has been spread over more than thirty years, I cannot refrain from expressing my gratitude to three commentators who have helped me greatly in different ways. Bengel's notes always serve as a kind of standard of spiritual insight ; and there is no one from whom I differ on a serious question of interpretation with more regret or more misgiving. Huther (4th edition, 1880) has given a most careful review of the opinions of previous editors to which I have been much indebted in revising my own notes. And Haupt has drawn at length a connected view of the Epistle which brings out into a clear light its theological significance. On many points of importance I am unable to accept his conclusions, but no one, I think, has shewn more impressively the true spirit of an interpreter of the New Testament.

There is a feeling of sadness in looking at that which must stand with all its imperfections as the accomplishment of a dream of early youth. The work might have answered better to the opportunity. But however greatly I have failed in other respects, I trust that at least I may have been allowed to encourage some students to linger with more devout patience, with more frank questionings than before, over words of ST JOHN.

CAMBRIDGE,
June 22, 1883.

WESTCOTT'S SIGNIFICANCE

TO the text which he annotates or expounds a commentator brings himself—in his own generation, environment and culture, with his own qualities, presuppositions and interests. Most commentators, whether they deal with books of the Bible or with any other literature, are so conditioned by their age and setting that, however helpful they are to their contemporaries, they speak a strange language to readers of later date and fail to make the text relevant. True, it should always be important to serious students of Scripture to know what was thought of its meaning by serious students who have gone before; but the serious students who appreciate the importance of this sufficiently to do something about it are few, and they need no reprints, for they know where to go to find what they want.

Westcott, like his colleagues Lightfoot and Hort, remains a standard commentator for the twentieth-century readers, for all his nineteenth-century qualities. He and his illustrious colleagues were not merely children of their age; by their work they helped to make their age what it was and set the impress of their minds upon it. Whatever they wrote in the field of biblical exegesis is still diligently examined by students of the books with which they dealt, and they continue to enrich our minds as we read them.

Following the injunction of an earlier commentator (J. A. Bengel), Westcott applied himself wholly to the text. Even if he was the junior partner in the textual partnership of Westcott and Hort, he and Hort were in complete sympathy as regards the principles and conclusions of their critical studies, and the acumen with which he prosecuted these studies marks his exegesis as well as his criticism. His knowledge of the whole Greek Bible was related to his knowledge of the whole range of ancient Greek literature, from the beginning of the classical age to the end of the patristic age. It is much rarer for commentators to come to the study of the Greek New Testament today with such a rich linguistic equipment as his—an equipment which was accompanied by a rare feeling for the sense of the Greek. His minute attention to the finer points of the language—particles, prepositions, tenses and so forth—may have been overdone, but if so, it was a fault in the right direction. It was not the pedantry of a mere lexicographer, but the devotion of one to whose sensitive mind classical Greek was still a living language.

To this sensitivity he added another quality, indispensable in a true biblical exegete—sympathy with the writers on whose works he commented. It is no accident that Westcott's greatest commentaries were written on the works of two biblical authors with whose minds his own was closely attuned—St. John and the writer to the Hebrews. He could see what they were getting at and convey their meaning and purpose to others because of his capacity for entering into their minds and thinking their thoughts after them. And he was thoroughly convinced of the permanent validity and relevance of what they thought and said. If (as he says on p.vi he set himself to interpret the Epistles of John as he would interpret any other book, he was led by this procedure to a firmer conviction than ever that these Epistles, with the other apostolic writings, have a quality unshared by "any other book".

For such reasons as these, while we cannot confine ourselves to Westcott nowadays, we can never dispense with him.

F. F. Bruce

University of Manchester

B. F. WESTCOTT: A Biographical Note

Brooke Foss Westcott was born 12 January 1825 in Birmingham. He was educated at King Edward VI's School in that city, and later at Trinity College, Cambridge, of which he became a fellow in 1849. He was ordained in 1851 by his former headmaster J. Prince Lee, who had become Bishop of Manchester. The following year he became assistant master at Harrow under C. J. Vaughan, and there Westcott began his literary work. Among the books he wrote while at Harrow were his *History of the New Testament Canon* and his *History of the English Bible*. In 1869 he was appointed a residentiary canon at Peterborough, and the year after he was made Regius Professor of Divinity at Cambridge.

In 1881 there appeared the Westcott and Hort critical edition of the Greek New Testament, which he had prepared with F. J. A. Hort. In the same year he produced the first of his distinguished commentaries, which he had planned as a series with Hort and his schoolfriend, former Cambridge pupil and then fellow professor, J. B. Lightfoot. Two years later he published his commentary on the Johannine Epistles which is reprinted in this volume, and in 1889 the commentary on Hebrews followed. His concern for pastoral as well as academic work was shown both by his interest in training ordinands at what is now known as Westcott House, Cambridge and by his enthusiastic support of missions, especially the Cambridge Mission to Delhi.

In 1890 he was appointed Bishop of Durham, an episcopate which continued until his death on 27 July 1901. He continued to write smaller theological works, but his fame rests chiefly on his commentaries and textual work. His son Arthur published the only sizeable biography, *Life and Letters of Brooke Foss Westcott*, in 1903, though surprisingly enough the two volumes make little mention of Westcott's greatest work—his commentating.

CONTENTS

Contents

INTRODUCTION
TO THE FIRST EPISTLE

I. TEXT.

THE text of the Epistle is contained in the following authorities:

1. GREEK MSS.

    (a) *Primary uncials :*

        א, Cod. Sin. sæc. IV.

        A, Cod. Alex. sæc. V.

        B, Cod. Vatic. sæc. IV.

        C, Cod. Ephr. sæc. V. from i. 1—iv. 2 ἐκ τοῦ θεοῦ.

    Secondary uncials :

        K, Cod. Mosq. sæc. IX.

        L, Cod. Angel. sæc. IX.

        P, Cod. Porphyr. sæc. IX.

    (β) *Cursives.* More than two hundred in number, including 13 (Cod. Colbert. sæc. XI. = 33 Gosp.), and 31 (Cod. Leicestr. sæc. XIV. = 69 Gosp.).

D, *Codex Bezæ*, sæc. VI., has lost 67 leaves after Mark xvi. 15 (Gk.), in which there can be no doubt that the Epistle was contained, for after this gap follows the Latin translation of 3 John 11—15. The Book of the Acts comes immediately afterwards.

2. VERSIONS.

    (a) *Latin. Old Latin.*

               A large and important fragment, iii. 8—end, has been published by L. Ziegler (1876) from a Munich MS. (cent. VII.), which gives an African text closely akin to that of Fulgentius (quoted as F or *Fris.*).

[margin note:] Authorities in which the Epistle is contained.

A nearly complete text of a different (Italic?) type has been preserved by Augustine in his Expository discourses on the Epistle (i. 1—v. 12). Many other fragments are preserved in quotations.

Vulgate Latin (V. lat. vg and vg).

(β) *Syriac.*

    Peshito (syr. vg).

    Harclean (syr. hl).

(γ) *Egyptian.*

    Memphitic (Coptic) (me).

    Thebaic (Sahidic) (the).

To these may be added the *Armenian* and the *Æthiopic*[1].

Character of the text. The text does not present many difficult problems (ii. 20; iv. 3; v. 10). It was exposed to far fewer disturbing influences than that of the Gospels. There were no parallel texts or parallel traditions at hand (unless probably in iv. 3) to supply additions to the original words, or modifications of their form. The utmost amount of variation likely to find favour with critics of the most opposite schools is practically of very small extent, and, though no variation is without real significance, of comparatively small moment.

Collation with Stephens, 1550. In the following table I have set down all the changes from the text of Stephens (1550) which I have adopted generally in accordance with the clear balance of the most ancient authority. The reader will be able to judge of their importance.

i. 3 add καὶ ὑμῖν, *also to you* (אABC).

    4 γρ. ἡμεῖς, write *we* (אA*B), for γρ. ὑμῖν, we write *to you*.

       ἡ χ. ἡμῶν, *our* joy (אB), for ἡ χ. ὑμῶν (AC), *your* joy (doubtful).

    5 ἔστιν αὕτη (אBC), for αὕτη ἐστίν (A).

       ἀγγελία, *message* (אAB), for ἐπαγγελία (C), *promise.*

---

[1] I have given below the text a fairly complete view of the readings of the primary uncials and of the most ancient versions, but this limited summary, though it shews clearly the sources of the later texts, cannot supersede the study of a full *apparatus criticus.*

οὐκ ἔστιν ἐν αὐτῷ (B), for ἐν αὐτῷ οὐκ ἔστιν (אAC).

7 Ἰησοῦ, Jesus (אBC), omit Χριστοῦ, Christ.

ii.   4 add ὅτι΄ ἔγνωκα (אAB).

6 om. οὕτως΄ περιπ. (AB) to walk, for so to walk.

7 ἀγαπητοί, Beloved (אABC), for ἀδελφοί, Brethren.

om. ἀπ᾽ ἀρχῆς (2°) (אABC), ye heard, for ye heard from the beginning.

14 ἔγραψα, I wrote (אABC), for γράφω, I write.

18 om. ὁ΄ ἀντίχριστος (א*BC).

19 ἐξ ἡμῶν ἦσαν (BC), for ἦσαν ἐξ ἡμῶν.

20 οἴδατε πάντες (B), ye all know, for καὶ οἴδατε πάντα, and ye know all things (doubtful).

23 add ὁ ὁμολογῶν τὸν υἱὸν καὶ τὸν πατέρα ἔχει (אABC), he that confesseth the Son hath the Father also.

24 om. οὖν (אABC), therefore.

27 μένει ἐν ὑμῖν (א(A)BC), for ἐν ὑμῖν μένει.

τὸ αὐτοῦ χρίσμα ((א)BC), his unction, for τὸ αὐτὸ χρ. the same unction.

μένετε ((א)ABC), abide, for μενεῖτε, ye shall abide.

28 ἐάν (אABC), if he shall, for ὅταν, when he shall.

σχῶμεν (אᶜABC), for ἔχωμεν.

iii.   1 add καὶ ἐσμέν (אABC), and such we are.

2 om. δέ (אABC), but.

5 om. ἡμῶν (AB), sins, for our sins.

13 om. μου (אABC), brethren, for my brethren.

14 om. τὸν ἀδελφόν (אAB), he that loveth not, for he that loveth not his brother.

16 θεῖναι (אABC) for τιθέναι.

18 om. μου (אABC), little children, for my little children.

add τῇ΄ γλώσσῃ (ABC).

add ἐν΄ ἔργῳ (אABC).

19 ἐν τούτῳ γνωσόμεθα (om. καὶ AB, γνωσόμεθα אABC), in this we shall perceive, for and in this we perceive.

τὴν καρδίαν (A*B), our heart, for τὰς κ. our hearts.

21 om. ἡμῶν (twice) (1. AB, 2. BC).

22 ἀπ᾽ αὐτοῦ (אABC) for παρ᾽ αὐτοῦ.

iv. 3 om. Χριστὸν ἐν σαρκὶ ἐληλυθότα (AB), *Christ come in flesh.*

10 ἠγαπήκαμεν (B), *have* loved, for ἠγαπήσαμεν, loved (doubtful).

12 ἐν ἡμῖν ἐστίν (אB) for ἐστὶν ἐν ἡμῖν.

15 add Χριστὸς (B), *Christ* (doubtful).

16 add μένει (אB), God *abideth* (doubtful).

19 om. αὐτόν (AB), we love, for we love *him.*

20 οὐ (אB) for πῶς, cannot love, for *how can he* love?

v. 1 om. καί (B), *also.*

2 ποιῶμεν (B), *do,* for τηρῶμεν, *observe.*

5 τίς ἐστιν δέ (B), *but* who is? for who is? (doubtful).

6 om. ὁ (אAB), Jesus Christ, for Jesus *the* Christ.

add ἐν᾽ τῷ αἷμ. and *in* the blood, for and the blood.

6, 7 om. ἐν τῷ οὐρανῷ...ἐν τῇ γῇ (אAB), *in heaven, the Father, the Word, and the Holy Ghost; and these three are one. And there are three that bear witness in earth.*

9 ὅτι (אAB), *that,* for ἦν, *which.*

10 αὐτῷ or αὐτῷ for ἑαυτῷ.

11 ὁ θεὸς ἡμῖν (B), for ἡμῖν ὁ θεός.

13 ἵνα...αἰώνιον, τοῖς πιστ...θεοῦ (א*B) for τοῖς πιστ...θεοῦ, ἵνα ...αἰώνιον, *that ye may know that ye have eternal life,* even *unto you that believe on the name of the Son of God,* for *unto you...God, that ye may...life.*

om. καὶ ἵνα πιστ. εἰς τὸ ὄν. τοῦ υἱοῦ τοῦ θεοῦ (אAB), *and that ye may believe on the name of the Son of God.*

15 ὃ ἐάν for ὃ ἄν.

ἀπ᾽ αὐτοῦ (אB) for παρ᾽ αὐτοῦ.

18 τηρεῖ αὐτόν (A*B), keepeth *him,* for τηρεῖ ἑαυτόν, keepeth *himself.*

20 γινώσκομεν (אAB) for γινώσκωμεν.

om. ἡ (אAB).

21 ἑαυτά (א*B) for ἑαυτούς.

om. Ἀμήν (אAB).

To these may be added a few variations which are more or less probable :

ii.   2 μόνων (B) for μόνον.

     10 οὐκ ἔστιν ἐν αὐτῷ (order) (אAC).

     25 ὑμῖν (B) for ἡμῖν.

     29 add καὶ πᾶς (אAC).

iii.   7 παιδία (AC) τεκνία.

     23 πιστεύωμεν (אAC) for πιστεύσωμεν.

iv.   2 ἐληλυθέναι (B) for ἐληλυθότα.

     3 λύει for μὴ ὁμολογεῖ.

v.   6 μόνῳ (B) for μόνον.

In v. 10 it may be questioned whether ὁ μὴ πιστεύων should not stand absolutely, τῷ θεῷ and τῷ υἱῷ being two attempts to define the sense.

It will be seen that there is in the majority of cases a clear preponderance if not a complete agreement of the most ancient Greek MSS. for the reading adopted. The mass of later Greek MSS. give in most cases the reading which is rejected, but not unfrequently they are fairly divided between the rival readings (*e.g.* ii. 4, 7, 13, 23, 24 ; iii. 1, 13, 16, &c.). The reading of the most ancient Greek MSS. is generally supported by important representatives of the early versions and by some later MSS. But in a very few cases a reading is taken on small ancient authority alone which would be inadequate if the reading were considered by itself (iv. 10, 15 ; v. 5). *{Superiority of the most ancient text.}*

But not to enter now into the details of evidence it will be obvious upon a consideration of the contexts that the most ancient reading gives in very many cases that shade of colouring to the passage which at once approves itself to be original (*e.g.* i. 7 ; ii. 7, 19, 27; iii. 1, 2, 5, 14; iv. 3, 19; v. 6, 18). In other cases the most ancient reading easily explains the origin of the recent reading while the converse change is unintelligible (*e.g.* ii. 23 ; v. 13 ; see also i. 4, 5 ; ii. 4, 13, 18, 20, 24, 27, 28; iii. 13, 18 ; v. 2, 9). In

one place only (iv. 20) does the reading of the more recent type of
Greek MSS. appear at first sight to be intrinsically more likely.

The variants offer good examples of conflate readings (ii. 15 τοῦ
θεοῦ καὶ πατρός; comp. 3 John 12 ὑπὸ αὐτῆς τῆς ἐκκλησίας καὶ τῆς
ἀληθείας) ; of omissions by *homœoteleuton* (ii. 27 f. ; iv. 6, 21 ; v. 2 f. ;
and especially ii. 23) ; of the addition and omission of the final Ν,
represented by a line over the vowel (ii. 13, 14) ; of *itacism* (iv. 2).

The text of Cod. Vat. B.   The text of B is, as elsewhere, of paramount excellence. It
appears to be in error in very few cases :

i.   2 + ὃ′ ἑωράκαμεν.

ii. 14 τὸ ἀπ᾽ ἀρχῆς.

    25 ὑμῖν, comp. iii. 1.

    27 χάρισμα.

iii. 21 ἔχει.

Some of the readings which it gives are more or less doubtful :

ii. 2 μόνων. Comp. v. 6.

    14 om. τοῦ θεοῦ.

    24 om. ἐν before τῷ πατρί.

    27 ἀλλά for ἀλλ᾽ ὡς.

    29 om. καί.

iii. 15 ἑαυτοῦ for αὐτοῦ.

    23 πιστεύσωμεν.

iv. 2 ἐληλυθέναι.

    10 ἠγαπήκαμεν.

    15 add Χριστός.

v.   5 τίς ἐστιν δέ.

    6 μόνῳ. Comp. ii. 2.

It is not, as far as I can judge, ever in error (unless in iii. 7)
when it is supported by some other primary uncial or version :

i.   5 οὐκ ἔστιν ἐν αὐτῷ B 13 31 syr. vg me the.

ii. 6 om. οὕτως AB syr. vg latt the.

    20 om. καί (2°) B the.

    πάντες ΝB the.

iii. 5 om. ἡμῶν ΑΒ 13 lat. vg syr. hl me.

   19 om. καί (1°) ΑΒ lat. vg syr. hl me.

      τὴν καρδίαν Α*Β syr. vg the.

   21 om. ἡμῶν (1°) ΑΒ 13.

      om. ἡμῶν (2°) ΒΟ.

iv. 3 om. Χρ. ἐν σ. ἐλ. ΑΒ lat. vg me.

   12 ἐν ἡμῖν ἐστίν אΒ.

   19 om. αὐτόν ΑΒ (the).

   20 οὐ δύναται אΒ syr. hl the.

v. 1 om. καί (2°) Β 13 (lat. vg) the.

   2 ποιῶμεν Β lat. vg syr me the.

   18 αὐτόν Α*Β.

(iv. 21 is not a case in point.)

The text of א contains many errors, some of which remain un- The text of Cod. Sin. א. corrected, and not a few peculiar false readings:

i. 3 ὃ ἀκηκ. καὶ ἑωρ. καὶ ἀπαγγέλλ.

   5 η απαγγελιας corrected to ἡ ἀγάπη τῆς ἐπαγγελίας.

ii. 3 φυλαξωμεν (1ᵃ m.).

   4 om. ἐν τούτῳ.

      ἡ ἀλ. τοῦ θεοῦ.

   8 ἀλ. καὶ ἐν.

   9 μισῶν, ψευστής ἐστιν καὶ ἐν τ. σκ.

   13 τὸ πονηρόν. Comp. v. 8 τὸν ἀλ.; v. 1.

   24 ἀκηκόατε (twice).

      ἐν τῷ π. καὶ ἐν τῷ υἱῷ.

   26 ταῦτα δέ.

   27 πνεῦμα (1ᵃ m.).

      ἀληθής.

   28 om. καὶ νῦν...αὐτῷ.

      ἐν τῇ παρ. αὐ. ἀπ' αὐτοῦ.

iii. 5 οἴδαμεν.

      οὐκ ἔ. ἐν αὐτῷ.

   14 μεταβέβηκεν.

21 ἀδελφοι.

22 αἰτώμεθα.

iv.   2 γινώσκομεν.

3 ὁμ. Ἰησοῦν κύριον.   Comp. 1 Cor. xii. 3.

ὅτι ἀκηκ. ὅτι.

8 om. ὁ μὴ ἀγ....θεόν (1ᵃ m.) : om. τὸν θ. (אᶜ).

9 ζῶμεν.

17 μεθ᾽ ἡμῶν ἐν ἡμῖν.

τῇ ἀγάπῃ τῆς κρ.

ἐσόμεθα.

20 om. ὅτι.

v.   1 τὸ γεγεννημένον.   Comp. v. 20; ii. 13.

7 οἱ τρεῖς.

9 τὴν μαρτ. τοῦ θεοῦ (1ᵃ m.).

10 οὐκ ἐπίστευκεν.

ἐμαρτύρηκεν.

20 τὸ ἀληθινόν (1ᵃ m.).

In several cases it has false readings in common with A and with C respectively :

אA.

iii. 21 add ἡμῶν after καταγινώσκῃ.

v.   6 add καὶ πνεύματος after αἵματος.

אC.

i.   9 add ἡμῶν after ἁμαρτίας (2°).

ii.   6 add οὕτως.

iii.   5 add ἡμῶν after ἁμαρτίας.

11 ἐπαγγελία.

13 add καί.

19 add καί.

21 add ἡμῶν after καρδία.

The text of Cod. Alex. A.   The text of A, which represents a far more ancient type in this Epistle than in the Gospels, contains many peculiar readings, in which it has often the support of the Vulgate :

i.   6 ἐὰν + γάρ.
   7 μετ' αὐτοῦ (some lat).

ii. 2 ἐστ. ἰλ. lat. vg.
   8 σκιά.
   ἐν αὐτ. ἀλ.
   27 om. καί before καθώς.

iii. 20 om. ὅτι 2° lat. vg me the.
   23 τῷ ὀν. αὐτοῦ' I. X.

iv. 6 ἐν τούτῳ lat. vg me the.
   7 add τὸν θεόν.
   8 οὐ γινώσκει.
   10 ἐκεῖνος for αὐτός.
   15 ὁμολογῇ.
   16 πιστεύομεν (lat. vg) me.
   19 add οὖν lat. vg.
   ὁ θεός for αὐτός lat. vg.
   21 ἀπὸ τοῦ θεοῦ lat. vg.

v.   6 πνεύματι for αἵματι.
   10 add τοῦ θεοῦ lat. vg me.
   τῷ υἱῷ lat. vg.
   οὐκ ἐπίστευσεν.
   11 αὕτη ἐστὶν ἡ ζ.
   14 ὄνομα for θέλημα.
   16 μὴ ἁμαρτ. ἁμ. μὴ πρ. θ.
   20 ἀληθινὸν θεόν lat. vg me.
   om. Ἰησοῦ Χριστῷ lat. vg.

The peculiar readings of C have no appearance of genuineness: The text of
Cod. Eph.
i.   4 add in fin. ἐν ἡμῖν.   C.
   9 om. ἡμᾶς.

ii. 21 om. πᾶν.

iii. 20 κύριος (for θεός).

iv. 2 Χριστὸν Ἰησοῦν.

In several places it gives a correction which was adopted widely:

i.   3 om. δέ.

    5 ἐπαγγελία.

ii.   4 om. ὅτι.

iii. 14 add τὸν ἀδελφόν.

The *Latin Vulgate*. The Vulgate Latin Version is for the most part very close to the early Greek text. It represents however in some cases readings which are not now noted from Greek MSS. :

ii.   1 *sed et si*: καὶ ἐὰν δέ (Did).

    12 *remittuntur* (? ἀφίονται).

iii. 17 *qui habuerit* : om. δέ.

iv.   3 *qui solvit* (λύει) *Jesum Christum.*

    hic est antichristus, quod.

    4 *eum*: αὐτόν.

    16 *caritati* + *Dei.*

v.   6 *Christus* for τὸ πνεῦμα.

    7 *unum sunt* for εἰς τὸ ἕν εἰσιν.

    9 *test. Dei* + *quod majus est.*

    15 *et scimus* (ℵ*A omit καὶ ἐάν).

Other readings are preserved in some later copies:

ii.   10 *in nobis non est.*

    27 *maneat*: μενέτω.

iii. 6 + *et omnis.*

    16 + *Dei.*

iv.   2 *cognoscitur*: γινώσκεται.

v.   16 *scit*: εἰδῇ.

    ut roget quis: ἵνα ἐρωτήσῃ τις.

    17 om. οὐ.

It agrees with ℵ alone in ii. 8 (+ *et in ipso*), and with B 31* in ii. 25 (*vobis*).

Some peculiarities of order may perhaps represent real variations:

i.   9 *fidelis et iustus est.*

ii.   5 *verbum eius.*

iv.   3 *nunc iam in mundo est.*

12 *vidit umquam.*

17 *nobiscum caritas.*

In three places '*sicut est*' represents ὡς, καθώς, i. 7; iii. 3, 7.

Variations in other passages may be simply due to interpretation: i. 4 *scripsimus*, ii. 18 *nunc autem, id.* 20 *sed vos*, iii. 19 *suademus*, iv. 20 *videt* (2).

The peculiarities of interpretation in the following places are worthy of remark.   Many of them are touched upon afterwards:

i.   3 *ut...sit.*

ii.   2 *pro totius mundi* [*peccatis*].

16 *conc. carnis est...quæ non est.*

21 *non...quasi ignorantibus...sed quasi scientibus...*

iii.   1 *ut nominemur et simus.*

10 *qui non est iustus.*

14 *translati sumus.*

v.   4 *quæ vincit.*

15 *quas postulamus.*

16 *petit.*

18 *generatio dei* (? ἡ γέννησις τοῦ θεοῦ).

20 *ut cognoscamus...ut simus.*

But caution is necessary in constructing the Greek text which the version represents.   The same words are not always rendered in the same way in like contexts.   Thus παράγεται is rendered *transierunt* in ii. 8 and *transibit* (*transit*) (though both forms may possibly represent *transiit*) in ii. 17; τηρεῖν is rendered in three consecutive verses by *observare, custodire, servare* (ii. 3, 4, 5); φῶς is rendered by *lux* (i. 5, 7; ii. 9), and by *lumen* (ii. 7, 10); γινώσκομεν in the same connexion is translated *scimus* (ii. 3, 5, 18; iii. 24), *cognoscimus* (iii. 19; iv. 6; v. 2), and *intellegimus* (iv. 13).

II. TITLE.

In *Cod. Vat.* B and *Cod. Alex.* A the title is simply Ἰωάνον
(-άννου) ᾱ, *Of John* 1. In *Cod. Sin.* א this is further defined
Ἰ. ἐπιστολὴ ᾱ, *The first Epistle of John;* and in *Cod. Angelicus* L
(saec. IX.) it becomes ἐπιστολὴ καθολικὴ τοῦ ἁγίου ἀποστόλου Ἰ., *The
Catholic Epistle of the holy Apostle John ;* while *Cod. Porphyr.* P
(saec. IX.) gives Ἰ. ·τοῦ εὐαγγελιστοῦ καὶ ἀποσ[τόλου ἐπιστολὴ] ᾱ, *The
first Epistle of John the Evangelist and Apostle.*

One heading from a later MS. (f^scr) is worth quoting : βροντῆς
υἱὸς Ἰ. τάδε χριστιανοῖσιν, *John, a son of thunder,* [*saith*] *these things
to Christians.*

The Epistle is commonly spoken of as ἐπιστολὴ καθολική, 'a
catholic, general, epistle.' The meaning of the epithet is well given
by Œcumenius (saec. X.). Καθολικαὶ λέγονται αὗται οἱονεὶ ἐγκύκλιοι.
Οὐ γὰρ ἀφωρισμένως ἔθνει ἑνὶ ἢ πόλει ὡς ὁ θεῖος Παῦλος, οἷον Ῥωμαί-
οις ἢ Κορινθίοις, προσφωνεῖ ταύτας τὰς ἐπιστολὰς ὁ τῶν τοιούτων τοῦ
κυρίου μαθητῶν θίασος, ἀλλὰ καθόλου τοῖς πιστοῖς, ἤτοι Ἰουδαίοις τοῖς
ἐν τῇ διασπορᾷ, ὡς καὶ ὁ Πέτρος, ἢ καὶ πᾶσι τοῖς ὑπὸ τὴν αὐτὴν πίστιν
Χριστιανοῖς τελοῦσιν (*Praef. ad Comm. in Ep. Jac.*).

The word occurs in this connexion from the close of the second
century onwards. Thus Clement of Alexandria (*Strom.* IV. c. 15,
§ 99, p. 606 P.) speaks of the letter contained in Acts xv. 23 ff. as
ἡ ἐπιστολὴ ἡ καθολικὴ τῶν ἀποστόλων ἁπάντων...διακομισθεῖσα εἰς
τοὺς πιστούς... Origen uses the epithet of the First Epistle of St
Peter (cf. Euseb. *H. E.* VI. 25), 1 John, Jude (in the Latin translation), and of the (apocryphal) letter of Barnabas (*c. Cels.* I. 63).
So also the word is used of letters with a general application
(though specially addressed) which made no claim to canonical
authority (Euseb. *H. E.* IV. 23; comp. v. 18).

In this sense the word was appropriately applied to the letters
of James, 1 Peter, 1 John, which formed the centre of the collection
of non-Pauline Epistles. It was then extended to 2 Peter and Jude,

which are perfectly general in their address; and so (less accurately) to 2, 3 John, which were taken in close connexion with 1 John.

By a singular error the group of letters was called in the later The title Western Church 'canonical' (*canonicæ*) in place of 'catholic.' *Canonical.* Junilius (c. A.D. 550) had spoken of the letters of James, 2 Peter, Jude, 2, 3 John as added by very many to the collection of Canonical books (quæ apostolorum Canonicæ nuncupantur). Cassiodorus following shortly afterwards adopted the epithet apparently as a peculiar title of the whole group (*de inst. div. Litt.* 8), though he extends it also to the whole collection of apostolic epistles. From him it passed into common use in this limited sense (comp. *Decr. Gelas.* § 6 *vv. ll., Hist. of N. T. Canon,* p. 572).

III.   FORM.

In catalogues of the Books of the New Testament the writing The writing is always called a 'letter,' but the question arises In what sense can has no it be so called? It has no address, no subscription; no name is con- specific marks of tained in it of person or place: there is no direct trace of the a letter; author, no indication of any special destination. In these respects it is distinguished from the Epistle of St James and from the Epistles to the Ephesians and to the Hebrews, which come nearest to it. The Epistle of St James ends abruptly, but it has a formal salutation. The Epistle to the Ephesians has a salutation, though it is probable that in different copies the names of different churches were inserted, and it has a formal close: the Epistle to the Hebrews has a formal close with several personal details. The writing of St John is destitute of all that is local or special.

But while this is so, the writing is at the same time instinct but is full of personal from first to last with intense personal feeling. The author is not relation- dealing with abstractions but with life and living men. He is ship. bound to them and they to him: the crown of his joy and their joy is the fulness of their faith (i. 4). He appeals to them as one who is acquainted both with their position and with their history (ii. 12 ff.).

He speaks in teaching and in counsel with the directness of personal experience (i. 1 ff.). He has a clear view of the dangers and of the strength of those whom he addresses (ii. 12 ff.; 7, 22, 27; iii. 2, 13 f.; iv. 1, 4 ff.; v. 13, 18 ff.). But all individual relationship and sympathy is seen in the light of a fellowship spiritual and eternal to which it is contributory.

A Pastoral.

Thus perhaps we can best look at the writing not as a Letter called out by any particular circumstances, but as a Pastoral addressed to those who had been carefully trained and had lived long in the Faith; and, more particularly, to those who were familiar either with the teaching contained in the Fourth Gospel or with the record itself. The substance of the Gospel is a commentary on the Epistle: the Epistle is (so to speak) the condensed moral and practical application of the Gospel.

IV. AUTHORSHIP, DATE, PLACE OF WRITING.

The authorship inseparable from that of the Gospel.

The question of the authorship of the Epistle cannot be discussed as an isolated question. The writing is so closely connected with the Fourth Gospel in vocabulary, style, thought, scope, that these two books cannot but be regarded as works of the same author (see § viii)[1]. The proofs which are given elsewhere to establish the fact that the Fourth Gospel was written by the Apostle St John extend to the Epistle also. Every paragraph of the Epistle reveals to the student its underlying dependence upon the record preserved in the Gospel. The teaching which it conveys is in every part the outcome of the life which is quickened by the Evangelist's witness to Christ. It is not that the author of the

---

[1] The arguments which have been alleged to support the opinion that the Books were by different authors, do not seem to me to need serious examination. They could not be urged if the books were not detached from life and criticised without regard to their main characteristics. Huther has examined them in detail. *Einl.* § 3.

Epistle directly uses the materials contained in the Gospel: he has found in them his starting-point and his inspiration, but at once he goes on to deal independently with problems which are before him.

A single illustration will suffice to shew the general relations of the two Books. Let any one compare the Introduction to the Gospel (John i. 1—18) with the Introduction to the Epistle (1 John i. 1—4), and it will be seen how the same mind deals with the same ideas in different connexions. No theory of conscious imitation can reasonably explain the subtle coincidences and differences in these two short crucial passages. And here a close comparison can be fairly made, because the Evangelist writes in this case not as a narrator of the Lord's words, but in his own person[1]. *The connexion between the two one of life not of external dependence*

It may be added that the writer of the Epistle speaks throughout with the authority of an Apostle. He claims naturally and simply an immediate knowledge of the fundamental facts of the Gospel (i. 1; iv. 14), and that special knowledge which was possessed only by the most intimate disciples of the Lord (i. 1 ἐψηλαφή-σαμεν).

But while the two writings are thus closely connected, there is no sufficient evidence to determine the relative dates of the Epistle and of the Gospel as written. The difference in the treatment of common topics and in the use of common language leads to no certain conclusion. Such variations are sufficiently accounted for by the different nature of the two writings; and there is every reason to believe that the Fourth Gospel was shaped by the Apostle in oral teaching long before it was published or committed to writing. It can only be said with confidence that the Epistle presupposes in those for whom it was composed a familiar acquaintance with the characteristic truths which are preserved for us in the Gospel. *The relative dates of the two Books uncertain.*

The conclusion as to the authorship of the Epistle which is obtained from internal evidence is supported by external evidence *External evidence.*

---

[1] Compare also i. 3 f., v. 13 with John xx. 31. See § ix.

as strong as the circumstances allow us to expect. It was used by Papias (Euseb. *H. E.* III. 39), by Polycarp (*ad Phil.* c. 7), and by Irenæus, the disciple of Polycarp (III. 16, 18). It is mentioned in the Muratorian fragment 'as received in the Catholic Church,' according to the more probable rendering, or as 'reckoned among the Catholic Epistles[1].' It was included in the oldest Versions of the East (Syriac) and West (Latin). It was quoted by the earliest fathers of Africa and Alexandria, whose writings have been preserved, Tertullian and Clement; and till recent times was 'universally acknowledged' (Euseb. *H. E.* III. 25; Hieron. *de virr. ill.* 9).

Probably written late and at Ephesus. There is no direct evidence to shew, when and where it was written. The circumstances of the Christian Society point clearly to a late date, and this may be fixed with reasonable likelihood in the last decade of the first century. The later years of St John were spent at Ephesus; and, in the absence of any other indication, it is natural to suppose that it was written there.

The specific form of false teaching which is directly condemned in the Epistle (iv. 3) suggests the same conclusion. Cerinthus, who is known to have maintained it, taught in Asia Minor at the end of the first century, and is placed by tradition in immediate connexion with St John (comp. § vi).

V. DESTINATION.

Addressed to a circle of Asiatic Churches. This being so, it seems to follow that the writing was addressed primarily to the circle of Asiatic Churches, of which Ephesus was the centre. Universal tradition and such direct evidence as there is from Asiatic writings alike confirm this view. Nor is there any evidence against it, for the strange statement which gained currency through Augustine (*Quæst. Evang.* II. 39) that the Epistle was addressed 'to the Parthians' (*epistola ad Parthos*) is obviously a blunder, and is wholly unsupported by any independent authority[2].

---

[1] Superscripti Johannis duas in catholica (all. catholicis) habentur. Comp. *Hist. of N. T. Canon*, p. 537.

[2] In one Latin MS., referred to by Sabatier, the Epistle is said to bear the title, *Epistola ad Sparthos*. This

VI. CHARACTER.

The exact destination of the Letter is however of no real moment. The colouring is not local but moral; and it offers a vivid picture of a Christian Society which is without parallel in the New Testament. The storm which St Paul foretold in his Pastoral Epistles (2 Tim. iii. 1; iv. 3), and in his address to the Ephesian elders (Acts xx. 29 f.), had broken over the Church. Jerusalem had been destroyed. The visible centre of the Theocracy had been removed. The Church stood out alone as the Body through which the Holy Spirit worked among men. And in correspondence with this change the typical form of trial was altered. Outward dangers were overcome. The world was indeed perilous; but it was rather by its seductions than by its hostility. There is no trace of any recent or impending persecution. Now the main temptations are from within. Perhaps a period of tranquillity gave occasion for internal dissensions as well as for internal development.

The Book answers to a new age of the Church.

Two general characteristics of the Epistle are due to this change in the position of the Church. On the one side the missionary work of the Society no longer occupies a first place in the Apostle's thoughts; and on the other, the topics of debate are changed.

At first sight there is something almost unintelligible in the tone in which St John speaks of ' the world.' He regards it without wonder and without sorrow. For him ' love ' is identical with ' love of the brethren.' The difficulty however disappears when his

The world overcome.

---

has led to the conjecture that it was originally *epistola ad Sparsos* (comp. 1 Pet. i. 1). It is however more probable that the title is a corruption of πρὸς παρθένους. In a fragment of the Latin translation of the *Outlines* of Clement of Alexandria, it is said: *secunda Johannis epistola quæ ad virgines scripta simplicissima est* (p. 1010 P.); and a late cursive MS. (62) has for the subscription of the second Epistle, 'I. β πρὸς Πάρθους. This title may easily have been extended to the

first Epistle, and then misinterpreted. So Cassiodorus extends the title *ad Parthos* to the Epistles of St John generally: Epistolæ Petri ad gentes ...Johannis ad Parthos (*de instit. div. litt.* XIV.). Bede's statement that ' Athanasius, bishop of Alexandria,' was ' among the many ecclesiastical writers who affirm that it was written to the Parthians' (*Prol. super vii. Canon. Epp.*), cannot be accepted without corroborative evidence.

point of sight is realised. According to his view, which answers to the eternal order of things, the world exists indeed, but more as a semblance than as a reality. It is overcome finally and for ever. It is on the point of vanishing. This outward consummation is in God's hands. And over against 'the world' there is the Church, the organised Christian society, the depository of the Truth and the witness for the Truth. By this therefore all that need be done to proclaim the Gospel to those without is done naturally and effectively in virtue of its very existence. It must overcome the darkness by shining. There is therefore no need for eager exhortation to spread the word. St Paul wrote, while the conflict was undecided. St John has seen its close.

The Jewish controversy closed. This paramount office of the Church to witness to and to embody the Truth, concentrated attention upon the central idea of its message in itself and not in its relation to other systems. The first controversies which fill the history of the Acts and St Paul's Epistles are over. There is no trace of any conflict between advocates of the Law and of the Gospel, between champions of works and faith. The difference of Jew and Gentile, and the question of circumcision, have no place in the composition. The names themselves do not occur (yet see 3 John 7). There is nothing even to shew to which body the readers originally belonged, for v. 21 cannot be confined to a literal interpretation. The main questions of **The main question that of the Person of Christ.** debate are gathered round the Person and Work of the Lord. On the one side He was represented as a mere man (Ebionism): on the other side He was represented as a mere phantom (Docetism): a third party endeavoured to combine these two opinions, and supposed that the divine element, Christ, was united with the man Jesus at His Baptism and left Him before the Passion (Cerinthianism).

The Epistle gives no evidence that St John had to contend with Ebionistic error. The false teaching with which he deals is Docetic **Docetism.** and specifically Cerinthian. In respect of the Docetic heresy generally Jerome's words are striking : apostolis adhuc in sæculo superstitibus, adhuc apud Judæam Christi sanguine recenti, phantasma

Domini corpus asserebatur (*Dial. adv. Lucifer.* § 23). Ignatius writes against it in urgent language :

Ad Trall. 9, 10, Κωφώθητε οὖν ὅταν ὑμῖν χωρὶς Ἰησοῦ Χριστοῦ λαλῇ τις, τοῦ ἐκ γένους Δαυίδ, τοῦ ἐκ Μαρίας, ὃς ἀληθῶς ἐγεννήθη, ἔφαγέν τε καὶ ἔπιεν, ἀληθῶς ἐδιώχθη ἐπὶ Ποντίου Πιλάτου, ἀληθῶς ἐσταυρώθη καὶ ἀπέθανεν...ὃς καὶ ἀληθῶς ἠγέρθη ἀπὸ νεκρῶν...Εἰ δέ, ὥσπερ τινὲς ἄθεοι ὄντες...λέγουσιν τὸ δοκεῖν πεπονθέναι αὐτὸν αὐτοὶ τὸ δοκεῖν ὄντες, ἐγὼ τί δέδεμαι ;

Ad Smyrn. 2, ἀληθῶς ἔπαθεν ὡς καὶ ἀληθῶς ἀνέστησεν ἑαυτόν· οὐχ ὥσπερ ἄπιστοί τινες λέγουσιν τὸ δοκεῖν αὐτὸν πεπονθέναι, αὐτοὶ τὸ δοκεῖν ὄντες. Comp. cc. 1, 5, 12.

Ad Ephes. 7, εἷς ἰατρός ἐστιν, σαρκικός τε καὶ πνευματικός, γεννη-τὸς καὶ ἀγέννητος, ἐν σαρκὶ γενόμενος θεός, ἐν θανάτῳ ζωὴ ἀληθινή, καὶ ἐκ Μαρίας καὶ ἐκ θεοῦ πρῶτον παθητὸς καὶ τότε ἀπαθής. Comp. c. 18.

So also Polycarp :

Ad Phil. c. 7, πᾶς γὰρ ὃς ἂν μὴ ὁμολογῇ Ἰησοῦν Χριστὸν ἐν σαρκὶ ἐληλυθέναι ἀντίχριστός ἐστι· καὶ ὃς ἂν μὴ ὁμολογῇ τὸ μαρτύριον τοῦ σταυροῦ ἐκ τοῦ διαβόλου ἐστί[1].

Irenæus characterises in particular the opinions of Cerinthus very clearly : [Cerinthus] Jesum subjicit non ex Virgine natum, impossibile enim hoc ei visum est ; fuisse autem eum Joseph et Mariæ filium...et plus potuisse justitia et prudentia et sapientia præ omnibus, et post baptismum descendisse in eum Christum ab ea principalitate quæ est super omnia...in fine autem revolasse iterum Christum de Jesu, et Jesum passum esse et resurrexisse : Christum autem impassibilem perseverasse existentem spiritalem[2]. *Cerinthianism.*

In the presence of these false views St John unfolds the Truth, *Against this false*

---

[1] The so-called 'Gospel according to Peter' is said to have favoured their views (Serapion, ap. Euseb. *H. E.* VI. 12).

[2] Iren. *adv. hær.* I. 26. 1. Comp. Epiph. *Hær.* XXVIII. 1. For the story of St John's refusal to be under the same roof with Cerinthus, see Iren. ap. Euseb. *H. E.* IV. 14 (Iren. *adv. hær.* III. 3. 4, on the authority of Polycarp). It is strange that either

St John or Cerinthus should have visited the baths at Ephesus. This difficulty however was not felt by Irenæus. The Christology of Nestorianism pressed to its logical consequences is not distinguishable, as it appears, from that of Cerinthus. The more extreme *Docetæ* regarded the manifestation of the Lord as being in appearance only (φαντασία), like the Theophanies in the Old Testament.

teaching St John proclaims again the Gospel

not in the form of argument but of announcement. He declares that Jesus Christ has come (iv. 2), and is coming (2 Ep. 7) in the flesh (comp. v. 6). He shews that the denial of the Incarnate Son is practically the denial of the Father, the denial of God (ii. 22; v. 20). It is the rejection of that power by which alone true life is possible through a divine fellowship (i. 2 f.).

as the old Truth.

But in insisting on these truths St John disclaims all appearance of bringing forward new points. His readers know implicitly all that he can tell them. He simply pleads that they should yield themselves to the guidance of the Spirit which they had received. So they would realise what in fact they already possessed (ii. 7, 24; iii. 11). Perhaps it may be inferred from the stress which St John lays on the identity of the original word with the teaching which he represented, that some had ventured to charge him also with innovation. Such an accusation would have superficial plausibility; and the Epistle deals with it conclusively either by anticipation or in view of actual opponents.

The letter specially applicable at present from its circumstances, and

Thus this latest of the Epistles is a voice from the midst of the Christian Church revealed at last in its independence. Many who read it had, in all probability, grown up as Christians. A Christianity of habit was now possible. The spiritual circumstances of those to whom it was first sent are like our own. The words need no accommodation to make them bear directly upon ourselves.

from its teaching.

And while the Christological errors which St John meets exist more or less at all times, they seem to have gained a dangerous prevalence now. Modern realism, which has found an ally in art, by striving to give distinctness to the actual outward features of the Lord's Life, seems to tend more and more to an Ebionitic Christology. Modern idealism, on the other hand, which aims at securing the pure spiritual conception free from all associations of time and place, is a new Docetism. Nor would it be hard to shew that popular Christology is largely though unconsciously affected by Cerinthian tendencies. The separation of Jesus, the Son of Man, from Christ, the Son of God, is constantly made to the destruction of the One, indivisible Person of our Lord and Saviour. We have indeed no power to follow such revelations of Scripture into supposed consequences, but our strength is to hold with absolute firmness the apostolic words as St John has delivered them to us.

The teaching of St John in his Epistle thus turns upon the Person of Christ. Under this aspect it is important to observe that it is intensely practical. St John everywhere presents moral ideas resting upon facts and realised in life. The foundation on which conviction is based is historical experience (i. ₁ ff.; iv. 14). This, as furnishing the materials for that knowledge which St John's readers had 'heard from the beginning,' is set over against mere speculation (ii. 24). Truth is never stated in a speculative form, but as a motive and a help for action. The writer does not set before his readers propositions about Christ, but the Living Christ Himself for present fellowship. And yet while this is so, the Epistle contains scarcely anything in detail of Christ's Life. He came in the flesh, 'by water and blood'; the Life was manifested; He walked as we are bound to walk. He laid down His Life for us; He is to be manifested yet again; this is all. There is no mention of the Cross or of the Resurrection. But Christ having died lives as our Advocate. (Compare Addit. Note on v. 6.) *The facts of the Gospel the basis and motive for action.*

The apprehension of the historical manifestation of the Life of Christ is thus pressed as the prevailing and sufficient motive for godlike conduct; and at the same time mere right opinion, apart from conduct, is exposed in its nothingness. Simply to say, 'we have fellowship with God,' 'we are in the light,' we 'know God,' is shewn to be delusion if the corresponding action is wanting (i. 6, ii. 9, 4). *Intellectual assent in itself insufficient.*

The Epistle, as has been already said, comes from the midst of the Christian Church to the members of the Church. It is the voice of an unquestioned teacher to disciples who are assumed to be anxious to fulfil their calling. In virtue of the circumstances of its composition it takes the widest range in the survey of the Gospel, and completes and harmonises the earlier forms of apostolic teaching. St John's doctrine of 'love' reconciles the complementary doctrines of 'faith' and 'works.' His view of the primal revelation 'that *Wide range of the Epistle.*

which was from the beginning...concerning the word of life,' places
Judaism in its true position as part of the discipline of the world,
and vindicates for Christianity its claim to universality. His doctrine of 'Jesus Christ come in flesh' affirms at once the historical
and the transcendental aspects of His Person. His exhibition of
a present divine fellowship for man, issuing in a future transfiguration of man to the divine likeness, offers a view of life able to meet
human weakness and human aspiration.

Silence as
to Old
Testament
and eccle-
siastical
organisa-
tion.

Two other peculiarities of the Epistle seem to be due to the
same causes which determined this catholicity of teaching. Alone
of all the writings of the New Testament except the two shorter
letters and the Epistle to Philemon, it contains no quotations or
clear reminiscences of the language of the Old Testament (yet see
iii. 12). And again, while the Christian Society is everywhere
contemplated in its definite spiritual completeness, nothing is said
on any detail of ritual or organisation.

VII. OBJECT.

The object
of the
Epistle (as
of the
Gospel)
positive.

The object of the Epistle corresponds with its character. It is
presented under a twofold form :

(i) i. 3, f. ὃ ἑωράκαμεν καὶ ἀκηκόαμεν ἀπαγγέλλομεν καὶ ὑμῖν, ἵνα
καὶ ὑμεῖς κοινωνίαν ἔχητε μεθ' ἡμῶν, καὶ ἡ κοινωνία δὲ ἡ ἡμετέρα μετὰ
τοῦ πατρὸς καὶ μετὰ τοῦ υἱοῦ αὐτοῦ Ἰησοῦ Χριστοῦ· καὶ ταῦτα γράφομεν
ἡμεῖς ἵνα ἡ χαρὰ ἡμῶν (v. ὑμῶν) ᾖ πεπληρωμένη.

*That which we have seen and heard declare we unto you also,
that ye also may have fellowship with us: yea, and our fellowship
is with the Father, and with his Son Jesus Christ : and these
things we write, that our joy may be fulfilled.*

(ii) v. 13 ταῦτα ἔγραψα ὑμῖν ἵνα εἰδῆτε ὅτι ζωὴν ἔχετε αἰώνιον, τοῖς
πιστεύουσιν εἰς τὸ ὄνομα τοῦ υἱοῦ τοῦ θεοῦ.

*These things have I written unto you, that ye may know that ye
have eternal life, even unto you that believe on the name of the Son
of God.*

With these must be compared the account given of the object of the Gospel :

(iii) John xx. 31 ταῦτα δὲ γέγραπται ἵνα πιστεύσητε ὅτι Ἰησοῦς ἐστὶν ὁ Χριστὸς ὁ υἱὸς τοῦ θεοῦ, καὶ ἵνα πιστεύοντες ζωὴν ἔχητε ἐν τῷ ὀνόματι αὐτοῦ.

But these are written, that ye may believe that Jesus is the Christ, the Son of God ; and that believing ye may have life in his name.

There is a complete harmony between the three. The acceptance of the revelation of Jesus—the Son of man—as the Christ, the Son of God (iii), brings the power of life (ii), and this life is fellowship with man and with God in Christ (i). Life, in other words, life eternal, is in Christ Jesus, and is realised in all its extent in union with Him : it is death to be apart from Him.

The pursuit of such a theme necessarily involves the condemnation and refutation of corresponding errors. But St John's method is to confute the error by the exposition of the truth realised in life. His object is polemical only so far as the clear unfolding of the essence of right teaching necessarily shews all error in its real character. In other words St John writes to call out a welcome for what he knows to be the Gospel and not to overthrow this or that false opinion.

VIII.   STYLE AND LANGUAGE.

The style of the Epistle bears a close resemblance to that of the Gospel both in vocabulary and structure. There is in both the same emphatic repetition of fundamental words and phrases,—'truth,' 'love,' 'light,' 'in the light,' 'being born of God,' 'being' or 'abiding in God'—and the same monotonous simplicity of construction. *General resemblance to the Gospel.*

The particles are singularly few. For example γάρ occurs only three times: ii. 19; iv. 20; v. 3 (2 John 11; 3 John 3, 7); δέ nine times (about one-third of its average frequency); μέν τε and οὖν (3 John 8) do not occur at all (the last is twice wrongly in common *Scantiness of particles.*

text). The absence of οὖν is the more remarkable because it is the characteristic particle of the narrative of the Gospel, where St John seems to dwell on the connexion of facts which might be overlooked; ὅτι, 'that' and 'because,' is very frequent; and it is constantly found where γάρ might have been expected.

The common particle of connexion is καί. This conjunction takes its peculiar colour from the sentences which are thus added one to the other : e.g. i. 5 ; ii. 3 ; and it is used not uncommonly when a particle of logical sequence might have been expected : e.g. iii. 3, 16.

Very frequently the sentences and clauses follow one another without any particles : e.g. ii. 22—24 ; iv. 4—6 ; 7—10 ; 11—13. See also ii. 5, 6 ; 9, 10 ; iii. 2 ; 4, 5 ; 9, 10.

Sometimes they are brought into an impressive parallelism by the repetition of a clause :

   i. 6, 8, 10 (ἐὰν εἴπωμεν).

   v. 18—20 (οἴδαμεν).

St John develops an idea by parallelism.
These different usages are different adaptations of St John's characteristic principle of composition : he explains and develops his ideas by parallelism or (which answers to the same tone of thought) by antagonism.

It is not of course maintained that this method of writing is the result of studied choice. It is, as far as we may presume to judge, the spontaneous expression of the Apostle's vision of the Truth, opening out in its fulness before the eye of the believer, complete in its own majesty, requiring to be described and not to be drawn out by processes of reasoning.

In this respect and generally it will be felt that the writing is thoroughly Hebraistic in tone, and yet it does not contain one quotation or verbal reminiscence from the Old Testament.

Characteristic words.
Of significant verbal coincidences of language between the Epistles and Gospel the following may be noticed. The words are either exceptionally frequent in these writings or peculiar to them :

   κόσμος (moral) (John i. 10 note).

φῶς (1 John i. 5 note).

σκοτία (σκότος) (i. 6 note).

φανεροῦν (i. 2 note).

φαίνειν (ii. 8 note).

ἑωρακέναι (i. 1 note).

θεᾶσθαι (θεωρεῖν only once in the Epistles : 1 John iii. 17 (John i. 14 note).

θάνατος (spiritual) (iii. 14 note).

ζωὴ αἰώνιος (ἡ αἰώνιος ζ., ἡ ζ. ἡ αἰ.) (Add. note on v. 20).

ἡ ἀλήθεια (i. 6 note).

ὁ ἀληθινὸς θεός (v. 20 note).

τὸ πνεῦμα τῆς ἀληθείας (iv. 6 note).

μαρτυρεῖν, μαρτυρία (i. 2 note).

τεκνία (ii. 1 note).

παιδία (ii. 14 note).

ὁ μονογενὴς υἱός (Add. note on iv. 9).

ἀγαπᾶν ἀλλήλους, τὸν ἀδελφόν, τοὺς ἀδ. (iii. 11 note).

νικᾶν (ii. 13 note).

μένειν, εἶναι, ἔν τινι (ii. 5 note).

τὴν ψυχὴν τιθέναι (iii. 16 note).

The frequent use of ἵνα when the idea of purpose is not directly obvious, and the elliptical use of ἀλλ' ἵνα, are both characteristic of these books (iii. 11 ; ii. 19 notes).

In addition to these verbal coincidences there are also larger coincidences of expression. Of these the most important are the following : Verbal co-incidences with the Gospel.

1 Epistle of St John.	Gospel of St John.
i. 2, 3 ἡ ζωὴ ἐφανερώθη καὶ ἑωράκαμεν καὶ μαρτυροῦμεν...ὃ ἑωράκαμεν καὶ ἀκηκόαμεν ἀπαγγέλλομεν καὶ ὑμῖν.	iii. 11 ὃ ἑωράκαμεν μαρτυροῦμεν.
id. 4 ταῦτα γράφομεν ἡμεῖς ἵνα ἡ χαρὰ ὑμῶν ᾖ πεπληρωμένη.	xvi. 24 αἰτεῖτε καὶ λήμψεσθε ἵνα ἡ χαρὰ ὑμῶν ᾖ πεπληρωμένη.

1 Epistle of St John.

ii. 11 ὁ μισῶν τὸν ἀδελφὸν αὐτοῦ
...ἐν τῇ σκοτίᾳ περιπατεῖ καὶ
οὐκ οἶδεν ποῦ ὑπάγει.

id. 14 ὁ λόγος τοῦ θεοῦ ἐν ὑμῖν
μένει.

id. 17 ὁ ποιῶν τὸ θέλημα τοῦ
θεοῦ μένει εἰς τὸν αἰῶνα.

iii. 5 ἁμαρτία ἐν αὐτῷ οὐκ ἔστιν.

id. 8 ἀπ' ἀρχῆς ὁ διάβολος ἁμαρτάνει.

id. 13 μὴ θαυμάζετε, ἀδελφοί,
εἰ μισεῖ ὑμᾶς ὁ κόσμος.

id. 14 οἴδαμεν ὅτι μεταβεβήκαμεν ἐκ τοῦ θανάτου εἰς τὴν
ζωὴν ὅτι ἀγαπῶμεν τοὺς ἀδελφούς.

id. 16 ἐκεῖνος ὑπὲρ ἡμῶν
τὴν ψυχὴν αὐτοῦ ἔθηκεν.

id. 22 ὃ ἂν αἰτῶμεν λαμβάνομεν
...ὅτι...τὰ ἀρεστὰ ἐνώπιον αὐτοῦ ποιοῦμεν.

id. 23 αὕτη ἐστὶν ἡ ἐντολὴ αὐτοῦ
ἵνα...ἀγαπῶμεν ἀλλήλους καθὼς ἔδωκεν ἐντολὴν ἡμῖν. Comp.
iv. 11.

iv. 6 ἡμεῖς ἐκ τοῦ θεοῦ ἐσμέν·
ὁ γινώσκων τὸν θεὸν ἀκούει ἡμῶν,
ὃς οὐκ ἔστιν ἐκ τοῦ θεοῦ   (a)
οὐκ ἀκούει ἡμῶν.   (b)

Gospel of St John.

xii. 35...
ὁ περιπατῶν ἐν τῇ σκοτίᾳ οὐκ
οἶδεν ποῦ ὑπάγει.

v. 38 τὸν λόγον αὐτοῦ οὐκ ἔχετε
μένοντα ἐν ὑμῖν.

viii. 35 ὁ υἱὸς
μένει εἰς τὸν αἰῶνα.

viii. 46 τίς ἐξ ὑμῶν ἐλέγχει με
περὶ ἁμαρτίας;

viii. 44 ἐκεῖνος [ὁ διάβολος]
ἀνθρωποκτόνος ἦν ἀπ' ἀρχῆς.

xv. 18
εἰ ὁ κόσμος ὑμᾶς μισεῖ γινώσκετε ὅτι ἐμὲ πρῶτον ὑμῶν μεμίσηκεν.

v. 24 ὁ τὸν λόγον μου ἀκούων...
μεταβέβηκεν ἐκ τοῦ θανάτου
εἰς τὴν ζωήν.

x. 15
τὴν ψυχήν μου τίθημι ὑπὲρ
τῶν προβάτων.

viii. 29 οὐκ ἀφῆκέν με μόνον
ὅτι ἐγὼ τὰ ἀρεστὰ αὐτῷ ποιῶ
πάντοτε.

xiii. 34 ἐντολὴν καινὴν δίδωμι
ὑμῖν
ἵνα ἀγαπᾶτε ἀλλήλους καθὼς
ἠγάπησα ὑμᾶς ἵνα...

viii. 47 ὁ ὢν ἐκ τοῦ θεοῦ τὰ
ῥήματα τοῦ θεοῦ ἀκούει·
ὑμεῖς οὐκ ἀκούετε   (b)
ὅτι ἐκ τοῦ θεοῦ οὐκ ἐστέ   (a)

1 EPISTLE OF ST JOHN.

iv. 15 ὃς ἐὰν ὁμολογήσῃ ὅτι
'Ιησοῦς [Χριστός] ἐστιν ὁ υἱὸς τοῦ
θεοῦ,
ὁ θεὸς ἐν αὐτῷ μένει καὶ αὐτὸς ἐν
τῷ θεῷ. Comp. v. 16; iii. 24.

id. 16 ἐγνώκαμεν καὶ πεπιστεύκαμεν.

id. 16
ὁ μένων ἐν τῇ ἀγάπῃ ἐν τῷ θεῷ
μένει.

v. 4, f. αὕτη ἐστὶν ἡ νίκη
ἡ νικήσασα τὸν κόσμον, ἡ πίστις
ἡμῶν.
τίς ἐστιν ὁ νικῶν τὸν κόσμον...

id. 9 ἡ μαρτυρία τοῦ θεοῦ μείζων
ἐστίν, ὅτι αὕτη ἐστὶν ἡ μαρτυρία
τοῦ θεοῦ, ὅτι μεμαρτύρηκεν περὶ
τοῦ υἱοῦ αὐτοῦ.

id. 20 δέδωκεν ἡμῖν διάνοιαν
ἵνα γιγνώσκομεν τὸν ἀληθινόν·
καί ἐσμεν ἐν τῷ ἀληθινῷ, ἐν τῷ υἱῷ
αὐτοῦ ['Ιησοῦ Χριστῷ]. οὗτός ἐστιν ὁ ἀληθινὸς θεός, καὶ ζωὴ αἰώνιος.

GOSPEL OF ST JOHN.

vi. 56 ὁ τρώγων μου τὴν σάρκα
καὶ πίνων μου τὸ αἷμα

ἐν ἐμοὶ μένει κἀγὼ ἐν αὐτῷ. Comp.
xiv. 17.

vi. 69 πεπιστεύκαμεν καὶ
ἐγνώκαμεν.

xv. 10 ἐὰν τὰς ἐντολάς μου τηρή-
σητε
μενεῖτε ἐν τῇ ἀγάπῃ μου. Comp.
v. 9 μείνατε ἐν τῇ ἀ. τῇ ἐμῇ.

xvi. 33 θαρσεῖτε
ἐγὼ νενίκηκα τὸν κόσμον.

v. 32 ἄλλος ἐστὶν ὁ μαρτυρῶν
περὶ ἐμοῦ καὶ οἶδα ὅτι ἀληθής ἐστιν
ἡ μαρτυρία ἣν μαρτυρεῖ περὶ ἐμοῦ.

xvii. 3 αὕτη ἐστὶν ἡ αἰώνιος
ζωὴ
ἵνα γινώσκωσι σὲ τὸν μόνον
ἀληθινὸν θεὸν καὶ ὃν ἀπέστειλας
'Ιησοῦν Χριστόν.

IX. THE EPISTLES AND THE GOSPEL.

The last two passages (1 John v. 20; John xvii. 3), which General
have been quoted, illustrate vividly the relation between the of the
Epistles and the Gospel. Both passages contain the same fundamental ideas: Eternal life is the progressive recognition (ἵνα γινώ- Gospel.
σκωσι) of God; and the power of this growing knowledge is given
in His Son Jesus Christ. But the ideas are presented differently

in the two places. The Gospel gives the historic revelation ; the
Epistle shews the revelation as it has been apprehended in the life
of the Society and of the believer.

The two complementary.   This fundamental difference can be presented in another form.
In the Epistle the aim of St John is to lay open what is the
significance of the spiritual truths of the Faith for present human
life.   In the Gospel his aim is to make clear that the true human
life of the Lord is a manifestation of divine love, that 'Jesus is the
Christ, the Son of God.'   Or, to put the contrast in an epigrammatic form, the theme of the Epistle is, 'the Christ is Jesus'; the
theme of the Gospel is, 'Jesus is the Christ.'   In the former the
writer starts from certain acknowledged spiritual conceptions and
points out that they have their foundation in history and their
necessary embodiment in conduct.   In the latter he shews how the
works and words of Jesus of Nazareth establish that in Him the
hope of Israel and the hope of humanity was fulfilled.   So it is
that the Gospel is a continuous record of the unfolding of the
'glory' of Christ.   In the Epistles alone of all the books of the
New Testament (except the Epistle to Philemon), the word 'glory'
does not occur.   Perhaps too it is significant that the word 'heaven'
also is absent from them.

The differences answer to differences between a History and a Pastoral.   Several differences in detail in the topics or form of teaching
in the books have been already noticed.   These belong to the
differences in the positions occupied by a historian and a preacher.
The teaching of the Lord which St John has preserved was given, as
He Himself said, 'in proverbs'; through the experience of Christian
life, the Spirit, 'sent in His Name,' enabled the Apostle to speak
'plainly' (John xvi. 25).

The Coming (παρουσία).   Some other differences still require to be noticed.   These also
spring from the historical circumstances of the writing.   The first
regards the doctrine of 'the Coming,' 'the Presence' (ἡ παρουσία)
of Christ.   In the Gospel St John does not record the eschatological discourses of the Lord—they had found their first fulfilment
when he wrote—and he preserves simply the general promise of a
'Coming' (xiv. 3 ; xxi. 22).   By the side of these he records the

references to the 'judgment' (v. 28 f.), and to 'the last day' (vi. 40, 44). In the Epistle he uses the term 'the Presence' (ii. 28), which is found in all the groups of New Testament writings, and speaks of a future 'manifestation' of the Ascended Christ (*l. c.* : iii. 2). As He 'came in flesh' (iv. 2), so He is still 'coming in flesh' (2 John 7). And the importance of this fact is pressed in its spiritual bearing. By denying it 'Antichrists' displayed their real nature. They sought to substitute a doctrine for a living Saviour.

St John's treatment of the present work of Christ stands in close connexion with this view of His future work. As the Holy Spirit is sent to believers as their Advocate on earth, so He is their Advocate with the Father in heaven (c. ii. 2). The two thoughts are complementary; and the heavenly advocacy of Christ rests upon His own promise in the Gospel (John xiv. 13 f.), though it must not be interpreted as excluding the Father's spontaneous love (John xvi. 26 f.). *The Advocacy of Christ.*

The exposition of the doctrine of 'propitiation' and 'cleansing' which is found in the Epistle (c. ii. 2 ; iv. 10 ἱλασμός; i. 7, 9 καθαρίζειν) is an application of the discourse at Capernaum (see especially John vi. 51, 56 f.); and it is specially remarkable that while the thoughts of the discourse are used, nothing is taken from the language. So again the peculiar description of the spiritual endowment of believers as an 'unction' (χρίσμα, c. ii. 20) perfectly embodies the words in John xx. 21 ff. ; the disciples are in a true sense 'Christs' in virtue of the Life of 'the Christ' (John xiv. 19 ; comp. Apoc. i. 6). Once more, the cardinal phrase 'born of God' (c. ii. 29, &c.), which occurs in the introduction to the Gospel (i. 13), but not in the record of the Lord's words, shews in another example how the original language of the Lord was shaped under the guidance of the Spirit to fullest use. *The doctrine of Propitiation.*

It seems scarcely necessary to remark that such differences between the Epistles and the Gospel are not only not indicative of any difference of authorship, but on the contrary furnish a strong proof that they are the products of one mind. The Epistles give later *These differences shew the working of life.*

growths of common and characteristic ideas. No imitator of the Gospel could have combined elements of likeness and unlikeness in such a manner ; and on the other hand, the substance of the Gospel adequately explains the more defined teaching of the first Epistle. The one writing stands to the other in an intelligible connexion of life.

X. PLAN.

No plan can be complete. It is extremely difficult to determine with certainty the structure of the Epistle. No single arrangement is able to take account of the complex development of thought which it offers, and of the many connexions which exist between its different parts. The following arrangement, which is followed out into detail in the notes, seems to me to give on the whole the truest and clearest view of the sequence of the exposition.

Outline followed. INTRODUCTION.

The facts of the Gospel issuing in fellowship and joy (i. 1—4).

A. THE PROBLEM OF LIFE AND THOSE TO WHOM IT IS PROPOSED (i. 5—ii. 17).

    I.   The Nature of God and the consequent relation of man to God (i. 5—10).

    II.   The remedy for Sin and the sign that it is effectual (ii. 1—6).

    III.   Obedience in love and light in actual life (ii. 7—11).

    IV.   Things temporal and eternal (ii. 12—17).

B. THE CONFLICT OF TRUTH AND FALSEHOOD WITHOUT AND WITHIN (ii. 18—iv. 6).

    I.   The revelation of Falsehood and Truth (ii. 18—29).

    II.   The children of God and the children of the Devil (iii. 1—12).

    III.   Brotherhood in Christ and the hatred of the world (iii. 13—24).

    IV.   The rival spirits of Truth and Error (iv. 1—6).

C. The christian life : the victory of faith (iv. 7—v. 21).

    I. The spirit of the Christian life : God and Love (iv. 7—21).

    II. The power of the Christian life: the Victory and Witness of Faith (v. 1—12).

    III. The activity and confidence of the Christian life : Epilogue (v. 13—21).

The thought of a fellowship between God and man, made possible and in part realised in the Christian Church, runs through the whole Epistle. From this it begins: *Our fellowship is with the Father, and with His Son, Jesus Christ* (i. 3). In this it closes : *We are in Him that is True, in His Son Jesus Christ* (v. 20). `The main thought.`

In the additional Notes I have endeavoured to illustrate the main points in the development of this thought. These notes when taken in proper order will serve as an introduction to the study of the doctrine of St John. For this purpose they are most conveniently grouped in the following manner: `Systematic illustration of its development`

    I. The doctrine of God.

        The idea of God: note on iv. 8; comp. iv. 12.

        The Divine Name: 3 John 7.

        The Holy Trinity: v. 20.

        The Divine Fatherhood: i. 2.

    II. The doctrine of Finite Being.

        Creation: note on ii. 17.

        God and man: ii. 9.

        The nature of man: iii. 19.

        The Devil: ii. 13.

        Sin: i. 9; comp. v. 16.

        The world (note on Gospel of St John i. 10).

        Antichrist: ii. 18.

    III. The doctrine of Redemption and Consummation.

        The Incarnation: note on iii. 5.

        The titles of Christ: iii. 23 ; comp. iv. 9; v. 1.

        Propitiation: ii. 2.

The virtue of Christ's Blood: i. 7.

Divine Sonship: iii. 1.

The titles of believers: iii. 14.

Divine Fellowship: iv. 15.

Eternal Life: v. 20.

For St John's view of the Bases of Belief I may be allowed to refer to what I have said in regard to his teaching on 'the Truth,' 'the Light,' 'the Witness' in the Introduction to the Gospel, pp. xliv. ff.

INTRODUCTION

TO

THE SECOND AND THIRD EPISTLES

I. TEXT.

THE authorities for the text of the Epistles are enumerated in Authori- the Introduction to the first Epistle, § 1 (including the MSS. ties. אAB(C)KLP). The text of *Cod. Ephr.* (C) is preserved for the third Epistle from *v.* 3—end.

The variations from the text of Stephens (1550) which I have Variations from Stephens, 1550. 2 JOHN. adopted are set down in the following table :

THE SECOND EPISTLE.

3 om. Κυρίου, 'Jesus Christ' (AB), for '*the Lord* Jesus Christ.'

5 γράφων for γράφω (apparently an error).

6 αὕτη ἡ ἐντολή ἐστιν (AB), for αὕτη 'ἐστὶν ἡ ἐντολή.

7 ἐξῆλθαν, *are gone forth* (אAB), for εἰσῆλθον, *are entered.*

8 ἀπολέσητε, *ye* lose (א°AB), for ἀπολέσωμεν, *we* lose.
ἀπολάβητε, *ye* receive (אAB), for ἀπολάβωμεν, *we* receive.

9 προάγων, *goeth onward* (אAB), for παραβαίνων, *transgresseth.*
om. τοῦ χριστοῦ (2°), 'the teaching' (אAB), for 'the teaching *of the Christ.*'

11 ὁ λέγων γάρ (אAB), for ὁ γὰρ λέγων.

12 γενέσθαι (אAB), for ἐλθεῖν.
ὑμῶν (probably) (AB), for ἡμῶν.
πεπληρωμένη ᾖ (אB), for ᾖ πεπληρωμένη.

13 om. Ἀμήν (אAB).

THE THIRD EPISTLE.

3 JOHN.

4 χάριν (probably), *favour* (B), for χαράν, *joy.*
ἐν + τῇ ἀληθείᾳ (ABC*), 'in *the* truth,' for 'in truth.'

5 τοῦτο, *this* (אABC), for εἰς τούς, *to the.*

7 ἐθνικῶν (אABC), for ἐθνῶν.

8 ὑπολαμβάνειν (𝐍ABC*), *to welcome,* for ἀπολαμβάνειν, *to receive.*

9 ἔγραψά + τι´ (𝐍*ABC), 'I wrote *somewhat*,' for 'I wrote.'

11 om. δέ, *but* (𝐍ABC).

12 οἶδας, *thou knowest* (𝐍ABC), for οἴδατε, *ye know.*

13 γράψαι σοι for γράφειν (𝐍ABC).

γράφειν for γράψαι (𝐍ABC).

14 σὲ ἰδεῖν for ἰδεῖν σε (ABC).

The text of B. The text of B maintains the first place as before. It has only one error in 2 John, the omission of τοῦ before πατρός in *v.* 4; and one error in 3 John, ἔγραψας for ἔγραψα in *v.* 9, in addition to two faults of writing, μαρτυρουν for μαρτυρούντων, *v.* 3 (at the end of a line), and ον for οὕς, *v.* 6.

The text of 𝐍. The text of 𝐍 has numerous errors and false readings:

2 JOHN. THE SECOND EPISTLE.

3 ἀπὸ θεοῦ...καὶ 'I. X. 𝐍*.

+ αὐτοῦ´ τοῦ πατρός, 𝐍* corr. 𝐍ᶜ.

4 ἔλαβον.

5 ἀλλ᾽ + ἐντολὴν´ ἦν.

6 ἡ ἐντολὴ + αὐτοῦ´.

περιπατήσητε.

7 om. ὁ´ ἀντίχριστος.

8 ἀπόλησθε 𝐍* corr. 𝐍ᶜ.

12 ἔχω 𝐍* A*.

στόμα + τι´ 𝐍*.

JOHN. THE THIRD EPISTLE.

8 ἐκκλησίᾳ for ἀληθείᾳ 𝐍* (so A).

10 om. ἐκ.

15 ἄσπασαι.

The text of A. There are, as in the first Epistle, many peculiar readings in A, some found also in the Latin Vulgate:

2 JOHN. THE SECOND EPISTLE.

1 οὐκ ἐγὼ δέ.

2 ἐνοικοῦσαν for μένουσαν.

3 om. ἔσται μεθ᾽ ὑμῶν.

4 ἀπό for παρά.

9 τὸν υἱὸν καὶ τὸν πατέρα vg.

12 γράψαι.

ἐλπίζω γάρ vg.

THE THIRD EPISTLE.   3 JOHN.

3 om. σύ.

5 ἐργάζῃ.

8 ἐκκλησίᾳ (so ℵ*).

10 ἄν.

13 οὐκ ἐβουλήθην.

(15 οἱ ἀδελφοί).

There is also an unusual number of peculiar readings in the *The text* part of the third Epistle preserved in C: *of C.* *3 JOHN.*

4 τούτων χαρὰν οὐκ ἔχω.

6 ποιήσας προπέμψεις.

7 ἐθνικῶν om. τῶν.

10 φλυαρῶν εἰς ἡμᾶς.

(ἐπιδεχομένους).

12 ὑπὸ αὐτῆς τῆς ἐκκλησίας καὶ τῆς ἀληθείας.

The readings of the Latin Vulgate do not offer anything of *The text* special interest: *of the Latin Vulgate.* *2 JOHN.*

THE SECOND EPISTLE.

3 *Sit* nobiscum (vobiscum) gratia.

a Christo Jesu.

THE THIRD EPISTLE.   3 JOHN.

4 majorem horum non habeo gratiam.

5 et hoc *in.*

9 *scripsissem forsitan.*

Some Latin copies have a singular addition after 2 John 11 : *ecce prodixi vobis ne in diem domini condemnemini.*

II. AUTHORSHIP.

The second and third Epistles of St John are reckoned by *These* Eusebius among 'the controverted books' in the same rank as the *Epistles reckoned* among 'the controverted Books.'

Epistles of St James, St Jude and 2 Peter[1], 'as well known and recognised by most.' He does not give the authority or the exact ground of the doubt, but states the question generally as being 'whether they belong to the Evangelist, or possibly to another of the same name[2].'

External evidence.

The Epistles are not contained in the Peshito Syriac Version, nor are they accepted by the Syrian Church. Origen was aware that 'all did not allow them to be genuine[3].' There is however no other ante-Nicene evidence against their authenticity. They are noticed as 'received in the Catholic Church' in the Muratorian Canon. This at least appears to be the most probable explanation of the clause. Comp. *Hist. of N. T. Canon*, p. 537. They were included in the Old Latin Version. Clement of Alexandria wrote short notes upon them[4]. Irenæus quotes the second Epistle as St John's, and once quotes a phrase from it as from the first Epistle[5]. There are no quotations from either of the Epistles in Origen, Tertullian, or Cyprian, but Dionysius of Alexandria clearly recognises them as the works of St John; and Aurelius, an African Bishop, quoted the second Epistle as 'St John's Epistle' at a Council where Cyprian was present.

The title 'the Elder' likely to create confusion.

It is not difficult to explain the doubt as to their authorship, which was felt by some. They probably had a very limited circulation from their personal (or narrow) destination. When they were carried abroad under the name of John, the title of 'the elder' was not unlikely to mislead the readers. Papias had spoken of 'an elder John'; and so it was natural to suppose that the John who so styled himself in the Epistles was the one to whom Papias referred, and not the Apostle. Eusebius may refer to this conjecture, though it does not appear distinctly before the time of

---

[1] *H. E.* III. 25 τῶν δὲ ἀντιλεγομένων γνωρίμων δ' οὖν ὅμως τοῖς πολλοῖς.

[2] *l. c.* εἴτε τοῦ εὐαγγελιστοῦ τυγχάνουσαι εἴτε καὶ ἑτέρου ὁμωνύμου ἐκείνῳ. He argued from them himself as being written by St John: *Demonstr. Ev.* III. 5.

[3] *In Joh.* Tom. v. ap. Euseb. *H. E.*

VI. 23.

[4] Euseb. *H. E.* VI. 14. Cf. *Strom.* II. 15.

[5] *Adv. hær.* III. 16. 8, in prædicta Epistola, having quoted in § 5, 1 John ii. 18 ff. Comp. I. 16. 3 Ἰωάννης ὁ τοῦ κυρίου μαθητής.

Jerome[1]. But this view of the authorship of the Epistles is purely conjectural. There is not the least direct evidence external or internal in its favour; and it is most unlikely that 'the elder John' would be in such a position as to be described by the simple title 'the elder,' which denotes a unique preëminence.

On the other hand, there is nothing in the use of the title *Not inapplicable to St John.* ὁ πρεσβύτερος, 'the elder,' by the writer of the Epistles inconsistent with the belief that he was the Apostle St John. For too little is known of the condition of the Churches of Asia Minor at the close of the apostolic age to allow any certain conclusion to be formed as to the sense in which he may have so styled himself. The term was used by Irenæus of those who held the highest office in the Church, perhaps through Asiatic usage, as of Polycarp, and of the early Bishops of Rome[2]; and the absolute use of it in the two Epistles cannot but mark a position wholly exceptional. One who could claim for himself the title 'the elder' must have occupied a place which would not necessarily be suggested by the title of 'an apostle'; and it is perfectly intelligible that St John should have used the title in virtue of which he wrote, rather than that which would have had no bearing upon his communication. As an illustration of the superintendence exercised in the Asiatic Churches by St John, see Euseb. *H. E.* III. 23.

Internal evidence amply confirms the general tenor of external *Internal evidence.* authority. The second Epistle bears the closest resemblance in language and thought to the first. The third Epistle has the closest affinity to the second, though from its subject it is less like the first in general form. Nevertheless it offers many striking parallels to constructions and language of St John: *v.* 3 ἐν ἀληθείᾳ; 4 μειζοτέραν τούτων...ἵνα...; 6, 12 μαρτυρεῖν τινι, 11 ἐκ τοῦ θεοῦ ἐστίν...οὐχ ἑώρακεν τὸν θεόν, 12 οἶδας ὅτι ἡ μαρτ. ἡ. ἀληθής ἐστιν.

The use of the Pauline words προπέμπειν, εὐοδοῦσθαι and ὑγιαίνειν, and of the peculiar words φλυαρεῖν, φιλοπρωτεύειν, ὑπολαμβάνειν (in the sense of 'welcome'), has no weight on the other side.

[1] Jerome however speaks of the opinion as widely held in his time: opinio a plerisque tradita (*de virr. ill.* 18).

[2] Iren. ap. Euseb. *H. E.* v. 20. 24.

The complexion of the third Epistle is not Pauline ; and the exceptional language belongs to the occasion on which it was written.

III. CHARACTER.

The letters contain no direct indication of the time or place at which they were written. They seem to belong to the same period of the Apostle's life as the first Epistle ; and they were therefore probably written from Ephesus.

The destination of the second Letter is enigmatic. No solution of the problem offered by Ἐκλεκτῇ Κυρίᾳ is satisfactory. Nor does the Letter itself offer any marked individuality of address.

Picture of the Church in the third Epistle.
The third Letter, on the other hand, reveals a striking and in some respects unique picture of the condition of the early Church. There is a dramatic vigour in the outlines of character which it indicates. Gaius and Diotrephes have distinct individualities ; and the reference to Demetrius comes in with natural force. Each personal trait speaks of a fulness of knowledge behind, and belongs to a living man. Another point which deserves notice is the view which is given of the independence of Christian societies. Diotrephes, in no remote corner, is able for a time to withstand an Apostle in the administration of his particular Church. On the other side, the calm confidence of St John seems to rest on himself more than on his official power. His presence will vindicate his authority. Once more, the growth of the Churches is as plainly marked as their independence. The first place in them has become an object of unworthy ambition. They are able and, as it appears, for the most part willing to maintain missionary teachers.

Altogether this last glimpse of Christian life in the apostolic age is one on which the student may well linger. The state of things which is disclosed does not come near an ideal, but it witnesses to the freedom and vigour of a growing faith.

JOHANNINE STUDIES SINCE WESTCOTT'S DAY

by F. F. BRUCE, D.D.

Rylands Professor of Biblical Criticism and Exegesis in the
University of Manchester

JOHANNINE STUDIES SINCE WESTCOTT'S DAY

by F. F. BRUCE, D.D.

Rylands Professor of Biblical Criticism and Exegesis in the
University of Manchester

Westcott's Commentaries

To do justice to the course of Johannine studies since B. F. Westcott published his commentaries on the Gospel and Epistles of John would require a work of the dimensions of the late W. F. Howard's *The Fourth Gospel in Recent Criticism and Interpretation* (1931); indeed, so well did Dr. Howard survey the field that, for the period up to 1955 (when a posthumous edition of the work appeared, brought up to date by C. K. Barrett), no further survey is necessary. It will be sufficient here to mention some of the lines along which the study of the Gospel and Epistles has been conducted since Westcott. The Apocalypse will not come within our purview; Westcott did not comment on it, and because of its distinctive character its criticism and interpretation are largely independent of the criticism and interpretation of the other Johannine writings.

The background of Westcott's commentaries on the Johannine Gospel and Epistles has recently been filled in for us in two Bishop Westcott Memorial Lectures—*Westcott as Commentator*, by C. K. Barrett (1958), and *The Vindication of Christianity in Westcott's Thought*, by H. Chadwick (1960). About 1860, with the encouragement of Macmillan the publisher, Westcott agreed with J. B. Lightfoot and F. J. A. Hort that the three of them should collaborate in writing commentaries on the whole of the New Testament. Westcott proposed to reserve for himself the Johannine writings (including the Apocalypse, on which, as has been said, he wrote no commentary) and the Epistle to the Hebrews. These commentaries were part of the exercise of studying and interpreting the history and literature of early Christianity in response to the challenge with which the traditional account had been confronted by the Tübingen school. This exercise, if it was to achieve its purpose, had to be carried through in accordance with the most rigorous canons of critical scholarship, and the three Cambridge scholars were exceptionally well equipped to do so. Granted that Westcott in particular reached conclusions that were in remarkable accord with the traditional account (as indeed he expected they would be), he could not justly be suspected of unscientific methods, or of cooking the evidence so as to produce the desired answer. The attempt made in the work entitled *Supernatural Religion* to fix the charge of intellectual dishonesty on him broke down ignominiously. No doubt Professor Chadwick is right in suggesting that Westcott (and Lightfoot) looked at the Early Church too much through the spectacles of Irenaeus, without taking adequately into account Irenaeus's apologetic interests; but when Westcott examined the evidence, he judged that Irenaeus's interpretation of it was the most probable.

Westcott's first commentary on *The Gospel according to St. John* appeared in 1880 as a volume in the 'Speaker's Commentary' series, published by John Murray. In accordance with the plan of this series, the text printed was the Authorized Version. A reprint of this commentary was published in 1958 by James Clarke, with a new introduction by Canon Adam Fox.

When he consented to prepare this work for the Speaker's Commentary, Westcott reserved the right to use the material in it for a later commentary on the Greek text of the Gospel. For this commentary he prepared a considerable amount of material, but it was unfinished at his death in 1901. It was completed on the basis of material in the earlier commentary, and published (also by John Murray) in two volumes in 1908.

The commentary on the Epistles of John was published by Macmillan in 1883. The commentary on Hebrews followed in 1889. An incomplete work on Ephesians was edited after Westcott's death by J. M. Schulhof and published (also by Macmillan) in 1906.

Linguistic Studies

In all his commentaries Westcott paid the minutest attention to the language of the biblical writers. Professor Barrett illustrates Westcott's gift for word study by referring to the additional note on 1 John ii.2 ('The use of *hilasmos* and cognates in the Greek Scriptures') which appears on pp. 85–87 of this commentary. Of equal importance is the additional note on 1 John iv. 9 ('The use of the term *monogenēs*'). More theological than lexical is his influential note on 1 John i. 7 ('The idea of Christ's Blood in the New Testament'); he acknowledges his indebtedness to William Milligan, but it is mainly to Westcott himself that we owe the wide diffusion of the idea that sacrificial blood 'includes the thought of the life preserved and active beyond death'.

In his word studies, and in his meticulous attention to the finest details of construction in the text, Westcott was unable to avail himself of the knowledge of the Hellenistic vernacular which was just beginning to come to light in his later years. But even if it had come to light earlier, it is doubtful if Westcott would have been greatly impressed by it. As appears from his remarks on pp. v and vi of the preface to this commentary, he had satisfied himself by long experience that the method of calling attention to 'the minutest points of language, construction, order, as serving to illustrate the meaning of St. John', verified itself by its results. Had he been shown that the *koinē* of New Testament times was

marked by considerable looseness in choice of particles, prepositions, pre-
fixes, tenses and word-order, he would probably have replied that this
might well be so, but that his own painstaking studies had assured him
that it was not so in the New Testament writings. It is, no doubt, better
to err on the side of excessive precision than on the other side, but the
fact is that many of the refinements which Westcott detected in the Greek
of the New Testament writers had long since disappeared from Greek of
any kind.

Where Westcott was faced with a non-classical construction, he was
apt to seek a special theological reason for it. Where, for example, 1 John
i.2 speaks of 'the eternal life which was with the Father' and expresses
'with' by the Greek preposition *pros*—used similarly in the prologue to
the Gospel where the Word is said to have been with (*pros*) God (John
i.1, 2)—Westcott explains this non-classical use of *pros* as denoting that
the eternal life was realized with the Father 'for its object and law'. But
within the New Testament itself we have evidence for the contemporary use of *pros* in the most everyday sense of 'with'—in Mark
vi.3, where our Lord's neighbours in Nazareth, speaking quite colloquially,
say: 'are not his sisters here with (*pros*) us?' We can value Westcott's
insights in theological exegesis without basing them so confidently as he
did on the minutiae of linguistic usage.

A Question of Presuppositions

It is not principally in linguistic matters, however, that much treatment of the Johannine literature since Westcott's day has followed
different lines from his.

His Series of concentric arguments ascribing the authorship of the
Fourth Gospel (*a*) to a Jew, (*b*) to a Jew of Palestine, (*c*) to an eyewitness,
(*d*) to an apostle, (*e*) to John the son of Zebedee, was cogent enough to
those who shared his presuppositions, as at the time the majority of
British exegetes did. But those who approached the question with other
presuppositions could account for the evidence which formed the basis of
Westcott's arguments by suggesting that the author wrote a fictitious
narrative under the guise of an apostolic eyewitness, relying on some local
colour to give his account verisimilitude. The arguments for identifying
the Beloved Disciple of the Fourth Gospel with the son of Zebedee could
be weakened if that disciple were regarded not as an individual but as an
ideal figure representing one who is a 'disciple indeed'.

Westcott's position, moreover, was unacceptable to those engaged
in the old 'quest of the historical Jesus' who relied on Mark's Gospel
as their basic source. Not only were some of them acutely conscious of
the difficulty of reconciling the Johannine and Markan portraits of Jesus;
there was also a tendency to regard the Markan outline of the ministry
as so consecutive and watertight that Johannine material which could not
be fitted into it must be rejected for historical purposes. This extreme
form of the 'Markan hypothesis' was increasingly rejected from the end

of the nineteenth century onwards, but as late as 1907, in his preface to
the second edition of *The Gospel History and its Transmission*, F. C.
Burkitt gives as his chief reason for doubting the historicity of the Johannine narrative of the raising of Lazarus the impossibility of explaining
'how and where the tale as told in the Fourth Gospel can possibly be
inserted into the framework given by S. Mark' (pp. vii f.). That no
scholar of Burkitt's calibre would think of appealing to such an argument
today is a measure of the difference that form criticism has made to our
thinking. In the hands of many of its exponents, indeed, form criticism
has been far from rehabilitating Westcott's position; it has tended rather
to emphasize that chronological sequence can no more be found in Mark
than in John, that Mark's record is as much theologically conditioned as
is John's, and that for many parts of both records the life-setting is to be
looked for in the experience of the primitive church. In the hands of
others, as we shall see, form criticism can yield more positive conclusions; but at least the Markan record is no longer treated as the norm
by which the Johannine record is to be judged and found wanting. This
consideration may even relieve, though it does not resolve, the discrep-
ancy between the 'Messianic secret' of Mark and the open avowal of
Jesus' Messiahship from the beginning in John. The difference in idiom
between the Synoptic and Johannine accounts of Jesus' teaching (even
when we take into account Matt. xi. 25-27 and its parallel Luke x.21, 22)
must, however, be accounted for on other than form-critical lines.

Composite Authorship ?

At the beginning of a discussion of 'The Riddle of the Fourth Gospel' C. A. Anderson Scott asserted: 'The famous proof of the Johannine
authorship with which Westcott made some of us familiar has broken
down. He began by assuming that the Gospel was all written by one hand,
and when that assumption had to be given up, some essential steps in
his argument went too' (*Living Issues in the New Testament*, 1933, p.86).
But Westcott's 'assumption' —even if that was all it was—has tended to
be confirmed rather than weakened by the inadequacy of those theories
that have envisaged more hands than one in the composition of the
Fourth Gospel. Anderson Scott mentions the studies of R. H. Strachan
(*The Fourth Gospel, its Significance and Environment*, 1917; *The Fourth
Evangelist: Dramatist or Historian?*, 1925) and A. E. Garvie (*The Beloved
Disciple*, 1922) which, though their authors are not 'extreme critics', find
at least three hands in the Gospel. But when Strachan in 1941 produced
the third edition of *The Fourth Gospel, its Significance and Environment*,
he was so dissatisfied with his earlier views that he found it necessary to
rewrite the book almost completely, and proclaimed that he had joined
the ranks of those 'who are convinced that the Gospel is essentially a
literary unity' (p. v). Garvie distinguished (i) the Witness, identified with
the beloved disciple but not with the son of Zebedee, (ii) the evangelist,
perhaps to be identified with John the elder, and (iii) the redactor, who

was responsible for the sixth and twenty-first chapters and a few other passages. This was a modification of the theory of B. W. Bacon (*Introduction to the New Testament*, 1900; *The Fourth Gospel in Research and Debate*, 1910), except that Bacon gave a larger part to the redactor, dismissed the figure of John the elder as too shadowy to merit serious consideration, and regarded the beloved disciple as an ideal portrait, based (in so far as it was based on any historical person) on Paul, in the light of his words in Gal. ii.20. It was the second-century redactor who, in the twenty-first chapter, hinted at the identification of the beloved disciple with the son of Zebedee in order to invest the Gospel with the prestige of apostolic authorship.

Such criticism is more ingenious than convincing; to distinguish between one hand and another in the body of the Gospel is an almost entirely subjective exercise. The twenty-first chapter indeed, coming as an appendix or epilogue after the concluding sentence of the previous chapter, does raise a question of literary criticism; and some exegetes have recognized a problem of composition in the discourse on the bread of life in the sixth chapter. But for the most part, the Gospel defies analysis of this kind.

G. H. C. Macgregor in his Moffatt Commentary on the Gospel (*The Gospel of John*, 1928) distinguishes between the evangelist (John the elder, who knew and admired the beloved disciple) and the redactor, who was responsible for the twenty-first chapter and certain other passages, giving the work its final shape. In a later work, *The Structure of the Fourth Gospel* (1961), in which Macgregor enjoyed the collaboration of A. Q. Morton, the conclusion was reached that Macgregor's earlier analysis was largely confirmed by the method of literary statistics.

The most interesting of recent attempts to analyse the Gospel has taken quite a different form. In his commentary in the Meyer series, *Das Evangelium des Johannes*, first published in 1941 (several subsequent editions have appeared since then), Rudolf Bultmann finds two main sources in the Gospel—one consisting of revelatory discourses and the other a book of signs—together with a good deal of redactional material, all of which the Evangelist has brought together to serve a purpose of his own (see p. lxvi below).

But few of these theories which envisage a variety of hands in the Gospel have convinced many apart from their proponents. For many readers the simile of D. F. Strauss is still valid—the Gospel is like its own seamless robe, woven in one piece throughout. The discourses which follow the 'signs' in the earlier part of the work are meditations which bring out their significance; the upper room discourses and high-priestly prayer which precede the passion narrative similarly bring out the significance of what follows them. The whole work expounds the successive themes which are briefly introduced in the prologue. And whatever is the precise relation of the epilogue of chapter xxi to all that goes before it, it is completely in character with the body of the Gospel.

Dislocation of Text ?

Theories of primitive dislocation of the text of the Gospel do not affect its unity as the aforementioned theories do. A number of attempts to restore the Gospel to what editors conceive to have been its original order have been published from time to time; the best known of these are those which are followed in Moffatt's translation of the New Testament. A specially strong case can be made out for the view that chapter vi originally preceded chapter v (although this is not one of the rearrangements adopted by Moffatt). It is indeed conceivable that at an early stage, antedating our earliest manuscript evidence for the Gospel, some of its sheets were wrongly arranged. But our ideas of the logical order of the material in the Gospel may not have been the Evangelist's, and a large question-mark must be set against even the most probable of the suggested rearrangements. (The relegation of the incident about the woman taken in adultery, John vii.53–viii.11, to a footnote, as in R.S.V., or to an appendix, as in N.E.B., is in a different case; this incident did not originally belong to any part of the Fourth Gospel.)

Early Death of John the Apostle

The change in the climate of opinion regarding the Fourth Gospel that followed Westcott's conservatism was not due in any substantial degree to the discovery of fresh evidence. One alleged piece of evidence that was pressed by some scholars about the beginning of the twentieth century was that John the Apostle died early, perhaps at the same time as his brother James (Acts xii.2), and must on this ground as well as others be ruled out as author of the Gospel. This was the interpretation placed by Wellhausen on the oracle of Jesus about the sons of Zebedee in Mark x.39, and it was held to be confirmed by the De Boor fragment of the Epitome of the History of Philip of Side (c. A.D.450), published in 1888, according to which 'Papias in his second book says that John the theologian and James his brother were killed by the Jews' (cf. the statement of the ninth-century Georgios Hamartolos, according to the *codex Coislinianus*, that John 'was deemed worthy of martyrdom, for Papias, in the second book of his *Dominical Oracles*, says that he was killed by the Jews'). Although this evidence for the early martyrdom of John, marshalled by E. Schwartz (*Uber den Tod der Söhne Zebedaei*, 1904), was accepted by many scholars, including F. C. Burkitt, R. H. Charles, J. Moffatt and B. W. Bacon, others have regarded it as tenuous in the extreme and contradicted by implication by writers much nearer to the time of Papias than Philip of Side or Georgios Hamartolos; W. F. Howard quotes A. S. Peake as saying (in the *Holborn Review* 19, 1928, p. 394) that 'the slenderness of this evidence . . . would have provoked derision if it had been adduced in favour of a conservative conclusion'. But certainty as to what Papias really said must await the rediscovery of his *Exegesis of the Dominical Oracles*, lost since the fourteenth century.

A Hellenizing Gospel ?

But whatever the truth about this evidence might be, the acceptance of the apostolic authorship of the Gospel seemed impossible to those who adopted the religio-historical method of New Testament interpretation, which was becoming very popular around the turn of the century, and saw in the Fourth Gospel an advanced stage in that acute Hellenization of Christianity which developed on the one hand into the full-blown Gnostic systems of the second century and on the other hand into the theological definitions which culminated in Chalcedonian orthodoxy.

Even the shadowy 'Elder John' of the well-known Papias fragment preserved by Eusebius (*Hist. Eccl.*iii.39.4) was a doubtful candidate for the authorship of such a work. F. von Hügel might speak of 'the very real and substantial Presbyter' who certainly lived at Ephesus (article 'John, Gospel of' in *Enc. Brit.*, edn. 11, 1911), and B. H. Streeter might provide him with something of a biography (*The Four Gospels*, 1924, pp. 365 ff.); but W. R. Inge, who shared their mystical exegesis of this Gospel, regarded the Elder as 'nebulous' (*Cambridge Biblical Essays*, ed. H. B. Swete, 1909, p. 253), and B. W. Bacon scornfully dismissed the whole reconstruction of the Elder John of Ephesus as 'a higher critical mare's nest of the purest breed' (*Hibbert Journal* 29, 1930–31, p. 321).

It is interesting to note that Von Hügel's *Encyclopaedia Britannica* article (which, it is said, he contributed after Alfred Loisy had been invited and declined) moved William Sanday from the rather conservative position which he had maintained in *The Criticism of the Fourth Gospel*, 1905 (see his *The Divine Overruling*, 1920, p.61).

Whether the Fourth Gospel was interpreted as a mystical meditation on the life of Jesus in the mind of a creative artist, or as a reinterpretation of His story in terms of Hellenistic culture, its value as a historical document was reckoned as rather small, although its value as a work of spiritual devotion remained unimpaired. While a few sturdy souls, like H. P. V. Nunn (*The Son of Zebedee*, 1927), refused to be influenced by the climate of opinion, others who dissented from it, like C. E. Raven, were so conscious of its pervasive strength that they thought twice before endangering their scholarly reputations by setting pen to paper and defying the 'Johannine taboo' (cf. Raven, *Jesus and the Gospel of Love*, 1931, p. 165).

A new and welcome note was struck with the posthumous publication of Sir Edwyn C. Hoskyns' *The Fourth Gospel*, edited by F. N. Davey (1940). The translator of Barth's *Römerbrief* and joint-author of *The Riddle of the New Testament* (1931) was a pioneer in the new Biblical Theology movement in England, and his work on John's Gospel is a major contribution to this Biblical theology. Questions of authorship and the like are regarded as not particularly important, or indeed as entirely elusive; what is important is the interpretation of the history of Jesus provided by this Gospel, an interpretation which makes sense of the contents of the Synoptic Gospels. To read the Fourth Gospel is to find oneself 'at the very heart of that Apostolic Christianity which must be radically distinguished from mysticism on the one hand and from mere historical reminiscences on the other' (p. 122). *Mutatis mutandis,* Hoskyns is in substantial agreement with Calvin's approach: 'I am accustomed to say that this Gospel is a key to open the door to the understanding of the others. For whoever grasps the power of Christ as it is here graphically portrayed, will afterwards read with advantage what the others relate about the manifested Redeemer' (Argument to Calvin's *Commentary on the Gospel of John*).

Among contemporary scholars, Rudolf Bultmann has continued to maintain with high distinction the Hellenizing character of the Fourth Gospel. His views on its teaching may be found not only in his commentary in the Meyer series but also in the section on the theology of the Johannine Gospels and Epistles in his *Theology of the New Testament,* Vol. II (1955). He attaches special importance to the revelatory discourses, in which he finds Jesus portrayed as the heavenly Revealer and Redeemer of Gnostic mythology. The Evangelist demythologizes the Gnostic substance while retaining the Gnostic framework; in other words, he transforms the cosmological dualism of Gnosticism into a dualism of decision. The coming of Jesus as the True Light is 'the judgment (*krisis*) of the world' (John iii.19; xii.31) in the sense that it makes possible for man the decision which sets him free from bondage to a world shrouded in darkness. Thus the message of the Fourth Gospel turns out to be almost identical with Professor Bultmann's existential interpretation of Christianity.

His reconstruction of the Gnostic myth as he envisages it in the Mandaic documents which are some centuries later than the Fourth first century A.D. is extremely precarious, especially when he draws upon Gospel. But his exegesis of this Gospel is basic to his whole New Testament theology; his interpretation of the Fourth Evangelist goes far to supply the presuppositions with which he undertakes the interpretation of other New Testament writers, and reveals a deep-seated sympathy with the mind of the Evangelist.

One interesting argument of Professor Bultmann's is that all the sacramental elements in the Fourth Gospel are later accretions. This represents the opposite pole of interpretation from Oscar Cullmann, who finds the whole Gospel permeated with sacramental teaching, so much so that it becomes a source of considerable value in investigating the sacramental faith and life of the early Church ('The Gospel according to St. John and Early Christian Worship,' *Early Christian Worship,* 1953, pp. 37 ff.).

R. H. Lightfoot's posthumous work, *St. John's Gospel: A Commentary* (1956), edited for publication by C. F. Evans, remarks that the traditional identification of the Evangelist with the son of Zebedee 'still receives support, and has never been shown to be impossible' (p. 2); it notes, however, that 'it has been increasingly realized that the value and importance of the book within the fourfold gospel does not stand or fall with its authorship by the son of Zebedee' and apparently endorses 'the growing conviction that not the fourth gospel only but all the gospels have been affected by the momentous events which took place in the development and expansion of the Church's life and thought in the first century' (p. 7). At the time of his death Lightfoot had practically completed the exposition and notes, based on the text of the Revised Version; they are a valuable help to the study of the Gospel.

Of recent English commentaries on the Fourth Gospel the most important, and the one most worthy to rank with Westcott's, is that by C. K. Barrett (1955). 'The most illuminating background of the fourth gospel is Hellenistic Judaism', he finds (p. 33). Like Philo, the Evangelist was familiar with basic Hellenistic ideas, and set out to present persuasively to a new public an originally Semitic faith. John was concerned to root the truth unfolded in Jesus not so much in individual incidents as in the total fact of the Incarnation. For example, instead of recording the institution of the Eucharist, he gives us the discourse of the sixth chapter in order to teach just what is meant by Christian belief in Jesus as the bread of life. While superficially he differs from the Synoptists (of which he was probably acquainted with two), yet at a deeper level he is theologically akin to them, expressing the significance of their narratives in other terms, as he clarifies Jesus' relation to God and 'universalizes the manhood of Jesus' (p. 45)—i.e. he represents Jesus not simply as *a man* but as the Son of God who has taken on Himself *humanity*.

Professor Barrett suggests that John the apostle migrated to Ephesus, where he lived to old age and composed apocalyptic works, which one of his disciples incorporated about A.D. 96 in the book of the Revelation. Another (or two others) of his disciples wrote the Johannine Epistles; yet another disciple, of profounder mind than that to be discerned in the Epistles, composed the first twenty chapters of the Gospel, to which the twenty-first chapter was added when the Gospel was published in orthodox circles.

'What does emerge from the evidence,' says Professor Barrett, 'is, not that the gospel as it stands is a first-hand historical document but that those responsible for it were seriously concerned about the meaning and authority of the apostolic witness to the history of Jesus' (p. 101). When it was composed, the problems which had beset the Church in the Pauline age were largely things of the past; the Fourth Evangelist and his contemporaries had to face the problems of Christian eschatology (preeminently the deferment of the parousia) and of Gnosticism. The treatment of the latter problem in the Fourth Gospel caused orthodox Christians at first to view it with considerable reserve (cf. J. N. Sanders, *The Fourth Gospel in the Early Church*, 1943). It took some time for them to realize that the Fourth Evangelist had provided the most effective refutation of Gnosticism. 'In an age when the first formulations of the Christian faith were seen by some to be unsatisfactory, when gnosticism in its various forms was perverting the Gospel and adopting it for its own uses, he attempted and achieved the essential task of setting forth the faith once delivered to the saints in the new idiom, for the winning of new converts to the Church, for the strengthening of those who were unsettled by the new winds of doctrine, and for the more adequate exposition of the faith itself' (Barrett, *op. cit.*, p. 21).

It is true that some Gnostics made use of the Fourth Gospel for their own purposes, although a Gospel which bore witness to the Word made flesh must in the end prove fatal to Gnosticism. But in view of this early tendency to use the Gospel in Gnostic interests, it is interesting to observe J. A. T. Robinson's view that the characteristic emphases of the Johannine Epistles 'can best . . . be understood if they are seen as necessary correctives to deductions drawn from the teaching of the fourth Gospel by a gnosticizing movement within Greek-speaking Diaspora Judaism' ('The Destination and Purpose of the Johannine Epistles,' *NTS* 7, 1960-61, pp. 56 ff.).

Palestinian Background

Even when the Hellenistic character of the Gospel was being most strongly pressed, however, there were not lacking those who persisted in reminding their colleagues of the pervasive Jewish element in the Gospel, and their number and influence have tended to increase. From the publication in 1902 of *Die Sprache und Heimat des vierten Evangelisten* Adolf Schlatter continued for upward of thirty years to show that not only is the Gospel's topography Palestinian but also that its thought can be paralleled time and time again from the literature of rabbinic Judaism. Israel Abrahams, an outstanding rabbinist in his day, referred in 1909 to 'the cumulative strength of the arguments adduced by Jewish writers favourable to the authenticity of the discourses in the Fourth Gospel, especially in relation to the circumstances in which they are reported to have been spoken' (*Cambridge Biblical Essays*, ed. H. B. Swete, p. 181), and spoke some years later of his 'own general impression, without asserting an early date for the Fourth Gospel', as being that 'the Gospel enshrines a genuine tradition of an aspect of Jesus' teaching which has not found a place in the Synoptics' (*Studies in Pharisaism and the Gospels*, i, 1917, p. 12). Another scholar who gave due weight to the rabbinic affinities of the Gospel was H. Odeberg (*The Fourth Gospel interpreted in its Relation to Contemporaneous Religious Currents*, 1929); it is to the detriment of his work, however, that he included Mandaism among the 'contemporaneous religious currents' to be reckoned with in the study of the Gospel.

The discovery and publication of the Syriac version of the long lost *Odes of Solomon* by J. Rendel Harris in 1909 suggested that here was a body of faintly Gnostic literature much more relevant to the Fourth Gospel than were the Mandaic texts; A. Jülicher is said to have remarked, in view of their religious idiom, that if Rendel Harris's early dating of the *Odes* could be established, 'all our criticism of the Fourth Gospel is *kaput*'.

The Jewishness of the Fourth Gospel was pressed to its utmost extreme by those scholars who saw in it the Greek translation of a document originally written in Aramaic. Foremost among these was C. F.

Burney (*The Aramaic Origin of the Fourth Gospel*, 1922); substantially the same position was maintained by C. C. Torrey (*The Four Gospels*, 1933; *Our Translated Gospels*, 1936) and J. de Zwaan ('John wrote in Aramaic', *JBL* 57, 1938, pp. 155 ff.). The thesis in this form can scarcely be sustained; G. R. Driver, reviewing Burney's book, suggested that the evidence could be satisfied if 'St. John was mentally translating as he wrote *logia*, handed down by tradition and current in Christian circles in Aramaic, from that language into the Greek in which he was actually composing his Gospel' (*The Original Language of the Fourth Gospel*, reprint from *The Jewish Guardian*, Jan. 1923).

In her pioneer study *The Fourth Gospel and Jewish Worship* (1960), Aileen Guilding has argued that the discourses in the Gospel are based on the biblical passages prescribed in the triennial Jewish lectionary for the periods of the year at which, according to the Evangelist, the discourses were delivered.

Every discovery pertaining to the religious history of the Near East around the beginning of the Christian era has been hailed as providing the key to unlock the mystery of the Fourth Gospel, and this has been so with the Qumran literature, discovered in 1947 and the following years. Among the scholars who have discussed the affinities of the Gospel with the Qumran texts have been W. F. Albright ('Recent Discoveries in Palestine and the Gospel of St. John', in *The Background of the New Testament and its Eschatology*, ed. W. D. Davies and D. Daube, 1956, pp. 153 ff.), Lucetta Mowry ('The Dead Sea Scrolls and the Gospel of John', *The Biblical Archæologist* 17, 1954, pp. 78 ff.), G. Baumbach (*Qumran und das Johannes-Evangelium*, 1958), and L. Morris (*The Dead Sea Scrolls and St. John's Gospel*, 1960). The principal points of contact are found in a comparison of the distinctive vocabulary and concepts of the Gospel with those of the Qumran texts. Such characteristic Johannine expressions as 'the sons of light', ' the light of life ', ' walking in darkness ', ' doing the truth ', ' the works of God ', turn up in the writings of the Qumran community. Like the men of Qumran, the Fourth Evangelist sees the world in terms of sharply contrasted light and darkness, good and evil, truth and falsehood. Professor Albright's contention is that John—and not John alone among New Testament writers—draws 'from a common reservoir of terminology and ideas which were well known to the Essenes and presumably familiar also to other Jewish sects of the period '. These affinities, however, should not be allowed to overshadow the new element in John's use of these concepts. When John speaks of the true light, he is not thinking in abstractions or referring primarily to a body of teaching or a holy community; for him the true light is identical with the Word made flesh. Professor Albright rightly emphasizes the 'wide gulf between the doctrines of the Essenes and the essentials of Johannine teaching '—essentials which relate to the function of the Messiah, the salvation of sinners, the ministry of healing, and the gospel of love.

In trying to account for the Qumran affinities of the Johannine writings, some have bethought themselves of the high probability that the beloved disciple of the Fourth Gospel was at one stage of his career a follower of John the Baptist, who in turn may have had some contact with an Essene group before he began his baptismal ministry (cf. especially J. A. T. Robinson, 'The Baptism of John and the Qumran Community', *HTR* 50, 1957, pp. 175 ff.). But these particular affinities belong to the larger question of the more general affinities between Qumran and early Christianity, a question which has been dealt with conspicuously well by M. Black (*The Scrolls and Christian Origins,* 1961). Professor Black explores certain affinities which have emerged between the Qumran community and the Samaritans, as representatives of a wider strand of nonconformity in Israel. The reference to Samaritans in the Fourth Gospel (e.g. the Jews' designation of Jesus as a Samaritan in John viii. 48, because of the trend of His teaching in the discourse immediately preceding) calls for further consideration in the light of recent research into Samaritan theology (cf. J. Macdonald, *The Theology of the Samaritans,* 1964).

The Samaritan narrative of John iv, also, can now be recognized as having its proper life-setting in an earlier phase of Jesus' ministry than that recorded by the synoptists. John the Baptist, according to John iii. 23, engaged in a brief baptismal ministry in the neighbourhood of Shechem (cf. W. F. Albright, *op.cit.,* p. 159), and when Jesus, visiting the same area a little later with His disciples, told them that they had entered into the labour of 'others' (John iv. 38), we may reasonably see a reference to this earlier ministry, and not a reading back into the ministry of the situation created by Philip's Samaritan mission of Acts viii (see J. A. T. Robinson, 'The "Others" of John 4:38', *Twelve New Testament Studies,* 1962, pp. 61 ff., against O. Cullmann, 'Samaria and the Origins of the Christian Mission', *The Early Church,* 1956, pp. 185 ff.).

The New Look

Among papers read at the 'Four Gospels Congress' held in Oxford in 1957, special importance attaches to contributions by W. C. van Unnik and J. A. T. Robinson. Discussing 'The Purpose of St. John's Gospel' (see *The Gospels Reconsidered,* 1960, pp. 167 ff.), Professor van Unnik revived the thesis of K. Bornhäuser (*Das Johannesevangelium eine Missionsschrift für Israel,* 1928), that this Gospel was basically a missionary document calculated to bring Jewish readers to faith in Christ. Bishop Robinson, presenting 'The New Look on the Fourth Gospel' (see *The Gospels Reconsidered,* pp. 154 ff.), took issue with 'five generally agreed presuppositions' on which current critical orthodoxy regarding this Gospel has been accustomed to rest. 'These are: (1) That the fourth Evangelist is dependent on sources, including (normally) one or more of the Synoptic Gospels. (2) That his own background is other than that of the events and teaching he is purporting to record. (3) That he is not to be regarded, seriously, as a witness to the Jesus of history, but simply to the Christ of faith. (4) That he represents the end-term of theological development in first-century Christianity. (5) That he is not himself the Apostle John nor a direct eyewitness.' The 'new look' challenges these propositions, and instead of accepting the view that the distinctive tradition of the ministry of Jesus preserved in the Fourth Gospel came 'out of the blue' at the end of the first century, affirms that there is 'a real continuity not merely in the memory of one old man, but in the life of an ongoing community, with the earliest days of Christianity.' The Bishop of Woolwich thus stands in the authentic succession of his uncle, J. Armitage Robinson (author of *The Historical Character of St. John's Gospel*, 1929). Not many readers of *Honest to God* (1963) have noticed that, for all its iconoclasm, it takes a conservative line on the authorship of the Fourth Gospel (see p. 52).

Independent Authority

In 1938 there appeared a little book entitled *Saint John and the Synoptic Gospels*, by P. Gardner-Smith, which pioneered the challenge to the first presupposition listed above by Bishop Robinson—that the Fourth Evangelist was dependent on one or more of the Synoptic Gospels. This presupposition had shown itself in a great variety of ways; for some, John deliberately avoided covering much of the ground which he knew to have been covered adequately by his predecessors; for others, he deliberately set himself to correct at point after point the statements or impressions which they made; for others again, he constructed parabolic narratives and meditative discourses out of incidents which he found in their records. Mr. Gardner-Smith exposed what he called 'the false assumption of St. John's dependence upon the Synoptists' and pointed out two consequences that followed if his thesis were established—(i) that the Fourth Gospel could now be regarded as an *independent* authority for the life of Jesus and (ii) that its historical value might be very great. It is a measure of the influence of this little book that its thesis, which few would have treated seriously before 1938, is now accepted by many New Testament scholars and is a well-known and respected thesis even to those who do not accept it.

If the Markan and Johannine narratives are independent, then the greater importance attaches to those features which they have in common —such as the central and crucial place occupied in Jesus' ministry by the feeding of the multitude and its aftermath, including Peter's confession.

In *The Historicity of the Fourth Gospel* (1960) A. J. B. Higgins, accepting Mr. Gardner-Smith's thesis, strengthens it with arguments of his own and presents a strong case for recognizing this Gospel as an independent historical document, which is not even necessarily the fourth in chronological sequence.

Mr. Gardner-Smith's thesis has been further strengthened by certain form-critical arguments. Form-critical analysis has even brought to light in the Fourth Gospel hidden 'parables' of a kind which were formerly believed to be absent from it—parables not derived from the Synoptic parables, but sharing a common origin with them (cf. J. A. T. Robinson,

'The Parable of the Shepherd', *ZNW* 46, 1955, pp. 233 ff.; C. H. Dodd, 'Une parabole cachée dans le quatrième Evangile', *Revue d'histoire et de philosophie religieuses*, 42, 1962, pp. 107 ff.). Again, in a lecture on 'The Dialogue Form in the Gospels' (*BJRL* 37, 1954–55, pp. 54 ff.) C. H. Dodd compared the dialogues in the Synoptic Gospels with those in John and showed how they differed in form; yet alongside the diversity in form there could be traced a community of theme suggesting that the Synoptic and Johannine traditions go back to an earlier 'unformed' tradition. He added that more of this 'unformed' tradition of Jesus' teaching might lie behind those Johannine dialogues which have no parallel in the Synoptic tradition, although they can be integrated with it. He conceded that the recognition of such material must call for very delicate judgment, but considered the quest to be far from hopeless.

Of all contemporary British scholars who have contributed to the Johannine debate, none has done so in a more distinguished manner than Professor Dodd. In his inaugural lecture as Norris-Hulse Professor of Divinity at Cambridge in 1936 he declared that the interpretation of the Fourth Gospel was not only one of the outstanding tasks of the time but the crucial test of success or failure in solving the problem of the New Testament as a whole, since this Gospel was like the keystone of an arch which was failing to hold together. How thoroughly he gave himself to this task in the years that followed may be seen in his two great works: *The Interpretation of the Fourth Gospel* (1953) and *Historical Tradition in the Fourth Gospel* (1964).

The Fourth Gospel was written, Professor Dodd holds, for a Hellenistic public far removed in time and place from the people among whom the evangelic events took place. The climate of thought in which this public lived he finds most clearly indicated by the literature of rabbinic Judaism, Philo, and the Hermetic writings, and the distinctive character of Johannine Christianity may be gauged by observing the transformation which it wrought in ideas which in a general way it shares with contemporary religious movements. While personal links between the Evangelist and the ministry of Jesus may be rather tenuous, he is recognized to be faithful to the main outline of the early apostolic preaching, and to have access to an independent tradition of the ministry.

> He makes use of the strongest expressions for union with God that contemporary religious language provided, in order to assure his readers that he does seriously mean what he says: that through faith in Christ we may enter into a personal community of life with the eternal God, which has the character of *agapē*, which is essentially supernatural and not of this world, and yet plants its feet firmly in this world, not only because real *agapē* cannot but express itself in practical conduct, but also because the crucial act of *agapē* was actually performed in history, on an April day about A.D.30, at a supper-table in Jerusalem, in a garden across the Kidron Valley, in the headquarters of Pontius Pilate, and on a Roman cross at Golgotha. So concrete, so actual, is the nature of the divine *agapē*; yet none the less for that, by entering into the relation of *agapē* thus opened up for men, we may dwell in God and He in us (*Interpretation*, pp. 199 f.).

In his *Historical Tradition in the Fourth Gospel,* Professor Dodd examines in detail the independent tradition which he believes the Evangelist to have followed. His conclusions are these. This tradition contained a fuller account of John the Baptist's ministry than that which was available to the Synoptic Evangelists, and included testimonies on his part to the messianic status of Jesus. It transmitted a credible account of an early ministry of Jesus in southern Palestine, and preserved a considerable body of topographical information about this region. It probably had more to say about the Galilaean ministry than survives in the Fourth Gospel in its present form, and contained information about Jesus's healing activities in Galilee and Judaea alike. It had a full and detailed passion narrative. It preserved a body of sayings, parables and dialogues drawn from the same general reservoir as those in the Synoptic Gospels; and in respect of those sayings which predict the return of Christ, it reaches back to an earlier stage than anything found in the other Gospels. The implications of these findings, based as they are on long and meticulous examination of the data, for the worth of the Fourth Gospel as a source for the story of Jesus, need no underlining.

The Johannine Epistles

On the relation between the First Epistle of John and the Fourth Gospel, Westcott says above (p. xxx, n. 1): 'The arguments which have been alleged to support the opinion that the Books were by different authors do not seem to me to need serious examination. They could not be urged if the books were not detached from life and criticised without regard to their main characteristics.' Over a quarter of a century later Dom John Chapman could dismiss the matter curtly with the remark that 'no sane critic will deny that the Gospel and the first Epistle are from the same pen' (*John the Presbyter and the Fourth Gospel,* 1911, p. 72). By this remark he presumably meant to exclude from the category of 'sane critics' those writers (mainly German) who had denied this identity of authorship, but his prediction (whether it was meant as one or not) was falsified when C. H. Dodd, a 'sane critic' if ever there was one, deviated from what he acknowledged to be 'the unvarying tradition from early times' ('The First Epistle of John and the Fourth Gospel', *BJRL* 21, 1937, pp. 129 ff.).

Professor Dodd's arguments for diversity of authorship are partly linguistic and party material. One of the linguistic arguments is that the Epistle contains none of the Aramaisms which characterize the Greek of the Gospel. Among the material arguments he sees differences between the two writings with regard to the parousia, the atonement and the Paraclete. The Gospel presents a realized eschatology, the Epistle a futurist eschatology.

A few British scholars had previously expressed some scepticism about the identity of authorship of the two documents (cf. E. F. Scott,

The Fourth Gospel, 1906, pp. 88f., 94; J. Moffatt, *Introduction to the Literature of the NT*[3], 1918, pp. 589 ff.). More outright denials of the identity had come from a number of German scholars (cf. H. Windisch, *Die katholischen Briefe*[2], 1930, pp. 109 ff.). But none had supported the case against the identity with such a careful array of evidence as Professor Dodd. Since 1937 a few other British scholars have been disposed to follow him; in particular C. K. Barrett (*The Gospel according to St. John*, p. 113) ascribes the First Epistle to a pupil of the Apostle John, but not the pupil (a 'bolder thinker' than his fellow-pupils) who wrote John i–xx. On the other hand, identity of authorship has been maintained by W. F. Howard ('The Common Authorship of the Johannine Gospel and Epistles', *JTS* 48, 1947, pp. 12 ff., reprinted in *The Fourth Gospel in Recent Criticism and Interpretation*[4], 1955, pp. 282 ff.) and T. W. Manson (*On Paul and John*, 1963, pp. 85 ff.); Manson is so sure that the Gospel and the Epistle present 'the theology of a single school or quite probably of a single author' that he goes to 1 John in the first instance to determine the Evangelist's distinctive lines of thought, since in the Gospel it is difficult to distinguish between the Evangelist's own thought and the teaching of Jesus which he reproduces.

In his volume on *The Johannine Epistles* in the Moffatt series (1946), C. H. Dodd suggests that when the author says 'we' in his introduction ('That which . . . we have heard, which we have seen with our eyes . . .'), he is not claiming to be an eyewitness but using the pronoun corporately, meaning 'we Christians'; he compares 'I brought you up out of the land of Egypt' in Amos ii. 10, centuries after the Exodus. But the contrast between 'we' and 'you' in 1 John i. 3 ('that which we have seen and heard we proclaim also to you, so that you may have fellowship with us') suggests that an eyewitness is communicating what he knows to younger fellow-Christians who were not eyewitnesses, so that they may share his experience as far as possible.

Professor Dodd's commentary, however, has carried the study of 1 John forward quite substantially. Its doctrinal basis, he shows, is common apostolic Christianity, the *kerygma* and *didache* of which appear here as 'the gospel' and 'the commandment'. The gospel proclaims the manifestation of divine love in the historic fact that 'God sent his only Son into the world, so that we might live through him' 1 John iv. 9); the commandment applies the practical lesson to the lives of believers: 'if God so loved us, we also ought to love one another' (iv. 11).

A number of writers have concentrated attention on the series of apodictive antitheses in 1 John ii. 29–iii. 10, and some have characterized them as belonging to an earlier Gnostic document (cf. R. Bultmann, 'Analyse des ersten Johannesbriefes', *Festgabe für A. Jülicher*, 1927, pp. 138 ff.). W. Nauck (*Die Tradition und der Charakter des ersten Johannesbriefes*, 1957) denies the Gnostic character of the antitheses, and while he recognizes them as constituting a previously-existing document, he considers this document to be the work of the author of the Epistle, who later used the series of antitheses as the basis of a baptismal homily addressed to his 'little children'. From this last viewpoint he studies the reference in

1 John v. 8 to 'the Spirit, the water and the blood', and takes the language here to reflect a situation (attested for Syria, by contrast with the Christian West) where the accepted order in Christian initiation was (1) the reception of the Spirit, (2) baptism, (3) the first Eucharist. He finds affinities between this primitive Christian order and the practice of certain Jewish communities, as witnessed by the Qumran literature, the *Testament of Levi* and the treatise *Joseph and Aseneth* (first century A.D.).

In the light of recent study of 1 John, it is reasonable to recognize its occasion in a crisis created by a considerable secession from the churches in the province of Asia in favour of an attractive and 'advanced' form of teaching, characterized by a docetic Christology and an anti-nomian ethic. The writer, who was in the Christian movement 'from the beginning', was in a position to expose this new teaching as a deviation from the apostolic gospel, since it denied the reality of the incarnation of the Son of God and set little store by the dominical commandment of love. Such a deviation was not the teaching of Christ; it was rather the teaching of Antichrist. Its exponents and devotees might claim to constitute a spiritual élite, but their claim was false: the writer can assure his rank-and-file Christian readers: 'you, no less than they, are among the initiated; this is the gift of the Holy One, and by it you all have knowledge' (1 John ii. 20, N.E.B.).

In 2 John the author, who calls himself 'the elder' (and is almost certainly identical with the author of 1 John), urges one of the churches of the province ('the elect lady') to give no countenance or hospitality to people who come propagating this subversive teaching. That this refusal of hospitality was a two-edged weapon is evident from 3 John, where the elder has to complain that in a certain church (which may or may not be the church addressed in 2 John) his own messengers have been refused hospitality (although on this occasion personal rivalry rather than doctrinal divergence was to blame). In respect of theological debate and church administration alike the Johannine epistles stand on the threshold of second-century developments. The call for care in receiving itinerant teachers reminds us of the *Didache*. It is uncertain whether Diotrephes, who rejected the elder's messengers, is the first monarchical bishop known to Christian literature or (which is more probable) should be seen as 'a symptom of the disease which the quasi-apostolic ministry of monarchical bishops was designed to relieve' (C. H. Dodd, *The Johannine Epistles*, p. 164).

Conclusion

The Johannine Gospel and Epistles, in short, stand alongside other aspects of the apostolic witness in the New Testament as enshrining a witness of independent value, derived not from the Synoptic or Pauline witness, but (like them) from the living revelation itself. Such a recognition does not put an end to all questions; rather it raises a number of new ones. But as these questions are posed by C. H. Dodd and some other Johannine interpreters of the present day, they may well find more satisfying answers than have been given since Westcott's time.

Abbreviations

BJRL	Bulletin of the John Rylands Library
JBL	Journal of Biblical Literature
JTS	Journal of Theological Studies
HTR	Harvard Theological Review
NTS	New Testament Studies
ZNW	Zeitschrift für neutestamentliche Wissenschaft

ΙΩΑΝΟΥ Α

ΙΩΑΝΟΥ Α

Ο. ΗΝ ΑΠ' ΑΡΧΗC, ὃ ἀκηκόαμεν, ὃ ἑωράκαμεν τοῖς ὀφθαλμοῖς ἡμῶν, ὃ ἐθεασάμεθα καὶ αἱ χεῖρες ἡμῶν

1. Tertullian twice quotes the verse (omitting ὃ ἦν ἀπ' ἀρχῆς) as if he read ὃ ἑωράκαμεν, ὃ ἀκηκόαμεν, τοῖς ὀφθαλμοῖς ἡμῶν ἐθεασάμεθα καὶ αἱ χεῖρες......(adv. Prax. 15, quod vidimus, quod audivimus, oculis nostris vidimus et manus......; de An. 17). Probably the transposition came from v. 3. This being adopted, the omission of ὃ before ἐθεασάμεθα became necessary. The same transposition occurs in the free quotation contained in the Muratorian Fragment, quæ vidimus oculis nostris et auribus audivimus et manus nostræ palpaverunt hæc scripsimus vobis (N. T. Canon, p. 535). In v. 3 ℵ harl transpose conversely and read ὃ ἀκηκ. καὶ ἑωρ.

INTRODUCTION. THE FACTS OF THE GOSPEL ISSUING IN FELLOWSHIP AND JOY. (I. 1—4.)

This preface to the Epistle corresponds in a remarkable manner with the preface to the Gospel (John i. 1—18); but the two passages are complementary and not parallel. The introduction to the Gospel treats of the personal Word (ὁ λόγος), and so naturally leads up to the record of His work on earth: the introduction to the Epistle treats of the revelation of life (ὁ λόγος τῆς ζωῆς) which culminated in the Incarnation, and leads up to a view of the position and privileges and duties of the Christian. In the former the Apostle sets forth the Being of the Word in relation to God and to the world (John i. 1, 2—5), the historic manifestation of the Word generally (6—13), the Incarnation as apprehended by personal experience (14—18). In the latter he states first the various parts which are united in the fulness of the apostolic testimony (1 John i. 1); then he dwells specially on the historic manifestation of the Life (i. 2); and lastly, he points out the personal results of this manifestation (i. 3, 4).. Thus there is a harmonious correspondence between the two sections regulated by the primary difference of subject. In each the main subject is described first (John i. 1, 2—5: 1 John i. 1): then the historical manifestation of it (John i. 6—13: 1 John i. 2): then its personal apprehension (John i. 14—18: 1 John i. 3 f.). Comp. Introd. § 7. The parallel was noticed by Dionysius of Alexandria (Euseb. H. E. vii. 25. 14 f.).

¹ *That which was from the beginning, that which we have heard, that which we have seen with our eyes, that which we beheld and our hands handled, concerning the word of life--² and the life was manifested, and we have. seen, and bear witness, and declare unto you the life,* even *the* life *eternal, which was with the Father and was manifested to us—³ that which we have seen and heard* (I say) *declare we unto you also, that you also may have fellowship with us; yea and our fellowship is with the Father, and with his Son Jesus Christ;* ⁴ *and these things write we that our* (your) *joy may be fulfilled.*

St John throughout this section uses the plural (contrast ii. 1, 7, &c.) as speaking in the name of the apostolic body of which he was the last surviving representative.

1—3. *That which was...that which we have seen and heard declare we...* The construction of the passage is broken by the parenthesis of *v.* 2, which may for the moment be dismissed from consideration. The beginning of *v.* 3 (ὃ ἑωράκ. καὶ ἀκήκ.) thus stands out clearly as a resumption of the construction and (in part) of the words of *v.* 1. The relatives in the two verses (ὃ ἀκήκ., ὃ ἑωράκ.) must therefore be identical in meaning; and the simple resumptive clause gives the clue to the interpretation of the original more complex clause. Now in *v.* 3 there can be no doubt that the relative ὅ is strictly neuter, 'that which': it can have no direct personal reference. The sense is perfectly simple: '*that which we have... heard, we declare...*' If to such a sentence the phrase, '*concerning the word of life*' (περὶ τοῦ λόγου τῆς ζωῆς) be added, there can still be no doubt as to the meaning. '*The word of life*' is the subject as to which the Apostle has gained the knowledge which he desires to communicate to others: '*that which we...have heard concerning the word of life we declare...*' So far the general interpretation of the passage appears to be quite clear; nor can the addition of other clauses in *v.* 1 alter it. Whatever view be adopted as to the meaning of the phrase, '*the word of life,*' it can only be taken, according to the natural structure of the sentence, as the object of the various modes of regard successively enumerated. The apparent harshness of combining the clause '*concerning the word of life*' with '*that which was from the beginning,*' and '*that which...our hands handled,*' is removed by the intervening phrases; and the preposition (περί) 'concerning,' 'in regard to,' is

comprehensive in its application. The ordinary construction by which the clause is treated as co-ordinate with the clauses which precede: '*that which was from the beginning, that which we have heard...even concerning the word of life...we declare to you,*' seems to be made impossible (1) by the resumptive words in *v.* 3, (2) by the break after *v.* 1, (3) by the extreme abruptness of the change in the form of the object of *we declare*.

1. The contents of this verse correspond closely with John i. 1, 9, 14 *In the beginning was the Word... There was the Light, the true Light, which lighteth every man, coming into the World... And the Word became flesh...* But, as has been already noticed, here the thought is of the revelation and not of the Person.

ὃ ἦν...ὃ ἀκηκ., ὃ ἑωρ., ὃ ἐθ...ἐψηλά-φησαν] *That which was...that which ...,that which...that which...handled.* These four clauses, separated by the repeated relative, which follow one another in a perfect sequence from the most abstract (ὃ ἦν ἀπ' ἀρχῆς) to the most material aspect of divine revelation (ὃ ἐθ...αἱ χ. ἐψηλάφησαν), bring into distinct prominence the different elements of the apostolic message. Of this, part extended to the utmost limits of time, being absolutely when time began: part was gradually unfolded in the course of human history. The succession of tenses marks clearly three parts of the message: *that which was* (ἦν)... *that which we have heard* (ἀκηκόαμεν) ..., *that which we beheld...*(ἐθεασά-μεθα...). That which we understand by the eternal purpose of God (Eph. i. 4), the relation of the Father to the Son (John xvii. 5), the acceptance of man in the Beloved (Eph. i. 6), *was* already, and entered as a factor into the development of finite being, when the succession of life began (ἦν ἀπ' ἀρχῆς, *was from the beginning*). But these truths were gradually realised in the course of ages, through the teaching of patriarchs, lawgivers, and prophets, and lastly of the Son Himself, Whose words are still pregnant with instruction (ὃ ἀκηκόαμεν, *which we have heard*); and above all, through the Presence of Christ, the lessons of Whose Life abide unchangeable with the Church and are realised in its life (ὃ ἑωράκαμεν τοῖς ὀφθαλμοῖς ἡμῶν, *which we have seen with our eyes*). And this Presence of Christ itself, as a historic fact, was the presence of One truly man. The perfection of His manhood was attested by the direct witness of those who were sensibly convinced of it (ὃ ἐθεασά-μεθα, κ.τ.λ., *which we beheld and our hands handled*). All the elements which may be described as the eternal, the historical, the personal, belong to the one subject, to the fulness of which they contribute, even '*the word of life.*'

As there is a succession of time in the sequence of the clauses, so there is also a climax of personal experience, from that which was remotest in apprehension to that which was most immediate (*that which was from the beginning...that which our hands handled*).

ἀπ' ἀρχῆς] *from the beginning.* Comp. c. ii. 7 note. '*From the beginning*' is contrasted with *in the beginning* (John i. 1). The latter marks what *was* already at the initial point, looking to that which is eternal, supra-temporal: the former looks to that which starting at the initial point has been operative in time. The latter deals with absolute being (ὁ λόγος ἦν πρὸς τὸν θεόν); the former with temporal development. Compare ἀπὸ καταβολῆς κόσμου (Apoc. xiii. 8, xvii. 8; Heb. iv. 3, ix. 26) as contrasted with πρὸ κατ. κ. (John xvii. 24; 1 Pet. i. 20).

The absence of the definite article both here and in John i. 1 is to be traced back finally to Gen. i. 1 (LXX.). The beginning is not regarded as a

definite concrete fact, but in its character, according to man's apprehension, 'that to which we look as beginning.' The use of ἐσχάτη ὥρα in c. ii. 18, ἔσχαται ἡμέραι 2 Tim. iii. 1 is similar. Compare iii. 10 ποιεῖν δικ. note.

The Greek commentators justly dwell on the grandeur of the claim which St John makes for the Christian Revelation as coeval in some sense with creation: θεολογῶν ἐξηγεῖται μὴ νεώτερον εἶναι τὸ καθ' ἡμᾶς μυστήριον, ἀλλ' ἐξ ἀρχῆς μὲν καὶ ἀεὶ τυγχάνειν αὐτὸ νῦν δὲ πεφανερῶσθαι ἐν τῷ κυρίῳ, ὃς ἔστι ζωὴ αἰώνιος καὶ θεὸς ἀληθινός (Theophlct. *Argum.*). And again in a note upon the verse: τοῦτο καὶ πρὸς Ἰουδαίους καὶ πρὸς Ἕλληνας οἳ ὡς νεώτερον διαβάλλουσι τὸ καθ' ἡμᾶς μυστήριον (id. *ad loc.*).

The 'hearing' 'concerning the word of life' is not to be limited to the actual preaching of the Lord during His visible presence, though it includes this. It embraces the whole divine preparation for the Advent provided by the teaching of Lawgiver and Prophets (comp. Heb. i. 1) fulfilled at last by Christ. This the Apostles had 'heard' faithfully when the Jewish people had not heard (John v. 37; Luke xvi. 29). So also the 'seeing,' as it appears, reaches beyond the personal vision of the Lord. The condition of Jew and Gentile, the civil and religious institutions by which St John was surrounded (Acts xvii. 28), the effects which the Gospel wrought, revealed to the eye of the Apostle something of 'the Life.' 'Hearing' and 'seeing' are combined in the work of the seer: Apoc. xxii. 8.

The clear reference to the Risen Christ in the word '*handled*,' makes it probable that the special manifestation indicated by the two aorists (ἐθεασάμεθα, ἐψηλάφησαν) is that given to the Apostles by the Lord after the Resurrection, which is in fact the revelation of Himself as He remains with His Church by the Spirit. The two words are united with one relative, and they express in ascending order the ground of the Apostle's personal belief in the reality of the true humanity of Christ as He is (*we beheld...and handled*).

Thus there is a survey of the whole course of revelation in the four clauses, more complete than has been already indicated. The personal experience of the Presence of Christ is crowned by the witness to the Risen Christ. This witness of what he had actually experienced is part of the message which the Apostle had to give (comp. Acts i. 22). The Resurrection was the final revelation of life. At the same time the four clauses bind together inseparably the divine and human. There is, as we have seen, but one subject whether this is revealed as eternal (*that which was from the beginning*), or through the experience of sense (*that which our hands handled*).

ἀκηκόαμεν] *have heard*, vv. 3, 5, iv. 3; John iv. 42, v. 37, xviii. 21. The perfect in every case preserves its full force.

ἑωράκ. τ. ὀφθ.] *have seen with our eyes.* The addition *with our eyes*, like *our hands* below, emphasises the idea of direct personal outward experience in a matter marvellous in itself. The vision was not of the soul within, but in life. Comp. Deut. iii. 21, iv. 3, xi. 7, xxi. 7; Zech. ix. 8; Ecclus. xvi. 5. See also John xx. 27.

On sight and hearing, see Philo, *de Sacr. A. et C.* § 22, i. 178.

ὃ ἑωράκαμεν...ὃ ἐθεασάμεθα...] *quod vidimus...quod perspeximus* V., *which we have seen...which we beheld.* The general relation of these clauses has been touched upon already. They offer also contrasts in detail. The change of tense marks the difference between that which was permanent in the lessons of the manifestation of the Lord, and that which was once shewn to special witnesses. The change of the verbs also is sig-

nificant. Θεᾶσθαι, like θεωρεῖν, expresses the calm, intent, continuous contemplation of an object which remains before the spectator. Comp. John i. 14 n. On the other hand the emphatic addition of τοῖς ὀφθαλμοῖς ἡμῶν to ἑωράκαμεν emphasises the personal nature of the witness as ἐθεασάμεθα emphasises its exactness. Generally the first two verbs (*heard, seen*) express the fact, and the second two (*beheld, handled*) the definite investigation by the observer.

Bede (*ad loc.*) brings out the moral element in ἐθεασάμεθα : Non solum quippe corporalibus oculis sicut ceteri Dominum viderunt sed et perspexerunt, cujus divinam quoque virtutem spiritualibus oculis cernebant.

ἐψηλάφησαν] *contrectaverunt* V. (all. *tractaverunt, palpaverunt, perscrutatæ sunt*), *handled.* There can be no doubt that the exact word is used with a distinct reference to the invitation of the Lord after His Resurrection: *Handle me...* (Luke xxiv. 39 ψηλαφήσατέ με). The tacit reference is the more worthy of notice because St John does not mention the fact of the Resurrection in his Epistle; nor does he use the word in his own narrative of the Resurrection. From early times it has been observed that St John used the term to mark the solid ground of the Apostolic conviction: οὐ γὰρ ὡς ἔτυχε συγκατεθέμεθα τῷ ὀφθέντι (Theophlct. *ad loc.*).

περὶ τοῦ λόγου τῆς ζωῆς] *de verbo vitæ* V. (*de sermone vitæ*, Tert.), *concerning the word of life*, that is *the message of life*, or, according to the more modern idiom, *the revelation of life. The word* (ὁ λόγος) conveys the notion of a connected whole (*sermo*), and is not merely an isolated utterance (ῥῆμα· comp. John vi. 68 ῥήματα ζωῆς αἰωνίου). Hence *the word of life* is the whole message from God to man, which tells of life, or, perhaps, out of which life springs, which beginning to be spoken by the prophets, was at last fully proclaimed by one who was His Son (Hebr. i. 1, 2). Christ is, indeed, Himself THE WORD, but in the present passage the obvious reference is to the whole *Gospel*, of which He is the centre and sum, and not to Himself personally. This follows both from the context and from the appended genitive (τῆς ζωῆς). It is *the life* and not *the word* which is said to have been manifested; and again in the four passages where ὁ λόγος is used personally (John i. 1 *ter*, 14) the term is absolute. On the other hand we have ὁ λόγος τῆς βασιλείας (Matt. xiii. 19), ὁ λόγος τῆς σωτηρίας ταύτης (Acts xiii. 26), ὁ λόγος τῆς χάριτος αὐτοῦ (Acts xx. 32), ὁ λόγος ὁ τοῦ σταυροῦ (2 Cor. i. 18), ὁ λόγος τῆς καταλλαγῆς (2 Cor. v. 19), ὁ λόγος τῆς ἀληθείας τοῦ εὐαγγελίου (Col. i. 5), ὁ λόγος τῆς ἀληθείας (2 Tim. ii. 15; comp. λόγ. ἀληθείας James i. 18), in all of which the genitive describes the subject of the tidings or record. There can then be no reason for departing from the general analogy of this universal usage here, since it gives an admirable sense, and the personal interpretation of ' *the word of life*' is not supported by any parallel. Moreover, a modification of the phrase itself occurs in St Paul, λόγον ζωῆς ἐπέχειν (Phil. ii. 16: compare also Titus i. 2, 3 ἐπ' ἐλπίδι ζωῆς αἰωνίου ἦν ἐπηγγείλατο...ἐφανέρωσεν δέ... τὸν λόγον αὐτοῦ...: John vi. 68; Acts v. 20). The personal interpretation could not fail to present itself to later readers, in whose speculation 'the Word' occupied a far larger place than it occupies in the writings of St John, and to become popular. In a most true sense Christ is the gospel; and the name of the triumphant conqueror in Apoc. xix. 13 (ὁ λόγος τοῦ θεοῦ· comp. Acts vi. 7, xv. 6 &c.) shews the natural transition in meaning from 'the Word of God' to Him who is 'the Word of God.' Comp. John x. 35.

The Peshito Syriac (not Harcl.) appears to support the interpretation which has been given; *that which is the word of life.*

The sense of the genitive τῆς ζωῆς, *of life*, is doubtful. According to general usage noticed above, it would specify the contents of the message : ' the revelation which proclaims and presents life to men.' It must however be noticed that in other connexions St John uses the words (τῆς ζωῆς) to describe the character of that to which they are applied, as life-giving, or life-sustaining: τὸ ξύλον τῆς ζωῆς (Apoc. ii. 7 &c.), ὁ στέφανος τῆς ζωῆς (Apoc. ii. 10), ζωῆς πηγαὶ ὑδάτων (Apoc. vii. 17), τὸ ὕδωρ τῆς ζωῆς (Apoc. xxi. 6 &c.), ἡ βίβλος τῆς ζωῆς (Apoc. iii. 5 &c.), and more particularly ὁ ἄρτος τῆς ζωῆς (John vi. 35), τὸ φῶς τῆς ζωῆς (John viii. 12), which suggest such a sense as 'the life-containing, life-communicating word.' The context here, which speaks of the manifestation of *the life*, appears at first sight to require the former interpretation; for it is easy to pass from the idea of *the life* as the subject of the divine revelation to *the life* made manifest, while the conception of *life* as characteristic of the word does not prepare the way for the transition so directly. On the other side the usage of the Gospel is of great weight; and it is not difficult to see how the thought of the revelation, which from first to last was inspired by and diffused life, leads to the thought that the life itself was personally manifested.

It is most probable that the two interpretations are not to be sharply separated. The revelation proclaims that which it includes; it has, announces, gives life. In Christ life as the subject and life as the character of the Revelation were absolutely united. See Additional Note on v. 20.

The preposition (περί) is used in a wide sense, 'in regard to,' 'in the ἐψηλάφησαν, περὶ τοῦ λόγου τῆς ζωῆς,—²καὶ ἡ ζωὴ

matter of.' Comp. John xvi. 8. The subject is not simply a message, but all that had been made clear through manifold experience 'concerning' it.

If we now look back over the verse it is not difficult to see why St John chose the neuter form (*that which was* and not *Him that was*), and why he limited the record of his experience by the addition *concerning the word of life*. He does not announce Christ or the revelation of life, but he announces something relating to both. Christ is indeed the one subject of his letter, yet not the Person of Christ absolutely but what he had himself come directly to know of Him. Nor yet again does the apostle write all that he had come to know of Christ by manifold intercourse, but just so much as illustrated the whole revelation of life (comp. John xx. 30 f.). His pastoral is not a Gospel nor a dogmatic exposition of truth, but an application of the Truth to life.

2. The whole verse is parenthetical. Elsewhere St John interrupts the construction by the introduction of a reflective comment (*v.* 3 b; c. ii. 27, John i. 14, 16, iii. 1, 16 ff., 31 ff., xix. 35, 2 John 2), and pauses after some critical statement to consider and realise its significance. And so here the mention of the whole 'revelation of life,'which extends throughout time, leads him to rest for a moment upon the one supreme fact up to which or from which all revelation comes. 'Concerning the word of life,' he seems to say, 'Yes, concerning that revelation which deals with life and which brings life in all its manifold relations; and yet while our thoughts embrace this vast range which it includes, we may never forget that the life itself was shewn to us in a personal form. What we have to declare is not a word (λόγος) only: it is a fact.'

The simple statement is given first (*the life was manifested*), and then subject and predicate are more fully explained ('*the life eternal which was with the Father,' 'was manifested to us*'). The phrase, *the life was manifested*, recals the corresponding phrase in the prologue to the Gospel, *the Word became flesh*. The latter regards the single fact of the Incarnation of the Word Who 'was God'; this regards the exhibition in its purity and fulness of the divine movement. And yet further, in the Gospel St John speaks directly of a Person: here he is speaking of the revelation which he had received of the energy of a Person. The full difference is felt if for a moment the predicates are transferred. The reality of the Incarnation would be undeclared if it were said: 'the Word was manifested'; the manifoldness of the operations of life would be circumscribed if it were said: 'the life became flesh.' The manifestation of the life was a consequence of the Incarnation of the Word, but it is not co-extensive with it.

καὶ ἡ ζωή] *and the life....* This use of the simplest conjunction (καί) is characteristic of St John. It seems to mark the succession of contemplation as distinguished from the sequence of reasoning. Thought is added to thought as in the interpretation of a vast scene open all at once before the eyes, of which the parts are realised one after the other.

ἡ ζωή] *the life*, John xiv. 6 n., xi. 25 n. The usage of the word in John i. 4 is somewhat different. Here life is regarded as final and absolute: there life is the particular revelation of life given in finite creation. Christ *is* the life which He *brings*, and which is realised by believers *in* Him. In Him 'the life' became visible. Comp. c. v. 11, 12, 20; Col. iii. 4; Rom. v. 10, vi. 23; 2 Cor. iv. 10;

ἐφανερώθη, καὶ ἑωράκαμεν καὶ μαρτυροῦμεν καὶ ἀπαγ-

2. καὶ ὃ ἑωράκαμεν, B (ἑορ.); καὶ ὃ ἑωρ. μαρτ. Dion Alex. (Migne, P. Gr. x. 1248). The insertion or omission of ο before εορακαμεν (so B) was equally easy; but ἐφανερώθη seems to require the direct connexion of ἑωράκαμεν with τὴν ζ. τ. αἰ.

2 Tim. i. 1. But the term 'the life' is not to be regarded as simply a personal name equivalent to the Word: it expresses one aspect of His Being and Working. Looking to Him we see under the conditions of present human being the embodied ideal of life, which is fellowship with God and with man in God.

ἐφανερώθη] manifestata est V. (below apparuit), was manifested. The word is used of the revelation of the Lord at His first coming (c. iii. 5, 8; John i. 31; comp. c. iv. 9; John vii. 4; 1 Pet. i. 20; 1 Tim. iii. 16; Heb. ix. 26); of His revelation after the Resurrection (John xxi. 14, 1; [Mark] xvi. 12, 14); and of the future revelation (c. ii. 28; comp. 1 Pet. v. 4; Col. iii. 4). In all these ways the Word Incarnate and glorified is made known as 'the Life.'

ἑωράκαμεν...μαρτυροῦμεν...ἀπαγγέλλομεν...] seen...bear witness...declare... The three verbs give in due sequence the ideas of personal experience, responsible affirmation, authoritative announcement, which are combined in the apostolic message. The first two verbs are probably used absolutely, though the object of the third (the life eternal) is potentially included in them. Comp. John i. 34, xix. 35. So Augustine, et vidimus et testes sumus.

ἑωράκαμεν] John xix. 35, i. 34, xiv. 7, 9. It is worthy of notice that this is the only part of the verb which is used by St John in the Gospel and Epistles (ὅρα μή, Apoc. xix. 10; xxii. 9: not xviii. 18; nor John vi. 2); and in these books it is singularly frequent.

Severus (Cramer Cat. ad loc.), comparing these words with iv. 12 θεὸν

οὐδεὶς πώποτε τεθέαται, no man hath beheld God at any time, remarks: τῷ σεσαρκῶσθαι καὶ ἐπηνθρωπηκέναι θεατὸς καὶ ψηλαφητὸς γενέσθαι εὐδόκησεν [ὁ λόγος], οὐχ ὃ ἦν θεαθεὶς καὶ ψηλαφηθεὶς ἀλλ' ὃ γέγονεν· εἰς γὰρ ὑπάρχων καὶ ἀδιαίρετος ὁ αὐτὸς ἦν καὶ θεατὸς καὶ ἀθέατος καὶ ἀφῇ μὴ ὑποπίπτων καὶ ψηλαφώμενος...

μαρτυροῦμεν] Comp. iv. 14; John xxi. 24. For the characteristic use of the idea of witness in St John see Introd. to Gospel of St John, pp. xliv. ff.

Augustine dwells on the associations of the Greek μάρτυρες which were lost in the Latin testes: Ergo hoc dixit Vidimus et testes sumus: Vidimus et martyres sumus; testimonium enim dicendo...cum displiceret ipsum testimonium hominibus adversus quos dicebatur, passi sunt omnia quæ passi sunt martyres (ad loc.).

ἀπαγγέλλομεν] adnunciamus V., we declare. The word occurs again in St John's writings in John xvi. 25 (it is falsely read iv. 51, xx. 18). In the Synoptists and Acts it is not uncommon in the sense of 'bearing back a message from one to another.' This fundamental idea underlies the use here and in John xvi. 25. The message comes from a Divine Presence and expresses a divine purpose.

Comp. 1 Cor. xiv. 25; Heb. ii. 12 (LXX.); v. 5 note.

The application of the words must not be confined to the Epistle, which is in fact distinguished from the general proclamation of the Gospel (v. 4, καὶ ταῦτα γράφομεν), but rather understood of the whole apostolic ministry. More particularly perhaps we may see a description of that teaching which St John embodied in his Gospel.

γέλλομεν ὑμῖν τὴν ζωὴν τὴν αἰώνιον ἥτις ἦν πρὸς τὸν

τὴν ζ. τὴν αἰ.] the eternal life, more exactly, the life, even the life eternal. The phrase used in the beginning of the verse is first taken up and then more fully developed. This form of expression in which the two elements of the idea are regarded separately is found in the N. T. only here and in ii. 25. The simpler form ἡ αἰώνιος ζωή is also very rare (John xvii. 3; Acts xiii. 46; 1 Tim. vi. 12), and in each case where it occurs describes the special Messianic gift brought by Christ (the eternal life) as distinguished from the general conception (ζωὴ αἰώνιος, life eternal).

This 'eternal life' is seen in this passage to be the divine life, the life that is and which was visibly shewn in Christ, and not merely an unending continuance (Heb. vii. 16, ζ. ἀκατάλυτος). Comp. John xvii. 3. The equivalent phrase appears to occur first in Dan. xii. 2 (עוֹלָם לְחַיֵּי). Comp. 2 Macc. vii. 9 εἰς αἰώνιον ἀναβίωσιν ζωῆς ἡμᾶς ἀναστήσει.

For the use of the article (ἡ ζ. ἡ αἰ.) see c. ii. 7 (ἡ ἐντ. ἡ π.) note; and for the idea of 'eternal life' the Additional Note on v. 20.

ἥτις ἦν...] which was.... This clause not only defines but in part confirms the former statement. The relative is not the simple relative (ἥ), but the 'qualitative' relative (ἥτις). Comp. John viii. 53 (ὅστις ἀπέθανεν); Apoc. i. 7; ii. 24; xi. 8; xx. 4. 'We declare with authority'—such is the apostle's meaning—'the life which is truly eternal, seeing that the life of which we speak was with the Father, and so is independent of the conditions of time; and it was manifested to us apostles, and so has been brought within the sphere of our knowledge.'

ἦν πρὸς τ. π.] erat apud patrem V., was with the Father. Comp. John i. 1, 2. The life was not 'in the Father,' nor in fellowship (μετά) or in

combination (σύν) with Him, but realised with Him for its object and law (ἦν πρός). That which is true of the Word as a Person, is true necessarily of the Word in action, and so of the Life which finds expression in action. The verb (ἦν) describes continuous and not past existence; or rather, it suggests under the forms of human thought an existence which is beyond time (Apoc. iv. 11 ἦσαν; John i. 3 f.).

τὸν πατέρα] The Father, the title of God when regarded relatively, as the 'One God, of whom (ἐξ οὗ) are all things' (1 Cor. viii. 6). The relation itself is defined more exactly either in reference to the material world: James i. 17 ὁ πατὴρ τῶν φώτων; or to men: Matt. v. 16 ὁ πατὴρ ὑμῶν, &c.; or, more commonly and peculiarly, to our Lord, 'the Son': Matt. vii. 21 ὁ πατήρ μου, &c. The difference of the paternal relation of the One Father to Christ and to Christians is indicated in a very remarkable manner in John xx. 17 (ἀναβαίνω πρὸς τὸν πατέρα μου καὶ πατ. ὑμῶν) where the unity of the Person is shewn by the one article common to the two clauses, and the distinctness of the relations by the repetition of the title with the proper personal pronoun. The simple title ὁ πατήρ occurs rarely in the Synoptic Gospels, and always with reference to 'the Son': Matt. xi. 27 || Luke x. 22; Matt. xxiv. 36 || Mark xiii. 32; Luke ix. 26; Matt. xxiii. 19. (But comp. Luke xi. 13 ὁ π. ὁ ἐξ οὐρανοῦ; the usage in Matt. xi. 26 || Luke x. 21; Mark xiv. 36 is different.) In the Acts it is found only in the opening chapters; i. 4, 7; ii. 33. In St Paul only Rom. vi. 4 (ἠγέρθη...διὰ τῆς δόξης τοῦ π.); 1 Cor. viii. 6 (εἷς θεὸς ὁ πατήρ); Eph. ii. 18 (τὴν προσαγωγὴν...πρὸς τὸν πατέρα); Col. i. 12 ?; (Rom. viii. 15 || Gal. iv. 6) and not at all in the Epistles of St Peter, St James or St Jude, or in the Apocalypse. In St John's Gospel, on the contrary, and in

πατέρα καὶ ἐφανερώθη ἡμῖν,—³ὃ ἑωράκαμεν καὶ ἀκηκόαμεν ἀπαγγέλλομεν καὶ ὑμῖν, ἵνα καὶ ὑμεῖς κοινωνίαν

3. ὃ ἀκηκ. καὶ ἑωρ. ℵ harl: see v. 1.　　+καὶ' ἀπαγγ. ℵ am.　　- καὶ'
ὑμῖν, ς vg me.　　- δὲ ς C*.　　Hence Aug. Ambr. vg et societas nostra sit
(ἵνα...ἔχητε καὶ ᾖ ἡ κοινωνία ἡ ἡμετέρα...).

his Epistles (i. ii.) the term is very frequent (1 Ep. i. 2 f.; ii. 1, 13, 15, 18, 22 ff.; iii. 1; iv. 14. 2 Ep. 3, 4, 9). Comp. John iv. 21 add. note; and the additional note on this passage.

In this place the idea of Fatherhood comes into prominence in connexion with life (the life was with the Father). In the Gospel the absolute idea of Godhead is placed in connexion with the Word (John i. 1 ὁ λ. ἦν πρὸς τὸν θεόν, the Word was with God). In both passages a glimpse is given of the essential relations of the Divine Persons, and we learn that the idea of Father lies in the Deity itself and finds fulfilment in the Deity. The simplest conception which we can form of God in Himself as absolutely perfect and self-sufficing includes Tripersonality.

ἐφαν. ἡμῖν] apparuit nobis V. (manifestata est in nobis Aug., palam facta est, &c. all.) was manifested to us. The general statement given before (was manifested) is made personal. Actual experience is the foundation of St John's testimony.

3. In the parenthesis (v. 2) St John has described the subject of his message as 'the life eternal': he now describes it as 'that which we have seen and heard.' The fulness of apostolic experience, the far-reaching knowledge of the Son of God, is indeed identical with the life. By appropriating that knowledge of the Son the life is appropriated.

Life is manifested in fellowship; and in regarding the end of his message St John looks at once to a twofold fellowship, human and divine, a fellowship with the Church and with God. He contemplates first the fel-

lowship which exists in the Christian body itself, and then rises from this to the thought of the wider privileges of such fellowship as resting on a divine basis. Manifeste ostendit B. Johannes quia quicunque societatem cum Deo habere desiderant primo ecclesiæ societati debent adunari.... (Bede).

ὃ ἑωρ. καὶ ἀκηκ.] that which we have seen and heard... The transposition of the verbs in this resumptive clause (v. 1 heard...seen...) is natural and significant. Before the Apostle was advancing up to the Incarnation, now he is starting from it. At the same time the two elements of experience are brought together and not (as before) separated by the repeated relative (v. 1 that which...that which...).

καὶ ὑμῖν] unto you also. The revelation was not for those only to whom it was first given; but for them also who 'had not seen.' The message was for 'them also' that 'they also' might enjoy the fruits of it. There is no redundance in the repeated καί.

This thought is well brought out by Augustine, who asks the question: Minus ergo sumus felices quam illi qui viderunt et audierunt? and answers it by recalling the history of St Thomas (John xx. 26 ff.) who rose by Faith above touch: Tetigit hominem, confessus est Deum. Et Dominus consolans nos qui ipsum jam in cælo sedentem manu contrectare non possumus sed fide contingere, ait illi Quia vidisti credidisti, beati qui non viderunt et credunt. Nos descripti sumus, nos designati sumus. Fiat ergo in nobis beatitudo quam Dominus prædixit futuram: manifestata est

ἔχητε μεθ᾽ ἡμῶν· καὶ ἡ κοινωνία δὲ ἡ ἡμετέρα μετὰ τοῦ
πατρὸς καὶ μετὰ τοῦ υἱοῦ αὐτοῦ Ἰησοῦ Χριστοῦ· ⁴καὶ

ipsa vita in carne...ut res quæ solo
corde videri potest videretur et oculis,
ut corda sanaret (Aug. *ad loc.*).

ἵνα...μεθ᾽ ἡμῶν] *ut et vos societatem
habeatis nobiscum* V., *that ye also
may have fellowship with us, i.e.*
'may be united with us, the apostolic
body, in the bonds of Christian communion' (comp. *vv.* 6, 7; iv. 6) by the
apprehension of the fulness of the truth;
that you may enjoy to the uttermost
by spiritual power what we gained in
the outward experience of life (John
xx. 29). The last of the apostles
points to the unbroken succession of
the heritage of Faith. It will be
observed that St John always assumes
that 'knowledge' carries with it the
corresponding action (*e.g.* ii. 3). The
words cannot without violence be
made to give the sense: 'that ye may
have the same fellowship [with God
and Christ] as we have.'

The phrase κοινωνίαν ἔχειν, as distinguished from the simple verb κοινωνεῖν (2 John 11; 1 Pet. iv. 13; Phil.
iv. 15), expresses not only the mere
fact, but also the enjoyment, the conscious realisation, of fellowship. Comp.
v. 8 (ἁμαρτίαν ἔχειν) note.

κοιν. μεθ᾽ ἡμῶν] *fellowship with.*
The preposition (μετά) emphasises the
mutual action of those who are united.
Κοινωνία is also used with a genitive
of the person (1 Cor. i. 9), as in the
case of things (1 Cor. x. 16; Phil. iii.
10), when the thought is of a blessing
imparted by fellowship in the person,
or of a fellowship springing from the
person (2 Cor. xiii. 13). The word is
also used absolutely Acts ii. 42.

καὶ ἡ κοιν. δέ...] *et societas nostra sit*
V., Aug., *yea and our fellowship...*
The connecting particles (καί...δέ) and
the possessive pronoun (ἡ κ. ἡ ἡμετέρα) are both emphatic. The particles
lay stress on the characteristics of the
fellowship which are to be brought

forward: the possessive in place of
the personal pronoun marks that
which peculiarly distinguishes Christians rather than simply that which
they enjoy. 'And the fellowship itself
in fact to which we call you, the fellowship which is truly Christian fellowship, &c.'

For καί...δέ... compare John vi. 51;
viii. 16, 17; xv. 27; 3 John 12. The
combination occurs sparingly throughout the N. T. The δέ serves as the
conjunction, while καί emphasises the
words to which it is attached.

For ἡ κοιν. ἡ ἡμετέρα compare John
xv. 9 n. (ἡ ἀγ. ἡ ἐμή), 11, 12; xvii. 13,
24; xviii. 36, &c.; c. ii. 7 note.

The insertion of the δέ makes the
false construction (*Latt.*) 'and that
our fellowship may be...' impossible.
The whole clause is like *v.* 2 (see
note), a development of the preceding idea over which the apostle lin-
gers as it were in personal reflection.
For the foundation of the thought see
John xvii. 20 f.

μετὰ τοῦ π...Ἰ. Χ.] *with the Father...
his Son Jesus Christ....* The thought
prepared in *vv.* 1, 2 now finds full expression. The revelation of 'the life'
had brought men into connexion with
'the Father.' 'The life' was apprehended in a true human personality
in virtue of the Incarnation, and so
men could have fellowship with the
life and with the source of life.
Through the Son God was revealed
and apprehended as Father. It must
also be observed that 'fellowship
with the Father' and 'fellowship
with His Son' are directly co-ordi-
nated (*with...and with...*). Such coordination implies sameness of essence. And yet further: the fellowship with the Father is not only said
to be established *through* the Son:
the fellowship with the Father is involved in fellowship with the Son

ταῦτα γράφομεν ἡμεῖς ἵνα ἡ χαρὰ ἡμῶν ᾖ πεπληρωμένη.

4. ἡμεῖς ℵA*B the: ὑμῖν ς A**C vg syrr me. In such a case the evidence of verss. is of little weight.

(ἡ χ.) ἡμῶν ℵB the; ὑμῶν ς AC me. The later MSS. and the Latin and Syriac verss. are divided. The confusion of ἡμ. and ὑμ. in the best authorities is so constant that a positive decision on the reading here is impossible. It may be noticed that C*, reading ὑμῶν, adds ἐν ἡμῖν and some verss. reading ἡμῶν add ἐν ὑμῖν at the end of the clause. Comp. ii. 8, 25; iii. 1; v. 4.

Some copies of Vulg. read ut + gaudeatis et' gaudium vestrum (nostrum) sit plenum.

(comp. ii. 23). The consummation of this fellowship is the 'being in God' (c. v. 20) 'a quo fontaliter omnia procedunt, in quo finaliter omnes sancti fruibiliter requiescunt' (Th. Kemp. i. 15. 2).

τοῦ υἱοῦ αὐ. 'I. X.] His Son Jesus Christ. By the use of this full title St John brings out now both aspects of the Lord's Person ('His Son,' 'Jesus Christ') which he had indicated before ('which was with the Father,' 'our hands handled'). The full title is found again in iii. 23; v. 20 (?); 2 John 3; 1 Cor. i. 9; 2 Cor. i. 19. Compare also i. 7 (iv. 15; v. 5); 1 Thess. i. 10; Heb. iv. 14. In each case it will be seen to be significant in all its elements.

4. καὶ ταῦτα] and these things. The apostolic message which had been regarded before in its unity (ὅ that which) is now regarded in some special aspects of its manifold power. St John embraces in 'the vision of his heart' (Eph. i. 18) all that his letter contains, though it was then unwritten.

The phrase, these things, is not however co-extensive with that which. St John has present to his mind both the general revelation of the Gospel (we declare) of which the end was to create spiritual fellowship between God and man and men; and the particular view of it which he purposes to lay before his readers (we write) with a view to establishing the fulness of joy in the Church.

γράφομεν ἡμεῖς] write we. Both

the pronoun and the verb are emphatic. The proclamation (vv. 2, 3) was presented in an abiding form: not spoken only but written, so far as there was need, that it might work its full effect. And it was written by those who had full authority to write. Nor is it fanciful to suppose that by the stress laid on the word write, which is emphasised by the absence of a personal object (the to you of the common text is to be omitted), St John looks forward to his apostolic service to later ages.

The plural (γράφομεν) which belongs to the form of the apostolic message stands in contrast with the personal address (γράφω) which immediately follows in c. ii. 1. Elsewhere in the epistle the verb occurs only in the singular (ii. 7 f., 12 ff., 21, 26; v. 13).

ἵνα ἡ χ. ἡμῶν (v. ὑμῶν) ᾖ πεπληρ.] that our (or your) joy may be fulfilled. The fulfilment of Christian joy depends upon the realisation of fellowship. The same thought underlies the other passages where the phrase occurs (see next note). Fellowship with Christ, and fellowship with the brethren, fellowship with Christ in the brethren, and with the brethren in Christ, is the measure of the fulness of joy. Both readings (ἡμῶν and ὑμῶν) are well supported and both give good sense. The object of the apostle may be regarded either as to the fulfilment of his work relatively to himself, or as to the fulfilment of his work relatively to his disciples. The joy of the apostle as well as the joy

⁵ Καὶ ἔστιν αὕτη ἡ ἀγγελία ἣν ἀκηκόαμεν ἀπ᾽ αὐτοῦ

5. καὶ ἔστιν αὕτη ℵBC; καὶ αὕτη ἐστίν ⸉ A vg.
ἡ ἀγγελία ℵᶜAB vg: ἡ ἐπαγγελία ⸉ C me the.
ℵ had originally η απαγγελιας, which the scribe himself altered by letters
written above to ἡ ἀγάπη τῆς ἐπαγγελίας. Comp. iii. 11; ii. 25.

of the disciples is secured by the same result.

ἡμῶν γὰρ ὑμῖν (Œcum. ὑμῶν…ἡμῖν) κοινωνούντων πλείστην ἔχομεν τὴν χάριν (l. χαρὰν) ἡμῶν, ἣν τοῖς θερισταῖς ὁ χαίρων σπορεὺς ἐν τῇ τοῦ μισθοῦ ἀπολήψει βραβεύσει χαιρόντων καὶ τούτων ὅτι τῶν πόνων αὐτῶν (l. αὐτοῦ) ἀπολαύουσι (Theophlct.).

πεπληρωμένη]plenum (V., Aug.), fulfilled. The phrase is 'characteristic. Comp. 2 John 12; John iii. 29, xv. 11, xvi. 24; xvii. 13. For the use of the resolved form see iv. 12 n. Gaudium doctorum fit plenum cum multos prædicando ad sanctæ ecclesiæ societatem...perducunt (Bede). Comp. Phil. ii. 2.

A. THE PROBLEM OF LIFE AND THOSE TO WHOM IT IS PROPOSED (i. 5— ii. 17).

I. 5—10. THE NATURE OF GOD AND THE CONSEQUENT RELATION OF MAN TO GOD.

The section contains 1 the description of the Being of God (v. 5); and then 2 the description of man's relation to God as thus made known (6—10), in answer to the three typical false pleas (i) of the indifference of moral action in regard to spiritual fellowship (6, 7); (ii) of the unreality of sinfulness as a permanent consequence of wrong action (8, 9); and (iii) of actual personal freedom from sinful deeds (10). These pleas are shewn to depend (1) on immediate denial of what is distinctly known (6); (2) on self-deception (8); and (3) on disregard of divine revelation (10).

1. The Nature of God (i. 5).

5. ⁵And this is the message which we have heard from him and

announce to you, that God is light, and in him is no darkness at all. The connexion of this verse with what precedes is not at once obvious. The declaration which it contains as to the nature of God is not, as far as we know, a direct repetition of any words of the Lord; nor is it clear at first sight how it gathers up what has been already said of 'the revelation of life' as apprehended in apostolic experience. Fuller consideration appears to shew that the idea of spiritual fellowship furnishes the clue to the course of St John's thought. Fellowship must repose upon mutual knowledge. If we have fellowship with God we must know truly what He is and what we are, and the latter knowledge flows from the former. The revelation of life from first to last is the progressive manifestation of God and the progressive assimilation to God. The revelation through the Incarnation completes all that was revealed before: Christ came 'not to destroy but to fulfil': and this revelation is briefly comprehended in the words 'God is light,' absolutely pure, glorious, self-communicating from His very nature. He imparts Himself, and man was made to receive Him; and, in spite of sin, man can receive Him. Thus the fundamental ideas of Christianity lie in this announcement: 'God is light'; and man turns to the Light as being himself created in the image of God (Gen. i. 27; 1 Cor. xi. 7) and re-created in Christ (Eph. ii. 10; Col. iii. 10). This message is really 'the Gospel.'

Hac sententia B. Johannes...divinæ puritatis excellentiam monstrat quam nos quoque imitari jubemur dicente *καὶ ἀναγγέλλομεν ὑμῖν, ὅτι ὁ θεὸς φῶς ἐστιν καὶ σκοτία*

ipso: *Sancti estote quoniam ego sanctus Dominus Deus vester* Lev. xix. 2 (Bede).

καί...] *And*... The declaration is the simple development of the statement in *v.* 3: 'We declare unto you what we have seen and heard, in order to establish your fellowship with us, and to fulfil our joy. And this *is* the message which has such divine power.'

ἔστιν αὕτη] *this is the message.* The original order (lost in V. *et hæc est*) in which the substantive verb stands first with unusual emphasis (*καὶ ἔστιν αὕτη*, comp. Hebr. xi. 1 note), marks the absoluteness, the permanence, of the message. The '*is*' is not merely a copula, but predicates existence in itself. Comp. c. v. 16, 17; ii. 15 note; John v. 45, viii. 50, 54. The exact form of expression is unique. On the other hand see c. ii. 25; iii. 11, 23; v. 4, 9, 11, 14 and 2 John 6.

ἀγγελία] *adnuntiatio* V., *message.* The word occurs only here and iii. 11 in the N.T., and it is rare in the LXX. The corresponding verb occurs in the N.T. only in John xx. 18. The simplest word appears to be chosen to describe the divine communication. The announcement as to the nature of God is a personal revelation and not a discovery. God gives tidings of Himself and so only can man know Him.

ἀπ᾽ αὐτοῦ] *from him*, that is, the Son of the Father, Jesus Christ, in whom the life was manifested, and who has been the main subject of the preceding verses.

The 'from' (*ἀπ᾽ αὐτοῦ*) marks the ultimate and not necessarily the immediate source (*παρ᾽ αὐτοῦ*). The phrase *ἀκούειν ἀπό* is not found elsewhere in St John (but see Acts ix. 13) while *ἀκούειν παρά* is frequent: John i. 40; vi. 45; vii. 51; viii. 26, 38, 40: xv. 15. The 'message' which the Apostle announces had been heard not only from the lips of Christ but in fact also from all those in whom

He had spoken in earlier times (1 Pet. i. 11). He was the source even where He was not the speaker. Comp. 1 Cor. xi. 23 *παρέλαβον ἀπό*, and c. ii. 27 note.

ἀναγγέλλομεν] *adnuntiamus*, V., *we announce.* The simple verb and its derivatives convey shades of meaning which cannot be preserved in a version. Ἀγγέλλειν simply '*to bring tidings*' occurs only John xx. 18. Ἀναγγέλλειν to report, with the additional idea of bringing the tidings *up to* or *back to* the person receiving them. Ἀπαγγέλλειν to announce with a distinct reference to the *source* or *place from* which the message comes. Καταγγέλλειν to proclaim with authority, as commissioned to spread the tidings *throughout* those who hear them. In *ἀναγγέλλειν* the recipient, in *ἀπαγγέλλειν* the origin, in *καταγγέλλειν* the relation of the bearer and hearer of the message, are respectively most prominent. (1) Thus *ἀναγγ.* has in nine cases a personal pronoun (*ὑμῖν, ἡμῖν*) after it, and in the two remaining places where it occurs (Acts xv. 4; xix. 18) the persons to whom the announcement is made are placed in clear prominence. The word is not found in the Synoptic Gospels (Mark v. 14, 19 false readings). For its meaning compare 1 Pet. i. 12 *ἃ νῦν ἀνηγγέλη ὑμῖν*, tidings which were lately brought as far as up to you. Acts xx. 20, 27 *τοῦ μὴ ἀναγγεῖλαι ὑμῖν*, not to extend my declaration of the Gospel even to you; John xvi. 13, 14, 15; Acts xv. 4; 2 Cor. vii. 7; Acts xiv. 27. (2) The proper sense of *ἀπαγγ.*, again, is seen clearly Matt. ii. 8 *ἀπαγγ. μοι*, from the place where you find the Christ, Mark xvi. 13 *ἀπηγγ. τοῖς λοιποῖς*, from Emmaus where the revelation was made; [John iv. 51 *ἀπηγγ. λέγοντες*, from his house where the sick child lay;] 1 Cor. xiv. 25 *ἀπαγγ.*, from the assembly at which he was moved. The word is frequent in the Synoptic

Gospels and in the Acts; elsewhere, in addition to the places quoted, it occurs only 1 Thess. i. 9; 1 John i. 2, 3. (Heb. ii. 12 LXX.) Comp. v. 2 note. (3) Καταγγέλλειν is found only in Acts (καταγγελεύς Acts xvii. 18) and St Paul. Its force appears Acts xvi. 21 καταγγέλλουσιν ἔθη, xvii. 3 ὃν ἐγὼ καταγγέλλω, &c.

In connexion with these words it may be noticed that St John never uses in his Gospel or Epistles εὐαγγέλιον (or cognates). Cf. Apoc. xiv. 6; x. 7.

ὅτι...ἐστὶν καί...οὐκ ἔστιν...] The combination of the positive and negative statements brings out (1) the idea of God's nature, and (2) the perfect realisation of the idea: He is light essentially, and in fact He is perfect, unmixed, light. The form of the negative statement is remarkable: 'Darkness there is not in Him, no, not in any way.' Οὐδείς is added similarly to a sentence already complete in John xix. 11 (vi. 63; xii. 19). The double negative is lost in the Latin: tenebræ in eo non sunt ullæ.

Positive and negative statements are combined vv. 6, 8; ii. 4, 27; v. 12; John i. 3, 5, 20; ii. 25; iii. 16 (20).

ὁ θεὸς φῶς ἐστίν] Deus lux est, V., God is light. The statement is made absolutely as to the nature of God, and not directly as to His action: as to what He is, and not as to what He does. It is not said that He is 'a light,' as one out of many, through Whom or from Whom illumination comes; nor again, that He is 'the light,' in relation to created beings. But it is said simply 'He is light.' The words are designed to give us some conception of His Being. Comp. Philo de Somn. i. p. 362 πρῶτος μὲν ὁ θεὸς φῶς ἐστί...καὶ οὐ μόνον φῶς ἀλλὰ καὶ παντὸς ἑτέρου φωτὸς ἀρχέτυπον, μᾶλλον δὲ ἀρχετύπου πρεσβύτερον καὶ ἀνώτερον....

Thus the phrase is at once distinguished from the cognate phrases which are defined by some addition; as

when creation, so far as it is a manifestation of the life of the Word, that is, as Life, is spoken of as being 'the light of men' (John i. 4 f.): or when 'the light, the true light, which lighteth every man' is spoken of as 'coming into the world' (John i. 9; comp. c. ii. 8); or when Christ—the Incarnate Word—declares Himself to be 'the light of the world' (John viii. 12; ix. 5; comp. xii. 46); or 'the light' (John iii. 19 f., xii. 35 f.); or when Christians, as representing Christ, are also called by Him 'the light of the world' (Matt. v. 14).

On the other hand it is closely parallel with two other phrases in St John's writings with which it must be compared and combined: God is spirit (John iv. 24) and God is love (c. iv. 8, 16).

To a certain degree this phrase unites the two others. It includes the thought of immateriality, which finds its most complete expression in the idea of 'spirit,' and that of 'diffusiveness,' which finds its most complete expression in the idea of 'love.' But to these thoughts it adds those of purity and glory, which find their most complete expression in relation to man as he is in the idea of 'fire' (Heb. xii. 29).

In order to enter into the meaning of the revelation given in the words, it is necessary to take account both of the biblical application of the term 'light' and of the thoughts which are naturally suggested by a consideration of the nature of light.

In each region of being 'light' represents the noblest manifestation of that energy to which it is applied. Physically 'light' embodies the idea of splendour, glory: intellectually of truth: morally of holiness.

Again: in virtue of light, life and action become possible. Light may exist close beside us and yet we ourselves be in darkness, wholly unconscious of its presence, unless some object intervene and itself become visible by reflecting into our eyes that which we had not before seen. Comp. Philo *de prœm. et pœn.* ii. 415 ὁ θεὸς ἑαυτοῦ φέγγος ὢν δι᾽ αὐτοῦ μόνου θεωρεῖται. See also Ps. xxxvi. 10. As light it cannot but propagate itself; and, as far as its own nature is concerned, propagate itself without bound. All that limits is darkness.

It must not however be supposed that in speaking of God as 'light' St John is speaking metaphorically, as if earthly 'light' were the reality to which God is likened. On the contrary according to his thought the earthly light, with all its associations, is but a reflection in the finite and sensible world of the heavenly light. Through the reflection we rise, according to our power, to the reality.

This being so, the description of God as 'light' is fitted to bring before us the conception that He is in Himself unapproachable, infinite, omnipresent, unchangeable, the source of life, of safety, of the transfiguration of all things.

And yet more than this the phrase has a direct bearing upon the economy of Redemption. It implies that God in Himself is absolutely holy; and at the same time that it is His nature to impart Himself without limit.

The first fact carries with it the condition of man's fellowship with Him. The second fact suggests that He will make some provision for the redemption and atonement of man fallen, in accordance with the purpose of creation.

The revelation of the Word, the Life, of 'Jesus, the Son of God,' fulfils the condition and the hope. By this we apprehend in all fulness that God is light, self-communicating, making the darkness felt to be what it is, conquering the darkness, while He claims from man complete self-surrender to His influence.

Here then as in every other place the revelation of the nature of God is not a satisfaction of speculative questionings: it is the groundwork of practical results.

God is light : therefore men must walk in the light.

God is spirit : therefore men must worship in spirit (John iv. 24).

God is love : therefore the manifestation of love is the sign of divine childship (iv. 7, 8, 16).

Comp. Heb. xii. 29.

See Additional Note on iv. 8.

The general opposition of light and darkness, which occurs throughout all Scripture, as throughout all literature, in its manifold partial applications, gives additional meaning to the phrase.

Category of Light.	*Category of Darkness.*
truth	falsehood.
good	evil.
joy	sorrow.
safety	peril.
life	death.

Compare Matt. iv. 16; Luke i. 79; xi. 35 f.; John iii. 19, 20; 1 Pet. ii. 9; 2 Cor. iv. 6; vi. 14; Ps. xxvii. 1 (and Hupfeld's note).

καὶ σκοτία...] The light which God is, is infinite, unbounded by any outline, and absolutely pure. It follows that all that is in darkness, all that is darkness, is excluded from fellowship with God by His very nature. There is in Him nothing which has affinity to it.

In speaking of 'light' and 'darkness' it is probable that St John had before him the Zoroastrian speculations on the two opposing spiritual powers which influenced Christian thought at a very early date. Comp. Basilides, *fragm.* Quidam enim [barbarorum] dixerunt initia omnium duo esse quibus bona et mala associaverunt, ipsa dicentes initia sine initio esse et ingenita: id est, in principiis lucem fuisse ac tenebras, quæ ex semetipsis essent non quæ esse dicebantur (ap. Iren. Stieren, i. p. 901).

οὐκ ἔστιν ἐν αὐτῷ οὐδεμία.   ⁶Ἐὰν εἴπωμεν ὅτι

οὐκ ἔστιν ἐν αὐτῷ B me the: ἐν αὐτῷ οὐκ ἔστιν ϛ ℵAC vg.   6. ἐὰν + γάρ A.

2.   *The relation of men to God* (i.
6—10).

The revelation of what God is determines man's relation to Him ; for
it is assumed that man knows (or can
know) what he himself is in himself.
The declaration of the majesty of
God therefore raises the question of
the possibility of man's fellowship
with Him; of the possibility, that is,
of the fulfilment of the Apostle's purpose (*v.* 3). How can the message
'*God is light*' issue in our *communion with the Father and with
His Son Jesus Christ?* The answer
lies, as we have seen, in the fact that
it is of the essence of light-nature to
communicate itself. The true sense
of what God is takes us out of ourselves. He gives Himself : we must
welcome Him ; and so reflecting His
glory we become like Him (2 Cor. iii.
18; 1 John iii. 2).

But this 'assimilation to God'
(ὁμοίωσις τῷ θεῷ κατὰ τὸ δυνατόν) requires a frank recognition of what
we are. St John therefore considers
the three false views which man is
tempted to take of his position. He
may deny the reality of sin (6, 7), or
his responsibility for sin (8, 9), or
the fact of sin in his own case (10).
By doing this he makes fellowship
with God, as He has been made
known, impossible for himself. On
the other hand, God has made provision for the realisation of fellowship
between Himself and man in spite of
sin.

The contrasts and consequences
involved in this view of man's relation
to God can be placed clearly in a
symmetrical form (*vv.* 6, 8, 10):
⁶*If we say We have fellowship with
Him, and walk in the darkness,
we lie, and
we do not the truth.*

⁸*If we say We have no sin,
we deceive ourselves and
the truth is not in us.*
¹⁰*If we say We have not sinned,
we make Him a liar and
His word is not in us.*

On the other hand (*vv.* 7, 9):
*But if we walk in the light, as He is
in the light,
we have fellowship one
with another, and
the blood of Jesus His
Son cleanseth us from
all sin.*
⁹*If we confess our sins,
He is faithful and right-
eous to forgive us our
sins, and
to cleanse us from ˙all
unrighteousness.*

The third contrast passes into a
different form (ii. 1 f.).
The whole description refers to the
general character and tendency of
life, and not to the absolute fulfilment
of the character in detail.
The progress in the development
of the thought is obvious from the
parallelisms. '*We lie,*' '*we deceive
ourselves,*' '*we make Him a liar*': we
are false, that is, to our own knowledge ; we persuade ourselves that
falsehood is truth; we dare to set ourselves above God. And again: '*we
do not the truth,*' '*the truth is not
in us,*' '*His word is not in us*': we
do not carry into act that which we
have recognised as our ruling principle; the Truth, to which conscience
bears witness, is not the spring and
law of our life; we have broken off
our vital connexion with the Truth
when it comes to us as '*the Word of
God*' with a present, personal force.
Corresponding to this growth of
falsehood we have a view of the
general character of the Christian

Κοινωνίαν ἔχομεν μετ᾽ αὐτοῦ καὶ ἐν τῷ σκότει περιπατῶμεν, ψευδόμεθα καὶ οὐ ποιοῦμεν τὴν ἀλήθειαν.

life, a life of spiritual fellowship and
sanctification; and then of its detailed
realisation in spite of partial failures.

6. ἐὰν εἴπωμεν] St John considers only the case of professing
Christians. In doing this he unites
himself with those whom he addresses; and recognises the fact that
he no less than his fellow-Christians
has to guard against the temptations
to which the three types of false doctrine correspond.

The exact form of expression (ἐὰν
εἴπωμεν) is found only in this passage
(vv. 6, 8, 10; comp. iv. 20 ἐάν τις εἴπῃ).
It contemplates a direct assertion of
the several statements, and not simply
the mental conception of them.

ὅτι] The particle here and in vv.
8, 10 seems to be recitative. Comp.
ii. 4; iv. 20; John i. 20, 32; iv. 17,
25; vi. 14; vii. 12; ix. 9, 23, 41.

κοιν. ἔχομεν μετ᾽ αὐτοῦ] *with Him,*
i.e. with God (the Father), the subject which immediately precedes.

The statement is the simple assertion of the enjoyment of the privileges
of the Christian faith, *v.* 3, note: "If
we claim to have reached the end of
Christian effort..."

καὶ ἐν τῷ σκ. περ.] The compati-
bility of indifference to moral action
with the possession of true faith has
ᴜ ᴊen maintained by enthusiasts in all
times oᶠ religious excitement. Comp.
c. ii. 4; iii. 6; 3 John 11.

For early forms of the false teach-
ing see Iren. i. 6, 2; Clem. Alex.
Sᵗᵛom. iii. 4 §§ 31 f.; 5 § 40. Comp.
Jude *v.* 4.

ἐν τῷ σκ. περ.] *walk in the darkness,* choose and use the darkness
as our sphere of action. The question is not directly of the specific
character of special acts, but of the
whole region of life outward and inward. The darkness (τὸ σκότος) is
the absolute opposite of 'the light.'

To choose this as our sphere of movement is necessarily to shun fellowship
with God. Part of the thought included in 'walking in darkness' may
be expressed by saying that we seek
to hide part of our lives from ourselves, from our neighbour, from God.
Comp. John iii. 20.

For the phrase see Is. ix. 2; John
viii. 12 (ἐν τῇ σκοτίᾳ). Comp. Matt. iv.
16; Luke i. 79; Rom. ii. 19. Σκότος
occurs in St John only here and John
iii. 19 note.

The image of 'walking,' resting on
the Old Testament ־ הֲלַךְ, LXX. περιπατεῖν, is not found applied to conduct
in classical writers, but is common in
St John and St Paul. The word is
not found in this sense in St James
or St Peter, and in the Synoptic
group of writings only in Mark vii. 5;
Acts xxi. 21. St John, it may be
added, does not use ἀναστροφή, ἀνα-
στρέφεσθαι, which are common in St
Peter and occur in St Paul and St
James; nor πορεύεσθαι, which is found
in St Luke (Gosp. Acts), St Peter (1,
2), and St Jude. Such 'walking' is
not to be limited to mere outward
conduct, but covers the whole activity
of life.

ψευδόμεθα...οὐ ποιοῦμεν...] The combination of the positive and negative
expressions here again (*v.* 5) presents
the two sides of the thought. Men
who profess to combine fellowship
with God with the choice of darkness
as their sphere of life, actively affirm
what they know to be false; and on
the other hand, they neglect to carry
out in deed what they claim to hold.
The two clauses (*lie...do*) correspond
with the two which precede (*say...
walk*).

ψευδόμεθα] The assertion is not
only false in fact, but known to be
false: it is at variance with man's
nature. Comp. James iii. 14.

^{7}ἐὰν δὲ ἐν τῷ φωτὶ περιπατῶμεν ὡς αὐτός ἐστιν ἐν τῷ

οὐ ποιοῦμεν τὴν ἀλήθειαν] *non facimus veritatem* V., *we do not the truth* (syr vg gives *do not advance in...*). Truth is not only in thought and word, but also in action. 'The Truth' (ἡ ἀλήθεια) which reaches to every part of human nature—the sum of all that 'is'—must find expression in a form answering to the whole man. 'I act,' in the words of Whichcote, 'and therefore I am.' Comp. John iii. 21 note; Neh. ix. 33 (LXX.). In the Old Testament the phrase 'to do mercy and truth' (LXX.) occurs not unfrequently: Gen. xlvii. 29; Josh. ii. 14; 2 Sam. ii. 6; xv. 20, &c. Contrast ποιεῖν ψεῦδος, Apoc. xxi. 27.

7. 'Walking in the darkness' is fatal to fellowship with God, but such fellowship is still possible. The Christian can in his measure imitate God (Eph. v. 1); and as he does so, he realises fellowship with the brethren, which is the visible sign of fellowship with God. At the same time Christ's Blood cleanseth him constantly, and little by little, from all sin. The chosen rule of life—the 'walking in light'—is more and more perfectly embodied in deed. The failure which is revealed in the presence of God is removed.

God *is* in the light absolutely and unalterably: man moves in the light from stage to stage as he advances to the fulness of his growth; and under the action of the light he is himself transfigured.

The process of this great change is written significantly in the N. T. Christ by resurrection from the dead first proclaimed light (Acts xxvi. 23), that is life reflecting the divine glory; to this God has called us (1 Pet. ii. 9); and opened our eyes *to look on the illumination of the gospel of the glory of Christ who is the image of God* (2 Cor. iv. 4); who *made us meet to be partakers of the inheritance of the*

saints in the light (Col. i. 12). By *believing on the light* we *become sons of light* (John xii. 36: comp. Luke xvi. 8; 1 Thess. v. 5); and finally are ourselves *light in the Lord* (Eph. v. 8).

'Walking in the light' brings two main results in regard to our relation to men and to God. We realise fellowship one with another, and in the vision of God's holiness we become conscious of our own sin. That fellowship is the pledge of a divine fellowship: that consciousness calls out the application of the virtue of Christ's life given for us and to us.

ἐὰν δέ...] *but if we walk...* There is a sharp contrast between the vain profession of fellowship and godlike action. *But*, setting aside mere words, *if we walk in the light...*

ἐν τῷ φ. περιπ.] The one absolute light is opposed to the darkness. To choose the light as the sphere of life is to live and move as in the revealed presence of God. Comp. Is. ii. 5; li. 4. The thought of walking in light and in darkness soon found expression in the allegory of 'The two ways.' Barn. *Ep.* xviii. ff. *Doctrine of the Apostles*, 1—6.

ὡς αὐτός...] *sicut et ipse* Latt., *as He Himself is in the light.* God is light, and He is in the light. Being light He radiates (as it were) His glory and dwells in this light unapproachable (1 Tim. vi. 16). The realm of perfect truth and purity in which He is completely corresponds to His own nature. Under another aspect light is His garment (Ps. civ. 2), which at once veils and reveals His Majesty.

Bede expresses well the contrast of περιπατεῖν and εἶναι: Notanda distinctio verborum... Ambulant...justi in luce cum virtutum operibus servientes ad meliora proficiunt... Deus autem sine aliquo profectu semper bonus, justus, verusque existit.

φωτί, κοινωνίαν ἔχομεν μετ᾽ ἀλλήλων καὶ τὸ αἷμα
᾽Ιησοῦ τοῦ υἱοῦ αὐτοῦ καθαρίζει ἡμᾶς ἀπὸ πάσης ἁμαρ-

7. μετ᾽ ἀλλήλων: A* (appy) tol Cl Al Tert (followed by J. C. domini nostri)
read μετ᾽ αὐτοῦ; harl has cum deo. The readings are evidently interpretative
glosses.
᾽Ιησοῦ ℵBC syrr the: +χριστοῦ ⸔ A vg me.
καθαρίζει: some auths., including A, read the future (καθαρίσει or καθαριεῖ).

αὐτός] He Himself, our Lord and
King. Comp. Deut. xxxii. 39; Is.
xli. 4 (Cheyne); xliii. 10; Jer. v. 12;
Ps. cii. 28 (הנא).
  κοιν. ἔχ. μετ᾽ ἀλλ.] societatem habemus ad invicem V., we have fellowship one with another, that is, brother
with brother : we enjoy the fulness of
Christian communion. The transcendental fellowship with God which the
false Christian claimed becomes for us
a practical fellowship in actual life.
True fellowship with God comes
through men. Love of the brethren is
the proof of the love of God : fellowship with the brethren is the proof of
fellowship with God.
  St John does not repeat the phrase
which he has quoted from the vain
professors of Christianity (we have
fellowship with Him, v. 6), but gives
that which is its true equivalent according to the conditions of our being.
Comp. v. 3.
  The supposition that μετ᾽ ἀλλήλων
means 'we with God and God with
us' is against the apostolic form of
language (John xx. 17), and also a-
gainst the genera form of St John's
argument, for he takes the fellowship
of Christians as the visible sign and
correlative of fellowship with God :
iv. 7, 12. Comp. iii. 11, 23.
  καὶ τὸ αἷμα...] and the blood...
This clause is coordinate with that
which goes before. The two results
of 'walking in the light' are inti-
mately bound together. Active fellowship shews the reality of that
larger spiritual life, which is life in
God ; and at the same time the action
of Christ upon the members of His

Body brings about that real sinlessness
which is essential to union with God.
  The case taken is that of those who
are in Christ's Body. The question
is not of 'justification,' but of 'sanctification.' 'Walking in the light' is
presupposed, as the condition for this
application of the virtue of Christ's
Life and Death. See Additional Note.
  ᾽Ιησοῦ τοῦ υἱοῦ αὐτοῦ] Jesus His
Son. The union of the two natures
in the one Person is clearly marked
by the contrast 'Jesus' (not Jesus
Christ), 'His Son.' Compare (iv. 15);
v. 5; Heb. iv. 14; (Gal. iv. 4 ff.);
and for the full title v. 3 note. Here
the human name (Jesus) brings out the
possibility of the communication of
Christ's Blood ; and the divine name
brings out its all-sufficing efficacy.
  Mire...ait et sanguis Jesu filii
ejus : Filius quippe Dei in divinitatis
natura sanguinem habere non potuit;
sed quia idem Filius Dei etiam Filius
hominis factus est recte propter unitatem personæ ejus Filii Dei sanguinem appellat ut verum eum corpus
assumpsisse, verum pro nobis sanguinem fudisse demonstraret (Bede).
So Ignatius (ad Eph. 1) ventures to
write ἐν αἵματι θεοῦ. Comp. Lightfoot on Clem. Rom. i. 2 παθήματα
αὐτοῦ, and the Additional Note in the
Appendix, pp. 400 ff.
  For the title see Additional Note
on iii. 23.
  καθαρίζει] emundat V., purgabit
Aug., cleanseth. Comp. John xiii. 10.
The thought is not of the forgiveness
of sin only, but of the removal of sin.
The sin is done away ; and the purifying action is exerted continuously.

τίας.   ⁸ Ἐὰν εἴπωμεν ὅτι ᾿Αμαρτίαν οὐκ ἔχομεν, ἑαυτοὺς

The idea of 'cleansing' is specially
connected with the fitting preparation
for divine service and divine fellowship. Ritual 'cleanness' was the
condition for the participation in the
privileges of approach to God, under
the Old Covenant. So 'the blood of
Christ' cleanses the conscience for
service to Him Who is a Living God
(Heb. ix. 13 f., 22 f.). He gave Himself for us, to cleanse for Himself
a peculiar people (Tit. ii. 14). He
cleansed the Church to present it to
Himself in glory (Eph. v. 26 f.).
The fulness of the thought is expressed in Matt. v. 8, where the blessing of 'the clean (καθαροί) in heart'
is that they shall see God (comp. 1
John iii. 2).

ἀ. πάσης ἁμ.] from all sin, so that
men are made like to God, in Whom
is no darkness (v. 5). The thought
here is of 'sin' and not of 'sins':
of the spring, the principle, and not
of the separate manifestations. For
the singular compare c. iii. 8 f.; John
i. 29: for the plural v. 9; ii. 2, 12;
iv. 10; Apoc. i. 5.

The sing. and plur. are used in significant connexion, John viii. 21, 24.

For the ·use of πᾶς with abstract
nouns (π. ἁμ. 'sin in all its many
forms') see James i. 2 πᾶσα χαρά, 2
Cor. xii. 12 πᾶσα ὑπομονή, Eph. i. 8
πᾶσα σοφία, 2 Pet. i. 5 πᾶσα σπουδή.
Contrast 1 Pet. v. 7 πᾶσα ἡ μέριμνα,
John v. 22 (τὴν κρίσιν πᾶσαν), xvi. 13
(τὴν ἀλήθειαν πᾶσαν).

The apostle describes the end and
consummation of Christ's work, towards which the believer is ever
moving. There is no promise that
the end will be reached on earth.

8. The mention of sin at the end
of v. 7 leads on to a new thought and
a new plea. 'How,' it may be asked,
'has the Christian anything more to
do with sin? How does it still continue?' The question has real difficulty.

Some who do not venture to affirm
the practical indifference of action,
may yet maintain that sin does not
cleave to him who has committed it,
that man is not truly responsible for
the final consequences of his conduct.
This is the second false plea: We have
no sin; sin is a transient phenomenon
which leaves behind no abiding issues:
it is an accident and not a principle
within us.

The issue of this second false plea
is also presented in a positive and
negative form. By affirming our practical irresponsibility 'we lead ourselves astray' positively, and negatively we shew that 'the truth is not
in us' as an informing, inspiring
power.

ἁμ. οὐκ ἔχομεν] we have no sin.
The phrase ἁμαρτίαν ἔχειν is peculiar
to St John in the N. T. Like corresponding phrases ἔχειν πίστιν (Matt.
xvii. 20; xxi. 21, &c.), ζωὴν ἔχειν (John
v. 26, 40, &c.), λύπην ἔχειν (John xvi.
21 f.), &c., it marks the presence of
something which is not isolated but a
continuous source of influence (comp.
κοινωνίαν ἔχειν v. 3).

Thus 'to have sin' is distinguished
from 'to sin' as the sinful principle is
distinguished from the sinful act in
itself. 'To have sin' includes the
idea of personal guilt: it describes a
state both as a consequence and as a
cause.

Comp. John ix. 41; xv. 22, note,
24; xix. 11.

The word 'sin' is to be taken quite
generally and not confined to original
sin, or to sin of any particular type.
A tempting form of this kind of error
finds expression in a fragment of
Clement of Alexandria (Ecl. Proph.
§ 15, p. 993 P.) ὁ μὲν πιστεύσας ἄφεσιν
ἁμαρτημάτων ἔλαβεν παρὰ τοῦ κυρίου,
ὁ δ' ἐν γνώσει γενόμενος ἅτε μηκέτι
ἁμαρτάνων παρ' ἑαυτοῦ τὴν ἄφεσιν τῶν
λοιπῶν κομίζεται.

πλανῶμεν καὶ ἡ ἀλήθεια οὐκ ἔστιν ἐν ἡμῖν. ⁹ἐὰν ὁμολογῶμεν τὰς ἁμαρτίας ἡμῶν, πιστός ἐστιν καὶ δίκαιος

8. οὐκ ἔστιν ἐν ἡμῖν ℵB me the: ἐν ἡμῖν οὐκ ἔστιν ⸂ AC vg.   Comp. v. 10.

ἑαυτοὺς πλαν.] ipsi nos seducimus
V., we deceive ourselves, or rather,
we lead ourselves astray. Our fatal
error is not only a fact (πλανώμεθα
Matt. xxii. 29; John vii. 47), but it is
a fact of which we are the responsible
authors. The result is due to our
own efforts. We know that the assertion which we make is false (ψευδόμεθα); and, more than this, we persuade ourselves that it is true.

The phrase does not occur again in
N. T. For the use of ἑαυτοὺς with
the first person see Acts xxiii. 14;
Rom. viii. 23; xv. 1; 1 Cor. xi. 31;
2 Cor. i. 9, &c. St John uses it with
the second person c. v. 21; 2 John 8;
John v. 42; vi. 53; xii. 8.

The idea of πλάνη (c. iv. 6) is in all
cases that of straying from the one
way (James v. 19 f.): not of miscon-
ception in itself, but of misconduct.
Such going astray is essentially ruin-
ous.

The cognate terms are used of
the false christs and prophets (Matt.
xxiv. 4 ff.; Apoc. ii. 20; xiii. 14; xix.
20; comp. c. iv. 6; 2 Ep. 7); of
Satan (Apoc. xii. 9; xx. 3 ff.), of
Babylon (Apoc. xviii. 23), of Balaam
(Jude 11).

Ἀπατάω, ἀπάτη (φρεναπατάω, φρενα-
πάτης) are not found in the writings
of St John. In this group of words
the primary idea is that of 'decep-
tion,' the conveying to another a false
belief.

καὶ ἡ ἀλ. οὐκ ἔ. ἐν ἡμ.] and the truth
is not in us. According to the true
reading the pronoun is unemphatic
(so v. 10). The thought of 'the Truth'
prevails over that of the persons. In
St John 'the Truth' is the whole
Gospel as that which meets the re-
quirements of man's nature. Comp.
John viii. 32 ff.; xviii. 37.   Introd.
to Gospel of St John, p. xliv.

The same conception is found in
the other apostolic writings; 2 Thess.
ii. 12; Rom. ii. 8; 2 Cor. xiii. 8;
(Gal. v. 7); 1 Tim. iii. 15; iv. 3; vi. 5;
2 Tim. ii. 15, 18; (Tit. i. 1); Heb. x.
26; 1 Pet. i. 22; James iii. 14; v. 19.

The Truth may therefore in this
most comprehensive sense be regarded
without us or within us: as something outwardly realised (v. 6 do the
truth), or as something inwardly efficacious (the truth is in us). Comp. v.
10 note. With this specific statement
ἡ ἀλ. οὐκ ἔστιν ἐν ἡμῖν (comp. ii. 4) contrast the general statement οὐκ ἔστιν
ἀλ. ἐν αὐτῷ John viii. 44 ('there is no
truth in him').

9. How then, it may be asked, can
consequences be done away? If sin
is something which clings to us in this
way, how can it be 'effaced'? The
answer is that the same attributes of
God which lead to the punishment of
the unrepentant lead to the forgiveness and cleansing of the penitent. He
meets frank confession with free blessing. And the divine blessing connected with the confession of sins is
twofold. It includes (1) the remission
of sins, the remission of the consequences which they entail, and (2)
the cleansing of the sinner from the
moral imperfection which separates
him from God: 1 Cor. vi. 9; Luke
xiii. 27.

ἐὰν ὁμολ.] There is no sharp opposition in form between this verse and
v. 8, as there is between 7 and 6 (if
we say—but if (ἐὰν δέ) we walk). Open
confession and open assertion are acts
of the same order.

ὁμολ. τὰς ἁμ.] confess our sins, not
only acknowledge them, but acknowledge them openly in the face of men.
Comp. ii. 23; iv. 2, 3, 15; Apoc. iii. 5;
John i. 20; ix. 22; xii. 42; Rom. x. 9,
&c. The exact phrase is not found else-

ἵνα ἀφῇ ἡμῖν τὰς ἁμαρτίας καὶ καθαρίσῃ ἡμᾶς ἀπὸ

9. τὰς ἁμ. (2) AB: + ἡμῶν אC vg syrr the me. om. ἡμᾶς C.

where in N.T.; but the kindred phrase ἐξομολογεῖσθαι ἁμαρτίας (παραπτώματα) occurs Matt. iii. 6 ‖ Mk i. 5; James v. 16. Comp. Acts xix. 18.

Comp. Ecclus. iv. 26 μὴ αἰσχυνθῇς ὁμολογῆσαι ἐφ' ἁμαρτίαις σου, Sus. v. 14 ὡμολόγησαν τὴν ἐπιθυμίαν.

Nothing is said or implied as to the mode in which such confession is to be made. That is to be determined by experience. Yet its essential character is made clear. It extends to specific, definite acts, and not only to sin in general terms. That which corresponds to saying 'we have no sin' is not saying 'we have sin,' but 'confessing our sins.' The denial is made in an abstract form: the confession is concrete and personal.

Augustine says with touching force: Ista levia quæ dicimus noli contemnere. Si contemnis quando appendis, expavesce quando numeras. And again: Vis ut ille ignoscat? tu agnosce.

πιστός ἐστιν...] The subject (God) is necessarily supplied from the context, vv. 5 ff. The form of the sentence (πιστός...ἵνα) presents the issue as that which is, in some sense, contemplated in the divine character. Forgiveness and cleansing are ends to which God, being what He is, has regard. He is not, as men are, fickle or arbitrary. On the contrary, He is essentially 'faithful' and 'righteous.' Comp. 1 Clem. ad Cor. c. 27.

Ἵνα is construed with adjectives in other cases: John i. 27 ἄξιος ἵνα...; Luke vii. 6 ἱκανὸς ἵνα..., but these are not strictly parallel; see c. iii. 11 note.

The epithet 'faithful' (πιστός) is applied to God not unfrequently in the Pauline epistles as being One who will fulfil His promises (Heb. x. 23; xi. 11), and complete what He has begun (1 Thess. v. 24; 1 Cor. i. 9),

and guard those who trust in Him (1 Cor. x. 13; comp. 1 Pet. iv. 19), because this is His Nature (2 Tim. ii. 13). With these passages those also must be compared in which Christ is spoken of as 'faithful' (2 Thess. iii. 3), and that both in regard to God (Heb. iii. 2) and to man (Heb. ii. 17).

God (the Father) again is spoken of in the New Testament as 'righteous' (δίκαιος) in Apoc. xvi. 5; John xvii. 25; Rom. iii. 26; and so also Christ, c. ii. 1, iii. 7; 1 Pet. iii. 18 (the usage in Matt. xxvii. 19, 24; Luke xxiii. 47 is different). The subject in c. ii. 29 is doubtful.

The essence of righteousness lies in the recognition and fulfilment of what is due from one to another. Truth passing into action is righteousness. He is said to be righteous who decides rightly, and he also who passes successfully through a trial.

Righteousness is completely fulfilled in God both in respect of what He does and of what He is. Here action and character (as we speak) absolutely coincide. And yet further, the 'righteousness' of God answers to His revealed purpose of love; so that the idea of righteousness in this case draws near not unfrequently to the idea of 'mercy.' Compare the use of 'righteousness' in the second part of Isaiah (e.g. xlii. 6, Cheyne).

It may indeed be said most truly that the righteousness of God is His love seen in relation to the discipline of man; and that love is righteousness seen in relation to the purpose of God.

So far as righteousness is manifested in the life of one whose powers and circumstances change, the principle, which is unchanging, will receive manifold relative embodiments from time to time.

The forgiveness and the cleansing

πάσης ἀδικίας.   ¹⁰'Ἐὰν εἴπωμεν ὅτι Οὐχ ἡμαρτήκαμεν,

of those who 'confess their sins' are
naturally connected with God's faithfulness and righteousness. They answer to what He has been pleased
to make known to us of His being
in Scripture and life and history.
He has laid down conditions for fellowship with Himself which man can
satisfy and which He will satisfy.

It is not difficult to see how this
view of God's action is included in
the fundamental message: *God is
light.* Light necessarily imparts itself (πιστός), and imparts itself as
light (δίκαιος).

The two epithets are applied to
God as 'a righteous and faithful witness,' Jer. xlii. 5.

ἀφῇ ἡμῖν τὰς ἁμ.] The verb ἀφιέναι
occurs in this connexion in St John
c. ii. 12; John xx. 23.   The phrase
ἄφεσις ἁμαρτιῶν (Synn., Acts, Eph.,
Col., Heb.) is not found in his writings.
The image of 'remission,' 'forgiveness,' presents sin as a 'debt,' something external to the man himself in
its consequences, just as the image of
'cleansing' marks the personal stain.

The repetition of the pronoun (ἡμῖν,
ἡμᾶς) is to be noticed.

ἀφῇ...καθαρίσῃ] remittat...emundet
ab... V., dimittat...purget ex... Aug.,
forgive...cleanse...   Both acts are
here spoken of in their completeness.
The specific sins (αἱ ἁμαρτίαι) are
forgiven (see Additional Note): the
character (ἀδικία) is purified.   The
Christian character (righteousness) depends on a distinct relation to God in
Christ.   This admits of no degree;
but there is a progressive hallowing
of the Christian which follows after
to the end of life (v. 7).

The two parts of the divine action
answer to the two aspects of righteousness already noticed.   As judg-
ing righteously God forgives those
who stand in a just relation to Himself: as being righteous He commu-

nicates His nature to those who are
united with Him in His Son.

Hence it is said that 'God cleanses'
—there can be no doubt as to the
subject—as before that 'the blood of
Christ cleanses.'   The Father, the one
Fountain of Godhead, cleanses by
applying the blood of the Son to
believers.   It is significant also that
'sin' (as distinguished from 'sins')
is here regarded under the relative
aspect of duty as 'unrighteousness'
(c. v. 17).

ἀδικίας] iniquitate V., unrighteousness.   The word occurs elsewhere in
St John only in c. v. 17; John vii. 18.

Generally the kindred words (δικαιοσύνη, &c.) are rare in his writings.
Righteousness and unrighteousness
are regarded by him characteristically
under the aspect of truth and falsehood: that is, under the form of being
rather than under the form of manifestation.

The correspondence of *righteous*
and *unrighteousness* is lost in the
Latin (justus...iniquitate), and hence
in A.V.

10.   So far the Apostle has dealt
with the two main aspects of the
revelation *God is light.*   He has
shewn what is the character which it
fixes for the man who is to have fellowship with Him (*if we walk in the
light*); and he has shewn also how
that character can be obtained (*if we
confess our sins*).   Man must become
like God; and to this end he must recognise his natural unlikeness to Him.

A third plea still remains.   He who
recognises the true character of sin,
and the natural permanence of sin as
a power within, may yet deny that
he personally has sinned.   This plea
is suggested by the words 'our sins'
in v. 9, just as the plea in v. 8 was
suggested by 'all sin' in v. 7.   Conviction in this case is sought not
primarily in consciousness (*we lie, v. 6*;

ψεύστην ποιοῦμεν αὐτὸν καὶ ὁ λόγος αὐτοῦ οὐκ ἔστιν
ἐν ἡμῖν.

we deceive ourselves, v. 8), but in the
voice of God (*we make Him a liar*).
The consequences of this assertion
of sinlessness are stated in the same
form as before (*vv.* 6, 8). By making
it we affirm (positively) that God
deals falsely with men; and (negatively) we are without the voice of God
within us which converts His revelation for each one into a living Word.
Thus divine revelation is regarded
first from without and then from
within. God speaks; and (it is implied) His word enters into the soul
of the believer, and becomes in him a
spring of truth (John iv. 14) and a
power of life (c. ii. 14). By claiming
sinlessness we first deny generally
the truth of the revelation of God;
and, as a consequence of this denial,
we lose the privilege of 'converse'
with Him: *His word is not in us.*

Philo in an interesting passage
(*Leg. Alleg.* i. 13: i. p. 50 M.) notices
the grounds on which men seek to
escape the charge of sin: ὁ μὴ ἐμ-
πνευσθεὶς (Gen. ii. 7) τὴν ἀληθινὴν
ζωὴν ἀλλ' ἄπειρος ὢν ἀρετῆς κολαζό-
μενος ἐφ' οἷς ἥμαρτεν εἶπεν ἂν ὡς ἀδίκως
κολάζεται, ἀπειρίᾳ γὰρ τοῦ ἀγαθοῦ σφάλ-
λεσθαι περὶ αὐτό...τάχα δὲ μηδ' ἁμαρτάνειν φήσει τὸ παράπαν εἴ γε τὰ ἀκούσια
καὶ τὰ κατὰ ἄγνοιαν οὐδὲ ἀδικημάτων
λόγον ἔχειν φασί τινες.

οὐχ ἡμαρτήκαμεν] *we have not sinned.*
The statement is quite unlimited. It
is an absolute denial of the fact of
past sin as carrying with it present
consequences.

ψ. ποιοῦμεν αὐτόν] *mendacem facimus eum* V., *we make Him a liar,*
that is God (the Father) who is the
main subject of the whole section
6—10 (*with Him, v.* 6; *as He is, v.* 7;
He is faithful, v. 9). The conclusion
follows from a consideration of the
nature of divine revelation. Revelation is directed in the first instance

to making clear the position of man
towards God. Such an office St Paul
assigns to law, and to the Law particularly. And generally all the com-
munications of God to men presuppose that the normal relations between earth and heaven have been
interrupted. To deny this is not only
to question God's truth in one particular point, but to question it altogether; to say not only 'He lieth'
in the specific declaration, but 'He is
a liar' in His whole dealing with
mankind. Comp. c. v. 10.

The peculiar phrase ψ. ποιοῦμεν is
characteristic of St John (John v. 18;
viii. 53; x. 33; xix. 7, 12), and carries
with it the idea of overweening, un-
righteous self-assertion.

ὁ λόγος αὐτοῦ] *His word,* the word
of God, ii. 14. Comp. John viii. 55;
x. 35; xvii. 6, 14, 17.

The phrase is used specially for the
Gospel message, which is the crown of
all revelation: Luke v. 1; viii. 11, 21;
xi. 28; and habitually in the Acts:
iv. 31; vi. 2, 7; viii. 14; xi. 1; xii.
24; xiii. 5, 7, 44, 46, &c.

The 'word' here differs from the
'truth' in *v.* 8 as the process differs
from the result. The 'truth' is the
sum considered objectively of that
which the 'word' expresses. The
word as a living power makes the
truth real little by little to him who
receives it (John viii. 31, 32). And
further, the 'word' is personal: it
calls up the thought of the speaker:
it is 'the word of God.' The truth on
the other hand is abstract, though it
is embodied in a Person.

The word, like the truth, can be
regarded both as the moving principle
which stirs the man and as the sphere
in which the man moves. The 'word
abides in him' (John v. 38, comp. viii.
37), and conversely he 'abides in the
word' (John viii. 31).

Additional Note on i. 2.   The Fatherhood of God.

The idea of the Divine Fatherhood, answering to that of human sonship *The Divine*
and childship (see Additional Note on iii. 1), occupies an important place *Father-*
in the writings of St John.   It cannot be rightly understood without *hood.*
reference to its development in the Old Testament and in the Synoptic
Gospels.

In the Old Testament the general notion of Fatherhood was made *i. In the*
personal by the special covenants which He was pleased to establish with *Old Testa-*
representative men.   He thus became the 'Father' of the chosen people *ment.*
in a peculiar sense (Ex. iv. 22; Deut. xxxii. 6; comp. i. 31, viii. 5; Is. lxiii.
16, lxiv. 8; comp. xliii. 1, 6, 21, xliv. 2, 24, xlvi. 3 ff.; Jer. xxxi. 9, 20; Hos.
xi. 1; Mal. ii. 10; comp. i. 6); and each member of the nation was His
child (Deut. xiv. 1; Is. i. 2, xxx. 1, 9, xliii. 6, lxiii. 8; Jer. iii. 4, 19; comp.
Matt. xv. 24, 26).   But this sonship was regarded as an exceptional blessing.
It belonged to the nation as 'priests and kings' to the Lord; and so we
find that the relationship of privilege, in which all the children of Israel
shared in some manner, was in an especial degree the characteristic of the
theocratic minister (comp. Ps. lxxii. 6).   Of the king, the representative
head of the royal nation, God said ' *Thou art my Son, this day,*' that is at
the moment of the solemn consecration, '*have I begotten thee*' (Ps. ii. 7):
and again, '*He shall cry unto me: Thou art my Father, my God, and the
rock of my salvation.   Also I will make him my firstborn, higher than
the kings of the earth*' (Ps. lxxxix. 26 f.; comp. 2 Sam. vii. 12 ff.).   Comp.
Ecclus. xxiii. 1, 4.

It will however be observed on a study of the passages that the idea of *This idea*
Fatherhood in the Old Testament is determined by the conceptions of an *limited.*
Eastern household, and further that it is nowhere extended to men generally.   God is the great Head of the family which looks back to Him as its
Author.   His 'children' owe Him absolute obedience and reverence: they
are 'in His hand': and conversely He offers them wise counsel and protection.   But the ruling thought throughout is that of authority and not
of love.   The relationship is derived from a peculiar manifestation of God's
Providence to one race (Ex. iv. 22; Hos. xi. 1), and not from the original
connexion of man as man with God.   If the nobility of sonship is to be
extended to Gentiles, it is by their incorporation in the chosen family (Ps.
lxxxvii.).

So far the conception of a Divine Fatherhood is (broadly speaking) *ii. The*
national among the Jews as it was physical in the Gentile world.   But in *idea of*
the Gospels the idea of Sonship is spiritual and personal.   God is revealed as *Father-*
the Giver and Sustainer (Matt. vii. 9 ff.) of a life like His own, to those who *hood in the*
were created in His image, after His likeness, but who have been alienated *Synoptic*
from Him (Luke xv. 11 ff.).   The original capacity of man to receive God is *Gospels.*
declared, and at the same time the will of God to satisfy it.   Both facts
are set forth once for all in the person of Him who was both the Son of
man and the Son of God.

This idea realised in Christ.

The idea of the Divine Fatherhood and of the Divine Sonship as realised in Christ appears in His first recorded words and in His dedication to His public ministry. The words spoken in the Temple: ' *Wist ye not that I must be in my Father's house?*' (Luke ii. 49 ἐν τοῖς τοῦ πατρός) appear to mark in the Lord, from the human side, the quickened consciousness of His mission at a crisis of His life, while as yet the local limitations of worship are fully recognised (contrast John iv. 21). The voice at the Baptism declares decisively the authority of acknowledged Sonship as that in which He is to accomplish His work (Matt. iii. 17 and parallels; comp. John i. 34).

Declared in the Sermon on the Mount.

In the Sermon on the Mount the idea of God's Fatherhood in relation both to Christ and to the disciples is exhibited most prominently. The first notice of the sonship of men is remarkable and if rightly interpreted most significant· ' *Blessed are the peacemakers for they shall be called sons of God*' (Matt. v. 9). This benediction is seen in its true light by comparison with the angelic hymn: ' *On earth peace among men of well-pleasing*' (Luke ii. 14). The peace of which Christ speaks is that of reunited humanity (comp. Eph. ii. 14 ff.). The blessing of sonship is for those who, quickened by God's Spirit (Rom. viii. 14), help to realise on earth that inward brotherhood of which He has given the foundation and the pledge.

The teaching which follows the beatitude enforces and unfolds this thought. The sign of Sonship is to be found in god-like works which cannot but be referred at once to their true and heavenly origin (Matt. v. 16). These are to be in range no less universal than the most universal gifts of God, the rain and the sunshine (v. 44 ff.; Luke vi. 35 ff.), in order that the fulness of divine sonship may be attained and manifested (*v.* 45 ὅπως γένησθε υἱοὶ τοῦ π. ὑ. τοῦ ἐν οὐρ.; Luke vi. 35 ἔσεσθε υἱοὶ ὑψίστου). At the same time the standard of judgment, even all-knowing love, impresses a new character upon action (Matt. vi. 1, 4, 6, 18). The obligations of kindred to others follow from the privilege of kindred with the common Father (Matt. vi. 14 f.; Mark xi. 25 f.). The Father's knowledge anticipates the petitions of the children (Matt. vi. 8; Luke xii. 30), and duly provides for their wants (Matt. vi. 26 ff.; Luke xii. 24 ff.). Here and elsewhere the laws of natural affection are extended to spiritual relations (Matt. vii. 9 ff.; Luke xi. 11 ff.).

The elevation of the idea in the New Testament.

From these passages it will be seen how immeasurably the conception of Fatherhood is extended by the Lord beyond that in the Old Testament. The bond is moral, and not physical: it is personal and human, and not national. It suggests thoughts of character, of duty, of confidence which belong to a believer as such and not peculiarly to those who stand in particular outward circumstances. In the few other passages in the Synoptic Gospels in which the title 'your Father' occurs, it has the same force: it conveys implicitly grounds of trust and the certainty of future triumph (Mat. x. 20, 29; Luke xii. 32). The 'name' of Him whom the Lord made known was, it may be said truly, 'the Father,' even as the name of Him who sent Moses was 'Jehovah,' 'the absolute,' 'the self-existent[1].' And in this con-

---

[1] There is really no strict representative of the name Jehovah in the New Testament except in the ὁ ὤν of the Apocalypse, and even there it is modified: Apoc. i. 4, 8, iv. 8 (ὁ ὤν καὶ ὁ ἦν καὶ ὁ ἐρχ.), xi. 17, xvi. 5 (ὁ ὤν καὶ ὁ ἦν).

nexion the first petition of the Lord's Prayer gains a new meaning: *Our Father which art in heaven, hallowed be Thy name*—the supreme revelation of Fatherhood (Matt. vi. 9; comp. Luke xi. 2).

The revelation of the Father is indeed distinctly claimed by the Lord for Himself alone (Matt. xi. 27; Luke x. 22). True discipleship to Him is the fulfilment of 'His Father's' will (Matt. vii. 21). He pronounces with authority upon the divine counsels and the divine working, as being of 'His Father' (Matt. xv. 13, xvi. 17, xviii. 10, 14, 19, 35, xxv. 34, xxvi. 29; Luke xxii. 29). He speaks of 'His Father's promise' (Luke xxiv. 49), and of 'His Father's presence' (Matt. x. 32 f.) with the confidence of a Son. But with the confidence of a Son the Lord maintains also the dependence of a Son. Every prayer which He makes will be answered (Matt. xxvi. 53), yet He places Himself wholly in 'His Father's' hands (Matt. xxvi. 39, 42); and He reserves some things for His Father alone (Matt. xx. 23). *The revelation of the Father by the work of Christ.*

Such a revelation of the Divine Fatherhood through the Son to sons definitely distinguishes the Christian doctrine of God from Pantheism and Theism. As against Pantheism it shews God as distinct from and raised immeasurably above the world; as against Theism it shews God as entering into a living fellowship with men, as taking humanity into personal union with Himself. The unseen King of the divine Kingdom is made known as One to whom His people can draw near with the confidence of children[1]. *Distinctive features of the revelation.*

The revelation of God as the Father is specially brought out by St John; but in a somewhat different form from that in which it is found in the Synoptists. Two titles occur commonly in the Gospel in relation to Christ: (a) The Father; and (β) My Father. Both of these occur in the Synoptists each nine or ten times. But on the other hand St John never uses the phrases ὁ πατήρ μου ὁ ἐν οὐρανοῖς (ὁ οὐράνιος), ὁ πατὴρ ὑμῶν ὁ ἐν οὐρανοῖς, which occur each nine times in the Synoptic Gospels; nor does he use the phrase ὁ πατὴρ ὑμῶν except xx. 17 (in contrast); nor yet the Pauline phrase ὁ πατὴρ ἡμῶν in his own writings. In the Epistles he uses *iii. The revelation of Fatherhood in St John,*

---

[1] The simple title 'my Father' is comparatively rare in the Synoptic Gospels. It is not found in St Mark (comp. viii. 38‖Matt. xvi. 27). It occurs in St Luke:

ii. 49 (ἐν τοῖς τοῦ π. μ.)
x. 22 (parallel to Matt. xi. 27)
xxii. 29 (καθὼς διέθετό μοι ὁ π. μ. βασιλείαν)
xxiv. 49 (τὴν ἐπαγγελίαν τοῦ π. μ.)

In St Matthew it is found more frequently

xi. 27 πάντα μοι παρεδόθη ὑπὸ τοῦ π. μ.
xx. 23 οἷς ἡτοίμασται ὑπὸ τοῦ π. μ.
xxv. 34 οἱ εὐλογημένοι τοῦ π. μ.
xxvi. 29 ἐν τῇ βασιλείᾳ τοῦ π. μ.
—— 39, 42 Πάτερ μου

xxvi. 53 παρακαλέσαι τὸν πατέρα μου.

But most frequently with the addition ὁ ἐν (τοῖς) οὐρανοῖς (ὁ οὐράνιος).

vii. 21, xii. 50 τὸ θέλημα τοῦ π. μ. τοῦ ἐν (τοῖς) οὐρ.
x. 32, 33 ἔμπροσθεν τοῦ π. μ. τοῦ ἐν (τοῖς) οὐρ.
xv. 13 ἣν οὐκ ἐφύτευσεν ὁ π. μ. ὁ οὐράνιος
xvi. 17 οὐκ ἀπεκάλυψέν ἀλλ' ὁ π. μ. ὁ ἐν οὐρ.
xviii. 10 τὸ πρόσωπον τοῦ π. μ. τοῦ ἐν οὐρ.
—— 19 γενήσεται αὐτοῖς παρὰ τοῦ π. μ. τοῦ ἐν οὐρ.
—— 35 οὕτως καὶ ὁ π. μ. ὁ οὐράνιος ποιήσει ὑμῖν.

uniformly the absolute title ὁ πατήρ (comp. 2 John 3) without any addition; and in the Apoc. ὁ πατὴρ αὐτοῦ (μου) but not ὁ πατήρ.

in contrast with that in the Synoptists. These differences though minute are really significant. St John in his latest writings regards the relation of the Divine Fatherhood in its eternal, that is, in its present, realisation, and not in regard to another order. Or to look at the truth from another point of view, St John presents to us the Sonship of Christ, the foundation of the sonship of men, from its absolute side, while the Synoptists connect it with the fulfilment of the office of the Messianic King.

The title 'the Father.' The full sense of the title 'the Father' will be seen by an examination of the passages in which the titles ὁ πατήρ and ὁ θεός occur in close connexion:

John i. 18 θεόν...εἰς τὸν κόλπον τοῦ πατρός.

— iii. 34 ff. ὁ θεός...τὰ ῥήματα τοῦ θεοῦ...ὁ πατὴρ ἀγαπᾷ...ἡ ὀργὴ τοῦ θεοῦ.

— iv. 21 ff. τῷ πατρί...τῷ πατρί...ὁ πατήρ...πνεῦμα ὁ θεός.

— vi. 27 ὁ πατήρ, ὁ θεός.

— 45 f. θεοῦ...τοῦ πατρός...τὸν πατέρα...τοῦ θεοῦ...τὸν πατέρα.

— xiii. 3 ὅτι πάντα ἔδωκεν αὐτῷ ὁ πατήρ...καὶ ὅτι ἀπὸ θεοῦ ἐξῆλθεν καὶ πρὸς τὸν θεὸν ὑπάγει.

— xiv. 1, 2, 9 τὸν θεόν...τοῦ πατρός μου...τὸν πατέρα.

1 John ii. 13 ff. τὸν πατέρα...τοῦ θεοῦ...τοῦ πατρός...τοῦ πατρός...τοῦ θεοῦ.

— iii. 1 ὁ πατήρ...θεοῦ.

— iv. 14 ff. ὁ πατήρ...τοῦ θεοῦ...ὁ θεός...τῷ θεῷ.

The title 'my Father.' The title 'my Father' as used by the Lord marks the special relation of God to the Son Incarnate, and so, mediately, to man in virtue of the Incarnation, and to all revelation as leading up to it. It is found John ii. 16, v. 17, 43, vi. 32, 40, viii. 19, 49, 54, x. 18, 25, 29, 37, xiv. 2, 7, 20, 21, 23, xv. 1, 8, 15, 23, 24, xx. 17.

The relation of the two titles. As to the relation of the two titles 'the Father' and 'my Father,' it may be said generally that 'the former suggests those thoughts which spring from the consideration of the moral connexion of God and man in virtue of the creation of man 'in the image of God,' while the latter points to those which spring from what has been made known to us in the course of the history of the world, the revelation of the connexion of the Incarnate Son with God and with man. 'The Father' corresponds under this aspect with the group of ideas gathered up in the Lord's title 'the Son of man' (comp. John vi. 27, viii. 28); and 'my Father' with those which are gathered up in the titles, 'the Son of God,' 'the Christ.'

The first instances in which the Lord uses the two titles seem to mark their meaning.

ii. 16 ὁ οἶκος τοῦ π. μου, comp. Luke ii. 49.

iv. 21, 23 προσκυνεῖν τῷ πατρί, comp. Matt. xi. 27.

And the first great discourse which lays the foundation of the Lord's claims unfolds the relation of the Son to the Father and to men, and so of men to the Father (John v. 19 ff.).

In this discourse it will be noticed that the title 'my Father' is found at the beginning and the end (*vv.* 17, 43), but elsewhere only the absolute titles 'the Father,' 'the Son.'

The two titles occur not unfrequently in close connexion, *e.g.*:

John v. 43 ἐλήλυθα ἐν τῷ ὀνόματι τοῦ πατρός μου.

— 45 μὴ δοκεῖτε ὅτι ἐγὼ κατηγορήσω ὑμῶν πρὸς τὸν πατέρα.

— vi. 27 τοῦτον ὁ πατὴρ ἐσφράγισεν.

— 32 ὁ πατήρ μου δίδωσιν ὑμῖν τὸν ἄρτον ἐκ τοῦ οὐρανοῦ.

— x. 27 διὰ τοῦτό με ὁ πατὴρ ἀγαπᾷ.

— 28 ταύτην τὴν ἐντολὴν ἔλαβον παρὰ τοῦ πατρός μου.

— 29 ὁ πατήρ μου ὃ δέδωκεν...ἁρπάζειν ἐκ τῆς χειρὸς τοῦ πατρός.

— xiv. 7 τὸν πατέρα μου ἂν ᾔδειτε.

— 9 ὁ ἑωρακὼς ἐμὲ ἑώρακεν τὸν πατέρα.

— xx. 17 οὔπω ἀναβέβηκα πρὸς τὸν πατέρα.

— ἀναβαίνω πρὸς τὸν πατέρα μου...

They are found also in phrases otherwise identical to which they give a sensible difference of colour.

John xiv. 11 ἐγὼ ἐν τῷ πατρὶ καὶ ὁ πατὴρ ἐν ἐμοί.

— 20 ἐγὼ ἐν τῷ πατρί μου καὶ ὑμεῖς ἐν ἐμοί.

— 31 ἐντολὴν ἔδωκέν μοι ὁ πατήρ.

— x. 18 ταύτην τὴν ἐντολὴν ἔλαβον παρὰ τοῦ πατρός μου.

If we try to go a little further into detail we notice the title 'the Father': Use of the title 'the Father.'

(1) In relation to men:

John iv. 21—3 προσκυνεῖν τῷ πατρί.

— v. 45 μὴ δοκεῖτε ὅτι ἐγὼ κατηγορήσω ὑμῶν πρὸς τὸν π.

— vi. 45 πᾶς ὁ ἀκούσας παρὰ τοῦ π.

— 46 οὐχ ὅτι τὸν π. ἑώρακέν τις.

— 65 ἐὰν μὴ ᾖ δεδομένον αὐτῷ ἐκ τοῦ π.

— x. 29 ἁρπάζειν ἐκ τῆς χειρὸς τοῦ π.

— 32 ἔδειξα ὑμῖν καλὰ ἐκ τοῦ π.

— xii. 26 τιμήσει αὐτὸν ὁ π.

— xiv. 6 οὐδεὶς ἔρχεται πρὸς τὸν π.

— 8 δεῖξον τὸν π....ἑώρακεν τὸν π.

— xv. 16 ὅτι ἂν αἰτήσητε τὸν π.

— xvi. 23 ἄν τι αἰτήσητε τὸν π.

— 26 ἐρωτήσω τὸν π. περὶ ὑμῶν.

— 27 ὁ π. φιλεῖ ὑμᾶς.

1 John ii. 1 παράκλητον ἔχομεν πρὸς τὸν π. (note).

— 14 ἐγνώκατε τὸν π.

— 15 ἡ ἀγάπη τοῦ π.

— 16 οὐκ ἔστιν ἐκ τοῦ π.

— iii. 1 δέδωκεν ἡμῖν ὁ π.

2 John 4 ἐντολὴν ἐλάβομεν παρὰ τοῦ π.

(2) In relation to the Son absolutely:

John i. 18 ὁ ὢν εἰς τὸν κόλπον τοῦ π.

— iii. 35 ὁ π. ἀγαπᾷ τὸν υἱόν (comp. xv. 9).

— v. 26 ὁ π....τῷ υἱῷ ἔδωκεν.

John vi. 46 οὗτος ἑώρακεν τὸν π.
— 57 κἀγὼ ζῶ διὰ τὸν π.
— x. 29 ἐγὼ καὶ ὁ π. ἕν ἐσμεν.
— xiv. 28 ὁ π. μείζων μού ἐστιν.
— xvi. 15 πάντα ὅσα ἔχει ὁ π. ἐμά ἐστιν.
1 John i. 2 ἥτις ἦν πρὸς τὸν π.
2 John 3 τοῦ υἱοῦ τοῦ π.
— 9 καὶ τὸν π. καὶ τὸν υἱὸν ἔχει (comp. 1 John ii. 22 ff.).

(3) In relation to the Mission of the Son—'the Father that sent me':

John v. 23 ὁ π. ὁ πέμψας αὐτόν.
— 36 ἃ δέδωκέν μοι ὁ π....μαρτυρεῖ ὅτι ὁ π. με ἀπέσταλκεν.
— 37, viii. 16, 18, xii. 49, xiv. 24 ὁ πέμψας με πατήρ.
— vi. 44 ὁ π. ὁ πέμψας με.
— x. 36 ὃν ὁ π. ἡγίασεν καὶ ἀπέστειλεν.
— xx. 21 καθὼς ἀπέσταλκέν με ὁ π.
Comp. xvi. 27 f. παρὰ τοῦ π., ἐκ τοῦ π. ἐξῆλθον.
1 John iv. 14 ὁ π. ἀπέσταλκεν τὸν υἱόν.
— i. 3, ii. 22, 23, 24 ὁ π., ὁ υἱός.

(4) More particularly in relation to the form of the Mission:

John v. 36 ἃ δέδωκέν μοι ὁ π. ἵνα τελειώσω αὐτά.
— vi. 27 ὁ υἱὸς τοῦ ἀνθρώπου...τοῦτον ὁ π. ἐσφράγισεν.
— viii. 28 καθὼς ἐδίδαξέν με ὁ π. ταῦτα λαλῶ.
— 38 ἃ ἐγὼ ἑώρακα παρὰ τῷ π. λαλῶ.
— xii. 50 καθὼς εἴρηκέν μοι ὁ π. οὕτως λαλῶ.
— xiv. 31 καθὼς ἐντολὴν ἔδωκέν μοι ὁ π. οὕτως ποιῶ.
— xv. 10 καθὼς ἐγὼ τοῦ π. τὰς ἐντολὰς τετήρηκα.
— xviii. 11 τὸ ποτήριον ὃ δέδωκέν μοι ὁ π.

(5) And also to the active communion between the Father and the Son in the accomplishment of it:

John v. 19 ff. ἂν μή τι βλέπῃ τὸν π. ποιοῦντα, ὁ π. πάντα δείκνυσιν αὐτῷ.
— vi. 37 ὃ δίδωσίν μοι ὁ π.
— x. 15 γινώσκει με ὁ π. κἀγὼ γινώσκω τὸν π.
— 38 ἐν ἐμοὶ ὁ π. κἀγὼ ἐν τῷ π.
— xiv. 10 ὁ π. ἐν ἐμοὶ μένων ποιεῖ τὰ ἔργα αὐτοῦ.
— 11 ἐγὼ ἐν τῷ π. καὶ ὁ π. ἐν ἐμοί.
— 31 ἀγαπῶ τὸν π.
— xvi. 32 ὁ π. μετ’ ἐμοῦ ἐστίν.

(6) And to the consummation of the Mission:

John x. 17 διὰ τοῦτό με ὁ π. ἀγαπᾷ ὅτι ἐγὼ τίθημι τὴν ψυχήν μου.
— xiv. 12 ἐγὼ πρὸς τὸν π. πορεύομαι.
— 13 ἵνα δοξασθῇ ὁ π. ἐν τῷ υἱῷ.
— 16 ἐρωτήσω τὸν π. καὶ ἄλλον παράκλητον δώσει.
— 28, xvi. 28 πορεύομαι πρὸς τὸν π.
— xvi. 10 πρὸς τὸν π. ὑπάγω.
— 17 ὑπάγω πρὸς τὸν π.
Comp. xiii. 1 ἵνα μεταβῇ...πρὸς τὸν π.

(7) And to the Mission of the Spirit :

John xiv. 26 τὸ πνεῦμα τὸ ἅγιον ὃ πέμψει ὁ π. ἐν τῷ ὀνόματί μου.
— xv. 26 ὁ παράκλητος ὃν ἐγὼ πέμψω ὑμῖν παρὰ τοῦ π., τὸ πνεῦμα...ὃ παρὰ τοῦ π. ἐκπορεύεται.
— xvi. 25 περὶ τοῦ π. ἀπαγγελῶ ὑμῖν.

In each respect the particular relation is traced up to the primal relation of the perfect divine love expressed in the idea of Fatherhood and Sonship.

The title 'my Father' is far more rare than 'the Father,' though it has been not unfrequently substituted for it in the later texts in order to bring out a more obvious sense. It fixes attention, as has been already remarked, upon the actual circumstances of Christ as the Incarnate Son, as serving to convey the true idea of God as Father.

Use of the title 'My Father.'

Hence it is used

(1) Specially in connexion with the office of Christ as the Fulfiller of the old Covenant, the Interpreter of the God of Israel Who had been misunderstood by the Jews. Looking to Christ, to His acts and words, Israel might see the true character of the Lord. The Son was the revelation of His Father :

John ii. 16 τὸν οἶκον τοῦ π. μ.
— v. 17 ὁ π. μ. ἕως ἄρτι ἐργάζεται.
— vi. 32 ὁ π. μ. δίδωσιν ὑμῖν τὸν ἄρτον ἐκ τοῦ οὐρανοῦ.
— viii. 19 οὔτε ἐμὲ οἴδατε οὔτε τὸν π. μ.   '
— 49 τιμῶ τὸν π. μ.
— 54 ἔστιν ὁ π. μ. ὁ δοξάζων με.
— x. 37 εἰ οὐ ποιῶ τὰ ἔργα τοῦ π. μ.
— xv. 1 ὁ π. μ. ὁ γεωργός ἐστιν.
— 8 ἐν τούτῳ ἐδοξάσθη ὁ π. μ.
— 23 ὁ ἐμὲ μισῶν καὶ τὸν π. μ. μισεῖ.
— 24 μεμισήκασιν καὶ ἐμὲ καὶ τὸν π. μ.

(2) And more widely of the particular aspect under which Christ presented the divine character in His own Person and Life :

John vi. 40 τὸ θέλημα τοῦ π. μ.
— x. 18 ταύτην τὴν ἐντολὴν ἔλαβον παρὰ τοῦ π. μ.
— 29 ὁ π. μ. ὃ δέδωκέν μοι.
— xiv. 2 ἐν τῇ οἰκίᾳ τοῦ π. μ.
— 7 εἰ ἐγνώκειτέ με καὶ τὸν π. μ. ἂν ᾔδειτε.
— 20 γνώσεσθε ὅτι ἐγὼ ἐν τῷ π. μ.
— 21 ἀγαπῶν ἐμὲ ἀγαπηθήσεται ὑπὸ τοῦ π. μ.
— 23 ὁ π. μ. ἀγαπήσει αὐτόν.
— xv. 15 ἃ ἤκουσα παρὰ τοῦ π. μ. ἐγνώρισα ὑμῖν.
— xx. 17 ἀναβαίνω πρὸς τὸν π. μ. καὶ πατέρα ὑμῶν.

Thus we can see the full force of the phrase 'I came in My Father's name,' and not simply 'in the Father's name.' Christ consummated the

earlier teaching and presented in a pattern of complete sacrifice the fulfilment of that love which is the source of being :

John v. 43 ἐλήλυθα ἐν τῷ ὀνόματι τοῦ π. μ.

— x. 25 τὰ ἔργα ἃ ἐγὼ ποιῶ ἐν τῷ ὀνόματι τοῦ π. μ.

Comp. xvii. 6, 11, 12, 26 (τὸ ὄνομα τοῦ π.).

'My Father' in the revelation of Christ brings 'the Father' close to
us (comp. Heb. ii. 11 ff.).

'The living   Still one other title must be noticed, 'the living Father,' John vi. 57.
Father.'   This phrase is unique, though it corresponds to the common title 'the
living God' (Apoc. vii. 2 θεοῦ ζῶντος, xv. 7 τοῦ θεοῦ τοῦ ζῶντος εἰς τοὺς αἰ.,
Matt. xvi. 16 ὁ υἱὸς τοῦ θ. τοῦ ζ. &c.). In the view which it gives of the
continuous activity of the divine love it completes the view of the divine
sovereignty given by the phrase ὁ βασιλεὺς τῶν αἰώνων, 1 Tim. i. 17; Apoc.
xv. 3.

*Additional Note on i. 7. The idea of Christ's Blood in the
New Testament[1].*

The idea   The interpretation of the passages in the New Testament which refer
of Blood in to the blessings obtained by the 'Blood' of Christ must rest finally upon
the O. T.   the interpretation given to the use of Blood in the sacrificial system of the
O. T. Our own natural associations with Blood tend, if not to mislead, at
least to obscure the ideas which it suggested to a Jew.

And here it is obvious that the place occupied by Blood in the Jewish
sacrifices was connected with the general conception attached to it through-
The seat of out the Pentateuch. The Blood is the seat of Life in such a sense that it
Life; and   can be spoken of directly as the Life itself (נֶפֶשׁ Gen. ix. 4; Deut. xii. 23).
More exactly the Life is said to be 'in the Blood' (Lev. xvii. 11). Hence it
was forbidden to eat flesh with the blood (Gen. ix. 4; Lev. vii. 26 f.; xvii.
11 ff.; Deut. xii. 23 f.): a man might not use another's life for the support
of his physical life.

living   For it must be observed that by the outpouring of the Blood the life
when shed. which was in it was not destroyed, though it was separated from the
organism which it had before quickened: Gen. iv. 10; comp. Heb. xii.
24 (παρὰ τὸν Ἄβελ); Apoc. vi. 10.

Appointed   This prohibition of the use of Blood as food gave occasion for the
for an   clearest declaration of its significance in sacrifice (Lev. xvii. 10 f.): *I will
atone-   even set my face against that soul that eateth blood, and will cut him off
ment.   from among the people. For the soul—life—(נֶפֶשׁ) of the flesh is in the
blood; and I have given it to you upon the altar to make an atonement
for your souls—lives (עַל־נַפְשֹׁתֵיכֶם), for the Blood, it atones through
the soul—life (בַּנֶּפֶשׁ יְכַפֵּר), i.e.* its atoning virtue lies not in its material
substance but in the life of which it is the 'vehicle.' Moreover, the

---

[1] On the subject of this note I may
refer to the very suggestive note of Dr
Milligan, *The Resurrection of Our Lord,*   pp. 263 ff. Compare Additional Note
on Hebr. ix. 12.

Blood already shed is distinctly treated as living. When it is sprinkled 'upon the altar' it makes atonement in virtue of the 'life' which is in it.

Thus two distinct ideas were included in the sacrifice of a victim, the death of the victim by the shedding of its blood, and the liberation, so to speak, of the principle of life by which it had been animated, so that this life became available for another end[1]. The ritual of sacrifice took account of both these moments in the symbolic act. The slaughtering of the victim, which was properly the work of the offerer, was sharply separated from the sprinkling of the blood, which was the exclusive work of the priest. The death was inflicted by him who in his representative acknowledged the due punishment of his sin; the bringing near to God of the life so rendered up was the office of the appointed mediators between God and men. Death and life were both exhibited, death as the consequence of sin, and life made by the divine appointment a source of life. And it is worthy of notice that these two thoughts of the shedding and of the sprinkling of the Blood, which embrace the two elements in the conception of atonement, were equally expressed by the one word αἱματεκχυσία, *sanguinis effusio (fusio)* V., *outpouring of blood* (Heb. ix. 22). Thus the life was first surrendered and then united with God. *Two aspects of its use: (1) shedding, (2) sprinkling.*

So far the thoughts suggested by the Jewish animal sacrifices seem to be clear; but they were necessarily imperfect and transitional. The union between the offerer and the offering was conventional and not real. The victim was irrational, so that there could be no true fellowship between it and the offender. Its death was involuntary, so that it could not embody in the highest form surrender to the divine will. *The Levitical use necessarily symbolical and imperfect.*

All that was foreshadowed by the Mosaic sacrificial system, all that was from the nature of the case wanting in it, Christ supplied. With Him, the Son of Man, all men are made capable of vital union: in Him all men find their true life. His sacrifice of Himself, through life and through death, was in every part a reasonable service. He endured the Cross at the hands of men. He was at once 'offered' and 'offered Himself' (Heb. ix. 14, 28); *and by His own blood He entered in once for all into the holy place, having obtained eternal redemption for us* (Heb. ix. 12). *The idea fulfilled in Christ.*

Thus in accordance with the typical teaching of the Levitical ordinances the Blood of Christ represents Christ's Life (1) as rendered in free self-sacrifice to God for men, and (2) as brought into perfect fellowship with God, having been set free by death. The Blood of Christ is, as shed, the Life of Christ given for men, and, as applied, the Life of Christ now given to men, the Life which is the spring of their life (John xii. 24). In each case the efficacy of the Life of Christ depends, from man's side, on the incorporation of the believer 'in Christ.' *Christ's Blood (1) shed (Death), (2) brought to God (Life).*

It will be evident from what has been said that while the thought of Christ's Blood (as shed) includes all that is involved in Christ's Death, the Death of Christ, on the other hand, expresses only a part, the initial part, *The idea of Christ's Blood always includes that of Christ's Life. Usage of St John.*

---

[1] Compare Philo, *qu. det. pot. ins.* § 23, i. 207 M.: ἡ μὲν οὖν κοινὴ πρὸς τὰ ἄλογα δύναμις οὐσίαν ἔλαχεν αἷμα· ἡ δὲ ἐκ τῆς λογικῆς ἀπορρευεῖσα πηγῆς, τὸ πνεῦμα... τύπον τινὰ καὶ χαρακτῆρα θείας δυνάμεως, ἣν ὀνόματι κυρίῳ Μωυσῆς εἰκόνα καλεῖ...

of the whole conception of Christ's Blood. The Blood always includes the
thought of the life preserved and active beyond death.

This conception of the Blood of Christ is fully brought out in the fundamental passage, John vi. 53—56. Participation in Christ's Blood is participation in His life (v. 56). But at the same time it is implied throughout
that it is only through His Death—His violent Death—that His Blood
can be made available for men.

In the other passages of St John's writings, where reference is made to
the Blood of Christ, now one part of the whole conception and now the
other predominates. In Apoc. i. 5 τῷ ἀγαπῶντι ἡμᾶς καὶ λύσαντι ἡμᾶς ἐκ
τῶν ἁμαρτιῶν [ἡμῶν] ἐν τῷ αἵματι αὐτοῦ, and in Apoc. v. 9 ὅτι ἐσφάγης καὶ
ἠγόρασας τῷ θεῷ ἐν τῷ αἵματι, the idea of the single act, the pouring out
of blood in death, is most prominent and yet not exclusively present.
In the one case the present participle (ἀγαπῶντι) seems to extend the act
beyond the moment of accomplishment; and in the other ἐν τῷ αἵματι
is felt to add something to ἐσφάγης which is not included in it. The
Blood is not simply the price by which the redeemed were purchased but
the power by which they were quickened so as to be capable of belonging
to God.

On the other hand in Apoc. xii. 11 ἐνίκησαν αὐτὸν διὰ τὸ αἷμα τοῦ
ἀρνίου, Apoc. vii. 14 ἐλεύκαναν αὐτὰς [τὰς στολάς] ἐν τῷ αἵματι τοῦ ἀρνίου,
1 John i. 7 τὸ αἷμα Ἰησοῦ τοῦ υἱοῦ αὐτοῦ καθαρίζει ἡμᾶς ἀπὸ πάσης ἁμαρτίας,
the conception of the Blood as an energetic power, as a fountain of life,
opened by death and flowing still, is clearly marked.

This latter thought explains the stress which St John lays on the issue
of the blood and the water from the side of the Lord after the Crucifixion
(John xix. 34; 1 John v. 6 ff. notes). That which was outwardly, physically, death, was yet reconcileable with life. Christ lived even in Death
and through Death.

The simple idea of the Death of Christ, as separated from His Life,
falls wholly into the background in the writings of St John (John xi. 50 f.;
xviii. 14; xii. 24 f., 33; xviii. 32). It is only in the words of Caiaphas that
the virtue of Christ's death is directly mentioned. In this respect his
usage differs from that of St Paul and St Peter (πάσχειν). If the Good
Shepherd 'lays down His life for the sheep' (John x. 11), this last act only
reveals the devotion of His care for them.

Usage of
the Epistle
to the
Hebrews.
In the Epistle to the Hebrews the manifold efficacy of Christ's Blood is
directly illustrated by a parallel with two representative sacrifices, the
Covenant Sacrifice by which Israel was brought into fellowship with God
(Heb. ix. 15 ff.), and the Service of the Day of Atonement, by which the
broken fellowship was again restored (Heb. ix. 11 ff.).

The Blood of Christ is the Blood of the New Covenant: Heb. ix. 15 ff.
See Matt. xxvi. 28; Mk. xiv. 24; Lc. xxii. 20; 1 Cor. xi. 25, 27 (comp. 1 Cor.
x. 16); and it is the Blood through which He as our High Priest enters
into the Presence of God for us: Heb. ix. 12, 23 ff.; comp. xiii. 12, i. 3.
These two aspects of the truth need to be carefully regarded. By 'sprink-
ling' of Christ's Blood the believer is first brought into fellowship with
God in Christ; and in the imperfect conduct of his personal life, the life of
Christ is continually communicated to him for growth and cleansing. He

himself enters into the Divine Presence 'in the Blood of Jesus' (Heb. x. 19) surrounded, as it were, and supported by the Life which flows from Him[1].

Similar thoughts find expression in the other writings of the New Testament. Thus we read with predominant reference to the initial act of salvation: *Usage in other books of N. T.*

Acts xx. 28 τὴν ἐκκλησίαν τοῦ θεοῦ ἣν περιεποιήσατο διὰ τοῦ αἵματος τοῦ ἰδίου.

1 Pet. i. 18 f. ἐλυτρώθητε...τιμίῳ αἵματι ὡς ἀμνοῦ ἀμώμου καὶ ἀσπίλου Χριστοῦ.

Col. i. 20 εἰρηνοποιήσας διὰ τοῦ αἵματος τοῦ σταυροῦ αὐτοῦ.

But even in such cases the first act is not regarded as an isolated act of forgiveness. It is the beginning of a state which continues:

Rom. v. 9 δικαιωθέντες νῦν ἐν τῷ αἵματι αὐτοῦ σωθησόμεθα δι᾽ αὐτοῦ.

Eph. i. 7 ἐν ᾧ ἔχομεν τὴν ἀπολύτρωσιν διὰ τοῦ αἵματος αὐτοῦ.

Eph. ii. 13 ἐγενήθητε ἐγγὺς ἐν τῷ αἵματι τοῦ Χριστοῦ.

In other places the thought of the continuous efficacy of Christ's Blood as a power of life is even more conspicuous:

1 Pet. i. 2 (ἐκλεκτοῖς) εἰς ὑπακοὴν καὶ ῥαντισμὸν αἵματος Ἰησοῦ Χριστοῦ.

Heb. ix. 14 τὸ αἷμα τοῦ Χριστοῦ...καθαριεῖ τὴν συνείδησιν ἡμῶν ἀπὸ νεκρῶν ἔργων εἰς τὸ λατρεύειν θεῷ ζῶντι.

Heb. x. 19 ἔχοντες ..παρρησίαν εἰς τὴν εἴσοδον τῶν ἁγίων ἐν τῷ αἵματι Ἰησοῦ...προσερχώμεθα...

Heb. xii. 24 (προσεληλύθατε) αἵματι ῥαντισμοῦ κρεῖττον λαλοῦντι παρὰ τὸν Ἄβελ.

The two elements which are thus included in the thought of Christ's Blood, or, in the narrower sense of the word, of Christ's Death and Christ's Blood, that is of Christ's Death (the Blood shed) and of Christ's Life (the Blood offered), are indicated clearly in *v.* 9 [*God*] *is faithful and righteous to forgive us our sins* (the virtue of Christ's Death); *and to cleanse us from all unrighteousness* (the virtue of Christ's Life). *1 John i. 9.*

Additional Note on i. 9. The idea of sin in St John.

The treatment of the doctrine of sin by St John requires to be considered briefly in its main features for the understanding of many details in the Epistle. 'Sin,' St John says in a phrase of which the terms are made convertible, 'is lawlessness' (c. iii. 4 ἁμαρτία ἐστὶν ἡ ἀνομία, *peccatum est iniquitas* V.). The description is absolutely exhaustive. Man is constituted with a threefold relation, a threefold obligation to self, to the world, to God. To violate the 'law' by which this relation is defined in life is 'to sin.' Each conscious act by which the law is broken *The idea of sin in St John.*

---

[1] Compare a remarkable passage of Clement of Alexandria: διττὸν δὲ τὸ αἷμα τοῦ κυρίου, τὸ μὲν γάρ ἐστιν αὐτοῦ σαρκικόν, ᾧ τῆς φθορᾶς λελυτρώμεθα, τὸ δὲ πνευματικόν, τουτέστιν ᾧ κεχρίσμεθα. καὶ τοῦτ᾽ ἔστι πιεῖν τὸ αἷμα τοῦ Ἰησοῦ τῆς κυριακῆς μεταλαβεῖν ἀφθαρσίας· ἰσχὺς δὲ τοῦ λόγου τὸ πνεῦμα, ὡς αἷμα σαρκός (*Pæd.* ii. 2, § 19).

is 'a sin': the principle which finds expression in the special acts is 'sin' (ἡ ἁμαρτία, John i. 29)[1].

Sin is self-assertion, selfishness, hatred. When traced back to its last form this 'sin' is the self-assertion of the finite in violation of the limits which guide the harmonious fulfilment of the idea of its being. Every such act, being in its essence self-regarding, self-centred, must be a violation of 'love.' Thus lawlessness is under another aspect selfishness; or as it is characterised by St John, 'hatred' in opposition to love (1 John ii. 9; iii. 14 f.; iv. 20). There can be essentially no middle term.

The revealed law. The 'law' which determines man's right conduct finds manifold declaration, through special divine utterances (John xvii. 8, ῥήματα), commandments (c. ii. 3 ἐντολαί), which are gathered up in the unity of one revelation (λόγος) without and within (c. ii. 7, 14). To disregard any of these is to sin.

'Sin,' 'sins.' It follows that ἁμαρτία ('a sin,' 'sin') and ἁμαρτάνειν ('to sin') have two distinct meanings. Ἁμαρτία may describe a single act impressed by the sinful character (1 John v. 16 f.), or sin regarded in the abstract (John xvi. 8 f.). And again ἁμαρτάνειν may be 'to commit a sinful act' (c. i. 10) or 'to present a sinful character' (c. iii. 6). The plural ἁμαρτίαι offers no ambiguity (John viii. 24; xx. 23; 1 John i. 9; ii. 2, 12; iii. 5; iv. 10; comp. Apoc. i. 5; xviii. 4 f.).

The sinful character. This distinction between the principle, the power, of sin and the manifestation of the power in individual sins is of primary importance. The wrong-doer embodies sin in deed (c. iii. 4, 8 ὁ ποιῶν τὴν ἁμαρτίαν, comp. John viii. 34), just as the right-doer embodies the Truth (c. i. 6 ποιεῖν τὴν ἀλήθειαν); and by so doing he contracts a character corresponding to his deeds (c. i. 8 ἔχει ἁμαρτίαν).

All men as sinful need salvation. Sin, as a fact, is universal (1 John i. 10); and the end of sin is death (James i. 15). Or, as St John states the case, looking at the eternal relations of things, man in his natural state is 'in death' (1 John iii. 14 μεταβεβήκαμεν ἐκ τοῦ θανάτου εἰς τὴν ζωήν; comp. John v. 24, 40; Matt. viii. 22 ‖ Lc. ix. 60; Lc. xv. 24). 'The wrath of God abideth upon him' (John iii. 36 μένει ἐπ᾽ αὐτόν; comp. Eph. ii. 3 τέκνα φύσει ὀργῆς). He needs 'salvation' (σώζειν John iii. 17; v. 34; x. 9; xii. 47; σωτήρ John iv. 42, 1 John iv. 14; ἡ σωτηρία John iv. 22; comp. Apoc. vii. 10; xii. 10; xix. 1).

It may come to pass that 'sin' and 'sins' surround the sinner and become as it were the element in which he exists (John viii. 21 ἐν τῇ ἁμαρτίᾳ, 24 ἐν ταῖς ἁμαρτίαις, comp. 1 John v. 19 ἐν τῷ πονηρῷ κεῖται). He who sins 'has not seen God' (1 John iii. 6). 'Darkness' not only hinders the use of sight but destroys the organ of sight (1 John ii. 11). There is even in the Christian body a sin unto death (c. v. 16 ἁμαρτία πρὸς θάνατον,

---

[1] This use of ἡ ἁμαρτία is not found in the Synoptic Gospels nor in the Acts. It occurs in St Paul: Rom. v. 12, &c.

Many of the special terms which are used for sin in different aspects in other writings of the New Testament, are wanting in St John, e.g. ἀσεβεῖν, ἀσέβεια (St Paul, St Peter, St Jude), παραβαίνειν, παράβασις, παραβάτης (St Matthew, St Paul, Hebrews, St James; in 2 John 9 read προάγων); (παρανομεῖν, παρανομία); παράπτωμα (παραπίπτειν) (St Matthew, St Mark, St Paul). He commonly speaks of sin under the terms 'darkness,' 'hatred,' 'wandering.' Compare the very interesting enumeration of typical forms of sin in Ecclus. xli. 17 f.

peccatum ad mortem V.) which excludes from the privileges of the Christian society, the natural forces of the Christian life.

The efficacy of Christ's work extends both to sin and sins. As 'the Christ Lamb of God' 'He taketh away the sin of the world' (John i. 29 ὁ ἀμνὸς deals with τοῦ θεοῦ, ὁ αἴρων τὴν ἁμαρτίαν τοῦ κόσμου, V. *Agnus Dei...qui tollit peccatum mundi*); and again ' He was manifested that He may take away sins,' sins. not simply 'our sins' (1 John iii. 5 ἐφανερώθη ἵνα ἄρῃ τὰς ἁμαρτίας, *apparuit ut peccata tolleret* V.). Under another aspect this 'removal of sins' is an 'undoing,' an 'abrogation of the works of the devil' (c. iii. 8 ἐφανερώθη ὁ υἱὸς τοῦ θεοῦ ἵνα λύσῃ τὰ ἔργα τοῦ διαβόλου, *apparuit Filius Dei ut dissolvat opera diaboli* V.).

The consequences of sin once committed place the need of the sinner in Sin brings a clear light. Sin unless it be taken away 'abideth' (John ix. 41); and debt, its consequences fall under three main heads. The sinner incurs a debt; bondage, he falls into bondage; and he is estranged from God. The particular act from God. calls for a proportionate reparation, the moral discipline of the debtor coinciding with the satisfaction due to the broken law; the wrong-doing impairs so far the powers of the doer; and it also places a barrier between him and God. The notion of debt (Matt. vi. 12) is recognised in that of the 'remission' of sins (c. i. 9; John xx. 23): the notion of bondage finds a most emphatic exposition in John viii. 32 ff.: 'the love of the Father' is incompatible with the love of the world, out of which sin springs (1 John ii. 15 ff.; comp. Eph. iv. 18; Col. i. 21).

Thus it is that man needs forgiveness, redemption, reconciliation. For- Forgive-giveness in order to be complete involves not only the remission of the ness. penalty of the deed but the removal of the direct results of the act on the doer. As long as a debtor finds that his debt is remembered though the payment of it will not be exacted, forgiveness is not complete. The exercise of such a power of forgiveness corresponds with a new creation. Thus when the Lord claims as Son of man the power of the forgiveness of sins He offers as a sign of it a creative act (Matt. ix. 5 f.; comp. John v. 14). And so St John appeals to the divine promise assured to the penitent to 'forgive their sins and cleanse them from all unrighteousness' (1 John i. 9).

Redemption again includes two elements, the deliverance of the sinner Redemp-from thraldom to a foreign power, and the restoration of his lost strength. tion. St John does not use the group of words connected with λύτρον (λυτροῦσθαι, λυτρωτής, λύτρωσις, ἀντίλυτρον), but he has the simple λύω (Apoc. i. 5); and in the Apocalypse he carries out the notion yet further, representing Christians as 'bought' for God (v. 9; xiv. 3 f.).

Man's estrangement from God by sin can also be regarded in two ways. Reconcili-Sin cannot but be a bar to God's love; and conversely man as sinful ation. cannot love God. He requires a change in condition and a change in feeling, propitiation and reconcilement. The latter thought finds its plainest expression in the group of words καταλλάσσειν, ἀποκαταλλάσσειν, καταλλαγή, which are peculiar to St Paul: the former in the group ἱλάσκομαι, ἱλασμός, ἱλαστήριον. The change in the personal relation of man to God, from the side of man, indicated by 'reconcilement' (2 Cor. v. 18—20; Rom. v. 10 f.), is referred to its source by St John, who shews that the love of God in the Mission of His Son calls out man's love (1 John iv. 10). On the other hand God looks with good pleasure on man in Christ: Christ is 'the propitiation for our sins' (c. ii. 2). 'He loosed us from our sins in His blood' (Apoc. i. 5). 'His blood cleanseth from all sin' (i. 7; comp. Heb. i. 3 καθαρισμὸν ἀμ. ποιησάμενος, Acts xxii. 16 ἀπόλουσαι τὰς ἀμ.)[1].

All flow from fellowship in Christ.
The last phrases lead at once to St John's view of the way in which the work of the Word Incarnate avails for forgiveness, for redemption, for reconcilement. By dying on the Cross He made His Life—His blood— available for all who believe in Him. The gift of God is eternal, divine, life, 'and this life is in His Son' (1 John v. 11 f.). The possession of such life is the destruction of past sin, and safety from sin to come (1 John iii. 9). By incorporation with Christ the believer shares the virtue of His humanity (John vi. 51, 57). Thus finally unbelief in Him is the test of sin (John xvi. 9).

Compare additional notes on i. 7; ii. 2, 13.

It may be added that it will be evident from this sketch of the teaching of the N.T. on sin, according to which the fundamental conception of sin is the self-assertion of the finite against the infinite, that the relation of good to evil is not one which exists of necessity in the nature of things. The difference is not metaphysical, inherent in being, so that the existence of evil is involved in the existence of good; nor physical, as if there were an essential antagonism between matter and spirit; but moral, that is recognised in the actual course of life, so that evil when present is known to be opposed to good.

---

[1] It will be of interest to put together without any discussion the various phrases which describe the action of Christ with regard to sin and sins.

(1) As to sin itself, He brought
condemnation by His Incarnation; Rom. viii. 3 ὁ θεὸς τὸν ἑαυτοῦ υἱὸν πέμψας...κατέκρινε τὴν ἁμαρτίαν ἐν τῇ σαρκί.
disannulling by His sacrifice: Heb. ix. 26 εἰς ἀθέτησιν τῆς ἁμαρτίας, διὰ τῆς θυσίας αὐτοῦ πεφανέρωται... Comp. Rom. vi. 7 ὁ ἀποθανὼν δεδικαίωται ἀπὸ τῆς ἁμ.

(2) As to the sins of men Christ
makes propitiation for them: Heb. ii. 17...ἀρχιερεύς...εἰς τὸ ἱλάσκεσθαι τὰς ἁμαρτίας τοῦ λαοῦ.

forgives them: Matt. ix. 2 ff.: ἀφίενταί σου αἱ ἁμαρτίαι. Comp. Col. ii. 13 χαρισάμενος τὰ παραπτώματα.
takes them away, by bearing them: 1 John iii. 5 ἵνα ἄρῃ τὰς ἁμαρτίας; John i. 29 ὁ αἴρων τὴν ἁμαρτίαν τοῦ κόσμου. Comp. Heb. x. 4 ἀφαιρεῖν ἁμ.; x. 11 περιελεῖν ἁμ.
looses men from them: Apoc. i. 5 τῷ...λύσαντι ἡμᾶς ἐκ τῶν ἁμ. ἐν τῷ αἵματι αὐτοῦ. Comp. Rom. vi. 22 ἐλευθερωθέντες ἀπὸ τῆς ἁμ.
cleanses men from all sin: 1 John i. 7 τὸ αἷμα Ἰησοῦ...καθαρίζει ἡμ. ἀπὸ π. ἁμ.
saves from sins: Matt. i. 21 σώσει ...ἀπὸ τῶν ἁμ.

II.   ¹Τεκνία μου, ταῦτα γράφω ὑμῖν ἵνα μὴ ἁμάρ-

II. THE REMEDY FOR SIN AND
THE SIGN THAT IT IS EFFECTUAL (ii.
1—6).

Having dealt with the fact of sin
and the false pleas by which man en-
deavours to do away with its significance, St John states

1 The divine remedy for sin (vv. 1, 2).

2 The sign that the remedy is effectual in any particular case (vv. 3—6).

The first sub-section answers to the
counter-statements made in relation to
the first two pleas of men (i. 7, 9), but
it has a prominent distinctness of form,
as giving the complete answer to the
problem raised in i. 5—10. The assurance of the forgiveness of sin when
combined with the fact of its universality might lead some to underrate
its evil. In order to remove the last
semblance of support for such an
error, St John shews that the nature of the remedy for sin is such as
to move men most powerfully to
shrink from all sin and to help them
to avoid it.

This connexion is partly indicated
by Augustine: Male vis esse securus,
sollicitus esto. Fidelis enim est et
justus ut dimittat nobis delicta nostra
si semper tibi displiceas et muteris
donec perficiaris. Ideo quid sequitur?
*Filioli mei, hæc scribo vobis ut non
peccetis.*

1. *The divine remedy for sin*
(ii. 1, 2).

¹*My little children, these things I
write to you that ye may not sin.
And if anyone sin, we have an advocate with the Father, Jesus Christ,
the righteous; ²and himself is a
propitiation for our sins, and not
for ours only, but also for the whole
world.*

The fact of sin as something which
is irreconcileable with God and fruitful in consequences raises the questions of propitiation and mediation.

How, it may be asked, is that forgiveness, that cleansing, already spoken
of (i. 7, 9), brought about? The answer
is given in the summary description
of Christ's work. Christ is a universal
propitiation for sins; and He is an
advocate for the Christian. He has
accomplished a work on earth for all:
He is accomplishing a work in heaven
for those who are united with Him.
Both in Person (*righteous*) and in
work (*propitiation*) He is fitted to
fulfil the office which our necessities
require. These thoughts are treated
in the inverse order, because the Apostle approaches the subject from the
side of believers (*we have*).

It has been already noticed that
the third plea (i. 10, *we have not
sinned*) is not treated exactly as the
two former. Symmetry would have
required a clause answering to the
assertion '*we have not sinned.*' St
John might, for example, have continued: 'if we sin....' But he shrinks
naturally from regarding sin as a
normal element in the Christian life;
and therefore he changes the mode
of dealing with the subject. Before
touching on the fact of sin, as indeed
part of the believer's experience to
the last, he asserts the end of his
teaching, which is sinlessness. This
is the end; and even if it cannot be
gained by the believer's effort and
directly, it can be gained through the
Saviour's work. That which is true
of the past (i. 9) is true throughout.

1. τεκνία μου] *filioli mei* V., *my
little children.* The form adopted in
i. 7, 9 is changed for one more direct
and personal. The thought of sin as a
reality for each one moves the Apostle
to address with the utmost tenderness
those to whom he stands in the relation of a father. The title τεκνία occurs in John xiii. 33 and c. ii. 12, 28;
iii. 7, 18; iv. 4; v. 21 (Gal. iv. 19 τεκνία
μου is uncertain). The full title τεκνία

τητε. καὶ ἐάν τις ἁμάρτῃ, παράκλητον ἔχομεν πρὸς

μου is found only here (c. iii. 18 is a
false reading). A commentary on St
John's use of the word is given by
the story (μῦθος οὐ μῦθος) of the
young Robber (Euseb. *H. E.* iii. 23).

ταῦτα γράφω] *these things I write*,
not only all that has been already said
as to the nature of God and as to the
reality, the nature, and the fact of sin
(i. 5—10), but, as i. 4, all that is present to the mind of the Apostle as the
substance of his letter, though indeed
the preceding section includes all by
implication.

The use of the singular, *I write (vv.*
7, 8, 12, 13, 14, 21, 26; v. 13; contrast
i. 4) follows from 'my dear children.'

ἵνα μὴ ἁμάρτητε] *ut non peccetis* V.,
that ye may not sin. The phrase
is absolute. The thought is of the
single act (ἁμάρτητε) not of the state
(ἁμαρτάνητε); and the tense is decisive
against the idea that the Apostle is
simply warning his disciples not to
draw encouragement for licence from
the doctrine of forgiveness. His aim
is to produce the completeness of the
Christ-like life (*v.* 6).

The difference of the aor. and pres.
conj. in connexion with ἵνα is well
illustrated by John v. 20, 23; vi. 28 f.

καὶ ἐάν τις...] *sed et si quis* V., *i.e.* ἐὰν
δὲ καί, *si quis* Aug., *and if any...* The
declaration of the remedy for sin is
placed as part of the main declaration of St John. It is not set as a
contrast (i. 7 ἐὰν δέ), nor simply as a
parallel clause (i. 9 ἐὰν ὁμολογῶμεν);
but as a continuous piece of the one
message. Here again the thought is
of the single act (ἁμάρτῃ) regarded
as past, into which the believer may
be carried against the true tenor of
his life (i. 7), as contrasted with the
habitual state (ἁμαρτάνει iii. 6, 8, 9; v.
18). Nothing is said in one direction
or the other of the possibility of a
Christian life actually sinless.

The change of construction in the

sentence is remarkable. St John
writes *if any one...we...* and not *if
ye sin...ye...*, nor yet *if we sin...
we...*or *if any one...he...*, in order
to bring out the individual character
of the offence, and then to shew that
he is speaking of the Christian body
with which he identifies himself,
and to which Christ's promises are
assured. This is forcibly pointed out
by Augustine: Non dixit *habetis,* nec
me habetis dixit, nec *ipsum Christum
habetis* dixit; sed et Christum posuit
non se, et *habemus* dixit non *habetis.*
Maluit se ponere in numero peccatorum ut haberet advocatum Christum quam ponere se pro Christo advocatum et inveniri inter damnandos
superbos. Comp. Hebr. x. 26 n.

ἔχομεν] *we have* as a divine gift.
Comp. ii. 23; v. 12; 2 John 9.

παράκλητον] *advocatum* V., *an advocate.* This is the uniform rendering of the Latin and English Versions in this place, and is unques-
tionably correct, although the Greek
fathers give to it, as in the Gospel, an
active sense, 'consoler,' 'comforter.'
Christ as Advocate pleads the cause
of the believer against his 'accuser'
(κατήγωρ Apoc. xii. 10; comp. Zech.
iii. 1; ἀντίδικος 1 Pet. v. 8). In this
work the 'other Advocate' (John xiv.
16), the Spirit of Christ, joins (Rom.
viii. 26, 34).

One aspect of the Advocate's office
was foreshadowed by the entrance of
the High Priest into the Holy of
Holies on the Day of Atonement
(Heb. ix. 11 ff., 24; vii. 25).

For the meaning of the term παράκλητος in the Gospel of St John (xiv.
16, 26; xv. 26; xvi. 7) see note on
xiv. 16.

It will be noticed that in the context of the passage in which the Lord
promises 'another Advocate' (John
xiv. 16), He sets forth His own advocacy (xiv. 12 ff.).

τὸν πατέρα Ἰησοῦν Χριστὸν δίκαιον, ²καὶ αὐτὸς

Augustine applies the legal image in a striking parallel: Si aliquando in hac vita committit se homo disertæ linguæ et non perit, committis te Verbo et periturus es? The reference to the Advocate implies that the Christian on his part has effectually sought His help. This is assumed, and indicated by the change of person (we Christians have). Clement of Rome (i. 36) speaks of the Lord under a corresponding title: ...εὕρομεν τὸ σωτήριον ἡμῶν Ἰησοῦν Χριστόν, τὸν ἀρχιερέα τῶν προσφορῶν ἡμῶν, τὸν προστάτην (patronum) καὶ βοηθὸν τῆς ἀσθενείας ἡμῶν.· πρὸς τὸν πατέρα] apud patrem V., ad patrem Aug. (apud deum patrem Tert.), with the Father, not simply in His Presence, but turned toward Him, addressing Him with continual pleadings. Comp. c. i. 2; John i. 1.

Christ's advocacy of man is addressed to God in that relation of Fatherhood which has been fully revealed in the Son who has taken manhood to Himself (πρὸς τὸν πατέρα not πρὸς τὸν θεόν).

Comp. i. 2 ἦν πρὸς τὸν πατέρα; i. 3 μετὰ τοῦ πατρὸς καὶ μετὰ τοῦ υἱοῦ αὐτοῦ; ii. 14 ἐγνώκατε τὸν πατέρα; ii. 15 ἡ ἀγάπη τοῦ. πατρός; ii. 16 οὐκ ἔστιν ἐκ τοῦ πατρός; ii. 22 ὁ ἀρνούμενος τὸν πατέρα καὶ τὸν υἱόν; ii. 23 ὁ ὁμολογῶν τὸν υἱὸν καὶ τὸν πατέρα ἔχει; ii. 24 ἐν τῷ υἱῷ καὶ [ἐν] τῷ πατρί; iii. 1 δέδωκεν ἡμῖν ὁ πατήρ; iv. 14 ὁ πατὴρ ἀπέσταλκεν τὸν υἱόν.

In every case this special conception is important for the fulness of the argument. See Additional Note on i. 2.

And on the other side man's Advocate is described by that compound name Jesus Christ, which presents Him in His humanity and also as the promised Saviour and King of mankind, the Son of man, and the Son of David. See Additional Note on iii. 23.

δίκαιον] the righteous. The adjective is not a simple epithet but marks predicatively ('being as He is righteous') that characteristic of the Lord which gives efficacy to His advocacy of man.

This rests (so to speak) not on His divine nature as Son of God, but on His human character (comp. 1 Pet. iii. 18).

He has Himself fulfilled and pleads for the fulfilment of that which is right according to the highest law. He is not an advocate who wishes to set aside the law but to carry it out and apply it. In Him the idea of manhood has obtained its absolute satisfaction, and in turn He claims that the virtue of this satisfaction be extended to all in fellowship with Himself.

The righteousness of Christ as presented here answers to the righteousness of the Father brought forward in i. 9: He accomplishes perfectly all that is set forth in the revelation of the Father's Nature. By this righteousness He fulfils in fact the conditions which the High Priest fulfilled in symbol. Comp. Heb. vii. 26.

The thought of righteousness as a divine attribute belongs peculiarly to St John: John xvii. 25 πατὴρ δίκαιε; c. i. 9; ii. 29; iii. 7. Comp. Rom. iii. 26.

Nothing is said of the manner of Christ's pleading: that is a subject wholly beyond our present powers. It is enough that St John represents it as the act of a Saviour still living (Heb. vii. 25) and in a living relation with His people. His work for them continues as real as during His earthly life (Lc. xxii. 32; xxiii. 34; John xvii. 24), though the conditions of it are changed. He is still acting personally in their behalf, and not only by the unexhausted and prevailing power of what He has once done. He Himself uses for His people the virtue of

ἰλασμός ἐστιν περὶ τῶν ἁμαρτιῶν ἡμῶν, οὐ περὶ τῶν
ἡμετέρων δὲ μόνον ἀλλὰ καὶ περὶ ὅλου τοῦ κόσμου.

2 ἰλ. ἐστιν ℵBC: ἐστ. ἰλ. A vg.
Rom. iii. 29.

μόνον ℵAC vg: μόνων B me the; comp.

that work which He accomplished on earth.

Bede says well: Unigenito Filio pro homine interpellare est apud coæternum Patrem se ipsum hominem demonstrare; eique pro humana natura rogasse est eandem naturam in divinitatis suæ celsitudine suscepisse. Interpellat ergo pro nobis Dominus non voce sed miseratione, quia quod damnare in electis noluit suscipiendo servavit.

2. καὶ αὐτός...] et ipse V., and He, or rather, and He Himself (Matt. i. 21). The emphatic pronoun enforces the thought of the efficacy of Christ's advocacy as 'righteous.' He who pleads our cause, having fulfilled the destiny of man, is at the same time the propitiation for our sins. Comp. v. 25; c. i. 7; iv. 10, 19 (3 John 10); John ii. 25; iv. 44; v. 20; vi. 6 (xii. 49); 1 Pet. ii. 24.

The ideas of 'advocacy' and 'propitiation' are distinct, and yet in close connexion. The latter furnishes the basis of the former: the latter is universal, while the former, so far as it is revealed, is exercised for believers. It is to be noticed further that the 'propitiation' itself is spoken of as something eternally valid (He is) and not as past (He was; comp. iii. 16 τὴν ψυχὴν ἔθηκεν).

ἰλασμός] propitiatio V., a propitiation. Comp. iv. 10. The Latin renderings are unusually numerous. Besides propitiatio which prevailed, exoratio, deprecatio, placatio are found, and also the verbal renderings (ipse) exorat, interpellat, postulat pro... And Augustine has in some places propitiator. Christ is said to be the 'propitiation' and not simply the 'propitiator' (as He is called

the 'Saviour' iv. 14), in order to emphasise the thought that He is Himself the propitiatory offering as well as the priest (comp. Rom. iii. 25). A propitiator might make use of means of propitiation, outside himself. But Christ is our propitiation, as He is 'our life' (Col. iii. 4), our 'righteousness, sanctification and redemption' (1 Cor. i. 31). He does not simply guide, teach, quicken: He is 'the Way, the Truth, the Life' (John xiv. 6). It follows that the efficacy of His work for the individual depends upon fellowship with Him. See Additional Note.

Qui per humanitatem interpellat pro nobis apud Patrem idem per divinitatem propitiatur nobis cum Patre (Bede ad loc.).

περὶ τῶν ἁμ. ἡ.] pro peccatis nostris V., peccatorum nostrorum Aug., for our sins. The privilege of Christians (ἡμῶν) is noticed first. And it is natural that in the first case the stress is laid on 'sins' (περὶ τῶν ἁμ. ἡμῶν) and in the second case on 'our' (περὶ τῶν ἡμετέρων).

The propitiation of Christ is here described as being 'for,' 'in the matter of (περί) our sins' (comp. כִּפֶּר עַל), and not as 'in behalf of us' (ὑπὲρ ἡμῶν). On the phrases περὶ (ὑπὲρ) ἁμαρτίας (-ιῶν) see Hebr. xiii. 11 note.

οὐ π. τ. ἡ. δέ] The particle (δέ) marks the clause as guarding against error, not merely adding a new thought.

περὶ ὅλου τοῦ κόσμου] pro totius mundi [sc. peccatis] V., (sed et) totius mundi Aug., for the whole world. The variation in the construction (for our sins...for the whole world) is full of meaning (comp. Heb. ix. 7). Christians as such are holy but still not

³ Καὶ ἐν τούτῳ γινώσκομεν ὅτι ἐγνώκαμεν αὐτόν, ἐὰν

3 Aug. reads simply *et in hoc cognoscimus eum.*   φυλάξωμεν (for τηρῶμεν) א*.

unstained by sins contracted 'in the walk of life' (John xiii. 10); the world, all outside the Church, as such is sinful (c. v. 19). But for all alike Christ's propitiation is valid. The propitiation extends as far as the need of it (*l.c.*), through all place and all time. Comp. iv. 14 (John iv. 42; xii. 32; xvii. 22—24).

The supposition that περὶ ὅλου τοῦ κόσμου is an elliptical expression for περὶ τῶν ἁμαρτιῶν ὅλου τοῦ κόσμου (so Latt.) is not justified by usage, and weakens the force of the passage. Contrast Hebr. vii. 27.

Philo in a noble passage (*de Monarch.* ii. 6, ii. p. 227 M.) contrasts the special offerings of other forms of worship with the universal intercession of the Jewish High-priest: ὁ τῶν Ἰουδαίων ἀρχιερεὺς οὐ μόνον ὑπὲρ ἅπαντος ἀνθρώπων γένους ἀλλὰ καὶ ὑπὲρ τῶν τῆς φύσεως μερῶν, γῆς ὕδατος ἀέρος καὶ πυρός, τάς τε εὐχὰς καὶ τὰς εὐχαριστίας ποιεῖται, τὸν κόσμον, ὅπερ ἐστὶ ταῖς ἀληθείαις, πατρίδα εἶναι ἑαυτοῦ νομίζων, ὑπὲρ ἧς ἱκεσίαις καὶ λιταῖς εἴωθεν ἐξευμενίζειν τὸν ἡγεμόνα ποτνιώμενος τῆς ἐπιεικοῦς καὶ ἵλεω φύσεως αὐτοῦ μεταδιδόναι τῷ γενομένῳ.

Comp. 1 Clem. R. c. 7 ἀτενίσωμεν εἰς τὸ αἷμα τοῦ Χριστοῦ καὶ ἴδωμεν ὡς ἔστιν τίμιον τῷ θεῷ καὶ πατρὶ αὐτοῦ, ὅτι διὰ τὴν ἡμετέραν σωτηρίαν ἐκχυθὲν παντὶ τῷ κόσμῳ μετανοίας χάριν ὑπήνεγκεν.

2. *The signs of the personal efficacy of the divine remedy for sin* (ii. 3—6).

³ *And in this we perceive that we know him, if we observe his commandments.* ⁴ *He that saith I know him and observeth not his commandments, is a liar, and in this man the truth is not;* ⁵ *but whosoever observeth his word, verily in this man the love of God hath been perfected.*

The first two verses of the chapter declare the nature of the divine remedy for sin; in these next four St John indicates the sign of its personal efficacy. The sign is twofold, and corresponds with two aspects of the spiritual life; there is the sign of knowledge (*vv.* 3—5 *a*); and there is the sign of union (*vv.* 5 *b*, 6). The sign of knowledge is (shortly) obedience; and the sign of union is imitation.

3. The new form of false doctrine which St John meets corresponds with and grows out of the first of those which he has already analysed. Some claimed a knowledge of God, as some claimed fellowship with God (i. 6), irrespective of a Christ-like life. Knowledge no less than fellowship involves real likeness (comp. John viii. 32; c. iii. 7).

vv. 3—5 *a. The sign of knowledge.* The sign of knowledge is developed characteristically by the Apostle. He first states generally that it lies in obedience (*v.* 3), and then follows out this statement further negatively and positively, shewing the issues of the want of obedience (*v.* 4), and of the activity of obedience (*v.* 5 *a*).

3. Under one aspect this verse is connected with i. 5. But between the declaration of God's nature and man's knowledge of Him there comes in the episode of sin. This fatal interruption breaks the natural development of thought. The connexion of i. 1, 3, 5 (καί), ii. 3 (καί), corresponds with that of John i. 1, 14.

ἐν τούτῳ γινώσκομεν] *in hoc scimus* V., *in hoc cognoscimus* Aug., *in this we perceive.* The phrase '*in this*' is characteristic of the Epistle and occurs with slight variations of form.

(1) *In this* (ἐν τούτῳ) *we perceive* (γινώσκομεν): ii. 5; iii. 24; iv. 13; v. 2 and so also '*in this we know*

(ἐγνώκαμεν)' iii. 16; and '*in this we
shall know* (γνωσόμεθα)' iii. 19; and
'*in this ye perceive* (γινώσκετε)' iv. 2.
Comp. John xiii. 35 (xv. 8; xvi. 30).

(2) *From this* (ἐκ τούτου) *we perceive :* iv. 6.

(3) *Whence* (ὅθεν) *we perceive :*
ii. 18.

Generally '*this*' (τοῦτο) marks something which has been already expressed, though it is further developed in
what follows (comp. *e.g.* διὰ τοῦτο...
ὅτι, iii. 1; John v. 16, 18; vi. 65;
viii. 47; x. 17; xii. 18; xvi. 15). But
here the reference appears to be to
that which is clearly apprehended in
the mind of the Apostle and present
to him, though it has not yet been
brought forward ; *in this*...namely *if
....* Perhaps however even here the
'*this*' really rests upon the whole
relation of the Christian to Christ
which is implied in *vv.* 1, 2. That
relation furnishes the test of knowledge ; if the relation be vital it will
include obedience. Comp. *v.* 2.

The experience to which the A-
postle appeals here and in the parallel passages (γινώσκομεν) is present
and immediate, confirmed from moment to moment in the actual course
of life. So far it is distinguished
from the knowledge of an absolute
fact (οἴδαμεν, iii. 2, note).

ἐγνώκαμεν...] *cognovimus* V., *know
Him*, or more exactly, *have come to a
knowledge of Him*. Knowledge of a
person involves sympathy (c. iii. 1 n.);
and in this particular case includes
the striving after conformity with
Him who is known. To know God as
God is to be in vital fellowship with
Him, to love Him, to fulfil that relation towards Him for which we are
born. And conversely to be known
by God, to be the object of His knowledge, is to be in harmony with Him.
Comp. Gal. iv. 9; 1 Cor. viii. 2; xiii.
12; John x. 14 f.; and negatively
Matt. vii. 23; 2 Cor. v. 21.

This knowledge of God gained by
experience (γινώσκειν), and so contrast-

ed with the knowledge which is immediate and absolute (οἶδα), is presented
in its different stages in the Gospel and
Epistles of St John. It is regarded

(1) In reference to the point of
acquisition (ἔγνων John i. 10; x. 38 ;
xvi. 3; xvii. 8, 25; c. iii. 1; iv. 8).

(2) As a result of the past realised
in the present (ἔγνωκα, John viii. 55;
xiv. 9; xvii. 7; *vv.* 4, 13, 14; iii. 6, 16;
2 John 1). And

(3) As being actually realised at
the moment (γινώσκω, John viii. 43;
x. 14 f., 27, 38; xiv. 7, 17; xvii. 3, 23;
c. iv. 2, 6, 7; v. 20).

These three aspects of the knowledge of God offer a view of the beginning, the strength and the aim of life.

It is worthy of remark that St John
nowhere uses γνῶσις (St Luke, St
Paul, St Peter), nor the compound
forms ἐπιγινώσκειν (Synn., Acts, St
Paul, 2 Peter), ἐπίγνωσις (St Paul,
Heb., 2 Peter). He confines himself,
as he does almost exclusively in dealing with faith (πιστεύειν εἰς), to the
simple verb. This form of expression
brings out most distinctly the personal character of the energy.

In this context it is not clearly defined to Whom the pronoun (ἐγν. αὐτόν) refers. The Divine Being fills
the apostle's vision, but the Person
is not distinctly named. It has been
supposed that the reference is to
Christ, the main subject of the preceding verses. In favour of this view
it is urged that in i. 6 ff. the αὐτοῦ
refers to the last subject of i. 5, and
that the construction of this section is
similar ; that the occurrence of the
phrase the *love of God* in *v.* 5 implies
a reference of the preceding αὐτοῦ to
the Son and not to the Father; that
Christ Himself speaks of the 'keeping of His Commandments' as the
proof of love (John xiv. 15, &c.). On
the other hand it is said that in this
Epistle 'the Commandments' referred
to are always the Commandments of
God (*i.e.* the Father) as iii. 22, 24; v.
2, 3; and that God is the great under-

τὰς ἐντολὰς αὐτοῦ τηρῶμεν. ⁴ὁ λέγων ὅτι ῎Εγνωκα
αὐτόν καὶ τὰς ἐντολὰς αὐτοῦ μὴ τηρῶν ψεύστης
ἐστίν, καὶ ἐν τούτῳ ἡ ἀλήθεια οὐκ ἔστιν· ⁵ὃς δ' ἂν τηρῇ

4 ὁ λέγων ὅτι ℵAB syrr: – ὅτι ϚC.   – καὶ' ἐν τ. A.   – ἐν τούτῳ ℵ:
ἡ ἀλ. + τοῦ Θεοῦ ℵ.

lying subject of all, the 'He' (αὐτός) which is self-defined; so that in point of fact αὐτός generally refers to 'God,' while ἐκεῖνος always refers to Christ (v. 6 note).

The sense remains substantially the same in both cases. It is in the Son that the Father is known (John xiv. 9). And perhaps it is best to suppose that St John assumes a general antecedent 'Him to whom we turn as God' without special distinction of Persons. In other places he does not seem to draw any sharp distinction between the Father and the Son, but in the One God looks now to the revelation of the Father in the Son and now to the revelation of the Son (comp. iii. 1—3, 5, 6: v. 20).

ἐάν...τηρῶμεν] si observemus V., si servaverimus Aug., if we keep His commandments. Comp. v. 4; iii. 22, 24; v. 3; John xiv. 15, 21; xv. 10; Apoc. xii. 17; xiv. 12. The phrase (τηρεῖν τὰς ἐντολάς) is only found elsewhere in New Testament in Matt. xix. 17; 1 Tim. vi. 14 (τηρεῖν τὴν ἐντ.). Comp. 1 Cor. vii. 19. It appears to be distinguished from the phrase which follows 'keep His word' as being an observance of definite instructions, while that is the observance of a principle which is ever taking a new embodiment in the very process of life.

The phrase ποιεῖν τὰς ἐντολάς, which is found in the common text of Apoc. xxii. 14, is a false reading.

The idea of τηρεῖν, as distinguished from φυλάσσειν in this connexion (John xii. 47; Matt. xix. 20; Luke xi. 28), appears to be that of watchful heed to an object which claims, so to speak, a living observance, a service

not of the letter but of the spirit. A definite, unchangeable, deposit is 'guarded' (φυλάσσεται, 1 Tim. vi. 20): a vital, growing, word is 'observed' (τηρεῖται, John xiv. 22). The two verbs occur in juxtaposition in John xvii. 12 (note).

4. ὁ λέγων] He that saith. This individualising of the statement stands in contrast with the comprehensive form cited before If we say (i. 6, 8, 10) and that used in v. 5. It occurs again vv. 6, 9. The clause is an interesting example of a compound subject ὁ [λέγων ὅτι...καὶ...μὴ τηρῶν].

ἔγνωκα αὐτόν] se nosse eum V., quia cognovit (cognovi) eum Aug., I know Him. The direct personal assertion (ὁ λέγων ὅτι) is bolder in form than the oblique construction in vv. 6, 9 (ὁ λέγων μένειν, εἶναι). Comp. Hos. viii. 2.

In the words which follow St John significantly takes up again phrases which he has used already in connexion with the three false pleas in regard to sin [ψεύστης ἐστίν ‖ ψευδόμεθα i. 6; ἐν τούτῳ ἡ ἀλ. οὐκ ἔστιν ‖ ἡ ἀλ. οὐκ ἔστιν ἐν ἡμῖν v. 8; (ὃς δ' ἂν τηρῇ) αὐτοῦ τὸν λόγον ‖ ὁ λόγος αὐτοῦ (οὐκ ἔστιν ἐν ἡμῖν) v. 10].

ψεύστης...ἐν τούτῳ...] a liar...in this man.... The whole character is false. See i. 10 note. The clause is very similar to i. 6 b, but differs from it in being general while that is special. Here we have two characteristics of a permanent state (is a liar, the truth is not in him), and there two separate manifestations of the state (we lie, we do not the truth).

ἐν τούτῳ...οὐκ ἔστιν] in him the truth is not. Or more literally in this man thus definitely characterised αὐτοῦ τὸν λόγον, ἀληθῶς ἐν τούτῳ ἡ ἀγάπη τοῦ θεοῦ

and brought before us. See v. 5. This use of the demonstrative pronoun is characteristic of St John (John v. 38; i. 2 note); and the emphatic order adds to its force.

The truth is said to be in a man as an active principle within him regulating his thoughts and judgments (c. i. 8; John viii. 44; comp. John viii. 32); and again a man is said to be in the truth, as the sphere in which he moves (2 John 4; 3 John 3, 4; John viii. 44; comp. John xvii. 17).

5. ὃς δ᾽ ἂν τηρῇ...] qui autem servat V., qui a. servaverit Aug., but whosoever keepeth. The indefinite form (iii. 17; iv. 15) marks the breadth of the assertion. The Apostle does not here, as before and after, either single out a special example (ὁ λέγων, v. 4), or join himself with others (ἐὰν εἴπωμεν, i. 6). He makes the statement in the most general terms.

It will be noticed that the opposite to the vain assertions of false claimants to the Christian name is not given in a counter assertion but, as always, in action (i. 7 if we walk; i. 9 if we confess; v. 10 he that loveth).

τηρῇ αὐτοῦ τὸν λόγον] keepeth his word. The phrase expresses not only the fulfilment of specific injunctions (keep His commandments, v. 3) but also the heedful regard to the whole revelation made by Christ as a living and active power, of which the voice is never silent. The unity of the many 'commandments' is not in a 'law' but in a 'word': it answers to the spirit and not to the letter. Comp. John viii. 51 f., 55; xiv. 23; xv. 20; xvii. 6. The passage John xiv. 21—24 is of singular interest as illustrating the full meaning of the phrase.

The position of the pronoun here (αὐτοῦ τὸν λόγον), as contrasted with that which it has in v. 3 (τὰς ἐντολὰς αὐτοῦ), emphasises the personal idea. The main thought is that the word is His word, the word of God. There is

emphasis also on the 'keeping' ὃς δ᾽ ἂν τηρῇ contrasted with ὁ...τὰς ἐντ. μὴ τηρῶν).

ἀληθῶς ἐν τούτῳ] verily in him, in this man, v. 4 note.

In the description of the state of the watchful believer the form of expression is changed significantly. St John does not say of him (v. 4) that 'he is true and the truth is in him'; but he rather regards his character from the divine side, and points out not what such a man is, but what such a man has received from Him who is unchangeable: in this man the love of God hath been perfected. By doing this he passes at the same time from that which may be a part of life to the fulness of life. Truth may be only a right conception realised in thought: love is the Truth realised in a personal relation. The love which God gives (iii. 1) becomes an active, divine power in the man who welcomes it.

ἡ ἀγάπη τοῦ θεοῦ] caritas Dei V., dilectio Dei Aug., the love of God. The phrase, which occurs in the Epistle first here and henceforth throughout it, is ambiguous and may mean, according as the gen. is taken subj. or obj., either (1) the love which God shews, or (2) the love of which God is the object. It may also mean more generally (3) the love which is characteristic of God whether it is regarded as shewn by God or by man through His help. Generally the genitive after ἀγάπη in the N. T. is subj., and defines those who feel or shew love: 1 Thess. iii. 6; 2 Thess. i. 3; Phil. i. 9; Col. i. 8; Philem. 5, 7; Apoc. ii. 4, 19. Once it marks the object of love: 2 Thess. ii. 10 ἡ ἀγ. τῆς ἀληθείας. But the object is more commonly expressed by εἰς: 1 Thess. iii. 12; Col. i. 4; 1 Pet. iv. 8. Comp. Ign. Mart. 1; [Clem. R.] fragm. 1 (Jacobson).

In St Paul 'the love of God,' with

τετελείωται. Ἐν τούτῳ γινώσκομεν ὅτι ἐν αὐτῷ ἐσμέν·

5 ἐν τούτῳ...ἐσμέν : Aug. reads *in hoc cognoscimus quia in ipso sumus si in ipso perfecti fuerimus.*

the doubtful exception of 2 Thess. iii. 5, always means the love which is shewn by God, which comes from God : 2 Cor. xiii. 13 ; Rom. v. 5 ; viii. 39 ; Eph. ii. 4 ; and so also 'the love of Christ' is the love which Christ has shewn and shews : 2 Cor. v. 14 ; Rom. viii. 35 ; Eph. iii. 19. Comp. Ign. *ad Trall.* 6 ; *ad Rom.* inscr. In like manner 'the love of the Spirit' (Rom. xv. 30) is that love which the Spirit kindles and sustains. The phrase 'the love of God' does not occur in the LXX.

The usage of St John is less simple than that of St Paul. In 1 John iv. 9 '*the love of God*' is evidently the love which God has shewn (comp. c. v, 9 ἡ μαρτυρία τοῦ θεοῦ), and this love is declared to be the spring of all love. '*His love*' (*v.* 12) becomes effective in man. This conception of the love of God as communicated by God to man is plainly expressed in 1 John iii. 1 *the Father hath given to us love* (comp. c. iv. 7, 16). Love such as God Himself feels—'divine love'— becomes therefore an endowment of the Christian. In this sense 'the love of God' in the believer calls for deeds of love to the brethren (c. iii. 17). At the same time God is Himself the object of the love of which He is the source and the rule : c. v. 3 (comp. John xiv. 15, 31); ii. 15 (ἡ ἀγ. τοῦ πατρός).

It appears therefore most probable that the fundamental idea of 'the love of God' in St John is 'the love which God has made known, and which answers to His nature.' This love communicated to man is effective in him towards the brethren and towards God Himself. But however it may be manifested the essential conception that it is a love divine in its origin and character is not lost. Comp. John xv. 9 f.

According to this interpretation the phrase corresponds with the 'righteousness of God' (Rom. i. 17, &c.), the 'peace of God' (Phil. iv. 7). The phrase occurs twice only in the Gospels : Luke xi. 42 ; John v. 42. In each case the rendering 'love to God' is admissible, but this rendering does not seem to exhaust the meaning (comp. Clem. R. 1 *Cor.* 49).

In the present passage there can be little doubt that c. iv. 9 defines the meaning. 'The love of God' is God's love towards man welcomed and appropriated by man. The thought of action is throughout connected with the thought of what God has done. The Christian 'knows the love of God' and it becomes in him a spring of love, attaining its complete development in human life through vital obedience.

On 'the use of ἀγάπη by St John see additional note on c. iii. 16.

ἀληθῶς] *vere* V., *verily*, in very truth, and not in word only (c. iii. 18). Comp. John i. 47 (48) ; viii. 31. The word qualifies the whole clause which follows. This practical result is contrasted by implication with the idle assertions of false Christians.

The perfection of love is conditioned by the completeness of obedience.

τετελείωται] *perfecta est* V., *consummata est* Lucf., *hath been perfected.* Comp. c. iv. 12 (note), 17, 18 where the thought is presented in different lights. Comp. Clem. R. 1 *Cor.* 50 οἱ ἐν ἀγάπῃ τελειωθέντες. *Doctr. Apost.* x. 5 μνήσθητι, κύριε, τῆς ἐκκλησίας σου...τελειῶσαι αὐτὴν ἐν τῇ ἀγάπῃ σου. The potential fulfilment of the love of God in the Christian lies in his absolute readiness to learn and to do God's will (comp. Rom. xiii. 10). Each Christian according to his

^{6}ὁ λέγων ἐν αὐτῷ μένειν ὀφείλει καθὼς ἐκεῖνος περιε-
πάτησεν καὶ αὐτὸς περιπατεῖν.

6 καὶ αὐτὸς περιπ. AB vg the: καὶ αὐτ. + οὕτως' περιπ. ⲋℵC me syr hcl.

measure is perfected as a member of
Christ (Eph. iv. 16). He receives
from Christ what Christ has Himself
received. Comp. John xvii. 25 f. On
this idea of 'perfection,' 'consummation,' see Heb. ii. 10; ix. 9; xii. 23 and
notes. Contrast τελεῖται 2 Cor. xii. 9.
Both τελειοῦν and ἐπιτελεῖν are used
of Christian action (Phil. iii. 12 ; Gal.
iii. 3). But in τελειοῦν there is the
idea of a continuous growth, a vital
development, an advance to maturity
(τελειότης, Heb. v. 13; vi. 1). In
ἐπιτελεῖν the notion is rather that of
attaining a definite end (τέλος). Contrast James ii. 22 ἐκ τῶν ἔργων ἡ πίστις ἐτελειώθη with 2 Cor. vii. 1 ἐπιτε-
λοῦντες ἁγιωσύνην, and Acts xx. 24
τελειῶσαι τὸν δρόμον with 2 Tim. iv. 7
τὸν δρόμον τετέλεκα. In 2 Cor. xii. 9
τελειοῦται has been substituted in
later authorities for τελεῖται.

v. 5 b, 6. The sign of union. The
sign of union with God is found in
the imitation of Christ. As the sign
of knowledge is to be seen in the
keeping of the divine commandments
in their unity (*v.* 3) and in the keeping of the divine word in its unity
(*v.* 5), so the sign of fellowship is to
be seen in the copying the divine life.

*In this we perceive that we are in
him: ⁶he that saith he abideth in
him, ought himself also to walk even
as he walked.*

'Εν τούτῳ] *Hereby, in this,* in the
realisation of this spirit of obedience
which is the gift of love : *v.* 3 note.

γινώσκομεν] Comp. *v.* 3 ; c. v. 2 notes.

ἐν αὐτῷ ἐσμέν] *are in him.* The
idea finds a full expression in Acts
xvii. 28 ἐν αὐτῷ ζῶμεν καὶ κινούμεθα
καὶ ἐσμέν. It is prominent in St John's
writings in its spiritual form, and is
presented under several different aspects. The fellowship of believers

with God is accomplished in Christ
(John xiv. 20 ; xvii. 21, 23). They
have in Him the unity and foundation of their being, even as 'the
world' 'lies in the evil one' (c. v.
19 f.). The connexion finds a twofold
fulfilment in 'heaven' and on 'earth,'
'we in Him and He in us' (iv. 15
note).

For the phrase 'being in God' St
John more commonly, as in the following clause, uses the phrase 'abiding in God,' which adds the conception of personal determination and
effort : *vv.* 24, 27, 28 ; iii. 6, 24 ; iv.
12 f.; 15 f. John vi. 56 note ; xv. 4 ff.

Thus there is a progressive close-
ness of relation in the three phrases
used in this section : ἐγνωκέναι αὐτόν,
εἶναι ἐν αὐτῷ, μένειν ἐν αὐτῷ ('cognitio,
communio, constantia,' Bengel).

6. ὁ λέγων] *he that saith.* *v.* 4.
The open, personal profession carries
with it a paramount obligation.

ἐν αὐτῷ μένειν] *v.* 5 note.

The construction of λέγω with the
infin. occurs again in *v.* 9. Comp.
2 Tim. ii. 18; and *v.* 4 note.

ὀφείλει] *debet* V., *ought,* is bound.
The obligation is represented as a
debt (Luke xvii. 10). The life which
is from God and in God must be
manifested after the pattern of the
divine life which has been shewn
upon earth. As contrasted with δεῖ,
an obligation in the nature of things
(John xx. 9), which is not found in
the Epistles of St John, though it is
not unfrequent in the Gospel (c. iii.
14 note) and the Apocalypse, ὀφείλειν
expresses a special, personal obligation.

Comp. c. iii. 16; iv. 11 ; 3 John 8 ;
Hebr. ii. 17 note.

The image is frequent in St Paul.
Comp. Rom. i. 14 ; Gal. v. 3.

καθὼς ἐκεῖνος] *even as he*, i.e. Christ. The pronoun ἐκεῖνος occurs iii. 3, 5, 7, 16; iv. 17, and is always used of Christ. He stands out as the one figure seen in full perfection of His humanity. Comp. John i. 18; 2 Tim. ii. 13. For the omission of οὕτως see c. iv. 17 note.

περιεπάτησεν] *walked*, i. 6 note. Even in the contemplation of the loftiest thoughts St John fixes a practical standard. The divine fellowship to which he points is realised on earth in corresponding action.

The pattern of Christ, as set before us in the New Testament, is in every case a pattern of humiliation, suffering, sacrifice. Comp. Matt. xi. 29; John xiii. 15; Rom. xv. 2 f.; Eph. v. 1 ff.; Phil. ii. 5 ff.; 1 Pet. ii. 21; Heb. xii. 2.

Augustine points out that 'walking' may be 'bearing' only: [Christus] fixus in cruce erat et in ipsa via ambulabat : ipsa est via caritatis.

III. Obedience in love and light in actual life (ii. 7—11).

The declaration of the test of knowledge of God and fellowship with God, which St John has given in *vv.* 3—6, leads to a view of the practical fulfilment of the test indicated already in *v.* 6. The Life of Christ, a Life of complete love, of complete self-sacrifice, is the type of the Christian's Life; and the significance of Christ's Life in this aspect is gathered up in the one commandment of love, which expresses what is meant by 'keeping His commandments' (*v.* 3) and 'walking even as He walked' (*v.* 6). This commandment is first set forth in its twofold character as old and yet new (*vv.* 7, 8); and then traced out in its issues (*vv.* 9—11).

i. *The Commandment old and new* (ii. 7, 8).

The commandment, which is the rule of the Christian Life, is as old as the first message of the Gospel and

yet as new as the latest realisation of its power. It lies included in what we first hear, and is illuminated by the growing experience of life.

⁷*Beloved, it is no new commandment I write to you, but an old commandment which ye had from the beginning : the commandment, the* old commandment, *is the word which ye heard.*

⁸*Again, a new commandment I write to you*, even *that which is true in him and in you, because the darkness is passing away and the light, the true* light, *already shineth.*

The 'commandment' to which the Apostle refers has not been formally stated, but it is implied in the 'ought' ('is bound' ὀφείλει of *v.* 6. The idea of the imitation of Christ is identical with the fulfilment of love. And the word ὀφείλει carries us back to the Lord's interpretation of His example : John xiii. 14 (ὑμεῖς ὀφείλετε). We have already seen that the many 'commandments' (*v.* 3) are included in 'the word' (*v.* 5). Now the 'commandments' are summed up in the one 'commandment' (John xiii. 34; comp. c. iii. 22 f.).

This commandment is spoken of as 'not new but old.' In this connexion 'old' may mean either (1) old relatively : one which belonged to the first stage of the Christian Church, while perhaps as yet it was unseparated from the old order: one of which believers had been in possession *from the beginning*, from the first origin of their faith ; or (2) old absolutely : one which was included in the very constitution of man *from the beginning:* one which the Jew had recognised in the injunctions of the Law, and the Gentile in the promptings of his heart.

The clause which immediately follows, and the identification of the commandment with 'the word' which the disciples heard, seem to determine that the first sense is undoubtedly right.

⁷Ἀγαπητοί, οὐκ ἐντολὴν καινὴν γράφω ὑμῖν, ἀλλ᾽
ἐντολὴν παλαιὰν ἣν εἴχετε ἀπ᾽ ἀρχῆς· ἡ ἐντολὴ ἡ

7 ἀγαπητοί ℵABC vg the me syrr : ἀδελφοί ⸖.

7. Ἀγαπητοί] *Carissimi* V., *Dilec-
tissimi* Aug., *Beloved.* This is the first
occurrence of the title. It is suggested by the thought of the last few
verses, just as the paternal address
My little children (v. 1) was suggested by i. 10. The love of God and
the love of Christ calling out man's
love presents Christians in their new
relation one to another. St John
while enforcing the commandment of
love gives expression to love. Comp.
iii. 2, 21; iv. 1, 7 note, 11; and in
the sing. 3 John 2, 5, 11. In each
case the use of the title illustrates the
apostle's thought. So also the title
ἀδελφοί brings out the point of his
teaching in the one place where he
adopts it : iii. 13. Comp. Hebr. vi. 9 note.
With ἀγαπητοί contrast ἠγαπημένοι
Col. iii. 12; 1 Thess. i. 4; 2 Thess. ii.
13. Comp. Eph. i. 6.

οὐκ ἐντ. κ. γ.] Comp. 2 John 5 οὐχ
ὡς ἐντ. γράφων σοι κ.

ἀπ᾽ ἀρχῆς] *ab initio* V., *from the
beginning.* The words are, as has
been already indicated, ambiguous.
The phrase is used both absolutely
and relatively.

1. It is used absolutely : c. iii. 8
ἀπ᾽ ἀρχῆς ὁ διάβολος ἁμαρτάνει, when
first the present order of being is
disclosed.

  vv. 13, 14 ὁ ἀπ᾽ ἀρχῆς.
  c. i. 1 ὁ ἦν ἀπ᾽ ἀρχῆς.
  Matt. xix. 4, 8 ἀπ᾽ ἀρχῆς. ‖ Mc. x. 6
ἀπ᾽ ἀρχῆς κτίσεως. 2 Pet. iii. 4.

2. Again it is used relatively in
different connexions :
  John xv. 27 ἀπ᾽ ἀρχῆς μετ᾽ ἐμοῦ
ἐστέ, from the beginning of my public
ministry. Comp. ἐξ ἀρχῆς John vi. 64,
xvi. 4; Acts xxvi. 4 τὴν ἀπ᾽ ἀρχῆς
γενομένην [βίωσιν] from the beginning
of my life.

Luke i. 2 οἱ ἀπ᾽ ἀρχῆς αὐτόπται.
Comp. Acts i. 22.
  c. ii. 24 ὁ ἀπ᾽ ἀρχῆς ἠκούσατε, from
the beginning of your Christian faith.
Comp. c. iii. 11; 2 John 6.

These last passages, which are closely
parallel, decide that the reference here
is to the beginning of the Christian
faith of the readers.
  Comp. Is. lxiii. 16 (LXX.).

The article is omitted as in the corresponding phrases ἀπὸ καταβολῆς
κόσμου, πρὸ καταβολῆς κόσμου. See
c. i. 1 note.

ἡ ἐντολὴ...ἠκούσατε] *the commandment,* the commandment of which I
speak, *the old* commandment, *is the
word which ye heard.* The form of
expression used emphasises the two
thoughts which have gone before (*the
commandment, the old* commandment). Comp. i. 2, ii. 25 ἡ ζωὴ ἡ αἰώνιος
(*the life, the eternal* life); i. 3 ἡ κοινωνία ἡ ἡμετέρα (the fellowship of which
I speak, the fellowship which is our
blessing); v. 8 τὸ φῶς τὸ ἀληθινόν; iv.
9 ὁ υἱὸς ὁ μονογενής: 2 John 11 τοῖς
ἔργοις αὐτοῦ τοῖς πονηροῖς: 13 τῆς ἀδελφῆς σου τῆς ἐκλεκτῆς.

On the other hand St John writes
c. iv. 18 ἡ τελεία ἀγάπη: 3 John 4 τὰ
ἐμὰ τέκνα.

ὁ λόγος] The old commandment,
the commandment of love, was included in the 'Gospel' which the
apostles proclaimed. The record of
the Lord's work, *the word of life,* was
a continuous call to love.

ὃν ἠκούσατε] *which ye heard,* v. 24,
iii. 11. Contrast the perfect: i. 1, 3,
5, iv. 3. The change of tenses in εἴχετε,
ἠκούσατε, is significant. The commandment was a continuous power :
the hearing of the word was at once
final in its obligation.

παλαιά ἐστιν ὁ λόγος ὃν ἠκούσατε.   ⁸ πάλιν ἐντολὴν
καινὴν γράφω ὑμῖν, ὅ ἐστιν ἀληθὲς ἐν αὐτῷ καὶ ἐν ὑμῖν,

ἠκούσατε ℵABC vg the me syrr : +ἀπ᾽ ἀρχῆς ς.   8 ἀλ. καὶ ἐν αὐτῷ ℵ :
ἐν αὐτῷ ἀλ. A.   ἐν ὑμῖν ℵBC vg the me syrr : ἐν ἡμῖν A syr hcl mg (lat).

8. πάλιν] *iterum* V., *again*. The
Apostle has given one side of the
Truth: he now turns to the other.
The πάλιν answers exactly to our
'again' when we enter on a new line
of argument or reflection, starting
afresh. Comp. John xvi. 28; 1 Cor.
xii. 21; 2 Cor. x. 7; xi. 16.

ἐντολὴν καινήν] *mandatum novum*
V., *a new commandment*. Comp.
John xiii. 34. The commandment of
love was new to the disciples who
had followed Christ when He gave it
them on the eve of the Passion in a
new form and with a new sanction.
It was new also to the believers whom
St John addressed in proportion as
they were now enabled to apprehend
with fresh power the Person and Life
of Christ. The 'newness' is relative
to the position of those to whom St
John writes. While life advances the
Gospel must be always new. Contrast
Hebr. viii. 13.

ὅ ἐστιν ἀληθές...] *quod verum est...*
V., even *that which is true...* The
whole sentence admits of several different translations: (1) As a new
commandment I write unto you that
which is true... (2) A new commandment write I unto you, namely, that
which is true... (3) A new commandment write I unto you, a fact (i.e.
that it is new as well as old) which is
true... The symmetry of the structure seems to be decisive against (1):
Ἐντολὴν καινὴν γράφω cannot but be
strictly parallel to οὐκ ἐντολὴν καινὴν
γράφω—'a new commandment do I
write,' 'not a new commandment do
I write.' It is more difficult to decide
between (2) and (3). If (2) be taken
the sense will be: 'A new commandment write I unto you, new no less
than old, new in its shape and in its

authority, even that which, while it was
enjoined upon us from the first, has
been found to correspond more closely
than we then understood with the facts
of Christ's Life, with the crowning
mystery of His Passion, and with the
facts of the Christian life.' If on the
other hand (3) be taken then we have
this line of thought: 'A new commandment write I unto you, new, I
say, as well as old, an assertion which
is proved true in Christ, so far as His
works and words have become more
fully known; and in you, so far as the
actual experience of life has shewn
this duty of love in a new light,
more comprehensive and more constraining.'

On the whole the second interpretation appears to fall in best with the
context and with the reason which follows (*because...the true light already
shineth*). That which gave novelty to
the commandment was found in the
larger and deeper views of Christ's
Person and of the work of the Church
which had been unfolded since 'the
beginning.' Old words, St John could
affirm, and appeal to his readers for
the confirmation of the statement, had
become new. Comp. 2 Cor. v. 17.

ὅτι ἡ σκοτία...] *because the darkness...* The Apostle justifies his paradox
by calling attention to the change
which had taken place in the face of
the world since the Gospel was first
preached. The outward establishment
of the Church gave a clearer distinctness to the Christian character. It had
become possible to point to that which
was openly before men's eyes. At the
same time the Person of Christ Himself, with its infinite significance, was
illuminated by the experience of believers. The meaning of 'the word'

ὅτι ἡ σκοτία παράγεται καὶ τὸ φῶς τὸ ἀληθινὸν ἤδη

σκιά Α.

(for example) was made clearer than before by the Gospel of St John as compared with the earlier Gospels.

The clause may be taken as an explanation of the reason for which the Apostle is repeating the command, even that it was the 'last hour.' But this interpretation appears improbable.

παράγεται...φαίνει]   transierunt... lucet V., is passing away...already shineth. The change is pictured as n process. The darkness is being withdrawn (παράγεται) as a curtain from the face of the world, and the light is beginning (ἤδη) to have free course.

For παράγεται see v. 17. The intrans. παράγει occurs 1 Cor. vii. 31; Ps. cxliv. (cxliii.) 4. The idea seems to be that God is removing the veil in order to lay open the better things which it conceals.

τὸ φῶς τὸ ἀληθινόν] verum lumen V., lux vera Aug., the light, the true light. The addition of the epithet ἀληθινόν (c. v. 20) which is found only here and John i. 9 (note) with φῶς, marks the light as that which fulfilled all that had been promised by the preparatory, partial, even fictitious, lights which had existed in the world before. If we endeavour to fix the meaning of 'the light' here it can be best done by the help of the parallel John i. 9. Before the Incarnation 'the Word,' 'the true Light' was ever 'coming into the world.' Now by the mission of the Holy Spirit, sent in His name, He was shining with a steady beam. The darkness had not eclipsed it. In the Christian Society, seen in the midst of the world, there was an evident manifestation of the light defining the lines of Christian conduct.

God 'is light' absolutely (i. 5): the revelation of God in Christ by the

Spirit is 'the light, the true light' for men; and in His light the believer is enabled to see all things.

φαίνει] lucet V., shineth. Comp. John i. 5 (note). The idea is of a luminary giving out its brightness: Apoc. i. 16, viii. 12, xxi. 23; 2 Pet. i. 19.

For the image generally compare Rom. xiii. 11 ff.; Tit. ii. 11; iii. 4.

2.   The issues of the commandment of love (ii. 9—11).

The fulfilment of the commandment of love is regarded in its general nature (v. 9) and then more in detail in the effects of love and hatred (vv. 10, 11). A state of love is the condition of being in light; and this state carries with it a clear certainty of right action which is otherwise unobtainable. Hatred on the other hand involves complete ignorance of the way and of the end of life. This must be so; for dwelling in darkness destroys the very power by which the light is discerned.

9He that saith he is in the light and hateth his brother is in the darkness until now. 10He that loveth his brother abideth in the light, and there is none occasion of stumbling in him; 11but he that hateth his brother is in the darkness, and walketh in the darkness, and knoweth not whither he goeth, because the darkness hath blinded his eyes.

9.   The link of transition lies in the last words of v. 8. The thought of 'the light already shining' naturally suggests the question, Who then is in the light? St John's account of the obligations and issues of love explains this and is an answer to the false claims of knowledge separated from the action which embodies it (comp. v. 4).

Ὁ λέγων...] He that saith. v. 4. It

φαίνει.   9Ὁ λέγων ἐν τῷ φωτὶ εἶναι καὶ τὸν
ἀδελφὸν αὐτοῦ μισῶν ἐν τῇ σκοτίᾳ ἐστὶν ἕως ἄρτι.

9 μισῶν : + ψεύστης ἐστὶν καὶ ℵ Cypr Lcfr.

is always easy to mistake an intellectual knowledge for a spiritual knowledge of the Truth. Real knowledge
involves, at least potentially, corresponding action.

ἐν τῷ φωτὶ εἶναι] is in the light,
surrounded, as it were, by an atmosphere of divine glory. Comp. i. 7 (iv.
15 note).

μισῶν...] hateth.... Indifference is
impossible. Comp. Luke xi. 23. There
is no twilight in this spiritual world.
'The brother' stands in a relation
towards us which makes some feeling
on our part inevitable. In such a case
there is a simple choice between 'for'
and 'against,' that is essentially between 'love' and 'hatred.' 'Hatred'
is the expression of a want of sympathy. Where sympathy exists hatred
is impossible (John vii. 7); where
sympathy does not exist hatred is
inevitable (John xv. 18 ff., xvii. 14,
iii. 20).

There is however a certain ambiguity
in the word 'hate' for it serves as the
opposite both to the love of natural
affection (φιλεῖν), and to the love of
moral judgment (ἀγαπᾶν). In the
former case 'hatred,' which may become a moral duty, involves the subjection of an instinct (John xii. 25,
xv. 18 f.; comp. Luke xiv. 26); in
the latter case 'hatred' expresses a
general determination of character (c.
iii. 15, iv. 20; comp. Matt. v. 43, vi.
24; Eph. v. 28 f.).

τὸν ἀδελφόν] his brother, that is,
his fellow-Christian, and not more
generally his fellow-man. It is only
through the recognition of the relation to Christ that the wider relation
is at last apprehended. The idea of
brotherhood under the new dispensation (comp. Acts ii. 37, iii. 17, vi. 3,
ix. 30, &c.: Rom. i. 13, &c.) is nor

mally thus limited (yet see Acts xxii.
1, xxviii. 17; Rom. ix. 3). 'Brethren'
are those who are united together in
Christ to God as their Father (John
xx. 17, xxi. 23; comp. Matt. xii. 50).
The title occurs significantly in the
first record of the action of the Church
(Acts i. 15 ἐν μέσῳ τῶν ἀδελφῶν;
comp. ix. 30, &c.) and then throughout
the apostolic writings (1 Thess. v. 26;
Gal. i. 2; 1 Cor. v. 11; Rom. xvi. 14
&c.; 1 Tim. vi. 2; James i. 9; 1 Pet. v.
12 &c.; c. iii. 14, 16; 3 John 3, 5, 10).
The singular is characteristic of this
epistle (vv. 10, 11, iii. 10, 15, 17, iv.
20 f., v. 16). Comp. Rom. xiv. 10 ff.;
1 Cor. viii. 13. Compare Additional
Note on c. iii. 14.

There is, as far as it appears, no
case where a fellow-man, as man, is
called 'a brother' in the N. T. Such
passages as Matt. v. 22 ff., Luke vi.
41 ff., presuppose a special bond of
'brotherhood.' The 'love' of the
brotherhood' (φιλαδελφία· 1 Thess. iv.
9; Rom. xii. 10; Heb. xiii. 1; 1 Pet.
i. 22 (iii. 8); 2 Pet. i. 7) leads up to
'love' (ἀγάπη). But this widest love
is expressly assigned in its full extent
only to God (John iii. 16, c. iv. 10 f.).

Augustine makes a striking application of the words to the Donatists:
Offendit te nescio quis sive malus,
sive ut tu putas malus, sive ut tu
fingis malus, et deseris tot bonos?
Qualis dilectio est fraterna? Qualis
apparuit in istis [Donatistis]. Cum
accusant Afros deseruerunt orbem
terrarum.

And again he points out the ground
of the Christian's love of enemies: Sic
dilige inimicos ut fratres optes. Sic
dilige inimicos ut in societatem tuam
vocentur. Sic enim dilexit ille qui in
cruce pendens ait Pater ignosce illis,
quia nesciunt quid faciunt.

¹⁰ὁ ἀγαπῶν τὸν ἀδελφὸν αὐτοῦ ἐν τῷ φωτὶ μένει, καὶ
σκάνδαλον ἐν αὐτῷ οὐκ ἔστιν· ¹¹ὁ δὲ μισῶν τὸν ἀδελφὸν
αὐτοῦ ἐν τῇ σκοτίᾳ ἐστὶν καὶ ἐν τῇ σκοτίᾳ περιπατεῖ,

10 ἐν αὐτῷ οὐκ ἔστιν B vg: οὐκ ἔστιν ἐν αὐτῷ אAC (me) the.

ἐν τῇ σκ. ἐστίν] is in the darkness.
Comp. i. 6 note. The assertion is not
simply characterised as false (i. 6 we
lie) or as revealing a false nature (v. 4
he is a liar): it involves the existence
of a moral state the exact opposite of
that which is claimed.

ἕως ἄρτι] usque adhuc V., until
now, though the light is actually
shining, and he affirms that he is in
it, yea even that he has been in it
from the first.

10. ὁ ἀγαπῶν...] He that loveth...
The reality of the fact is set against
the assertion in v. 9 (He that saith...).
Comp. vv. 4, 5 note.

ἐν τῷ φωτὶ μένει] abideth (and not
simply is as in v. 9) in the light.
The idea of stability is added to that
of simple 'being' (comp. vv. 5, 6).
The position of the false brother and
of the true brother is referred to the
initial point of faith. Love testifies
to the continuance of a divine fellowship on man's part but does not create
it: the absence of love shews that the
fellowship has never been realised.
For the use of 'abide' in various
connexions see v. 6, iii. 14, iv. 16; 2
John 9; John xii. 46.

By love the disciple 'follows' his
Master and has 'the light of life'
(John viii. 12).

σκάνδαλον...ἔστιν] scandalum in eo
non est V., there is none occasion of
stumbling in him. The image occurs
elsewhere in St John's writings in
John vi. 61, xvi. 1; Apoc. ii. 14;
comp. John xi. 9 f. It is at first
sight doubtful whether the occasion of
stumbling is that which may be in the
way of others or in the way of the
believer himself. A man may cause
others to fall through want of love or

he may by the same defect create
difficulties in his own path.

The parallel in v. 11 favours the
second view. Love gives the single
eye which commands a clear prospect
of the course to be followed, while if
love be absent doubts and questionings arise which tend to the overthrow of faith (2 Pet. i. 10). But on
the other hand the general use of
σκάνδαλον points to the first meaning,
and it is quite in St John's manner to
regard love in its twofold working in
relation to the man who loves and to
others, while he regards hatred only
in its subject. The triumph of love is
that it creates no prejudice against
the Truth. Want of love is the most
prolific source of offences.

ἐν αὐτῷ] in him. If the 'offence'
is that which stands in a man's own
way, then he is regarded as offering
in himself the scene of his spiritual
advance: his progress, his dangers, are
spiritual, internal. If the offence is
that which lies in another's way, then
he who gives the offence presents
the cause of stumbling in his own
person.

11. Of the fruits of love it is sufficient to say that 'he that loveth
abideth in the light, and there is
none occasion of stumbling in him.'
The issues of hatred are traced in different directions. They are regarded
both in respect of present being (is
in) and action (walketh in) and in
respect of the final goal (knoweth
not whither) to which life is directed.
He who hates has lost the faculty of
seeing, which requires light and love,
'so that his whole life is a continual
error' (Howe).

ἐστίν...περιπατεῖ...] Comp. i. 7. The

καὶ οὐκ οἶδεν ποῦ ὑπάγει, ὅτι ἡ σκοτία ἐτύφλωσεν

phrase πορεύεσθαι ἐν σκότει is used in a different sense in Is. J. 10.

οὐκ οἶδεν...] *knoweth not*... John xii. 35; Prov. iv. 19. On the other hand that which was true of Christ (John viii. 12, xiii. 3) is true also of the believer (comp. John xiv. 4, 5). He knows what is the end of life.

ὑπάγει] *goeth.* The idea is not that of proceeding to a definite point (πορεύεσθαι), but of leaving the present scene.

ἐτύφλ. τοὺς ὀφθαλμούς] The image comes from Is. vi. 10 (John xii. 40), which is the fundamental description of God's mode of dealing with the self-willed. Comp. Rom. xi. 10 (Ps. lxix. 24); and for the opposite Eph. i. 18 πεφωτισμένους τοὺς ὀφθ. τῆς καρδίας. (Clem. 1 *Cor.* 36.)

ἐτύφλωσεν] The English idiom will not bear the exact rendering *blinded.* The original tense (comp. 2 Cor. iv. 4 and contrast John xii. 40) marks the decisive action of the darkness at the fatal moment when it once for all 'overtook' the man (John xii. 35 ἵνα μὴ καταλάβῃ, i. 5 οὐ κατέλαβεν). This darkness not only hindered the use of vision but (as darkness does physically) destroyed the spiritual organ.

IV.   THINGS TEMPORAL AND ETERNAL (ii. 12—17).

Hitherto St John has stated briefly the main scope of his Epistle. He has shewn what is the great problem of life, and how the Gospel meets it with an answer and a law complete and progressive, old and new. He now pauses, as it were, to contemplate those whom he is addressing more distinctly and directly, and to gather up in a more definite form the charge which is at once the foundation and the end of all he writes.

The section is divided into two parts. The Apostle first gives the ground of his appeal (*vv.* 12—14); and then he gives the appeal itself (15—17).

1.   *The ground of the appeal* (ii. 12—14).

The ground of the Apostle's appeal lies in the character and position of those whom he is addressing. He regards his readers first under their common aspect as all alike believers, and then under a twofold aspect as 'fathers' and 'young men,' separated one from another by the length of their Christian experience. This he does twice, first in respect of the actual work in which he is at the moment engaged, and then again in respect of a work looked upon as finished and complete. He shews with an impressive iteration that from first to last, in all that he writes or has written, one unchanging motive is supreme. Because his readers are Christians and have in part experienced the power of their faith he moves them to nobler efforts; his object is that their 'joy may be fulfilled' (c. i. 4).

The exact relation of γράφω to ἔγραψα has been variously explained. It may be a reference to some other writing which has not been preserved, or, as some think, to the Gospel (comp. 3 John 9; 1 Cor. v. 9; 2 Cor. ii. 3 f., vii. 12); but the use of ἔγραψα in *vv.* 21, 26 is unfavourable to this view.

It may mark a contrast between the former part of the letter, and that part which the Apostle is now writing, as if he resumed his work after an interval and looked back upon the words already written (comp. 1 Cor. ix. 15; Rom. xv. 15).

Or it may indicate simply a change of mental position in accordance with which St John transfers himself to the place of his readers, and regards the whole letter as they would do, as belonging to a past date.

Or yet again, to put this mode of

τοὺς ὀφθαλμοὺς αὐτοῦ.   ¹²Γράφω ὑμῖν, τεκνία,

explanation in another form, St John
may look at his letter first as it is in
the process of transcription still incomplete (1 Cor. xiv. 37; 2 Cor. xiii.
10), and then as it is ideally complete. This appears to be the true
explanation of the 'epistolary aorist.'
Comp. *vv.* 21, 26, v. 13; 2 John 12;
1 Pet. v. 12; Gal. vi. 11; Philem. 19, 21.

The Latin renderings of γράφω and
ἔγραψα are alike *scribo.*

The symmetry of the corresponding
clauses is remarkable.

(1) *I write to you*, little children
(τεκνία), *because*

> your sins are forgiven you
> for His name's sake.

(a) *I write to you, fathers, because*

> *ye know Him that is from the
> beginning.*

(β) *I write to you, young men,
because*

> *ye have overcome the evil
> one.*

(2) *I have written (I wrote) to
you*, little ones (παιδία), *because*

> ye know the Father.

(a) *I have written (I wrote) to
you, fathers, because*

> *ye know Him that is from
> the beginning.*

(β) *I have written (I wrote) to
you, young men, because*

> ye are strong and the word
> of God abideth in you and
> *ye have overcome the evil
> one.*

The common title of address is
different in the two cases (1) *little
children;* (2) *little ones.* And in
correspondence with this the aspect
of the common ground of addressing
those who are thus designated is also
different (1) *because your sins are
forgiven for His name's sake;* (2)
because ye know the Father. The
special ground of addressing 'the
fathers' is the same in each case:

that of addressing 'the young men' is
not changed in the second case but
more fully developed.

The causes of these variations will
appear as we examine the text.

Augustine, like many others, supposes that three classes of readers are
addressed. On this assumption he
characterises them vigorously:

Filii sunt, patres sunt, juvenes sunt.
Filii quia nascuntur: patres quia
principium agnoscunt: juvenes, quare?
Quia vicistis malignum. In filiis
nativitas, in patribus antiquitas, in
juvenibus fortitudo.

12. Γράφω] *I write.* Compare *v.* 1,
and contrast i. 4 (*we write*). For the
present tense compare Gal. i. 20;
1 Cor. xiv. 37; 2 Cor. i. 13; 1 Tim.
iii. 14.

τεκνία] *filioli* V., *little children.*
Comp. *v.* 1 *my little children.* The
simple title occurs again *v.* 28 (iii. 7),
iv. 4, v. 21. The word which expresses fellowship of nature is connected with that which is the sign of
it, the forgiveness of sins. Comp.
John iii. 5. Both from the symmetry
of the structure (*little children,
fathers, young men*), and from the
general scope of the passage, it is
evident that the title (here as elsewhere) is addressed to all St John's
readers and not to a particular class
of children in age.

ὅτι] *quoniam* V., *quia* Aug., *because.* There can be no doubt that
the particle is causal (*because*) and
not declarative (*that*). St John does
not write to make known the privileges of Christians, but to enforce
the duties which follow from the enjoyment of them.

ἀφέωνται ὐ. αἱ ἀμ.] *remittuntur
vobis peccata* V., *your sins are forgiven*, i.e. have been forgiven. The
present of the Latin is misleading
though the past forgiveness of sin
carries with it the constant applica-

ὅτι ἀφέωνται ὑμῖν αἱ ἁμαρτίαι διὰ τὸ ὄνομα αὐτοῦ.

tion of the grace to which it was due :
John xiii. 10. In parallel narratives, it may be added, ἀφίενται is
used by St Matthew (ix. 2, 5) and St
Mark (ii. 5, 9), and ἀφέωνται by St
Luke (v. 20, 23). In Luke vii. 47 f.
ἀφέωνται is practically undisturbed.
The reading in John xx. 23 is somewhat doubtful (ἀφέωνται, ἀφίενται).

The proclamation of the forgiveness
of sins was the message of the Gospel:
Luke xxiv. 47; Acts xiii. 38. This
includes potentially the fulfilment of
man's destiny as man. Comp. i. 9 note.
For Christ's sake the Father (v. 14) forgives those who are united with Him.

διὰ τὸ ὄνομα αὐτοῦ] propter nomen
ejus V., per n. e. Aug., for His name's
sake. There is no direct antecedent ;
but from v. 6 the thought of Christ as
the perfect exemplar of divine love
has been present to the mind of the
apostle; and the pronoun clearly refers to Him. Forgiveness is granted
to men because Christ is indeed what
He is revealed to be and what His
'name' expresses. It is of course
assumed that Christians acknowledge
Him as being what He is (Matt. xxviii.
19).

Redemption is referred to Christ as
He has been made known, both in
respect of the fact that that revelation
contains the force through which as
the means (διά gen.) and the ground
for the sake of which as the cause
(διά acc.) it is accomplished. See c. iv.
9 ζήσωμεν δι' αὐτοῦ; John vi. 57 ζήσει
δι' ἐμέ. The latter construction is
very rare. Comp. John xv. 3 καθαροί
ἐστε διὰ τὸν λόγον; Apoc. xii. 11 ἐνίκησαν διὰ τὸ αἷμα τοῦ ἀρνίου.

For διὰ τὸ ὄνομα see Matt. x. 22,
xxiv. 9 and parallels; John xv. 21;
Apoc. ii. 3.

διὰ τοῦ ὀνόματος Acts iv. 30, x. 43;
1 Cor. i. 10.

In two other places of the Epistle
'the name' of Christ is mentioned as
the object of faith in different aspects.
The commandment of God is that we
believe the name (πιστεύειν τῷ ὀν.) of
His Son Jesus Christ (iii. 23), that
is, that we accept the revelation conveyed in that full title as true. And
again those who believe in the name
(πιστεύειν εἰς τὸ ὄν.) of the Son of
God (v. 13), who cast themselves
wholly upon the revelation, are assured of the possession of life eternal
(comp. John i. 12 note). With these
passages must be compared John xx.
31, where St John says that the object of his Gospel was that his readers
may believe that Jesus is the Christ,
the Son of God, and believing may
have life in His name (ἐν τῷ ὀν.), in
fellowship with Him as He has thus
been made known.

The pregnant use of 'the name' as
summing up that which is made known
of Christ, explains how it came to be
used as equivalent to 'the faith': 3
John 7 ὑπὲρ τοῦ ὀνόματος ἐξῆλθαν.
See Additional Note on iii. 23.

13. Believers, who are one in the
possession of the gift of forgiveness,
are distinguished by the circumstances of life. Differences of experience correspond generally to differences of age. Mature Christians, in
a society like that which St John addressed, would be 'fathers' in years.
The difference of 'fathers' and 'young
men' answers to that of 'the thinkers,
and the soldiers in the Christian
army,' to the two main applications of
the Faith. It is a spring of wisdom;
and it is also a spring of strength. In
the natural sequence action is the
way to that knowledge through which
wisdom comes. Christian wisdom is
not speculative but first the fruit of
work and then the principle of work.

The characteristic of 'fathers' is
knowledge, the fruit of experience
(ἐγνώκατε): that of 'young men,'
victory, the prize of strength. St

¹³γράφω ὑμῖν, πατέρες, ὅτι ἐγνώκατε τὸν ἀπ᾽ ἀρχῆς·
γράφω ὑμῖν, νεανίσκοι, ὅτι νενικήκατε τὸν πονηρόν.

13 τὸ πονηρόν ℵ.

John bases his appeal to each class on that which they had severally gained.

πατέρες] The word, like אָב, Abba, pater, papa, is used naturally of those who stand in a position of responsible authority. Thus it is applied in the O.T. to prophets (2 K. ii. 12 ; vi. 21 ; xiii. 14), priests (Jud. xvii. 10; xviii. 19), teachers (Prov. i. 8). Comp. Matt. xxiii. 9; (1 Cor. iv. 15;) Acts vii. 2 ; xxii. 1. Here the natural characteristic of age is combined with that of eminence in the Christian body.

ὅτι ἐγνώκατε] quoniam (quia) cognovistis V., because ye know.... The essence of wisdom lies in the recognition of the unity of purpose which runs through the whole development of being, and of that unity of life which exists in all. This truth is brought home through the deeper understanding of the age-long revelation of God consummated in the Incarnation and interpreted by the Spirit.

For the idea of knowledge see v. 3 note. God can be known only in His Son. The knowledge here spoken of is that which is the result of the past still abiding (ἐγνώκατε) and not that which marked a crisis in growth (ἔγνωτε) or which is still in continuous advance (γινώσκετε).

τὸν ἀπ᾽ ἀρχῆς] eum qui ab initio (a principio Aug.) est V., Him that is from the beginning, the Word, that is, brought near to us in the Person of Christ Jesus. The title sums up shortly what is expressed in its successive stages in John i. 1—14, the Word through Whom all things were made, and in Whom all things consist, Who, as Life, was the Light of men, Who was ever coming into the world which He

made, Who became Flesh. The word of life (c. i. 1) is the record of the revelation of Him that is from the beginning. The whole course of history is, when rightly understood, the manifestation of one will. To know this in Christ is the prerogative of a 'father,' and the knowledge is the opportunity for the completest life.

νεανίσκοι] adulescentes V., juvenes Aug., young men in the full vigour of opening life. Comp. Matt. xix. 20; Luke vii. 14.

νενικήκατε] have overcome, not 'overcame' simply (c. v. 4 ἡ νίκη ἡ νικήσασα). The past remains effective. The image, based on John xvi. 33, is characteristic of the Apocalypse (ii. 7 ff., xii. 11, xxi. 7) and of this Epistle : v. 14, iv. 4, v. 4 f.

τὸν πονηρόν] malignum V., the evil one, v. 14, iii. 12, v. 18 f.; John xvii. 15; Matt. vi. 13, xiii. 19, 38 (v. 37, 39). The personal aspect of the Christian conflict on its spiritual side is naturally brought out now. Darkness has its prince: John xii. 31, xiv. 30, xvi. 11. It is assumed that a conflict is inevitable unless men passively yield to the power of evil (c. v. 19). Comp. Eph. ii. 2, vi. 12. The abruptness with which the idea of 'the evil one' is introduced shews that it was familiar. See Additional Note.

14. At the close of v. 13 there is a pause in thought if not a break in the composition of the letter. Looking back on the record of his purpose the apostle appears to resume the thread of his argument: 'I write, yea I have written, because you have had experience of the Faith.'

παιδία] infantes V., pueri Aug., little ones. This title, little ones, which like τεκνία is applied to the whole

^{14}ἔγραψα ὑμῖν, παιδία, ὅτι ἐγνώκατε τὸν πατέρα·
ἔγραψα ὑμῖν, πατέρες, ὅτι ἐγνώκατε τὸν ἀπ᾽ ἀρχῆς·
ἔγραψα ὑμῖν, νεανίσκοι, ὅτι ἰσχυροί ἐστε καὶ ὁ λόγος

14 ἔγραψα ὑ. π. ℵABC the me syrr : γράφω ὑ. π. ϛ.   τὸ ἀπ᾽ ἀρχῆς B.
ὁ λόγος τοῦ θεοῦ ℵAC vg syrr : – τοῦ θεοῦ B the.

Christian body, differs from *little children* by emphasising the idea of subordination and not that of kinsmanship. St John speaks not as sharing the nature of those to whom he writes, but as placed in a position of authority over them. Comp. *v.* 18 (John xxi. 5).

In correspondence with this difference in the address St John gives a different reason for his writing: *because ye know the Father.*

The sense of an immediate personal relationship to God (comp. John xiv. 7) gives stability to all the gradations of human authority. In this respect 'knowing the Father' is different from 'knowing Him that is from the beginning.' The former involves a direct spiritual connexion: the latter involves besides an intellectual apprehension of the divine 'plan.' The knowledge 'of the Father' is that of present love and submission: the knowledge of Him 'that is from the beginning' is sympathy with the Divine Thought which is fulfilled in all time.

At the same time the two titles 'little children,' 'little ones,' indicate a twofold spiritual position. As 'little children' we are all bound one to another by the bond of natural affection: as 'little ones' we all recognise our equal feebleness in the presence of the One Father. It may be added that the relation of the readers of the letter to the Apostle really determined their relation to God (c. i. 3).

There is a difference in the general ground for writing (*v.* 12 *because your sins are forgiven..., v.* 14 *because ye*

know the Father), but in writing to 'the fathers' specially there is no change, no development, in St John's language. The knowledge of Christ as the Word, active from the beginning of Creation, includes all that we can know. At the same time this knowledge is regarded in two different aspects corresponding to the two general ideas of forgiveness and Fatherhood (*vv.* 12, 14); even as the Incarnation satisfies man's need of redemption and his need of consummation.

In writing to 'the young men' St John makes no change in his reason (*because ye have overcome the evil one*) but he develops what he has said. He adds the twofold permanent ground of the Christian's victory to the assertion of the fact which he made before. The young soldier is '*strong*' (ἰσχυρός comp. Eph. vi. 10; Matt. vii. 29) as having the personal qualifications for his work ; and '*the word of God abideth in him,*' so that he is in living contact with the source of life. The natural endowment of energetic vigour is consecrated to a divine end by a divine voice.

ὁ λόγος...μένει...] *the word...abideth...* Comp. *vv.* 24, 27; John xv. 7 (*v.* 3). The converse thought occurs John viii. 31. Comp. c. i. 10 note.

2.   *The appeal* (ii. 15—17).

In the preceding verses St John has set forth the privileges of Christians both generally in their sense of forgiveness and of a Divine Fatherhood, and specially in the far-reaching wisdom of the old, and the victorious strength of the young: he now goes [τοῦ θεοῦ] ἐν ὑμῖν μένει καὶ νενικήκατε τὸν πονηρόν.

on to enforce the consequence which is made possible. A great 'love not' follows on the command to love. The structure of the passage is simple and regular. The prohibition (15 *a*) is followed by a view of its overwhelming necessity. The love of the world is incompatible with the love of the Father (15 *b*), for the objects of love determine its character (16). And further: there is between them the contrast of time and eternity, of transition and abiding (17).

¹⁵*Love not the world nor the things in the world. If any one love the world, the love of the Father is not in him:* ¹⁶*because all that is in the world, the desire of the flesh, and the desire of the eyes, and the vainglory of life, is not of the Father, but is of the world.* ¹⁷*And the world is passing away, and the desire thereof, but he that doeth the will of God abideth for ever.*

The three false tendencies under which St John ranges 'all that is in the world' cover the whole ground of worldliness, of the temptation to set up the creature as an end. They offer typical tests of man's real state as to himself, as to things external, and (specially) as to his fellow-men. Or, if we follow the division suggested by the words (ἐπιθυμία, ἐπιθυμία, ἀλαζονία), they indicate prevailing false views in regard to want and to possession. We desire wrongly and we glory wrongly in what we have.

The 'wants' which man feels can be divided into two great classes. Some things he desires to appropriate personally: some things he desires to enjoy without appropriation. The desire of the flesh embraces the one class (*e.g.* gratification of appetites); the desire of the eyes the other (*e.g.* pursuit of art as an end). The wrong use of possession lies in

the empty and ostentatious assertion of advantages which are placed in a wrong light. A superiority is asserted on external grounds which cannot be justified in the face of the true issues of life. The ἀλάζων is in this case 'one who lays claim to blessings which are not truly his for the sake of renown' (comp. Theophr. *Char.* § 23; [Plat.] *Def.* p. 416 ἀλαζονεία ἕξις προσποιητικὴ ἀγαθοῦ ἢ ἀγαθῶν τῶν μὴ ὑπαρχόντων).

The three tendencies naturally recall the three Temptations of the Lord, with which they have obvious points of contact. The first Temptation corresponds to the first and most elementary form of ἐπιθυμία τῆς σαρκός, the desire of the simplest support of natural life. A divine word is sovereign over this: the means which God uses are not limited to one form (Luke iv. 4). The offer of the kingdoms of the civilized world (τῆς οἰκουμένης) and their glory, which is placed second in St Luke's order seems to answer in the loftiest shape to ἐπιθυμία τῶν ὀφθαλμῶν, the power of commanding all that is fairest and most attractive in the world. Here also Scripture shews that no aim however true and noble can be allowed to trench on the absolute homage due to God (Luke iv. 8). And again the call to claim an open manifestation of God's protecting power touches the root of ἀλαζονία τοῦ βίου, in which endowments and gifts are used arbitrarily for personal ostentation. Such use is a tempting of God from Whom man dares to isolate himself (Luke iv. 12).

It has been felt no less natural to look for some correspondence between the threefold worldly tendencies of St John and the three master vices which occupy a prominent place in ancient and mediæval ethics, φιληδονία, πλεονεξία, φιλοδοξία, voluptas, avaritia, superbia.

¹⁵ Μὴ ἀγαπᾶτε τὸν κόσμον μηδὲ τὰ ἐν τῷ κόσμῳ. ἐάν
τις ἀγαπᾷ τὸν κόσμον, οὐκ ἔστιν ἡ ἀγάπη τοῦ πατρὸς

15 ἡ ἀγάπη τοῦ πατρός ℵB vg syrr the me : ἡ ἀγ. τοῦ θεοῦ AC.

The correspondence is so far real, though not direct, that the germs of these special vices lie in the feelings which St John characterises. Comp. Just. M. *Dial.* 82, p. 308 D διὰ δέος οὖν [Ezech. iii. 17 ff.] καὶ ἡμεῖς σπουδάζομεν ὁμιλεῖν κατὰ τὰς γραφάς, οὐ διὰ φιλοχρηματίαν ἢ φιλοδοξίαν ἢ φιληδονίαν· ἐν οὐδενὶ γὰρ τούτων ἐλέγξαι ἡμᾶς ὄντας δύναταί τις.

The enumeration does not include spiritual sins. These are not, under the present aspect, 'of the world' or 'in the world.' St John has dwelt before on the relation of man to man —love and hatred; and he dwells afterwards on the relation of man to true opinion. Here he is considering the relation of man to the κόσμος as an external system which has lost its true character: Rom. viii. 19 f.

15. Μὴ ἀγαπᾶτε] *Nolite diligere* V., *Love not.* The command is not given to any particular class (as to the young) but to all. That which man may not do, being what he is, God can do, John iii. 16 (ἠγάπησεν τὸν κόσμον). God looks through the surface of things by which man is misled to the very being which He created.

τὸν κόσμον] *mundum* V., *the world,* the order of finite being regarded as apart from God. The Roman empire with its idolatry of the Emperor as the representative of the State, presented the idea in a concrete and impressive form.

The system as an organised whole (κόσμος) is in other places considered as the dominant form of life, the age (ὁ αἰὼν οὖτος, ὁ νῦν αἰών). Comp. Rom. xii. 2; 2 Tim. iv. 2.

For the use of κόσμος see John i. 10 note.

With 'the world' are joined 'the things in the world,' all, that is, which

finds its proper sphere and fulfilment in a finite order and without God. 'To be in the world' is the opposite to 'being in God.' The question is not of the present necessary limitations of thought and action but of their aim and object. Whatever is treated as complete without reference to God is so far a rival to God. This thought is brought out in the words which follow.

Augustine illustrates the idea in respect of the love of nature : Non te prohibet Deus amare ista sed non diligere ad beatitudinem, sed ad hoc probare et laudare ut ames creatorem. Quemadmodum......si sponsus faceret sponsæ suæ annulum et illa acceptum annulum plus diligeret quam sponsum qui illi fecerit annulum ; nonne in ipso dono sponsi anima adultera deprehenderetur quamvis hoc amaret quod dedit sponsus?

ἐάν τις...] There can be but one supreme object of moral devotion. All secondary objects will be referred to this. The love of the finite as an absolute object necessarily excludes the love of the Creator (*the Father*). Comp. Rom. i. 25; James iv. 4 (ἡ φιλία τοῦ κόσμου). Unum cor duos tam sibi adversarios amores non capit : Matt. vi. 24 (Bede, *ad loc.*).

Here as elsewhere St John places the contrast before his readers in its ultimate essential form, as of light and darkness, love and hatred. He assumes that there cannot be a vacuum in the soul. So Augustine writes :̄ Noli diligere mundum. Exclude malum amorem mundi ut implearis amore Dei. Vas es sed adhuc plenus es ; funde quod habes ut accipias quod non habes.

It will be observed also that he speaks here of *the love of the Father* ἐν αὐτῷ· ¹⁶ὅτι πᾶν τὸ ἐν τῷ κόσμῳ· ἡ ἐπιθυμία τῆς

and not of *the love of God* (c. ii. 5 note). The phrase is unique (comp. Col. i. 12 f.), and suggests as the object of man's love God as He has been pleased to bring Himself within the range of man's knowledge (John xiv. 9; comp. c. i. 2 note). Thus it expresses primarily the love of 'the children' of God to God; but this love answers to and springs out of the love shewn to them by 'the Father' whom 'they know' (*v.* 14).

By the 'love of the world, and of the things in the world' the sense of the personal relationship to God is lost, and not merely the sense of a divine presence. Of the man who is swayed by such a passion it must be said that *the love of the Father is not in him* as an animating, inspiring power (c. i. 10). This phrase expresses more than 'he loveth not God' or 'he loveth not the Father.' That form of expression would describe a simple fact: this presents the fact as a ruling principle. The exact order of the Greek is remarkable: 'there exists not, whatever he may say, the love of the Father in him.' Comp. c. i. 5 ; iv. 16 f.; John v. 45; vi. 45; vii. 28; viii. 44, 50, 54; ix. 16; x. 12, 34; xiii. 10, 16.

The thought finds a striking expression under the imagery of St John in a fragment of Philo quoted by John of Damascus (*Parall. Sacra* A, *Tit.* xxx. p. 370): ἀμήχανον συνυπάρχειν τὴν πρὸς κόσμον ἀγάπην τῇ πρὸς τὸν θεὸν ἀγάπῃ, ὡς ἀμήχανον συνυπάρχειν ἀλλήλοις φῶς καὶ σκότος.

16. ὅτι...] *because...* In moral and spiritual things there is a law of equilibrium. Nothing rises higher than its source. The desire of things earthly as ends in themselves comes from the world and is bounded by the world. It is therefore incompatible with the love of the Father.

The point of sight from which 'all that is in the world' is regarded here

is more distinctly defined than in *v.* 15. In themselves all finite objects, 'the things that are in the world,' are 'of the Father.' It is the false view of them which makes them idols. Hence St John defines 'that which is in the world,' that which, as now regarded, finds its consummation 'in the world,' from the human side. The feeling which misuses the object determines and shews by its misuse what there is defective in the object which gives occasion to the wrongdoing.

This general aspect of the question determines the exact form of language. St John writes πᾶν τὸ ἐν τ. κ. and not πάντα τὰ ἐν τ. κ. He looks at 'all' in its unity in relation to the feeling man. Comp. c. v. 4: Eph. v. 13 (πάντα, πᾶν). The world as such has nothing more to offer than what is summed up in the three typical phrases by which πᾶν is defined. This thought has been made wrongly the main thought of the sentence by the Latin versions: *omne quod in mundo est concupiscentia (desiderium) carnis est et....*

ἡ ἐπιθυμία τῆς σαρκός] *concupiscentia (desiderium* Aug.) *carnis* V., *the desire of the flesh,* the desire of which the flesh is the seat. The genitive with ἐπιθυμία is in the N. T. characteristically subjective (John viii. 44; Rom. i. 24; Apoc. xviii. 14). Comp. Gal. v. 16, 24; Eph. ii. 3; 1 Pet. ii. 11 (αἱ σαρκικαὶ ἐπιθυμίαι, Rom. xiii. 14; 1 Pet. iv. 2 (ἀνθρώπων ἐπιθυμίαις); Tit. ii. 12 (αἱ κοσμικαὶ ἐπιθυμίαι).

Under this category are included all desires which involve the appropriation of the object to which they are directed. By the separate mention of οἱ ὀφθαλμοί the sense of σάρξ is proportionately limited.

In St John generally σάρξ is used to express humanity under the present

σαρκὸς καὶ ἡ ἐπιθυμία τῶν ὀφθαλμῶν καὶ ἡ ἀλαζονία
τοῦ βίου, οὐκ ἔστιν ἐκ τοῦ πατρός, ἀλλὰ ἐκ τοῦ κόσ-

conditions of life (c. iv. 2; 2 John 7; John i. 14; vi. 51—55; xvii. 2). Once the θέλημα σαρκός is set by the side of θέλημα ἀνδρός as distinct from it (John i. 13); twice σάρξ is opposed to πνεῦμα (John iii. 6; vi. 63); and once κατὰ τὴν σάρκα is used to describe a judgment which is external, superficial, destitute of moral insight (John viii. 15). The desire of the σάρξ as σάρξ is necessarily for that which is like itself. It cannot include any spiritual element.

Compare Additional Note on iii. 19.

ἡ ἐπιθ. τῶν ὀφθ.] concupiscentia (desiderium Aug.) oculorum V., the desire of the eyes, the desire of which the eyes are the organ: not the pleasure of the miser only or characteristically (Eccles. iv. 8; v. 11), but all personal vicious indulgence represented by seeing. The desire of appropriation enters into 'the desire of the flesh': the 'desire of the eyes' is satisfied by enjoyment which comes under the general form of contemplation. So far it is true that in the former the thought of physical pleasure is dominant, as the object of desire, while in the latter forms of mental ('psychical') pleasure find place. The 'eyes' are the typical example of the organs to which art ministers.

Augustine gives a singular illustration of what he holds to be 'the desire of the eyes,' which is worth quoting as giving a vivid trait in the Christian feeling of his time: Aliquando tentat etiam [curiositas] servos Dei, ut velint quasi miraculum facere: tentare utrum exaudiat illos Deus in miraculis. Curiositas est; hoc est desiderium oculorum; non est a patre.

ἡ ἀλαζ. τοῦ βίου] superbia vitæ V., ambitio sæculi Aug. (other Latin authorities give jactantia hujus vitæ, vitæ humanæ), the vainglory of life, the vainglory which springs out of and belongs to our visible earthly life. The genitive is subjective, as in the two other cases. The ἀλαζών (comp. Rom. i. 30; 2 Tim. iii. 2) is closely connected with the ὑπερήφανος; but his vice centres in self and is consummated in his absolute self-exaltation, while the ὑπερήφανος shews his character by his overweening treatment of others. 'The ἀλαζών sins most against truth: the ὑπερήφανος sins most against love.' Ἀλαζονία may be referred to a false view of 'what things are in themselves, empty and unstable: ὑπερηφανία to a false view of what our relations to other persons are. Comp. Mk. vii. 22; Luke i. 51; James iv. 6; 1 Pet. v. 5. See also Wisd. v. 8; xvii. 7; 2 Macc. ix. 8, xv. 6; Prov. xxv. 6.

Such 'vainglory,' such a false view of the value of our possessions, belongs to life (ὁ βίος) in its present concretè manifestation and not to life in its essential principle (ἡ ζωή). Comp. Luke viii. 14 (ἡδοναὶ τοῦ βίου); 1 Tim. ii. 2 (βίον διάγειν); 2 Tim. ii. 4 (ταῖς τοῦ βίου πραγματείαις); (in 1 Pet. iv. 3 τοῦ βίου is an addition, but βιῶσαι occurs in v. 2). Hence ὁ βίος is used for 'the means of life': Mk. xii. 44; Luke [viii. 43], xv. 12, 30; c. iii. 17. Compare also βίωσις, Acts xxvi. 4; and βιωτικός, Luke xxi. 34; 1 Cor. vi. 3 f.

These characteristic feelings of want and of wealth, the desire of the flesh and the desire of the eyes, and the vainglory of life, are said to be, as man now is naturally, of the world (c. iv. 5 note; John xv. 19; xvii. 14, 16; xviii. 36). The declaration marks the false position into which man has come. In his original

μου ἐστίν· ¹⁷καὶ ὁ κόσμος παράγεται καὶ ἡ ἐπιθυμία
[αὐτοῦ], ὁ δὲ ποιῶν τὸ θέλημα τοῦ θεοῦ μένει εἰς τὸν
αἰῶνα.

17 ἡ ἐπιθ. αὐτοῦ : − αὐτοῦ A.   Many Latin authorities and (in sense) the The-
baic version add : *quomodo (sicut et) deus (ipse) manet in æternum.*

constitution the desire was good, because it was directed consciously towards the fulfilment of his office in
regard to the whole order and to God:
the exultation was good, because it
was an acknowledgment of divine
bounty. Now the desire is suggested
by the creature and not by the Creator, by the object separated from the
Living Author of all, not by the Living
Author to whom the child should
look (ἐκ τοῦ πατρός not simply ἐκ τοῦ
θεοῦ). Thus each typical false tendency is the corruption of a noble
instinct, the longing for support and
for beauty, the joy of thankfulness.

Est ergo triplex amor qui tria illa
excludat quæ non sunt ex Patre.......
Et forte hæc sunt de quibus in Lege
præcipitur : *Diliges Dominum Deum
tuum ex toto corde tuo et ex tota
anima tua et ex tota virtute tua*
(Deut. vi. 5), id est diliges dulciter sive
affectuose, diliges prudenter, diliges
fortiter (Bern. *Serm. de div.* xxix. 1).

The phrase εἶναι ἐκ (*v.* 21 ; iii. 19;
iv. 5) *to be of* is characteristic of St
John expressing derivation and dependence. Compare John iii. 31 note;
and Additional Note on iii. 1.

17. This clause contains a second
ground for the prohibition in *v.* 15.
Not only is the love of the world irreconcileable with the love of the Father; but also, yet further, the fate
of the world is included in its essential character. The world—the external system which occupied the
place of God—was already when St
John wrote in the act of dissolution
and vanishing.

The words can also be taken as a
second proof of the antagonism of the
love of the Father and of the love of

the world, so far as these are at variance in their issue no less than in their
source. But this connexion appears
to be less natural than the other.

παράγεται] *is passing away:* see
v. 8. The word describes not the
general character of the world as
transitory but its actual condition in
the face of the Church, 'the Kingdom
of God.' The whole sum of finite
things, regarded in itself as complete,
is (as it were) a screen which hides
the presence of God. By the declaration of the Truth this was in St John's
time beginning to be removed. Compare *v.* 8 ; 1 Cor. vii. 31 ; and contrast
the ideal view from the divine side:
τὰ ἀρχαῖα παρῆλθεν, ἰδοὺ γέγονεν καινά
(2 Cor. v. 17 : comp. Apoc. xxi. 4).

In the thanksgiving after the
Eucharist in *The Doctrine of the
Apostles* the clause occurs: ἐλθέτω
χάρις καὶ παρελθέτω ὁ κόσμος οὗτος (c.
x. 6).

ἡ ἐπιθυμία αὐτοῦ] *concupiscentia*
(*desideria* Aug.) *ejus* V., *the desire
thereof,* the desire which belongs to
it and which it stimulates. Comp.
Tit. ii. 12 αἱ κοσμικαὶ ἐπιθυμίαι. The
gen. is subjective as in *v.* 16, though
it is true that the desire which the
world fosters is in turn directed to
the world as its object. A verb corresponding to παράγεται must be supplied. The world which is the source
and the object of the desire is shewn
to be by itself unsubstantial and evan-
escent. The desire therefore is shewn
in its utter vanity (καταργεῖται). But
the desire remains as an aching void.

The contrast to this 'desire' which
is earth-born and empty is 'the will
of God.' That alone is permanent of
which this will is the ground.

ὁ δὲ ποιῶν...μένει...] *qui autem
facit (fecerit* Aug.) V., *but he that
doeth...abideth...* While the fabric of
'the world' is being removed the
Christian suffers no disturbance. The
present in this sense is eternal. When
all else changes the obedience of love
continues unchanged. This abides
in the new order to which indeed it
properly belongs. The contrast to
the world converted into an idol is
not God, but the believer who in
action strives to do God's will. Hence
St John does not say 'he that loveth
God,' which might have been suggested by *v.* 15, but *he that doeth the
will of God abideth for ever.* Such a
one is truly akin to the Son of man:
Mk. iii. 35.

Compare John iv. 34; vi. 38; vii.
17; ix. 31.

The will of God expresses the true
end of all things, and is opposed to
'the desire' which springs from a
finite source as its ultimate origin.
At the same time 'the will of God'
includes the right use of all natural
powers, faculties, instincts, which in
their essential nature answer to it:
Apoc. iv. 11. Compare 1 Thess. iv. 3.
In speaking of the divine will St
John says 'the will of God' and not
'the will of the Father' as might
seem to be suggested by *v.* 16. Stress
is laid upon the divine majesty rather
than upon the divine love. 'The will
of the Father' is found only in St
Matthew (vi. 10 *our Father,* vii. 21;
xii. 50 *my Father;* comp. xviii. 14;
xxvi. 42). *The will of our God and
Father* occurs Gal. i. 4 (comp. Eph.
i. 5, 9, 11). *The will of God* is not
unfrequent: 1 Pet. ii. 15; iii. 17; iv.
19; Rom. i. 10; xii. 2; Heb. x. 36.
In the Gospel of St John the phrase
which is always used by the Lord is
the will of Him that sent me: iv. 34;
v. 30; vi. 38 ff. (vii. 17).

μένει εἰς τ. αἰ.] *abideth for ever.*
Comp. John viii. 35; xii. 34; 2 Cor.
ix. 9 (LXX.); 1 Pet. i. 25 (LXX.). The

absolute use of μένειν is not unfrequent: John xv. 16; 1 Pet. i. 23;
Heb. x. 34.

εἰς τὸν αἰῶνα] *in æternum* V. This
is the only form in which αἰών occurs
in the Epistles (here and 2 John 2)
and Gospel (12 times) of St John,
except the correlative ἐκ τοῦ αἰῶνος
(John ix. 32). The phrase occurs independently of the LXX. (1 Pet. i. 25;
2 Cor. ix. 9; Hebr. v. 6; vi. 20; vii.
17 ff.) only (with negative) in Matth.
xxi. 19‖Mk. xi. 14; Mk. iii. 29; 1
Cor. viii. 13 (Jude 13 εἰς αἰῶνα). [1 Pet.
i. 23 and 2 Pet. ii. 17 are false readings.] It is very common in the LXX. as
the rendering of עַד עוֹלָם, לְעוֹלָם, עוֹלָם.
The thought contained in the words
here is given by the addition which is
found in *Theb.* and *Old Lat.* 'as God
also abideth for ever' (*sicut et ipse
manet in æternum*). Augustine reads
the addition and remarks on the
whole passage: Voluit te amor mundi, tene Christum. Propter te factus
est temporalis ut tu fias æternus;
quia et ille sic factus est temporalis
ut maneret æternus.

And again: Terram diligis, terra
eris. Deum diligis: quid dicam, Deus
eris? Non audeo dicere ex me:
scripturas audiamus *Ego dixi, dii estis
et filii altissimi omnes.*

B. THE CONFLICT OF TRUTH AND
FALSEHOOD WITHOUT AND WITHIN
(ii. 18—iv. 6).

The broad contrast which has been
drawn in the last section between
things temporal and eternal, between
the world and the Church, leads to
the central subject of the Epistle, the
great conflict of life, which is treated
of in ii. 18—iv. 6. In this the hostile
power is seen to arise from within
the Christian society. The world has
found expression in an anti-Christian
system which lays claim to spiritual
endowment and authority. False
prophetic power (Apoc. xiii. 1 ff.)
takes its place by the side of the

^{18} Παιδία, ἐσχάτη ὥρα ἐστίν, καὶ καθὼς ἠκούσατε

imperial power (Apoc. xii. 1 ff.). These false teachers, this 'spirit of anti-christ,' are 'of the world' (iv. 4 f.).

Characteristic marks of this conflict appear throughout: ἀντίχριστος ii. 18, 20; τὸ πνεῦμα τοῦ ἀντιχρίστου iv. 3; ψευδοπροφῆται iv. 1; οἱ πλανῶντες ii. 26, comp. iii. 7; τὸ πνεῦμα τῆς πλάνης iv. 6. And underneath the false spiritual teaching lies 'the hatred' of the world: iii. 13. The question is no longer of false opinion or. vicious practice within the Church, but of temptations to yield allegiance to a rival power.

The view which St John gives of the Christian conflict falls into four sections:

I. THE REVELATION OF FALSEHOOD AND TRUTH (ii. 18—29).

II. THE CHILDREN OF GOD AND THE CHILDREN OF THE DEVIL (iii. 1—12).

III. BROTHERHOOD IN CHRIST AND THE HATRED OF THE WORLD (iii. 13—24).

IV. THE RIVAL SPIRITS OF TRUTH AND ERROR (iv. 1—6).

Step by step the strength of the Christian is shewn in his firm hold upon the Truth, in the consciousness and the character of Sonship, in the activity of Love, in the power of Spiritual Discernment. So the conflict passes to victory.

I. THE REVELATION OF FALSEHOOD AND TRUTH (ii. 18—29).

This section is separable into three parts:

1. *Antichrists and Christians* (18—21).

2. *The essence and the power of the Truth* (22—25).

3. *Abiding in the Truth* (26—29).

The progress of thought is simple. The fact of apostasy from the Christian body is recognised as a characteristic of the crisis. This fact serves to

remind Christians of the gift which they have received for the discernment of the Truth. The essence of the Truth lies in the acknowledgment of the Messiahship of Jesus. The confession of the Son gives fellowship with the Father; issuing in the life eternal. This knowledge of God then Christians have to keep firmly, that they may face their Lord at His appearance. And true knowledge has the seal of righteousness, likeness to God, the mark of divine sonship.

1. *Antichrists and Christians* (18—21).

The necessity of conflict which has been laid down on general grounds in *vv.* 15—17 is enforced by the special circumstances of the age. It is 'a last hour,' and as such marked by divisions, errors, temptations in the Christian society itself (18, 19). At the same time, as answering to this special peril, Christians have a gift of spiritual discernment which it is their privilege to use as a decisive criterion of error (20, 21).

^{18}*My little ones, it is a last hour, and as ye heard that Antichrist cometh, even now many Antichrists have arisen; whence we perceive that it is a last hour.* ^{19}*They went out from us, but they were not of us; for if they had been of us, they would have remained with us; but they went out that they may be made manifest that they all are not of us.* ^{20}*And ye have an unction from the Holy One; and ye all know—*^{21}*I have not written to you because ye know not the truth, but because ye know it, and because no lie is of the truth.*

18. Παιδία] *Filioli* (*Pueri*) V., *My little ones*. See *v.* 14. The Apostle addresses his readers with the authority of age and experience, and not as dwelling on the thought of spiritual kinship (τεκνία).

In the sentence which precedes he had spoken of 'the world' as 'passing away.' He now points out the decisive sign of the coming change in the condition of the Christian society. It is 'a last hour.'

The conception of 'a last time,' 'a last season,' the 'last days,' rests upon the O. T., in which the phrase אַחֲרִית הַיָּמִים is used for the distant future, on which the prophet's eye is fixed. Thus in Gen. xlix. 1; Num. xxiv. 14 (ἐπ' ἐσχάτων [-του] τῶν ἡμερῶν) it points to the time when Israel had entered upon the possession of Canaan, the first stage in the fulfilment of the divine promise. In Is. ii. 2; Mic. iv. 1; Hos. iii. 5; Jerem. xxiii. 20; xxx. 24; xlviii. 47; xlix. 39, it describes the time when Zion shall be restored and the people shall fear and obey the Lord. In Ezek. xxxviii. 16 it regards some particular season of signal deliverance. Thus the phrase in its biblical sense includes in part the notion of 'the age to come' and the immediate preparation for it.

In post-biblical times 'the age to come' was sharply distinguished from the period of trial by which it was to be ushered in; and 'the latter days' came to be regarded as a season of conflict and suffering through which the divine victory should be accomplished. This appears to be the ruling idea of the phrase in the N. T.: Acts ii. 17 ἐν ταῖς ἐσχ. ἡμ. (Joel iii. 1, ἐσχάταις being an explanatory gloss); James v. 3 ἐν ἐσχ. ἡμ.; 1 Pet. i. 20 ἐπ' ἐσχάτων τῶν χρόνων.

But in this interpretation the successive partial dawnings of 'the age to come' give a different force to the words 'the last days' which usher in the age according to the context in which they occur. In one sense 'the age to come' dated from Pentecost; in another from the destruction of Jerusalem; in another it was still the object of hope. So also 'the last days' are found in each of the seasons of fierce trial which precede the several

comings of Christ. The age in which we live is, under one aspect, 'the last days,' and in another it is 'the age to come,' which was prepared by the travail-pains of the old order. As we look forward a season of sore distress separates us from that which is still to be revealed (2 Tim. iii. 1; 2 Pet. iii. 3; Jude 18; 1 Pet. i. 5, contrast v. 20): as we look back we have entered on an inheritance now through struggles of 'a last time.'

But while the great counsel of God goes forward to fulfilment the date of the consummation is not revealed: Acts i. 7; Matt. xxiv. 36.

The calculation which Severus (Cramer, *Cat.* in loc.) makes is interesting in the face of our present knowledge of the world's history: πεντακισχιλίων ἐνιαυτῶν παραδραμόντων ἐξ οὗ γέγονεν ὁ κόσμος...καὶ ἀπὸ τῆς Χριστοῦ παρουσίας οὔπω πεπληρωμένων ἑξακοσίων ἡγοῦν ἑπτακοσίων ἢ χιλίων ἐτῶν, δῶμεν γὰρ οὕτω, πῶς [οὐκ] (*dele*) ἔξω λόγου φανήσεται τῶν ἑξακοσίων ἐτῶν ἢ χιλίων, εἰ τύχοι, τὰς ἡμέρας πρὸς τὰς τῶν πεντακισχιλίων παρεξεταζομένας ἐσχάτας καλεῖν;

In this passage the anarthrous phrase ἐσχάτη ὥρα, *novissima hora* V., seems to mark the general character of the period and not its specific relation to 'the end.' It was a period of critical change, 'a last hour,' but not definitely 'the last hour.' The exact phrase is not found elsewhere in the N.T. (comp. 1 Pet. i. 5; 2 Tim. iii. 1). The use of 'hour' recals that in the Gospel: iv. 21, 23; v. 35, 38; xvi. 2, 4, 25, 32. Compare ii. 4; vii. 30; viii. 20; xii. 23, 27; xiii. 1; xvii. 1; and the idea of 'a last hour' corresponds with the characteristic phrase of St John 'the last day' (vi. 39 f., 44, 54; xi. 24; xii. 48). The definiteness of this latter phrase (ἡ ἐσχ. ἡ.) justifies the wider sense given to the former (comp. iv. 17, ἡ ἡμέρα τῆς κρίσεως note). Comp. Ign. *ad Ephes.* c. 11. The true reading in 1 Thess. v. 2 (ἡμ. not ἡ ἡμ.) illustrates ἐσχ. ὥρα here.

καθὼς ἠκούσατε] *as ye heard* in

ὅτι ᾿Αντίχριστος ἔρχεται, καὶ νῦν ἀντίχριστοι πολλοὶ

18 ὅτι ᾿Αντ.: – ὅτι A.   ᾿Αντίχριστος א*BC: ὁ ἀντίχριστος אᶜA.

general terms as part of the evangelic message (Mk. xiii. 6 ff.; Matt. xxiv. 5, 24), and in the teaching of apostles (Acts xx. 30). Comp. 1 Tim. iv. 1. These general predictions of false Christs and false teachers were concentrated in the thought of a typical adversary: 2 Thess. ii. 3.

᾿Αντίχριστος] The term *Antichrist* is peculiar to St John in the N.T. It occurs again *v.* 22; iv. 3 and 2 John 7. The absence of the article shews that it had become current as a technical (proper) name.

The word means far more than simply 'an adversary of Christ.' As far as the form is concerned it may describe 'one who takes the place of Christ' (ἀντιβασιλεύς, ἀντιταμίας, ἀνθύπατος), or 'one who under the same character opposes Christ' (ἀντιδιδάσκαλος, ἀντιστρατιώτης). There is a similar ambiguity in the word ἀντιστράτηγος, which means both 'one who occupies the place of στρατηγός, *proprætor,*' and also 'an opposing general.' It seems to be most consonant to the context to hold that ᾿Αντίχριστος here describes one who assuming the guise of Christ opposes Christ. In this sense it embodies an important truth. That hostility is really formidable in which the adversary preserves the semblance of the characteristic excellence which he opposes (comp. 2 Cor. xi. 13; Apoc. ii. 2). The Antichrist assails Christ by proposing to do or to preserve what He did while he denies Him (comp. John v. 43). The false Christ on the other hand (ψευδόχριστος Matt. xxiv. 24) is simply a pretender to the Messianic office. In St John's use of 'Antichrist' it will be seen that the sense is determined by the full Christian conception of 'Christ' and not by the Jewish conception of the promised Saviour.

Under one aspect it may be said that the work of the Incarnation was

to reveal the true divine destiny of man in his union with God through Christ; while the lie of Antichrist was to teach that man is divine apart from God in Christ.

The passages in which the term occurs are not decisive as to St John's teaching in regard to the coming of one great Antichrist, of which the others were preparatory embodiments. As far as his words are concerned 'Antichrist' may be the personification of the principle shewn in different antichrists, or the person whose appearance is prepared by these particular forms of evil. The former is however the most natural interpretation: *v.* 22; 2 John 7. The spirit of evil comes in those whom he inspires. Contrast 2 Thess. ii. 3 ff.

The essential character of 'Antichrist' lies in the denial of the true humanity of Messiah (*v.* 22 ὁ ἀρνούμενος ὅτι Ἰησοῦς οὐκ ἔστιν ὁ χριστός. iv. 3 πν. ὁ μὴ ὁμολογεῖ (λύει) τὸν Ἰησοῦν. 2 John 7 οἱ μὴ ὁμολογοῦντες Ἰησοῦν Χριστὸν ἐρχόμενον ἐν σαρκί). This denial involves the complete misunderstanding of Christ's past and future work, and takes away the knowledge of the Father, which is brought to us by the Incarnate Son. The teaching of Antichrist leaves God and the world still ununited. The proclamation of the union is the message of the Gospel.

It may be added that St John's description of 'Antichrist' (c. iv. 3) is made use of by Polycarp (*ad Phil.* 7); and Irenæus, the disciple of Polycarp, first developed the teaching. The word does not occur in the other Apostolic Fathers, or Justin Martyr, who does however refer to ὁ τῆς ἀνομίας ἄνθρωπος (*Dial.* 32, p. 250 A ὁ τῆς ἀποστασίας ἄνθρωπος, *Dial.* 110, p. 336 D). It appears therefore to be characteristic of the school of St John. See Additional Note.

γεγόνασιν· ὅθεν γινώσκομεν ὅτι ἐσχάτη ὥρα ἐστίν.
¹⁹ἐξ ἡμῶν ἐξῆλθαν, ἀλλ᾽ οὐκ ἦσαν ἐξ ἡμῶν· εἰ γὰρ ἐξ

19 ἐξ ἡμῶν ἦσαν (2⁰) BC syrr me the: ἦσαν ἐξ ἡμῶν ℵA vg.

ἔρχεται] *venit* (*sit venturus*) V.,
cometh. The same term is used of
Christ and of His adversary. Comp.
c. iv. 3; John xiv. 3; xxi. 22 f.; Apoc.
xxii. 20. In both cases it implies
something more than one advent,
though it includes this. The rival
power finds a personal expression as
often as Christ comes. Comp. v. 6
note.

καθώς...καὶ νῦν] *as...even so now*.
Comp. John xv. 9; xvii. 18; xx. 21.

γεγόνασιν] *facti sunt* V., *have
arisen*, and fulfilled the expectation.
The use of a different word for their
advent (γεγόνασιν not ἐληλύθασιν) connects their appearance with the actual conditions of the development of
the Church. Comp. Heb. ii. 17 note.
The use is the more remarkable as the
verb is not used elsewhere in the
epistle (yet 3 John 8). The tense
shews that these antichrists are
spoken of as being still active. They
are not simple types of Antichrist but
revelations of him in many parts: c.
iv. 3.

For the absolute use of γίνεσθαι see
2 Pet. ii. 1; John i. 6; Mk. i. 4.

ὅθεν γινώσκομεν...] *whence we perceive*... because this form of trial is
connected with each critical conflict
which comes before an end. A full
manifestation of (good and) evil is the
condition of a divine judgment.

Ὅθεν is found here only in the
writings of St John. It is characteristic of the Epistle to the Hebrews
(see ii. 17 note), but is not found in
the Epistles of St Paul.

19. ἐξ ἡμ. ἐξ.] *Ex nobis prodierunt*
(*exierunt*) V., They went out from us,
they proceeded from our midst. They
belonged at first to our outward communion and shared all our privi-

leges. Till the moment of separation
they were undistinguishable from the
rest of the Christian society; *but they
were not of us*, they did not draw
their life from our life (c. i. 3) and so
form living members of the body.
Comp. Heb. vi. 4 ff.

The change in the position of ἐξ
ἡμῶν in the successive clauses varies
the emphasis: 'From us, it is true,
they went out, but they were not *of*
us; for if they had been of *us* really...'
For εἶναι ἐκ see v. 16 note.

The phrase ἐξελθεῖν ἐξ may describe
either removal (Apoc. xviii. 4; John
viii. 59) or origin (Apoc. ix. 3; xiv.
13 ff.; xix. 5, 21; John iv. 30). The
correspondence with οὐκ ἦσαν ἐξ ἡμῶν
decides here in favour of the latter
sense (comp. Acts xx. 30), though it
necessarily leads to the other. This
trait in the Antichrists indicates one
ground of their influence. They professed to speak with the voice of the
Christian Body. Διὰ τί ἀπὸ τῶν τοῦ
Κυρίου μαθητῶν οἱ ἀντίχριστοι; ἵν᾽ ἔ-
χοιεν τὸ πιστὸν τοῖς πλανωμένοις κο-
μίζειν ὡς ἀπὸ τῶν μαθητῶν ὄντες...
(Theophlct.)

εἰ γὰρ...] If they had in the truest
sense shared our life, the life would
have gone forward to its fruitful consummation (μεμενήκεισαν ἄν *perman-
sissent utique* V.). The fact of separation revealed the imperfection of their
fellowship. The words will not admit
of any theoretical deductions. The test
of experience is laid down as final.
Non audio quid sonet, Augustine
says, sed video quid vivat. Opera
loquuntur ; et verba requirimus ?

Here, looking upon the manifest
apostasy, St John denies the truth of
the life; from another point of sight,
in regard to the uncertain future, the

ἡμῶν ἦσαν, μεμενήκεισαν ἂν μεθ᾽ ἡμῶν· ἀλλ᾽ ἵνα φανερω-

life is presented as real, but liable to
an abrupt close (John xv. 1 ff.). The
two views are perfectly harmonious.
The end of life is fruitfulness. The life
which is barren or worse than barren is
not life and yet potentially it was life.

Thus Augustine can say truly in
reference to the actual Church: Si
antequam exirent non erant ex nobis,
multi intus sunt, non exierunt, et
tamen Antichristi sunt. And again:
Sic sunt in corpore Christi quomodo
humores mali. Compare also the
striking language of Ignatius, *ad
Trall.* 11 οὗτοι οὐκ εἰσὶ φυτεία πατρὸς
ἀλλ᾽ ἔγγονα κατηραμένα. πᾶσα δέ, φη-
σὶν ὁ κύριος, φυτεία ἣν οὐκ ἐφύτευσεν ὁ
πατήρ μου ὁ ἐπουράνιος ἐκριζωθήτω. εἰ
γὰρ ἦσαν τοῦ πατρὸς κλάδοι οὐκ ἂν ἦσαν
ἐχθροὶ τοῦ σταυροῦ τοῦ Χριστοῦ ἀλλὰ
τῶν ἀποκτεινάντων τὸν τῆς δόξης κύριον.
It may be added that γάρ, *for*, is
very rarely used in the Epistles; c. iv.
20; v. 3; 2 John 11; 3 John 3, 7.
As distinguished from ὅτι, *because*, it
will be seen that γάρ expresses a
reason or explanation alleged (subjective), while ὅτι marks a distinct
fact (objective) which is itself an adequate cause or explanation of that
with which it is connected. Comp.
c. v. 3, 4; John ii. 25; iii. 16—21;
iii. 23 f.; ix. 22, &c.

μεθ᾽ ἡμῶν] It might have been expected that St John would have
written ἐν ἡμῖν, according to his characteristic usage which is all but universal in his Epistles; but the thought
is not of absolute unity in one body
but of personal fellowship one with
another: John xiv. 16; Luke xxiv.
29.

ἀλλ᾽ ἵνα...] *but they went out* (or
this separation came to pass) *that
they may be made manifest* (*ut
manifesti sint* [*manifestarentur*] V.),
that they all are not of us i.e. that
none of them are of us. For this
ellipse see John i. 8; ix. 3; xiii. 18; xiv.

31; xv. 25. The departure of these
false teachers after a temporary
sojourn in the Christian society was
brought about that they might be shewn
in their true character, and so seen
to be not of it. The last clause is
rather irregular in form. The πάντες
is inserted as it were by an afterthought; 'they went out that they
may be made manifest that they are
not, no not in any case, however fair
their pretensions may be, of us.'

The separation of these teachers
from the Christian Body was, without exception, a decisive proof that
they did not belong truly to it. The
clear revelation of their character was
a divine provision for the avoidance
of further evil. By 'going out' they
neutralised the influence which they
would otherwise have exercised. Comp.
1 Cor. xi. 19.

When the πᾶς is separated by the
verb from the οὐ the negation, according to the usage of the New Testament,
is always universal (*all...not*), and not
partial (*not all*). Comp. *v.* 21; iii. 15;
Apoc. xxii. 3; Matt. xxiv. 22 (οὐ...
πᾶς); Luke i. 37 (οὐ πᾶς); Acts x.
15; Rom. iii. 20 (οὐ...πᾶς); Gal. ii.
16 (οὐ...πᾶς); Eph. v. 5; and in dependent negations, John iii. 16 (πᾶς
...μή); vi. 39 (πᾶς...μή); xii. 46 (*id.*);
1 Cor. i. 29 (μή...πᾶς); Eph. iv. 29
(πᾶς...μή). Comp. Apoc. xxi. 27 (οὐ
μή...πᾶς).

On the other hand see Matt. vii. 21;
Rom. ix. 6; 1 Cor. x. 23; xv. 39 (οὐ
πᾶς).

In the face of this usage it is impossible to translate the words '*that
they may be made manifest* themselves, and that it may be made manifest in them *that not all* who are outwardly united with the Church *are of
us*, in true fellowship with Christ.'

For φανερ. ὅτι οὐκ εἰσίν compare
2 Cor. iii. 3 φανερούμενοι ὅτι ἐστέ.

20. Even without this revelation

θῶσιν ὅτι οὐκ εἰσὶν πάντες ἐξ ἡμῶν. ²⁰καὶ ὑμεῖς χρίσμα
ἔχετε ἀπὸ τοῦ ἁγίου· οἴδατε πάντες—²¹οὐκ ἔγραψα

20 οἴδατε πάντες: καὶ οἴδατε πάντα ς. See Additional Note.

in outward fact, the readers of the
Epistle had the power of discerning
the real character of 'Antichrists.'
'Christians' are themselves in a true
sense 'Christs,' anointed ones, consecrated to God as 'prophets,' 'priests,'
and 'kings' (1 Pet. ii. 5 (9); Apoc. i.
6; v. 10; xx. 6); and in virtue of that
consecration endowed with corresponding blessings. So Severus (Cramer, Cat. in loc.) writes: χριστοί εἰσιν
οὐχ οἱ προφῆται μόνον...ἀλλ' ἐξαιρέτως
καὶ πάντες οἱ εἰς τὸν μέγαν καὶ μόνον
καὶ ἀληθῆ Χριστὸν καὶ σωτῆρα Θεὸν
πιστεύσαντες...καὶ ἐν τῷ θείῳ...βαπτίσ-
ματι συμβολικῶς τῷ μύρῳ χριόμενοι...
καὶ ὑμεῖς...] Sed (et) vos... V., And
further you yourselves, in virtue of
your position as contrasted with them,
have an unction (comp. v. 27 χρίσμα
ὃ ἐλάβετε) from the Holy One. Comp.
vv. 24, 27; iv. 4.

χρίσμα] unctionem V. (unguentum
Hier.), an unction. The word, which
expresses not the act of anointing,
but that with which it is performed
('anointing oil' Ex. xxix. 7; xxx. 25;
xl. 15 (LXX.); comp. Dan. ix. 26), marks
the connexion of Christians with their
Head. As He was 'anointed' for His
office (Luke iv. 18 [Is. lxi. 1]; Acts iv.
27 [Ps. ii. 2]; x. 38; Heb. i. 9 [Ps. xlv.
7]); so too are they (2 Cor. i. 21 f.). The
verb χρίω (answering to מָשַׁח) in LXX.
is employed generally, though not exclusively, of the anointing of things
for sacred use. In the New Testament
it is found only in the places quoted
above, and thus always of the impart-
ment of a divine grace.

Here the outward symbol of the
Old Testament—the sacred oil—is used
to signify the gift of the Spirit from
the Holy One which is the characteristic endowment of Christians. This
gift is referred to a definite time (v.

27 ὃ ἐλάβετε); and the narrative of the
Acts fixes this normally at the im-
position of hands which followed on
Baptism (Acts viii. 14 ff.). But the
context shews that the word χρίσμα is
not to be understood of the material
sign, but of the corresponding spiritual
reality. There is not indeed any evidence to shew that 'the chrism' was
used at confirmation in the first age.
Perhaps, as has been suggested, St
John's language here may have tended to fix the custom, which represented the communication of the divine
grace in an outward rite. Tertullian
speaks of the custom as habitual in
his time: Egressi de lavacro perun-
gimur benedicta unctione de pristina
disciplina, qua ungi oleo de cornu in
sacerdotium solebant (de Bapt. 7).

Unctio spiritualis ipse Spiritus Sanctus est cujus sacramentum est in unctione visibili (Bede).

This 'unction,' this gift of the Spirit,
is said to come finally (ἀπό, see c. i. 5,
note) from the Holy One. The title
is chosen with direct reference to the
gift, for all hallowing flows from 'the
Holy One,' but in itself it is ambiguous, and has been understood of God
(the Father) and of Christ. In support of the former view reference is
made to 1 Cor. vi. 19; John xiv. 16;
comp. Baruch iv. 22, 37; but ὁ ἅγιος
seems to be more naturally referred to
Christ; Apoc. iii. 7; John vi. 69; Acts
iii. 14; iv. 27, 30; and Christ Himself
'sends' the Paraclete (John xvi. 7).

οἴδατε πάντες] ye all know, i.e. the
Truth. If this reading be adopted
the statement must be taken in close
connexion with the clause which follows: 'ye all know—I have not written
to you because ye do not know—the
Truth.' With οἴδατε τὴν ἀλ. contrast
2 John 2 οἱ ἐγνωκότες τὴν ἀλ.

ὑμῖν ὅτι οὐκ οἴδατε τὴν ἀλήθειαν, ἀλλ᾽ ὅτι οἴδατε
αὐτήν, καὶ ὅτι πᾶν ψεῦδος ἐκ τῆς ἀληθείας οὐκ
ἔστιν.   ²² Τίς ἐστιν ὁ ψεύστης εἰ μὴ ὁ ἀρ-

21 – πᾶν C.

The common reading καὶ οἴδατε πάντα gives an explanation of the actual force of χρίσμα ἔχετε : 'ye have an unction, and, in virtue of that gift of the Holy Spirit, ye know all things ; ye have potentially complete and certain knowledge: no false teaching can deceive you if ye are faithful to yourselves.' Comp. v. 27; Jude 5 (εἰδότας ἅπαξ πάντα); John xiv. 26, xvi. 13. See Additional Note.

21. The object of the Apostle in writing was not to communicate fresh knowledge, but to bring into active and decisive use the knowledge which his readers already possessed. For ἔγραψα see vv. 14 note, 26.

ἀλλ᾽ ὅτι...καὶ ὅτι...] sed quasi scientibus...et quoniam...(sed quia... quia) V., but because...and because... The ὅτι in the second clause appears to be coordinated with that in the first clause. St John gives two grounds for his writing :

1. Because his readers know the truth.

2. Because no lie is of the truth.

The first witnesses to the necessary sympathy between writer and readers : the second explains the occasion of the particular warning.

The second ὅτι can however also be translated 'that' thus defining a second feature in Christian knowledge : 'ye know the truth and know that no lie is of the truth.' In this case the words indicate the practical consequences which follow from the revelation of the antichrists.

According to both views the absolute irreconcileableness of any falsehood with 'the Truth' is laid down as a clear rule for the protection of Christians in the presence of seductive teachers. It was, on the other hand,

the office of the Paraclete to guide them 'into all the Truth' (John xvi. 13).

πᾶν ψ....οὐκ ἔστιν] see v. 19 note.

ψεῦδος] mendacium V. Error is regarded in its positive form as part of 'the lie' (τὸ ψεῦδος) which is the opposite of 'the Truth.' Compare John viii. 44; 2 Thess. ii. 11; Rom. i. 25; Eph. iv. 25. See also Apoc. xxi. 27, xxii. 15.

ἐκ τῆς ἀλ. οὐκ ἔστιν] c. iii. 19; John xviii. 37. See v. 16 note. The source of falsehood is marked in John viii. 44.

2. The essence and the power of the Truth (22—25).

The mention of 'lies' in v. 21 leads directly to the question as to the essential character of him who maintains them, and by contrast of him who holds the Truth (22, 23). Then follows the portraiture of the power of the Truth firmly held, which brings fellowship with God, even eternal life (24, 25).

²² Who is the liar but he that denieth that Jesus is the Christ? This is the Antichrist, even he that denieth the Father and the Son. ²³ Every one that denieth the Son hath not even the Father: he that confesseth the Son hath the Father also. ²⁴ As for you, let that which ye heard from the beginning abide in you. If that abide in you which ye heard from the beginning, ye also shall abide in the Son and in the Father. ²⁵ And this is the promise that he himself promised us, even the life eternal.

22. τίς ἐστιν...] Quis est mendax ...? V. Who is the liar...? The abrupt question (comp. c. v. 5) corresponds with a brief mental pause after

νούμενος ὅτι Ἰησοῦς οὐκ ἔστιν ὁ χριστός; οὗτός
ἐστιν ὁ ἀντίχριστος, ὁ ἀρνούμενος τὸν πατέρα καὶ τὸν

v. 21. 'I have spoken of lies : *what*, nay rather, *who* is their source ? Who is the liar?' The abruptness of *vv.* 22 f. is remarkable. Clause stands by clause in stern solemnity without any connecting particles.

ὁ ψεύστης] *the liar*, who offers in his own person the sum of all that is false ; and not simply 'a liar' who is guilty of a particular sin. The denial of the fact 'Jesus is the Christ' when grasped in its full significance—intellectual, moral, spiritual—includes all falsehood: it reduces all knowledge of necessity to a knowledge of phenomena: it takes away the highest ideal of sacrifice: it destroys the connexion of God and man.

τίς...εἰ μή] c. v. 5; 1 Cor. ii. 11; 2 Cor. ii. 2, &c.

ὁ ἀρνούμενος ὅτι...οὐκ ἔστιν] *that denieth that...* The insertion of the negative in the original (preserved in the Old Latin, *qui negat quod Jesus non est Christus*) gives a positive, aggressive, character to the negation. The adversary denies that Jesus is the Christ when the claim is made ; and on his own part he affirms that He is not. Comp. Luke xx. 27; Gal. v. 7; Heb. xii. 19. For the converse see John i. 20.

The phrase by which St John describes the master-falsehood as the 'denial that Jesus is the Christ,' itself marks the progress of Christian thought. In the earliest stage of the Church the words would have expressed a denial of the Messiahship of Jesus from the Jewish point of view (Acts v. 42, ix. 22, xvii. 3, xviii. 28). They now answer to a later form of opinion. A common 'Gnostic' theory was that 'the æon Christ' descended upon the man Jesus at His Baptism, and left Him before the Passion. Those who held

such a doctrine denied that 'Jesus was the Christ'; and in so denying, denied the union of the divine and human in one Person. This heresy then St John signalises here, the direct contradiction to the fundamental truth which he proclaimed, *the Word became flesh.*

οὗτος] *this* liar, this maintainer of the central falsehood in regard to revelation, as to God and man, *is the antichrist*, even *he that denieth the Father and the Son.* The denial of the personal union of true manhood and true Godhead in Christ involves the denial of the essential relations of Fatherhood and Sonship in the Divine Nature. The conception of this relation in the immanent Trinity prepares the way for the fact of the Incarnation; and conversely, the fact of the Incarnation gives reality to that moral conception of God as active Love without which Theism becomes a formula.

ὁ ἀντίχριστος] The term expresses the embodiment of a principle, and is not to be confined to one person. The character of 'the antichrist' is described in the words which follow (even *he that...Son*), which are not simply a resumption of οὗτος.

ὁ ἀρνούμενος τ. π.] To deny the Father is to refuse to acknowledge God as Father. Comp. Matt. x. 33; Acts iii. 13 f.; 2 Tim. ii. 12; 2 Pet. ii. 1; Jude 4.

τὸν πατέρα] The title *the Father* occurs in the Epistles of St John, as in the Gospel, in connexion with 'the Son' (*vv.* 22, 23, 24, i. 3, iv. 14; 2 J. 3, 9), and in relation to men (ii. 1, 14, 15 f., iii. 1; 2 J. 4) in virtue of the revelation of Christ. It is used also in relation to 'the Life' (i. 2 note).

The title always stands in the Epistles in its simple form. 'His Father'

υἱόν. ²³πᾶς ὁ ἀρνούμενος τὸν υἱὸν οὐδὲ τὸν πατέρα ἔχει.
ὁ ὁμολογῶν τὸν υἱὸν καὶ τὸν πατέρα ἔχει. ²⁴Ὑμεῖς ὁ

23 ὁ ὁμολ....ἔχει ‭ℵ‬ABC me syrr. om. ς.
Other conjunctions are inserted in versions.

24 ὑμεῖς ‭ℵ‬ABC vg: ὑμ.+οὖν ς.

or 'our Father,' or 'the Father in heaven' do not occur. See Additional Note on i. 2.

τὸν υἱόν] By the use of the absolute term *the Son* (comp. John v. 19 note), which occurs in the Epistle first here (comp. iv. 14, v. 12), St John brings out distinctly what is involved in the fact that the Christ and Jesus are personally one. There is no passage in the mind of the Apostle from one personality to another, from the human to the divine, nor yet from the conception of 'the man Christ Jesus' to that of 'the Word': the thought of 'the Son' includes both these conceptions in their ideal fulness.

23. πᾶς ὁ ἀρν. τ. υἱ....] *Qui negat Filium nec Patrem habet* V. The original is compressed: *Every one that denieth the Son hath not even the Father* (οὐδὲ τ. π. ἔ.) or, according to our idiom, *No one that denieth the Son hath even the Father.* Such a one hath not the Son, whom he rejects, nor yet the Father, whom he professes to regard. The translation quoted by Augustine completes the sentence: *qui negat Filium nec Filium nec Patrem habet.*

The 'denial of the Son' expresses in another form that which has been more fully described before as 'the denial of Jesus as the Christ.'

The denial of the Son involves the loss of the Father, not only because the ideas of sonship and fatherhood are correlative, but because the Son alone can reveal the Father (Matt. xi. 27; John xiv. 9), and it is, in other words, only in the Son that we have the revelation of God as Father.

The οὐδέ retains its full force 'has *not even* the Father,' though this result may seem to be against expecta-

tion, and contrary to the claim of the false teachers. Comp. John v. 22, viii. 42; Gal. ii. 3; 1 Tim. vi. 7.

For the use of πᾶς ὁ ἀρν. in place of the simple ὁ ἀρν. see c. iii. 3 note.

οὐδὲ ἔχει...ἔχει] *hath not even... hath...* The second clause in each case is more than a simple repetition of the first (comp. Wisd. x. 8). It is not said of him 'that denieth the Son' that he denieth the Father also; but that he 'hath not even the Father.' Such a man might shrink from denying the Father in words, and even claim to do Him honour, but yet St John says 'he hath not even the Father,' as one who enjoys the certain possession of a living Friend. And conversely he 'that confesseth the Son' not only confesses the Father in an act of faith, but also lives in conscious communion with Him.

ἔχει] Comp. v. 12; 2 John 9.

Augustine has an interesting discussion on the application of the test to Catholics and Donatists. His conclusion is: 'Quisquis factis negat Christum Antichristus est,' adding the words quoted on *v.* 19. And Bede says of this confession: confessionem hic cordis vocis et operis inquirit qualem quærebat Paulus (1 Cor. xii. 3).

ὁ ὁμολογῶν τὸν υἱόν] *qui confitetur Filium* V., *he that confesseth the Son,* he that openly acknowledges that Jesus is the Christ, the Son of God. The constructions of ὁμολογεῖν in N.T. are numerous. The simplest are those with the *infin.* and with ὅτι which serve for the affirmation of a definite fact past, present or future (*infin.* c. iv. 2; Tit. i. 16; Matt. xiv. 7; ὅτι c. iv. 15; John i. 20; Acts xxiv. 14; Heb. xi. 13). From the construction with the *infin.* that with the *accus.*

ἠκούσατε ἀπ᾽ ἀρχῆς, ἐν ὑμῖν μενέτω· ἐὰν ἐν ὑμῖν μείνῃ
ὃ ἀπ᾽ ἀρχῆς ἠκούσατε, καὶ ὑμεῖς ἐν τῷ υἱῷ καὶ [ἐν]

ἀκηκόατε (bis) ℵ.　　ὃ ἀπ᾽ ἀρχ. ἀκηκ. ℵ (vg) mg the.　　ἐν τῷ π. ℵAC : – ἐν B vg.
ἐν τῷ π. καὶ ἐν τῷ υἱῷ ℵ syr vg.

follows, either a simple *accus*. Acts xxiii. 8 (comp. c. i. 9); or an *accus*. with a secondary predicate 2 John 7; John ix. 22. Here and in c. iv. 3 the predicate which gives the substance of the confession is supplied from the context. Elsewhere the verb is used absolutely: John xii. 42 ; with cogn. accus. 1 Tim. vi. 12 ; with the substance of the confession added in the direct: Rom. x. 9 (Κύριος Ἰησοῦς). More remarkable is the construction with ἐν Matt. x. 31 f.; Luke xii. 8, which suggests the idea of an acknowledged fellowship.

To know the Son as Son is to have such knowledge as we can have at present of the Father (John xiv. 7 ff.). Hence *he that confesseth the Son hath the Father also* as well as the Son whom he directly acknowledges.

24 f. The view of the true nature of the confession and denial of Christ is followed by a view of the power of the confession. The knowledge to which it witnesses carries with it eternal life.

24. Ὑμεῖς...] *As for you*... The pronoun stands at the head of the sentence in contrast with the false teachers of whom the Apostle has spoken (*v.* 22): comp. Matt. xiii. 18. For the irregular construction see *v.* 27; John vi. 39; vii. 38 ; xiv. 12 ; xv. 2 ; Luke xxi. 6, &c.

The construction is broken, because the thought of St John is turned from that which the disciples had to do to that which was done for them. 'As for you, do you keep' is changed to 'As for you, let that abide in you.' The final strength of the Christian lies not in his own effort, but in the Truth by which he is inspired. That is the power of life which he is charged

not to hinder. Comp. John xv. 7. For the double divine fellowship, 'God in us, we in God,' see iv. 15 note.

ὃ ἠκούσατε...] *that which ye heard*...(*v.* 7). The first simple message of the Gospel apprehended in its unity (ὃ not ἅ; comp. John xiv. 23). This 'word' taken into the heart becomes a power fashioning the whole man (John viii. 31 f.; xv. 7).

ἐν ὑμῖν μενέτω] *let that...abide in you*. The Gospel is described both as a medium in which the believer lives (John viii. 31), and as a quickening spirit which dwells in him (Col. iii. 16; 2 John 2).

ὃ ἠκ. ἀπ᾽ ἀρχῆς...ὃ ἀπ᾽ ἀρχ. ἠκ....] The change of order marks a change of emphasis. In the first clause the stress lies on the fact that the readers had received a divine message (*ye heard*): in the second, on the coincidence of that message in time with the origin of their faith (*from the beginning*). Comp. iii. 8 note.

καὶ ὑμεῖς...] *ye also*...i.e. 'then ye on your side...' not 'ye as well as others....' The presence of the divine life carries with it of necessity the possession of divine fellowship. Thus one fact is correlative to the other (comp. i. 3). This correlation is made clearer by the correspondence in the pronouns: ἐὰν ἐν ὑμῖν...καὶ ὑμεῖς. Comp. iii. 24.

For the use of καί to mark a corresponding issue, see iv. 11.

ἐν τῷ υἱῷ καὶ ἐν τ. π.] The order, as contrasted with that in *v.* 22 (τ. π. καὶ τ. υἱ.), is significant. Here the thought is that of rising through the confession of the Son to the knowledge of the Father; there the thought is of the issue of denial culminating in the denial of the Father.

τῷ πατρὶ μενεῖτε. ²⁵καὶ αὕτη ἐστὶν ἡ ἐπαγγελία
ἣν αὐτὸς ἐπηγγείλατο ἡμῖν, τὴν ζωὴν τὴν αἰώνιον.   ²⁶ Ταῦτα ἔγραψα ὑμῖν περὶ τῶν πλα-

25 ἡμῖν: ὑμῖν B (lat).   26 ταῦτα + δέ ℵ syrvg.

25. καὶ αὕτη ἐστίν...] *And this is...*
The pronoun may refer either to that
which precedes or to that which follows. The promise may be that of
abiding communion with the Father
and the Son (John xvii. 21), which is
explained by the words added in apposition 'the life eternal'; or it may
be simply 'the life eternal.' In either
case 'the life eternal' consists in union
with God by that knowledge which is
sympathy (John xvii. 3), so that there
is no real difference of sense in the
two interpretations.   The usage of
St John in the Epistle is decidedly in
favour of the second view (i. 5, iii. 23,
v. 11, 14), nor is there any sufficient
reason for departing from it.

ἐπαγγελία] *repromissio* V., *polli-
citatio* Aug. This is the only place
where the word occurs in the writings
of St John (not c. i. 5).   Contrast
ἐπάγγελμα (*promissum* V.) 2 Pet. i. 4;
iii. 13.

ἣν αὐτός...] *that He...* He himself,
Christ our Master.   The *nom.* (αὐτός)
is always emphatic : see *v.* 2 note.
There is not any special saying of the
Lord recorded in which this promise
is expressly contained (yet comp.
James i. 12 ; Apoc. ii. 10); but it was
the whole aim and scope of His
teaching to lead men to seek 'life.'
And a divine charge is a divine
promise.

τὴν ζ. τὴν αἰ.] See c. i. 2 note. For
the attraction compare Phil. iii. 18.
Winer, p. 665.

3. *Abiding in the Truth* (ii. 26—29).
The view which St John has given
of the nature and power of the Truth
is followed by a fresh application of
the teaching to the readers of the
Epistle. An affirmation (μένετε, *indic.*,

v. 27) leads to a command (μένετε,
imper., *v.* 28). Thus the paragraph
falls into two parts which deal (1)
with the divine teaching as permanent and progressive (*vv.* 26 f.) and
(2) with human effort directed to the
future (*vv.* 28 f.).

²⁶ *These things have I written to
you concerning them that would lead
you astray.* ²⁷ *And as for you, the
unction which ye received from him
abideth in you, and ye have no need
that any one teach you ; but as his
unction teacheth you of all things
(and it is true and is no lie), and
even as it taught you, ye abide in
him.* ²⁸ *And now, little children, abide
in him, that, if he shall be manifested,
we may have boldness and not shrink
in shame from him at his presence.*
²⁹ *If ye know that he is righteous,
know (notice) that every one that doeth
righteousness hath been begotten of
him.*

26 f.   In the preceding verses (*vv.*
24 f.) St John had appealed to the
original apostolic message which his
readers had received (ὃ ἠκούσατε) in
contrast with all false teaching.   He
now appeals to the inward voice of the
Spirit whose first teaching (ἐδίδαξεν)
and whose present teaching (διδάσκει)
is one.

26. Ταῦτα] *These things*, the clear
unfolding of the true character and
significance of the false teachers in
relation to the Church (*vv.* 18—25).

ἔγραψα] See *v.* 14 note.

τῶν πλανώντων] *qui seducunt vos*
V., *them that would lead you astray*,
who are actively engaged in the effort:
c. iii. 7; Apoc. xiii. 14, xii. 9.

St John has spoken of the false

νώντων ὑμᾶς. ²⁷καὶ ὑμεῖς τὸ χρίσμα ὃ ἐλάβετε ἀπ᾽ αὐτοῦ μένει ἐν ὑμῖν, καὶ οὐ χρείαν ἔχετε ἵνα τις διδάσκῃ ὑμᾶς· ἀλλ᾽ ὡς τὸ αὐτοῦ χρίσμα διδάσκει ὑμᾶς περὶ

27 χρίσμα (1): χάρισ μα B.　　　　　　μέν. ἐν ὑμ. ℵABC vg me the: ἐν ὑμ. μέν. ς:
μενέτω vg.　　　　　ἀλλ᾽ ὡς ℵAC vg the: ἀλλά B.　　　τὸ αὐτοῦ ℵBC vg the
syr hl.: τὸ αὐτό ςA me.　　　χρίσμα (2): πνεῦμα ℵ* me (χρεῖσμα B).

teachers under their spiritual aspect as 'antichrists'; he now speaks of them under their outward aspect as leading men away from the fellowship of the Christian Society.

27. καὶ ὑμεῖς...] And as for you... The construction is like that in v. 24. The pronoun is set at the head of the sentence in order to bring out sharply the contrast between believers and their adversaries.

τὸ χρίσμα] v. 20 note.

ὃ ἐλάβ. ἀ. αὐ.] which ye received from Him 'the Holy One' (v. 20), even Christ (v. 25). The gift which before (v. 20) was simply described as a possession (ἔχετε) is now referred to its source. The personal relation to which it witnesses is a ground of confidence.

ἐλάβ. ἀπ᾽ αὐ.] The use of ἀπό to mark the source in this connexion has been already touched on (c. i. 5). The distinction of the 'source' (ἀπό) and the 'giver' (παρά) is illustrated by the combination of the prepositions ἀπό and παρά with different verbs:

(1) λαμβάνειν παρά John v. 41, 44; x. 18; 2 John 4; Apoc. ii. 27; Mk. xii. 2; Acts ii. 33; iii. 5; xvii. 9; xx. 24; James i. 7; 2 Pet. i. 17. λαμβάνειν ἀπό 1 John iii. 22; 3 John 7; Matt. xvii. 25.

(2) παραλαμβάνειν παρά 1 Thess. ii. 13; iv. 1; 2 Thess. iii. 6; Gal. i. 12; παραλαμβάνειν ἀπό 1 Cor. xi. 23.

(3) ἔχειν παρά Acts ix. 14. ἔχειν ἀπό c. ii. 20; iv. 21; 1 Tim. iii. 7. ἔχειν ἐκ 1 Cor. vii. 7; 2 Cor. v. 1.

For ἀκούειν παρά, ἀπό see c. i. 5 note.

μένει] abideth. The apostle so writes as looking at the divine side of the

truth. The gifts of God are sure on His part.

οὐ χρείαν ἔχ....] ye have no need... The outpouring of the Spirit, the characteristic of the last days (Jer. xxxi. 34; Joel ii. 28; Heb. viii. 11; Acts ii. 17 ff.), gave to each one who received it a sure criterion of truth. Christians needed not fresh teaching even from apostles, still less from those who professed to guide them into new 'depths.'

οὐ χρ. ἔχ. ἵνα...] non necesse habetis ut V., non habetis necessitatem ut Aug. The same construction occurs in John ii. 25, xvi. 30. The phrase χρείαν ἔχειν is used absolutely in several places: Mk. ii. 25; Acts ii. 45, iv. 35; 1 Cor. xii. 24; Eph. iv. 28, as in this Epistle c. iii. 17. This usage supplies a probable explanation of the construction: 'Ye are not in need such that you require....'

ἀλλ᾽ ὡς...καὶ καθὼς...ἐν αὐτῷ] but as His unction teacheth you...and even as it taught you, ye abide in Him. These words serve to establish the statement just made. 'You need no one to teach you, but on the contrary you remain firm in that direct divine fellowship established by the teaching which you are continually receiving and which at first you received once for all.' Impatience drives men to look without for the guidance which in due time will be recognised within. Such impatience is the opposite to the steadfastness of the Christian.

But while so much is clear the construction of the sentence is uncertain. The last clause (and even as...in Him) may be either a resumption or πάντων, καὶ ἀληθές ἐστιν καὶ οὐκ ἔστιν ψεῦδος, καὶ

27 ἀληθής ℵ.   καὶ καθώς: om. καὶ A the.

rather a continuation of the former words (*as His...no lie*), or a new and distinct clause. In the latter case the first apodosis will be in the words '*so is it true and no lie*,' '*but as His unction teacheth you, even so is it true and no lie*.' This use of καὶ in the apodosis is however rare in St John; nor does there appear to be any special force in making the affirmation of the perfect truth of the divine teaching a substantive conclusion. It is therefore more natural to suppose that there is only one apodosis (*ye abide in Him*), and that the sentence as originally shaped (*but, on the contrary, as His unction teacheth you concerning all things, ye abide in Him*) was afterwards enlarged by the addition of the reflection '*and it is true and is no lie*,' which again led to the further statement that the present progressive teaching is essentially the same as the first teaching *as His unction teacheth...and even as it taught you, ye abide in Him.*

The reading of B gives a plain and simple sense, but it is difficult to understand how it could have been altered if it had been the original reading.

τὸ αὐ. χρ.] *His unction,* the unction which ye received from Christ. Comp. John xvi. 7.

The most unusual order τὸ αὐ. χρ. (for τὸ χρ. αὐ.) throws a strong emphasis on the pronoun. Comp. 1 Thess. ii. 19 (contrast 1 Cor. xv. 23; 2 Cor. vii. 7); Rom. iii. 24 (in 2 Pet. iii. 7 τῷ αὐτοῦ λ. is probably a false reading). As might be expected this is the normal order with ἐκεῖνος: John v. 47; 2 Pet. i. 16; 2 Cor. viii. 9, 14; 2 Tim. ii. 26; Tit. iii. 7.

διδ. ὑ. π. π.] *teacheth you of all things.* The application and interpretation of the truth is continuous.

The Spirit of Truth sent in Christ's name (John xiv. 26), sent, that is, to make the meaning of the Incarnation fully known, is ever bringing out something more of the infinite meaning of His Person and Work, in connexion with the new results of thought and observation (περὶ πάντων). Comp. John xvi. 13 f.

καὶ ἀληθές ἐστιν...] *and it is true...* The 'unction,' the gift of the Spirit, is now identified with the results of the gift. The Spirit is the Spirit of Truth (John xiv. 17); and its teaching is true, and admits no element of falsehood (*v.* 21).

Parenthetical reflections like this are found elsewhere in St John's writings. Comp. c. i. 2 note.

οὐκ ἔ. ψεῦδος] *non est mendacium* V., *is no lie.* By the use of ψεῦδος (not ψευδές) St John implies that the false teachers practically represented the Gospel as 'a lie' in its concrete form, and not simply as 'false' (comp. *v.* 21 note).

The combination of the positive and negative is characteristic of St John: i. 5 note.

καὶ καθὼς ἐδίδαξεν...] *and even as it taught....* The first teaching contained implicitly all that is slowly brought to light in later times (comp. ii. 7). The believer abides in Christ as the Spirit makes Him known, and even as it made Him known in the simple Gospel 'Jesus is the Christ.' This clause excludes all 'developments' of teaching which cannot be shewn to exist in germ in the original message; and at the same time leaves no room for the inventions of fanaticism. That which was taught first is the absolute standard.

The use of καθώς marks this idea of a definite and fixed standard: *vv.* 6, 18, iii. 2, 3, 7, 12, &c.

καθὼς ἐδίδαξεν ὑμᾶς, μένετε ἐν αὐτῷ. ²⁸Καὶ νῦν,
τεκνία, μένετε ἐν αὐτῷ, ἵνα ἐὰν φανερωθῇ σχῶμεν παρ-

μένετε ℵABC vg syrr me the: μενεῖτε ϛ.   28 – καὶ νῦν...αὐτῷ ℵ.
ἵνα ἐάν ℵABC the: ἵνα ὅταν ϛ syrr.   σχῶμεν ℵᶜABC: ἔχωμεν ϛ ℵ*.

μένετε ἐν αὐτῷ] *ye abide in Him*,
i.e. Christ. The verb may be indicative or imperative (as in v. 28, so
Vulg. *manete in eo*), but the parallelism with μένει (*the unction abideth...ye abide*) is decisive in favour of
the indicative. In this verse St John
assumes the fulfilment of the conditions which he presses upon his
readers in v. 28.

For the general thought compare
John vi. 56, xv. 4 ff. Elsewhere the
Christian is said to 'abide in God':
iii. 24, iv. 12 ff. So in *vv.* 28 f. 'Christ'
and 'God' are treated as interchange-
able.

At first sight it might appear most
natural to take ἐν αὐτῷ of the 'teaching of the Spirit' (χρίσμα) as is done
by the Latin translation used by
Augustine (*permanete in ipsa* sc.
unctione) according to John viii. 31 ;
but the personal reference cannot be
questioned in v. 28, and that must decide the interpretation here. Christ—
God in Christ—is the subject constantly present to the mind of the
Apostle.

Augustine contrasts finely the human and divine teachers : Sonus verborum nostrorum aures percutit,
magister intus est. Nolite putare
quemquam hominem aliquid discere
ab homine. Admonere possumus per
strepitum vocis nostræ ; si non sit intus qui doceat inanis fit strepitus
noster.... Magisteria forinsecus ad-
jutoria quædam sunt et admonitiones.
Cathedram in cælo habet qui corda
docet.

28 f. St John turns from the ideal
view of the believer to the practical
enforcement of duty : ' I have said
that God's gift is unchangeable ; and
that the Christian continues living in

that which he received, and so abides
in his Lord ; and now, in the face of
your enemies, realise your life : do
you abide in Him, and prove your fellowship by your action.'

The verses serve also to prepare
the way for the next section, introducing ideas which are afterwards developed (φανεροῦσθαι, παρρησίαν ἔχειν,
ποιεῖν τὴν δικ., γεγεννῆσθαι ἐξ αὐτοῦ).

28. καὶ νῦν...] *And now...* For this
connexion see John xvii. 5 ; 2 John
5; Acts iii. 17, x. 5, xiii. 11, xx. 25,
xxii. 16.

τεκνία] *filioli* V., *my little children*.
The tenderness of the address (τεκνία)
commends the charge.

ἐν αὐτῷ] *in Him*, i.e. in Christ, v. 27.

ἐὰν φανερωθῇ] *cum apparuerit* V.,
cum manifestatus fuerit Aug., *if he
shall be manifested*, c. iii. 2. The hy-
pothetic form does not throw doubt
upon the fact in itself (see v. 29), but
marks the uncertainty of the circumstances under which the fact will be
realised : the manifestation might be
while they all still lived. Comp. John
xxi. 22 f. ; c. iv. 17 ἐν τῇ ἡμ. τῆς κρίσεως.

The same word φανερωθῆναι is used
for the first manifestation of the Lord
in the flesh (c. i. 2, iii. 5, 8 ; 1 Tim. iii.
16 ; 1 Pet. i. 20); and for that manifestation which is still looked for (c.
iii. 2; Col. iii. 4 ; 1 Pet. v. 4). It is
used also for the manifestations of the
Risen Lord ([Mark] xvi. 12, 14; John
xxi. 14 (1)), and for His 'manifestation to Israel' (John i. 31 : comp. vii.
4).

It is worthy of notice that St John
nowhere uses ἀποκαλύπτεσθαι of the
revelation of Christ.

σχῶμεν παρρ.] *we may...* St John
again identifies himself with his

ρησίαν καὶ μὴ αἰσχυνθῶμεν ἀπ' αὐτοῦ ἐν τῇ παρουσίᾳ
αὐτοῦ.　²⁹ἐὰν εἰδῆτε ὅτι δίκαιός ἐστιν, γινώσκετε ὅτι
πᾶς ὁ ποιῶν τὴν δικαιοσύνην ἐξ αὐτοῦ γεγέννηται.

28 ἐν τῇ παρ. ἁ. ἀπ' αὐτοῦ ℵ.　　　29 εἰδῆτε ℵBC vg syrr: ἴδητε A me.　　− ὅτι
πᾶς B me syr hl: ὅτι+καί' πᾶς ℵAC the syr vg.

children : comp. *v.* I. All form one
body. It is possible to understand
the words as referring to the Apostle's
joy in the crown of his work (comp.
I Thess. ii. 19 f.; Phil. iv. I). The
parallel with I Thess. ii. 19 f. is certainly close ; but it seems to be more
natural to suppose that the apostle
made himself one with those who
shared his life, and the absence of
the personal pronoun seems to exclude
the notion of any contrast between
him and them.

The use of ἔχειν παρρησίαν (c. iii.
21, iv. 17, v. 14; comp. Heb. iii. 6,
x. 19; Phil. 8) in connexion with the
manifestation of Christ suggests St
Paul's thought of the judgment-seat
of Christ (2 Cor. v. 10) or of God
(Rom. xiv. 10), where man must
'render account' (Rom. xiv. 12) of his
life. The idea of open, unreserved
utterance is never lost. See John vii.
4 note. The difference in order here
(σχ. παρρ.) and in iii. 21, iv. 17 (παρρ.
ἔχειν) indicates a different emphasis
on the elements of the phrase : comp.
Eph. iii. 12.

μὴ αἰσχυνθῶμεν ἀπ' αὐτοῦ] *non con-
fundamur ab eo* V., *not shrink with
shame from Him,* 'as a guilty thing
surprised.' The same thought of
separation is found more plainly expressed 2 Thess. i. 9. The construction αἰσχύνεσθαι ἀπό is used in the
same sense in the LXX: Is. i. 29;
Jer. ii. 36, xii. 13 (וּבֹשׁ מֵ); Ecclus.
xxi. 22, xli. 17 ff.

παρουσίᾳ] *adventu* V., *presence*
(coming). The word does not occur
elsewhere in St John's writings. Its
single occurrence here, where it might
easily have been omitted, in exactly

the same sense as it bears in all the
other groups of apostolic writings
(Matt., James, 2 Peter, 1, 2 Thess., I
Cor.) is a signal example of the danger
of drawing conclusions from the negative phenomena of the books of the
New Testament. The fact is the more
worthy of notice as the subject of
eschatology falls into the background
in the Gospel and Epistles of St John.
Comp. John xxi. 22.

It may be added that St John does
not use the Pauline word ἐπιφάνεια
(2 Thess., 1, 2 Tim., Tit.).

29. ἐὰν εἰδῆτε...γινώσκετε...] *si scitis
...scitote* (Vig. Taps. *scitis*)... V. *If
ye know...perceive, observe, notice....*
Knowledge which is absolute (εἰδῆτε)
becomes the basis of knowledge which
is realised in observation (γινώσκετε).
Comp. John ii. 24 note. The distinction is lost in the Latin and can
hardly be preserved in an English
version.

The second verb (γινώσκετε) may be
either indicative or imperative. Both
renderings are found in early Latin
authorities. In favour of the imperative it is urged that it stands between two imperatives (μένετε; and
iii. I ἴδετε). On the other hand it is
said that *v.* 29 contains a general
reason for the command in *v.* 28.
'Abide in Him in fruitful well-doing,
for the first article of your faith teaches
you that right action is the sign of a
divine birth.'

A decision is difficult ; but upon
the whole the general structure of *vv.*
28 f. favours the imperative. It seems
to be more in accordance with the
context that St John should here
charge his readers to apply practi-

cally the truth which they had inwardly mastered, than that he should appeal to them as having done thus.

The use of ἐάν with the subj. (ἐὰν εἰδῆτε), when there is no intention of questioning the fact or treating it as uncertain, often serves to turn the thoughts of the hearer or reader upon it in the way of self-interrogation: 'if, as I assume to be the case, as you profess, as by silent inquiry you can assure yourselves....' Comp. c. iv. 12 (v. 15); John xiv. 15.

δίκαιος...ἐξ αὐ. γεγένν.] *He is righteous...begotten of Him....* Great difficulty has been felt in determining whether the pronoun refers to 'God' or to 'Christ.' There can be no doubt that Christ is the subject in *v.* 28 (*abide in Him...at His presence*). It is therefore most natural to suppose that He is the subject in this verse also, unless the context makes such an interpretation impossible. This probability is strengthened by the fact that no personal pronoun is introduced in *v.* 29. And there is a further presumption that the same subject is continued from the fact that in iii. 1 a new subject is distinctly named (*the Father*). The application of the epithet 'righteous' to Christ is supported by *v.* 1. But it is argued on the other side that the Christian cannot be said '*to be born of Christ.*' It is certainly true that the exact phrase does not occur elsewhere, while '*to be born of God*' (who is called 'righteous' c. i. 9) is a characteristic phrase of St John (γενν. ἐκ θεοῦ John i. 13, γενν. ἐκ τοῦ θεοῦ c. iii. 9; iv. 7; v. 1, 4, 18). But this argument does not seem to be conclusive. Christians are said equally to '*abide in God*' and to '*abide in Christ*' (*v.* 27). They are also said to be '*born of the Spirit*' (John iii. 6, 8). The word of Christ is in them as a quickening power (comp. 1 Pet. i. 23; James i. 18). There is then nothing against the tenour of Scripture in saying that Christians are 'born of

Christ,' who is 'God only-begotten' (John i. 18).

The true solution of the difficulty seems to be that when St John thinks of God in relation to men he never thinks of Him apart from Christ (comp. c. v. 20). And again he never thinks of Christ in His human nature without adding the thought of His divine nature. Thus a rapid transition is possible from the one aspect of the Lord's divine-human Person to the other. Here the passage is from 'Christ' to 'God' (ἐὰν φανερωθῇ, ἐν τῇ παρουσίᾳ αὐτοῦ, δίκαιός ἐστιν, ἐξ αὐτοῦ γεγέννηται); and conversely in iii. 1—4 the passage is from 'God' to 'Christ' (τέκνα θεοῦ, οὐκ ἔγνω αὐτόν, ἐὰν φανερωθῇ, ὅμοιοι αὐτῷ ἐσόμεθα, καθὼς ἐκεῖνός), yet without any change of Person.

This appears to be the view of Augustine who writes: ex ipso natus est, ex Deo, ex Christo. Bede writes simply 'id est, ex Christo.'

δίκαιος] *righteous.* The epithet is used of Christ ii. 1; iii. 7. Comp. Acts iii. 14, vii. 52, xxii. 14; and of God (the Father) c. i. 9 (see note); John xvii. 25; Apoc. xvi. 5.

ὅτι πᾶς...γεγέννηται] *that every one...hath been begotten of Him.* The presence of righteous action is the sure sign of the reality of the divine birth. We are often tempted, according to our imperfect standards of judgment, to exclude some (comp. *v.* 23 πᾶς ὁ ἀρν. note), but the divine law admits no exception. It must be further observed that righteousness is not the condition but the consequence of Sonship. God is the one source of righteousness. Apart from God in Christ there is no righteousness. It follows therefore that the presence of active righteousness is the sign of the divine Sonship, and the sign of that abiding power of Sonship which brings final confidence. Other tests of Sonship are offered in the Epistle: 'love' (iv. 7) and belief 'that Jesus is the

Christ' (v. 1). Each one, it will be found, includes the others. See v. 1 note.

The apostle's argument might have appeared more direct if the clauses had been inverted: 'know (take note of the fact) that every one that is born of God doeth righteousness.' But the present order includes a promise, and leaves the power of Sonship in its amplitude. The outwardly witnessed fact of righteousness points to the reality of a relation which includes blessings not yet fully grasped.

ὁ ποιῶν τὴν δικ.] *qui facit justitiam* V., *who doeth righteousness*, who realises in action little by little the righteousness which corresponds with the Divine Nature (τὴν δικ. compare c. iii. 7 note). The tense (ποιῶν) is full of meaning, as Theophylact observes: ἐπισημαντέον ὅτι οὐκ εἶπε Πᾶς

ὁ ποιήσας δικαιοσύνην ἤ, Ὁ ποιήσων ἀλλ' Ὁ ποιῶν. πρακτικαὶ γὰρ [αἱ] ἀρεταὶ καὶ ἐν τῷ γίνεσθαι ἔχουσι τὸ εἶναι· παυσάμεναι δὲ ἢ μέλλουσαι οὐδὲ τὸ εἶναι ἔχουσι.

Bede thus marks the beginning and the end of this realisation of righteousness: Cœpisti non defendere peccatum tuum, jam inchoasti justitiam. Perficietur autem in te quando te nihil aliud facere delectabit.

Compare also ποιεῖν τὴν ἀλήθειαν c. i. 6 note.

ἐξ αὐτοῦ γεγέννηται] *ex ipso natus est* V., *is begotten of Him*. Comp. c. iii. 9 note. The phrase occurs here first in the Epistle. The order emphasises the fact that such a one has *God* for his Father, and not that he has a new life. Compare iii. 9 b; iv. 7; v. 1; John i. 13.

Additional Note on ii. 2.　*The use of* ἱλασμός *and cognates in the Greek Scriptures.*

The word ἱλασμός occurs in the N.T. only here and in a parallel passage iv. 10.

In the LXX. it is found with the corresponding ἐξιλασμός more frequently, where one or other of the two words is the usual representative of כִּפֻּרִים:

Lev. xxv. 9 ἡ ἡμέρα τοῦ ἱλασμοῦ.
— xxiii. 27 f. ἡ ἡμέρα τοῦ ἐξιλασμοῦ.
Num. v. 8 ὁ κριὸς τοῦ ἱλασμοῦ δι᾽ οὗ ἐξιλάσεται.
— xxix. 11 τὸ περὶ τῆς ἁμαρτίας τῆς ἐξιλάσεως.
Exod. xxix. 36 ἡ ἡμέρα τοῦ καθαρισμοῦ.
Vat. A. Σ. Θ. ἐξιλασμοῦ.
— xxx. 10 ἀπὸ τοῦ αἵματος τοῦ καθαρισμοῦ.
Vat. A. ἐξιλασμοῦ.

The two words used also for חַטָּאת:
xlv. 19 λήψεται ἀπὸ τοῦ αἵματος τοῦ ἐξιλασμοῦ.
xliv. 27 προσοίσουσιν ἱλασμόν.
Comp. Ezek. xliii. 23 (Amos viii. 14 is a false rendering of אַשְׁמָה).

2 Macc. iii. 33 ποιουμένου τοῦ ἀρχιερέως τὸν ἱλασμόν (the sacrifice offered for the recovery of Heliodorus).

2 Macc. xii. 45 περὶ τῶν τεθνηκότων τὸν ἐξιλασμὸν ἐποιήσατο τῆς ἁμαρτίας ἀπολυθῆναι.

In Ps. cxxix. (cxxx.) 4 and Dan. ix. 9 ἱλασμός (-οί) is used to translate סְלִיחָה.

The words are always used absolutely without any addition to mark the person to or for whom, or the offence for which the propitiation is offered.

In Ecclus. xviii. 12 ἐπλήθυνε (κύριος) τὸν ἐξιλασμὸν αὐτοῦ the sense is that of Ps. cxxix. 4 'mercifulness.' Comp. c. xvi. 11 ἐξιλασμοί.

The corresponding verb ἱλάσκομαι is found twice in the N.T.:

(1)　With the dat. of person sinning,
　　　Luke xviii. 13 ἱλάσθητί μοι τῷ ἁμαρτωλῷ.
(2)　With the accus. of the sin,
　　　Heb. ii. 17 εἰς τὸ ἱλάσκεσθαι τὰς ἁμαρτίας τοῦ λαοῦ.

Ἱλάσκομαι is comparatively rare in the LXX. It occurs as a translation of כִּפֶּר:
(1)　With accus. of the sin,
　　　Ps. lxiv. 3 ἱλάσῃ τὰς ἀσεβείας (all. ταῖς ἀσ.).
(2)　With dat. of the sin,
　　　Ps. lxxvii. 38 ἱλάσεται ταῖς ἁμαρτίαις.
　　　— lxxviii. 9 ἱλάσθητι ταῖς ἁμ.

It occurs also as a translation of סָלַח for which ἵλεως εἶναι is commonly used:
(1)　With the dat. of person,
　　　4 (2) K. v. 18 ἱλάσεται [ἱλασθήσεται] τῷ δούλῳ.

Use of ἱλασμός in N. T. and LXX.

Use of ἱλάσκομαι.

(2) With the dat. of the sin,

Ps. xxiv. 12 ἱλάσθητι τῇ ἁμαρτίᾳ.

(3) Absolutely,

Lam. iii. 42 οὐχ ἱλάσθης.

Dan. ix. 19 ἱλάσθητι.

And once as a translation of נָחַם which is commonly rendered by μετανοεῖν :

Ex. xxxii. 14 ἱλάσθη κύριος περιποιῆσαι τὸν λαὸν αὐτοῦ.

The use of the aor. ἱλασθῆναι of God corresponds with the sense of ἱλάσκεσθαι, 'to be propitious,' and does not involve the sense 'to propitiate.'

ἐξιλάσ-
κομαι.
The compound ἐξιλάσκομαι, which is the usual representative of כִּפֶּר, is more common. This is found

(1) With the accusative

(a) of the object cleansed :

Ezek. xliii. 26 τὸ θυσιαστήριον.

— xlv. 18 τὸ ἅγιον.

— xlv. 20 τὸν οἶκον.

— xliii. 20, 22 τὸ θυσιαστήριον (חִטֵּא).

(b) and specially of sin,

Dan. ix. 24 τοῦ ἐξιλάσασθαι ἀδικίας.

Ecclus. iii. 30 ἁμαρτίας.

Comp. Ps. lxiv. 4.

In this case the subject (he who expiates, atones, cleanses) may be either

(a) God,

Ecclus. v. 6 πλῆθος ἁμαρτιῶν.

— xxxi. (xxxiv.) 23 οὐδὲ ἐν πλήθει θυσιῶν ἐξιλάσκεται ἁμαρτίας,

or

(b) the human agent,

Ecclus. iii. 3 ὁ τιμῶν πατέρα ἐξιλάσεται ἁμαρτίας.

— xx. 28, xxviii. 5.

So also the word is found in the passive,

1 Sam. iii. 14 εἰ ἐξιλασθήσεται ἡ ἀδικία...ἐκ θυσίας (יִתְכַּפֵּר).

Comp. Deut. xxi. 8 ἐξιλασθήσεται αὐτοῖς τὸ αἷμα.

(2) With περί gen.

(a) of the sin,

Ex. xxxii. 30, &c.

or

(b) of the person sinning,

Lev. i. 4.

— iv. 20, &c.

Comp. Ecclus. xvi. 7 οὐκ ἐξιλάσατο περὶ τῶν ἀρχαίων γιγάντων.

So also with ὑπέρ,

Ezek. xlv. 17.

The word is also used absolutely,

Lev. xvi. 17. Comp. Lam. iii. 42 ; Dan. ix. 19.

(3) Passive with ἀπό,

Num. xxxv. 33 οὐκ ἐξιλασθήσεται ἡ γῆ ἀπὸ τοῦ αἵματος.

(4) The accusative of the person 'propitiated' is found only,

Gen. xxxii. 20 (כָּפַר) ἐξιλάσομαι τὸ πρόσωπον αὐτοῦ ἐν τοῖς δώροις (for ἐν comp. Levit. vi. 37; 1 Sam. iii. 14).

Zech. vii. 2 (חָלָה) ἐξιλάσασθαι τὸν κύριον.

These constructions stand in remarkable contrast with the Classical and Hellenistic[1] usage in which the accus. of the person propitiated is the normal construction from Homer downwards; a usage which prevails in patristic writers. Contrast
of Biblical
and
Classical
usage.

They shew that the scriptural conception of ἱλάσκεσθαι is not that of appeasing one who is angry, with a personal feeling, against the offender; but of altering the character of that which from without occasions a necessary alienation, and interposes an inevitable obstacle to fellowship. Such phrases as 'propitiating God' and God 'being reconciled' are foreign to the language of the N. T. Man is reconciled (2 Cor. v. 18 ff.; Rom. v. 10 f.). There is a 'propitiation' in the matter of the sin or of the sinner. The love of God is the same throughout; but He 'cannot' in virtue of His very Nature welcome the impenitent and sinful: and more than this, He 'cannot' treat sin as if it were not sin.

This being so, the ἱλασμός, when it is applied to the sinner, so to speak, neutralises the sin. In this respect the idea of the efficacy of Christ's propitiation corresponds with one aspect of the Pauline phrase 'in Christ.' The believer being united with Christ enjoys the quickening, purifying, action of Christ's 'Blood,' of the virtue of His Life and Death, of His Life made available for men through Death.

Compare Additional Note on i. 9.

Additional Note on ii. 9. *St John's view of the state of man.*

St John assumes that the actual state of man and of the world is known by experience, from what we see about us and from history and from consciousness.

Naturally 'darkness' (comp. c. i. 5, note) is the sphere in which man abides (John xii. 46; 1 John ii. 9 ἕως ἄρτι) until it is dispelled. (Comp. John viii. 12; 1 Pet. ii. 9; Eph. vi. 12; Col. i. 13.) Under one aspect this darkness has wrought its work, and the crisis is past (c. ii. 11, ἐτύφλωσεν, note). Under another aspect there are times when the darkness falls afresh over men with a thicker gloom (John xii. 35, ἵνα μὴ σκ. ὑ. καταλάβῃ). Viewed from a different point of sight this darkness is death (John v. 24). Man by
nature in
darkness
and death.

---

[1] E.g. Clem. ad Cor. i. 7 οἱ δὲ (the Ninevites) μετανοήσαντες ἐπὶ τοῖς ἁμαρτήμασιν ἐξιλάσαντο τὸν θεὸν ἱκετεύσαντες. Herm. Vis. i. 2 πῶς ἐξιλάσομαι τὸν θεὸν περὶ τῶν ἁμαρτιῶν μου τῶν τελείων; Test. xii. Patr. Levi 3 οἱ ἄγγελοι...οἱ λειτουργοῦντες καὶ ἐξιλασκόμενοι πρὸς Κύριον ἐπὶ

πάσαις ταῖς ἀγνοίαις τῶν δικαίων. Philo, de plantat. § 39 (i. 354) εὐξάμενοι καὶ θυσίας ἀναγαγόντες, καὶ ἱλασάμενοι τὸ θεῖον. Comp. Leg. Alleg. iii. § 61 (i. 121 M.). Joseph. Antt. viii. 4, 3 τίνι ἄλλῳ μᾶλλον ἱλάσασθαι μηνίοντα [τὸν θεόν]...δεξιώτερόν ἐστιν ἡμῖν ἢ φωνῇ...;

This state due to external influence.　　This present state of man is due to a mysterious interruption of the Divine plan which is noticed abruptly (John i. 5) and came from another order (c. iii. 8). It is not due to a physical or metaphysical necessity, and is foreign to the essence of man. As the creature of God man was made good not absolutely but relatively. Sin has disturbed his normal development (c. iii. 4). Nothing however is said by St John of the Fall; nor does he mention Adam (yet comp. Apoc. xii. 9 ff.; xx. 2 ὁ ὄφις ὁ ἀρχαῖος). The sin of Cain, the manifestation of sin in the realm of human life, and not the sin of Adam, is treated as the archetypal sin (c. iii. 12).

Man failed to see God.　　As a necessary consequence of his state, man failed of himself to gain a knowledge of God in the way of nature (John i. 10; comp. iii. 3), though he was not left unvisited (John i. 4, 9).

The mission of the Son of God revealed man to himself.　　Under these circumstances God sent his Son to save the world, giving in this the measure of His love (John iii. 16 f.; c. iv. 10). But the coming of Christ was in effect a judgment, shewing to men what they had become (John ix. 39; comp. Apoc. iii. 17 ff.; Luke ii. 34 f.). For they were not without the power of recognising this Divine revelation (John xv. 22, 24; v. 36). The will to recognise God and not the capacity was wanting (John v. 40; vii. 17; viii. 44; xii. 48 ἔχει τὸν κρίνοντα; comp. iii. 18; vi. 67; ix. 41). The manifestation of love called out, as a necessary consequence, the opposition of selfishness, hatred (John iii. 19 f.; vii. 7; xv. 18 f., 23 f.; xvii. 14; comp. c. ii. 9, 11; iii. 10, 15; iv. 20). But this hatred was in despite of man's real nature. It is true still that if he violates moral law he 'lies,' and 'deceives himself' (c. i. 6, 8; ii. 4, 22; iv. 20).

The actual state of man shewn in contrasts.　　These several traits combine to give a striking view of the grandeur and powerlessness of man ('un roseau pensant'). He is made for God: he is unable of himself to attain to God: God claims his concurrence with the activity of Divine love. And it is most worthy of notice that St John simply declares the antithetic facts in their simple solemnity. He shews no desire to resolve the discords which he accentuates. He leaves them for a state of fuller knowledge and larger life.

Man is in darkness and death (John v. 24; c. iii. 14). On the other side the true Light shineth (John i. 5; xii. 36; c. ii. 8); and Christ offers 'His flesh for the life of the world' (John vi. 51).

The world 'lieth in the Evil One' (c. v. 19). On the other side 'the Prince of the world' is judged and cast out (John xii. 31; xvi. 11; comp. xiii. 40; c. v. 4 ἡ νίκη ἡ νικήσασα). There is a human will which is responsible and therefore in that sense 'free' (John v. 40; iii. 19 ff.; vii. 17). On the other side there is a Divine will which we cannot conceive to be finally ineffective (vi. 44 ff., 65; v. 21).

In the opening of the Gospel, John i. 12 f., these contrasts find a concurrent affirmation. On the one side the human element is seen in ἔλαβον, πιστεύουσιν, γενέσθαι. On the other side the Divine element is seen in ἐγεννήθησαν, ἔδωκεν ἐξουσίαν, τέκνα θεοῦ. Comp. John vi. 27 ff. (ἐργάζεσθε, δώσει).

The wide extent of these contrasts.　　The same clear assertion of truths which appear to be in opposition extends to other parts of the region of Divine and human relations. There is one absolute message (John xii. 48); and yet concessions are made that men may embrace it more readily (John v. 34; comp. viii. 17). There is a group whom Christ speaks of as His own (John x. 27, 4); and yet He appeals generally to all, for the image of thirst expresses a universal want which Christ alone can satisfy (John vii. 37). A new birth is necessary for the perception of the Divine Kingdom and entrance into it (John iii. 3 ff.); and yet there are, as still without it, those who 'are of the truth' (John xviii. 37), who 'do the truth' (iii. 21), who are 'children of God' (xi. 52).

In part we can see perhaps where the reconciliation of these statements can be found. In part they finally go back to the fundamental antithesis of the finite and infinite before which our present powers fail. The teaching of St John helps us to see that it is enough that we hold the fulness of the truth as it is presented to us in complementary fragments.

Additional Note on ii. 13. *The powers of evil.*

St John speaks comparatively little of subordinate spiritual powers in his Gospel and Epistles. The ministry of angels is essential to the whole structure of the Apocalypse, which contains also characteristic references to 'the Serpent,' 'the ancient Serpent,' 'the dragon' (xii. 3 ff.; xiii. 2 ff.; xvi. 13; xx. 2), 'who is called the Devil and Satan' (xii. 9); compare also ix. 20 (τὰ δαιμόνια); xvi. 14 (πν. δαιμονίων). But into these notices we do not now inquire. Few references to subordinate powers of good and evil in St John.

The only references to angels in the Gospel are in i. 51 (52); xx. 12 (v. (3) 4, embodies an early tradition, but is no part of the original text). They have no place in the Epistles. In the Gospel 'demons' are only spoken of by the Jews or in direct reference to their words (vii. 20; viii. 48 ff.; x. 20 f.). In the first epistle 'spirits' of antichrist are described as influencing men (c. iv. 2 ff. note, 6).

But the notices of the representative power of evil are of great importance. He is spoken of as 'the Devil' (ὁ διάβολος John viii. 44; xiii. 2; c. iii. 8, 10), the false accuser (John vi. 70 note); 'Satan' (ὁ Σατανᾶς John xiii. 27), the adversary (comp. ὁ κατήγωρ Apoc. xii. 10); 'the evil one' (ὁ πονηρός xvii. 15, note; c. ii. 13 f.; iii. 12; v. 18 f.); 'the ruler of this (the) world' (ὁ ἄρχων τοῦ κόσμου τούτου John xii. 31; xvi. 11; ὁ τοῦ κ. ἄρχ. John xiv. 30). The Evil One.

Of his origin nothing is specially said. But enough is laid down to exclude the notion of two coordinate or absolute or original beings, good and evil. He was originally good, but 'he stood not (John viii. 44 οὐκ ἕστηκεν, note) in the truth.' This is all that we are concerned to know. For the rest he appears 'from the beginning' on the scene of human activity (c. iii. 8). Thus he stands in opposition to the Word (c. i. 1), and finally to the Incarnate Son (c. iii. 8 note; v. 18 f.; John xiv. 30 f.). A fallen being.

In this respect he is directly at variance with Christ in His essential character. Christ is 'the truth' (John xiv. 6): the devil is a liar (John viii. 44; comp. c. ii. 22). Christ is 'the life' (John xiv. 6): the devil is a murderer (John viii. 44; comp. c. iii. 15). In each case a personal an- The antagonist of the Son.

tagonist is set over against the absolute idea. In relation to the reality of things, and in relation to human fellowship: in the regions of thought, feeling, action; the devil conflicts with the Son of God.

His present influence on men.

For the present, as the title 'the ruler of this world' implies, the devil exercises a wide influence over men (c. iii. 8 ff.; John viii. 44; xiii. 2, 27). They may become his 'sons,' his 'children' (c. iii. 10 note); they may be 'of him' (c. iii. 8). But they are never said to be 'born of him,' as they are born of God (c. ii. 29 &c.). And in relation to the work of Christ he is already finally defeated (John xvi. 11; xii. 31; xiv. 30; c. v. 4, 18). It remains to secure the fruits of the victory.

Already overthrown.

Additional Note on ii. 17. *St John's teaching on creation.*

St John's conception of creation.

The main conception of creation which is present in the writings of St John is expressed by the first notice which he makes of it: '*all things came into being* (ἐγένετο) *through* [the Word]' (John i. 3). This statement sets aside the notions of eternal matter and of inherent evil in matter. 'There was when' the world 'was not' (John xvii. 5, 24); and, by implication, all things as made were good. The agency of the Word 'who was God' again excludes both the Gnostic idea of a Demiurge, a creator essentially inferior to God; and the idea of an abstract Monotheism, in which there is no living relation between the creature and the Creator; for as all things come into being 'through' the Word, so they are supported 'in' Him (John i. 3 ὁ γέγ. ἐν αὐτῷ ζωὴ ἦν note; comp. Col. i. 16 f.; Heb. i. 3). And yet more the use of the term ἐγένετο, 'came into being,' as distinguished from ἐκτίσθη 'were created,' suggests the thought that Creation is to be regarded (according to our apprehension) as a manifestation of a Divine law of love. Thus Creation (πάντα ἐγένετο δι' αὐτοῦ) answers to the Incarnation (ὁ λόγος σὰρξ ἐγένετο). All the unfolding and infolding of finite being to the last issue lies in the fulfilment of His will Who is love.

An order unfolded in spite of the irruption of darkness. A Divine 'must.'

The irruption of darkness, however, has hindered the normal progress of the counsel of God. This is obvious in 'the world' which falls within the range of man's observation. But in spite of the violation of the Divine order by man there is still a fulfilment of the counsel of God in the world. This is seen most distinctly in the record of the Lord's work. In the accomplishment of this there is a Divine necessity, a 'must' and a 'cannot' in the very nature of things; and also a Divine sequence in the unfolding of its parts.

This Divine 'must' (δεῖ) extends to the relation of the Forerunner to Christ (iii. 30); to the fulfilment of the work of God during an allotted time (ix. 4); to the Passion and Exaltation (iii. 14; xii. 34); to the Rising again (xx. 9); to the execution of a wider office (x. 16) (comp. Apoc. i. 1; iv. 1; xxii. 6; xvii. 10; xx. 3).

A Divine 'cannot.'

On the other hand there is also a 'cannot,' a moral, and not an external or arbitrary, impossibility in life. This defines, while it does not limit, the action of the Son: v. 19, 30 (comp. Mark vi. 5). And so also it fixes the conditions of discipleship (iii. 5; vi. 44, 65; vii. 34, 36; viii. 21 f.; comp. xiii. 33, 36); of understanding (iii. 3; viii. 43 f.; xiv. 17); of faith (xii. 39; comp. v. 44); of fruitfulness (xv. 4 f.); of progress (xvi. 12); of character (1 John iii. 9).

These terms ('must,' 'cannot') lay open the conditions (so to speak) of A Divine the Lord's life. The Divine sequence in the course of its events is no less 'hour.' distinctly marked by the term 'hour.' The crises of the manifestations of the Lord are absolutely fixed in time (ii. 4; comp. xi. 9 f.; ix. 4). Till this hour comes His enemies are powerless (vii. 30; viii. 20). When it has come He recognises its advent (xii. 27; xvii. 1); and it is appointed with a view to the issue to which it leads (xii. 23; xiii. 1 ἵνα).

Compare iv. 21, 23; v. 25, 28; 1 John ii. 18; Apoc. xiv. 7, 15 (ὥρα; John vii. 6, 8 (καιρός); Eph. i. 10 τὸ πλήρωμα τῶν καιρῶν; Gal. iv. 4 τὸ πλήρωμα τοῦ χρόνου.

Under this same aspect the 'works' of the Lord are said to have been The life of 'given' to Him (v. 36; xvii. 4). The circumstances which furnished Christ, occasion for them are shewn to enter into the scheme of providence (ix. 3 ἵνα; xi. 4 ἵνα). Even unbelief was a necessity in regard of the history of mankind (xii. 38; xiii. 18; xv. 25; xvii. 12). This being so, Christ knew all 'the things that were coming upon Him' (xviii. 4; comp. xiii. 1, 11; vi. 64; comp. xviii. 9, 32). He laid down His life 'in order to take it again' (x. 17). This was His Father's will.

The whole life of Christ was thus a 'fulfilment,' 'a bringing to a perfect accomplishment' of all that had been shadowed forth or begun[1].

The same Divine appointment is extended to the discipline of the Church. and the The extremity of persecution is part of the revelation of the counsel of God life of the (John xvi. 2 ἵνα, note), as even was the failure of the disciples at their according Master's suffering (John xvi. 32 ἵνα, note). The birth of the Church has a to law. real correspondence with the birth of the man (John xvi. 21 ff.). And in the work of service there is an appointed difference of function with a common end (John iv. 36 ff.).

The life of Christ and the life of the Church, as presented by St John, thus A true become revelations of a perfect order even in the disorder of the world nature lying beneath the surface of things, and veiled by suffering and by the under- workings of evil. In the same way he seems to indicate that below the neath ap- transitory appearances of nature there is that which is Divine and abiding. pearances. '*The world passeth away* (παράγεται) *and the desire thereof*' (1 John ii. 17, 8), but at the same time he looked for a new heaven and a new earth (Apoc. xxi. 1).

He recognised most sharply the difference between the natural and the unnatural in what we call Nature as a whole, and saw in the complete

---

[1] The use of the two words πληρόω, τελειόω is worth study:

(a) πληρῶσαι
vii. 8 ὁ ἐμὸς καιρὸς οὔπω πεπλήρωται.
Of Holy Scripture and Divine words: ἵνα πληρωθῇ xii. 38; xiii. 18; xv. 25; xvii. 12; xviii. 32; xix. 24, 36. Comp. Apoc. vi. 11.

(b) τελειῶσαι
iv. 34 τελ. αὐτοῦ τὸ ἔργον; v. 36 τὰ ἔργα ἃ δέδ. ἵνα τελ.; xvii. 4 τὸ ἔργον τελ. ὃ δέδωκάς μοι.
Of Holy Scripture: xix. 28 ἵνα τελ. ἡ γρ. Comp. τετέλεσται, xix. 28, 30; and Apoc. x. 7.

destruction of the unnatural, the restoration of Nature. In this position he stands alike removed from the Hellenic worship of nature and from the Gnostic degradation of nature. (Comp. Lutterbeck, *Lehrb. d. Apost.* ii. 270 f.)

Additional Note on ii. 18. Antichrist.

Elements in the conception of Antichrist.

Different elements entered into the conception of 'Antichrist' in early patristic literature. Of these the chief were Dan. vii. 7 ff.; Matt. xxiv. 23 ff.; 2 Thess. ii. 3 ff.; Apoc. xiii.

But the aspects under which the opposing power is presented by St Paul and St John (Epistle) are distinct. The portraiture in St Paul is based on that of Daniel and presents a single adversary claiming personal worship, while St John dwells upon the spiritual element in his claims, and the spiritual falsehood which gave him the semblance of strength.

Irenæus.

IRENÆUS, the earliest writer who treats of the subject in detail, combines the name of Antichrist with the description in 2 Thess. ii. 3 ff. and the cognate passages in Daniel, St Matthew and the Apocalypse (Iren. v. 25 ff.; compare iii. 6, 4; 7, 2; 16, 5, 8; 23, 7).

CLEMENT OF ALEXANDRIA is silent on Antichrist. But the teaching on Antichrist attracted the attention of CELSUS, though Origen says that he had not read what was said of him by Daniel or Paul (*c. Cels.* vi. 45). In reply

Origen.

to Celsus ORIGEN explains his own view, which is briefly that the Son of God and the son of the evil one, of Satan, of the devil, stand at the opposite poles of humanity, presenting in direct opposition the capacity of man for good and for evil. Elsewhere Origen draws out at length a comparison of Christ and Antichrist. All that Christ is in reality Antichrist offers in false appearance (*Comm. Ser. in Matt.* § 27); and so all false teaching which assumes the guise of truth, among heretics and even among heathen, is in some sense 'Antichrist' (*id.* § 47).

Tertullian.

TERTULLIAN speaks several times of Antichrist and Antichrists. Quoting 2 Thess. ii. 3 he writes '*homo delinquentiæ,* id est, *antichristus*' (*de Res. carnis,* 24; cf. 27). Again referring to Matt. xxiv. 24, he asks: ' qui pseudoprophetæ sunt nisi falsi prædicatores? qui pseudapostoli nisi adulteri evangelizatores? qui antichristi nisi Christi rebelles? (*de præscr. hær.* 4). And again in reference to 1 John ii. 18 he writes: in epistola sua eos maxime antichristos vocat qui Christum negarent in carne venisse, et qui non putarent Jesum esse filium dei. Illud Marcion, hoc Ebion vindicavit (*id.* 33).

Balaam.

One feature in the conception of Antichrist ought not to be overlooked. Just as Moses was the type of the Christ in His prophetic character, Balaam, 'the anti-Moses,' was regarded as a type of the Antichrist. This explains the enigmatic references in Apoc. ii. 14 (6); Jude 11; 2 Pet. ii. 15.

Armillus.

In late Rabbinic traditions an Antichrist (Armillus, Armalgus) was represented as killing the Messiah of the stock of Ephraim, and then himself slain by the Messiah of the stock of David (Targ. on Is. xi. 4; comp. 2 Thess. ii. 8).

The Epistles to the Seven Churches form a commentary on the idea of The Apocalypse. the many antichrists.

Apoc. ii. 2 (Ephesus) τοὺς λέγοντας ἑαυτοὺς ἀποστόλους. *id.* 6 τὰ ἔργα τῶν Νικολαιτῶν.

ii. 9 (Smyrna) τῶν λεγόντων ᾿Ιουδαίους εἶναι.

ii. 13 (Pergamum) ὅπου ὁ θρόνος τοῦ Σατανᾶ. 14 τὴν διδαχὴν Βαλαάμ. 15 τὴν διδαχὴν Νικολαιτῶν.

ii. 20 (Thyatira) ᾿Ιεζέβελ, ἡ λέγουσα ἑαυτὴν προφῆτιν. 24 τὰ βαθέα τοῦ Σατανᾶ (cf. 1 Cor. ii. 10).

iii. 3 (Sardis) μνημόνευε πῶς εἴληφας καὶ ἤκουσας καὶ.τήρει.

iii. 8 f. (Philadelphia) τῆς συναγωγῆς τοῦ Σατανᾶ, τῶν λεγόντων ἑαυτοὺς ᾿Ιουδαίους εἶναι.

Additional Note on the reading of ii. 20.

There is a remarkable variety of readings in the last words of this verse :

(1) καὶ οἴδατε πάντα
    AC MSS mss
    Memph Vulg.

The Syriac reads πάντα but translates it as if it were masc. (*and know every man*).

(2) καὶ οἴδατε (-αι ℵ) πάντες ℵP 9.

Hesych. Presb. (sæc. vii) *in Lev.* i. 5 ff. (Migne *P. Gr.* XCIII. p. 796) Et vos unctionem habetis a sancto et scitis omnes.

(3) οἴδατε πάντες B Theb.

The rendering which is given without variation in the Discourses of Augustine (ad loc.) *ut ipsi vobis manifesti sitis* can hardly be correct. His comment suggests πάντες : hanc unctionem Christi dicit omnes qui habent cognoscere malos et bonos; nec opus esse ut doceantur quia ipsa unctio docet eos.

The Latin translation of Irenæus, in a continuous quotation of *vv.* 18—22, omits *v.* 20 and part of *v.* 21: ...sed ut manifestarentur quoniam non sunt ex nobis. Cognoscite ergo quoniam omne mendacium extraneum est et non est de veritate. Quis est mendax...(Iren. iii. 16. 5).

The combination for πάντες ℵBP 9 Theb. is very strong; and the shorter reading without καί readily explains how the others arose. When once the connexion of οἴδατε with τὴν ἀλήθειαν was lost, the insertion of καί and the change of πάντες to πάντα was almost inevitable, especially with the apparent parallel in *v.* 27 περὶ πάντων.

The occurrence of 9 (Cambr. Univ. Libr. Kk. vi. 4) in the small group of authorities which have preserved the main element of the true reading may serve as an excuse for directing attention to that remarkable MS, which has been strangely overlooked.

It was pointed out by Porson and Marsh that this MS is that marked ιγ΄ in Stephens' edition of 1550; and apparently the capricious selection of readings quoted from it by Stephens has been the limit of the knowledge of the MS preserved by later editors. Mill's generalisations from the readings in Stephens (*Proleg.* 1170) might well have caused it to be more carefully examined.

The following readings in I John are worthy of notice :

i. 2 ἐφανερώθη ἐν ἡμῖν.
    — 4 ἡμῶν.
    — 9 τὰς ἁμαρτίας ἡμῶν.
ii. 1 γράφομεν.
    — 8 ἐν ἡμῖν.
    — 11 ἐτύφλωσεν αὐτὸν καὶ τοὺς ὀφθαλμοὺς αὐτοῦ.
    — 17 ἡ ἐπιθυμία om. αὐτοῦ.
    — 18 νῦν om. καί.
    — 20 καὶ οἴδατε πάντες.
iii. 1 ἔδωκεν.
    — — κληθῶμεν καὶ ἐσμέν.
    — 5. τὰς ἁμαρτίας ἡμῶν.
    — 7 τέκνα.
    — 8 τοῦ διαβόλου ἐστίν om. ἐκ.
    — — ὁ διάβολος ἀπ᾽ ἀρχῆς.
    — 19 γινωσκόμεθα.
    — 21 καταγινώσκῃ om. ἡμῶν.
    — 23 πιστεύωμεν.
iv. 2 γινώσκομεν.
    — 3 Ἰησοῦν om. τόν.
    — 8 ὁ μὴ ἀγαπῶν ἐκ τοῦ θεοῦ οὐκ ἔστιν.
    — 10 ἠγαπήκαμεν.
v.   4 ὑμῶν.
    — 20 ἡ ζωὴ ἡ αἰώνιος.

The title of the Epistle is ἐπιστολὴ Ἰωάννου ᾱ and the subscription τοῦ ἁγίου ἀπ. Ἰω ἐπιστολὴ ᾱ.

III.   ¹Ἴδετε ποταπὴν ἀγάπην δέδωκεν ἡμῖν ὁ πατὴρ

1 δέδωκεν אBC: ἔδωκεν A.   ἡμῖν: ὑμῖν B.

II. The children of God and the children of the devil (iii. 1—12).

The section seems to fall most naturally into three parts:

1. *The position present and future of the children of God* (iii. 1—3).

2. *The essential character of the children of God* (4—9).

3. *The outward manifestation of the children of God* (10—12).

The thoughts are unfolded throughout in contrast with the corresponding thoughts as to the position, character, and manifestation of 'the children of the devil.' The world knows not Christians. Sin is incompatible with Sonship of God. Active hatred is the sign of hostility to right.

1. *The position present and future of the children of God* (1—3).

The position of Christians is considered in regard both to the present (*v.* 1) and to the future (*v.* 2). They stand now to 'the Father' in the relation of 'children of God' in title and in reality: on the other hand 'the world' fails to recognise them. Their future is as yet unrevealed; but so much is known that it will answer to the open, transfiguring vision of God in Christ. Meanwhile therefore the thought of this transfiguration is the rule and inspiration of Christian effort (*v.* 3).

¹ *Behold (See) what manner of love the Father hath given to us, that we should be called children of God:—and such we are. For this cause the world knoweth us not, because it knew him not.* ² *Beloved, now are we children of God, and it is not yet manifested what we shall be. We know that if he shall be manifested, we shall be like him, because we shall see him even as he is. And every one that hath this hope*

on him purifieth himself even as he is pure.

1. Ἴδετε] *Videte* V., *Ecce* Aug., *Behold, See.* The use of the plural is remarkable, and elsewhere it is used only of something actually visible (Gal. vi. 11; yet comp. Acts xiii. 41, LXX). The image at the close of the last chapter (*born of Him*) seems to fill St John's vision, and, as he pauses to dwell upon it himself, he invites his readers to contemplate the same truth as present before them in an intelligible shape.

ποταπὴν ἀγάπην] *qualem caritatem (dilectionem* Aug.) V., *what manner of love* truly divine in its nature. The word ποταπός, which is not found in the LXX, is rare in the New Testament. It is used to call attention to the character both of persons (Matt. viii. 27; Luke vii. 39; 2 Pet. iii. 11) and of things (Mk. xiii. 1; Luke i. 29).

ὁ πατήρ] *the Father.* This title is chosen in order to illustrate and (in some degree) to explain the gift of love which God has bestowed on men.

δέδωκεν ἡ.] *dedit nobis* V., *hath given to us.* Comp. John xiv. 27. The love is not simply exhibited towards believers, but imparted to them. The divine love is, as it were, infused into them, so that it is their own, and becomes in them the source of a divine life (Rom. xiii. 10). In virtue of this gift therefore they are inspired with a love which is like the love of God, and by this they truly claim the title of children of God, as partakers in His nature. Comp. c. iv. 7, 19. See also Leo, *Serm.* xii. § 1 (Migne, *Patrol. Lat.* LIV. p. 169): Diligendo itaque nos Deus ad imaginem suam nos reparat et, ut in nobis formam suæ bonitatis inveniat, dat unde ipsi quoque quod operatur operemur, accendens ἵνα τέκνα θεοῦ κληθῶμεν, καὶ ἐσμέν. διὰ τοῦτο ὁ

καὶ ἐσμέν ℵABC vg me the syrr: om. ϛ. The Latt. by a natural error read *et*
simus (as depending on *ut*). Compare c. v. 20.

scilicet mentium nostrarum lucernas, et igne nos suæ caritatis inflammans, ut non solum ipsum sed etiam quidquid diligit diligamus.

With δέδωκεν, which regards the endowment of the receiver, contrast κεχάρισται (Gal. iii. 18), ἐχαρίσατο (Phil. ii. 9) which regards the feeling of the giver.

ἡμῖν (ὑμῖν)] St John is here considering the blessing of love as actually realised in the Christian society. Contrast John iii. 16 ἠγάπησεν ὁ θεὸς τὸν κόσμον.

ἵνα...κληθᾶμεν...] *ut...nominemur* (*vocemur* Aug.) V., *that we should be called*. The final particle has its full force. The divine gift of love which is appropriated by the believer forms the basis, the justification, of the divine title. The end of the blessing is that sonship may be real. For ἵνα compare *v*. 11 note.

Pelagii...condemnatur hæresis in eo quod dicitur a Deo nobis caritatem... dari qua adoptionem filiorum accipiamus (Bede).

τέκνα θεοῦ] *filii Dei* V., *children of God* not *sons of God* which comes from the Latin. The thought here is of the community of nature with the prospect of development (τέκνον, comp. 2 Pet. i. 4), and not of the position of privilege (υἱός). The only place in St John's writings where 'son' is used of the relation of man to God is Apoc. xxi. 7 in a free quotation from Zech. viii. 8.

The use of υἱός is characteristic of St Paul's Epistles to the Romans and Galatians: Rom. viii. 14, 19; Gal. iii. 26; iv. 6, 7. Comp. Heb. ii. 10, xii. 5 ff.; Rom. ix. 26; 2 Cor. vi. 18; Matt. v. 9, 45, xvii. 26; Luke xi. 35, xx. 36.

On the other hand the idea of 'children of God' (τέκνα θεοῦ) is not un-

frequent in St John: *vv*. 2, 10, v. 2; John i. 12, xi. 52. See Additional Note.

By using θεοῦ in place of the simple pronoun αὐτοῦ St John, reciting the full name of Christians (*v*. 10; v. 2; John i. 12, xi. 52; Rom. viii. 16 ff., ix. 8; Phil. ii. 15), emphasises the idea of the nobility of the Christian's position ('children of Him who is God').

κληθῶμεν] *be called*. The privilege is already enjoyed in the present and not only anticipated in the future. Christians are outwardly recognised as 'God's children' in their services and intercourse with others. Such an open recognition of the title gives a solemn dignity to it.

It is worthy of notice that St John never uses καλεῖν of the Divine 'call' (John x. 3 φωνεῖ). Comp. John ii. 2.

καὶ ἐσμέν] *and such we are*. This parenthetical addition is an emphatic expression of the Apostle's own faith. He has stated the historic position of Christians in the world, which depends on the Father's gift of love. He affirms now that that historic position corresponds with a real fact. The name represents an absolute truth. For such an introduction of a reflective comment see i. 2 note; 2 John 2. The Latin by a natural error connects the ἐσμέν with ἵνα, *ut nominemur...et simus*.

διὰ τοῦτο] *propter hoc* V., *For this cause* (iv. 5), i.e. because we are children of God, and so share His nature, *the world knoweth us not*, seeing that it has shewn decisively its inability to recognise Him. The reference to the world at first sight seems to interrupt the current of thought, but St John's whole argument proceeds on the supposition that men stand between two powers, God and the

κόσμος οὐ γινώσκει ἡμᾶς ὅτι οὐκ ἔγνω αὐτόν.   ²Ἀγα-
πητοί, νῦν τέκνα θεοῦ ἐσμέν, καὶ οὔπω ἐφανερώθη τί

ἡμᾶς: ὑμᾶς ℵ*.

world. He has shewn the relation
in which they stand to God: he now
shews the relation in which they stand
to the world. At the same time the
clause meets an objection which is
likely to rise from a consideration of
the character of Christians. If they
are children of God, righteous and
loving, may they not look for an immediate and decisive victory? So we
are inclined to argue; and therefore
the Apostle at once points out that
their likeness to God becomes the occasion of misunderstanding.

οὐ γινώσκει...οὐκ ἔγνω...] non novit...non novit... V., non cognoscit...
non cognovit...Aug., the world knoweth us not, does not enter into, come
to understand, our principles and
methods and character, for true knowledge of men requires sympathy (c. ii.
3 note). The conduct of Christians
must be more or less a riddle to those
who do not take account of that
which is to them the spring of action.
This follows from the fact that when
the opportunity was given to the
world for recognising the great features of the divine character it knew
Him not (comp. c. iv. 8 note). The
world failed to recognise God so far
as He was manifested in creation and
history (1 Cor. i. 21); and its failure
was still more conspicuous when He
was manifested in His Son (John xvi.
3). It is to this revelation specially
that the Apostle refers. The 'Him'
is God in Christ, as in ii. 29.

Augustine says, using an impressive
image: [homines] amando delecta-
tiones peccatorum non agnoscebant
Deum: amando quod febris suadebat
injuriam medico faciebant.

2. Ἀγαπητοί] Carissimi V., Di-
lectissimi Aug., Beloved. The title
(ii. 7 note) embodies the thought

which has been just expressed. St
John in the spirit of love addresses
those who with him look forward to
the issue of love. In doing this he
takes up the words which he has just
used, half in personal reflection (καὶ
ἐσμέν); 'Yes, now are we children,
children with the promise of mature
development.' The change to which
he thus looks forward will not be in
the position of children, but in the
conditions under which the relation
will be shewn. The Christian has now,
even in the present life, that which
carries with it potentially infinite
blessings, but the manifestation of his
sonship is hindered by the circumstances in which he is placed. He
will not be anything essentially different hereafter, but he will be what he
is now essentially more completely,
though in ways wholly beyond our
powers of imagination.

νῦν...ἐσμέν, καὶ...] now are we...
and... The thought of what Christians
are and the thought of what they will
be are treated as parts of the same
thought and not placed in contrast.
The fact and the hope are both power-
ful for life.

οὔπω ἐφανερώθη...ἐὰν φανερωθῇ...]
nondum apparuit...cum apparuerit...V., nondum manifestatum est
(and apparuit)...cum apparuerit
(and manifestatum fuerit) Aug.,
manifestatum est...si manifestaverit
(one ms. manifestatus fuerit) Tert.,
nondum revelatum est...cum revelatum fuerit Ambr.

The main difficulty in this passage
lies in the interpretation of the clause
ἐὰν φανερωθῇ. The subject is not
expressed; and the clause can be
rendered either (1) if it shall be
manifested i.e. what we shall be;
or (2) if he shall be manifested. In

ἐσόμεθα. οἴδαμεν ὅτι ἐὰν φανερωθῇ ὅμοιοι αὐτῷ ἐσόμεθα, ὅτι ὀψόμεθα αὐτὸν καθώς ἐστιν. ³καὶ πᾶς ὁ

2 οἴδαμεν ℵABC vg the syr hl: +δέ ς me syr vg.

favour of the first interpretation it is
urged that the clause must refer back
to the corresponding words (οὔπω
ἐφανερώθη) which have immediately
gone before: *it is not yet manifested…
if it shall be manifested…;* unless
such an explanation be obviously
excluded by other considerations;
and on the other hand it is answered
rightly, I think, that this is in fact
the case; that the words *if it shall
be manifested* are altogether without
force; or rather that they obscure the
meaning. The knowledge which is
affirmed is not dependent on any
manifestation, but absolute. Christians
already possess it; and their certainty
so far is not conditioned by anything
future. Or to put the thought somewhat differently: it cannot be said
that the knowledge that we shall be
like Christ (which is assumed) depends upon the manifestation of what
we shall be. On the other hand there
is an inspiring power in the assurance
that our likeness to the Lord will be
a likeness to His glorified Being,
which will hereafter be shewn, though
as yet we cannot understand what it
is.

And further in support of the rendering *if he shall be manifested* it is to
be noticed that the same phrase has
been used in ii. 28 where the meaning
is beyond all doubt. It may be added
that this use of φανεροῦσθαι appears
to rule the whole line of the Apostle's
thought (ii. 28, iii. 8). Christ has been
(was) manifested and He will be
manifested. The past manifestations
made some things clear and left some
things dark (iii. 5, 8). The future
manifestation will remove this darkness (comp. Col. iii. 4).

Even in the foregoing clause there
is, as will be seen, something of this

same thought. The manifestations of
the Risen Christ have not completely
illuminated our future.

οὔπω ἐφανερώθη] *it is not yet made
manifest.* The aorist (ἐφανερώθη) appears to point back to some definite
occasion on which the revelation
might have been expected (compare
ἔγνω *v.* 1). Perhaps it is best to
refer the word to the manifestations
(comp. ii. 28 note) of the Risen Lord.
These revelations of a changed and
glorified humanity do not make
known to us what we shall be. They
only serve to shew that the limitations of the present mode of ·existence
will be removed.

τί ἐσόμεθα] For the use of the
direct interrogation, see Moulton's
Winer, pp. 210 f.

οἴδαμεν] *We know.* Comp. c. v. 2, 18
notes. There is no opposition between
this clause and that which immediately precedes such as is suggested
by the δέ of the common text. The
knowledge corresponds with the
whole consciousness of the position
of children.

ὅμοιοι αὐτῷ] *similes ei* V., *like him,*
like God in Christ. The image in which
we were made will then be consummated in the likeness to which it was
the divine purpose that we should
attain. Compare the Essay on *The
Gospel of Creation,* III. 1 (*a*).

This likeness of man redeemed and
perfected to God is the likeness of
the creature reflecting the glory of
the Creator. Contrast Phil. ii. 6 τὸ
εἶναι ἴσα θεῷ, said of the Son. Dispar
est res, sed *sicut* ad similitudinem
dicitur. Habemus ergo et nos imaginem Dei, sed non illam quam habet
Filius æqualis Patri (Aug.).

ὅτι ὀψόμεθα…] *quoniam videbimus…*V., *because we shall see….* The

causal particle is ambiguous.... The likeness to God may be either (1) the necessary condition, or (2) the actual consequence of the Divine Vision. The argument may be: We shall see God, and therefore, since this is possible, we must be like Him; or, We shall see God, and in that Presence we shall reflect His glory and be transformed into His likeness. Both thoughts are scriptural; and perhaps the two thoughts are not very sharply distinguished here. It is true that likeness is, in this case, the condition of vision; and it is true also that likeness is the consequence of vision. We see that which we have the sympathetic power of seeing and we gain greater power of seeing, that is greater sympathy with the object of sight, by exercise of the power which we have. Augustine dwells upon this idea: Tota vita Christiani boni sanctum desiderium est. Quod autem desideras nondum vides; sed desiderando capax efficeris ut cum venerit quod videas implearis. ......Deus differendo extendit desiderium, desiderando extendit animum, extendendo facit capaciorem. And again: Hæc est vita nostra ut desiderando exerceamur.

At the same time it may be urged that the verb (ἐσόμεθα), which describes a being and not a becoming (γενησόμεθα 1 Cor. xv. 37, 54; John x. 16), appears to mark a state which co-exists with the divine manifestation at the first, and does not follow from it. On the other hand the thought of the transfiguring virtue of the divine vision is familiar. Comp. 2 Cor. iii. 18; v. 4; Iren. IV. 38. 3 (a very fine passage).

In either case the central truth is the same. The great confidence of the believer is that he will see the full revelation of the glory of God in Christ, and therefore that when that is made he will be like Him. Time, indeed, before and after, has no place in the eternal.

Augustine strives to emphasise the thought of the verse: Ergo visuri sumus quandam visionem...præcellentem omnes pulcritudines terrenas, auri, argenti, nemorum atque camporum, pulcritudinem maris et aeris, pulcritudinem solis et lunæ, pulcritudinem stellarum, pulcritudinem angelorum: omnia superantem quia ex ipsa pulcra sunt omnia. Quid ergo nos erimus quando hæc videbimus? Quid nobis promissum est? *Similes ei erimus, quoniam videbimus eum sicuti est.* Quomodo potuit lingua sonuit: cetera corde cogitentur.

Philo in a remarkable passage (*de Abr.* § 12, ii. pp. 9 f. M.) speaks of the vision of the 'Father of all things,' as man's highest blessing: ὅτῳ ἐξεγένετο μὴ μόνον τὰ ἄλλα ὅσα ἐν τῇ φύσει δι' ἐπιστήμης καταλαμβάνειν ἀλλὰ καὶ τὸν πατέρα καὶ ποιητὴν τῶν συμπάντων, ὁρᾶν, ἐπ' ἄκρον εὐδαιμονίας ἴστω προεληλυθώς. οὐδὲν γὰρ ἀνωτέρω θεοῦ πρὸς ὃν εἴ τις τὸ τῆς ψυχῆς τείνας ὄμμα ἔφθακε μονὴν εὐχέσθω καὶ στάσιν.

The main elements in the idea of the 'vision' of God seem to be a real knowledge, a direct knowledge, a continuous knowledge, a knowledge which is the foundation of service. The seat of the organ of spiritual sight is the 'heart,' the part of man which is representative of personal character (Eph. i. 18; Matt. v. 8). The 'vision' of God's face appears in the hope of the righteous in the Psalms (Ps. xvii. 15; xi. 7 Hupfeld), while it is recognised as unattainable and unbearable by man in the present earthly life (Ex. xxxiii. 18 ff.). In the new Jerusalem it finds accomplishment, Apoc. xxii. 4, *His servants* (δοῦλοι) *shall do Him service* (λατρεύσουσιν) *and they shall see His face and His name shall be on their foreheads.* As He is light, they shall be made light (comp. Eph. v. 13), and when the sons of God are thus revealed the end of creation will be reached (Rom. viii. 18 ff.).

In treating of this final transfiguἔχων τὴν ἐλπίδα ταύτην ἐπ᾿ αὐτῷ ἀγνίζει ἑαυτὸν καθὼς

ration the Greek Fathers did not scruple to speak of men as being 'deified' (θεοποιεῖσθαι), though the phrase sounds strange to our ears (Athan. *de Inc. Verbi* iv. § 22).

καθώς ἐστιν] *sicuti est* V., *even as He is.* Hitherto the Divine in Christ has been veiled. Hereafter the Godhead will be plain as the Manhood, when, according to Christ's prayer, His disciples shall see His Glory (John xvii. 24). It may be doubted whether it could be said of the Father that men shall see Him 'as He is.' Comp. 1 Cor. xiii. 12, ἄρτι δι᾿ ἐσόπτρου ἐν αἰνίγματι τότε πρόσωπον πρὸς πρόσωπον. Thomas Aquinas discusses at length (*Sum. Theol. Suppl. Qu.* xcii. art. 1) the question whether the human intellect can attain to seeing God in essence (ad videndum Deum per essentiam), and concludes in the affirmative.

'The last words with which [Dr Arnold] closed his last lecture on the New Testament were in commenting on [this verse]. "So too," he said, "in the Corinthians, *For now we see through a glass darkly, but then face to face.* Yes," he added, with marked fervency, "the mere contemplation of Christ shall transform us into His likeness"' (*Life* ii. 329 f.).

3. καὶ πᾶς...ἐπ᾿ αὐτῷ] *et omnis qui habet hanc spem in eo* (*ipso* Aug.) V., *And every one that hath this hope on Him.* The practical conclusion from the great Christian hope of the assimilation of the believer to his Lord is given as a coordinate thought (καί). The conclusion itself is involved in the hope. He who looks forward to becoming like God hereafter must strive after His likeness now: Matt. v. 8; Gal. v. 5, ἐλπίδα δικαιοσύνης ἀπεκδεχόμεθα.

By employing the universal form of expression (πᾶς ὁ ἔχων) instead of the simply descriptive (ὁ ἔχων), St John deals with the exceptional presumption of men who regarded themselves as above the common law. In each case where this characteristic form of language occurs there is apparently a reference to some who had questioned the application of a general principle in particular cases (*vv.* 4, 6, 9, 10, 15; c. ii. 23, 27; iv. 7; v. 1, 4, 18; 2 John 9).

It is remarkable that this is the only place in which St John speaks of the Christian 'Hope,' a characteristic thought of St Paul and St Peter. St Peter speaks of a 'living hope' as the result of a new birth (1 Pet. i. 3).

ἐπ᾿ αὐτῷ] *on Him,* that is, as before, on God in Christ.

The phrase ἔχειν ἐλπίδα ἐπί τινι is not found elsewhere in the N.T. It is distinguished from ἐλπ. ἔχειν εἰς (Acts xxiv. 15) by the idea of 'hope resting upon' in place of 'reaching unto': and from the simple 'hoping on' (ἐλπίζειν ἐπί Rom. xv. 12; 1 Tim. iv. 10) by that of the enjoyment of possession. Comp. i. 3 note (κοινωνίαν ἔχειν).

ἀγνίζει ἑαυτόν] *purifieth himself.* Personal effort is necessarily called out by a definite object of personal devotion. The believer's act is the using what God gives. So Augustine writes: Quis nos castificat nisi Deus? Sed Deus te nolentem non castificat. Ergo quod adjungis voluntatem tuam Deo castificas teipsum. Castificas te non de te sed de illo qui venit ut habitet in te. Tamen quia agis ibi aliquid voluntate ideo et tibi aliquid tributum est.

Comp. James iv. 8; 1 Pet. i. 22; 2 Cor. vii. 1; 1 Tim. v. 22.

ἀγνίζει] *sanctificat* V., *castificat* Aug., *purifieth.* The thought probably is derived from the ceremonial purification required before the appearance in the Divine presence. Comp. John xi. 55 (Acts xxi. 24 ff.); Ex. xix. 10. The spiritual correlative is marked Heb. x. 19 ff.

ἐκεῖνος ἁγνός ἐστιν.

It is not easy to lay down sharply the distinction between ἁγνός, ἁγνίζειν and καθαρός, καθαρίζειν. As far as the usage of the N.T. is concerned, ἁγνός has a personal, an internal, reference which is wanting in καθαρός. Ἁγνός suggests the notion of shrinking from contamination, of a delicate sensibility to pollution of any kind, while καθαρός expresses simply the fact of cleanness. Ἁγνός marks predominantly a feeling, and καθαρός a state. Ἁγνεία comes as the result of an inward effort, καθαρότης by the application of some outward means. He of whom it is said that he ἁγνίζει ἑαυτόν not only keeps himself actually 'pure,' but disciplines and trains himself that he may move more surely among the defilements of the world (1 Tim. v. 22; 1 Pet. iii. 2). Both ἁγνός and καθαρός differ from ἅγιος in that they admit the thought or the fact of temptation or pollution; while ἅγιος describes that which is holy absolutely, either in itself or in idea. God can be spoken of as ἅγιος but not as ἁγνός, while Christ can be spoken of as ἁγνός in virtue of the perfection of His humanity. A man is ἅγιος in virtue of his divine destination (Heb. x. 10; Is. iv. 3 LXX.) to which he is gradually conformed (ἁγιάζεται, Heb. x. 14); he is ἁγνός in virtue of earthly, human discipline. Comp. note on Hebr. vii. 26.

καθὼς ἐκ. ἁγνός ἐστιν] even as He (Christ) is pure. The pronoun ἐκεῖνος, as throughout the Epistle (ii. 6 note), refers to Christ. It is chosen here, though the preceding αὐτός refers to the same divine-human Person, in order to emphasise the reference to the Lord's human life. It is in respect of this only that He can be spoken of as ἁγνός; and in respect of His true humanity it can be said of Him that "He is pure," and not only that "He was pure." The result of the perfection of His earthly disci-

⁴ Πᾶς ὁ ποιῶν τὴν ἁμαρ-

pline (Heb. v. 7 ff.) still abides in His glorified state. For the change of pronouns compare v. 5; John v. 39; xix. 35.

2. The essential character of the children of God (iii. 4—9).

The character of children of God is seen in relation to sin and righteousness. Sin is in its nature irreconcileable with Christianity (vv. 4—6). Sin marks a connexion with the devil as righteousness with Christ (vv. 7, 8). Sin is impossible for the child of God (v. 9). The underlying thought of the action of false teachers (v. 7), who placed salvation in knowledge, is everywhere present.

4—6. The nature of sin is considered in itself as to its manifestation and its essence (v. 4); as to Christ both in His Work and in His Person (v. 5); and as to man negatively and positively (v. 6).

⁴Every one that doeth sin doeth also lawlessness; and sin is lawlessness. ⁵And ye know that he was manifested, that he may take away sins; and in him is no sin. ⁶Every one that abideth in him sinneth not; every one that sinneth hath not seen him neither knoweth him.

4. The transition of thought from vv. 1—3 lies in the idea of 'purification.' This effort corresponds with the fulfilment of man's true destiny, which Christ has again made possible. He who commits sin does in fact violate the divine law; and, more than this, sin and violation of the divine law are absolutely identical. The first clause deals with the practical manifestation of sin and the second with the innermost essence of it.

In vv. 4, 5 the successive clauses are coordinated by καί...καί...καί. In vv. 6—8 clause follows clause without any conjunction.

4. Πᾶς ὁ ποιῶν...] Every one that...

τίαν καὶ τὴν ἀνομίαν ποιεῖ, καὶ ἡ ἁμαρτία ἐστὶν ἡ

Comp. *v.* 3 note. The constant repetition of this form in this group of verses is very impressive.

ὁ ποιῶν τὴν ἁμ.] *qui facit peccatum* (*delictum* Tert.) V., *that doeth sin.* The phrase is distinguished from the simple term 'that sinneth' (ὁ ἁμαρτάνων *v.* 6) by adding the conception of the actual realisation of sin as something which is definitely brought about. This conception is emphasised by the addition of the article (τὴν ἁμαρτίαν). The man does not simply commit a sin (πᾶς ὁ ἁμαρτίαν ποιῶν comp. *v.* 9; I Pet. ii. 22; 2 Cor. xi. 7), but realises sin in its completeness. Comp. Eurip. *Andr.* fr. 150. Compare *vv.* 8, 9, John viii. 34 (τὴν ἁμ.); and contrast James v. 15 κἂν ἁμαρτίας ᾐ πεποιηκώς.

The corresponding phrase is ὁ ποιῶν τὴν δικαιοσύνην *v.* 7 (10), ii. 29. Sin as a whole (ἡ ἁμαρτία) answers to righteousness as a whole (ἡ δικαιοσύνη). For ἡ ἁμαρτία compare Rom. v. 12 (ἁμαρτία *v.* 13); 20 f., vi. 1 ff.

καὶ τὴν ἀνομ. ποιεῖ] *et iniquitatem facit* V., *doeth also lawlessness*, violates a law which claims his loyal obedience (comp. Matt. xiii. 41; vii. 23 οἱ ἐργαζόμενοι τὴν ἀνομ.). And, yet more than this,

ἡ ἁμαρτία ἐστὶν ἡ ἀνομία, *peccatum est iniquitas* V., *sin is lawlessness.* Sin and lawlessness are convertible terms. Sin is not an arbitrary conception. It is the assertion of the selfish will against a paramount authority. He who sins breaks not only by accident or in an isolated detail, but essentially the 'law' which he was created to fulfil.

This 'law' which expresses the divine ideal of man's constitution and growth has three chief applications. There is the 'law' of each man's personal being: there is the 'law' of his relation to things without him: there is the 'law' of his relation to God. To violate any part of this threefold law is to sin, for all parts are divine. (James ii. 10.)

The Mosaic Law was directed in a representative fashion to each of these spheres of duty. It touched upon man's dealing with himself: upon his treatment of creation (of men, animals and crops): upon his duty towards God. In this way it was fitted to bring home to men the divine side of all action.

The origin of sin in selfishness is vividly illustrated by St James (i. 14 f.), who shews also that the neglect of duty, the violation of the law of growth, is sin (James iv. 17). So St John lays down that 'unrighteousness,' the failure to fulfil our obligations to others, is sin (c. v. 17).

Other examples of the use of the article with both subject and predicate, when the two are convertible, occur: Apoc. xix. 10 ἡ μαρτυρία Ἰησοῦ ἐστὶν τὸ πνεῦμα τῆς προφητείας; Matt. vi. 22; I Cor. x. 4; xv. 56; Phil. iii. 19; comp. John i. 4; xv. 1; 2 Cor. iii. 17. The variations in Matt. xiii. 38 f. are instructive (ὁ ἀγρός ἐστιν ὁ κόσμος... ὁ θερισμὸς συντέλεια αἰῶνος).

It is interesting to notice that Bede observes the inadequacy of the Latin rendering: Virtus hujus sententiæ, he says, facilius in lingua Græcorum, qua edita est epistola, comprehenditur, siquidem apud eos *iniquitas* ἀνομία vocatur... Omnes enim qui peccant prævaricationis (Ps. cxix. 119 Lat.) rei sunt, hoc est non solum illi qui datam sibi scriptæ legis scientiam contemnunt, sed et illi qui innocentiam legis naturalis quam in protoplasto omnes accepimus sive infirmitate sive negligentia sive etiam ignorantia corrumpunt.

For the change of order in the two clauses see v. 2 note.

5. Not only is sin a violation of the law of man's being: it sets at

ἀνομία. ⁵καὶ οἴδατε ὅτι ἐκεῖνος ἐφανερώθη ἵνα τὰς
ἁμαρτίας ἄρῃ, καὶ ἁμαρτία ἐν αὐτῷ οὐκ ἔστιν. ⁶πᾶς

5 οἴδατε: οἴδαμεν א the (lat).　　τὰς ἁμ. AB vg me syr hl: +ἡμῶν ℭאC the (lat).
ἐν αὐ. οὐκ ἔ.: οὐκ ἔ. ἐν αὐ. א me the

naught Christ's mission. His work
was to take away sins : He Himself
was sinless. Thus the most elementary
knowledge shews that sin is utterly
alien from the faith.

οἴδατε] *scitis* V., *ye know*. This
appeal to the knowledge of Christians
is characteristic of St John, though it
is found also in St Paul: c. ii. 20 f.,
iv. 2, 14 f., v. 15, 18 f. note; 3 John 12.

ἐκεῖνος ἐφαν.] *ille apparuit* V.,
manifestatus est Aug., *He was manifested*. The subject is not defined
under any particular aspect (*Lamb of
God* John i. 29, *Son of God v.* 8), but
left in its fulness. For ἐκεῖνος see c.
ii. 6 note. It will be observed that in
this verse ἐκεῖνος and αὐτός are naturally referred to the same subject.
Comp. John xix. 35.

ἐφανερώθη] *was manifested*. Comp.
i. 2; ii. 28 notes. The 'manifestation'
of the Lord includes the whole of His
historical Life with its consequences :
His Birth, and Growth, and Ministry,
and Passion, and Resurrection, and
Ascension. Each part of the Revelation contributed in some way to the
removal of sins. The Redemption
and Atonement were wrought out by
His living as well as by His dying.
Compare Matt. viii. 17.

The idea of 'manifestation' in this
connexion involves a previous being.
Thus the term includes not only ὁ ἦν
ἀπ' ἀρχῆς but also ἦν ἐν ἀρχῇ.

For the different phrases used by
St John to describe the Incarnation
see Additional Note.

ἵνα...ἄρῃ] *ut peccatum* (*-ta* Tert.) *au-
ferat* Aug., *ut peccata nostra tolleret*
V., *that He may take away sins*, not
simply do away with the punishment
of them. Comp. i. 9 note.

Tollit autem et dimittendo quæ

facta sunt et adjuvando ne fiant et
perducendo ad vitam ubi fieri omnino
non possint (Bede).

For the sense of αἴρειν compare John
i. 29 note ; and Heb. x. 4 (ἀφαίρειν
ἁμ.); *id.* 11 (περιελεῖν ἁμ.) notes. The
dominant thought here is not that of
the self-sacrifice of Christ, but of His
utter hostility to sin in every shape.
He came to remove all sins even as
He was Himself sinless. It is true
that Christ 'took away' sins by
'taking them upon Him,' by 'bearing
them,' but the simple sense of 'bearing' appears to be foreign to the
context here, though it has found
strong support in the parallel passage
in the Gospel.

The use of the plural 'sins' (τὰς ἁμ.)
distinguishes the exact conception of
Christ's work here from that given in
John i. 29 ('the sin of the world').
The idea is that of the manifold personal realisations of the sin of humanity
which Christ takes away. The phrase
stands without further definition (*sins*
not *our sins*) in order to include the fulness of the truth expressed in c. ii. 2.

For the plural used absolutely see
Rom. vii. 5; Col. i. 14; Heb. i. 3;
(James v. 16 ; 1 Pet. ii. 24). [The com-
mon reading in Eph. ii. 1 is wrong.]

ἁμαρτία ἐν αὐτῷ οὐκ ἔστιν] The clause
is independent and not to be connected with ὅτι. For the statement
and the form of expression compare
John vii. 18 ἀδικία ἐν αὐτῷ οὐκ ἔστιν.
This fact at once explains how Christ
could take away sin, and how sin is incompatible with fellowship with Him.
The tense (*is* not *was*) marks the
eternal character of the Redeemer.
All that belongs to His 'perfected'
manhood (Heb. ii. 10, v. 9) 'is' in Him
no less than His unchanged Divinity.

ὁ ἐν αὐτῷ μένων οὐχ ἁμαρτάνει· πᾶς ὁ ἁμαρτάνων οὐχ

6 πᾶς ὁ ἁμ.:   + καί vg syr vg

The 'purity' of v. 3 is traced back to its inherent source.

The emphasis is thrown upon 'sin,' so that the literal rendering would be: 'sin in Him there is not.'

6. This verse flows directly from the last clause of v. 5. True fellowship with Christ, Who is absolutely sinless, is necessarily inconsistent with sin; and, yet further, the practice of sin excludes the reality of a professed knowledge of Christ. 'No one that abideth in Him sinneth.'

μένων] St John speaks of 'abiding' in Christ and not simply of 'being' in Christ, because his argument rests on the efficacy of continuous human effort. Comp. ii. 5 note.

οὐχ ἁμαρτάνει] sinneth not. The commentary on this phrase is found in c. i. 6. It describes a character, 'a prevailing habit' and not primarily an act. Comp. Tit. iii. 11; Hebr. x. 26. Each separate sinful act does as such interrupt the fellowship, and yet so far as it is foreign to the character of the man, and removed from him (ii. 1), it leaves his character unchanged. This is the truth which Augustine partially expresses when he says that the sin spoken of is the violation of love; for love may be taken fairly to express the essence of the Christian character. Comp. c. v. 18 note.

Compare John xiii. 10.

Bede describes the fact as it is practically embodied when he says: in quantum in eo manet in tantum non peccat; but he leaves out of sight the internal spiritual character.

πᾶς ὁ ἁμ....οὐδὲ ἔγνωκεν αὐτόν] The interruption of the formal parallelism is characteristic of St John. Instead of saying 'every one that sinneth abideth not in (is cut off from) Him,' he substitutes a predicative clause which carries back the mind of the reader to an earlier stage of the fatal

failure, as if he would say: 'In such a case there is no question of 'abiding.' The conditions of fellowship have never been satisfied. Such a one hath not seen Christ (God in Christ) nor yet come to know Him.'

Compare i. 6 f. ('fellowship with Him,' 'fellowship one with another'); i. 8, 9, ii. 4 f. ('the truth is not in us,' 'the love of God is perfected'); vv. 7, 8; iv. 5, 6 a; 7 b, 8; v. 10. In ii. 23 there is a perfect correspondence.

οὐχ ἑώρ....αὐτόν] non vidit eum nec cognovit eum V., hath not seen... neither knoweth. The first word describes the immediate and direct vision of Christ; and the second the personal and detailed appropriation of the truth so presented to the eyes. 'Seeing' expresses briefly the fullest exertion of our utmost faculties of gaining new elements of truth from without: 'knowing' (ἐγνωκέναι), the apprehension and coordination of the truth within. 'Knowing' is less direct and immediate and therefore forms the climax here.

ἑώρακεν] Comp. c. iv. 20; 3 John 11; John i. 18, v. 37, vi. 46, xiv. 7, 9 (Heb. xi. 27).

The use of the word here in connexion with Christ seems to point to some teachers who appealed to their personal sight of the Lord (comp. i. 1 ff.; John xix. 35, xx. 29) as giving authority to their false doctrine. Of such in spite of outward intercourse it could be said that 'they had not seen Christ' (comp. 2 Cor. v. 16).

οὐδὲ ἔγνωκεν] 'neither hath come to know,' i.e. neither knoweth. The point regarded is present and not past. Comp. ii. 3 note.

The statement leaves on one side the question of the indefectibility of grace. It deals with the actual state of the man. Past sight and past knowledge cease to be unless they go forward.

έώρακεν αὐτὸν οὐδὲ ἔγνωκεν αὐτόν. ⁷Τεκνία, μηδεὶς
πλανάτω ὑμᾶς· ὁ ποιῶν τὴν δικαιοσύνην δίκαιός ἐστιν,

7 τεκνία אּB vg syrr; παιδία AC me syrhlmg.   μή τις A.   − τὴν' δικ. אּ*.

Luther expressed the truth when he said 'He who is a Christian is no Christian.'

7, 8. From considering the nature of sin St John passes on to consider the personal spiritual source with which it is connected as righteousness is connected with Christ. Sin is the sign of dependence on the devil whose works Christ came to abolish.

⁷ *Little children, let no one lead you astray: he that doeth righteousness is righteous, even as he is righteous:* ⁸ *he that doeth sin is of the devil, because the devil sinneth from the beginning. Unto this end the Son of God was manifested that he may destroy the works of the devil.*

7. Τεκνία] *Filioli* V., *Little children.* See ii. 12 note. The tenderness of the address is called out by the peril of the situation.

μηδεὶς πλανάτω] *nemo vos seducat* V., *let no one,* even with the most plausible signs of authority (ii. 26), *lead you astray.* The question is one of action not of opinion. Comp. i. 8 note.

ὁ ποιῶν τὴν δικ.] *he that doeth righteousness,* he who gives effect to it in life, who realises it in conduct (c. ii. 29). Compare '*doeth sin*' (*v.* 4 note), '*doeth the truth*' (c. i. 6 note).

'To do righteousness' is more than 'to do righteous acts' (ποιεῖν δίκαια, comp. 1 Pet. iii. 12 ποιεῖν κακά, James iv. 17 καλὸν π.), or even than 'to do the acts of righteousness' (ποιεῖν τὰ δίκαια, comp. *v.* 22 π. τὰ ἀρεστά, Rom. iii. 8 π. τὰ κακά); and it differs from 'doing that which is righteous' (π. τὸ δίκαιον, comp. Rom. xiii. 3 f. π. τὸ ἀγαθόν, τὸ κακόν) by presenting the idea in a less abstract form. Compare Col. iv. 1 (τὸ δίκαιον, τὴν ἰσότητα); iii. 5 (ἀκαθαρσίαν, τὴν πλεονεξίαν).

The exact phrase is different in form from the negative phrase (*v.* 10 note). 'Righteousness' here is the virtue in its completeness and unity (τὴν δικαιοσύνην): in *v.* 10 δικαιοσύνη expresses any particular manifestation of righteousness. Comp. ii. 29; Matt. v. 5.

δίκαιός ἐστιν] Righteousness is the sign of divine sonship (c. ii. 29). The 'doing righteousness' reveals the character and does not create it. The man who is righteous is recognised by his actions. The personal character underlies the deeds. The form of the sentence may be compared with John iii. 31 *he that is of the earth is of the earth and speaketh of the earth.*

καθώς] *sicut* V., *even as.* Christ (ἐκεῖνος c. ii. 6 note) is the One Type of righteousness. The Christian's righteousness, like that of his Master, must extend to the fulness of life. Comp. *v.* 3; ii. 6; iv. 17; John xiii. 15; xv. 12; xvii. 14.

Augustine (whom Bede transcribes) remarks on this comparison between the righteousness of the believer and the righteousness of Christ (see *v.* 2): Videtis quia non semper *sicut* ad parilitatem et æqualitatem refertur... Habemus et nos imaginem Dei, sed non illam quam habet Filius æqualis Patri.

δίκαιός ἐστιν] ii. 29; iv. 17; *v.* 3 notes. Christ gave the complete example of the fulfilment of all man's offices. In Him righteousness was and is the expression of love.

8. The opposite to *v.* 7 is expressed with characteristic variations in the parallelism :

(a) ὁ π. τὴν δικ. ‖ ὁ ποιῶν τὴν ἁμ.
(b) δίκαιός ἐστιν ‖ ἐκ τοῦ διαβ. ἐστίν.
(c) καθὼς ἐ. δ. ἐ. ‖ ὅτι...ὁ διάβ. ἁμ.

The spiritual affinity (b) is in the

καθὼς ἐκεῖνος δίκαιός ἐστιν· ⁸ὁ ποιῶν τὴν ἁμαρτίαν ἐκ
τοῦ διαβόλου ἐστίν, ὅτι ἀπ᾽ ἀρχῆς ὁ διάβολος ἁμαρτάνει. εἰς τοῦτο ἐφανερώθη ὁ υἱὸς τοῦ θεοῦ ἵνα λύσῃ

8 ὁ ποιῶν : ὁ δὲ π. A me (lat).

one case described by the personal character, in the other, directly; while man's character is shewn to be in each case though under different relations (καθώς, ὅτι), a reflection of his spiritual master (c).

ὁ π. τὴν ἁμ.] v. 4 note.

ἐκ τοῦ διαβ. ἐστίν] ex (de, a, all.) diabolo est V., is of the devil, draws from him the ruling principles of his life, as his child. Comp. ii. 16 note; and Additional Note on v. 1. The phrase finds a parallel in was of the evil one, v. 12; and John viii. 44 ye are of your father, the devil. Compare 'to be of the things below' John viii. 23; to be of the world xvii. 16, &c., c. ii. 16. Additional Note on v. 1.

It will be noticed that as St Paul traces back sin to the act of the typical representative of mankind, Adam (Rom. v. 14; 1 Cor. xv. 22), so St John traces it back yet further to a spiritual origin.

Augustine remarks that the devil is not treated in Scripture as the author of any being: Neminem fecit diabolus, neminem genuit, neminem creavit. Sed quicunque fuerit imitatus diabolum quasi de illo natus sit filius diaboli imitando non proprie nascendo. In this connexion it is remarkable that Origen, while he distinctly notices that in relation to the devil St John says ἐστίν ἐκ and not γεγέννηται ἐκ (γεγεννημένος ἐστὶν ἐκ) (in Joh. xx. § 13, iv. 325), elsewhere gives ἐκ τοῦ διαβόλου γεγένηται (γεγέννηται) (Hom. ix. in Jer. § 4, iii. 181; Sch. in Jer. xii. 10, iii. 290; Hom. vi. in Ezech. § 3, iii. 377, Lat.) in quoting the verse freely.

For St John's teaching on the powers of evil see Additional Note on ii. 13.

ὅτι...ἁμαρτάνει] because...the begin-

ning. The force of the argument lies in the recognition of the state of things at the first dawn of human history. From the very beginning we see a power in action hostile to God. Between these two, as between light and darkness, there can be no middle term. He who does not belong to the one belongs to the other. Character reveals the choice. The position of ἀπ᾽ ἀρχῆς at the head of the clause emphasises the thought. Contrast i. 1; ii. 7; iii. 11; and compare ii. 24 note.

ἀπ᾽ ἀρχῆς] ab initio V., a primordio Tert., from the beginning. Comp. i. 1; ii. 7 notes. Sin exists before man.

ἁμαρτάνει] sinneth. See v. 6 note. His sinful action is continuous and present: subjunxit verbum præsentis temporis quia ex quo ab initio cœpit diabolus peccare nunquam desiit (Bede).

εἰς τοῦτο] in hoc V. (ideo, idcirco all.), unto this end, which has been included in the preceding clauses and is defined by what follows.

ἐφανερώθη] See v. 5 note.

ὁ υἱὸς τοῦ θεοῦ] the Son of God. The title of dignity is now expressed for the first time in the Epistle to bring out the nature of the conflict (c. iv. 4). Hitherto the Christ has been spoken of under the title 'the Son' (ii. 22, 23, 24), or more fully 'His (i.e. the Father's) Son' (i. 3). Henceforward 'the Son of God' is His most common name (iv. 15; v. 5, 9 ff., 20). The spiritual adversary of man has a mightier spiritual antagonist. A second Adam answers to the first Adam: the Son of God to the devil.

λύσῃ] dissolvat V., solvat Aug., destroy. 'The works of the devil' are

τὰ ἔργα τοῦ διαβόλου. ⁹πᾶς ὁ γεγεννημένος ἐκ τοῦ
θεοῦ ἁμαρτίαν οὐ ποιεῖ, ὅτι σπέρμα αὐτοῦ ἐν αὐτῷ

represented as having a certain con-
sistency, and coherence. They shew
a kind of solid front. But Christ by
His coming has revealed them in their
complete unsubstantiality. He has
'undone' the seeming bonds by which
they were held together.

The word λύειν occurs literally in
this sense Acts xxvii. 41. Comp.
Eph. ii. 14; John ii. 19, and 2 Pet. iii.
10—12; and Acts v. 38; Gal. ii. 18;
Rom. xiv. 20 &c. (καταλύειν).

The transition to the figurative
sense is seen in Acts xiii. 43 (λυθείσης
τῆς συναγωγῆς), ii. 24. Comp. Ign.
Eph. 13 καθαιροῦνται αἱ δυνάμεις τοῦ
Σατανᾶ καὶ λύεται ὁ ὄλεθρος αὐτοῦ ἐν
τῇ ὁμονοίᾳ ὑμῶν τῆς πίστεως.

The two objects of the 'manifestation' of Christ (vv. 5, 8) cover the
whole work of redemption, 'to take
away sins,' 'to destroy the works of
the devil.'

In this connexion 'the works of the
devil' are gathered up in 'sin' which
is their spring. This the devil has
wrought in men and in the world,
and men make his works their own.
Comp. John viii. 41. These works
under different aspects are spoken of
as 'works of darkness' (Rom. xiii. 12;
Eph. v. 11), and 'of the flesh' (Gal. v.
19). They stand opposed to 'the
works of God' (John ix. 3) and 'the
works of the Christ' (Matt. xi. 2). Augustine brings the thought of 'de-
stroying the works of the devil' into
connexion with man's natural and spiritual births: Si cum nullo peccato
nascimur, quid est quod cum infanti-
bus ad baptismum curritur ut absol-
vantur? Ergo duas nativitates at-
tendite fratres, Adam et Christi...
Nativitas illa trahit secum peccatum,
nativitas ista liberat a peccato.

9. The antagonism of the Christian
to sin is now placed in its last and decisive aspect. Two things are affirmed

of him: 'he doeth no sin' and 'he
cannot sin.' The first fact follows
from the permanence of the vital
power by which he is animated. The
second from the nature of that power,
that it is of God. In the second case
the ἐκ τοῦ θεοῦ is placed emphatically
first; 'he cannot sin, because it is of
God, and of no other, that he hath
been born.'

9 Every one that is begotten of God
doeth no sin, because his seed abideth
in him; and he cannot sin because he
is begotten of God.

ὁ γεγεννημένος ἐκ τοῦ θεοῦ] qui natus
est ex Deo V., that is begotten of God.
Comp. ii. 29. The phrase occurs here
first in the epistle in its full form.
Comp. iv. 7, v. 1 (4), 18.

John i. 13 (iii. 3, 5 ff.).

The exact form is important. The
perfect (ὁ γεγεννημένος) marks not only
the single act (aor. ἐγεννήθησαν John
i. 13;' c. v. 18) but the continuous
presence of its efficacy. 'He that
hath been born and still remains a
child of God.' See Additional Note
on v. 1.

ἁμαρτίαν οὐ ποιεῖ] Compare v. 4
note. A fine phrase of Athenagoras
will serve as a comment on this view
of the Christian life: οἷς ὁ βίος ὡς
πρὸς στάθμην τὸν θεὸν κανονίζεται
('Christians for whom the conception
of God is the ideal standard of life')
...ἵστε τούτους, μηδ' εἰς ἔννοιάν ποτε τοῦ
βραχυτάτου ἐλευσομένους ἁμαρτήματος
(Leg. pro Christ. c. 31).

σπέρμα αὐτοῦ] semen ipsius V., his
seed, the principle of life which He
has given continues to be the ruling
principle of the believer's growth.
God gives, as it were, of Himself to
the Christian. He does not only work
upon him and leave him. The germ
of the new life is that out of which
the mature man will in due time be
developed. Comp. John i. 13.

μένει, καὶ οὐ δύναται ἁμαρτάνειν, ὅτι ἐκ τοῦ θεοῦ γεγέννηται.   ¹⁰'Ἐν τούτῳ φανερά ἐστιν τὰ τέκνα τοῦ θεοῦ καὶ τὰ τέκνα τοῦ διαβόλου· πᾶς ὁ μὴ ποιῶν

The instrument by which this vital element is conveyed is the 'word': James i. 18; 1 Pet. i. 23; Luke viii. 12, 15.

The absence of the article (σπέρμα not τὸ σπέρμα) directs attention to the character of the divine principle and not to the divine principle communicated in the particular case. See v. 10 note.

οὐ δύναται ἁμ.] he cannot sin. The ideas of divine sonship and sin are mutually exclusive. As long as the relationship with God is real (ὅτι ἐκ θεοῦ γεγέννν.) sinful acts are but accidents. They do not touch the essence of the man's being. The impossibility of sinning in such a case lies in the moral nature of things. Comp. John v. 19, 30, xii. 39, xiv. 17, &c.

Augustine again insists that the reference is to the great commandment of love: Est quoddam peccatum quod non potest admittere ille qui natus est ex Deo, et quo non admisso solvuntur cetera, quo admisso confirmantur cetera. Quod est hoc peccatum? Facere contra mandatum Christi, contra testamentum novum (John xiii. 34). The explanation is true so far as love is the determining element in the Christian character.

3. The outward manifestation of the children of God (10—12).

The spiritual affinities of men are shewn by two patent signs, righteousness and love (v. 10); and these signs correspond to two archetypal patterns, the Gospel, that is, the Life of Christ (v. 11), and the history of Cain (v. 12).

¹⁰In this the children of God are manifest and the children of the devil: every one that doeth not

righteousness is not of God, and he that loveth not his brother. ¹¹Because this is the message which ye heard from the beginning that we should love one another: ¹²not as Cain was of the wicked one and slew his brother; and wherefore slew he him? because his own works were evil and his brother's righteous.

10. Life reveals the children of God. They bear characteristic marks which stamp their action and their feeling, their conduct and the motive of their conduct. They embody righteousness in deed. They acknowledge the ties which Christ has established among Christians and so potentially among men. They practically realise the law of man's original constitution, and the law of man's redemption.

Ἐν τούτῳ] In hoc V. (Ex hoc F.), In this, in this fact of the essential sinlessness of the Christian's life, which is followed out into its main aspects in the verse which follows (comp. c. ii. 3 note).

τὰ τέκνα τοῦ θεοῦ] filii Dei V., the children of God. See v. 1 note.

St John divides the world sharply into two classes. Looking at the spiritual characteristics of life he admits no intermediate class. For him there is only light and darkness, and no twilight. He sees only 'life' and 'death.'

φανερά] manifesti V., manifestati Aug., manifest, so that all men may see what they are: Matt. xii. 16; Acts vii. 13; 1 Cor. xi. 19. That which is in its essence secret is thus revealed before the eyes of men. Comp. Mark iv. 22; 2 Cor. v. 10 f.

τὰ τέκνα τοῦ διαβόλου] filii diaboli V., the children of the devil. The phrase is unique. Compare Eph. ii. 3 τέκνα φύσει ὀργῆς. 2 Pet. ii. 14 κατάρας τέκνα. And also: Matt. xiii. 38

δικαιοσύνην οὐκ ἔστιν ἐκ τοῦ θεοῦ, καὶ ὁ μὴ ἀγαπῶν
τὸν ἀδελφὸν αὐτοῦ. ¹¹ὅτι αὕτη ἐστὶν ἡ ἀγγελία ἣν

10 ὁ μὴ ποιῶν δικ. אABC me syrr (lat): ὁ μὴ ὢν δίκαιος vg the syr hl mg.
δικαιοσύνην אB : τὴν δικ. AC. Comp. v. 7.   11 ἀγγελία AB vg: ἐπαγγελία אC me
the syrr (lat). Comp. i. 5.

οἱ υἱοὶ τοῦ πονηροῦ; xxiii. 15 υἱὸς γεέν-
νης; Acts xiii. 10 υἱὲ διαβόλου.

πᾶς ὁ μὴ π. δ.] *Every one...* Compare *v.* 3 note. By expressing the
characterisation of Divine sonship in
a negative form, St John enforces the
necessary universality of the condition which he lays down, and gives a
pointed warning against those who
trusted in the Christian name. It is
not only true that every one that
doeth righteousness 'hath been born
of God' (ii. 29) and 'is of God' (3 John
11) and shares the character of Christ
(*v.* 7), but it is true also that to do
righteousness is a necessity for him
who is of God. A Christian must be
active and not passive only. To fail
either in deed or in word (c. iv. 3 ὁ μὴ·
ὁμολογεῖ) is fatal to the reality of the
divine connexion.

ὁ μὴ ποιῶν δικ.] *qui non est justus*
V. (*qui non facit justitiam* F.), *that
doeth not righteousness.* It has been
already noticed (*v.* 7 note) that the
phrase used here is different from
that used in *v.* 7, ii. 29. Here 'righteousness' (δικαιοσύνη) expresses that
which bears a particular character: in
the former passage 'righteousness'
(ἡ δικαιοσύνη) expresses the idea
realised in its completeness. The
same general distinction is to be
observed in the use of other like
words in the Epistle: ἁμαρτία *vv.*
5, 9, v. 16 f.; ἡ ἁμαρτία *vv.* 4, 8;
ἀγάπη iv. 8, 16; ἡ ἀγάπη (ii. 5, 15),
iii. 16, iv. 7, 10, 12, 16 ff. (v. 3); ζωή
v. 15, v. 11, 13, 16, 20; ἡ ζωή i. 2, ii.
25, iii. 14, v. 12; ἀλήθεια 3 John 3;
ἡ ἀλήθεια i. 6, 8, ii. 4, 21, iii. 19, iv. 6,
v. 6; 2 John 1, 2; 3 John 8.

The full force of the article will also
be felt in the following places: i. 6 ἐν

τῷ σκότει, ii. 9 ἐν τῷ φωτί, iii. 4 ἡ
ἀνομία, iv. 18 τῇ γλώσσῃ, v. 10 τὴν
μαρτυρίαν (v. 21 τῶν εἰδώλων). On the
other hand the absence of the article
in the following places is significant:
in ii. 18 ἐσχάτη ὥρα, *v.* 9 σπέρμα.
From the nature of the case anarthrous forms occur in predicates and
negative sentences : yet see iii. 4, v. 6.

οὐκ ἔ. ἐ. τ. θ.] Comp. iv. 3 note ;
Additional Note on *v.* 1.

καὶ ὁ μὴ ἀγ. τ. ἀδ.] *and he that loveth
not his brother.* Comp. ii. 10 note.
This clause is not a mere explanation
of that which precedes but the expression of it in its highest Christian
form. Righteousness involves the fulfilment of all law, of relations to God
and to man, both personally and
socially. The love of Christian for
Christian, resting on the sense of a
divine fellowship (c. i. 3) carries forward to its loftiest embodiment the
righteousness which man can reach.

Augustine says in striking words
which were adopted by Bede: Quidquid vis habe; hoc solum [caritatem]
non habeas : nihil tibi prodest. Alia
si non habeas hoc habe, et implesti
legem.

11, 12. The revelation of character
is traced back to the type given in
the portraiture of the first fulfilment
of man's ideal in the Gospel, and of
the first sin after the Fall.

11. ὅτι...] *Because...* The whole
aim of the Gospel is the creation and
strengthening of love. To this Christ's
life of sacrifice pointed from first to
last. The record of His life is the
message of the Gospel.

ἡ ἀγγελία] *adnuntiatio* V., *mandatum* F., *repromissio* (ἐπαγγελία) Lucf.,
the message. Comp. i. 5 note.

ἠκούσατε ἀπ' ἀρχῆς, ἵνα ἀγαπῶμεν ἀλλήλους· ¹²οὐ καθὼς Καὶν ἐκ τοῦ πονηροῦ ἦν καὶ ἔσφαξεν τὸν ἀδελφὸν
αὐτοῦ· καὶ χάριν τίνος ἔσφαξεν αὐτόν; ὅτι τὰ ἔργα
αὐτοῦ πονηρὰ ἦν, τὰ δὲ τοῦ ἀδελφοῦ αὐτοῦ δίκαια.

ἀπ' ἀρχῆς] *from the beginning.* See
ii. 7 note. The first tidings of Christianity contain this lesson.

ἵνα ἀγαπῶμεν ἀλλ.] *ut diligatis al-*
terutrum V., *diligamus invicem* Aug.,
that we love one another... The
words do not simply give the contents of the message, but its aim, its
purpose. The fundamental declaration of Christ's Life and Work is
directed to this end, that men should
be moved by it to self-sacrifice. For
this use of ἵνα see *v.* 23; iv. 21;
John xiii. 34; xv. 12, 17. The particle not unfrequently expresses an
effort or an aim suggested by the
words which precede: c. v. 3; iv.
17; 2 John 6; John iv. 34; vi. 29;
viii. 56; xv. 13; xvii. 3. Sometimes
it indicates a divine purpose which is
not at once obvious: *v.* 1; i. 9; John
xii. 23; xvi. 2, 32.

The phrase '*to love one another*'
(*v.* 23 note) differs in shade of meaning from 'loving the brethren' (*v.* 14).
'Loving one another' expresses the
full social energy of the Christian
life: 'loving the brethren' points to
the personal feeling of one towards
the body.

12. οὐ καθώς...] *not as*... The construction is irregular and elliptical.
Comp. John vi. 58. The clause without the negative would have run on
naturally with *v.* 10 ...'that loveth
not his brother, even as Cain was of
the evil one and slew his brother.'
Cain shewed his dependence on the
devil by want of love and hatred
of righteousness. But the insertion
of *v.* 11, the positive rule of Christians, leads to the insertion of the
negative before the typical example
of the opposite character. 'We do
not (or We shall not) present the

type of selfishness, even as Cain was
of the evil one...' 'The case is not
with us as it was with Cain; he
was of the evil one...' The use of
the direct negative οὐ requires that
the sentence should be treated as
independent and not connected with
ἵνα (μηδὲ ὦμεν ἐκ τοῦ πονηροῦ καθὼς
Καίν...).

The history of the first death naturally attracted wide attention as
presenting in a representative and impressive form the issues of selfishness,
self-will, sin. Comp. Jude 11; Heb.
xi. 4; xii. 24. Philo discusses the
history in a special book. In Clem.
Hom. iii. 25 it is said of Cain: φονεὺς
ἦν καὶ ψεύστης καὶ μετὰ ἁμαρτιῶν ἡσυ-
χάζειν μηδὲ ἐπὶ τῷ ἄρχειν θέλων.

ἐκ τοῦ πονηροῦ ἦν] *ex maligno erat*
V., *was of the evil one.* Comp. *v.* 8 ἐκ
τοῦ διαβόλου ἐστίν note; ii. 13 τὸν
πονηρόν note. The name is chosen
here in order to connect the works of
Cain (πονηρὰ ἦν) with their spiritual
source.

ἔσφαξεν] *occidit* V., *slew.* The word
occurs elsewhere in the N.T. only in the
Apocalypse. It expresses properly the
slaughter of a victim. Here it seems
to point to the deliberate determination of the murder.

καὶ χάριν τίνος...] *et propter quid*
V., *and wherefore*... This unusual
mode of expression (comp. *v.* 17),
appears to be adopted in order to bring
out sharply that the murder of a
brother came from hatred of righteousness. Cain lost practical sympathy
with his brother; and so in the end
he slew him.

This use of χάριν occurs in this
place only in the writings of St John.
Elsewhere in the N. T. it stands (as
generally) after its case. It expresses

¹³ Μὴ θαυμάζετε, ἀδελφοί, εἰ μισεῖ ὑμᾶς ὁ κόσμος.

13 μὴ θαυμ. ABC^{corr} vg me the syr hl: +καὶ' μὴ θαυμ. ℵC* syr vg.   ἀδελφοί
ℵABC vg: +μου ⲥ̄ me the syrr.

commonly an object aimed at (Eph. iii. 1, 14; 1 Tim. v. 14; Gal. iii. 19, Lgtft. &c.), but also an antecedent ground (Luke vii. 47).

ὅτι...] *because...* The explanation given is an interpretation of the history in Gen. iv. The sacrifices (Heb. xi. 4) answered to the characters of the brothers, and God's judgment upon them gave occasion for the open revelation of character which followed.

Augustine traces the temptation of Cain to envy: Qui invidet non amat. Peccatum diaboli est in illo... Cecidit enim et invidit stanti. Non ideo voluit dejicere ut ipse staret sed ne solus caderet.

III. BROTHERHOOD IN CHRIST AND THE HATRED OF THE WORLD (iii. 13—24).

There appear to be three main divisions of the section:

1. *Hatred and love* (13—15).
2. *The manifestation of love* (16—18).
3. *The fruit of love* (19—24).

St John starts from the thought of hatred as the characteristic of the world. Over against this is love, the necessary sign of the presence of the new life of Christians. This love must be moulded on the pattern of Christ's sacrifice, and extend to the fulness of life. And the fruit of love is confidence, which issues in perfect sympathy.

1. *Hatred and love* (13—15).

The thought of Cain leads to the consideration of the Cain-like character. Hatred is the mark of the world, which is 'dead' (13). Love among Christians is the sign of a new life (14). And consequently hatred among Christians is the sign not only of the absence of life but of the destruction of life (15).

¹³*Marvel not, brethren, if the world hateth you.* ¹⁴*We know that we have passed out of death into life, because we love the brethren: he that loveth not abideth in death.* ¹⁵*Every one that hateth his brother is a murderer; and ye know that no murderer hath eternal life abiding in him.*

13. Love has been presented as the necessary mark of the Christian. Still it is met by hatred. This however cannot but be so. Love is the sign of a change from death to life. They who remain in death must shew their real nature (hatred) towards the living. Terrible as Cain's history is, it is still realised in essence.

Μὴ θαυμάζετε] *Nolite mirari* V., *Marvel not.* For the thought compare John xv. 18 ff., xvi. 1 ff.

The words occur again John v. 28, and in another form John iii. 7 μὴ θαυμάσῃς. The latter place is the only example in the Gospel or Epistles (John xix. 24 is not strictly parallel) of the imperative construction of μή with aor. subj. which occurs more frequently than the construction with pres. imp. in the Apocalypse (vi. 6, vii. 3, x. 4, xi. 2, xxii. 10). A comparison of John iii. 7 with the present passage brings out the difference of meaning in the two constructions. There the thought is of the special feeling aroused by the single statement, here of the continuous feeling stirred by the whole temper of men (comp. ii. 15, iv. 1). Comp. 1 Pet. ii. 17; John ii. 16 note.

For θαυμάζειν εἰ see Mark xv. 44.

ἀδελφοί] *brethren.* This is the only place in the Epistle where this title of address is used (ii. 7 is a false reading). It contains an implicit argument. By emphasising the new relation in which Christians stand one to another it implies that this position of necessary

¹⁴ἡμεῖς οἴδαμεν ὅτι μεταβεβήκαμεν ἐκ τοῦ θανάτου εἰς
τὴν ζωήν, ὅτι ἀγαπῶμεν τοὺς ἀδελφούς· ὁ μὴ ἀγαπῶν

14 τοὺς ἀδ. + ἡμῶν ℵ syr vg.   ὁ μὴ ἀγ. ℵAB vg.: +τὸν ἀδελφόν [αὐτοῦ] ʓC
me syrr.

mutual affection is characteristic of
them as distinguished from other men
('the world'). The title is common
in St James (ἀδελφοί, ἀδελφοί μου),
and not unfrequent in St Paul and in
the Epistle to the Hebrews. It is not
found in the first Epistle of St Peter
or St Jude.

The three forms which St John
borrows from the family to express
Christian relations preserve each their
proper meaning. 'Brethren' expresses
the idea of Christian equality in virtue
of the common life: 'Children' (τεκνία)
that of spiritual dependence in the
order of the new life with the prospect of growth: 'Little ones' (παιδία)
that of subordination and immaturity.
In contrast with these 'Beloved' is
simply the personal manifestation of
feeling.

εἰ μισεῖ] si odit V., if...hateth you.
This is assumed as a fact (comp. c. iv.
11; v. 9; John xv. 18); and by the
order the stress is thrown here upon
the verb and not (as in John xv.
18 ff.) upon the pronoun or the subject. Hatred is characteristic of 'the
world' (mundus V., hic mundus F.).

14. ἡμεῖς οἴδαμεν] nos scimus V.
We (ἡμεῖς) as distinguished from the
world, know by the essential nature
of our faith, by our own inward experience....The fact that we are conscious
of a love for Christians as Christians
is a proof to us that we have entered
upon a new life: that we now first
truly live. The passage has been
made: the new sphere of being has
been gained. Life is not future but
present. Compare the simple οἴδαμεν
in v. 2.

μεταβεβήκαμεν] translati sumus V.,
have passed... Comp. John v. 24 (xiii.
1). This love was indeed the accept-

ance in faith of Christ's 'word' (c. ii.
7, iii. 11).

ἐκ τοῦ θ. εἰς τὴν ζ.] de morte in vitam
V., out of death into life. Death and
life are regarded as the two spheres
in which men move, and they are presented in their substantive fulness
'the death which is truly death,' 'the
life which is truly life' (ὁ θάνατος, ἡ
ζωή). Ὁ θάνατος is found here and
in the following clause in St John's
Epistles; in the Gospel it occurs only
in the parallel v. 24 (xi. 13 is different).
Ὁ θάνατος is personified in Apoc. i. 18;
vi. 8, ix. 6, xx. 13 f. (xxi. 4). Compare
Acts ii. 24; Rom. v. 12 ff., viii. 2; 1
Cor. xv. 21 ff.; 2 Cor. iv. 12; 2 Tim. i.
10 (opposed to ζωή); Heb. ii. 14. For
ἡ ζωή compare i. 2 note; John v. 24;
Matt. vii. 14 (opposed to ἡ ἀπώλεια),
xviii. 8 f., xix. 17; (Mark ix. 43, 45);
Acts iii. 15; 2 Cor. v. 4. The depth
of the expression is lost both in Latin
and in English.

'To enter into life' (εἰσελ. εἰς τὴν ζ.) is
a phrase characteristic of St Matthew
(xviii. 8 f., xix. 17; comp. vii. 14) and
of St Mark (ix. 43, 45). In this
largest sense 'life' (ἡ ζωή) is the fulfilment of the highest idea of being:
perfect truth in perfect action. Compare 2 Tim. i. 10 καταργήσαντος μὲν
τὸν θάνατον φωτίσαντος δὲ ζωὴν καὶ
ἀφθαρσίαν, where in the second member the thought is of 'life' in the
abstract and not of the Christian fulfilment of the whole conception of life.

ὅτι...ὅτι...] quoniam...quoniam...
V., that...because... Active love is the
sign of life and not the ground of life.
Comp. Luke vii. 47. The connexion
is 'we know because...' and not 'we
have passed because...'

τοὺς ἀδ.] the brethren. The simple
phrase (3 John 5, 10) is more expres-

μένει ἐν τῷ θανάτῳ. ¹⁵πᾶς ὁ μισῶν τὸν ἀδελφὸν
αὐτοῦ ἀνθρωποκτόνος ἐστίν, καὶ οἴδατε ὅτι πᾶς ἀνθρωποκτόνος οὐκ ἔχει ζωὴν αἰώνιον ἐν αὐτῷ μένου-

15 ἑαυτοῦ B.   αυτω B: ἑαυτῷ ℵAC.

sive than 'our brethren.' This is the
only place in which the exact words
occur (ἀγ. τοὺς ἀδελφούς). Elsewhere
St John says ἀγ. ἀλλήλους (v. 11 note).
'Αγ. τὸν ἀδ. occurs ii. 10; iii. 10; iv. 20.
See Additional Note.

In view of the imperfection of
Christians Augustine says: Viget
[gloria caritatis] sed adhuc in hieme:
viget radix sed quasi aridi sunt rami.
Intus est medulla quæ viget, intus
sunt folia arborum, intus fructus; sed
æstatem expectant.

ὁ μὴ ἀγαπῶν] qui non diligit V.,
he that loveth not. The omission of
his brother, according to the true
text, strengthens the thought. The
feeling is regarded in its completest
form.

μένει ἐν τῷ θ.] abideth (permanet
F.) in death. There is a moral vis
inertiæ. It is not said that he dies.
Death is his natural state. It follows that love and life are convertible
terms. Si in morte manet qui non
diligit, in qua morte manet qui odit?
(Petr. Ven. [ap. Bernard. Epp.] Ep.
229 § 5.)

Compare John iii. 36.

15. The hatred of 'the world' can
cause no marvel: it is, in a certain
sense, natural. But hatred may find
place among 'the brethren' (ii. 9, 11).
There are Cains in the new family.
Such hatred is essentially identical
with murder, not simply as being the
first step towards it but as involving
the same moral position. It is moreover in the man himself the destruction of that life which is love.

πᾶς ὁ...] Every one that hateth...
though he bear the name of Christ.
Comp. c. iii. 3.

ἀνθρωποκτόνος] homicida V., murderer. The word is used of the devil,

John viii. 44. Among men Cain is
the type.

οἴδατε] ye know. Comp. c. v. 18
note.

πᾶς...οὐκ...] Comp. ii. 19 note.

πᾶς ἀνθρωποκτόνος] Omnis inquit
homicida: scilicet non solum ille qui
ferro verum et ille qui odio fratrem
insequitur (Bede).

ζ. αἰ. ἐν αὐτῷ μέν.] eternal life
abiding in him. The addition of
the last words brings out the thought
that 'eternal life' must (under, the
circumstances of our present life) be
a continuous power, and a communicated gift (comp. John vi. 53).

The whole phrase is unique. Elsewhere 'the word' (ii. 14; John v. 38;
comp. xv. 7), the 'unction' (ii. 27), 'the
seed of God' (iii. 9), 'the love of God'
(iii. 17), 'the truth' (2 John 2) are
said to 'abide' in the believer; and so
also God (v. 24, iv. 12, 13, 15 f.) and
Christ (John vi. 56, xv. 5). Even to
the last man has not 'life in himself.'
This is the divine prerogative alone.

2. The manifestation of love (vv.
16—18).

It has been shewn that love is the
sign of the Christian life. It is now
shewn that love must be fashioned
after the pattern of Christ who made
it known in sacrifice (v. 16). Such
love extends to the common intercourse of life (v. 17); and must be at
once active and real (v. 18).

¹⁶ In this we know love, because he
laid down his life for us; and we
ought to lay down our lives for the
brethren. ¹⁷ But whosoever has the
world's goods, and beholdeth his
brother in need, and shutteth up his
heart from him, how abideth the love
of God in him? ¹⁸ Little children,

σαν.   16ʹΕν τούτῳ ἐγνώκαμεν τὴν ἀγάπην, ὅτι
ἐκεῖνος ὑπὲρ ἡμῶν τὴν ψυχὴν αὐτοῦ ἔθηκεν· καὶ ἡμεῖς
ὀφείλομεν ὑπὲρ τῶν ἀδελφῶν τὰς ψυχὰς θεῖναι.   17 ὃς
δ᾽ ἂν ἔχῃ τὸν βίον τοῦ κόσμου καὶ θεωρῇ τὸν ἀδελφὸν

16 τὴν ἀγ.+τοῦ θεοῦ vg.   θεῖναι ℵABC: τιθέναι ς.

let us not love in word, neither with
the tongue, but in deed and truth.

16. Ἐν τούτῳ] In this, see c. ii. 3
note. The truth which has been
enunciated, the self-sacrificing character of love, as opposed to the murder-
ous character of hatred, opens the way
to the most complete revelation of love.
The 'this,' as elsewhere, looks both
backwards and forwards.

ἐγνώκαμεν] cognovimus V., cognoscimus Aug., we know as the result of
divine teaching: we have learnt and
now hold the lesson for ever. This
knowledge of experience is contrasted
with the knowledge of intuition (οἴδατε) in v. 15. Comp. John xv. 13.

τὴν ἀγάπην] See Additional Note.

ἐκεῖνος] He, Christ. See ii. 6 note.

τὴν ψυχὴν αὐτοῦ ἔθηκεν] animam
suam posuit V., laid down His life.
The phrase is peculiar to St John,
John x. 11 (note), 15, 17 ff., xiii. 37 ff.,
xv. 13.

This is the only passage in the
Epistle in which St John uses ὑπὲρ in
behalf of (comp. 3 John 7). It occurs
in the Gospel in similar connexions not
unfrequently: vi. 51; x. 11, 15; xi. 50
ff.; xiii. 37 f.; xv. 13; xvii. 19; xviii.
14. Contrast περί c. ii. 2; iv. 10.

The image appears to be that of
divesting oneself of a thing (John xiii.
4). Compare 'animam ponere,' 'de-
ponere.'

καὶ ἡμεῖς ὀφείλομεν] and we ought…
as a consequence of this knowledge;
but St John regards the duty as included in the knowledge (and we
ought) and not as logically deduced
from it (wherefore we ought). Comp.
v. 3. The obligation lies in the perception of the relation in which we

stand to one another and to Christ.
That which constrains us is not only
His example, but the truth which
that example reveals. Comp. v. 7.
For ὀφείλομεν see ii. 6 note. Ignatius
speaking of himself in the spirit of
this passage says to the Ephesians:
ἀντίψυχον ὑμῶν ἐγώ (ad Eph. 21;
comp. ad Smyrn. 10; ad Polyc. 2, 6).
The words addressed by St John to
the young Robber sound like an echo
of it: ἂν δέῃ τὸν σὸν θάνατον ἑκὼν ὑπο-
μενῶ, ὡς ὁ Κύριος τὸν ὑπὲρ ἡμῶν· ὑπὲρ
σοῦ τὴν ψυχὴν ἀντιδώσω τὴν ἐμήν
(Euseb. H. E. iii. 23).

17. St John turns from considering
the greatness of our obligation to notice
the ordinary character of failure. By
the transition he suggests that there
is a danger in indulging ourselves in
lofty views which lie out of the way of
common experience. We may therefore try ourselves by a far more home-
ly test. The question is commonly
not of dying for another but of communicating to another the outward
means of living. If we are found
wanting here, we need look no further
for judgment.

ὃς δ᾽ ἂν ἔχῃ] Qui habuerit V. Comp.
ii. 5 note.

τὸν βίον τοῦ κόσμου] substantiam
vitæ V., facultates mundi Aug., the
life of the world, 'the substance of
the world,' as contrasted with 'life
eternal' (v. 15). Comp. Luke xv. 12
(τὸν βίον); ii. 16 note. The phrase
includes all the endowments which
make up our earthly riches, wealth,
station, intellect. It has been finely
said of a great teacher that 'he was
tender to dulness as to all forms of
poverty.'

αὐτοῦ χρείαν ἔχοντα καὶ κλείσῃ τὰ σπλάγχνα αὐτοῦ
ἀπ᾽ αὐτοῦ, πῶς ἡ ἀγάπη τοῦ θεοῦ μένει ἐν αὐτῷ;
¹⁸Τεκνία, μὴ ἀγαπῶμεν λόγῳ μηδὲ τῇ γλώσσῃ ἀλλὰ

18 τεκνία ℵABC (vg) syrhl: +μου ς syr vg me the (vg).　　τῇ γλ. ABC:
–τῇ ςℵ.

θεωρῇ] *behold* as a spectacle on
which he allows his eyes to rest. This
is the only place where the verb occurs in St John's Epistles; and elsewhere in the Epistles it is found only
in Heb. vii. 4. Comp. Apoc. xi. 11 f.
The word is common in the Gospel of
St John and is always used with its
full meaning. See John ii. 23 note.

χρείαν ἔχοντα] *necesse habere* V.,
egere F., *esurientem, egentem* Aug.
The rendering of the Vulgate is
suggested by ii. 27. See note there
for the absolute use of χρ. ἔχειν.

κλείσῃ τὰ σπλ.] *clauserit viscera sua
ab eo* V., *shuts up his heart from him*
so that the destitute brother can find
no access to his sympathy. The phrase
'to shut up the heart' is apparently
unique. It expresses the interposi-
tion of a barrier between the sufferer
and the tender feelings of his brother.
Comp. Ps. lxxvii. 10 (רח קפץ συνέχειν
τοὺς οἰκτιρμούς LXX.). Τὰ σπλάγχνα is
found here only in the writings of St
John (it occurs in St Luke and St
Paul).

πῶς...;] *how doth...?* The interro-
gative construction is similar to that
in *v.* 12.

ἡ ἀ. τοῦ θ.] *caritas Dei* V., *dilectio
Dei* Aug., *the love of God*, the love of
which God is at once the object and
the author and the pattern. Comp.
ii. 5 note.

μένει] *abide*...as a continuous active
power. Comp. *v.* 15.

18. Τεκνία] *Filioli* V., *Little children*. The word of address is changed
(*v.* 13). The father now pleads with
those who draw their being from him.

μὴ...λόγῳ μηδὲ τῇ γλ.] *not...with
word, neither with the tongue*, in
theory as opposed to action; with

mere outward expression as opposed
to the genuine movement of our whole
being.

λόγῳ...ἐν ἔργῳ...] *with word...in
deed*... The slight change of construction marks the difference between the
instrument and the sphere of the manifestation of love. It must find scope
in our true and full life. For ἐν ἔργῳ
καὶ ἀλ. compare John iv. 23 f. ἐν
πνεύματι καὶ ἀληθείᾳ.

'If love depends on a word, when
the word ceaseth the love ceaseth.
Such was the love of Balak and Balaam' (Jalkut Reub. 145. 4: Schoettgen). The passage quoted from *Aboth*
v. 22 is wholly different in sense.

3. *The fruit of love (vv.* 19—24).

As St John has spoken of the necessity and of the pattern of love so
now he goes on to speak of its fruit.
The fruit of love is confidence. Such
confidence stills the condemnation
which the heart pronounces against
the believer (*vv.* 19, 20). It finds
its expression in prayers, which are
necessarily answered, because they are
the voice of obedient love (*vv.* 21—23).
It issues in the fulness of sympathy
(*v.* 24).

¹⁹ *In this we shall know that we
are of the truth, and shall assure our
heart before him,* ²⁰ *whereinsoever
our heart may condemn us; because
God is greater than our heart and
knoweth all things.* ²¹*Beloved, if our
heart condemn us not, we have boldness towards God,* ²² *and whatsoever
we ask we receive from him, because
we observe his commandments and
do the things that are pleasing in his
sight.* ²³ *And this is his commandment, that we should believe the name*

ἐν ἔργῳ καὶ ἀληθείᾳ.   ¹⁹Ἐν τούτῳ γνωσόμεθα
ὅτι ἐκ τῆς ἀληθείας ἐσμέν, καὶ ἔμπροσθεν αὐτοῦ πείσομεν τὴν καρδίαν ἡμῶν ²⁰ὅτι ἐὰν καταγινώσκῃ ἡμῶν

ἐν ἔ. ℵABC: – ἐν ϛ.   19 ἐν τ. AB vg me syrhl: + καὶ΄ ἐν τ. ℵC the syrvg.
γνωσόμεθα ℵABC me the: γινώσκομεν ϛ vg syrr.   τὴν κ. A*B the syrvg: τὰς
κ. ℵA**C vg me syrhl.

of his Son Jesus Christ and love one
another, even as he gave us commandment. ²⁴ And he that observeth his
commandments abideth in him and
he in him; and in this we know that
he abideth in us, from the Spirit
which he gave us.

19. Ἐν τούτῳ] In this, the consciousness of active and sincere love
of the brethren, resting upon and
moulded by the love of Christ.

γνωσόμεθα] cognoscemus V., we shall
know, perceive. The future expresses
the dependence of the knowledge upon
the fulfilment of the specified condition. Again it is to be noticed that
the knowledge which comes through
outward experience stands in contrast
with the knowledge which belongs to
the idea of faith v. 14 (οἴδαμεν).

ἐκ τῆς ἀλ. ἐσμέν] ex veritate sumus
V., are of the truth, draw the power
of our being from the Truth as its
source. Comp. ii. 16. Christ Himself
is revealed as the Truth, in whom the
right relations of man to man and to
God and to the world are perfectly
presented (comp. John xviii. 37). So
far then as the Christian is like Him,
he is 'of the truth.' The conception
of being 'a child of the Truth' is different from that of being 'a child
of God,' though practically the two
are identical. In the latter case the
thought is of the presence of the divine
principle as divine: in the former, of
the fulfilment of all the offices of man.

καὶ ἔμπροσθεν αὐτοῦ...] and, as a
consequence of the knowledge of our
complete dependence upon the Truth,
we shall assure our hearts before Him,
i.e. in the presence of God. The antecedent is supplied by the reader.

The simple pronoun (αὐτός) naturally
describes the one Sovereign Lord,
just as the isolating and defining pronoun (ἐκεῖνος) describes Christ.

The phrase 'before Him' (in con-
spectu ejus V., coram ipso Aug.) stands
emphatically first in order to mark
the essential character of the Christian
life. It is lived out in the very sight
of God. The believer feels himself to
be always before His eyes. In that
Presence (comp. ii. 28), if not before,
he comes to find what he is. Comp.
2 Cor. v. 10 (φανερωθῆναι); 1 Thess.
iii. 13.

πείσομεν...ὅτι ἐὰν καταγινώσκῃ...ὅτι
μείζων...πάντα] suademus (suadeamus,
suadebimus) quoniam si reprehenderit nos (male senserit Aug.) cor nostrum major est Deus corde nostro et
novit omnia V., (we) shall assure our
heart before Him whereinsoever our
heart condemn us, because God is
greater than our heart and knoweth
all things. The many conflicting interpretations of this passage spring
out of the different translations of (1)
the verb πείσομεν, and (2) the double
conjunction or relative ὅτι (ὅ τι).

1. Thus if we take the sense persuade for the verb, there are two
groups of renderings possible: the
first (a) in which the clauses which
follow give the substance of that of
which we are satisfied; and the second (β) in which this substance is
supposed to be supplied by the reader.

(a) In the first case there are two
possible views:

(a) The second ὅτι may be simply
resumptive: We shall persuade our
heart, that, if our heart condemn us,
that, I say, God is greater...

ἡ καρδία, ὅτι μείζων ἐστὶν ὁ θεὸς τῆς καρδίας ἡμῶν

20 ὅτι μ. ℵBC syrvg: om. ὅτι A vg me the.   κύριος (for θεός) C.

(b) Or the first ὅτι may be taken as
the relative : *We shall persuade our
heart, whereinsoever our heart condemn us, that God is greater...*
Against both these interpretations
it may be urged, as it seems, with decisive force, that the conclusion is not
one which flows naturally from the
premiss. The consciousness of a sincere love of the brethren does not
furnish the basis of the conviction of
the sovereign greatness of God.

(β) If the substance of that of which
we shall be persuaded is mentally supplied, as, 'that we are of the truth,'
or 'that our prayers are heard,' there
are again two possible interpretations :

(a) The second ὅτι may be taken as
resumptive in the sense *because: we
shall persuade our heart, because if
our heart condemn us, because I say
God is greater...*

(b) Or again the first ὅτι may be
taken as the relative: *we shall persuade our heart whereinsoever our
heart condemn us, because God is
greater...*
It appears to be a fatal objection to
both these views that just that has to
be supplied which the sense given to
the verb leads the reader to expect to
be clearly expressed. And further it
may be remarked that while the use
of a resumptive ὅτι is quite intelligible
after the introduction of a considerable clause it is very unnatural after
the insertion of a few words.

2. If on the other hand the verb
be taken in the sense 'we shall assure,'
'we shall still and tranquillise the
fears and misgivings of our heart,'
there are yet two modes of completing
the sentence:

(a) The second ὅτι may be taken as
resumptive in the sense of *because:
we shall assure our hearts, because if
our heart condemn us, because, I say,*

God is greater. Such a resumptive
use of the particle has however been
shewn to be very harsh.

(β) There remains then the adoption of the first ὅτι as the relative :
*We shall assure our heart, wherein-
soever our heart condemn us, because
God is greater...*
This sense falls in completely with
the context and flows naturally from
the Greek.

But an ambiguity still remains. In
what sense is the superior greatness
of God to be understood ? Is it the
ground of our exceeding need? or of
our sure confidence ? Both interpretations can be drawn from the words.
(1) We shall then, and then only, still
our heart, in whatsoever it may condemn us, because we know that the
judgment of God must be severer than
our own judgment, and so apart from
fellowship with Him we can have no
hope. Or (2) We shall then still our
heart in whatsoever it may condemn
us, because we are in fellowship with
God, and that fact assures us of His
sovereign mercy. The latter sense
seems to be required by the whole
context. See below.

πείσομεν] The nearest parallel in
the N. T. to the sense of the word
which has been adopted here is Matt.
xxviii. 14. Comp. 2 Macc. iv. 45.

τὴν καρδίαν] *our heart*, the seat of
the moral character. It occurs only
in this passage in the Epistles of St
John. Comp. Rom. ii. 15 ; Eph. i. 18.
The singular (which St John always
uses in the Gospel and Epistle) fixes
the thought upon the personal trial in
each case. See Additional Note.

20. ὅτι ἐάν] *whereinsoever.* The
words balance the 'all things' which
follows. The form ὅτι ἐάν does not
occur as the true text elsewhere in
N. T. (Col. iii. 23 ὃ ἐάν), but always

καὶ γινώσκει πάντα. ²¹'Αγαπητοί, ἐὰν ἡ καρδία μὴ
καταγινώσκῃ, παρρησίαν ἔχομεν πρὸς τὸν θεόν, ²²καὶ

21 ἀγαπητοί: ἀδελφοί ℵ.   ἡ κ. AB (lat): +ἡμῶν ℭℵC vg syrr me the.
μὴ κατ. BC: +ἡμῶν ℭℵA vg me the syrr.   ἔχομεν: ἔχει B.

ὅτι ἄν (John ii. 5, xiv. 13, xv. 16). This
however does not appear to be a decisive objection. In John ii. 5, xv. 16
ἐάν is an early variant (ℵA).

καταγινώσκῃ] reprehenderit V.,
male senserit Aug., condemn. The
word is used of the internal judgment
of conscience (Ecclus. xiv. 2) as distinguished from the formal sentence
of the judge (κατακρίνω).
Comp. Gal. ii. 11.

μείζων ἐ. ὁ θ. τῆς κ. ἡ.] major est
Deus corde nostro V., God is greater
than our heart, justly able to sway
and control it. He is the Supreme
Sovereign over the whole man. Nothing in man can stand against His
judgment and will. The context requires that this sovereignty should be
regarded under the aspect of love, as
exercised for the calming of human
doubts. The supposition that 'greater'
means more searching and authoritative in condemnation than the heart
is at variance with the tenor of the
passage and also with the natural sense
of 'greater.'

γινώσκει π.] novit omnia V., knoweth all things, watches (to use human
language) the course and spring of
action (John ii. 25 note), not only this
failure and that on which the heart
dwells, but these and all else, and
with this knowledge offers us His
love and assures us of it.

Thus the meaning of the whole
passage will be: The sense within us
of a sincere love of the brethren, which
is the sign of God's presence with us,
will enable us to stay the accusations
of our conscience, whatever they may
be, because God, who gives us the
love, and so blesses us with His fellowship, is greater than our heart; and
He, having perfect knowledge, for-

gives all on which the heart sadly
dwells.

21. 'Αγαπητοί] Carissimi V., Dilec-
tissimi Aug. Comp. c. ii. 7 note. The
tender address follows naturally from
the thought of the fears and hopes of
Christians. The sense of misgiving
(the condemnation of the heart) and
the sense of duty done (the acquittal
of the heart) severally involve special
applications of the divine revelation.
In the one case this revelation brings
assurance, and in the other effectual
prayer.

ἐὰν ἡ καρδία μὴ καταγ.] si cor nostrum
non reprehenderit V. (male senserit
Aug.), if our heart condemn us not.
This evidently is the converse case to
'if our heart condemn us.' It does
not imply a claim to sinlessness, nor
yet an insensibility to the heinousness
of sin, but the action of a lively faith
which retains a real sense of fellowship with God, and this carries with it
confidence and peace.

The change in the order of the
words in the parallel clauses marks
a change of emphasis. In the first
clause stress is laid on the fact of
condemnation (ὅτι ἐὰν καταγινώσκῃ ἡ
καρδία): in the second on the moral
faculty which pronounces no condemnation (ἐὰν ἡ καρδία μὴ καταγ.).

παρρησίαν ἔχομεν] fiduciam habemus V., we have boldness, so as
to express without reserve all our
wants. Compare c. v. 14 (ii. 28, iv.
17); John vii. 4 note. The thought
here is of the boldness with which the
son appears before the Father, and
not of that with which the accused
appears before the Judge.

πρὸς τ. θ.] ad Deum V., towards
God. Compare Acts xxiv. 16; Rom. iv.
2 (πρὸς θ.), v. 1; 2 Cor. iii. 4; Phil. iv. 6.

ὃ ἂν αἰτῶμεν λαμβάνομεν ἀπ' αὐτοῦ, ὅτι τὰς ἐντολὰς
αὐτοῦ τηροῦμεν καὶ τὰ ἀρεστὰ ἐνώπιον αὐτοῦ ποιοῦμεν.
²³καὶ αὕτη ἐστὶν ἡ ἐντολὴ αὐτοῦ, ἵνα πιστεύσωμεν τῷ

22 αἰτώμεθα ℵ. Comp. v. 14 f.   λαμβάνωμεν A: comp. for similar confusion c. iv. 17 (ℵ) 13 : accipiemus vg the syr hl.   ἀπ' αὐ. ℵABC: παρ' αὐ. ς.
τηρῶμεν ℵA.   23 πιστεύσωμεν ςB: πιστεύωμεν ℵAC.   τῷ ὀν. τοῦ υἱ. αὐ.
'I. X. ℵBC vg me the syrr: τῷ ὀν. αὐ. 'I. Χριστῷ A (all. τῷ υἱῷ αὐ. 'I. X.).

22. καὶ ὃ ἂν αἰτῶμεν] et quodcunque
petierimus V., and whatsoever we
ask... The expression of our wants is
followed by the satisfying of them.
The words describe the actual present
experience of the believer (αἰτῶμεν)
and the assertion is absolute. Every
prayer is granted. But Augustine
rightly adds : Discernamus exaudi-
tiones Dei. Invenimus enim quosdam
non exauditos ad voluntatem exauditos ad salutem ; et rursus quosdam
invenimus exauditos ad voluntatem
et non exauditos ad salutem.

Here the thought is of the actual
perception of the gift by the believer
in time (λαμβάνομεν): in St Mark xi.
24 (ἐλάβετε) the thought is of the
divine response in the eternal order.
For λαμβ. ἀπό see c. ii. 27 note.

ὅτι...τηροῦμεν] because we observe...
Obedience is not alleged as the ground
but as the assurance of the fulfilment.
The answer to prayer is given not as
a reward for meritorious action, but
because the prayer itself rightly understood coincides with God's will
(comp. John viii 29, xi. 42). The sole
object of the believer is to do thoroughly the part which has been assigned
to him : his petitions are directed to
this end and so are necessarily granted.
Comp. John xv. 7.

τηροῦμεν...ποιοῦμεν] keep...do...The
eyes of the believer are turned watch-
fully to discern (τηροῦμεν) the will of
God for the future, and at the present
he is engaged in executing that which
is pleasing to Him. Under this twofold aspect right action is presented
both as a work of obedience and as a

work of freedom, as enjoined and also
as spontaneous.

For the sense of τηρεῖν see John
xvii. 12 note, and for τηρεῖν τ. ἐντ. c.
ii. 3 note.   Τηρεῖν and ποιεῖν occur
again together in v. 2. 3.

τὰ ἀρεστά] ea quæ sunt placita V.,
the things that are pleasing...not
simply 'things pleasing,' but definitely
those which correspond with our position and duty.

Compare John viii. 29.

ἐνώπιον αὐτοῦ] coram eo V., in His
sight.   Comp. Hebr. xiii. 21 ; Acts iv.
19; 1 Pet. iii. 4; 1 Tim. ii. 3 ; v. 4.
But we find ἀρεστὰ αὐτῷ John viii. 29.
The slight shade of difference between ἔμπροσθεν αὐτοῦ (v. 19) and ἐνώπιον αὐτοῦ seems to be expressed by
the phrases 'in His presence' and 'in
His sight.'   The latter phrase accentuates the thought of the Divine
regard.   Comp. John xii. 37 (ἔμπ. αὐ.)
and xx. 30 (ἐνώπ. τ. μ.).

23. καὶ αὕτη ἐ. ἡ ἐντ. αὐ.] And this
is his commandment.   The 'things
that are pleasing,' the many 'commandments' are summed up in one
commandment, which includes faith
and practice, the power of action and
the form of action, faith and love.
Comp. ii. 4 f.; 2 John 6.

ἡ ἐντολή...ἵνα...] Comp. John xiii.
34, xv. 12, 17.

ἵνα πιστεύσωμεν...] that we believe
...Faith also is a work, John vi. 29,
and therefore the proper object of
command; and it may be regarded
either as unceasingly continuous and
progressive (πιστεύωμεν) or as exercised at a critical moment when the

ὀνόματι τοῦ υἱοῦ αὐτοῦ Ἰησοῦ Χριστοῦ καὶ ἀγαπῶμεν

whole tenor of life is determined (πιστεύσωμεν). This is the first place in the Epistle in which the exercise of faith is mentioned. Afterwards πιστεύω occurs not unfrequently. On the whole the reading πιστεύσωμεν is the more likely here. In this case the decisive act of faith is treated as the foundation of the abiding work of love; at the same time the present πιστεύωμεν gives an excellent sense, faith and love being presented as simultaneous in their present development.

The tenses of the verb (πιστεύω) appear to be used with significant exactness by St John; and the instances of the occurrence of the different forms will repay examination.

1 *Present:* the immediate, continuous exercise of faith:
John x. 38 (dat.), vi. 29, xvi. 9 (εἰς), xx. 31 (ὅτι), iv. 42, x. 25 f., xii. 39 (xix. 35), xx. 31 (abs.).
imper.: John iv. 21, x. 37, xiv. 11; 1 John iv. 1 (dat.); John xii. 36, xiv. 1 (εἰς).
partic. (ὁ πιστεύων, οἱ πιστεύοντες): John v. 24; 1 John v. 10 (dat.); John iii. 16, 18, 36, vi. 35, 40, 47, vii. 38 f., xi. 25 f., xii. 44, 46, xiv. 2, xvii. 20; 1 John v. 10, 13 (εἰς), 1 John v. 1, 5 (ὅτι); John iii. 15, vi. 64 (abs.).

2 *Imperfect:* the continuous exercise of faith in the past:
John v. 46 (dat.), vii. 5, xii. 11, 37 (εἰς).

3 *Aorist:* the definite, decisive act of faith:
John ii. 22, iv. 50, vi. 30, x. 38; 1 John iii. 23 (dat.); John ii. 11, 23, iv. 39, vii. 31, 48, viii. 30, ix. 36, x. 42, xi. 45, xii. 42 (εἰς); John viii. 24, ix. 18, xi. 42, xiii. 19, xvii. 8, 21 (ὅτι); John i. 7, iv. 4, 53, v. 44, xi. 15, 40, xiv. 29 (abs.).

partic.: John xx. 29 (abs.).

4 *Perfect:* the past exercise of faith continued into the present:
John viii. 31 (dat.); John iii. 18, 1 John v. 10 (εἰς); John vi. 69, xi. 27, xvi. 27 (ὅτι); John xx. 29; 1 John iv. 16 (?) (abs.).

The differences come out clearly where different tenses stand in close connexion; e.g. John vi. 29 f., vii. 5, 31, xii. 37, 42; 1 John v. 10.

πιστ. τῷ ὀνόματι] *believe the name...* The phrase is remarkable. It is equivalent to 'believe as true the message which the name conveys.' The full title, *His Son Jesus Christ* (c. i. 3 note), is a compressed Creed. Contrast 'believe in the name' v. 13; John i. 12, ii. 23, iii. 18. Comp. v. 10. The translation of A. V. probably comes from the Vulgate which gives *credamus in nomine,* the rendering elsewhere of πιστεύειν εἰς τὸ ὄνομα (John i. 12, ii. 23, iii. 18). See Additional Note on the names of Christ in this Epistle.

ἀγαπῶμεν ἀλλ.] *diligamus alterutrum* V., *love one another: v.* 11 note, iv. 7, 11, 12; 2 John 5; John xiii. 34 (ἐντολὴν καινὴν δίδωμι); xv. 12, 17. The exact words are used (contrast *v.* 14) in which Christ Himself gave the commandment on the eve of His Passion, when He fulfilled the ideal of love. The subject to ἔδωκεν is supplied naturally from the preceding clause.

Compare Rom. xiii. 10.

Multum facit qui multum diligit... Bene facit qui communitati magis quam suæ voluntati servit (Thom. a Kempis, *De Imit.* I. 15, 2).

24. The obedience, which is the rule of the Christian life, issues in abiding fellowship with God. This verse is closely connected with *v.* 22, while *v.* 23 is in thought parenthetical.

ἀλλήλους, καθὼς ἔδωκεν ἐντολὴν ἡμῖν. ²⁴καὶ ὁ τηρῶν
τὰς ἐντολὰς αὐτοῦ ἐν αὐτῷ μένει καὶ αὐτὸς ἐν αὐτῷ.
καὶ ἐν τούτῳ γινώσκομεν ὅτι μένει ἐν ἡμῖν, ἐκ τοῦ πνεύματος οὗ ἡμῖν ἔδωκεν.

ἡμῖν ℵABC vg me the syrr: om. ς.   24 καὶ ἐν τ.: om. καὶ ℵ* the.   οὗ
ἡμ. ἔδ. ABC (lat): οὗ ἔδ. ἡμ. ℵ vg me the syrr.

καὶ ὁ τηρῶν...] *And he that obser-*
veth... These words take up ὅτι τὰς
ἐντολὰς αὐτοῦ τηρ. in *v.* 22, so that the
reference is to 'the commandments of
God,' and not directly to the one commandment of Christ *v.* 23. Our prayers
are granted because they spring out
of that spirit which strives after perfect sympathy; and, more than this,
our obedience is the pledge of a personal fellowship.

ἐν αὐτῷ μένει...] i.e. in God. See
c. iv. 15 note.

Bede says with singular force: Sit
ergo tibi domus Deus et esto domus
Dei: mane in Deo, et maneat in te
Deus.

ἐν τούτῳ γινώσκομεν] *in this we*
know, perceive... The love which the
Christian feels, and which is the spring
of his obedience, assures him of God's
fellowship with him. In other words,

God has given him of His Spirit.
The use of the two prepositions '*in*
(ἐν) *this,*' '*from* (ἐκ) the Spirit,' shews
that the two clauses are not in apposition. Γινώσκομεν is repeated in
thought before ἐκ τοῦ πν. c. iv. 6.

ἐκ τοῦ πνεύματος] This is the first
mention of the Spirit in the Epistle.
Afterwards the references are not unfrequent. It is remarkable that the
Name never occurs with the epithet
'Holy' in the Epistles or Apocalypse
of St John.

οὗ...ἔδωκεν] *which he gave* when
we became Christians. Comp. c. iv. 13;
John xiv. 16; Acts v. 32, viii. 18, xv.
8; 2 Cor. i. 21 f.

Augustine draws a striking conclusion from the truth that the Spirit of
God is the source of man's life: Con-
temne te cum laudaris. Ille in te
laudetur qui per te operatur.

Additional Note on iii. 1. Children of God.

The three phrases by which St John describes the new life.

St John uses several phrases to describe the relation of believers to God which require to be carefully considered in connexion with the contexts in which they occur.

The initial fact of the communication of the divine life is expressed by γεννηθῆναι ἐκ τοῦ θεοῦ (i). The essential connexion existing in virtue of this quickening is expressed by εἶναι ἐκ τοῦ θεοῦ (ii). In virtue of this connexion the believer becomes and is a τέκνον θεοῦ (iii).

i. 'To be born (begotten) of God,' (1) in the Perfect,

i. (1) The phrase γεννηθῆναι ἐκ τ. θ. is used commonly in the perfect (γεγέννηται, γεγεννημένος); that is, the initial fact of the new life is regarded in its abiding power.

This communicated life is

(a) shewn by certain signs, faith in Jesus as the Christ, righteousness and love:

1 John v. 1 πᾶς ὁ πιστεύων ὅτι Ἰησοῦς ἐστιν ὁ χριστὸς ἐκ τοῦ θεοῦ γεγέννηται.

— ii. 29 πᾶς ὁ ποιῶν τὴν δικαιοσύνην ἐξ αὐτοῦ γεγέννηται.

— iv. 7 πᾶς ὁ ἀγαπῶν ἐκ τοῦ θεοῦ γεγέννηται.

and

(β) carries with it certain consequences, freedom from sin and victory:

1 John iii. 9 πᾶς ὁ γεγεννημένος ἐκ τοῦ θεοῦ ἁμαρτίαν οὐ ποιεῖ ὅτι σπέρμα αὐτοῦ ἐν αὐτῷ μένει.

— οὐ δύναται ἁμαρτάνειν ὅτι ἐκ τοῦ θεοῦ γεγέννηται.

— v. 18 πᾶς ὁ γεγεννημένος ἐκ τοῦ θεοῦ οὐχ ἁμαρτάνει.

— 4 πᾶν τὸ γεγεννημένον ἐκ τοῦ θεοῦ νικᾷ τὸν κόσμον.

Compare

John iii. 6 τὸ γεγεννημένον ἐκ τοῦ πνεύματος.

— 8 ὁ γεγεννημένος ἐκ τοῦ πνεύματος.

(2) in the Aorist.

(2) The fact of the communication of the divine life is specially noticed:

John i. 12 f. ἔδωκεν αὐτοῖς ἐξουσίαν τέκνα θεοῦ γενέσθαι...οἳ...ἐκ θεοῦ ἐγεννήθησαν.

Compare

1 John v. 18 ὁ γεννηθεὶς ἐκ τοῦ θεοῦ.

— 1 πᾶς ὁ ἀγαπῶν τὸν γεννήσαντα...

Compare also

John iii. 3 (7) ἐὰν μή τις γεννηθῇ ἄνωθεν.

— 5 ἐὰν μή τις γεννηθῇ ἐξ ὕδατος καὶ πνεύματος.

The aorist and perfect occur together 1 John v. 18; John iii. 5—8. See also Gal. iv. 23, 29.

The form of expression is not found in any of the other writers of the N.T. Yet compare St Paul's use of γεννᾶν 1 Cor. iv. 15; Philem. 10; and St Peter's use of ἀναγεννᾶν, 1 Pet. i. 3, 23.

ii. The phrase εἶναι ἐκ τοῦ θεοῦ is connected with a considerable group ii. *'To be of similar phrases, εἶναι ἐκ τοῦ διαβόλου (c. iii. 8), ἐκ τοῦ πονηροῦ (iii. 12), ἐκ of God,* τοῦ κόσμου (ii. 16, note), ἐκ τῆς ἀληθείας (ii. 21, note), ἐκ τῆς γῆς (John iii. 31, note), ἐκ τῶν κάτω, ἐκ τῶν ἄνω (viii. 23). It expresses the ideas of derivation and dependence, and so of a moral correspondence between the issue and the source.

(1) The characteristics of him who is thus vitally dependent upon God (1) signs (1 John v. 19, iv. 4, 6) are expressed both in a positive and in a negative in men; form.

(a) positively:

3 John 11 ὁ ἀγαθοποιῶν ἐκ τοῦ θεοῦ ἐστίν.
John viii. 47 ὁ ὢν ἐκ τοῦ θεοῦ τὰ ῥήματα τοῦ θεοῦ ἀκούει.

(β) negatively:

1 John iii. 10 πᾶς ὁ μὴ ποιῶν δικαιοσύνην οὐκ ἔστιν ἐκ τοῦ θεοῦ.
— iv. 6 ὃς οὐκ ἔστιν ἐκ τοῦ θεοῦ οὐκ ἀκούει ἡμῶν.

(2) And corresponding declarations are made with regard to spirits (2) signs (1 John iv. 1): in spirits.

1 John iv. 2 πᾶν πνεῦμα ὃ ὁμολογεῖ Ἰησοῦν Χριστὸν ἐν σαρκὶ ἐληλυθότα ἐκ
τοῦ θεοῦ ἐστίν.
— 3 πᾶν πνεῦμα ὃ μὴ ὁμολογεῖ τὸν Ἰησοῦν ἐκ τοῦ θεοῦ οὐκ ἔστιν.

Compare

1 John iv. 7 ἡ ἀγάπη ἐκ τοῦ θεοῦ ἐστίν.
John vii. 17 ...περὶ τῆς διδαχῆς πότερον ἐκ τοῦ θεοῦ ἐστίν...
1 John ii. 16 πᾶν τὸ ἐν τῷ κόσμῳ...οὐκ ἔστιν ἐκ τοῦ πατρός...

The nearest parallels in other writings of the N.T. are:

Acts v. 38 f. εἰ ἐκ θεοῦ ἐστίν.
1 Cor. i. 30 ἐξ αὐτοῦ [τοῦ θεοῦ] ὑμεῖς ἐστὲ ἐν Χριστῷ Ἰησοῦ.
— xi. 12 τὰ δὲ πάντα ἐκ τοῦ θεοῦ.

iii. The familiar title τέκνον θεοῦ, which describes the relation established iii. *'Child* by the new life, is of rarer occurrence in St John's writings. *of God.'*

(1) The power of duly becoming a 'child of God' is given by the (1) The communication of the divine life. beginning.

John i. 12 f. ἔδωκεν αὐτοῖς ἐξουσίαν τέκνα θεοῦ γενέσθαι, τοῖς πιστεύουσιν
εἰς τὸ ὄνομα αὐτοῦ, οἱ...ἐκ θεοῦ ἐγεννήθησαν.

(2) The position is realised through the gift of love. (2) The
1 John iii. 1...ἀγάπην δέδωκεν ἡμῖν ὁ πατὴρ ἵνα τέκνα θεοῦ κληθῶμεν... growth
— 2 νῦν τέκνα θεοῦ ἐσμέν. and

(3) Thus 'the children of God' form a distinct body marked by right- (3) The eousness and love. signs.

1 John iii. 10 ἐν τούτῳ φανερά ἐστιν τὰ τέκνα τοῦ θεοῦ...

Comp. c. v. 2; John xi. 52.

The idea of τέκνον as it is thus presented by St John includes the two The idea notions of the presence of the divine principle and the action of human of 'chil- growth. The child is made to share in his Father's nature (comp. 2 Pet. i. dren' 4), and he uses in progressive advance the powers which he has received.

This thought of progress will be traced through the whole picture which St John draws of the spiritual life. 'From strength to strength' is the law by which it is shaped.

distinct from that of 'sons.'
It is therefore easily intelligible why St John never uses the title υἱός, the name of definite dignity and privilege, to describe the relation of Christians to God. He regards their position not as the result of an 'adoption' (υἱοθεσία), but as the result of a new life which advances from the vital germ to full maturity.

Additional Note on iii. 5. Aspects of the Incarnation.

Different aspects of the Incarnation.
The phrases which St John uses to describe the Incarnation fall into different groups corresponding with different aspects of the Fact. In regard to the Father, it is a 'Sending,' a 'Mission' (1). In regard to the Son, it is a 'Coming' (2). In regard to the form, it is in 'Flesh' (3). In regard to men, it is a 'Manifestation' (4).

1. MISSION.
1. The idea of the Mission of Christ, the Son, by the Father is expressed by two verbs, πέμπω, ἀποστέλλω. The former describes the simple relation of the Sent to the Sender: the last adds 'the accessory notions of a special commission and so far of a delegated authority in the person sent.'

(a) The use of πέμπω.
Πέμπω is not found in this connexion in the Epistles of St John (comp. Rom. viii. 3 only); and it is used in the Gospel only by the Lord in the participial form in three phrases ὁ πέμψας με (αὐτόν), ὁ πέμψας με πατήρ, ὁ πατὴρ ὁ πέμψας με.

i. ὁ πέμψας με.
Of these phrases the simple ὁ πέμψας με is by far the most common. It is used in two connexions to express (a) some relation of Christ to Him Who sent Him, and (β) some relation of men to Christ as so sent.

(a) John iv. 34 ἐμὸν βρῶμα...ἵνα ποιήσω τὸ θέλημα τοῦ π. μ.
— v. 30 ζητῶ...τὸ θέλημα τοῦ π. μ.
— vi. 38 καταβέβηκα...ἵνα ποιῶ...τὸ θέλημα τοῦ π. μ.
— 39 τοῦτό ἐστιν τὸ θέλημα τοῦ π. μ. ἵνα...μὴ ἀπολέσω...
— vii. 16 ἡ ἐμὴ διδαχή...ἐστίν...τοῦ π. μ.
— 26 ὁ π. μ. ἀληθής ἐστιν κἀγὼ ἃ ἤκουσα...λαλῶ.
— ix. 4 δεῖ ἐργάζεσθαι τὰ ἔργα τοῦ π. μ.
— viii. 29 ὁ π. μ. μετ᾽ ἐμοῦ ἐστιν.
— vii. 33, xvi. 5 ὑπάγω πρὸς τὸν π. μ.
Comp. vii. 18 ὁ ζητῶν τὴν δόξαν τοῦ π. αὐτὸν ἀληθής ἐστιν.

(β) John v. 24 ὁ...πιστεύων τῷ π. μ.
— xii. 44 ὁ πιστεύων εἰς ἐμέ...πιστεύει...εἰς τὸν π. μ.
— 45 ὁ θεωρῶν ἐμὲ θεωρεῖ τὸν π. μ.
— xiii. 20 ὁ ἐμὲ λαμβάνων λαμβάνει τὸν π. μ.
— xv. 21 ταῦτα ποιήσουσιν διὰ τὸ ὄνομά μου ὅτι οὐκ οἴδασιν τὸν π. μ.
Comp. vii. 28 ἔστιν ἀληθινὸς ὁ π. μ. ὃν ὑμεῖς οὐκ οἴδατε.

The phrase ὁ πέμψας με πατήρ adds to the notion of 'sending' that of ii. ὁ πέμψας με πατήρ.
the essential relation which gives authority to the mission.

John v. 37 ὁ π. μ. π. ἐκεῖνος μεμαρτύρηκεν.
— [viii. 16 (doubtful reading: comp. viii. 29) μόνος οὐκ εἰμί, ἀλλ' ἐγὼ καὶ ὁ π. μ. π.]
— viii. 18 μαρτυρεῖ περὶ ἐμοῦ ὁ π. μ. π.
— xii. 49 ὁ π. μ. π....ἐντολὴν δέδωκεν τί εἴπω...
— xiv. 24 ὁ λόγος ὃν ἀκούετε...ἐστίν...τοῦ π. μ. π.

In the phrase ὁ πατὴρ ὁ πέμψας με the two notions of natural authority iii. ὁ πατὴρ ὁ πέμψας με.
and mission are dwelt on separately. It occurs

John vi. 44 ἐὰν μὴ ὁ π. ὁ π. μ. ἑλκύσῃ αὐτόν.
Comp. v. 23 ὁ μὴ τιμῶν τὸν υἱὸν οὐ τιμᾷ τὸν π. τ. π. αὐτόν.

The use of ἀποστέλλω differs from that of πέμπω by the fact that in St (b) The
John (yet see Matt. x. 40; Mark ix. 37; Luke ix. 48, x. 16) it is found only use of
in the finite forms, ἀπέστειλα, ἀπέσταλκα. ἀποστέλλω.
The *aorist* is by far the most common tense. This is used to describe i. Aorist.
the fact of the specific Mission in some particular aspect:

John iii. 17 ἀπέστειλεν ὁ θεὸς τὸν υἱὸν εἰς τὸν κόσμον...ἵνα σωθῇ ὁ κόσμος δι' αὐτοῦ.
— x. 36 ὃν ὁ πατὴρ ἡγίασεν καὶ ἀπέστειλεν εἰς τὸν κόσμον.
1 John iv. 10 [ὁ θεὸς] ἀπέστειλεν τὸν υἱὸν αὐτοῦ ἱλασμὸν περὶ τῶν ἁμαρτιῶν ἡμῶν.

Compare
John vi. 57 καθὼς ἀπέστειλέν με ὁ ζῶν πατήρ...
— xvii. 18 καθὼς ἐμὲ ἀπέστειλας εἰς τὸν κόσμον...
— vii. 29 παρ' αὐτοῦ εἰμὶ κἀκεῖνός με ἀπέστειλεν.
— viii. 42 οὐδὲ ἀπ' ἐμαυτοῦ ἐλήλυθα ἀλλ' ἐκεῖνός με ἀπέστειλεν.

And this Mission is presented as the object (a) of recognition (know-ledge), or (β) of faith:

(a) John xvii. 3 ἵνα γινώσκωσιν...ὃν ἀπέστειλας Ἰησοῦν Χριστόν.
— 23 ἵνα γινώσκῃ ὁ κόσμος ὅτι σύ με ἀπέστειλας.
— 25 οὗτοι ἔγνωσαν ὅτι σύ με ἀπέστειλας.
(β) John v. 38 ὅτι ὃν ἀπέστειλεν ἐκεῖνος τούτῳ ὑμεῖς οὐ πιστεύετε.
— vi. 29 τὸ ἔργον τοῦ θεοῦ ἵνα πιστεύητε εἰς ὃν ἀπέστειλεν ἐκεῖνος.
— xi. 42 ἵνα πιστεύσωσιν ὅτι σύ με ἀπέστειλας.
— xvii. 21 ἵνα ὁ κόσμος πιστεύῃ ὅτι σύ με ἀπέστειλας.
Comp. John iii. 34 ...ἐσφράγισεν ὅτι...ὃν γὰρ ἀπέστειλεν ὁ θεός...

The *perfect*, which occurs but rarely, describes the Mission in its ii. Perfect.
abiding continuance:

John v. 36 τὰ ἔργα ἃ ποιῶ μαρτυρεῖ...ὅτι ὁ πατήρ με ἀπέσταλκεν.
1 John iv. 9 τὸν υἱὸν αὐτοῦ τὸν μονογενῆ ἀπέσταλκεν ὁ θεὸς εἰς τον κόσμον ἵνα ζήσωμεν δι' αὐτοῦ.
— 14 τεθεάμεθα καὶ μαρτυροῦμεν ὅτι ὁ πατὴρ ἀπέσταλκεν τὸν υἱὸν σωτῆρα τοῦ κόσμου.
John xx. 21 καθὼς ἀπέσταλκέν με ὁ πατήρ, κἀγὼ πέμπω ὑμᾶς.

2. COMING.   2. The Coming of Christ, like the Mission, is regarded both as a simple fact realised historically once for all (ἦλθον), and as an abiding fact (ἥκω, ἐλήλυθα). It is also set forth as a present fact being realised at the moment, and as a future fact of which the fulfilment is potentially begun (ἔρχομαι)[1].

(a) Aor. ἦλθον.

The simple fact of Christ's Coming is affirmed by St John both in respect of His true Divinity as the Word, and of His true humanity.

John i. 11 εἰς τὰ ἴδια ἦλθεν [τὸ φῶς τὸ ἀληθινόν].

1 John v. 6 ὁ ἐλθὼν δι' ὕδατος καὶ αἵματος Ἰησοῦς Χριστός.

In the discourses of the Lord the fact of His Coming, the fact of the Incarnation, is connected with the manifold issues which it involved:

John ix. 39 εἰς κρίμα ἐγὼ εἰς τὸν κόσμον τοῦτον ἦλθον ἵνα οἱ μὴ βλέποντες ...καὶ οἱ βλέποντες...

— x. 10 ἐγὼ ἦλθον ἵνα ζωὴν ἔχωσιν καὶ περισσὸν ἔχωσιν.

— xii. 47 οὐκ ἦλθον ἵνα κρίνω τὸν κόσμον ἀλλ' ἵνα σώσω τὸν κόσμον.

— xv. 22 εἰ μὴ ἦλθον καὶ ἐλάλησα οὐκ ἂν εἶχον ἁμαρτίαν.

And the Lord bases the truth of His witness on His consciousness of the fact:

John viii. 14 ἀληθής ἐστιν ἡ μαρτυρία μου ὅτι οἶδα πόθεν ἦλθον καὶ ποῦ ὑπάγω (contrasted with πόθεν ἔρχομαι).

ἐξῆλθον.

The divine relation implied in this use of 'came' is expressed more distinctly by the verb 'came forth' (ἐξῆλθον). This is used in the Lord's words with different prepositions (ἐκ, παρά):

John viii. 42 ἐγὼ ἐκ τοῦ θεοῦ ἐξῆλθον καὶ ἥκω.

— xvi. 28 ἐξῆλθον ἐκ τοῦ πατρὸς καὶ ἐλήλυθα εἰς τὸν κόσμον.

— 27 πεπιστεύκατε ὅτι ἐγὼ παρὰ τοῦ πατρὸς ἐξῆλθον.

— xvii. 8 ἔγνωσαν...ὅτι παρὰ σοῦ ἐξῆλθον.

And it is significant that St John and the disciples use the word with a yet different turn of thought (ἀπό):

John xiii. 3 εἰδὼς...ὅτι ἀπὸ θεοῦ ἐξῆλθεν.

— xvi. 30 πιστεύομεν ὅτι ἀπὸ θεοῦ ἐξῆλθες[2].

(b) Perf. ἐλήλυθα.

The perfect (ἐλήλυθα) serves to bring out the abiding significance of the fact of Christ's Coming, the necessary effects which it has as distinguished

---

[1] The usage in John i. 9 ἦν τὸ φῶς τὸ ἀληθινόν......ἐρχόμενον is unique. See note.

[2] It is of interest to compare the instances of the use of ἦλθον, ἐλήλυθα in the Synoptic Gospels:

Matt. v. 17 οὐκ ἦλθον καταλῦσαι ἀλλὰ πληρῶσαι.

—— ix. 13 ‖ Mark ii. 17 οὐκ ἦλθον καλέσαι δικαίους ἀλλὰ ἁμαρτωλούς·

Luke v. 32 οὐκ ἐλήλυθα κ. δ. ἁ. ἁ. εἰς μετάνοιαν.

—— x. 34 οὐκ ἦλθον βαλεῖν εἰρήνην ἀλλὰ μάχαιραν. ἦλθον γὰρ διχάσαι......

Luke xii. 49 πῦρ ἦλθον βαλεῖν ἐπὶ τὴν γῆν.

Matt. xi. 19 ‖ Luke vii. 33 ἦλθεν (Lk. ἐλήλυθεν) ὁ υἱὸς τοῦ ἀνθρώπου ἐσθίων καὶ πίνων.

—— xx. 28 ‖ Mark x. 45 ὁ υἱὸς τοῦ ἀνθρώπου οὐκ ἦλθεν διακονηθῆναι...

Luke xix. 10 ἦλθεν ὁ υἱὸς τοῦ ἀνθρώπου ζητῆσαι καὶ σῶσαι τὸ ἀπολωλός.

from its general issues. So St John uses the tense in connexion with the testing power of Christ revealed as 'light' and 'in flesh':

John iii. 19 τὸ φῶς ἐλήλυθεν εἰς τὸν κόσμον καὶ ἠγάπησαν οἱ ἄνθρωποι μᾶλλον τὸ σκότος...

1 John iv. 2 πᾶν πνεῦμα ὃ ὁμολογεῖ 'Ι. Χ. ἐν σαρκὶ ἐληλυθότα ἐκ τοῦ θεοῦ ἐστίν.

And the Lord thus speaks of the special character of His Coming:

John v. 43 ἐγὼ ἐλήλυθα ἐν τῷ ὀνόματι τοῦ πατρός μου.

— xii. 46 ἐγὼ φῶς εἰς τὸν κόσμον ἐλήλυθα.

— xviii. 37 ἐλήλυθα εἰς τὸν κόσμον ἵνα μαρτυρήσω τῇ ἀληθείᾳ.

and generally:

John vii. 28 καὶ ἀπ᾽ ἐμαυτοῦ οὐκ ἐλήλυθα (viii. 42 οὐδὲ ἀπ᾽ ἐμ. ἐλ.).

— xvi. 28 ἐξῆλθον ἐκ τοῦ πατρὸς καὶ ἐλήλυθα εἰς τὸν κόσμον.

The verb ἥκω is used in this connexion twice only: ἥκω.

John viii. 42 ἐκ τοῦ θεοῦ ἐξῆλθον καὶ ἥκω.

1 John v. 20 ὁ υἱὸς τοῦ θεοῦ ἥκει.

It occurs also in quotations from the LXX. Hebr. x. 7, 9 (ἥκω); Rom. x. 26; Heb. x. 37 (ἥξει); and of the future Coming of Christ; Apoc. ii. 25, iii. 3.

The present ἔρχομαι occurs to describe a Coming realised at the (c) Pres. moment: ἔρχομαι.

John viii. 14 πόθεν ἔρχομαι (contrasted with πόθεν ἦλθον),

and as a future fact potentially included in the present:

John xiv. 3 πάλιν ἔρχομαι.

— 18, 28 ἔρχομαι πρὸς ὑμᾶς.

— xxi. 22 f. ἕως ἔρχομαι.

2 John 7 οἱ μὴ ὁμολογοῦντες 'Ι. Χ. ἐρχόμενον ἐν σαρκί.

Comp. John iii. 31 f. ὁ ἄνωθεν (ἐκ τοῦ οὐρανοῦ) ἐρχόμενος.

See also Apoc. i. 7, ii. 6, iii. 11, xxii. 7, 12, 20.

The passages John viii. 14, 42, xvi. 27 f. will repay particular study as illustrating the different forms.

3. The mode of Christ's Coming is exhaustively set forth in the three 3. INCAR-phrases in which it is connected with 'flesh.' First there is the fundamental NATION. statement:

John i. 14 ὁ λόγος σὰρξ ἐγένετο.

And then this fact is connected with the past and present:

1 John iv. 2 (ὁμολογεῖν) 'Ιησοῦν Χριστὸν ἐν σαρκὶ ἐληλυθότα (ἐληλυ-θέναι),

and with the future:

2 John 7 (ὁμολογεῖν) 'Ιησοῦν Χριστὸν ἐρχόμενον ἐν σαρκί.

The 'manifestation' (φανερωθῆναι) of the Lord is noticed by St John 4. MANI-in regard to the great crises in His progressive revelation. Thus it is said FESTATION. that He was 'manifested' by the Incarnation:

1 John i. 2 ἡ ζωὴ ἐφανερώθη.

— iii. 5 ἐκεῖνος ἐφανερώθη ἵνα τὰς ἁμαρτίας ἄρῃ.

— 8 ἐφανερώθη ὁ υἱὸς τοῦ θεοῦ ἵνα λύσῃ τὰ ἔργα τοῦ διαβόλου.

and when He was openly presented to the people:

John i. 31 ἵνα φανερωθῇ τῷ Ἰσραὴλ διὰ τοῦτο ἦλθον.

So also 'He was manifested' and 'He manifested Himself' in the new life after the Resurrection:

John xxi. 14 ἐφανερώθη Ἰησοῦς τοῖς μαθηταῖς.

—   1 ἐφανέρωσεν ἑαυτὸν Ἰησοῦς τοῖς μαθηταῖς.

and Christians still look for a manifestation in the future:

1 John ii. 28 ἵνα ἐὰν φανερωθῇ σχῶμεν παρρησίαν...ἐν τῇ παρουσίᾳ αὐτοῦ.

—   iii. 2 ἐὰν φανερωθῇ ὅμοιοι αὐτῷ ἐσόμεθα.

Completeness of the teaching.   It is not necessary to draw out in detail the teaching of these pregnant words. They offer the fullest view which man can gain of the Person of the Lord in its absolute unity, truly human and truly divine. St John says both 'the Word became flesh' and 'Jesus Christ came in flesh'; and further he speaks of 'Jesus Christ coming in flesh.' Again he says equally 'the Life was manifested,' 'the Life which was with the Father,' and 'He [Jesus Christ] was manifested,' and 'the Son of God was manifested.' Now one aspect of the Lord's Person, now another is brought forward without change. There is nothing in the least degree formal in the different statements: they spring directly out of the immediate context as answering to one sovereign conception: and when put together they combine to produce a final harmony, the fulness of apostolic teaching, upon the central Truth of the Gospel. The least variation adds something to the completeness of the idea; and the minute correspondences bring an assurance that the result which the combination of the different phrases suggests answers to the thought of the Apostle which underlay all that he wrote.

Additional Note on iii. 14. Titles of believers.

The titles of believers in the New Test. Christians.   The different names which are given to Christians in the Apostolic writings offer an instructive study of the original conception of the Gospel. The origin of the historic Gentile name 'Christians' (Χριστιανοί, comp. Pompeiani) is noticed in Acts xi. 26; and it is used as familiarly known by Agrippa (Acts xxvi. 26) and by St Peter (1 Pet. ix. 16; comp. Tac. Ann. xv. 44). From the time of Ignatius this name, with the correlative for 'Christianity' (Χριστιανισμός), passed into general use (comp. Ign. ad Magn. 4, 10; ad Rom. 3; Mart. Polyc. 10); but it was natural that in the first age of the Church it should not be used by believers among themselves.

Four titles: disciples, brethren, saints, believers.   Four terms find more or less currency in the N. T. which express different aspects of the Christian view of the Christian position: 'the disciples' (οἱ μαθηταί), 'the brethren' (οἱ ἀδελφοί), 'the saints' (οἱ ἅγιοι), 'the believers' (οἱ πιστοί, οἱ πιστεύοντες). These fall into two pairs, of which the first pair, 'disciples,' 'brethren,' marks predominantly traits of personal relationship, and the second pair, 'saints,' 'faithful,' traits of general character.

The earliest title is that of 'the disciples.' This answers to 'master,' 1. *The disciples.*
'teacher' (διδάσκαλος), and passed from the Jewish schools to the followers
of Christ during His lifetime. It was used both in a wider sense for all
who attached themselves to Him (John ii. 11 ff.; vi. 61, 66; vii. 3) and also
in a narrower sense for 'the twelve' (John xiii. 5 ff.). After the Ascension
it is still employed absolutely in the narrative of the Acts to describe
believers generally (vi. 1, 2, 7; ix. 19, 25, 38; xi. 26, 29; xiii. 52; xiv. 20,
22, 28; xviii. 23, 27; xix. 9, 30; xx. 1; xxi. 4, 16); and so it is found in
the record of a speech of St Peter (xv. 10) and of a speech of St Paul (xx.
30). The discipleship is once connected with the human teacher (ix. 25 οἱ
μ. αὐτοῦ) and once with the Lord (ix. 19). It is remarkable that in one
place (xix. 1) those who had only received John's Baptism are spoken of as
disciples. The title does not occur in the Epistles or in the Apocalypse.

It is significant that the first title given to the body of believers after 2. *The brethren.*
the Ascension is 'the brethren' (Acts i. 15 true text); and from this time
onwards it occurs in all the groups of Apostolic writings. Thus in the Acts
it is found in the narrative: ix. 30; x. 23; xi. 29; xiv. 2; xv. 1, 3, 22, 32 f.,
40; xvi. 2, 40; xvii. 10; xviii. 18, 27; xxi. 7, 17; xxviii. 14 f.; and once in
the record of St Paul's words: xv. 36. Twice in the same book it is used
of unconverted Jews: xxii. 5 (St Paul's words); xxviii. 21. St Paul uses
the title throughout his Epistles: 1 Thess. iv. 10; v. 26 f.; 1 Cor. viii. 12;
xvi. 20; Gal. i. 2; Rom. xvi. 14; Phil. iv. 21; Eph. vi. 23; Col. iv. 15;
1 Tim. iv. 6; 2 Tim. iv. 21. In the writings of St John it occurs: 1 John iii.
14; 3 John 5, 10; John xxi. 23. St Peter uses the abstract term 'the
brotherhood' (ἡ ἀδελφότης, 1 Pet. ii. 17; v. 9). The singular is not
uncommonly used (*e.g.* Rom. xvi. 23; 1 Cor. vii. 15), and especially with a
personal pronoun, 'thy brother,' 'his brother' (*e.g.* Rom. xiv. 10; 1 John
ii. 9 ff.). Compare c. ii. 9 note. On 'the friends' see 3 John 15.

The general idea of 'the believers' is expressed in three different forms 3. *The believers.*
which convey shades of difference in the application of the common mean-
ing: 'the believers' (οἱ πιστοί), 'they that believe' (οἱ πιστεύοντες), 'they
that believed' (οἱ πιστεύσαντες). The first (οἱ πιστοί) is found Acts x. 45
(οἱ ἐκ περιτομῆς πιστοί); 1 Tim. iv. 12; comp. Eph. i. 1; 1 Tim. iv. 3;
1 Pet. i. 21. 'They that believe' (οἱ πιστεύοντες) occurs: 1 Pet. ii. 7; 1 Thess.
i. 7; ii. 10 f.; 1 Cor. i. 21; Rom. iii. 22; Eph. i. 19. 'They that believed'
(οἱ πιστεύσαντες) occurs: Acts ii. 44; iv. 32; 2 Thess. i. 10; Hebr. iv. 3.
In the two last phrases the historic reference to the act of belief still
remains.

The title 'the saints' is characteristic of St Paul and of the Apocalypse. 4. *The saints.*
It occurs four times in the Acts, twice in connexion with St Paul's conver-
sion (Acts ix. 13 τοὺς ἁγίους σου; xxvi. 10), and twice in connexion with the
episode of St Peter's visit to Lydda (ix. 32) and Joppa (ix. 41). It is found
also once in St Jude (Jude 3); but not in any other of the Catholic Epistles
(comp. 1 Pet. ii. 5, 9). In St Paul it is frequent and distributed throughout
his Epistles: 1 Thess. iii. 13; 2 Thess. i. 10; 1 Cor. vi. 1 f.; xiv. 33; xvi. 1,
15; 2 Cor. i. 1; viii. 4; ix. 1, 12; xiii. 12; Rom. xii. 13; xv. 25 f., 31;
xvi. 2, 15; Phil. i. 1; iv. 22; Eph. i. 1, 15, 18; iv. 12; vi. 18; Col. i. 2, 4,
12, 26; Philem. 5, 7. It is found also in Hebr. vi. 10; xiii. 24. In the

Apocalypse it is found: v. 8; viii. 3 f.; xi. 18; xiii. 7, 10; xiv. 12; xvii. 6; xviii. 20; xix. 8.

General relation of the titles. The main differences of conception between the four titles are evident. Christians stand in the position of learners in the school of their Lord. The lesson which they have to learn surpasses all others. But the relation to the Divine Master is at once embodied in a new relation to fellow-believers. So the title 'the disciples' is soon lost in that of 'the brethren.' In the same way the title of 'the faithful,' which corresponds to 'disciples,' is far less common and characteristic than 'the saints' ('the holy'), which marks the recognised consecration of believers.

The titles in connexion. But while these broad distinctions are obvious, it is not easy to seize the exact force of the particular titles except that of 'the faithful' on each occasion, or even when they come near together, as 'disciples' and 'brethren'; Acts xi. 29; xviii. 27; xxi. 16 f.: 'disciples' and 'saints'; Acts ix. 38, 41: 'brethren' and 'saints'; 1 Cor. xvi. 15, 20; Rom. xvi. 14 f.; Eph. vi. 18, 23. It seems not unlikely that the title 'the brethren' was carried over from the 'Israel according to the flesh' to the spiritual Israel, and was specially used of the Jewish congregations. This view is supported by Acts xxii. 5; xxviii. 21. But in any case the title was soon extended more widely: Acts xv. 1.

Additional Note on iii. 16. *St John's conception of love*
(ἀγάπη).

1. The verb ἀγαπᾶν occurs throughout Greek literature from Homer downwards. The noun ἀγάπη belongs to Biblical literature exclusively. It occurs first in the LXX. (for אַהֲבָה most commonly, which is also rendered by ἀγάπησις and rarely by φιλία), where it is found in 2 Sam. xiii. 15 (μέγα τὸ μῖσος ὃ ἐμίσησεν αὐτὴν ὑπὲρ τὴν ἀγάπην ἣν ἠγάπησεν αὐτήν [Θάμαρ]), thirteen times in Eccles. and Cant., and in Jer. ii. 2 (ἐμνήσθην...ἀγάπης τελειώσεώς σου). It is not found in the Pentateuch; nor is it quoted from Josephus (Philo, *Quod Deus immut.* 14 φόβον τε καὶ ἀγάπην). The word is used in all the books of the New Testament except the Gospel of St Mark, Acts, and the Epistle of St James (in the Synoptic Gospels only Matt. xxiv. 12; Luke xi. 42). The collateral form ἀγάπησις occurs in the LXX. and later Greek writers but not in the New Testament.

Ἔρως occurs twice in the LXX.: Prov. vii. 18; xxx. 16 (as also ἐρᾶν and ἐραστής), but it is not found in N. T. Comp. Ign. *Rom.* 7, ὁ ἐμὸς ἔρως ἐσταύρωται and Bp Lightfoot's note.

The one compound of ἀγαπ- which is recorded is the Homeric ἀγαπήνωρ.

2. The words ἀγαπᾶν, ἀγάπη are used to describe the feeling of

I. God (the Father) for

  (1) *The Son:*

    John iii. 35 ὁ πατὴρ ἀγαπᾷ τὸν υἱόν.

    — x. 17 διὰ τοῦτό με ὁ πατὴρ ἀγαπᾷ ὅτι...

John xv. 9 καθὼς ἠγάπησέ με ὁ πατήρ, κἀγώ...
— — 10 μένω αὐτοῦ ἐν τῇ ἀγάπῃ.
— xvii. 23 ...καθὼς ἐμὲ ἠγάπησας.
— — 24 ἠγάπησάς με πρὸ καταβολῆς κόσμου.
— — 26 ἵνα ἡ ἀγάπη ἣν ἠγάπησάς με ἐν αὐτοῖς ᾖ...

(2) *The world:*
John iii. 16 οὕτως ἠγάπησεν ὁ θεὸς τὸν κόσμον ὥστε...

(3) *Men:*
John xiv. 21 ὁ ἀγαπῶν με ἀγαπηθήσεται ὑπὸ τοῦ πατρός μου.
— — 23 ὁ πατήρ μου ἀγαπήσει αὐτόν.
— xvii. 23 ἠγάπησας αὐτοὺς καθὼς ἐμὲ ἠγάπησας.
1 John iv. 10 αὐτὸς [ὁ θεὸς] ἠγάπησεν ἡμᾶς.
— — 11 εἰ οὕτως ὁ θεὸς ἠγάπησεν ἡμᾶς...

Comp. Apoc. xx. 9 τὴν πόλιν τὴν ἠγαπημένην.

Φιλεῖν is found in a corresponding connexion in regard to

(1) *The Son:*
John v. 20 ὁ πατὴρ φιλεῖ (v. l. ἀγαπᾷ) τὸν υἱόν.

(2) *Men:*
John xvi. 27 ὁ πατὴρ φιλεῖ ὑμᾶς.

II. The Son, for

(1) *The Father:*
John xiv. 31 ἵνα γνῷ ὁ κόσμος ὅτι ἀγαπῶ τὸν πατέρα.

(2) *The disciples:*
severally
    xi. 5 ἠγάπα δὲ ὁ Ἰησοῦς τὴν Μάρθαν...
    xiii. 23; xix. 26; xxi. 7, 20 (εἰς τῶν μαθητῶν) ὃν ἠγάπα ὁ Ἰησοῦς.
    xiv. 21 ἐγὼ ἀγαπήσω αὐτόν...
    Apoc. iii. 9 ὅτι ἐγὼ ἠγάπησά σε.

generally
    xiii. 1 ἀγαπήσας τοὺς ἰδίους τοὺς ἐν τῷ κόσμῳ εἰς τέλος ἠγάπησεν αὐτούς.
    xiii. 34; xv. 9, 12 ἠγάπησα ὑμᾶς· μείνατε...
    [— 9 μείνατε ἐν τῇ ἀγάπῃ τῇ ἐμῇ]?
    — 10 μενεῖτε ἐν τῇ ἀγάπῃ μου καθώς...
    Apoc. i. 5 τῷ ἀγαπῶντι ἡμᾶς.

Compare the use of φιλεῖν for the feeling of Christ towards men severally.
    John xi. 3 ἴδε ὃν φιλεῖς ἀσθενεῖ.
    — — 36 ἴδε πῶς ἐφίλει αὐτόν.
    — xx. 2 μαθητὴς ὃν ἐφίλει ὁ Ἰησοῦς.
    Apoc. iii. 19 ἐγὼ ὅσους ἐὰν φιλῶ, ἐλέγχω.

III. Men for

(1) *God (the Father):*
John v. 42 τὴν ἀγάπην τοῦ θεοῦ οὐκ ἔχετε ἐν ἑαυτοῖς.

1 John ii. 15 οὐκ ἔστιν ἡ ἀγάπη τοῦ πατρὸς ἐν αὐτῷ.
  — iv. 10 οὐχ ὅτι ἡμεῖς ἠγαπήκαμεν τὸν θεόν.
  — — 20 f. ἐάν τις εἴπῃ ὅτι Ἀγαπῶ τον θεόν.
  — v. 1 πᾶς ὁ ἀγαπῶν τὸν γεννήσαντα...
  — — 2 ...ὅταν τὸν θεὸν ἀγαπῶμεν.

(2) *Christ*:
John viii. 42 εἰ ὁ θεὸς πατὴρ ὑμῶν ἦν ἠγαπᾶτε ἂν ἐμέ.
  — xiv. 15 ἐὰν ἀγαπᾶτέ με...
  — — 21 ...ἐκεῖνός ἐστιν ὁ ἀγαπῶν με· ὁ δὲ ἀγαπῶν με...
  — — 23 ἐάν τις ἀγαπᾷ με...
  — — 24 ὁ μὴ ἀγαπῶν με...
  — — 28 εἰ ἠγαπᾶτέ με ἐχάρητε ἄν...
  [— xv. 9 μείνατε ἐν τῇ ἀγάπῃ τῇ ἐμῇ...]?
  — xxi. 15 f. Σίμων Ἰωάνου ἀγαπᾷς με...;

(3) *The brethren*:
John xiii. 34; xv. 17 (ἐντολὴν) ἵνα ἀγαπᾶτε ἀλλήλους.
  — — 35 ...ἐὰν ἀγάπην ἔχητε ἐν ἀλλήλοις.
  — xv. 12 ἵνα ἀγαπᾶτε ἀλλήλους καθὼς ἠγάπησα ὑμᾶς.
1 John ii. 10; iv. 21 ὁ ἀγαπῶν τὸν ἀδελφόν...
  — iii. 10, 14; iv. 20 ὁ μὴ ἀγαπῶν τὸν ἀδελφόν.
  — — 11, 23; iv. 7, 11; 2 John 5 (ἀγγελία) ἵνα ἀγαπῶμεν ἀλλήλους.
  — — 14 ...ὅτι ἀγαπῶμεν τοὺς ἀδελφούς.
  — v. 1 ...ἀγαπᾷ καὶ τὸν γεγεννημένον ἐξ αὐτοῦ.
  — — 2 ὅτι ἀγαπῶμεν τὰ τέκνα τοῦ θεοῦ.
2 John 1 οὓς ἐγὼ ἀγαπῶ.
3 John 1 ὃν ἐγὼ ἀγαπῶ.

(4) *Life*:
Apoc. xii. 11 οὐκ ἠγάπησαν τὴν ψυχὴν αὐτῶν ἄχρι θανάτου.

(5) *Evil* (*darkness*):
John iii. 19 ἠγάπησαν...μᾶλλον τὸ σκότος ἢ τὸ φῶς.
  — xii. 43 ἠγάπησαν τὴν δόξαν τῶν ἀνθρώπων...
1 John ii. 15 μὴ ἀγαπᾶτε τὸν κόσμον μηδὲ τὰ ἐν τῷ κόσμῳ· ἐάν τις ἀγαπᾷ τὸν κόσμον...

So φιλεῖν is used of the feeling of men for

(1) *Christ*:
John xvi. 27 ὑμεῖς ἐμὲ πεφιλήκατε.
  — xxi. 15 ff. σὺ οἶδας (γινώσκεις) ὅτι φιλῶ σε.
  — — 17 φιλεῖς με ;
Comp. 1 Cor. xvi. 22 εἴ τις οὐ φιλεῖ τὸν κύριον.

(2) *Life*:
John xii. 25 ὁ φιλῶν τὴν ψυχήν.

(3) *Evil*:
Apoc. xxii. 15 ὁ φιλῶν...ψεῦδος.

Comp. John xv. 19 ὁ κόσμος ἂν τὸ ἴδιον ἐφίλει.

Φιλεῖν is not used by St John of the feeling of man for the Father or for man (Matt. x. 27; Tit. iii. 15).

Φιλία occurs only James iv. 4 ἡ φιλία τοῦ κόσμου ἔχθρα τοῦ θεοῦ ἐστίν.

3. The words ἀγαπᾶν, ἀγάπη are also used absolutely.

 1 John iii. 1 ποταπὴν ἀγάπην δέδωκεν ἡμῖν ὁ θεός...
 — — 16 ἐν τούτῳ ἐγνώκαμεν τὴν ἀγάπην...
 — — 18 μὴ ἀγαπῶμεν λόγῳ...
 — iv. 7 ἡ ἀγάπη ἐκ τοῦ θεοῦ ἐστίν.
 — — id. πᾶς ὁ ἀγαπῶν ἐκ τοῦ θεοῦ γεγέννηται.
 — — 8 ὁ μὴ ἀγαπῶν οὐκ ἔγνω τὸν θεόν.
 — — id., 16 ὁ θεὸς ἀγάπη ἐστίν.
 — — 10 ἐν τούτῳ ἐστὶν ἡ ἀγάπη, οὐχ ὅτι...
 — — 16 ὁ μένων ἐν τῇ ἀγάπῃ.
 — — 17 ἐν τούτῳ τετελείωται ἡ ἀγάπη μεθ᾽ ἡμῶν, ἵνα...
 — — 18 φόβος οὐκ ἔστιν ἐν τῇ ἀγάπῃ.
 — — id. ἡ τελεία ἀγάπη ἔξω βάλλει τὸν φόβον.
 — — id. ὁ φοβούμενος οὐ τετελείωται ἐν τῇ ἀγάπῃ.
 — — 19 ἡμεῖς ἀγαπῶμεν, ὅτι...
2 John 3 ἐν ἀληθείᾳ καὶ ἀγάπῃ.
 — 6 αὕτη ἐστὶν ἡ ἀγάπη, ἵνα...
3 John 6 ἐμαρτύρησάν σου τῇ ἀγάπῃ.

4. From a consideration of these passages it will be seen that ἀγαπᾶν, ἀγάπη are an expression of character, determined, as we are forced to conceive of things, by will, and not of spontaneous, natural emotion.

In this sense 'love' is the willing communication to others of that which we have and are; and the exact opposite of that passion which is the desire of personal appropriation (ἐρᾶν, ἔρως).

5. God Himself is love. The creation and preservation of the world are in essence a continuous manifestation of His love; but, as things are, His love is characteristically made known through redemption, that is the consummation of the divine counsel of creation in spite of the intrusion of sin (1 John iii. 16; iv. 9). So it is that the revelation of the divine love is referred to an absolute (eternal) moment (ἠγάπησας, ἠγάπησεν) both in relation to the Son and also to the world and to men.

6. At the same time God who is love is also the source of love (1 John iv. 7). He endows believers with love (1 John iii. 1, 16 f.; iv. 9, 12, 16; 2 John 6); and this love becomes in them a fountain of moral energy, issuing necessarily in self-sacrifice (John xv. 13; 1 John iii. 16).

On the other hand the love of evil is so far moral suicide.

7. It is of interest to notice that 'love' is connected by St Paul with each Person of the Holy Trinity:

ἡ ἀγάπη τοῦ θεοῦ· 2 Thess. iii. 5; 2 Cor. xiii. 13; Rom. v. 5; (Eph. ii. 4).
ἡ ἀγάπη τοῦ χριστοῦ· 2 Cor. v. 14; Rom. viii. 35; Eph. iii. 19.
ἡ ἀγάπη τοῦ πνεύματος· Rom. xv. 30.

In each case the thought appears to be of the love of which God is the source rather than the object. But the love of God in man becomes in him a spring of love. On the idea of 'the love of God' see c. ii. 5 note.

Additional Note on iii. 19. The nature of man.

Limitation of St John's view of man's nature.

St John does not, like St Paul, give any definite analysis of the constitution or of the spiritual experience of man. But he recognises the same elements in human nature. Like St Paul, he distinguishes 'the flesh,' 'the soul,' 'the spirit,' 'the heart.' But it is worthy of notice that the characteristic intellectual faculties are rarely noticed by him. 'Understanding' (διάνοια) occurs only once in the most remarkable passage 1 John v. 20; and 'mind' (νοῦς) is found only in the Apocalypse (xiii. 18; xvii. 9). 'Conscience' (συνείδησις) is nowhere mentioned by St John (contrast [John] viii. 8). In St Paul these words are not unfrequent. For St John's use of γινώσκειν see c. ii. 3 note.

i. *Flesh* (σάρξ).

The term 'flesh' (σάρξ) describes the element with the characteristics of the element (comp. 1 Cor. xv. 39). It includes all that belongs to the life of sensation, all by which we are open to the physical influences of pleasure and pain, which naturally sway our actions.

As applied to human nature 'flesh' describes humanity so far as it is limited and defined by earthly conditions. In 'flesh' lies the point of connexion between man and the lower world. Through flesh come the temptations which belong to sense.

The word is used of mankind (as in O. T.) John xvii. 2 (πᾶσα σάρξ) to describe them under the aspect of earthly transitoriness.

'Flesh' is contrasted with 'spirit,' not as evil with good, but as the ruling element of one order with the ruling element of another: John iii. 6; vi. 63.

By 'flesh' we are united to earth; and by 'spirit' to heaven.

'The will of the flesh' (John i. 13) is the determination which belongs to the earthly powers of man as such.

'The desire of the flesh' (1 John ii. 16) is the desire which, as it springs out of man's present earthly constitution, is confined within the earthly sphere and rises no higher.

'Judgment after the flesh' (John viii. 15) is external, superficial, limited by what catches the senses (comp. 2 Cor. v. 16).

Thus the idea of evil attaches to the flesh not in virtue of what it is essentially, but from the undue preponderance which is given to it. The flesh serves for the manifestation of character. It ministers to other powers. It becomes evil when it is made supreme or dominates. It does not include the idea of sinfulness, but it describes human personality on the side which tends to sin, and on which we actually have sinned.

The essential conception of σάρξ is seen in its application to Christ.

(1) in His Person :

John i. 14 ὁ λόγος σὰρξ ἐγένετο.

1 John iv. 2 ἐληλυθὼς ἐν σαρκί.

2 John 7 ἐρχόμενος ἐν σαρκί.

Compare 1 Tim. iii. 16 ἐφανερώθη ἐν σαρκί.

Col. i. 22 τὸ σῶμα τῆς σαρκὸς αὐτοῦ.

And

(2) in His Work :

John vi. 51 ἡ σάρξ μου ὑπὲρ τῆς τοῦ κόσμου ζωῆς.

— 53 φαγεῖν τὴν σάρκα τοῦ υἱοῦ τοῦ ἀνθρώπου καὶ πιεῖν αὐτοῦ τὸ αἷμα.

— 56 ὁ τρώγων μου τὴν σάρκα καὶ πίνων μου τὸ αἷμα.

Use of 'flesh' in relation to Christ.

In these passages 'flesh' is seen to describe the element of Christ's perfect humanity.

It may be added that while σῶμα is found in St John (John ii. 21 ; xx. 12, &c.), it is never used metaphorically, and it does not occur in the epistles (Apoc. xviii. 13 = *mancipiorum*). In the Apocalypse σάρξ is found only in the plural.

The sense of the word represented by '*soul*,' '*life*' (ψυχή) is often obscure in other apostolic writers from the complex nature of the living man ; but in St John it is used only for the personal principle of our present earthly life, the vital energy of the σάρξ (yet notice John x. 24).

ii. Soul 'life' (ψυχή).

It is used

(1) of men generally :

John xii. 25 (comp. Luke xiv. 26 ; xvii. 33).

— xiii. 37 f. τιθέναι τὴν ψυχήν.

— xv. 13 *id.*; 1 John iii. 16 *id.*; 3 John 2.

And

(2) of Christ :

John xii. 27 ; x. 11, 15, 17 τὴν ψ. τιθέναι.

1 John iii. 16 *id.*

With the phrase τιθέναι τὴν ψυχὴν ὑπέρ (x. 11, 15 ; comp. Matt. xx. 28) must be contrasted (δοῦναι) τὴν σάρκα ὑπέρ (vi. 51).

In the Apocalypse ψυχή is used in the most unusual sense of disembodied 'souls' ; vi. 9 ; xx. 4.

While the 'soul' (ψυχή) expresses the sum of man's present vital powers, the 'spirit' (πνεῦμα) describes the quickening element which belongs to a heavenly sphere (comp. Rom. viii. 10) as the flesh describes the earthly element : John iii. 6 (5) ; vi. 63.

iii. Spirit (πνεῦμα).

It is used of the Lord : John xiii. 21 (comp. xii. 27) ; xi. 33.

Compare the phrases 'to become in spirit,' 'in spirit,' found in the Apocalypse : i. 10 (ἐγενόμην ἐν πνεύματι) ; iv. 2 (*id.*) ; xvii. 13 (ἐν πνεύματι) ; xxi. 10 (*id.*).

The sense the 'breath of life' is wholly distinct : John xix. 30 (comp. Matt. xxvii. 50 ; Lk. viii. 55) ; Apoc. xi. 11 (πνεῦμα ζωῆς) ; xiii. 15 (δοῦναι πν. τῇ εἰκόνι).

iv. 'Heart' (καρδία).

The seat of individual character, of personal feeling and moral determination, is the 'heart' (καρδία). The elements already considered are morally colourless in themselves, they are generic and not individual. The mention of the heart is comparatively rare in St John. But he shews that it is the seat of sorrow (John xvi. 6), of joy (xvi. 22), of distress generally (xiv. 1, 27), and also of purpose (xiii. 2), and spiritual discernment (xii. 40, LXX.).

The most remarkable passage in which he describes the office of the heart is in 1 John iii. 19—21. In this the heart appears as representing the whole conscious moral nature of man. The heart in fact includes the conscience, and covers the whole range of life. It takes account not only of the abstract rule but of all the personal circumstances which go to characterise action.

Compare Apoc. ii. 23; xvii. 17; xviii. 7.

Additional Note on iii. 23. The Names of the Lord.

The names of the Lord in the Epistles.

Something has been already said on the use of the Divine Names in the Epistles of St John (Additional Note on i. 2). It is however of deep interest to study in detail the exact relation of the several Names of the Lord to the contexts in which they occur. Such an inquiry will leave, I believe, a strong conviction in the mind of the student that each Name is perfectly fitted to present that aspect of the Lord's Person which is dominant at the particular point in the Apostle's exposition of the Truth.

The idea of 'the Name.'

Here, as elsewhere in the Bible, the Name has two distinct and yet closely connected meanings. It may express the revelation of the Divine Being given by a special title; or the whole sum of the manifold revelations gathered up together so as to form one supreme revelation. It is used in the latter sense in regard to the revelation of God in Christ in 3 John 7 ὑπὲρ τοῦ ὀνόματος, where τὸ ὄνομα, 'the Name' absolutely, includes the essential elements of the Christian Creed, the complete revelation of Christ's Person and Work in relation to God and man (comp. Acts v. 41; John xx. 31). In ii. 12 διὰ τὸ ὄνομα αὐτοῦ the term is more limited. The Person Who is present to St John through the paragraph is Christ as He lived on earth and gave Himself for those whom He called brethren (ii. 6; comp. Hebr. ii. 11 ff.). In iii. 23, v. 13 the exact sense of 'the Name' is defined by the words which follow.

The special names: His Son Jesus Christ,

From the Name thus generally referred to or defined we pass to the actual Names used. The full title His Son Jesus Christ (ὁ υἱὸς αὐτοῦ Ἰησοῦς Χριστός) is found i. 3, iii. 23, v. 20. The divine antecedent is differently described in the three cases, and this difference slightly colours the phrase. In i. 3 it is 'the Father' (compare 2 John 3 παρὰ θεοῦ πατρός, καὶ παρὰ Ἰησοῦ Χριστοῦ τοῦ υἱοῦ τοῦ πατρός); in iii. 23, 'God'; and in v. 20, 'He that is true.' Thus in the three cases the Sonship of Jesus Christ is regarded in relation to God as the Father, to God as God, and to God as perfectly satisfying the divine ideal which man is able to form. Bearing these secondary differences in mind we see that the whole phrase includes the two elements of the confession, or the two confessions, which St John brings into prominence: 'Jesus [Christ] is the Son of God' (iv. 15, v. 5); and 'Jesus is the Christ' (v. 1; comp. ii. 22). It is in other words 'the Name' written out at length.

The constituents of this compressed phrase are all used separately by St John:

(1) *Jesus:*   *Jesus,*

    ii. 22 ὁ ἀρνούμενος ὅτι Ἰησοῦς οὐκ ἔστιν ὁ χριστός.

    v. 1 ὁ πιστεύων ὅτι Ἰησοῦς ἐστὶν ὁ χριστός.

    iv. 3 ὃ μὴ ὁμολογεῖ τὸν Ἰησοῦν.

In these passages it is obvious that the central thought is of the Lord in His perfect, historical, humanity. The use of the definite article in the last example probably conveys a reference to *v.* 2.

(2) *Christ:*   *Christ,*

    2 John 9 ἡ διδαχὴ τοῦ χριστοῦ.

The title seems to point back to the long preparation under the Old Covenant which checks impatience (προάγων) under the New.

(3) *Jesus Christ:*   *Jesus*

    ii. 1 παράκλητον ἔχομεν...Ἰησοῦν Χριστὸν δίκαιον.   *Christ,*

    v. 6 ὁ ἐλθὼν δι' ὕδατος καὶ αἵματος, Ἰησοῦς Χριστός.

    2 John 7 οἱ μὴ ὁμολ. Ἰησοῦν Χριστὸν ἐρχόμενον ἐν σαρκί.

Here the idea of the Messianic position of the Lord is no less important for the full sense than that of His true humanity.

In iv. 15 ὅτι Ἰησοῦς [Χριστός] ἐστιν ὁ υἱὸς τοῦ θεοῦ the reading is doubtful. The adoption of Χριστός adds to the completeness of the thought.

For the clause iv. 2 ὁμολ. Ἰησοῦν Χριστὸν ἐν σαρκὶ ἐλ. see note. In spite of the close verbal parallel of these words with 2 John 7 the use of Ἰησοῦς Χριστός here seems to be differentiated from the sense there by ἐληλυθότα as contrasted with ἐρχόμενον.

(4) *the Son:*   *the Son,*

    ii. 22 ὁ ἀρνούμενος τὸν πατέρα καὶ τὸν υἱόν.

    — 23 ὁ ἀρν. τὸν υἱὸν οὐδὲ τὸν πατέρα ἔχει.

    — 23 ὁ ὁμολογῶν τὸν υἱὸν καὶ τὸν πατέρα ἔχει.

    — 24 ἐν τῷ υἱῷ καὶ ἐν τῷ πατρὶ μενεῖτε.

    iv. 14 ὁ πατὴρ ἀπέσταλκεν τὸν υἱόν.

    v. 12 ὁ ἔχων τὸν υἱὸν ἔχει τὴν ζωήν.

In all these cases the central thought is that of the absolute relation of sonship to fatherhood. The argument turns upon essential conceptions of son and father. Comp. John v. 19 note.

(5) *the Son of God:*   *the Son*

    iii. 8 ἐφανερώθη ὁ υἱὸς τοῦ θεοῦ ἵνα λύσῃ τὰ ἔργα τοῦ διαβόλου.   *of God,*

    v. 10 ὁ πιστεύων εἰς τὸν υἱὸν τοῦ θεοῦ.

    — 12 ὁ μὴ ἔχων τὸν υἱὸν τοῦ θεοῦ.

    — 13 τοῖς πιστ. εἰς τὸ ὄνομα τοῦ υἱοῦ τοῦ θεοῦ.

    — 20 οἴδαμεν ὅτι ὁ υἱὸς τοῦ θεοῦ ἥκει.

With these passages must be compared

iv. 10 ἀπέστ. τὸν υἱὸν αὐτοῦ,

v. 9 ff. ὁ υἱὸς αὐτοῦ,

where the immediate antecedent is ὁ θεός. In all these cases the idea of Christ's divine dignity is equally prominent with that of sonship in relation to a father.

Compare also v. 18 ὁ γεννηθεὶς ἐκ τοῦ θεοῦ.

Jesus His Son,

(6)   *Jesus His* (God's) *Son:*

i. 7 τὸ αἷμα Ἰησοῦ τοῦ υἱοῦ αὐτοῦ.

The double title brings out the two truths that 'the blood' of Christ can be made available for men and is efficacious.

His Son, His only Son.

(7)   *His* (God's) *Son, His only Son:*

iv. 9 τὸν υἱὸν αὐτοῦ τὸν μονογενῆ.

The uniqueness of the gift is the manifestation of love.

In connexion with these titles it must be added that the title 'the Son' in various forms is eminently characteristic of the first and second Epistles, in which it occurs 24 (or 25) times (22 or 23 + 2), more times than in all the Epistles of St Paul.

It is remarkable that the title 'Lord' (κύριος) is not found in the Epistles (not 2 John 3). It occurs in the narrative of the Gospel and is frequent in the Apocalypse. It occurs also in all the other epistles of the N. T. except that to Titus.

The absence of the title may perhaps be explained by the general view of the relation of Christ to the believer which is given in the Epistles. The central thought is that of fellowship. For the same reason the conception of external organization is also wanting in the Epistle.

IV. ¹'Αγαπητοί, μὴ παντὶ πνεύματι πιστεύετε,
ἀλλὰ δοκιμάζετε τὰ πνεύματα εἰ ἐκ τοῦ θεοῦ ἐστίν,

IV. THE RIVAL SPIRITS OF TRUTH
AND ERROR (iv. 1—6).

This section is closely connected
both with what precedes and with
what follows; and corresponds with
the first section of this great division
of the Epistle : ii. 18—29. It contains
three main thoughts:

1 There are many spiritual influences at work (v. 1).

2 The test of spirits lies in the
witness to the incarnation (vv. 2, 3).

3 The test of men lies in the
recognition of the Truth (vv. 4, 5).

The progress of thought is parallel
to that in ii. 18—29 (see p. 67), but
the argument of St John has passed
to a new stage. There his teaching
was centred in the Messiahship, the
Sonship of Jesus: here in the Incarnation of Jesus Christ. There he
insisted on the original message of the
Gospel: here he appears to regard
the fuller interpretation of the message. This section in fact presents
the conflict of the Faith with its
counterfeits in the last form, as a conflict of spiritual powers, unseen and
real.

1   The many spiritual influences
(v. 1).

The 'many false prophets' stand
in a relation towards the Spirit like
that which the 'many Antichrists' occupy towards Christ (ii. 18). Through
them evil spiritual powers find expression. Spirits therefore must be
proved.

¹ Beloved, believe not every spirit,
but prove the spirits, whether they
are of God; because many false
prophets are gone out into the world.

1. 'Αγαπητοί] Comp. ii. 7 note. The
existence of a subtle spiritual danger
calls out the tenderness of love.

μὴ παντὶ πν. πιστ.] nolite omni

spiritui credere V., believe not every
spirit. The mention of a spirit as the
characteristic endowment of Christians leads to a definition of true and
false spirits. There are many spiritual
powers active among men, and our
first impulse is to believe and to obey
them. They evidently represent that
which is not of sight. But some of
these are evil influences belonging to
the unseen order. They come to us
under specious forms of ambition,
power, honour, knowledge, as distinguished from earthly sensual enjoy-
ments. All such spirits are partial
revelations of the one spirit of' evil
which become (so to speak) embodied
in men.

Comp. Doctr. App. 11 οὐ πᾶς ὁ
λαλῶν ἐν πνεύματι προφήτης ἐστίν, ἀλλ'
ἐὰν ἔχῃ τοὺς τρόπους κυρίου.

δοκιμάζετε τὰ πν.]probate spiritusV.,
prove the spirits. As we are charged
to 'prove' the season (Luke xii. 56),
ourselves (1 Cor. xi. 28; 2 Cor. xiii. 5),
what is the will of God (Rom. xii. 2 ;
Eph. v. 10), our work (Gal. vi. 4), our
fellow-workers (2 Cor. viii. 8, 22; 1
Cor. xvi. 3; 1 Tim. iii. 10), all things
(1 Thess. v. 21, notice vv. 19, 20), so
we are charged to 'prove the spirits.'
Elsewhere the discrimination of spirits
is referred to a special gift (1 Cor. xii.
10 διακρίσεις πνευμάτων). Here however the injunction to 'prove' them
is given to all Christians. Comp. ii.
20. Man maintains his personal supremacy and responsibility in the presence of these powers : 1 Cor. xiv. 32.

εἰ ἐκ τοῦ θ. ἐστίν] whether they are
of God, whether they derive from Him
their characteristic being and their
power.

For εἶναι ἐκ see ii. 16 note; and for
δοκιμ. εἰ compare 2 Cor. xiii. 5; Mk.
iii. 2; Lk. xiv. 28, 31 (Matt. xii. 10
parallels).

ὅτι πολλοὶ ψευδοπροφῆται ἐξεληλύθασιν εἰς τὸν κόσμον.   ²Ἐν τούτῳ γινώσκετε τὸ πνεῦμα

2 γινώσκετε ℵᶜABC me the syrhl: γινώσκεται vg syrvg: γινώσκομεν ℵ*

ὅτι π. ψευδ....] Such watchful care is required *because many false prophets*, through whom the false spirits speak, as the Spirit speaks through the true prophets (2 Pet. i. 21, ii. 1), *are gone out into the world*. 'The spirit of antichrist' inspires them. So 'false Christs' and 'false prophets' are joined together (Matt. xxiv. 24). The use of the term ψευδοπροφήτης in the N. T. is suggestive. It is applied to the rivals of the true prophets under the old dispensation (Luke vi. 26; 2 Pet. ii. 1); and to the rivals of the apostles under the new dispensation (Matt. vii. 15, xxiv. 11, 23, f. ‖ Mk. xiii. 22; Acts xiii. 6); and especially, in the Apocalypse, to the embodied power of spiritual falsehood (Apoc. xvi. 13, xix. 20, xx. 10). The false-prophet is not only a false-teacher (2 Pet. ii. 1 ψευδοπροφῆται, ψευδοδιδάσκαλοι), but a false-teacher who supports his claims by manifestations of spiritual power (Matt. xxiv. 24 δώσουσιν σημεῖα μεγάλα καὶ τέρατα; Acts xiii. 6 ἄνδρα τινὰ μάγον; Apoc. xix. 20 ὁ ποιήσας τὰ σημεῖα).

ἐξεληλύθασιν] *exierunt* V. (*prodierunt* F.), *are gone out* on a mission of evil from their dark home. The tense, as contrasted with ii. 19, 2 John 7, ἐξῆλθαν, expresses the continuance of their agency as distinguished from the single fact of their departure. Comp. John viii. 42, xiii. 3, xvi. 27 &c.

εἰς τὸν κόσμον] *into the world* as the scene of their activity. John iii. 17, ix. 39, x. 36 &c.

The words evidently refer to external circumstances vividly present to St John's mind. They point, as it appears, to the great outbreak of the Gentile pseudo-Christianity which is vaguely spoken of as Gnosticism, the endeavour to separate the 'ideas' of the Faith from the facts of the historic Redemption.

2. *The test of spirits lies in the witness to the Incarnation* (2, 3).

2, 3. The test of the presence of the Divine Spirit is the confession of the Incarnation, or, more exactly, of the Incarnate Saviour. The Gospel centres in a Person and not in any truth, even the greatest, about the Person. The Incarnate Saviour is the pledge of the complete redemption and perfection of man, of the restoration of 'the body' to its proper place as the perfect organ of the spirit. Hence the Divine Spirit must bear witness to Him. The test of spirits is found in the confession of a fact which vindicates the fulness of life. The test of antichrist was found in the confession of a spiritual truth (ii. 22 f.).

²*In this ye know the Spirit of God; every spirit which confesseth Jesus Christ come in flesh is of God;* ³*and every spirit which confesseth not Jesus is not of God. And this is the spirit*(revelation)*of Antichrist whereof ye heard that it cometh; and now is it in the world already.*

2. Ἐν τούτῳ] *In hoc* V. (*Hinc* F. Hereby. The idea of the process of testing passes directly into that of the test itself.

γινώσκετε] *cognoscitur* (*i.e.* γινώσκεται) V., *ye know*, *i.e.* perceive, recognise the presence of. The Vulgate rendering is evidently derived from a common itacism (-αι for -ε) and may be dismissed at once. Throughout the Epistle St John speaks personally (*we know, ye know*), and not in an abstract form (*it is known*). It is more difficult to decide whether γι-

τοῦ θεοῦ· πᾶν πνεῦμα ὃ ὁμολογεῖ 'Ιησοῦν Χριστὸν ἐν
σαρκὶ ἐληλυθότα ἐκ τοῦ θεοῦ ἐστίν, ³καὶ πᾶν πνεῦμα

Ῑν Χ̄ν : Χ̄ν Ῑν C.　　ἐληλυθότα ℵAC : ἐληλυθέναι B (vg).

νώσκετε is *indic. (ye know)*, or *imper.*
(know ye). In every other place in
the Epistle ἐν τούτῳ is joined with a
direct statement. On the other hand
it is always elsewhere used with the
first person in combination with γινώσκω (ἐν τούτῳ γινώσκομεν, ἐγνώκαμεν). The change of person may
therefore be connected with a change
of mood; and in this case the imperative carries on the charge *believe not,
prove.* Compare John xv. 18. So far
there is nothing in usage to determine
the question; but on the whole it
seems more likely that St John would
appeal to the results of actual experience which had been hitherto decisive *(ye discern, recognise)* than
seem to enjoin a new and untried
rule *(discern, recognise).* Comp. *v.* 4.

τὸ πν. τοῦ θ.] *the Spirit of God,* the
one Holy Spirit who reveals Himself
in many ways and in many parts. He
must be recognised as the inspirer of
all who speak from God; and all that
is truly spoken is from Him.

In *v.* 13 St John speaks of 'His
Spirit' *(i.e.* of God), and in c. v. 6, 8
of 'the Spirit,' but, as has been noticed,
the title 'the Holy Spirit' is not found
in the Epistles or in the Apocalypse.
Comp. *v.* 6.

πᾶν πν. ὃ...] *every spirit which...*
There is an endless variety in the
operations of the Spirit (1 Cor. xii. 4).
These severally appear to find cha-
racteristic organs in 'spirits' which
are capable of acting on man's spirit.
Comp. 1 Cor. xii. 10; xiv. 12, 32;
Hebr. i. 14, (xii. 9, 23), (1 Pet. iii. 19),
(Apoc. xxii. 6); τὰ ἑπτὰ πν. Apoc. i.
4; iii. 1; iv. 5; v. 6.

ὁμολογεῖ] *confitetur* V., *confesseth,*
openly and boldly acknowledges the
Person of the Incarnate Saviour and
not only the fact of the Incarnation.

Comp. ii. 23 note. The question
here is not of inner faith, but of outward confession. Faith, if it is real,
must declare itself. Active love must
be connected with a distinct recognition of its source. Ergo, Augustine
says, followed by Bede, ipse est spiritus Dei qui dicit Jesum in carne venisse; qui non dicit lingua sed factis;
qui dicit non sonando sed amando.

'Ι. Χ. ἐν σ. ἐλ.] The construction of
these words is not quite clear. Three
ways of taking them are possible. (1)
The direct object may be 'Ιησοῦν and
χριστὸν ἐν σ. ἐλ. a secondary predicate: 'confesseth Jesus as Christ and
a Christ come in flesh'; (2) The direct
object may be 'Ιησοῦν Χριστὸν and
ἐν σ. ἐλ. a secondary predicate: 'confesseth Jesus Christ, Him who is known
by this full name, as come in flesh';
(3) The whole phrase may form a compound direct object: 'confesseth Him,
whose nature and work is described
by the phrase, 'Jesus Christ come in
flesh'.' The corresponding clause in
v. 3 'Ιησοῦν which gives the person
and not any statement about the person as the object of confession is in
favour of the last view.

ἐληλυθότα] The construction with
the participle gives a different thought
from that with the infinitive (ἐληλυθέναι). It does not express the acknowledgment of the truth of the fact
but the acknowledgment of One in
whom this fact is fulfilled and of whom
it is predicated. Comp. 2 John 7 (ὁμολ.
ἐρχόμενον). For the sense of ἔρχεσθαι
see c. v. 6 note.

ἐν σαρκὶ ἐληλ.] *come in flesh,* manifested under this special form. The
order (ἐν σαρκὶ ἐλ.) and the tense of
the verb (ἐλη.) lay emphasis on the
mode rather than on the fact of
Christ's coming. 'The Word became

ὃ μὴ ὁμολογεῖ τὸν Ἰησοῦν ἐκ τοῦ θεοῦ οὐκ ἔστιν· καὶ

3 ὃ μὴ ὁμολογεῖ : ὃ λύει vg. See Additional Note.   τὸν Ῑν AB (vg) me syrr ;
Ῑν Χ̄ν (vg) (others read τὸν Ῑν Χ̄ν).   + ἐν σαρκὶ ἐληλυθότα ℵ syrr (lat): om. AB
vg me the.

flesh' (i. 14); and that not tempo-
rarily, but so that He is still coming
in it (2 John 7). The Christ 'who
should come' came, and coming in
this way fulfilled and still fulfils the
promises of the past. For the confession is not only of One who 'came'
(ἐλθόντα) but of One who 'is come'
(ἐληλυθότα), whose 'coming' is an
abiding fact. And yet further He
came 'in flesh,' as revealing the nature
of His mission in this form, and not
only 'into flesh' (εἰς σάρκα), as simply
entering on such a form of being.
ἐκ τοῦ θ. ἐ.] Comp. 1 Cor. xii. 3;
and Additional Note on iii. 1.
3. καὶ πᾶν πν.] The negative statement is here directly joined to the
positive. In ii. 23 the positive and
negative statements are placed in
simple parallelism.
ὃ μὴ ὁμ. τὸν Ἰ.] The substance of
the confession which has been given
in detail in the former verse is gathered up in the single human name of
the Lord. To 'confess Jesus,' which
in the connexion can only mean to
confess 'Jesus as Lord' (1 Cor. xii. 3,
Rom. x. 9), is to recognise divine
sovereignty in One Who is truly man,
or, in other words, to recognise the
union of the divine and human in one
Person, a truth which finds its only
adequate expression in the fact of the
Incarnation.
The very ancient reading ὃ λύει τὸν
Ἰησοῦν (qui solvit Jesum V., qui
destruit Lcfr.: see Additional Note)
expresses this view more directly.
The meaning which it is designed to
convey must be 'which separates the
divine from the human, which divides
the one divine-human Person.' But
it may well be doubted whether

Ἰησοῦς would be used in this comprehensive sense. In Scripture 'Jesus'
always emphasises the humanity of
the Lord considered in itself. The
thought would be conveyed by ὁ λύει
Ἰησοῦν Χριστόν or even by ὁ λύει τὸν
χριστόν. It seems likely that the
verb was transferred to this context
from some traditional saying of St
John in which it was applied to false
teachers, such as οἱ λύοντες τὸν χριστόν, or the like. The words of Polycarp which appear only indirectly, and
yet certainly, to refer to the phrase
in the Epistle indicate that St John
dwelt upon the thought in various
aspects: πᾶς γὰρ ὃς ἂν μὴ ὁμολογῇ Ἰησοῦν Χριστὸν ἐν σαρκὶ ἐληλυθέναι ἀντίχριστός ἐστι, καὶ ὃς ἂν μὴ ὁμολογῇ τὸ
μαρτύριον τοῦ σταυροῦ ἐκ τοῦ διαβόλου
ἐστί (ad Phil. c. vii.).
ὃ μὴ ὁμολογεῖ] The use of μή marks
the character of the spirit which leads
to the denial ('such that it confesseth
not') as distinguished from the simple
fact of the failure to confess (ὁ οὐχ
ὁμολογεῖ: v. 6 ὃς οὐκ ἔστιν).
τὸν Ἰ.] Comp. i. 7 note. For the use
of this simple human name of the Lord
in similar connexions see Rom. iii. 26;
(x. 9;) 2 Cor. xi. 4; Eph. iv. 21; Phil.
ii. 10; Hebr. ii. 9 note. Comp. 2 Cor.
iv. 10 f.
ἐκ τοῦ θεοῦ οὐκ ἔ.] The denial of
the Incarnation is in fact the denial
of that which is characteristic of
the Christian Faith, the true union of
God and man (comp. ii. 22 ff.). By
this form of statement (as distinguished from 'is of the devil,' or the
like) St John meets the specious
claims of the false prophets: such a
spirit, whatever appearances may be,
is not of God.

τοῦτό ἐστιν τὸ τοῦ ἀντιχρίστου, ὃ ἀκηκόατε ὅτι ἔρχεται, καὶ νῦν ἐν τῷ κόσμῳ ἐστὶν ἤδη.　　⁴Ὑμεῖς

ὃ ἀκηκ.: ὅτι ἀκηκ. א.

The antagonists regarded here are
not mere unbelievers but those who
knowing Christianity fashion it into a
shape of their own.

Augustine (ad loc.) remarks characteristically that the denial of the
Incarnation is the sign of the absence
of love: Caritas illum adduxit ad carnem. Quisquis ergo non habet caritatem negat Christum in carne venisse.
And so he goes on to interpret 'solvit'
of the spirit of the schismatic: Ille
venit colligere, tu venis solvere. Dis-
tringere vis membra Christi. Quomodo non negas Christum in carne
venisse qui disrumpis Ecclesiam Dei
quam Ille congregavit?

It is of interest to notice the two
negative signs which St John gives of
'not being of God.' In c. iii. 10 he
writes πᾶς ὁ μὴ ποιῶν δικαιοσύνην οὐκ
ἔστιν ἐκ τοῦ θεοῦ: here πᾶν πνεῦμα ὃ
μὴ ὁμολογεῖ τὸν Ἰησοῦν ἐκ τοῦ θεοῦ οὐκ
ἔστιν. In the case of men the proof
of the absence of the divine connexion
is found in the want of active righteousness: in the case of spirits in the
failure to confess the Incarnation.
The two tests exactly correspond to
one another in the two spheres to
which they severally belong. The
confession of the Incarnation embodied
in life must produce the effort after
righteousness which finds its absolute
spiritual support in the belief in the
Incarnation.

καὶ τοῦτο...] et hic est antichristus
quod audistis V., hoc est illius antichristi quod aud. F., 'and this whole
manifestation of false, ungodly, spiritual powers is the manifestation of
antichrist, whereof (ὃ not ὄν) ye have
heard....' The omission of πνεῦμα in
the phrase τὸ τοῦ ἀντιχρίστου gives
greater breadth to the thought, so
that the words include the many

spirits, the many forces, which reveal
the action of antichrist.

τοῦ ἀντιχρίστου] The spiritual influence is not only negatively 'not of
God': it is positively 'of antichrist.'

ἀκηκόατε] Compare καθὼς ἠκούσατε
ii. 18. The difference in tense places
the two warnings in a somewhat different relation to the hearers. For
the perfect see c. i. 1, 3, 5; for the
aorist, ii. 7, 18, 24, iii. 11; 2 John 6.

ἔρχεται] The same word is used of
the advent of the power of evil as of
the advent of the Lord. Comp. ii. 18;
v. 6, notes.

καὶ νῦν...ἤδη] et nunc jam V., and
now...already. For the position of ἤδη
see John ix. 27 (not iv. 35). The prophecy had found fulfilment before the
Church had looked for it.

3. *The test of men lies in the recognition of the Truth* (4—6).

4—6. In the verses which precede
(2, 3) St John has considered the
teaching of spirits as the test of their
character. He now regards the subject from another point of view and
considers the teaching of spirits as the
test of men.

⁴ *Ye are of God, little children, and
have overcome them, because greater
is he that is in you than he that is in
the world.* ⁵ *They are of the world:
for this cause speak they of the world
and the world heareth them.* ⁶ *We
are of God: he that knoweth God
heareth us; he who is not of God
heareth not us. By this we know
the spirit of truth and the spirit of
error.*

4. Ὑμεῖς] *You* as contrasted with
the world; *you* who are in possession
of spiritual endowments. Comp. ii. 20
καὶ ὑμεῖς χρίσμα ἔχετε, ii. 24, 27.

ἐκ τοῦ θεοῦ ἐστέ] Comp. Additional Note on iii. 1.

ἐκ τοῦ θεοῦ ἐστέ, τεκνία, καὶ νενικήκατε αὐτούς, ὅτι
μείζων ἐστὶν ὁ ἐν ὑμῖν ἢ ὁ ἐν τῷ κόσμῳ· ⁵αὐτοὶ ἐκ τοῦ

The hearers of St John have that divine connexion which the false spirits have not (v. 3 ἐκ τοῦ θ. οὐκ ἔ.).

τεκνία] c. iii. 18. The father in Christ speaks again. The address 'beloved' has been used twice in the interval (iii. 21, iv. 1).

νενικήκατε αὐτούς] vicistis eum V., eos F., have overcome them. The personal reference goes back to v. 1 (ψευδοπροφῆται). The intervening verses are structurally parenthetical, though they contain the ruling thought of the section.

The false spirits, whose characteristic has now been defined, must have their organs through whom to speak; and Christians must wage war against them. In this conflict the virtue of their Master's Victory (John xvi. 33) is granted to them. They have to claim the fruits of a triumph which has been already gained.

Comp. ii. 13 (νενικήκατε) note. The thought of a spiritual conflict is developed in Eph. vi. 12 ff.

ὅτι...] The ground and the assurance of the victory of Christians lie in the Power by which they are inspired (c. iii. 24). The strength of men is proportioned to the vital force of which they are the organs.

Vicistis eum, inquit. Sed unde vicerunt? Numquid liberi virtute arbitrii? Non utique. Taceat Pelagius, dicat ipse Johannes: Quoniam major est qui in vobis est... (Bede). So Augustine; ...qui audit Vicistis erigit caput, erigit cervicem, laudari se vult. Noli te extollere: vide quis in te vicit.

μείζων] greater. See iii. 20.

ὁ ἐν ὑμῖν] qui in vobis est V., he that is in you, that is in the Christian Society. The Church appears to be set over against the world; so that here the thought is of the body, and

not (as in iii. 24) of the individual. The Divine Person is undefined. We think naturally of God in Christ. Comp. John vi. 56, xiv. 20, xv. 4 f., xvii. 23, 26. Elsewhere 'the word of God' (c. ii. 14), 'the unction received from Him' (ii. 27), 'His seed' (iii. 9) is said to 'abide' in believers, as here He himself is in them. See note on v. 15. St Paul expresses the same thought in relation to the individual: Gal. ii. 20.

ὁ ἐν τῷ κόσμῳ] he that is in the world. The many false spirits represent one personal power of falsehood, 'the prince of the world' (John xii. 31, xiv. 30), the devil whose 'children' the wicked are (iii. 10). The world occupies in regard to him the same twofold position which Christians occupy with regard to God: 'the world lieth in the wicked one' (c. v. 19) and he 'is in the world.' The natural opposite to 'in you,' taken personally, would have been 'in them'; but St John wishes to shew that these false prophets are representatives of the world. The conflict, as has been said above, is regarded socially.

Comp. Eph. ii. 2.

5. αὐτοί...] ipsi V., they, the false prophets, through whom the false spirits work.

The nom. pl. αὐτοί, which occurs here only in the Epistles, emphasises the contrast. Comp. James ii. 6, 7; Hebr. xiii. 17; Luke xi. 48. See c. ii. 25 note.

ἐκ τ. κ. εἰσίν] de mundo sunt V., are of the world and not simply of the earth (John iii. 31). The 'earth' expresses the necessary limitations of the present order: the 'world' the moral characteristics of the order, as separated from God. For the phrase compare c. ii. 16; John xv. 19, xvii.

κόσμου εἰσίν· διὰ τοῦτο ἐκ τοῦ κόσμου λαλοῦσιν καὶ
ὁ κόσμος αὐτῶν ἀκούει. ⁶ἡμεῖς ἐκ τοῦ θεοῦ ἐσμέν· ὁ
γινώσκων τὸν θεὸν ἀκούει ἡμῶν, ὃς οὐκ ἔστιν ἐκ τοῦ

6 ὃς οὐκ...ἡμῶν : om. A.

14, 16 and the cognate phrase 'to be
of this world': John viii. 23, xviii. 36.
διὰ τοῦτο] *ideo* V., *for this cause.*
The character of their speech and the
character of their hearers are determined by their own character. They
draw the spirit and the substance of
their teaching from (out of) the world
and therefore it finds acceptance with
kindred natures. The words 'of the
world' answer to 'the world' in the
order of the original : '*it is of the
world they speak, and the world
heareth them.*'
For the threefold repetition of 'the
world' see John iii. 17, 31; 2 Macc.
vii. 11.
ἀκούει] Comp. John xv. 19.
6. ἡμεῖς ἐκ τ. θ. ἐ.] *we are of God.*
The apostle has spoken of Christian
hearers (*v.* 4 ὑμεῖς ἐκ τ. θ. ἐ.): he now
speaks of Christian teachers. In each
case living dependence upon God pro-
duces its full effect. The hearer dis-
cerns the true message. The teacher
discovers the true disciple. And this
concurrence of experience brings fresh
assurance and deeper knowledge.
The opposition of ἡμεῖς to ὑμεῖς and
the use of ἀκούει shew that St John is
not speaking here of Christians generally but of those whose work it is to
unfold the divine message.
The description of the true teachers
is not exactly parallel with that of the
false teachers. It is not directly said
of these that 'they speak of God' because the conclusion does not admit
of being put in the same form as in
the former case ('they speak of the
world and the world heareth them').
The world listens to those who express its own thoughts; the Christian
listens to those who teach him more

of God, new thoughts which he makes
his own. Thus the argument which
in the former clause lies in 'speak of
the world,' in this clause lies in ' he
that knoweth God.' The readiness to
hear springs from a living, growing,
knowledge, which welcomes and ap-
propriates the truth.
Comp. John viii. 47.
ὁ γινώσκων τ. θ.] *qui novit Deum*
V., *he that knoweth God.* The Latin
and English renderings both fail to
express the force of the original
phrase which describes a knowledge
apprehended as progressive and not
complete, a knowledge which answers
to the processes of life. Comp. *v.* 7,
v. 20; John xvii. 3. Contrast ii. 3 f.,
13 f., iii. 1.
So St Paul speaks of 'the call' of
God as continuous; 1 Thess. v. 24.
Comp. Phil. iii. 12 ff.
St John appears to choose this most
expressive phrase in place of the more
general one 'he that is of God' in
order to illustrate the position of the
true disciple as one who is ever advancing in the knowledge of God, and
whose power of hearing and learning
is given by this attitude of faithful
expectancy.
So it is that when he passes to the
negative side it is sufficient to say 'he
that is not of God' without bringing
into prominence the special energy
which flows from this divine dependence in regard to the fuller exposition of the Gospel.
The contrast which is marked here
between him 'that *knoweth God*' and
the man 'who *is not of God*' is given
under a slightly different form in *v.* 7
where it is said 'he that loveth *hath
been born of God* and *knoweth God,*'

θεοῦ οὐκ ἀκούει ἡμῶν. ἐκ τούτου γινώσκομεν τὸ πνεῦμα
τῆς ἀληθείας καὶ τὸ πνεῦμα τῆς πλάνης.

ἐκ τούτου אB syrr: ἐν τούτῳ A vg me the.

while 'he that loveth not *knew not God.'*

οὐκ ἀκούει] Comp. John xiv. 17 note.

ἐκ τούτου] *in hoc* V., *hereby, from this.* The phrase does not occur again in the Epistle and must be distinguished from the common ἐν τούτῳ (see c. ii. 3 note). It is found twice in the Gospel marking a connexion partly historical and partly moral (vi. 66, xix. 12). 'Εν τούτῳ seems to note a fact which is a direct indication in itself of that which is perceived: ἐκ τούτου suggests some further process by which the conclusion is obtained. The consideration of the general character of those who receive and of those who reject the message, and again of the teaching which is received and rejected by those who are children of God, leads to a fuller discernment of the spirit of the Truth and of the spirit of the opposing error. The power to recognise and accept the fuller exhibition of the Truth must come from the Spirit of Truth: the rejection of the Truth reveals the working of the spirit of error.

γινώσκομεν] *cognoscimus* V., *we know, recognise, perceive.* This power of recognition belongs to all believers. It is not limited to teachers by an emphatic pronoun as before; but expresses what is learnt in different ways by hearers and teachers.

τὸ πν. τῆς ἀλ.] *spiritum veritatis* V., *the Spirit of Truth.* Comp. John xiv. 17 note; 1 Cor. ii. 12 ff.

τὸ πν. τῆς πλάνης] *spiritum erroris* V., *the spirit of error.* The phrase is unique in the N. T. Comp. 1 Cor. ii. 12 τὸ πνεῦμα τοῦ κόσμου. 1 Tim. iv. 1 πνεύμασι πλάνοις. In contrast to ἡ ἀλήθεια 'the Truth' stands ἡ πλάνη (Eph. iv. 14) 'the error,' in which lie

concentrated the germs of all manifold errors. Compare τὸ ψεῦδος 2 Thess. ii. 11; Rom. i. 25; Eph. iv. 24 f.; John viii. 44.

'The seven spirits of error' occupy an important place in *The Testaments of the XII Patriarchs,* Reuben 2ff. The two spirits of truth and error are described as attending man, and it is added, τὸ πνεῦμα τῆς ἀληθείας μαρτυρεῖ πάντα καὶ κατηγορεῖ πάντων, καὶ ἐμπεπύρισται ὁ ἁμαρτήσας ἐκ τῆς ἰδίας καρδίας. Judah, 20.

C. THE CHRISTIAN LIFE: THE VICTORY OF FAITH.
(iv. 7—v. 21.)

The consideration of Antichrists and of the spirit of Antichrist and error is now over, and St John lays open the fulness of the Christian life. In doing this he takes up in a new connexion thoughts which he has before touched upon, and groups them in relation to the final revelation *God is love* (iv. 8, 16).

The whole division of the Epistle seems to fall most naturally into three sections:

I. THE SPIRIT OF THE CHRISTIAN LIFE: GOD AND LOVE.
(iv. 7—21.)

II. THE POWER OF THE CHRISTIAN LIFE: THE VICTORY AND WITNESS OF FAITH.
(v. 1—12.)

III. THE ACTIVITY AND CONFIDENCE OF THE CHRISTIAN LIFE: EPILOGUE.
(v. 13—21.)

I. THE SPIRIT OF THE CHRISTIAN LIFE: GOD AND LOVE (iv. 7—21).

This section deals in succession with

⁷ Ἀγαπητοί, ἀγαπῶμεν ἀλλήλους, ὅτι ἡ ἀγάπη ἐκ
τοῦ θεοῦ ἐστίν, καὶ πᾶς ὁ ἀγαπῶν ἐκ τοῦ θεοῦ γεγέν-

7 ὁ ἀγαπῶν: +τὸν θεόν A (*fratrem* is also added).

1. *The ground of love* (7—10).

2. *The inspiration of love*
⟨11—16 a⟩.

3. *The activity of love* (16 b—
21).

In the first paragraph the subject
is regarded mainly from its abstract,
and in the second mainly from its
personal side : ‾ in the third it is
treated in relation to action.

1. *The ground of love* (7—10).

The Christian Society has been
shewn to be clearly distinguished
from the world, even when the world
obtains the support of spiritual powers. St John therefore passes on to
consider the spirit of the Christian
life as seen in the Christian Body.
This spirit is love, the presence of
which is the proof of divine sonship,
seeing that God is love (*vv.* 7, 8);
and in the Incarnation we have set
before us the manifestation (*v.* 9)
and the essence of love (*v.* 10).

⁷ *Beloved, let us love one another,
because love is of God, and every one
that loveth is begotten of God and
knoweth God.* ⁸ *He that loveth not,
knoweth not (knew not) God, because
God is love.* ⁹ *In this was manifested the love of God in us, that God
hath sent his Son, his only Son, into
the world that we may live through
him.* ¹⁰ *In this is love, not that we
have loved God, but that he loved us,
and sent his Son a propitiation for
our sins.*

7. The transition of thought appears to lie in the implied efficiency
of love as a moral test of knowledge.
The twofold commandment of faith
and love is essentially one commandment (iii. 23 f.). Love in the region
of action corresponds to the confession

of the Incarnation in the region of
thought. The Christian spirit then
is proved by love. Comp. John x.
14 ff. note.

Ἀγαπητοί] The title and the charge
go together. See ch. ii. 7 note.

The title occurs comparatively frequently in 2 Peter, Jude, and sparingly
in the other Epistles of the New Testament: 2 Pet. iii. 1, 8, 14, 17;
Jude 3, 17, 20; 1 Pet. ii. 11; iv. 12;
2 Cor. vii. 1; xii. 19; Rom. xii. 19;
Phil. iv. 1; Hebr. vi. 9. Ἀγαπητοί
μου occurs 1 Cor. x. 14; and ἀδελφοί
μου ἀγαπητοί, James i. 16, 19; ii. 5;
1 Cor. xv. 58.

ἀγαπῶμεν ἀλλήλους] *diligamus invicem* V., *let us love one another.*
Comp. ch. iii. 11 note. St John deals
with the love of Christians for Christians (φιλαδελφία, St Paul, Hebr., St
Peter) as the absolute type of love.
There is no longer any distinction of
'ye' and 'we' (*vv.* 4 ff.); nor any emphasis on the pronoun. Compare iii.
14, 18, 23; iv. 12, 19; v. 2. St John
never says ἀγαπᾶτε, though he does
say μὴ ἀγαπᾶτε (ii. 15).

ὅτι...] *because...* The charge is
based upon a twofold argument: (1)
Love is of God, and therefore, since it
proceeds from Him, it must be characteristic also of those who partake
in His Nature, as His children ; and
again, (2) Active love becomes to
him who exercises it the sign of his
sonship (iii. 19).

ἐκ τ. θ. ἐ.] *is of God,* flows from
Him, as the one spring, and in such
a way that the connexion with the
source remains unbroken. See Additional Note on iii. 1.

πᾶς ὁ ἀγαπῶν...] *every one that
loveth...* The clause appears at first
sight to be inverted in form. It
might have seemed to be a more

νηται καὶ γινώσκει τὸν θεόν. ⁸ὁ μὴ ἀγαπῶν οὐκ ἔγνω
τὸν θεόν, ὅτι ὁ θεὸς ἀγάπη ἐστίν. ⁹ἐν τούτῳ ἐφανερώθη ἡ ἀγάπη τοῦ θεοῦ ἐν ἡμῖν, ὅτι τὸν υἱὸν αὐτοῦ

8 ὁ μὴ ἀγ....θεόν: om. ℵ* (om. τὸν θεὸν ℵᶜ).   οὐκ ἔγνω: οὐ γινώσκει A:
οὐκ ἔγνωκεν ℵᶜ.

direct argument to say 'let us love
one another because...every one that
is born of God loveth.' But as it is,
the words bring out the blessing as
well as the implied necessity of love.
Every one that loveth hath in the
consciousness of that spirit the proof
of his divine sonship. Comp. c. iii. 19.
πᾶς ὁ...] every one that... Comp.
iii. 3 note. St John does not say
simply 'he that loveth.' He insists
on the supreme characteristic of love
as overpowering in whomsoever it is
realised difficulties which men might
discover in subordinate differences.
ἐκ τοῦ θ. γεγέννηται] hath been begotten of God. Compare Additional
Note on iii. 1. The combination of
γεγέννηται with γινώσκει (not ἔγνωκεν)
is significant. Living knowledge is
regarded only in its present activity.
The active principle of sonship is
referred to its origin.
γινώσκει] cognoscit V., knoweth.
See v. 6 note. The present is sharply
contrasted with the aor. (ἔγνω, novit,
V.) which follows (v. 8).
The idea of 'knowledge' is introduced here in connexion with the action of the Spirit of Truth in the fuller
unfolding of the mystery of Christ's
Person. He that loveth derives his
spiritual being from God, and of
necessity therefore is in sympathy
with Him, and knows Him, that is,
recognises every revelation which
shews more of Him (v. 6).
8. As the presence of active love
is the pledge of advancing knowledge, so the absence of love is the
proof that apparent knowledge was
not real. 'He that loveth not, knew
not God' (οὐκ ἔγνω τ. θ., non novit V.,

ignorat F.) when he made profession
of knowing Him. His acknowledgment of God (as at Baptism) was
based on no true recognition of His
nature.
The aor. (ἔγνων) always has its full
force. Compare iii. 1; John x. 38,
xvi. 3.
ὅτι...] because. It is assumed that
knowledge involves practical sympathy. Compare ii. 3 note.
Bede puts well one side of the
truth; Quisquis [Deum] non amat,
profecto ostendit quia quam sit ama-
bilis non novit (ad c. ii. 5).
This conception of the nature of
knowledge corresponds with the view
of the Gospel as 'the Truth.'
ὁ θ. ἀγάπη ἐστίν] Deus caritas est
V. See Additional Note.
9. ἐν τούτῳ...ὅτι...] In hoc...quo-
niam... V. In this...that... So v. 10,
John ix. 30.
ἐν τ. ἐφαν....] The manifestation and
the essence of love (v. 10 ἐν τ. ἐστὶν
ἡ ἀ.) are distinguished, though both
are seen in the Incarnation. The
manifestation of love was shewn in
the fact (τ. υἱ. τ. μον. ἀπέστ.) and in
the end (ἵνα ζήσ.) of the Mission of
the Son. The essence of love was
shewn in this that the Mission of the
Son was absolutely spontaneous (αὐτὸς ἠγάπησεν ἡ.). Comp. Rom. viii. 32.
ἐφανερώθη]apparuit V.,manifestata
est Aug., was manifested. That which
'was' eternally was made known in
time. Compare c. i. 2 note. In the
retrospect of His completed work on
earth the Lord says: ἐφανέρωσά σου
τὸ ὄνομα (John xvii. 6), that is 'the
Father's name,' the revelation of love.
See also 2 Tim. i. 9 f.

τὸν μονογενῆ ἀπέσταλκεν ὁ θεὸς εἰς τὸν κόσμον ἵνα
ζήσωμεν δι' αὐτοῦ.   ¹⁰ ἐν τούτῳ ἐστὶν ἡ ἀγάπη, οὐχ

9 ζήσωμεν : ζῶμεν ℵ*.   10 ἡ ἀγ.: +τοῦ θεοῦ ℵ me the.

ἐν ἡμῖν] *in nobis* V., *in us:* not
simply 'towards us' as the objects
to whom the love was directed, but
'in us,' in us believers, as the medium in which it was revealed and
in which it was effective (*that we
may live through Him*). Comp. *v.*
16. The Christian shares the life of
Christ, and so becomes himself a
secondary sign of God's love. There
is a sense in which creation shews
God's love, but this revelation becomes clear through the new creation. The manifestation of the love
of God *to* man becomes a living power
as a manifestation of His love *in* man.

The sense *in our case*, or *among
us* (John i. 14), is excluded by the constant use of the preposition in the
context to express the presence of
God in the Christian body (*v.* 12).

τὸν υἱὸν αὐ. τὸν μον.] *filium suum
unigenitum* V., *His Son, His only
Son*. The exact form occurs only here
and John iii. 16. Comp. ii. 7; John i.
14 notes; and Additional Note on iii.
23. The order of the words in the
whole clause is most impressive: 'in
this that His Son, His only Son, hath
God sent into the world,' into the
world, though alienated from Him.

ἀπέσταλκεν] *He hath sent*, and we
now enjoy the blessings of the Mission:
v. 14; John v. 36, xx. 21. Comp.
John v. 33; Luke iv. 18; 2 Cor. xii.
17, &c. The aorist (ἀπέστειλα) occurs *v.* 10; John iii. 17, 34, vi. 29, &c.,
xvii. 3, &c. See Additional Notes on
iii. 5; John xx. 21.

Both here and in John iii. 16 the
Mission of the Son is referred to
'God' and not to 'the Father.' The
central idea is that of the divine
majesty of the Son and not that of
the special relation in which the

Father stands to the Son and, through
the Son, to men. Contrast *v.* 14, and
see Additional Note on i. 2.

ἵνα ζήσωμεν...] *that we may live*...
The natural state of men is that of
death: c. iii. 14. It is perhaps strange
that this is the only place in the
Epistles in which the verb ζῆν occurs.
Compare John v. 25; vi. 51, 57 f.;
xi. 25; xiv. 19. The term is used
because the Apostle lays stress upon
the activity of the Christian and not
upon his safety only (*that we may be
saved:* John iii. 17). In him, as he
lives, the love of God is seen visibly
working. As compared with John
iii. 16 f., which should be closely
examined with this passage, the object of the Mission of Christ is here
set forth in its personal working and
not in its general scope.

δι' αὐτοῦ] *per eum* V., *through
Him*, as the efficient cause of life.

Elsewhere the Christian is said to
live 'on account of' Christ; John vi.
57 (δι' ἐμέ).

St Paul speaks of Christ as living
in the Christian; Gal. ii. 20. 'The
life of Jesus' is that which the believer strives to manifest: 2 Cor. iv.
10 f.; and Christ is his life: Col. iii.
4 (comp. 1 John v. 12, 20); while
hereafter the Christian will live with
Him (σὺν αὐτῷ): 1 Thess. v. 10. So
Christ is the aim of the Christian's
life: Rom. xiv. 8 (τῷ κυρίῳ ζ.); comp.
Rom. vi. 10 f.; Gal. ii. 19; and the
substance of his life (τὸ ζῆν): Phil.
i. 21.

It is to be noticed that the Christian
is not said in the New Testament to
'live in Christ' (contrast Acts xvii.
28): though the Christian's life is
'in Him': 1 John v. 11; Rom. vi. 23;
2 Tim. i. 1. This phrase however

ὅτι ἡμεῖς ἠγαπήκαμεν τὸν θεόν, ἀλλ' ὅτι αὐτὸς ἠγάπησεν ἡμᾶς καὶ ἀπέστειλεν τὸν υἱὸν αὐτοῦ ἱλασμὸν
περὶ τῶν ἁμαρτιῶν ἡμῶν.   ¹¹ Ἀγαπητοί, εἰ
οὕτως ὁ θεὸς ἠγάπησεν ἡμᾶς, καὶ ἡμεῖς ὀφείλομεν ἀλλή-

ἠγαπήσαμεν אᶜA (ἠγάπησεν א*): ἠγαπήκαμεν B.   αὐτός: ἐκεῖνος A.
ἀπέστειλεν: ἀπέσταλκεν א.

occurs in Polyc. *ad Phil.* 8, δι' ἡμᾶς,
ἵνα ζήσωμεν ἐν αὐτῷ, πάντα ὑπέμεινε.

10. ἐν τούτῳ ἐστίν...ὅτι...] *in this
is...that...* In this we can see a
revelation of the true nature of love.
The source of love is the free will of
God Himself. He loved us because
'He is love,' and in virtue of that love
sent His Son. The origin of love lies
beyond humanity.

ἡ ἀγάπη] *caritas* V., *love*, in its
most absolute sense, not farther defined as the love of God or of man.

οὐχ ὅτι...ἀλλ' ὅτι...] *non quasi...sed
quoniam* V., *not that...but that...*
The negative clause is brought forward to emphasise the thought of
man's inability to originate love. For
somewhat similar forms of expression
see 2 John 5; John vi. 38; vii. 22;
xii. 6. Non illum dileximus prius:
nam ad hoc nos dilexit ut diligamus
eum (Aug., Bede).

αὐτός] *ipse* V., *He*, of His own free
will. Compare ii. 25 note.

ἠγάπησεν] *loved us.* The love is
viewed in regard to its historic manifestation, John iii. 16; Eph. ii. 4;
2 Thess. ii. 16. Comp. Gal. ii. 20;
Eph. v. 2, 25; Apoc. iii. 9.

ἱλασμόν] *propitiationem* V., *litatorem* Aug. ; in quibusdam codicibus...
legitur...*litatorem*... Bede; *expiatorem*
Lcfr., *a propitiation.* Comp. ii. 2 note.
The idea is introduced here to mark
the preparation of men for fellowship
with God. God was pleased to make
men fit to share His nature. The life
(*v.* 9) followed on the removal of sin.

2. *The inspiration of love* (11—16a).

St John has shewn that love must

come from God Who has revealed in
the Incarnation what it is essentially,
the spontaneous communication of the
highest good. He now considers what
must be the effect upon men of this
manifestation of love, which is the
assurance and the revelation of the
Divine Presence.

The character of God's love carries
with it an obligation to love (*v.* 11)
through the fulfilment of which by
the Spirit we gain the highest possible
assurance of fellowship with God (*vv.*
12, 13). And the experience of the
Church attests equally the love of
God and the effects of His love
among men (14—16 a).

¹¹ *Beloved, if God so loved us, we
also ought to love one another.* ¹²*No
man hath ever yet beheld God: if we
love one another, God abideth in us
and his love is perfected in us.* ¹³*In
this we know that we abide in him
and he in us, because he hath given
us of his Spirit.* ¹⁴*And we have
beheld and bear witness that the
Father hath sent the Son as Saviour
of the world.* ¹⁵*Whosoever shall
confess that Jesus [Christ] is the Son
of God, God abideth in him and he
in God.* ¹⁶*And we know and have
believed the love which God hath in us.*

11. Ἀγαπητοί] *v.* 7 note.

εἰ οὕτως...] *si sic Deus dilexit nos,
if it was so*, as we see in the mission
of His Son, *God loved us....* The
order of the words throws a stress
upon the particular manifestation of
God's love (ἠγάπησεν, John iii. 16);
and the repetition of ὁ θεός emphasises the Majesty of Him Who thus
revealed His love.

λους ἀγαπᾶν. ¹²θεὸν οὐδεὶς πώποτε τεθέαται· ἐὰν ἀγαπῶμεν ἀλλήλους, ὁ θεὸς ἐν ἡμῖν μένει καὶ ἡ ἀγάπη αὐτοῦ

καὶ ἡ. ὀφ.] *et nos debemus* V., *we also ought*... See iii. 16 note. The love which God has not only shewn but given to us (*v.* 1) becomes a constraining motive for action.

ἀλλ. ἀγ.] *alterutrum diligere* V., *invicem diligere* Aug. (F.). The phrase marks the mutual fulness of love. Comp. iii. 11 note. Of the love itself Augustine says: Noli in homine amare errorem, sed hominem: hominem enim Deus fecit, errorem ipse homo fecit.

It is of importance to observe that the obligation which St John draws from the fact of God's love is not that we should 'love God' but that we should 'love one another.' It is through human affections and duties that the spiritual, when once apprehended in its sublime purity, gains definiteness and reality under the conditions of our present state (comp. *v.* 20; c. i. 3 note). The thought of 'the love of God' (*i.e.* of which God is the object) as distinct from the 'love of Christ' (John xiv. 15, 21, 23 f., 28; xxi. 16; Eph. vi. 24) is very rare in the N. T. (*v.* 21; c. v. 2; Rom. viii. 28; 1 Cor. ii. 9, LXX.; viii. 3 εἴ τις ἀγαπᾷ τὸν θεόν, οὗτος ἔγνωσται ὑπ' αὐτοῦ). The command to love God is quoted from the Law (Matt. xxii. 37 and parr. from Deut. vi. 5). Gradually by the elevation of thought God seemed to be withdrawn from men; and then in the Person of His Son, who took humanity to Himself, God gave back to man that in which human feeling can find inspiration and rest.

12. θεόν...τεθέαται] *Deum nemo vidit unquam* V., *God hath no man ever beheld.* Comp. John i. 18 note. In both passages θεόν stands first and without the article, 'God as God'; and in both passages the object is

directly followed by the subject: *God hath no man ever* (seen). But the verbs are different. In John i. 18 the thought is of the vision which might be the foundation of revelation (ἑώρακεν): here the thought is of the continuous beholding which answers to abiding fellowship (τεθέαται). Comp. John xvi. 16 note. On θεός and ὁ θεός see Additional Note.

οὐδεὶς πώποτε...] *no man ever yet*... In these words St John seems to call up all the triumphs of the saints in past time. However close their fellowship with God had been, yet no one had beheld Him as He is. The question here is not one of abstract power but of actual experience.

ἐὰν ἀγαπῶμεν...] *if we love*...... Though God is invisible He yet is not only very near to us but may be in us, the Life of our lives. The words, as Bede points out, meet the implied question: Quo solatio utendum ubi divina visione nondum licet perfrui?

The manifestation of active love by men witnesses to two facts: (1) the abiding of God in them, and (2) the presence of divine love in them in its completest form. There is both the reality of fellowship and the effectiveness of fellowship.

ὁ θ. ἐν ἡμ. μένει] *abideth in us.* See Additional Note on *v.* 15. Generally this fellowship is described under its two aspects ('God in us, we in God'), but here the idea is that of the power of the divine indwelling. Comp. John xvii. 23, 26.

The question has been asked (Bede), How the highest blessedness is attached to the mutual love of Christians while in the Gospel the love of enemies is enjoined (Matt. v. 43 ff.)? The answer lies in the recognition of the essence of Christian love. This resting upon the Incarnation regards

τετελειωμένη ἐν ἡμῖν ἐστίν. ¹³ ἐν τούτῳ γινώσκομεν
ὅτι ἐν αὐτῷ μένομεν καὶ αὐτὸς ἐν ἡμῖν, ὅτι ἐκ τοῦ

12 τετ. ἐν ἡμῖν ἐ. אB: ἐν ἡμῖν τετ. ἐ. A vg: τετ. ἐ. ἐν ἡμῖν me the syrr.

all men in the light of that fact. The Christian can separate in man that which belongs to his true nature from the disease which corrupts it: Sævit in te homo. Ille sævit, tu deprecare: ille odit, tu miserere. Febris animæ ipsius te odit: sanus erit et gratias tibi aget (Aug. *in* 1 *Joh. Tract.* viii. § 11).

The love of the brethren is indeed the recognition of God in men by the exercise of that in man which is after the image of God. Ubi factus est ad imaginem Dei? Augustine asks on this passage, and replies: In intellectu, in mente, in interiore homine, in eo quod intelligit caritatem, dijudicat justitiam et injustitiam, novit a quo factus est, potest intelligere Creatorem suum, laudare Creatorem suum (*Tract.* viii. § 6).

He afterwards adds a profound test of love: Hoc naturale habes: semper melior eris quam bestia. Si vis melior esse quam alius homo, invidebis ei quando tibi esse videbis æqualem. Debes velle omnes homines æquales tibi esse (§ 8.)

ἡ ἀγ. αὐτοῦ] *caritas ejus* V., *His love*, the love which answers to His nature and with which He has endowed us. Comp. ii. 5 note. Man receives the love of God and makes it his own. Neither of the two specially defined senses, 'the love of God for man,' or 'the love of man for God,' suits the context.

τετελ....ἐστίν] The resolved form (i. 4; contrast *v.* 17, ii. 5) emphasises the two elements of the thought: 'the love of God is in us'; 'the love of God is in us in its completest form.' It is through man that 'the love of God' finds its fulfilment on earth.

The ideas of the perfection of love

in the believer and of the perfection of the believer in love are presented in several different forms in the epistle. In c. ii. 5 the sign of the perfection of 'the love of God' in man is found in the watchful regard which the believer pays to His revelation (ὃς ἂν τηρῇ αὐτοῦ τὸν λόγον). Here it is found in the love of Christians for one another. The two signs explain and indeed include each other. Love is the fulfilment of divine obedience. The commandment of Christ was love (cf. c. iii. 23).

In *vv.* 17, 18 the perfection of love is presented under another aspect. The fruit of the possession of 'love' is shewn in regard to the believer himself. 'Love hath been perfected with us' to the end that 'we may have boldness in the day of judgment.' And for the present, 'he that feareth hath not been made perfect in love.' Obedience, active love, confidence, these three, point to the same fact. Where the one is the other is. The source of all is the full development of the divine gift of love.

This characteristic thought of St John is found in the Thanksgiving after the Eucharist in the *Doctr. App.* 10 Μνήσθητι, Κύριε, τῆς ἐκκλησίας σου τοῦ...τελειῶσαι αὐτὴν ἐν τῇ ἀγάπῃ σου...

13. ἐν τούτῳ γινώσκομεν...] *in hoc intellegimus* V., *in this*, the possession of the spirit of love, which flows from God, *we perceive*, we are severally conscious of the fact of the divine indwelling which has been affirmed generally (*v.* 12, *God abideth in us*); and that by continuous and progressive experience (contrast ἐγνώκαμεν, *v.* 16).

ἐν αὐτῷ μένομεν...] See Additional

πνεύματος αὐτοῦ δέδωκεν ἡμῖν. ¹⁴Καὶ ἡμεῖς τεθεάμεθα
καὶ μαρτυροῦμεν ὅτι ὁ πατὴρ ἀπέσταλκεν τὸν υἱὸν
σωτῆρα τοῦ κόσμου. ¹⁵ὃς ἐὰν ὁμολογήσῃ ὅτι Ἰησοῦς

13 δέδωκεν ℵB: ἔδωκεν A.
15 ὁμολογήσῃ: ὁμολογῇ A.

14 τεθεάμεθα ℵB: ἐθεασάμεθα A.
Ἰησοῦς: +Χριστός B.

Note on v. 15. The believer feels in the enjoyment of this affection that the centre of his life is no longer within himself nor on earth; because the spirit by which it is inspired, by which alone it can be inspired, is the Spirit of God.

ἐκ τοῦ πν.] de spiritu suo V., of His Spirit, 'to each according to his several ability.' Under different aspects it can be said that God gives to Christians 'His Spirit' (1 Thess. iv. 8), or 'of His Spirit.' For the use of ἐκ (contrast iii. 24) see John vi. 11, i. 16. In the Holy Trinity we conceive of the perfect union of the Father and the Son as realised through the Spirit. So too it is through the same Spirit that the 'many sons' are united in the Son with God.

δέδωκεν] hath given. Contrast iii. 24, ἔδωκεν. The difference in tense corresponds to the difference in the sense of ἐκ τοῦ πνεύματος.

14. Καὶ ἡμεῖς τεθ....] Et nos vidimus V., And we have beheld.... The emphatic pronoun (v. 6, i. 4; John i. 16) brings into prominence the experience of the Christian Society gathered up in that of its leaders. The apostle does not speak of himself personally but as representing the Church for which he had a special work to do. His experience (John i. 14) was in another form the experience of all (John i. 16). The vision and witness of the immediate disciples correspond with the knowledge and belief of the disciples in all ages. Or, to express the same truth otherwise, that vision and witness remain as an abiding endowment of the living Body.

τεθεάμεθα] Strictly speaking the immediate objects of τεθεάμεθα and μαρτυροῦμεν are different. The object of contemplation was the revelation of the Lord's Life: the object of witness, the declaration of its meaning. In a wider sense spiritual facts can become the objects of direct vision (comp. John i. 33, μένον). Here however the thought is that the significance of the Lord's Mission was made known to those who carefully regarded His Life and observed the necessary tendency of all His actions. In this respect His Life was the object of contemplation (θεᾶσθαι) and not of vision. Compare John i. 34 (ἑώρακα) with John i. 32 (τεθέαμαι). See also c. i. 1, 2.

The use of τεθεάμεθα carries the mind back to v. 12, θεὸν οὐδεὶς τεθέαται. Though God Himself had not been the object of direct human regard, yet Christian faith rests upon a historic revelation of His Nature.

τεθεάμεθα καὶ μαρτυροῦμεν] Comp. i. 2, ἑωράκαμεν καὶ μαρτυροῦμεν, iii. 11, 32, and contrast John i. 34, ἑώρακα καὶ μεμαρτύρηκα, xix. 35. The continuous witness was based upon the abiding experience.

ὁ πατήρ] Comp. v. 10 (ὁ θεός) note.

ἀπέσταλκεν] hath sent. The testimony is borne not simply to the historic fact (v. 10, ἀπέστειλεν), but (as in v. 9) to the permanence of Christ's mission. Of this believers have direct knowledge. Comp. Additional Note on c. iii. 5.

σωτῆρα τοῦ κ.] salvatorem mundi V. (sœculi F.), as Saviour of the world. The full title occurs once again in the N. T. as the confession

[Χριστός] ἐστιν ὁ υἱὸς τοῦ θεοῦ, ὁ θεὸς ἐν αὐτῷ μένει καὶ αὐτὸς ἐν τῷ θεῷ. ¹⁶Καὶ ἡμεῖς ἐγνώκαμεν

of the Samaritans, John iv. 42; and the thought which it conveys is expressed in John iii. 17. St John nowhere else uses the title σωτήρ, which in other apostolic writings is applied both (1) to 'God': 1 Tim. i. 1 θεὸς σωτὴρ ἡμῶν καὶ X. 'I.; Tit. i. 3 ὁ σ. ἡμῶν θ., ii. 10, iii. 4; Jude 25 μόνος θεὸς σωτήρ; and more expressly 1 Tim. ii. 3 ὁ σ. ἡ. θ. ὃς πάντας ἀνθρώπους θέλει σωθῆναι, iv. 10 θεὸς ζῶν, ὅς ἐστιν σωτὴρ πάντων ἀνθρώπων, μάλιστα πιστῶν (comp. Luke i. 47); and (2) to Christ : Luke ii. 11 ἐτέχθη ὑμῖν σ. ὅς ἐστιν χριστὸς κύριος; Acts v. 31 ['Ιησοῦν] ὁ θεὸς ἀρχηγὸν καὶ σωτῆρα ὕψωσεν, xiii. 23 ὁ θεός...ἤγαγεν τῷ 'Ισραὴλ σωτῆρα 'Ιησοῦν; 2 Tim. i. 10 ὁ σ. ἡ. X. 'I.; Tit. i. 4 X. 'I. ὁ σ. ἡ. (comp. v. 3), ii. 13 ὁ μέγας θεὸς καὶ σ. ἡ. X. 'I., iii. 6 'I. X. ὁ σ. ἡ.; 2 Pet. i. 11 ὁ κύριος ἡ. καὶ σ. 'I. X., ii. 20, iii. 18 (comp. iii. 2 ὁ κ. καὶ σ.); and more particularly Phil. iii. 20 σ. ἀπεκδεχόμεθα κύριον 'I. X. (Eph. v. 23 αὐτὸς σωτὴρ τοῦ σώματος is doubtful). Thus the title is confined (with the exception of the writings of St Luke) to the later writings of the N. T., and is not found in the central group of St Paul's Epistles. The double application in Tit. i. 3 f. is very instructive.

The title is applied to God not unfrequently in the LXX.: Deut. xxxii. 15 θεὸς σ. (צוּר יְשֻׁעָתִי a Deo salutari V.); Ps. xxiv. (xxiii.) 5; xxv. (xxiv.) 5 (Deus salvator meus V.); xxvii. (xxvi.) 9 (אֱלֹהֵי יִשְׁעִי Deus salutaris meus V.); lxv. (lxiv.) 6; lxxix. (lxxviii.) 9; xcv. (xciv.) 1 || Deut. xxxii. 15; Is. xvii. 10; xlv. 15 (מוֹשִׁיעַ salvator V.). Comp. Wisd. xvi. 7; Ecclus. li. 1; 1 Macc. iv. 30. It is used also of human deliverers : Jud. iii. 9, 15 (מוֹשִׁיעַ salvator V.); and of the promised salvation (Saviour): Is. lxii. 11 (יֵשַׁע salvator V.).

In Classical writers the title is used of many deities, especially of Zeus; and it was given under later Greek dynasties to princes and benefactors. Comp. Pearson On the Creed, pp. 72 f. (136 ff.) notes, and Wetstein on Lk. ii. 11 for numerous examples. It had no Latin equivalent in Cicero's time. Cicero commenting on the title as applied to Verres adds : Hoc quantum est? ita magnum est ut Latine uno verbo exprimi non possit. Is est nimirum soter qui salutem dat (in Verr. ii. 2, 63).

The accus. (σωτῆρα) describes what Christ is and not simply what He is designed to be. Compare ii. 2 ἱλασμός ἐστιν, v. 10 ἀπέστειλεν ἱλασμόν. That which is yet partly future in its human application (Phil. iii. 20 σωτῆρα ἀπεκδεχόμεθα) is complete in the divine idea.

It is worthy of notice that the words σώζειν and σωτηρία are not found in the Epistles of St John.

15. ὃς ἐάν] See ii. 5 note. There is no limitation in the will of God (1 Tim. ii. 3).

ὁμολογήσῃ] See ii. 23 note; v. 2 note. The different forms of the confession require to be studied together. He that confesseth the Son hath the Father also (ii. 23); Every spirit that confesseth Jesus Christ come in the flesh is of God (iv. 2); Whosoever confesseth that Jesus [Christ] is the Son of God, God abideth in him and he in God. The exact point of the confession here prepares for the conclusion. The recognition of the revelation of God is the sign of the presence of God (comp. 1 Cor. xii. 3). The fruit of the confession characterised in v. 2 is now described fully.

'Ιησοῦς...ὁ υἱὸς τοῦ θ.] Comp. Hebr. iv. 14 note; and c. iii. 8 note.

ὁ θ. ἐν αὐ....αὐ. ἐν τῷ θ.] God in him ...he in God. See Additional Note.

καὶ πεπιστεύκαμεν τὴν ἀγάπην ἣν ἔχει ὁ θεὸς ἐν

16 πεπιστεύκαμεν אB (vg): πιστεύομεν A me.   ὁ θεός: —ὁ א.

The two clauses mark two aspects of the Christian's life. The believer has a new and invincible power for the fulfilment of his work on earth: 'God is in him.' And again he realises that his life is not on earth, that he belongs essentially to another order: 'he is in God.' The divine fellowship is complete and effective in each direction.

This complementary view of the fulness of the Christian life, as the believer lives in God and God in him, is presented by St John in several forms. *The love of God abideth in him* (iii. 17), and he *abideth in love* (iv. 16). *Eternal life abides in him* (iii. 15); and *this life is in the Son of God* (v. 11). *The Truth is in him* (i. 8; ii. 4), and he *walketh in the Truth* (2 Ep. 3). *The word of God is* and *abideth in him* (i. 10; ii. 14; cf. ii. 24), and he *abides in the word* (John viii. 31). He is and abides in the light (ii. 9 f.), and the unction of God abides in him (ii. 27), and guides him to all the Truth. Comp. Apoc. iii. 20.

Vicissim in se habitant qui continet et qui continetur. Habitas in Deo, sed ut continearis: habitat in te Deus, sed ut te contineat ne cadas (Aug., Bede).

16. Καὶ ἡμεῖς] *And we*, we who can speak from the fulness of Christian experience as confessors of Christ.... The case is taken from supposition (ὃς ἐὰν) to fact. For ἡμεῖς see *v.* 14 note.

ἐγνώκ. καὶ πεπιστ. τὴν ἀγ.] *cognovimus et credidimus caritati* V., *cogn. et credimus quam dilectionem Deus habet* Aug., *cogn. et credidimus in* [*caritate*] *quam habet Deus* F. The two verbs form a compound verb, in which the idea of belief qualifies and explains what is in this case the primary and predominant idea, know-

ledge. The Vulgate rendering throws the emphasis wrongly on *belief.* The same two verbs occur in John vi. 69 in the reverse order: ἡμεῖς πεπιστεύκαμεν καὶ ἐγνώκαμεν ὅτι σὺ εἶ ὁ ἅγιος τοῦ θεοῦ. Under different aspects knowledge precedes faith and faith precedes knowledge. We must have a true if limited knowledge of the object of faith before true faith can exist; and true faith opens the way to fuller knowledge. A general faith in Christ and self-surrender to Him prepared the disciples for a loftier apprehension of His character. The actual experience of love includes the promise of a larger manifestation of its treasures. This St John indicates here: 'We have perceived the divine love. To a certain extent we have realised what it is: but we have not exhausted its meaning. In knowing we have believed too; and in the conscious imperfection of knowledge we wait without doubt for future revelation.'

τὴν ἀγ. ἣν ἔχει ὁ θ. ἐν ἡμῖν] For the phrase ἀγάπ. ἔχειν see John xiii. 35 ἐὰν ἀγ. ἔχητε ἐν ἀλλήλοις; John xv. 13; 1 Pet. iv. 8 τὴν εἰς ἑαυτοὺς ἀγ. ἐκτενῆ ἔχοντες; 1 Cor. xiii. 1 ff.; Phil. ii. 2. It is clear from the context that the love here spoken of is the love which God has and shews towards man. But St John adds a second thought to that of God's love towards man (εἰς ἡμᾶς). The love of God becomes a power in the Christian Body (ἐν ἡμῖν). Believers are the sphere in which it operates and makes itself felt in the world (2 Cor. iv. 10 f.). Comp. *v.* 9 note.

3. *The activity of love* (16b—21).

In the two preceding sections St John has shewn what love is in its essence and origin, and how it neces-

ἡμῖν.   Ὁ θεὸς ἀγάπη ἐστίν, καὶ ὁ μένων ἐν
τῇ ἀγάπῃ ἐν τῷ θεῷ μένει καὶ ὁ θεὸς ἐν αὐτῷ [μένει].

ἐν αὐτῷ μένει ℵB me the syrhl: − μένει A vg.

sarily becomes an inspiring power in the believer, answering to a confession of the Incarnation. He now developes more fully the activity of love; and this in two relations, as to the believer in himself (16 *b*—18), and as to the believer in his dealings with his fellow-Christians (19—21). On the one side, it is by continuance in love that the divine fellowship is realised by the believer (16 *b*), while love is perfected in the divine fellowship, so that the last element of fear is cast out of the soul of him who loves (17, 18). And on the other side love, which is of a divine origin (19), must be fulfilled after a divine type, in love to the brethren (20), according to the divine commandment (21).

Ambrose has traced in a famous passage the progress of love till it finds its consummation in complete self-surrender. This he sees shadowed out in three passages of Canticles (ii. 16 f.; vi. 2; vii. 10). First there is the quickening of the divine affection in the soul by the revelation of the Word; next, the freedom of mutual intercourse between the soul and the Word; and at last the soul offers itself absolutely to the Word that He may rest there (Ambr. *de Isaac et anima,* c. viii. § 68).

God is love, and he that abideth in love abideth in God and God [abideth] in him. ¹⁷ *In this love is perfected with us, that we may have boldness in the day of judgment; because even as he is, so are we in the world.* ¹⁸ *There is no fear in love, but perfect love casteth out fear, because fear hath punishment; and he that feareth is not perfected in love.*

The words of *v.* 8 *God is love* are repeated as the subject of a new

development of thought. Before the idea was of birth and knowledge, now the idea is of growth and action. The revelation of the Nature of God as love calls out a response in answer to that which is necessarily regarded as a 'personal' call to men, and by suggesting the idea of unlimited self-communication as characteristic of God, it sets a type for human action. The nature of the believer must be conformed to the Nature of God.

καὶ ὁ μένων...] *and he that abideth* ... From the very Nature of God it follows as a necessary consequence that the life of self-devotion is a life in fellowship with Him. By the use of the conjunction in place of simple parallelism (*he that abideth*) the unity of the complex idea is emphasised.

ὁ μένων ἐν τῇ ἀγ.] *he that abideth in love* as the sphere in which his life is fulfilled. Compare John xv. 9 f. μ. ἐν τῇ ἀγάπῃ τῇ ἐμῇ, μ. ἐν τῇ ἀγ. μου. Here the feeling is regarded absolutely without any further definition of its object, as God or man. But the divine ideal made known through Christ is present to the mind of writer and reader.

Under different aspects St John presents elsewhere 'the light' (c. ii. 10), and 'the word' (John viii. 31), as the sphere in which the Christian 'abides,' 'loving his brother' and 'believing'; just as the unbeliever 'abides in darkness' (John xii. 46), and 'he that loveth not,' 'in death' (c. iii. 14).

ἐν τ. θ. μ. καὶ ὁ θ. ἐν αὐ. [μ.]] *abideth in God and God [abideth] in him.* See *v.* 15 Additional Note. He that so abideth in love hath risen to the heavenly order (Col. iii. 3) and found

¹⁷Ἐν τούτῳ τετελείωται ἡ ἀγάπη μεθ' ἡμῶν, ἵνα παρ-

17 ἡ ἀγάπη: +τοῦ θεοῦ the (lat).   μεθ' ἡμῶν: +ἐν ἡμῖν ℵ.

the power of divine fellowship for the accomplishment of earthly work.

It has been seen that this twofold blessing is connected with obedience (iii. 24) and confession (iv. 15). And love involves obedience (John xiv. 15 τηρήσετε, Rom. xiii. 10), and is the condition of fuller knowledge (John xiv. 21 ff.).

17. Ἐν τούτῳ...] *In this*... The reference has been variously explained. Some have connected *in this* with what follows, others with what precedes. In the former case two views have been held. The words have been taken closely with the second of the following clauses, ἐν τούτῳ...ὅτι...*in this...because...*, and again with the first, ἐν τούτῳ...ἵνα..., *in this...that* ... The former construction may be at once set aside. The intervening clause, ἵνα...κρίσεως, makes the connexion of ἐν τούτῳ with ὅτι most unnatural. The connexion of ἐν τούτῳ with ἵνα gives a true sense and is not foreign to St John's style, though the exact combination does not occur (not John xv. 8) in his writings; for it would not be strange that he should use a final particle (ἵνα) in place of a demonstrative particle (ὅτι), in order to bring out the idea of effort involved to the last in the realisation of confidence (comp. John xvii. 3; c. iii. 11 note). But the context and his general usage (comp. ii. 3 note) favour the conclusion that the reference is to that which precedes. The argument requires the affirmation of a fact from which a consequence is drawn, rather than a further explanation of how love is perfected. The fellowship of man with God and of God with man carries with it the consummation of love. *In this*— in this double communion—*love hath been perfected* already on the divine

side; and it is God's will that men should make its blessings their own in view of the close of earthly life.

Jerome has a strange inversion of the sense of the passage: In hoc perfecta est...caritas, si fiduciam habeamus...ut quomodo ille est sic et nos simus... (*c. Jovin.* i. c. 40).

τετελ. μεθ' ἡμῶν] *perfecta est nobiscum* V., *is* (*hath been*) *perfected with us*. There can be no doubt that μεθ' ἡμῶν is to be joined with the verb. The structure of the sentence is decisive against taking ἡ ἀγ. μεθ' ἡμῶν together in the sense 'the love which is realised between Christians,' or 'the love of God shewn among us.' The unique form of expression appears to have been chosen in place of the simple 'hath been perfected in us' in order to place the perfection clearly in the realised fellowship of God and man. Love is not simply perfected in man (ἐν ἡμῖν) by an act of divine power, but in fulfilling this issue God works with man (μεθ' ἡμῶν). Something of the same thought of cooperation is seen in Acts xv. 4, ὅσα ἐποίησεν ὁ θεὸς μετ' αὐτῶν. Comp. 2 John 3 ἔσται μεθ' ἡμῶν χάρις....

Philo calls attention to a use of the preposition not unlike in Gen. iii. 12 (LXX. ἡ γυνὴ ἣν ἔδωκας μετ' ἐμοῦ): εὖ τὸ μὴ φάναι ἡ γυνὴ ἣν ἔδωκας ἐμοὶ ἀλλὰ μετ' ἐμοῦ. οὐ γὰρ ἐμοὶ ὡς κτῆμα...ἔδωκας ἀλλὰ καὶ αὐτὴν ἀφῆκας ἄνετον καὶ ἐλευθέραν... (*Leg. Alleg.* iii. § 18; i. 98 M.).

τετελείωται] *v.* 12; c. ii. 5 note. The tense presents the perfection as dependent on a continuous fellowship between God and the Christian body. Contrast Clem. *ad Cor.* i. 50 οἱ ἐν ἀγάπῃ τελειωθέντες.

ἵνα παρρ. ἔχ.] *ut fiduciam habeamus* V. The fulness of love is given with a view to an end. The feeling ρησίαν ἔχωμεν ἐν τῇ ἡμέρᾳ τῆς κρίσεως, ὅτι καθὼς

ἔχωμεν: ἔχομεν ℵ.   ἡμέρᾳ: ἀγάπῃ ℵ.

which is active now will have its fullest effect in the supreme trial of existence. St John, who habitually regards the eternal aspect of things, regards the boldness as something which is possessed absolutely (τετε-λείωται...ἵνα ἔχωμεν...). In an earlier passage (ii. 28), he enjoined abiding in God in Christ as the source of confidence at Christ's Presence. He now points out how the confidence is established. To abide in God is to share the character of Christ under the conditions of earth. The sense of spiritual harmony with Him which this abiding brings necessarily inspires boldness in the believer; and it is the purpose of God that it should do so. So God fulfils His counsel of love. Thus the whole train of thought is brought to a natural conclusion. "God is love: he that abideth in love abideth in God...In this communion love finds consummation, in order that 'by conscious conformity with Christ' the last trial of life may be overcome, when 'the last fear is banished.'"

παρρ. ἔχωμεν] c. ii. 28 note.

ἐν τῇ ἡμ. τῆς κρ.] in die judicii V., in the day of judgment, when Christ shall come to execute judgment on the world (c. ii. 28). The definite phrase is found here only. The indefinite phrase, 'a day of judgment' (ἡμ. κρ.), occurs in Matt. x. 15; xi. 22, 24; xii. 36; 2 Pet. ii. 9; iii. 7. Compare also Apoc. vi. 17 ἡ ἡμ. ἡ μεγάλη τῆς ὀργῆς αὐτῶν; Rom. ii. 5 ἡμ. ὀργῆς καὶ ἀποκαλύψεως τῆς δικαιοκρισίας τοῦ θεοῦ; 1 Pet. ii. 12 ἡμ. ἐπισκοπῆς. In the Gospel St John speaks of 'the last day' (ἡ ἐσχάτη ἡμ.); vi. 39, 40, 44, 54; xi. 24; xii. 48; which is elsewhere styled simply 'that day' (ἐκείνη ἡ ἡμ., ἡ ἡμ. ἐκ.), Matt. vii. 22; Luke vi. 23; x. 12; xxi. 34; 2 Thess.

i. 10; 2 Tim. i. 12, 18; iv. 8. The phrase 'the judgment' (ἡ κρίσις) is found Matt. xii. 41 f.; Luke x. 14; xi. 31 f.

It is of interest to notice that the privilege which is here attributed to love is, under another aspect, attributed also to faith; John iii. 18; v. 24. The two cannot be separated.

ὅτι καθὼς ἐκεῖνος...] because even as He [Christ, c. ii. 6 note] is... The ground of boldness is present likeness to Christ. He has 'passed out of this world' (John xiii. 1), but His disciples are still 'in the world' (John xvii. 11), and have a work to do there (John xvii. 18). In fulfilling this work He is their ideal (c. ii. 6): conformity to Him is the rule of their judgment (John xv. 18 ff.). And the likeness of Christians to Christ is to His character as it is at present and eternally (καθὼς ἐκ. ἐστιν, comp. iii. 2, 7) and not to the particular form in which it was historically manifested (κ. ἐκ. ἦν).

The reference is not to any one attribute, as love or righteousness, but to the whole character of Christ as it is made known; and His high-priestly prayer serves as a commentary on the view which St John suggests of the position of Christians in the world.

Following Augustine (see iii. 7 note) Bede says forcibly: Non semper ad æqualitatem dicitur sicut, sed dicitur ad quandam similitudinem... Si ergo facti sumus ad imaginem Dei, quare non sicut Deus sumus? non ad æqualitatem sed pro modo nostro. Inde ergo nobis datur fiducia in die judicii, quia sicut ille est et nos sumus in hoc mundo, imitando videlicet perfectionem dilectionis in mundo cujus ille exemplum nobis quotidie præbet de cælo.

ἐκεῖνός ἐστιν καὶ ἡμεῖς ἐσμὲν ἐν τῷ κόσμῳ τούτῳ.
¹⁸φόβος οὐκ ἔστιν ἐν τῇ ἀγάπῃ, ἀλλ' ἡ τελεία ἀγάπη
ἔξω βάλλει τὸν φόβον, ὅτι ὁ φόβος κόλασιν ἔχει, ὁ

ἐσμέν: ἐσόμεθα א.

καθὼς...καὶ ἡμεῖς...] The οὕτως in the second member of the comparison is sometimes replaced by καὶ: c. ii. 6, 18; John xvii. 18; xx. 21 (xv. 9 is doubtful); sometimes it is omitted: c. ii. 27; and especially when the order of the clauses is inverted: John v. 23; Rom. xv. 7.

καὶ ἡμ. ἑ. ἐν τῷ κ. τ.] The likeness is conditioned by the circumstances of the present state. 'This world' (ὁ κ. οὗτος), as distinguished from 'the world,' emphasises the idea of transitoriness. The phrase is not found elsewhere in the Epistles of John. See John i. 10 note.

18. The thought of boldness necessarily calls up that of its opposite, fear. There is fear in man naturally; but love ever tends to expel it. Fear finds no place in love, and it cannot therefore co-exist with perfect love which occupies the whole 'heart.' The ideas are expressed in a general form and hold good absolutely, but they necessarily are specialised mentally from the context.

φόβος...ἐν τῇ ἀγ.] Love is the simple desire for the highest good of another or of others, and is the expression of a spirit of self-surrender. Fear therefore—the shrinking from another—cannot be an essential element in love. Here the reader at once feels that the abstract principle has found a typical embodiment in the self-sacrifice of Christ, towards the imitation of which Christians strive through His Spirit.

The fear of which St John speaks is, of course, not the reverence of the son (Hebr. v. 7 ff.), but the dread of the criminal or of the slave (Rom. viii. 15).

So Augustine says: Aliud est timere Deum ne mittat te in gehennam cum diabolo: aliud est timere Deum ne recedat a te.

ἀλλ'...] but, so far is it from being the case that fear has a place in love, it is of the nature of love to expel fear. Fear is an instrument of painful discipline; and when the end of perfect fellowship with God has been reached, the discipline is no longer needed. This sentence ἀλλ'...ἔχει is parenthetical.

ἡ τελ. ἀγάπη] perfect love, not 'perfected love' (ἡ τετελειωμένη ἀγ.). The thought is of love which is complete in all its parts, which has reached its complete development (Hebr. v. 14 note); of what it is and not of what it has become. Comp. James i. 4; iii. 2; Eph. iv. 13.

The arrangement ἡ τελ. ἀγ., which is common, for example, in 2 Pet., is unique in the Epistle (comp. 3 John 4 τὰ ἐμὰ τέκνα). See c. ii. 7 note. It expresses a shade of meaning, as distinct from ἡ ἀγ. ἡ τελ., which is evidently appropriate here.

ἔξω βάλλει] foras mittit V., casteth forth from the whole sphere of life. There is no longer scope for its operation. St John thus recognises the provisional presence of fear in the believer. It is found for a time with growing love, but mature love removes it. The phrase βάλλει ἔξω, which suggests the thought of a defined realm of spiritual activity (Apoc. xxii. 15), is more vivid than ἐκβάλλει. Comp. Matt. v. 13; xiii. 48; Luke xiv. 35 (βάλλειν ἔξω); John vi. 37; ix. 34 f.; xii. 31; xv. 6 (ἐκβάλλειν ἔξω).

ὅτι ὁ φ. κόλ. ἔχει] quoniam timor pœnam (tormentum Aug.) habet V.,

δὲ φοβούμενος οὐ τετελείωται ἐν τῇ ἀγάπῃ. ¹⁹ Ἡμεῖς
ἀγαπῶμεν, ὅτι αὐτὸς πρῶτος ἠγάπησεν ἡμᾶς. ²⁰ ἐάν

19 ἡμεῖς NB me the syrhl: +οὖν A vg syrvg.   ἀγαπῶμεν AB: +τὸν θεόν
N (vg) me syrr. (αὐτόν and invicem are also added.)   αὐτός NB me the syrr:
ὁ θεός A vg.

because fear hath punishment. Fear,
which is the expression of disharmony
and therefore the anticipation of suffering, at the same time must include
suffering. And the suffering which
comes from disharmony with God is
divine punishment which has a salutary office : Hebr. xii. 11. Such
punishment is not future only but
present. Comp. John iii. 18.

κόλ. ἔχει] includes, brings with it
punishment. Comp. Hebr. x. 35 (τὴν
παρρησίαν) ἥτις ἔχει μεγάλην μισθαπο-
δοσίαν. James ii. 17 (i. 4).
The word κόλασις occurs elsewhere
in the N. T. only in Matt. xxv. 46.
The verb κολάζεσθαι is found in Acts
iv. 21 ; 2 Pet. ii. 9 (not ii. 4). The noun
occurs in the LXX. of Ezekiel (for
מִכְשׁוֹל): xiv. 3, 4, 7; xviii. 30 (xliii.
11); xliv. 12; and both the noun and
verb occur not unfrequently in Wisdom : xi. 14, 17; xvi. 1, 2, &c.
The familiar classical distinction between τιμωρία, which regarded the re-
tributive suffering, and κόλασις, which
regarded the disciplinary chastisement
of the wrong-doer, was familiar to the
Alexandrine Greeks : e.g. Philo, de
confus. ling. § 34 (i. 431 M.) ἔστι δὲ
καὶ κόλασις οὐκ ἐπιζήμιον ἁμαρτημάτων
οὖσα κώλυσις καὶ ἐπανόρθωσις.

ὁ δὲ φοβούμενος...] and he that
feareth... This clause goes closely
with the first clause of the sentence:
'there is no fear in love, but he that
feareth hath not been made perfect
in love.' That which is stated first as an
abstract principle ('fear') is repeated
in a personal form (' he that feareth').
St John, while he lays down the full
truth, recognises the facts of life and
deals with them. There are those

who fear while yet they love: so far
their love though real is incomplete.

The second and third clauses of
the verse illustrate well the distinction of ἀλλά (sed) and δέ (autem). The
second clause (ἀλλ' ἡ τ. ἀ.) stands in
sharp opposition to the first, while
the third (ὁ δὲ φ.) deals with a limitation, or objection.

οὐ τετελείωται ἐν τῇ ἀγ.] This consummation of the believer is presented
in two complementary forms. He is
himself the sphere in which love finds
its perfection ; and love is the sphere
in which he finds his perfection. Love
is perfected in him (ii. 5): and he is
perfected in love. Comp. Additional
Note on v. 15.

Bengel in one of his unmatched
epigrams gives a history of the soul
through its relations to fear and love :
Varius hominum status : sine timore
et amore; cum timore sine amore;
cum timore et amore; sine timore
cum amore.

19—21. In the preceding verses
St John has shewn what love brings
to the believer. He now lays open
the obligation which it imposes upon
him. The love which is inspired by
God must be manifested towards the
brethren according to His commandment.

¹⁹ We love, because he first loved us.
²⁰ If any one say I love God, and
hate his brother, he is a liar ; for he
that loveth not his brother whom he
hath seen cannot love God, whom he
hath not seen. ²¹ And this commandment have we from him that he who
loveth God love his brother also.

19. Ἡμεῖς ἀγ.] Nos ergo diligamus
invicem V. The absence of any title of

τις εἴπη ὅτι Ἀγαπῶ τὸν θεόν, καὶ τὸν ἀδελφὸν αὐτοῦ
μισῇ, ψεύστης ἐστίν· ὁ γὰρ μὴ ἀγαπῶν τὸν ἀδελφὸν

20 – ὅτι ℵ.

address and the addition of the personal pronoun distinguish this phrase from *v.* 7 ἀγαπητοί, ἀγαπῶμεν ἀλλήλους, and seem to shew clearly that the verb is an indicative (*We love*), and not a conjunctive (*Let us love*). It is worthy of notice that the Latin and Pesh. Syriac which give the hortatory rendering add a connecting particle as many Greek authorities (οὖν).

The indicative also suits the context better. The fact of love is assumed, and then it is shewn in its workings. Comp. iii. 16.

According to the true reading the idea of love is left in its full breadth without any definition of the object, as God (αὐτόν or τὸν θεόν), or man (*invicem* V.). This is required by what follows, where it is falsely urged that the claims of 'love' can be satisfied by bare 'love of God.'

ὅτι αὐτὸς πρ. ἠγ. ἡμ.] Comp. *v.* 10. The thought here is different from that in the former context. There love was regarded in its essence: here it is regarded in its personal exercise. Our love is the light kindled by the love of God. And the divine origin of love determines its character and also assures its stability. Comp. John xv. 16.

πρῶτος ἠγ.] *prior dilexit* V. Comp. Rom. v. 8. The priority of the love of God to all love on man's part which is accentuated here, is a ground for the spontaneous exercise of love on the part of the believer towards those who do not seem to invite it.

20, 21. The consequences of the preceding statement are traced out in two ways from the nature of the case (*v.* 20), and from the direct commandment of God (*v.* 21). The love of God, which is assumed to exist at least in profession, must include love of the brethren, and so God has Himself enjoined. The thought of loving God is here first discussed (comp. *v.* 10).

20. ἐάν τις εἴπη] The form of expression differs slightly from that in i. 6 ff. (ἐὰν εἴπωμεν). There a view was given of the general position of Christians : here a particular case is taken, involving personal feeling. Contrast also 'he that [saith]' and 'every one that [saith],' c. iii. 3 note ; ii. 4 note.

εἴπη ὅτι Ἀγαπῶ...] For the use of the recitative ὅτι see i. 6 note. The claim is like those which have been noticed in ii. 4, 9 ; i. 6 ff., by which the faith is taken out of the sphere of practical life.

It is worthy of notice that in the Gospel of St John ἀγαπᾶν is not used of the feeling of man for God (the Father). It is so used in the other Gospels in a quotation from the LXX.

μισῇ] *hate*. St John admits no position of indifference. See ii. 9 note.

ψεύστης ἐστίν] Comp. ii. 4 ὁ λέγων ὅτι Ἔγνωκα αὐτὸν καὶ τὰς ἐντολὰς αὐτοῦ μὴ τηρῶν ψεύστης ἐστίν... The claim to the knowledge of God without obedience, and the claim to the love of God without action, involve not only the denial of what is known to be true (ψεύδεσθαι), but falseness of character. Comp. i. 10 note, and v. 10. See also John viii. 44, 55 ; and c. ii. 22.

ὁ γὰρ μὴ ἀγαπῶν...] *for he that loveth not*... The particular statement (ἐάν τις εἴπη) is refuted by a general principle. Sight is taken as the sign of that kind of limitation which brings objects within the range of our present powers. It is necessarily easier to love that which is like ourselves

αὐτοῦ ὃν ἑώρακεν, τὸν θεὸν ὃν οὐχ ἑώρακεν οὐ δύναται
ἀγαπᾷν. ²¹καὶ ταύτην τὴν ἐντολὴν ἔχομεν ἀπ᾽ αὐτοῦ,
ἵνα ὁ ἀγαπῶν τὸν θεὸν ἀγαπᾷ καὶ τὸν ἀδελφὸν αὐτοῦ.

οὐ δύν. אB the syrhl: πῶς δύν. A vg me syrvg.   21 ἀπ᾽ αὐτοῦ: ἀπὸ τοῦ
θεοῦ A vg.

than that which we cannot grasp in
a finite form. And the title 'brother'
brings out the idea of that which is
godlike in man to which love can be
directed. He therefore who fails to
recognise God as He reveals Himself
through Christ in man (Matt. xxv. 40
ἐνὶ τούτων τῶν ἀδελφῶν μου τῶν ἐλα-
χίστων) cannot love God. He has
refused the help which God has provided for the expression of love in
action.

Philo traces the thought through
the natural love of children for parents: φασί τινες ὡς ἄρα πατὴρ καὶ
μήτηρ ἐμφανεῖς εἰσὶ θεοί...ἀμήχανον δὲ
εὐσεβεῖσθαι τὸν ἀόρατον ὑπὸ τῶν εἰς
τοὺς ἐμφανεῖς καὶ ἐγγὺς ὄντας ἀσεβούν-
των (de decal. § 23, ii. p. 204 M.). The
love of parents involves the love of
brethren.

τὸν θ. ὃν οὐχ ἑώρ.] John i. 18 note;
v. 12 (τεθέαται); 1 Tim. vi. 16. The
inverted order in the corresponding
clauses is singularly expressive. There
is also a more solemn pathos in the
direct negative οὐ δύναται than in the
more rhetorical phrase of the common text πῶς δύναται.

ἑώρακεν...οὐχ ἑώρακεν...] videt...
non videt... V., hath seen...hath not
seen... It might have seemed more
natural to say 'seeth...cannot see...';
but the two perfects mark the fact
that a revelation with abiding consequences has and has not been made
in the two cases. The vision of 'the
brother' may in any particular case

be clouded but he has been seen, and
the idea of brotherhood abides for
constant use.

21. καὶ ταύτην τ. ἐ.] That which is
a spiritual necessity is also an express
injunction. The commandment of
love which has been implied in the
preceding verses is now defined.
Comp. c. iii. 23.

ἀπ᾽ αὐτοῦ] a Deo V., ab ipso Lat.
Vet., from Him, from God. The context makes it probable that, though
the Divine Person is not clearly defined, the reference is to the Father
(v. 19), Who by sending His Son
shewed the way of love. The commandment was given in substance by
Christ (John xiii. 34), but it came
from God (ἀπό) as its final source.
Compare i. 5; ii. 27 notes; and contrast the use of παρά Apoc. ii. 27;
John viii. 26, 40; x. 18.

ἵνα...] that... The final particle
gives more than the simple contents
of the commandment. It marks the
injunction as directed to an aim; and
implies that the effort to obtain it
can never be relaxed (ἵνα...ἀγαπᾷ).
Comp. John xiii. 34 note.

Augustine (on c. v. 3) uses the
words of the ascended Lord to Saul
to illustrate and enforce the lesson:
Persecutori Saulo [Christus] dixit de-
super: Saule, Saule, quid me perse-
queris? Ascendi in cælum, sed adhuc
in terra jaceo. Hic ad dexteram patris sedeo: ibi adhuc esurio, sitio et
peregrinus sum.

Additional Note on the reading of iv. 3.

The first clause in this verse is given in several different forms in existing Greek authorities. These are

General view of the variations.

π. πν. ὃ μὴ ὁμολογεῖ τὸν Ἰησοῦν   AB.

π. πν. ὃ μὴ ὁμολογεῖ   Ἰησοῦν Κύριον ἐν σαρκὶ ἐληλυθότα   ℵ.

π. πν. ὃ μὴ ὁμολογεῖ τὸν Ἰησοῦν Χριστὸν ἐν σαρκὶ ἐληλυθότα   L, &c.

π. πν. ὃ μὴ ὁμολογεῖ   Ἰησοῦν Χριστὸν ἐν σαρκὶ ἐληλυθότα   K, &c.

To these variations must be added another, which is represented by the Vulgate reading:

π. πν. ὃ λύει   τὸν Ἰησοῦν.

The main interest centres on the alternatives μὴ ὁμολογεῖ and λύει.

As the direct evidence now stands, μὴ ὁμολογεῖ is read by

(1) All Greek MSS, uncial and cursive,

(2) All the versions except the Latin, and by one important Old Latin MS (*Fris.*),

External evidence for (i) μὴ ὁμολογεῖ,

(3) The Greek Fathers who quote the passage with the exception of Socrates, from Cyril downwards, to whom Polycarp must probably be added : πᾶς γὰρ ὃς ἂν μὴ ὁμολογῇ Ἰησοῦν Χριστὸν ἐληλυθέναι ἀντίχριστός ἐστι (*ad Phil.* 7).

On the other hand

(1) Socrates gives λύει as having been the reading in 'the old copies.'

(ii) for λύει.

(2) All Latin MSS, with one exception, read *solvit;* and

(3) This reading, with the variant *destruit*, prevails in the Latin Fathers, being universal in the later writers.

The evidence of Socrates, the only Greek authority for λύει, is contained in a passage which presents several difficulties. Speaking of the error of Nestorius and of his general self-sufficiency and contempt for accurate learning, he goes on to say : 'for example he was ignorant of the fact that in the Catholic Epistle of John it was written in the ancient copies that *every spirit which divideth* (λύει) *Jesus is not from God.* For they that desired to separate the deity from the man of the dispensation [i.e. Christ Jesus] removed this thought [the condemnation of those who 'divide Jesus'] from the ancient copies. Wherefore also the ancient interpreters noted this very fact, that there were some who had tampered with the epistle wishing to divide the man from God[1].'

The evidence of Socrates.

It will be seen that Socrates does not say that the reading was found in copies which he had himself seen, but only that it once was found in the text: he writes that it 'had been written' (γέγραπτο) and not that 'it is written' (γέγραπται). Again it is a sign that he is not quoting any Greek

[1] *H. E.* vii. 32, αὐτίκα γοῦν ἠγνόησεν ὅτι ἐν τῇ καθολικῇ Ἰωάννου γέγραπτο ἐν τοῖς παλαιοῖς ἀντιγράφοις ὅτι πᾶν πνεῦμα ὃ λύει τὸν Ἰησοῦν ἀπὸ τοῦ θεοῦ οὐκ ἔστι. ταύτην γὰρ τὴν διάνοιαν ἐκ τῶν παλαιῶν ἀντιγράφων περιεῖλον οἱ χωρίζειν ἀπὸ τοῦ τῆς οἰκονομίας ἀνθρώπου βουλόμενοι τὴν θεότητα· διὸ καὶ οἱ παλαιοὶ ἑρμηνεῖς αὐτὸ τοῦτο ἐπεσημήναντο, ὥς τινες εἶεν ῥᾳδιουργήσαντες τὴν ἐπιστολήν, λύειν ἀπὸ τοῦ θεοῦ τὸν ἄνθρωπον θέλοντες.

MS that he writes ἀπὸ τοῦ θεοῦ for ἐκ τοῦ θεοῦ, a variant which has no Greek authority. His language is in fact perfectly satisfied by the supposition that he was acquainted with the Latin reading and some Latin commentary[1].

Quotations in texts of Greek Fathers.

In the Latin translation of IRENÆUS 2 John 7 and 1 John iv. 3 are quoted as from the same epistle (Iren. iii. 16, 8). After the quotation of the former passage the text continues...Johannes in prædicta epistola fugere eos præcepit dicens...*omnis spiritus qui solvit Jesum non est ex Deo sed de (ex) Antichristo est.* The context shews clearly in what sense Irenæus understood St John's words, but it is not decisive as to the reading which he had in his Greek text.

The Latin translation of CLEMENT's *Outlines* (Ὑποτυπώσεις) on 2 John gives as part of the substance of this Epistle : adstruit in hac epistola... ut nemo *dividat Jesum Christum*, sed unum credere *Jesum Christum venisse in carne.*

The reading 'solvit Jesum' is found in the Latin translation of ORIGEN : Hæc autem dicentes non solvimus suscepti corporis hominem, cum sit scriptum apud Johannem *omnis spiritus qui solvit Jesum non est ex Deo*, sed unicuique substantiæ proprietatem servamus (*in Matt. Com. Scr.* § 65). But the character of the translation is such as to give no satisfactory assurance that Origen's Greek text read λύει.

There is no indication, as far as I am aware, that the reading λύει was accepted by or known to any other Greek or Eastern father.

Latin Patristic evidence.

Yet the fact remains that the reading was found at a very early date. TERTULLIAN uses the phrases 'solvere Jesum' (*adv. Marc.* v. 16) and 'solvere Jesum Christum' (*de Jejun.* 1). In the former passage he appears to combine the language of 1 John iv. 3 and 2 John 7, as is done in the Latin translation of Clement : Johannes dicit processisse in mundum præcursores antichristi spiritus, *negantes Christum in carne venisse et solventes Jesum;* and it may be observed that the close connexion of the two verses in some of the Latin renderings (which give *venisse* for ἐρχόμενον in 2 John 7) makes it difficult to decide to which of the two reference is made in particular cases. The words of Tertullian *de Carne Chr.* 24 qui *negat Christum in carne venisse hic antichristus est; de Præscr. hær.* 33 in epistola sua [Johannes] eos maxime antichristos vocat *qui Christum negarent in carne venisse et qui non putarent Jesum filium Dei esse* (comp. *c. Marc.* iii. 8 negantes Christum in carne venisse); and of Cyprian (*Testim.* ii. 8) *qui autem negat in carne venisse de Deo non est sed est de antichristi spiritu*[2], were probably moulded by the passage in the second epistle.

AUGUSTINE in his explanation of the epistle first quotes the passage at length with the reading '*qui non confitetur Jesum Christum in carne venisse*,' which he explains (referring to c. ii. 19), and then without any remark he passes on to explain 'solvere': Adeo ut noveritis quia ad facta retulit : Et *omnis spiritus*, ait, *qui solvit Jesum;* and again afterwards he unites both phrases : ' *solvis Jesum et negas in carne venisse.*'

---

[1] Socrates was acquainted with Latin : *H. E.* i. 12.

[2] All. *de Deo natus non est sed est Antichristus.*

The variations in PRISCILLIAN are very instructive : Johannes ait *omnis spiritus...qui solvit Jesum de Deo non est...* (Tract. i. 37). Scriptum est : *omnis spiritus qui confitetur...qui autem non confitetur de Deo non est* (Tract. ii. 52). Illam apostolicam feramus jure sententiam *omnem spiritum qui negat Jesum de Deo non esse et omnem spiritum...* (Tract. iii. 67).

FULGENTIUS[1] and TICHONIUS[2] combine phrases from the two epistles with even greater freedom.

It is remarkable that BEDE, who was aware of the substance of Socrates' criticism, supposes that those who tampered with the epistle left out the whole clause : In tantum ex Deo non sunt ut quidam...hunc...versiculum quo dicitur *et omnis spiritus qui solvit Jesum ex Deo non est*, ex hac epistola eraserint, ne scilicet per auctoritatem beati Joannis convinceretur error eorum. Denique Nestorius nescire se prodidit hanc authenticis exemplaribus inditam fuisse sententiam...

This strange assertion is repeated by FULBERT of CHARTRES[3], and HINCMAR[4]. Such a misunderstanding offers a memorable example of the way in which critical statements are unintelligently perverted and made the ground of unjust charges.

From this review there can be no question as to the overwhelming weight of external evidence in favour of μὴ ὁμολογεῖ. To set this aside without the clearest necessity is to suspend all laws of textual criticism. No reading supported by such authority as λύει is, I believe, more than a very early gloss. And on careful consideration it seems that the internal evidence is not more favourable to λύει Ἰησοῦν than the external. It is scarcely possible that such a phrase could be used for separating the divine and human natures in Christ. The name Ἰησοῦς brings prominently forward the humanity of the Lord. Socrates evidently felt this, for he defines λύειν by the addition ἀπὸ τοῦ θεοῦ.

The language of Polycarp shews that St John's teaching upon the subject was current in various forms. It seems likely that he used two main phrases λύειν Ἰησοῦν Χριστόν and μὴ ὁμολογεῖν τὸν Ἰησοῦν (answering to Κύριος Ἰησοῦς Rom. x. 9). This being so, the λύει in the former phrase was added as a gloss on the phrase μὴ ὁμολογεῖ of the epistle in some early

Internal evidence.

[1] *Ad Trasim.* i. c. 5. De qua veritate...ille qui de pectore ipsius sapientiæ mysteriorum cælestium meruit intelligentiam illuminatus haurire fiducialiter dicit: *omnis spiritus qui confitetur Jesum Christum in carne venisse ex Deo est. Omnis spiritus qui non confitetur Jesum Christum in carne venisse ex Deo non est; et hic est Antichristus. Ep.* xvii. c. 10 Joannes...testatur quia *omnis spiritus qui solvit Jesum ex Deo non est, et hic est antichristus.*

[2] *Reg.* IV. Super Joannem *multi pseudoprophetæ prodierunt in hunc mundum. In isto cognoscite spiritus Dei. Omnis spiritus qui solvit Jesum et negat in carne venisse de Deo non est sed hic de Antichristo est. Quod audistis quoniam venit et nunc in isto mundo præsens est.*

[3] *Ep.* v. (i) Cujus [Arii] auditores quoniam Spiritum Sanctum Deum esse negabant de Evangelio eraserunt illud quod Salvator ait *Spiritus est Deus*, et de epistola Joannis eraserunt *et omnis spiritus qui solvit Jesum ex Deo non est.* Sicut Nestorius...

[4] *Opusc. et Epist.* xviii. (Migne, *Patr. Lat.* cxxvi. p. 351) quidam etiam de epistola Joannis eraserunt *et omnis spiritus qui solvit Jesum ex Deo non est.* The whole paragraph is very instructive.

copies, and so passed into the Latin version[1]. The additions to 'Ιησοῦν are easily intelligible, and the forms in which they occur shew that they are no part of the original text. At the same time it is not unreasonable to suppose that the unusual amount of variants indicates the influence of some traditional form of words upon the text. In 2 John 7 there is no variation in the corresponding phrase; nor is the characteristic word of that passage (ἐρχόμενον) introduced here by any authority.

Additional Note on iv. 8. The revelation of God.

Tendencies towards two conceptions of God in the Apostolic age, abstract and concrete.

Jewish thought in the age of St John represented in striking forms the two chief tendencies of religious speculation on the Being of God. On the one side there was the philosophic, theoretic tendency which leads to an abstract conception; and on the other the popular, practical tendency which leads to a concrete conception. The former found an exponent in Philo: the latter was embodied in the current creed of Palestine, which more and more reduced the God of the Covenant to the position of the God of the Jews.

St John unites them.

St John unites the truths which gave force to these tendencies, the transcendental and the personal truth, in a perfect harmony. He wholly avoids the Alexandrine terms—τὸ ὄν, ἐπέκεινα πάσης οὐσίας and the like— and yet he preserves the thoughts at which they aimed. He recognises most emphatically the privileges of Israel, and at the same time he places the 'One God' in a living, loving connexion with 'the world.'

His teaching rests on the Old Testament.

The foundation of his teaching lies in the Monotheism of the O. T., which is not rigid, sterile, final, like the Monotheism of Islam, but vital and progressive. The unity which it affirms is not numerical but essential (John x. 30 ἐγὼ καὶ ὁ πατὴρ ἕν ἐσμεν: comp. xvii. 3; 1 John v. 20).

Opposed to

Dualism,

In this sense the thought of 'the only God' (John v. 44) is opposed to all forms of Dualism, Polytheism, Pantheism. He is the One source of life (John v. 26); and through the Word, 'the Son,' to Whom 'he gave to have life in himself' (John l.c.), 'all things came into being' (John i. 3). All notion of coeternal matter or of a coeternal principle of evil, as antagonistic to or limiting the divine action, is set aside. God 'loved the world' (John iii. 16; comp. 1 John ii. 2) not as strange but as His own. All men need (John iii. 3) and all men are capable of (John xii. 32) union with Him. The devil left his first place 'in the Truth' (John viii. 44); and Christ 'came to undo his works' (1 John iii. 8) by taking 'flesh,' which could not therefore have been in essential opposition to His Nature.

Polytheism,

The allusions to Polytheism in St John are naturally less prominent than those in St Paul. Once in general terms he warns against 'the idols' which

---

[1] A passage of Cyril of Alexandria will shew how naturally the gloss might be introduced. He quotes the passage: πᾶν πνεῦμα ὃ μὴ ὁμολογεῖ τὸν 'Ιησοῦν ἐκ τοῦ θεοῦ οὐκ ἔστι and then in his interpretation adds ὁ τοίνυν οὐ λέγων θεὸν εἶναι ἀληθῶς τὸν Χριστὸν διαιρῶν δὲ καὶ κατασμικρύνων τὴν δόξαν αὐτοῦ τὸ τοῦ 'Αντιχρίστου πνεῦμα ἔχων ἀλώσεται (de recta fide ad. reg. p. 94). The Greek version of Leo's Letter to Flavian (c. v. p. 830) gives πᾶν πνεῦμα τὸ διαιροῦν 'Ιησοῦν Χριστὸν ἀπὸ θεοῦ οὐκ ἔστι καὶ οὗτός ἐστιν ὁ 'Αντίχριστος as the rendering of the Latin omnis spiritus qui solvit Jesum ex Deo non est et hic est Antichristus.

usurp the place of 'the true God' (1 John v. 21); and in the Apocalypse he marks the connexion between the empire and idolatry (xiii. 14 f.; and comp. xxi. 8; xxii. 15). But his teaching is directed rather against the spirit than against the form of polytheism. 'The only true God,' God revealed as Father in the Son, excludes polytheism of necessity both within and without the Christian Body.

St John, like St Paul, places Creation in close relation with the Creator, but he affirms the reality of the relation which the words imply. God is present in all things but He transcends them. They answered to His will in their beginning (Apoc. iv. 11), and are supported by His working (John v. 17). *Pantheism.*

For the most part St John, like the other writers of the Bible, leaves the reader to form his conception of God from what is recorded of His action; but in three phrases he has laid down once for all the great outlines within which our thoughts on the Divine Nature must be confined. The first sentence is in his narrative of the Lord's words: '*God is spirit*' (John iv. 24); the two others are in his first Epistle: '*God is light*' (1 John i. 5 note) and '*God is love*' (1 John iv. 8, 16). *St John's three statements as to the Divine Nature.*

To these may be added a fourth, in which he speaks of the revelation of 'Him that is true' made in 'Jesus Christ His Son': 'this,' he says, 'is the true God and eternal life' (1 John v. 20). So he passes from the idea of God to the revelation of God to man.

The three phrases which have been quoted do not simply specify properties of God (as 'God is loving'), but, so far as we can apprehend them, essential aspects of His Nature. The first, if we may venture to distinguish them, is metaphysical and describes God in Himself, in His Being: He is Spirit. The second is moral, and describes God in His character towards all created things: He is Light. The third is personal, and describes God in His action towards self-conscious creatures: He is Love. In this order they offer a progress of thought: each statement is taken up and developed in that which follows.

i. *God is spirit* (πνεῦμα ὁ θεός). The statement obviously refers to the divine nature and not to the divine personality. The parallel phrases are a sufficient proof of this. God is not 'a spirit,' as one of many, but 'spirit.' As spirit, He is absolutely raised above all limitations of succession (time and space) into which finally all thoughts of change and transitoriness are resolved. *i. God is spirit.*

There is no anticipation of this idea in the O. T. The 'Spirit of God' is constantly spoken of; but the loftiest descriptions of the Divine Majesty are always relative to space (Is. lxvi. 1; 1 K. viii. 27; Jer. xxiii. 24).

It follows that God as God is not cognisable by the senses (John i. 18 1 John iv. 12). The Theophanies of the O. T. were not manifestations of 'God' but of the Son of God (John xii. 41; Is. vi. 1; comp. Apoc. iv. 2 ff.).

But while the material vision of God is impossible, there is a spiritual and a moral vision of God through Christ (John xiv. 9; comp. xii. 45) and through love, which leads up to the transfiguring contemplation of the Divine Presence (1 John iii. 2).

ii. *God is light* (ὁ θεὸς φῶς ἐστίν). This statement again is absolute as to the Nature of God, and not as to His action (not 'a light' or 'the *ii. God is light.*

light of men'). The phrase expresses unlimited self-communication, diffusiveness. Light is by shining: darkness alone bounds. And further, the
communication of light is of that which is pure and glorious. Such is God
towards all finite being, the condition of life and action. He reveals Himself through the works of creation which reflect His perfections in a form
answering to the powers of man, and yet God is not to be fully apprehended
by man as He is.

The idea is not distinctly expressed in the O. T., though it underlies the
thought of the Divine 'glory' (Ex. xxiv. 17; Hab. iii. 3 f.). Compare also
Is. x. 17; Ps. xxxvi. 9; civ. 2; Ezek. i. 27. It is indicated in Wisdom
(vii. 26), and Philo uses the very words of St John: de Somn. i. p. 632,
πρῶτον μὲν ὁ θεὸς φῶς ἐστί...καὶ οὐ μόνον φῶς ἀλλὰ καὶ παντὸς ἑτέρου φωτὸς
ἀρχέτυπον μᾶλλον δὲ ἀρχετύπου πρεσβύτερον, καὶ ἀνώτερον, λόγον ἔχων παρα-
δείγματος. Compare also Philo de nom. mut. i. 579; de sacrif. ii. p. 254;
one remarkable phrase which Philo uses deserves to be quoted: ὁ θεὸς
ἑαυτοῦ φέγγος ὢν δι᾽ αὐτοῦ μόνου θεωρεῖται (de præm. et pœn. ii. 415).

The idea of Light, it may be added, passes into that of Fire; but this
thought is not brought out by St John (Hebr. xii. 29: Deut. iv. 24).

iii. God is
love.

iii. God is love (ὁ θεὸς ἀγάπη ἐστίν). In this declaration the idea of
'personality' is first revealed, and in the case of God necessarily of a self-
sufficing personality (see Additional Note on v. 20). The idea of God is not
only that of an unlimited self-communication, but a self-communication
which calls out and receives a response (1 John iv. 7 ff.), which requires the
recognition not only of glory but of goodness. And this love is original,
and not occasioned (1 John iv. 10). It corresponds to the innermost nature
of God, and finds its source in Him and not in man (1 John iv. 19, iii. 1),
non enim habet homo unde Deum diligat nisi ex Deo (Aug. De Trin. xv. 17,
32). It is not like the love which is called out in the finite by the sense of
imperfection (ἔρως Plat. Sympos. pp. 201 ff.), but is the expression of perfect benevolence. The only earthly image which answers to it is the love of
parents for children (Eph. iii. 15), while that of Christ for the Church is
likened to the love of husband for wife (Eph. v. 25); compare the view of
the relation of Jehovah to Israel in the Old Test. (Jer. ii.; Hos. ii.).

Augustine argues that the name 'Love' belongs characteristically in the
Holy Trinity to the Holy Spirit; who 'communicates to us that common
love by which the Father and His Son love one another' (de Trin. xv. 17,
27). Si ergo, he says, proprie aliquid horum trium caritas nuncupanda est,
quid aptius quam ut hoc sit Spiritus Sanctus? Ut scilicet in illa simplici
summaque natura non sit aliud substantia et aliud caritas, sed substantia
ipsa sit caritas, et caritas ipsa sit substantia, sive in Patre sive in Filio, sive
in Spiritu Sancto, ut tamen proprie Spiritus Sanctus caritas nuncupetur
(id. 17, 29).

As answering to this love of God, Creation in its essence and destiny
reveals not only the will but also the nature of God. As yet there is conflict and disorder, and St John does not, like St Paul (1 Cor. xv. 28),
distinctly contemplate the end. He lays down the eternal truths which
must find fulfilment.

For the same reason the thoughts of judgment and vengeance which are
prominent in the Apocalypse fall into the background in the Gospel and

Epistles. These lie, so to speak, rather in the necessity of things so far as they are apart from God than in the will of God.

In the O. T. love is an attribute of God, one of many exercised in particular relations: Deut. iv. 37, vii. 8, 13, x. 15, 18, xxiii. 5; 2 Sam. xii. 25; Is. xli. 8, xliii. 4, xlviii. 14; Mal. i. 2. In the N. T. first love can be shewn to be the very Being of God as answering to the Revelation in Christ; and we may see a certain fitness in the fact that this crowning truth is brought out in the latest of the apostolic writings.

In other passages St John speaks of God as 'living' (John vi. 57 ὁ ζῶν πατήρ), 'true' (ἀληθής John viii. 26, iii. 33; comp. 1 John i. 10), 'faithful' (πιστός 1 John i. 9; Apoc. i. 5, iii. 14, xix. 11), 'righteous' (δίκαιος John xvii. 25; 1 John i. 9; comp. Apoc. xvi. 5), 'holy' (ἅγιος John xvii. 11; comp. Apoc. vi. 10). And he records how His character is shewn to us in His action in Nature (John v. 17), History (xi. 4, xix. 11), and Grace (vi. 44 f.). Comp. John xii. 28, x. 29, xi. 41 f.

Additional Note on iv. 9. The use of the term μονογενής.

The term μονογενής is derived from the vocabulary of the LXX. It occurs there altogether eight times, three times in the Psalms, three times in Tobit, once in Judges and once in the book of Wisdom. The use of the word in Tobit is quite simple. Tobit and Sarah are two μονογενεῖς, *only children* of their parents (viii. 17): Sarah is μονογενής (or μία iii. 10) the *one daughter* of her father (iii. 15; cf. vi. 11 where the reading is doubtful). In the book of Wisdom the meaning of the term is less easy to express. It is said (vii. 22) that in Wisdom *there is a spirit intelligent, holy,* μονογενές, *manifold, subtle, versatile...* The epithet evidently describes the essential nature and not the derivation of this spirit: it is something absolutely one, unique (*unicus* in Latt.). The use of μονογενής, i. in the LXX.

In the three passages of the Psalms, as in Jud. xi. 34, the word represents the Hebrew יָחִיד, twice as a significant title of the soul, the *one single* irreparable life of man (Ps. xxii. (xxi.) 21; xxxv. (xxxiv.) 17, *unicam meam* Lat. Vet.; *solitariam meam* V.), and once of the sufferer left *alone and solitary* in his distress (Ps. xxv. (xxiv.) 16 *unicus* Lat. Vet.; *solus* V.; and so Aquila rightly in Ps. lxviii. (lxvii.) 6 [LXX. μονοτρόπους], but in the three other places he gives μοναχός, which is the rendering of Sym. and Theod. here).

In six other places the same original word (יָחִיד) is represented by ἀγαπητός (Gen. xxii. 2, 12, 16; Jer. vi. 26; Amos viii. 10; Zech. xii. 10), which also carries with it the notion of 'an only child'; once by ἀγαπώμενος, Prov. iv. 3. In Jud. xi. 34 Cod. A. gives the duplicate rendering μονογενής, ἀγαπητή.

In the New Testament μονογενής has the same meaning *only* (Lk. viii. 42 *unica*), or *only child* (Lk. vii. 12 *unicus*; ix. 38 *id.*; Hebr. xi. 17, *unicus* Vet. Lat. *unigenitus* V., comp. John i. 14, *unici* Tert., *unigeniti* most); and so the word is used of the Lord (John iii. 16 *unicus* Vet. Lat.; *unigenitus* V.; 1 John iv. 9 *unicum* Vet. Lat.; *unigenitum* V.; comp. John i. 14), and once, according to the most ancient authorities in connexion with the ii. in the N. T.

word 'God' (John i. 18 μονογενὴς θεός; unicus filius, Adim. ap. Aug.; unigenitus filius (Deus), rell.).

iii. in later   The one instance of the use of the word in the sub-apostolic writings
writings.   gives exactly the same sense.   Clement speaks of the Phœnix (*Ep.* i. 25) as
μονογενὲς ὑπάρχον, a bird 'absolutely unique, the only one of its kind.'
(Comp. Bp Lightfoot *ad loc.*)

The word next appears prominently in the system of Valentinus.   The
Mind (Νοῦς) the offspring of the ineffable Depth (Βυθός) and Silence
(Σιγή), which alone embraced the greatness of the First Father, itself 'the
Father and beginning of all things,' was also called ὁ Μονογενής, the only-
born.   And from this Being 'like and equal' to its Author, in conjunction
with Truth the other Æons proceeded (Iren. i. 1, 2).

These mystical speculations fixed attention upon the term; but perhaps
at the same time they checked its technical use in the Church.   It does
not in fact occur in the earlier types of the Creed, which are found in
Irenæus, Tertullian and Novatian; and in Tertullian the corresponding
Latin term *unicus* is used of God (the Father): *de virg. vel.* 1; *adv. Prax.* 2.
But it is worthy of notice that in the confession of Ignatius before Trajan,
which follows the great lines of a Baptismal Symbol, the phrase is found: εἷς
ἔστιν θεός...καὶ εἷς Χριστὸς Ἰησοῦς ὁ υἱὸς τοῦ θεοῦ ὁ μονογενής (*Ignat. Mart.* 2;
comp. *Polyc. Mart.* 20).   And it was apparently from Antioch that the
term spread as an element of the expression of the Catholic Faith.

Confes-   In the second half of the third century the word appears in the Con-
sions   fessions of Syria and Asia Minor (*Syn. Ant.* A.D. 269, Routh, iii. p. 290;
of Faith. Greg. Thaum. ap. Greg. Nyss. 3, p. 912; Lucian, Socr. 2, 10, 7; *Apost.
Const.* 7, 41; Marcellus, Epiph. *Hær.* 72, p. 836); and from that time it
gradually obtained a permanent place in the Creeds of the East and the
West.

The earliest certain example of the word in this connexion brings out
its force very plainly.   The Synod of Antioch (269), which condemned Paul
of Samosata, in giving the exposition of their ancient belief which they
addressed to him, write: 'We confess and proclaim the Son as begotten,
'an only Son (γεννητόν, υἱὸν μονογενῆ), the image of the unseen God, the
'firstborn of all creation, the Wisdom and Word and Power of God, who was
'before the ages not by foreknowledge but by essence and subsistence,
'God, Son of God, having recognised Him as such both in the Old and New
'Testament' (Routh, *Rell. Sacr.* iii. 290; comp. Alex. Alexandr. ap. Theodor.
H. E. 1. 4. 45, φύσις μονογενής).

The point which is emphasised by the word here is evidently the absolute oneness of the Being of the Son.   He stands to the Father in a
relation wholly singular.   He is the one only Son, the one to whom the
title belongs in a sense completely unique and peculiar.   The thought is
centred in the Personal existence of the Son, and not in the Generation of
the Son.   That mystery is dealt with in another phrase.   Consistently with
this view the earliest Latin forms of the Creed uniformly represent the
word by *unicus*, the *only son*, and not by *unigenitus* the *only-begotten son*,
and this rendering has maintained its place in the Apostles' Creed and in
our English version of it.   But towards the close of the fourth century in
translations from the Greek *unigenitus* came to be substituted for *unicus*,

and this interpretation has passed into our version of the Constantino-politan Creed (*only-begotten*).

The sense of *only Son* is preserved by the Syriac versions of the Nicene Creed, which go back to the original word which was rendered in the LXX. μονογενής and ἀγαπητός (ܝܚܝܕ) following in this the example of the Syriac translation of the N. T., where the word μονογενής is so rendered uniformly: Caspari, pp. 101, 116.

The exact phraseology of the true Nicene Creed separates distinctly these two thoughts of the generation of the Son, and of the unique being of the Son. 'We believe...in one Lord Jesus Christ, begotten of the Father 'an only Son' (γεννηθέντα ἐκ πατρὸς μονογενῆ)[1], where the uniqueness of nature is further defined by the addition 'that is to say of the essence of 'the Father.' And this proper sense of the word μονογενής, as marking the oneness of the sonship, preserves a close affinity in idea with ἀγαπητός *well-beloved*, the second translation of יָחִיד. Both words define that which is essentially singular in filial relationship: '*Only son* and *well-beloved*,' Athanasius writes, 'are the same' (*Or. c. Ar.* iv. 24).

But in the interval which elapsed before the council of Constantinople Later in-the important distinction between the sonship and the generation of the terpreta-Son was beginning to be obscured, and μονογενής was treated as equivalent tions. to μόνος γεννηθείς, so as to include both the fact of the uniqueness of the Nature of the Son and the ground (if we may so speak) of His uniqueness[2].

In this way the grand simplicity of the original idea of the word was lost. Other thoughts, true in themselves, were gathered round it, and at last the sense was given by Gregory of Nazianzus as describing 'not the 'only Son of an only Parent, at one only time, but also that He was (be-'gotten) in a singular way (μονοτρόπως)' (*Orat.* xxx. 20). And this conception, with which no fault can be found except that it is not contained in the word, became popularly current afterwards and was admirably expressed by John of Damascus: Μονογενὴς δὲ ὅτι μόνος ἐκ μόνου τοῦ πατρὸς μόνως ἐγεννήθη (*De Fid. Orthod.* i. 8. 135).

One other use of the word μονογενής, which is at first strange to our The ears, remains to be noticed. The true reading in John i. 18 is in all proba- phrase bility μονογενὴς θεός (*unigenitus Deus*), and this phrase occurs in some of μονογενὴς the Confessions of the fourth century. Thus it appears in a copy of the θεός. Nicene Creed addressed by Eustathius to Liberius (c. 366), (Socr. iv. 12, 14), and in a Creed set forth by the council of Antioch in 341 (πιστεύομεν ...εἰς ἕνα Κύριον Ἰν. Χν. τὸν υἱὸν αὐτοῦ τὸν μονογενῆ θεόν...τὸν γεννηθέντα... Socr. ii. 10, 12; Athan. *de Syn.* 23), which was said in fact to be the Creed of Lucian the Martyr; and again in the Synodical letter of the Synod of Ancyra (358) (Sozom. 3, 5, 9: Epiph. *Hær.* 73, 8).

The phrase is common in patristic writings both in connexion with the passage in St John's Gospel and independently. Didymus sets the phrase

---

[1] There can be no doubt that in this sentence μονογενῆ is (so to speak) a secondary predicate, and not a fresh epithet. The clause is so rendered in the Syriac version; Caspari, p. 101.

[2] The word μονογεννητός does not occur. The instance quoted by Bing-ham (3, 359) from Ussher is simply a false conjunction of the words...μονο-γενῆ τόν... See Heurtley, pp. 79, 82.

μονογενὴς θεὸς λόγος parallel with εἷς θεός. Alexander, who reads ὁ μονογενὴς υἱός in John i. 18 speaks afterwards of the 'ineffable subsistence of
God the only Son' (θεὸς μονογενής Theod. 1, 4, §§ 15, 19). Gregory of
Nyssa, who uses it most frequently, says 'the sum of the Christian religion
'is to believe in God the only Son (τὸν μονογενῆ θεόν) who is the Truth and
'the true Light and the Power of God and the Life' (c. Eunom. 12, p. 913,
Migne).

On the relation of μονογενής to πρωτότοκος as applied to the Son see
Lightfoot on Col. i. 15; and the typical passage of Athanasius: Orat. c.
Ar. ii. 21 § 9. In connecting πρωτότοκος with the Incarnate Lord, I
believe that the great Greek fathers wished to guard the truth which
I have sought to express in the Essay on 'The Gospel of Creation.'

For the use of the phrase μονογενὴς θεός see Dr Hort's Two Disserta-
tions, Cambridge, 1876.

Additional Note on iv. 12. On the use of θεός and ὁ θεός.

Differ-
ence of
ὁ θεός and
θεός.

A careful examination of the passages, relatively few in number, in
which θεός is used without the article in St John's writings leads to the
conclusion that the difference between ὁ θεός and θεός is such as might
have been expected antecedently. The former brings before us the Personal
God Who has been revealed to us in a personal relation to ourselves: the
latter fixes our thoughts on the general conception of the Divine Character
and Being.

i. Use in
St John,
θεός with-
out the
article.

i. Θεός occurs without the article (exclusively of cases where it occurs
with a preposition) in the following passages:

John i. 1 θεὸς ἦν ὁ λόγος.
  „   12 τέκνα θεοῦ. So 1 John iii. 1, 2.
  „   18 θεὸν οὐδεὶς ἑώρακεν. 1 John iv. 12 θεὸν οὐδεὶς πώποτε
            τεθέαται.
  „ vi. 45 διδακτοὶ θεοῦ (LXX).
  „ viii. 54 λέγετε ὅτι θεὸς ὑμῶν ἐστίν.
  „ x. 33 ποιεῖς σεαυτὸν θεόν.
  „   34 f. εἶπα θεοί ἐστε (LXX).
  „ xix. 7 υἱὸν θεοῦ ἑαυτὸν ἐποίησεν.
1 John iii. 1, 2 (above John i. 12).
  „   iv. 12 (above John i. 18).
2 John 9 θεὸν οὐκ ἔχει.
Apoc. vii. 2 σφραγῖδα θεοῦ ζῶντος (comp. 1 Thess. i. 9; 2 Cor. iii.
            3, vi. 16; 1 Tim. iv. 10; Hebr. ix. 14, x. 31, xii. 22).
  „ xxi. 3 ὁ θεὸς μετ' αὐτῶν ἔσται [αὐτῶν θεός].
  „   7 ἔσομαι αὐτῷ θεός.

It is clear that in these passages ὁ θεός either could not be used, or
could only be used with a serious change of sense.

Use with
prepo-
sitions.

The use of ὁ θεός and θεός with prepositions presents some marked
results.

  I. ἀπό.
    (a) With article:

Apoc. xii. 6 τόπον ἡτοιμασμένον ἀπὸ τοῦ θ.

„ xxi. 10 (πόλιν) καταβαίνουσαν ἐκ τοῦ οὐρανοῦ ἀπὸ τοῦ θ.

(β) Without article:

John iii. 2 ἀπὸ θ. ἐλήλυθας.

„ xiii. 3 ἀπὸ θ. ἐξῆλθεν.

„ xvi. 30 ἀπὸ θ. ἐξῆλθες.

2. εἰς.

John xiv. 1 πιστεύετε εἰς τὸν θ.

3. ἐκ.

(a) With article :

γεννηθῆναι ἐκ τοῦ θ. .1 John iii. 9, v. 1, 4, 18.

εἶναι ἐκ τοῦ θ. John vii. 17, viii. 47 ; 1 John iii. 10, iv. 1 ff., 6 f., v. 19 ; 3 John 11.

John viii. 42 ἐκ τοῦ θ. ἐξῆλθον.

Apoc. xi. 11 πνεῦμα ζωῆς ἐκ τοῦ θ.

(β) Without article :

John i. 13 ἐκ θεοῦ ἐγεννήθησαν.

4. ἐν.

(a) With article :

1 John iv. 15 αὐτὸς [μένει] ἐν τῷ θ.

„ 16 ἐν τῷ θ. μένει.

(β) Without article :

John iii. 21 ἐν θ. ἐστὶν εἰργασμένα.

5. παρά.

(a) With article :

John vi. 46 ὁ ὢν παρὰ [τοῦ] θ.

„ viii. 40 ἣν ἤκουσα παρὰ τοῦ θ.

(β) Without article :

John i. 6 ἀπεσταλμένος παρὰ θ.

„ ix. 16 οὐκ ἔστιν οὗτος παρὰ θ.

„ 33 εἰ ἦν παρὰ θ.

2 John 3 εἰρήνη παρὰ θ. πατρός.

6. πρός.

Uniformly with the article :

John i. 1 ἦν πρὸς τὸν θ.

„ xiii. 3 ὑπάγει πρὸς τὸν θ.

1 John iii. 21 παρρησίαν ἔχομεν πρὸς τὸν θ.

Apoc. xii. 5 ἡρπάσθη πρὸς τὸν θ.

„ xiii. 6 βλασφημίας πρὸς τὸν θ.

Throughout it will be seen that in θεός the general conception of divinity is dominant, and in ὁ θεός that of the One Being in personal relation to others.

ii. The same general difference is observable in the use of the terms in the other Books of the N. T. Thus it may be noticed that the article is uniformly found

(1) with ἐνώπιον (ἔναντι, κατενώπιον, κατέναντι) (31 times) except 2 Cor. ii. 17.

ii. Use in other Books, with prepositions.

(2) with πρός acc. (19 times).

(3) with ὑπό gen. (13 times) except Rom. xiii. 1; Gal. iv. 9.

On the other hand the article is never used with κατά acc. (6 times), while it is used in the two places where κατά is used with gen.

Examples of usage.   A few illustrations will serve to make this difference felt :

Acts v. 4 οὐκ ἐψεύσω ἀνθρώποις ἀλλὰ τῷ θεῷ.

„   29 πειθαρχεῖν δεῖ θεῷ μᾶλλον ἢ ἀνθρώποις.

„ vii. 55 εἶδεν δόξαν θεοῦ καὶ Ἰησοῦν ἑστῶτα ἐκ δεξιῶν τοῦ θεοῦ.

„ xiv. 15 ἐπιστρέφειν ἐπὶ θεὸν ζῶντα.

„ xv. 19 τοῖς ἀπὸ τῶν ἐθνῶν ἐπιστρέφουσιν ἐπὶ τὸν θεόν.

Comp. 1 Tim. iv. 10 and 2 Cor. i. 9.

Acts xx. 21 τὴν εἰς θεὸν μετάνοιαν.

„ xxiv. 15 ἐλπίδα ἔχειν εἰς τὸν θεόν.

1 Thess. i. 9 ἐπεστρέψατε πρὸς τὸν θεὸν ἀπὸ τῶν εἰδώλων δουλεύειν θεῷ ζῶντι καὶ ἀληθινῷ.

„ ii. 13 εὐχαριστοῦμεν τῷ θεῷ...ὅτι παραλαβόντες λόγον ἀκοῆς... τοῦ θεοῦ ἐδέξασθε οὐ λόγον ἀνθρ. ἀλλὰ ..λόγον θεοῦ.

1 Cor. iii. 19 μωρία παρὰ τῷ θεῷ ἐστίν.

„ vii. 24 ἐν τούτῳ μενέτω παρὰ θεῷ.

Rom. ii. 17 καυχᾶσαι ἐν θεῷ.

„ 11 καυχώμενοι ἐν τῷ θεῷ.

In this connexion also, though other considerations come in here, the following parallel phrases deserve notice : εὐαγγέλιον θεοῦ Rom. i. 1 ; τὸ εὐαγγ. τοῦ θ. Rom. xv. 16; δικαιοσύνη θεοῦ 2 Cor. v. 21; ἡ δικ. τοῦ θ. Rom. x. 3; ὀργὴ θεοῦ Rom. i. 18; ἡ ὀργὴ τοῦ θ. John iii. 36, Eph. v. 6; ἀλήθεια θεοῦ Rom. xv. 8; ἡ ἀλήθ. τοῦ θ. Rom. i. 25, iii. 7.

Additional Note on iv. 15.   Divine Fellowship.

The fact of the divine fellowship is presented by St John in different forms.

1. Sometimes it is set forth in its reciprocal fulness :

iii. 24, *he that keepeth* (ὁ τηρῶν) *His commandments abideth in Him* (ὁ θεός) *and He in him.*

iv. 13, *hereby we perceive that we abide in Him and He in us, because He hath given us of His Spirit.*

iv. 15, *whosoever shall confess that Jesus* [*Christ*] *is the Son of God, God abideth in him and he in God.*

iv. 16, *God is love, and he that abideth in love abideth in God, and God* [*abideth*] *in him.*

With these passages in which the divine fellowship is described as a fellowship with 'God,' must be compared those in which it is described as a fellowship with Christ :

John vi. 56, *he that eateth* (ὁ τρώγων) *my flesh and drinketh my blood abideth in Me and I in him.*

John xiv. 20, *in that day ye shall know* (γνώσεσθε) *that I am in my Father, and ye in Me, and I in you.*

John xv. 5 *he that abideth in Me and I in him, the same beareth much fruit.*

It will be observed that, with one exception (c. iv. 15), the 'dwelling' or 'being' of man in God is placed first (iii. 24, iv. 13, 16; comp. ii. 24; John vi. 56, xiv. 20, xv. 5). The ascension to heaven, if we may so speak, generally precedes the transfiguration of earth.

2. Sometimes again the divine fellowship is regarded in one of its two aspects :

    (a) The abiding (being) of man in God (or Christ) :

        ii. 5, *in this we know* (γινώσκομεν) *that we are in Him.*

        ii. 6, *he that saith he abideth in Him ought himself also to walk even as He walked.*

        iii. 6, *every one that abideth in Him sinneth not.*

        v. 20, *we know* (οἴδαμεν) *that the Son of God hath come...and we are in Him that is true* (ἐν τῷ ἀληθινῷ).

Compare John xv. 4 (ye cannot bear fruit) *except ye abide in Me.*

        ii. 28, *abide in Him that if He shall be manifested we may have boldness...*

    (β) The abiding (being) of God (or Christ) in man :

        iii. 24, *hereby we know* (γινώσκομεν) *that He abideth in us, from the Spirit which He gave us.*

        iv. 12, *if we love one another God abideth in us...*

        John xvii. 22 f., *the glory which Thou hast given Me I have given unto them ; that they may be one, even as We are one; I in them, and Thou in Me...*

        John xvii. 26, *I made known unto them Thy Name...that the love wherewith Thou lovedst Me may be in them and I in them.*

It is of interest to examine these several passages as illustrating the efficient cause, the conditions, the sign, the results of this fellowship of man with God.

    (a) The efficient cause : the recognition of the revelation of God in Christ, of the Glory and the Name of the Father: John xvii. 22 f., 26, xiv. 20 ; 1 John v. 20.

    (β) The conditions : confession, iv. 15 ; obedience, iii. 24, ii. 6 ; love, iv. 16. These are summed up in the thought of participation in Christ's Humanity, John vi. 56.

    (γ) The sign : the possession of the Spirit of God, iii. 24 ; which shews itself as the source of obedience, ii. 5 ; and of love, iv. 12 f.

    (δ) The results : fruitfulness, John xv. 4 f. ; confidence, 1 John ii. 28 ; guilelessness, iii. 6.

The use of the terms 'abiding' and 'being' is also suggestive :

    (a) abide : ii. 6, 28, iii. 6, 24, iv. 12 f., 15 f. ; John vi. 56, xv. 4 f.

    (b) be : ii. 5, v. 20 ; John xiv. 20, xvii. 23, 26.

In this connexion Basil's remark is of interest that the Spirit is spoken of 'as the place of those that are sanctified.' 'The Spirit,' he goes on to say, 'is the place of the saints; and the saint is a place appropriate to the 'Spirit...' (*de Spir. S.* xxvi. § 62).

V. ¹ Πᾶς ὁ πιστεύων ὅτι Ἰησοῦς ἐστὶν ὁ χριστὸς

II. THE POWER OF THE CHRISTIAN
LIFE : THE VICTORY AND WIT-
NESS OF FAITH (v. 1—12).

The whole of this section is closely
connected, but two main thoughts,
'Faith' and 'Witness,' respectively
prevail in the opening and closing
verses. Thus it may be divided into
two parts,

    1. *The victory of Faith* (1—5).
    2. *The Divine Witness* (6—12.)

    1. *The victory of Faith* (v. 1—5).
In the last section it has been seen
that the love of 'the brethren' is enjoined as an essential accompaniment
of the love of God. St John now
traces the foundations of spiritual
kinsmanship. 'Brethren' are united
by a common Divine Father. The
human condition of this union is faith
in Jesus as the Christ. This faith is
able to overcome and has potentially
overcome every force of the world.
The succession of thought is clearly
marked. Faith is the sign of a new
life, and the presence of this life involves love for all who share it (1).
The reality of this love is shewn by
active obedience (2, 3). Such obedience is made possible by the gift of a
Divine life, a truth which is affirmed
in the abstract, and also in regard to
the Life of Christ (4), and in regard to
the experience of the believer (5).

  ¹ *Every one that believes that Jesus
is the Christ is begotten of God, and
every one that loveth him that begat
loveth him that is begotten of him.
² In this we know that we love the
children of God, when we love God
and do his commandments;* ³*for this
is the love of God, that we observe his
commandments, and his commandments are not grievous;* ⁴ *because
everything that is begotten of God
overcometh the world; and this is
the victory that overcame the world,
even our faith.* ⁵[*Yea,*] *who is he*

that overcometh the world but he that
believeth that Jesus is the Son of God?
  1. The transition from the former
section lies in the thought of brotherhood. Brotherhood is founded on the
vital apprehension of the revelation of
Christ given by God. It is not then
an arbitrary command that he who
loves God love his brother also. He
must do so. For he consciously shares
with every brother the principle of
his new being.

  Πᾶς ὁ πιστεύων] Comp. c. iii. 3.
  The verb πιστεύειν is here used for
the first time in the epistle in its full
and definite sense. In iv. 16 it describes a general position with regard
to the Divine purpose. In iii. 23 it
expresses a belief in the truth of the
revelation as to Christ. Here it presents that belief in a direct and personal form. 'He that believeth that
Jesus is the Christ' not only admits
an intellectual truth but enters into a
direct relation with the powers of a
spiritual order. 'The command' of
God (iii. 23) finds so far an individual
accomplishment.

  In the former chapter (iv. 2, 15;
comp. ii. 23), St John has spoken of
the 'confession' of Christ in relation
to society : here he speaks of faith
in relation to the single believer.
The main thought there was of the
recognition, here of the essence of the
children of God. The forms of confession are given in the most explicit
form. The article of faith is given
more simply. A living faith carries
with it more than the exact terms of
specific belief convey (John xi. 27).

  Compare vv. 5, 10, 13.
  Such faith involves the present action of a new and Divine life, which
must have a Divine origin. Comp.
1 Cor. xii. 3. Faith here is regarded
simply as the sign of the life which
has been given. Nothing is said of
the relation between the human and

ἐκ τοῦ θεοῦ γεγέννηται, καὶ πᾶς ὁ ἀγαπῶν τὸν γεννήσαντα ἀγαπᾷ τὸν γεγεννημένον ἐξ αὐτοῦ. ²ἐν τούτῳ

1 ἀγ. τὸν γεγ. B vg the: ἀγ + καὶ' τὸν γεγ. (א) A syrr.   τὸν γεγ. : τὸ γεγ. א.

the Divine—the faith of man, and 'the
seed of God' (iii. 9)—in the first quickening of life. Comp. John i. 12 note.
ὅτι 'I. ἐστὶν ὁ χριστός] Comp. v. 5
ὅτι 'I. ἐστὶν ὁ υἱὸς τοῦ θεοῦ. John xx.
31 ὅτι 'I. ἐστὶν ὁ χριστὸς ὁ υἱὸς τοῦ
θεοῦ. For the choice of the exact
terms of belief here, see ii. 22.
ἐκ τοῦ θ. γεγ.] See c. iii. 9 note.
καὶ πᾶς ὁ ἀγ. τ. γενν.] et omnis qui
diligit eum qui genuit V., and every
one that loveth Him that begat... It
is assumed that the child will have
love for the Author of his being.
Love follows directly from life. And
in this spiritual connexion love must
be directed to the character, and not
to the Person apart from the character. It follows therefore that it will
be extended to all those to whom the
character has been communicated.
ὁ ἀγαπῶν] Augustine brings out the
necessary connexion between faith
and love (faith in action): cum dilectione, fides Christiani: sine dilectione,
fides dæmonis.
τὸν γενν.] The word is used also of
the human agent, Philem. 10.
τὸν γεγενν. ἐξ αὐτοῦ] eum qui natus est ex eo V., him that hath been
begotten of Him, the child who draws
from Him the abiding principle of
his life. The singular (contrast 'the
children' v. 2) emphasises the direct
relation of Father and child, and also
of brother and brother. This relation,
as here regarded, is personal and not
social.
Throughout the Epistle St John
individualises: ii. 4 ff., 9 ff., 15, 17,
22 f., 29; iii. 3 ff., 9 f., 15, 17.
The idea of Augustine that the reference is to Christ is foreign to the
context.
2. What then, it may be asked, is
the sign of this spiritual love which

is essentially different from a natural
preference? The love of the children
of God, such is the answer, is attested
by the love of God, that is, by obedience to God. At first sight this
answer seems simply to invert the
terms of the statement which has
been made already. The love of God
and the love of the children of God
do in fact include each the other. It
is equally true to say 'He who loves
God loves the children of God,' and
to say 'He who loves the children of
God loves God.' Either form of love
may be made the ground or the conclusion in the argument. But in reality the test of the love of the brethren given here introduces a new
idea. The will of Christians is essentially the will of God (comp. iii. 22).
The effort to fulfil the commandments
of God is consequently the effort to
do that which our 'brethren' most
desire to be done: the proof of love.
Bede says well: Ille solus recte
proximum diligere probatur qui et
Conditoris amore flagrare conspicitur.
It will also be further observed that
the passage stands in close connexion
with c. ii. 3 in this we perceive that
we know Him if we keep His commandments; and with iii. 23 this is
His commandment that we believe
the Name...and love one another...
(comp. iv. 20).
Obedience to the manifold commandments of God (αἱ ἐντολαί), the
active fulfilment of Christian duty, is
the sign of a knowledge of God: and
knowledge of God is love of God.
And again, the one commandment
of God (ἡ ἐντολή) is that we believe
the Name of His Son and love one
another.
Here the love of God and obedience in detail, which is identical with

γινώσκομεν ὅτι ἀγαπῶμεν τὰ τέκνα τοῦ θεοῦ, ὅταν
τὸν θεὸν ἀγαπῶμεν καὶ τὰς ἐντολὰς ·αὐτοῦ ποιῶμεν·

2 ποιῶμεν B vg (me the syrr): τηρῶμεν ℵ (lat).   2, 3 om. ποιῶμεν...αὐτοῦ A.

it (v. 3), is given as the sign of the reality of love for the brethren, who are the children of God.

This thought that the love of God is obedience to His commandments is the uniting thought in the three passages. It is clearly seen through this how we can say (now more completely than before): 'We love God and keep His commandments, and therefore we love the brethren'; or 'We love the brethren, and therefore we love God and keep His commandments.' Whichever proposition is established, the other follows from it. Comp. c. i. 3.

At the same time the transference of the test of the love of the brethren to a spiritual region enables the believer to discern (γινώσκομεν) the reality of his love in spite of the many differences which separate him from the object of it under the conditions of earthly life.

ἐν τούτῳ...] in this .. The perception comes not as a conviction drawn from a state of obedient love (ἐκ τούτου, from this), but in the very exercise of the feeling. The 'this,' as elsewhere, seems to look backward at once and forward, to the fact and to the manifestation of the love of God. Comp. ii. 3 note.

γινώσκομεν] cognoscimus V., we know, perceive. The conviction is brought home to us in the present interpretation of the facts of life. Compare ii. 3 note, 5, 18; iii. 24 (V. scimus); iv. 13 (V. intelligimus); and contrast the use of οἴδαμεν in iii. 2, 5, 14 f.; v. 15, 18 ff. (V. scimus, scitis). See v. 18 note. The use of ὅταν brings into prominence the immediate and continuous exercise of this power of knowledge.

ἀγαπῶμεν] The love which is spoken

of is that of Christian for Christian as Christian, a feeling which has to be distinguished from human affection. Of this love, which belongs to the spiritual sphere, love to God, that is obedience to God, is necessarily a final criterion.

τὰ τέκνα τοῦ θ.] natos Dei V., the children of God. Comp. iii. 1 note. St John does not say 'brethren' here, because the argument turns upon the relation of Christians to God and not upon their relation to one another. At the same time the plural follows naturally on the singular of v. 1. Then the thought was of the individual realisation of the divine sonship: here the thought is of the general, social, duty.

This is the only place where ὅταν occurs in the Epistles of St John. With the present conj. it expresses either an action repeated indefinitely (John viii. 44, ix. 5, &c.), or an action at an indefinite time regarded as actually going on (John vii. 27 ἔρχηται, contrast v. 31 ἔλθῃ; xvi. 21 τίκτῃ followed by γεννήσῃ). Comp. 1 Cor. xv. 24 (παραδιδοῖ, καταργήσῃ).

ὅταν...ἀγαπῶμεν] cum...diligamus, V. The literal rendering 'whenever we love' makes the meaning clear. Each act of love to God, that is practically, each act of obedience, carries with it the fresh conviction of true love to the children of God. Ἐάν (c. ii. 3; John xiii. 35) gives the general condition: ὅταν, the particular and repeated fulfilment of it.

The change of order (comp. iii. 4) in the objects (ἀγαπ. τὰ τέκνα, ὅταν τὸν θ. ἀγαπ. καὶ τὰς ἐντ. ποι.) corresponds with a natural change in emphasis: 'We know that we love the brethren, when God is the end of our affection and His commands the guide of our

³αὕτη γάρ ἐστιν ἡ ἀγάπη τοῦ θεοῦ ἵνα τὰς ἐντολὰς
αὐτοῦ τηρῶμεν, καὶ αἱ ἐντολαὶ αὐτοῦ βαρεῖαι οὐκ εἰσίν,
⁴ὅτι πᾶν τὸ γεγεννημένον ἐκ τοῦ θεοῦ νικᾷ τὸν κόσμον.

action.' In other cases where the object stands before the verb a similar shade of meaning is seen : *e.g.* ii. 20; iv. 9, 12; v. 9.

καὶ τὰς ἐντ. αὐτοῦ ποι.] *et mandata eius faciamus* V., and *do His commandments*. This clause brings the love of God into the region of active life. The phrase itself is unique (Apoc. xxii. 14 is a false reading); and seems to be chosen in order to express the active energy of obedience as positive and not only negative. Comp. c. i. 6 π. τὴν ἀλήθειαν note.

Augustine follows out his false interpretation of 'him that is begotten of Him' in *v.* 1 by a striking application here: Filios Dei dixit qui Filium Dei paulo ante dicebat, quia filii Dei corpus sunt unici Filii Dei; et cum ille caput nos membra unus est Filius Dei.

He also adds a wider application of the principle: Omnes homines, etiam inimicos vestros, diligatis, non quia sunt fratres, sed ut fratres sint; ut semper fraterno amore flagretis sive in fratrem factum, sive in inimicum ut frater fiat diligendo.

3. αὕτη γάρ...] *for this...* The words give an explanation of the second clause (*and do His commandments*) in the former verse. Love of God can only be shewn in the effort to fulfil His will. Comp. John xiv. 15, 21, 31.

ἵνα...τηρῶμεν καὶ...] *ut custodiamus* V. The love of God is not simply the keeping (τήρησις, τὸ τηρεῖν) of the commandments of God, but rather a continuous and watchful endeavour to observe them. Comp. John vi. 29 ἵνα πιστεύητε, xvii. 3 ἵνα γιν.: 2 John 6. And the nature of the commandments is not such as to crush the

freedom and spontaneity of love. They are not *grievous*, heavy (βαρεῖαι, *gravia* V.), an oppressive and exhausting burden. Compare Matt. xi. 30 τὸ φορτίον μου ἐλαφρόν ἐστιν, and contrast Matt. xxiii. 4 δεσμεύουσιν φορτία βαρέα.

4. ὅτι...] *because...* Comp. ii. 19 note. The fact that the divine commandments are not a burden is not established by a consideration of their character. In themselves they are difficult (Acts xiv. 22; John xvi. 33). To love the brethren is not a light thing. But with the commandment comes also the power of fulfilment. Natural taste, feeling, judgment may check spiritual sympathy; but every faculty and power which is quickened by God is essentially stronger than 'the world' and realises its victory at once.

In the development of the thought St John passes from the abstract (πᾶν τὸ γεγενν.) to the concrete and personal (τίς ἐστιν ὁ νικῶν), through the decisive history in which the truth was once for all absolutely realised (ἡ νίκη ἡ νικήσασα).

πᾶν τὸ γεγ.] St John chooses the abstract form (contrast *v.* 1 τὸν γεγ.) in order to convey an universal truth. The thought is not so much of the believer in his unity, nor of the Church, but of each element included in the individual life and in the life of the society. Compare John iii. 6 τὸ γεγ. and John iii. 8 πᾶς ὁ γεγ.

νικᾷ τὸν κ.] *conquers the world*— not 'hath conquered' (c. ii. 13 f., iv. 4), nor yet 'will conquer'—in a struggle which is present and continuous. Under the title 'the world' St John gathers up the sum of all the limited, transitory powers opposed to God which make obedience difficult. It

καὶ αὕτη ἐστὶν ἡ νίκη ἡ νικήσασα τὸν κόσμον, ἡ πίστις
ἡμῶν· ⁵τίς ἐστιν [δὲ] ὁ νικῶν τὸν κόσμον εἰ μὴ ὁ
πιστεύων ὅτι Ἰησοῦς ἐστιν ὁ υἱὸς τοῦ θεοῦ;

5 τίς ἐστιν δέ B (lat): τίς δέ ἐστιν ℵ (lat) syrhl me: τίς ἐστιν A vg.

is by the introduction of the spiritual, the eternal, that we obtain a true standard for things, and so can overcome the temptations which spring out of a narrow, earthly, temporal estimate. And this holds good not only of man as a whole but of each power and faculty with which he is endowed. Comp. John xvi. 33.

καὶ αὕτη...] The certainty of the victory of that which partakes of the Divine is illustrated by a view of the nature of the victory itself. The victory which the Christian is ever winning is the individual appropriation of a victory gained once for all.

ἡ νίκη...ἡ πίστις ἡμῶν] the victory ...our faith. The word νίκη occurs here only in the N.T., and πίστις here only in St John's Epistles. Πίστις is not found in St John's Gospel. It occurs in the Apocalypse: ii. 13, 19; xiii. 10; xiv. 12. In ii. 13, xiv. 12 it appears to be used objectively for 'the faith of Christ,' as embodied in a confession ('fides quæ creditur'): in ii. 19, xiii. 10, it is the subjective spirit of the true believer ('fides qua creditur'). Here the sense is fixed by the context. 'Our faith' is the faith which is summed up in the confession that Jesus is 'the Christ, the Son of God.' The Life represented by that creed was the victory over the world as Christ Himself interpreted it (John xvi. 33). To hold that faith, to enter into the meaning and the power of that conquest through apparent failure, is to share in its triumph. Our faith is not merely victorious: it is the embodiment of *the victory which overcame the world.* Thus the aorist (ἡ νικήσασα, *quæ vincit* V., inadequately) receives its full

force. The victory of Christ was gained upon a narrow field, but it was world-wide in its effects. Comp. Ign. *ad Sm.* 10 ἡ τελεία πίστις, Ἰησοῦς Χριστός, and Col. ii. 2 εἰς ἐπίγνωσιν τοῦ μυστηρίου τοῦ θεοῦ, Χριστοῦ.

5. τίς ἐστιν...] At length the question becomes directly personal. St John appeals to the experience of those whom he addresses. The single believer (ὁ νικῶν) takes the place of the abstract element (τὸ γεγεννημένον), and of the absolute force (ἡ πίστις). The victory of the divine principle is, as he triumphantly claims, actually realised in the victory of the Christian.

τίς...εἰ μή...] Compare ii. 22. The personal victory is regarded in its course (ὁ νικῶν), as the representative victory was regarded in its completion (ἡ ν. ἡ νικήσασα).

ὅτι Ἰ. ἐστὶν ὁ υἱ. τοῦ θ.] Comp. *v.* 1. By the use of the title 'the Son of God' in connexion with the human name, *Jesus,* the antithesis involved in the faith is expressed in the sharpest form. There is a similar passage from 'the Christ' to 'the Son' in ii. 22 ff.

2. *The Divine Witness* (v. 6—12).

The victory of Faith has been shewn to lie in the confession of Jesus as the Son of God. St John now goes on to unfold the character (6—8), and the effectiveness (9—12) of the witness by which this confession is sustained and justified.

6—8. The character of the witness to the substance of the Christian Faith is laid open by a consideration of the historical witness which is offered to men in the Life of Christ, and

⁶Οὖτός ἐστιν ὁ ἐλθὼν διʼ ὕδατος καὶ αἵματος, Ἰησοῦς

6 καὶ αἵματος B vg syrvg : +καὶ πνεύματος ℵA (lat) me the syrhl (others substitute πν. for αἵμ. and some read καὶ πν. καὶ αἵμ.).   Ἰς Χ̅ς ℵAB : Χ̅ς Ἰ̅ς the:
Ἰ̅ς ὁ Χ̅ς ϛ syrhl. See Additional Note.

in the life of the Church (6 *a*, *b*) ;
of the divine principle of witness
(6 *c*) ; and of the personal witnesses
(7, 8).

⁶ *This is He that came by water
and blood, Jesus Christ ; not in the
water only, but in the water and
in the blood. And the Spirit is that
which beareth witness, because the
Spirit is the Truth.* ⁷ *Because three
are they that bear witness,* ⁸*the Spirit
and the water and the blood; and the
three are for the one.*

6. The two parts of the historical
witness to Christ are distinguished
by the different forms in which the
common outward symbols are used in
corresponding clauses. He came ' *by
water and blood,*' and again ' *not in
the water only, but in the water and
in the blood.*'

Οὖτος...] The pronoun goes back to
the subject of the last sentence.
" *This* ' Jesus,' who has been affirmed
to be 'the Son of God,' *is He that
came...*" The compound title at the
end of the clause, *Jesus Christ*, emphasises the truth which is established by the manner of the ' coming '
of ' Jesus ': ' *This is He that came...*'
and whose Divine Office is expressed
by the full name which He bears,
even *Jesus Christ*.

ὁ ἐλθών...] *He that came...* The
verb is used with a clear reference to
the technical sense of ' he that cometh '
(ὁ ἐρχόμενος Matt. xi. 3 ; Luke vii.
19 f. ; comp. John i. 15, 27 ; vi. 14 ;
xi. 27 ; xii. 13 ; see also John i. 30 ;
x. 8). Thus ' He that came' is equivalent to ' He that fulfilled the promises to the fathers, as the Saviour
sent from God.' Comp. ii. 18 note.

διʼ ὕδατος καὶ αἵματος] *per aquam et*

sanguinem V., *by (through) water
and blood.* The sense of ' *He that
came*,' which distinctly points to a
past historic fact, determines that
these terms also must have a historic
meaning, and refer to definite events
characteristic of the manner in which
the Lord fulfilled His office upon
earth. ' He came—He was shewn
to be the Christ—by water and blood.'
' Water ' and ' blood ' contributed in
some way to reveal the nature and
the fulfilment of His work.

There can be no doubt that the
Death upon the Cross satisfies the
conception of ' coming by blood.'
By so dying the Lord made known
His work as Redeemer ; and opened
the fountain of His life to men. Comp.
Additional Note on i. 7.

The ' coming by water,' which naturally corresponds to this final act of
sacrifice, is the Baptism, whereby
the Lord declared His purpose ' *to
fulfil all righteousness*' (Matt. iii.
15). The water, by Christ's voluntary
acceptance of the Baptist's ministry,
became the means through which the
divine purpose was fulfilled (Matt. iii.
17). The Baptist was sent baptizing
in water that Christ might be made
manifest (John i. 31). Even in the
case of the Lord Baptism is shewn to
have been the external condition of
the ' descent and abiding of the Holy
Spirit ' (John i. 33 f.) ; and by His
Baptism Christ fulfilled for the humanity which He took to Himself,
though not for Himself, the condition
of regeneration.

But we cannot stop at the reference to the cardinal events in the
Lord's Life whereby He ' came by
water and blood ' in the fulfilment of

His historic work. While He hung upon the Cross, dead in regard to mortal life, but still living (see John xix. 34 note), He came again 'by water and blood.' The issue of 'blood and water' from His side evidently indicated that He henceforth became for men the source of blessing symbolised by the twofold stream, and realised in His own human life by Baptism and Death upon the Cross. The one historic coming was shewn to be the foundation of a continuous spiritual coming; and St John saw in this the subject of the crucial testimony which he had to give (John xix. 35).

Compare the fragment of Claudius Apollinaris (Routh, *Rell.* i. 161) ὁ ἐκχέας ἐκ τῆς πλευρᾶς αὐτοῦ τὰ δύο πάλιν καθάρσια ὕδωρ καὶ αἷμα, λόγον καὶ πνεῦμα (the Gospel of the Incarnate Word and the sanctifying presence of the Spirit).

This exceptional note of the Evangelist seems to place the reference here to the significant fact recorded in the Gospel beyond question. The readers of the Epistle could not but be familiar with the incident either from the oral or from the written teaching of the Apostle; and conscious of the stress which he laid upon it, as the confirmation of Christian faith, they could not fail to recall it here.

Compare Bede : Nec reticendum quod in hoc quoque sanguis et aqua testimonium illi dederunt quod de latere mortui vivaciter effluxerunt, quod erat contra naturam corporum mortuorum, atque ob id mysteriis aptum et testimonio veritatis fuit congruum, videlicet insinuans quia et ipsum Domini corpus melius post mortem esset victurum resuscitatum in gloria et ipsa mors illius nobis vitam donaret.

Such an extension of the meaning of 'water and blood' appears to be implied in the words that follow : *not in the water only, but in the water and in the blood,* followed by

the reference to the present witness of the Spirit. The change of the preposition, the use of the article, and the stress laid on actual experience, shew that St John is speaking of a continuation of the first coming under some new but analogous form. Further, it is to be noticed that what was before spoken of in its unity (δι' ὕ. καὶ αἵ.) is now spoken of in its separate parts (ἐν τῷ ὕ. καὶ ἐν τῷ αἵμ.). The first proof of the Messiahship of Jesus lay in His complete historical fulfilment of Messiah's work once for all in bringing purification and salvation : that proof is continued in the experience of the Church in its two separate parts.

Thus we are led to the ideas which underlie the two sacraments, and which are brought home to us in and through them : the ideas which in their most general form are laid open in John iii., vi. It is through Christ's 'coming by water and blood,' and His Life through Death, that the life of the Spirit and the cleansing and support of our human life in all its fulness are assured. The actual experience of these blessings is the abiding witness of the Church to Him.

Bede, probably following Augustine, whose Commentary is not extant after *v.* 3, well combines the historic and sacramental references : *Qui venit per aquam et sanguinem,* aquam videlicet lavacri et sanguinem suæ passionis : non solum baptizari propter nostram ablutionem dignatus est, ut nobis baptismi sacramentum consecraret ac traderet, verum etiam sanguinem suum dedit pro nobis, sua nos passione redimens, cujus sacramentis semper refecti nutriremur ad salutem.

διά...ἐν...] The historic Mission of Christ—the pledge of His Presence—was established 'through' the cardinal events of His Ministry. The abiding presence of Christ—the issue of His Mission—is realised 'in' that which is appointed to perpetuate

Χριστός· οὐκ ἐν τῷ ὕδατι μόνον ἀλλ᾽ ἐν τῷ ὕδατι καὶ
ἐν τῷ αἵματι· καὶ τὸ πνεῦμά ἐστιν τὸ μαρτυροῦν, ὅτι τὸ

μόνον: μόνῳ B.   αἵματι ℵB vg me the syrr: πνεύματι A (some add πνεύματι,
others read αἵματι...πνεύματι).   τὸ πνεῦμα (2°): Χριστός vg.   Perhaps x̄p̄c̄ for s̄p̄s̄.
(Not Ambr. Fulg.)

the power of His work. The one
preposition marks the means by
which Christ's office was revealed :
the other the sphere in which He
continues to exercise it.

δι᾽ ὕδατος καὶ αἵμ.] The order is
significantly changed from that in
the Gospel (blood and water). The
order in the Gospel is (so to speak)
the order of the divine gift: the full
power of human life comes first: that
in the Epistle is the order of the
human appropriation of the gift.

The symbolism of 'blood' as representing the natural human life
sacrificed and so made available for
others, has been already touched
upon.   In contrast with this, 'water'
represents the power of the spiritual
life : John iii. 5; iv. 14; vii. 38 (Zech.
xiv. 8). Comp. Apoc. xxi. 6; xxii. 1, 17.

οὐκ ἐν τῷ ὕδ. μ.] not in the water
only. The reference is probably to
such teachers as Irenæus mentions
(i. 26, 1) : [Cerinthus docuit] post
baptismum descendisse in eum (Iesum)
ab ea principalitate quæ est super
omnia Christum figura columbæ; et
tunc annunciasse incognitum Patrem
et virtutes perfecisse : in fine autem
revolasse iterum Christum de Jesu et
Jesum passum esse et resurrexisse;
Christum autem impassibilem perseverasse, existentem spiritalem.   In
some form or other the same kind of
error is always repeating itself. The
spiritual life is exalted into an undue
supremacy, to the neglect of the redemption of the earthly life.

For this reason St John says οὐκ
ἐν τῷ ὕδ. μόνον, and not οὐ δι᾽ ὕδ. μόνον.
He contradicts a false view of Christ's
abiding work and not only a false
view of Christ's Person in Himself.

καὶ τὸ πν....] and the Spirit...   In
the words which immediately precede
St John has indicated a present action
of Christ.   He now shews how the
reality of that action is established.
The Spirit—the Divine Spirit—is
that which witnesseth, not 'which
witnessed' (3 John 6), or 'which hath
witnessed' (v. 9).   His testimony is
given now and uninterruptedly. Such
'witness' is the peculiar office of the
Spirit (John xiv. 26; xv. 26; xvi.
8 ff).   By this it is that men are
enabled to pierce beneath the external phenomena and the external
rites to their innermost meaning.
Nothing is said of the substance of
the witness or of those to whom it is
given.   These details are included in
the idea of the Spirit's witness. He
speaks of Divine Truth; and He
speaks to the souls of believers.

Thus there is, as will be seen,
a striking parallelism between the
office of Christ and the office of the
Spirit.   Jesus is He that came, once
for all fulfilling the Messiah's work ;
and the Spirit is that which beareth
witness, ever applying and interpreting His Mission and His gifts.

ὅτι τὸ πνεῦμα...] quoniam (quod)
Christus V., because the Spirit...   The
conjunction (ὅτι) has been interpreted
both as giving the substance (that)
and as giving the reason (because) of
the testimony. The former translation
gives no tolerable sense unless the
Latin reading of Christ for the Spirit
is adopted. But the sense thus gained
is foreign to the context.   While then
we take the translation because as certainly right, the meaning of the word
is ambiguous here.   It may mean :
The Spirit gives the witness (1) be-

πνεῦμά ἐστιν ἡ ἀλήθεια.   ⁷ὅτι τρεῖς εἰσὶν οἱ μαρτυροῦντες, ⁸τὸ πνεῦμα καὶ τὸ ὕδωρ καὶ τὸ αἷμα, καὶ οἱ

7 τρεῖς: οἱ τρεῖς ℵ.   7, 8 See Additional Note.

cause it is essentially *fitted* to do so :
or (2) *because* by its essential nature
it is *constrained* to do so. Perhaps
the one idea passes into the other, so
that it is not necessary to distinguish
them sharply. In that which is Divine, nature and office coincide.

τὸ πν. ἐστιν ἡ ἀλ.] *the Spirit is the
Truth.* Just as Christ is the Truth
(John xiv. 6), so the Spirit sent in
Christ's name is the Truth. The Spirit
cannot but make known, as men can
bear the revelation, that which is
eternal and absolute in changing phenomena. That which 'is' is in virtue
of the Spirit, in virtue of Christ (Col.
i. 15 ff.).

Bede has a vigorous note on the
Latin reading (*Christus est veritas*):
Quia ergo Spiritus Jesum Christum
esse veritatem testatur, ipse se veritatem cognominat, Baptista illum veritatem prædicat, Filius tonitrui veritatem evangelizat : taceant blasphemi
qui hunc phantasma esse dogmati-
zant ; pereant de terra memoriæ eorum qui eum vel Deum vel hominem
esse verum denegant.

7, 8. ὅτι τρεῖς εἰσίν...] *Because
three are they...* This clause appears
to give the reason for the main proposition in *v.* 5, that 'Jesus is the
Son of God,' a truth briefly expressed
and affirmed by His full Name, 'Jesus
Christ.' What has been said in *v.* 6
—*this is He that came*—prepares
the way for the assertion of this
complete personal testimony, adequate according to the human standard: Deut. xix. 15; comp. John viii.
17 ff. The stress laid by the order
upon 'three' emphasises this thought
of the fulness of the number of the
witnesses, and the consequent certainty of that which they affirm. The
faith in Jesus as 'the Christ, the Son

of God' is reasonable according to the
ordinary laws of belief.

It seems to be less natural to regard
the clause as a confirmation of the
words which immediately precede.
The ground of the Spirit's witness
is given perfectly in the declaration
of His Nature and Office as 'the
Truth.' Yet it is possible that the
ὅτι may simply explain the addition
of the Spirit : "besides 'the Water'
and 'the Blood,' there is yet another
witness ; *because three are they that
bear witness.*"

τρεῖς...οἱ μαρτυροῦντες] The passage
from the neuter τὸ μαρτυροῦν to the
masculine οἱ μαρτυροῦντες marks the
different aspect under which the
witness is now regarded, as a personal witness. The transition is made
through the Spirit, who is regarded both as a power and as a person : comp. John xiv. 26; xv. 26,
τὸ πνεῦμα...ὅ...ἐκεῖνος. Just as the
Spirit is found to be personal in His
work with men, so also 'the water'
and 'the blood' speak personally
through those in whom their efficacy
is realised.

οἱ μαρτ.] The participle, as distinguished from the noun οἱ μάρτυρες
(Acts i. 8 ; ii. 32, &c.), expresses the
actual delivery of the witness, and
this is a present, continuous, action.
The witness here is considered mainly
as the living witness of the Church
and not as the historical witness of
the Gospels. Through believers these
three, 'the Spirit and the Water
and the Blood,' perform a work not
for believers only but for the world
(John xvii. 20 ff.).

8. τὸ πνεῦμα] The Spirit has a twofold office, one corresponding with
that of Christ (οὗτός ἐστιν ὁ ἐλθών...
τὸ πνεῦμά ἐστιν τὸ μαρτυροῦν...); and

τρεῖς εἰς τὸ ἕν. εἰσιν. ⁹ Εἰ τὴν μαρτυρίαν τῶν ἀνθρώπων
λαμβάνομεν, ἡ μαρτυρία τοῦ θεοῦ μείζων ἐστίν, ὅτι
αὕτη ἐστὶν ἡ μαρτυρία τοῦ θεοῦ ὅτι μεμαρτύρηκεν περὶ

9 τῶν ἀνθρ.: τοῦ θεοῦ ℵ*.   ὅτι (2°) ℵAB vg me the: ἦν ς.

the other coordinate with that of the power of spiritual life and the power of redemption brought by Christ (τὸ πν., τὸ ὕδωρ, τὸ αἷμα). In this latter connexion it must be remembered that the Spirit is the sign of the glory of the Risen Christ; John vii. 39; xvi. 7; Acts ii. 32 f. Thus the Spirit, with the Water and Blood, completes the witness to the Incarnation as a Fact no less than as an open source of blessing. For the witness of the Spirit see Acts v. 32.

οἱ τρεῖς εἰς τὸ ἕν εἰσιν] *the three are for the one.* The subject is emphatically repeated to mark the unity of the object. 'The three personal witnesses are turned to the one absolute end,' to establish the one Truth (τὸ ἕν, *the one,* not simply *one*), that definite Truth which is everywhere present through the Epistle. The idea is not that of simple unanimity in the witnesses (εἰς ἓν εἶναι), but that of their convergence (so to speak) on the one Gospel of 'Christ come in the flesh,' to know which is eternal life.

With the phrase εἰς τὸ ἕν εἶναι may be contrasted ἓν εἶναι John x. 30; xvii. 21 f.; 1 Cor. iii. 8; τελειοῦσθαι εἰς ἕν John xvii. 23; συνάγειν εἰς ἓν John xi. 52.

9—12. St John goes on from considering the character of the witness to Christ to consider its effectiveness. It is a divine witness (9): it is a human, internal witness (10): it is a witness realised in a present life (11), in fellowship with the Son (12).

⁹ *If we receive the witness of men, the witness of God is greater, because this is the witness of God, that He hath borne witness concerning His*

Son. ¹⁰ *He that believeth on the Son of God hath the witness in himself: he that believeth not God hath made Him a liar, because he hath not believed on the witness which God hath borne concerning His Son.* ¹¹ *And this is the witness, that God gave us eternal life, and this life is in His Son.* ¹² *He that hath the Son hath the life: he that hath not the Son of God hath not the life.*

9. Εἰ τὴν μ. τ. ἀνθρ. λαμβ.] *Si... accipimus* V., *If we receive...* This is assumed as unquestioned: c. iii. 13. The threefold witness of which St John has spoken, simply as being threefold, satisfies the conditions of human testimony. Much more then, he argues, does a threefold divine witness meet all claims; and such a witness, it is implied, we have in the witness of the Spirit, the water and the blood. This witness therefore is 'greater' than the witness of men in regard to its authority: John v. 36. Comp. c. iii. 20; iv. 4.

For μαρτ. λαμβ. see John iii. 11, 32 f.; v. 34.

The form of the argument is irregular. Instead of completing the sentence on the same type as he began, 'much more shall we receive the witness of God,' St John states that which is the ground of this conclusion, 'the witness of God is greater.'

ὅτι αὕτη ἐ....ὅτι...] *quoniam hoc est .. quia...* V., *because this is...that...* The words look backward and forward. This triple witness which has been described, and which is now defined further to be a witness of God concerning His Son: this is the final form of the witness of God.

The witness was open and visible

τοῦ υἱοῦ αὐτοῦ. ¹⁰ὁ πιστεύων εἰς τὸν υἱὸν τοῦ θεοῦ
ἔχει τὴν μαρτυρίαν ἐν αὐτῷ· ὁ μὴ πιστεύων τῷ θεῷ

10 τὴν μαρτ. ℵB the syrr: +τοῦ θεοῦ A vg me.   αυτω AB: ἑαυτῷ ℵ.
τῷ θεῷ ℵB me syrr: τῷ υἱῷ A vg syrhlmg (others read τῷ υἱῷ τοῦ θεοῦ, τῷ υἱῷ
αὐτοῦ, and Cod. Am. omits by the first hand).

to the world in the general effect of
Christ's death and the pouring out of
the Spirit: so much was unquestionable.

The first conjunction (*because*)
does not give the ground of the
superior authority of the divine witness, that is taken for granted, but
the ground for appealing to it. Such
a witness has been given, and therefore we appeal to it.

The second ὅτι is ambiguous. It
may be (1) parallel with the former
one: 'because this is the witness of
God, because, I say, He hath borne
witness...'; or, it may be (2) explanatory of the μαρτυρίαν: 'because this
is the witness of God, even that He
hath borne witness...'; or again (3)
the word may be the relative (ὅ τι):
'because this is the witness of God,
even that which He hath witnessed....'

No one of the explanations is without difficulty. Against (2) it may be
urged that it is strange to insist on
the idea that the witness of God lies
in the fact that He hath witnessed
concerning His Son.

The usage of St John and of the
Apostolic writers generally is against
(3); though perhaps reference may be
made to iii. 20; John viii. 25. [In
Matt. xviii. 28 εἴ τι.]

The usage of St John (c. i. 5; v.
11, 14) is equally against (1).

On the whole it is best to take the
clause as explanatory of αὕτη: 'because
this is the witness of God, even the
fact that He hath borne witness concerning His Son.' God has spoken;
and His message is the witness to the
Incarnation. Comp. *v.* 11.

μεμαρτύρηκεν] *testificatus est* V.,

hath witnessed. The form is to be
distinguished from 'witnesseth' and
'witnessed.'

μεμαρτύρηκα John i. 34; iii. 26; v.
33, 37; xix. 35. (Hebr. xi. 5; 3 John
12.)

ἐμαρτύρησα John i. 32; iv. 44;
xiii. 21; Acts xv. 8; 1 Cor. xv.
15; 1 Tim. vi. 13; 3 John 6; Apoc.
i. 2; Hebr. xi. 2, 4, 39.

It may be added that *vv.* 6—9
contain a testimony to the Holy
Trinity in the several works of the
Divine Persons: Christ 'comes,'
the Spirit 'witnesses,' God (the
Father) 'hath witnessed concerning
His Son.'

10. The witness is not of external
testimony only, but internal also.
Absolute self-surrender to the Son of
God brings to the believer a direct
consciousness of His Divine Nature
and work. *He that believeth on the
Son of God hath the witness in himself.* That which for others is external
is for the believer experimental. The
witness of Spirit and water and blood
becomes an inner conviction of life
and cleansing and redemption. The
title of divine dignity (*the Son of
God*) points to the assurance of this
effect. Moreover it is to be noticed
that here the condition laid down is
belief in the Person of Christ (πιστ.
εἰς), and not belief in a fact (πιστ. ὅτι
v. 1).

ὁ μὴ πιστ. τῷ θ.] *he that believeth
not God.* The direct antithesis to
'believing on the Son' is 'not believing God.' This follows from the fact
that 'believing on the Son' comes from
'believing God,' that is, welcoming
His testimony.

For the phrase μὴ πιστεύειν τῷ θεῷ

ψεύστην πεποίηκεν αὐτόν, ὅτι οὐ πεπίστευκεν εἰς τὴν
μαρτυρίαν ἣν μεμαρτύρηκεν ὁ θεὸς περὶ τοῦ υἱοῦ αὐτοῦ.
¹¹καὶ αὕτη ἐστὶν ἡ μαρτυρία, ὅτι ζωὴν αἰώνιον ἔδωκεν

οὐ πεπίστευκεν ϚB: οὐκ ἐπίστευσεν A (οὐκ ἐπίστευκεν א).   μεμαρτ.: ἐμαρτύρηκεν א.

(as distinguished from μὴ π. εἰς τὸν θ.)
see John v. 24; vi. 29 f.; viii. 30 f.
Comp. c. iii. 23 n.

ψεύστην πεπ. αὐ.] mendacem facit
V., hath made Him a liar, false in
all His dealings with men. See i.
10 n. The word marks the general
character and not only falsity in the
particular case. Comp. John viii. 44 ;
c. ii. 4, 22 ; iv. 20. The form of expression suggests the idea of an inward
conflict. A voice has been heard and
it has been deliberately rejected.

πεποίηκεν...πεπίστευκεν] These two
perfects definitely connect the present
position of the unbeliever with a past
act. When the crisis of choice came
he refused the message: he made
God a liar: he did not believe on
His testimony: and the result of that
decision entered into him and clings
to him. Compare, for a similar use of
πεπίστευκα, John iii. 18; vi. 69 (c. iv.
16); xi. 27 ; xvi. 27 ; xx. 29 ; 2 Tim.
i. 12 ; Tit. iii. 8.

ὅτι οὐ πεπίστ.] The negative expresses the direct fact. Contrast John
iii. 18 ὅτι μὴ πεπίστ. which presents
the conception. See John vi. 64.

οὐ πεπίστ. εἰς τὴν μαρτ.] non cre-
didit in testimonium V., hath not
believed on the witness, not simply
'believed the witness.' The phrase
is unique. Belief in the truth of the
witness (πιστ. τῇ μαρτυρίᾳ, compare
John v. 47) is carried on to personal
belief in the object of the witness,
that is, the Incarnate Son Himself.

The phrase is illustrated by πιστεύειν εἰς τὸ ὄνομα (v. 13 n.), in which
the 'name' represents the Person
under the particular aspect which it
expresses. In one other case πιστεύ-

ειν εἰς is used with an object not
directly personal, John xii. 36 πιστεύειν
εἰς τὸ φῶς, but here φῶς is used with
immediate reference to John viii. 12 ;
ix. 5.

So it stands out that the ultimate
object of faith is not a fact or a dogma
but a Person.

ἣν μεμαρτ....] It might have seemed
simpler to say 'the witness of God'
(v. 9); but St John repeats at length
what he has shewn that witness to be,
a witness concerning His Son.

11, 12. The witness, which has
been shewn to be divine and internal,
points also to the presence of a divine
life, which, given once for all, is enjoyed by fellowship with the Son.

11. καὶ αὕτη...] 'The witness of God'
(v. 9) is in part unfolded : the witness
that He hath given concerning His
Son is this, that He gave us eternal
life. The Mission of His Son, which
He attested, was the gift of life (John
x. 10, 28; xvii. 2), of life in His Son
(John xx. 31, ἐν τῷ ὀνόματι).

ζ. αἰ. ἔδωκεν] gave eternal life, not
hath given. Compare c. iii. 23 f.
(ἔδωκεν) with c. iii. 1; iv. 13; v. 20
(δέδωκεν). The reference is to the
historic facts by which this life was
communicated to humanity. That
which before Christ's coming was a
great hope, by His coming was realised and given. The gift, as far as
St John here regards it, was made to
Christians (ἡμῖν), who appropriate it.

ζωὴν αἰώνιον] vv. 13, 20; c. iii. 15.
This form is to be distinguished from
ἡ ζ. ἡ αἰών. (c. i. 2, note) and ἡ αἰώνιος
ζ. which occurs only John xvii. 3.
It simply defines the character of the
life, and does not identify it with the
only true life.

ὁ θεὸς ἡμῖν, καὶ αὕτη ἡ ζωὴ ἐν τῷ υἱῷ αὐτοῦ ἐστίν.
¹²ὁ ἔχων τὸν υἱὸν ἔχει τὴν ζωήν· ὁ μὴ ἔχων τὸν υἱὸν
τοῦ θεοῦ τὴν ζωὴν οὐκ ἔχει.   ¹³ Ταῦτα ἔγραψα

11 ὁ θ. ἡμ. B (the) syrhl: ἡμ. ὁ θ. אA vg me syrvg.   αὕτη ἐστὶν ἡ ζ. A.

ἐν τῷ υἱῷ] The life is not separate
from God but in God. Believers united
with Christ are in Him united with
God. Comp. Rom. vi. 23; 2 Tim.
i. 1.

12. ὁ ἔχων...] The variations from
exact parallelism in the two members
of the verse are significant. In the
second member τὸν υἱὸν τοῦ θεοῦ
stands for τὸν υἱόν, and the position
of τὴν ζωήν is changed.

ὁ ἔχων τὸν υἱόν] He that hath the
Son, in Whom the Father is known.
Comp. c. ii. 23; 2 John 9; and for
the use of ἔχειν, John iii. 29; iv. 17.

ἔχει τὴν ζ.] hath life, or rather
the life which God has given. Contrast v. 13; iii. 15; John v. 26;
x. 10; xx. 31. Comp. Col. iii. 4.

In the spirit of these words Ignatius speaks of Jesus Christ as τὸ
ἀδιάκριτον ἡμῶν ζῆν, 'our inseparable
life' (Eph. 3); and τὸ ἀληθινὸν ἡμῶν
ζῆν, 'our true life' (Smyrn. 4). Comp.
Magn. 5; Trall. 9.

ὁ μὴ ἔχων τ. υἱ. τοῦ θ.] he that hath
not the Son of God. The fuller title
seems to mark emphatically the necessity of failure in such a case. God
is the only source of life.

For the combination of the positive
and negative see c. i. 5; ii. 4, 27;
John i. 3; iii. 16.

III. The Activity and Confidence
of the Christian Life: Epilogue.

This last section of the Epistle is
symmetrical in structure:
  1. The aim re-stated (13).
  2. The confidence of spiritual
      action (14—17).
  3 The certainty of spiritual
      knowledge (18—20).

4. A final warning (21).
The progress of thought is clear.
Having reached the close of his
writing St John recals the main
purpose of writing it (i. 4), which he
has fulfilled (v. 13); and then illustrates the confidence of the Christian
life under two aspects, (1) as it finds
expression in spiritual action (14—17),
and (2) as it is realised in inward conviction (18—20). He concludes by a
warning against everything which
usurps the place of God (21).]

1. The aim of the Epistle re-
stated (13).

¹³ These things have I written, that
ye may know that ye have eternal life,
to you who believe on the name of the
Son of God.

13. Ταῦτα ἔγραψα] These things
have I written (I wrote)... In reviewing his Epistle St John indicates
the fulfilment of his purpose (i. 3, 4).
The consciousness of eternal life brings
divine fellowship and completed joy.
Comp. John xx. 30 f.

For the use of ἔγραψα (contrast
γέγραφα John xix. 22) see c. ii. 12
—14 note. The Apostle looks back
upon his work, and records the aim
which he set before himself.

ἵνα εἰδῆτε] ut sciatis V., that ye
may know with a knowledge final and
certain. Compare ii. 29 note; iii. 14
note. The eternal life may be present and yet not realised in its inherent power. The fruits may not be
referred to their source; and again
they may be delayed. But there is a
knowledge of life which is independent of external signs; and this St
John seeks to quicken.

The order ζωὴν ἔχ. αἰών. is not found

ὑμῖν ἵνα εἰδῆτε ὅτι ζωὴν ἔχετε αἰώνιον, τοῖς πιστεύουσιν
εἰς τὸ ὄνομα τοῦ υἱοῦ τοῦ θεοῦ. ¹⁴καὶ αὕτη ἐστὶν ἡ
παρρησία ἣν ἔχομεν πρὸς αὐτόν, ὅτι ἐάν τι αἰτώμεθα

13 ὑμῖν ℵAB vg me the syrr: +τοῖς πιστεύουσιν εἰς τὸ ὄνομα τοῦ υἱοῦ τοῦ θεοῦ ⸝.
ἔχ. αἰών. AB vg syrhl: αἰών. ἔχ. ℵ.　　τοῖς πιστεύουσιν ℵ*B syrr: οἱ πιστεύοντες ℵᶜA vg me the: καὶ ἵνα πιστεύητε ⸝.　　14 ἔχομεν: ἔχωμεν A.　　ὅτι
ἐάν τι ⸝ℵB syrhl the: ὅτι ἄν A: ὅτι ὃ ἐάν vg syrvg.

elsewhere : the epithet comes as an
afterthought: 'that ye have life—yes,
eternal life.'

τοῖς πιστεύουσιν] to you who believe.
The dative, which is added as a kind
of afterthought, defines the character
of the persons who are addressed : 'to
you, yes, to you who believe ..' Compare John i. 12; v. 16. The present
activity of faith (πιστεύουσιν) is the
sign of life (iii. 23 note).

τοῖς πιστ. εἰς τὸ ὄν....] qui creditis
in nomine...V., who believe in the
name of..., who believe in Him who
is revealed to us under this title as
being the Son of God. Contrast iii.
23 note (πιστ. τῷ ὄν.); and compare
John i. 12 note; ii. 23 note; iii. 18.
For similar uses of ὄνομα see c. ii. 12
(διὰ τὸ ὄνομα αὐτοῦ) note; 3 John 7
(τὸ ὄνομα) note.

τοῦ υἱοῦ τοῦ θεοῦ] the Son of God,
vv. 5, 10, 12, 20; iii. 8 note; iv. 15.
The title is the pledge of the certainty of the possession of life.

2.　The confidence of spiritual action
(14—17).

The consciousness of a divine life
brings to the believer perfect boldness in prayer, that is, in converse
with God (14, 15); and this boldness
finds characteristic expression in intercession for the brethren (16, 17).

¹⁴And this is the boldness which
we have towards Him, that, if we ask
anything according to His will, He
heareth us. ¹⁵And if we know that
He heareth us whatsoever we ask, we
know that we have the petitions which
we have asked from Him.

¹⁶If any one see his brother sinning
a sin not unto death, he shall ask, and
He (he) will give him life, even to them
that sin not unto death. There is
sin unto death: I do not say that he
should pray for that: ¹⁷all unrighteousness is sin, and there is sin
not unto death.

14. καὶ αὕτη...] It is implied that
the knowledge which the Christian
can gain is not for mere passive possession, nor yet for himself alone. It
finds scope in corresponding expression. The life is fruitful. Comp.
Matt. xviii. 15, 20.

ἡ παρρησία ἣν ἔχομεν...] fiducia
quam habemus... V., the boldness of
speech, utterance, which we have as
the consequence of our possession of
life. See c. ii. 28 note. The gift of
eternal life enables the believer to
come directly before God (Hebr. iv.
16) and speak every thought without
reserve. This he has strength to do
in the present trials of life (c. iii. 21);
and he looks forward to a like open-
ness of trust 'at the presence of
Christ' (ii. 28), and 'in the day of
judgment' (iv. 17).

πρὸς αὐτόν] ad eum V., towards
Him, that is, God, the main subject
of the passage.

αὕτη ... ὅτι ... ἀκούει ...] this...that
...He heareth. The fact (that He
heareth) and not the conviction of
the fact ('we know that He heareth'),
is identified with the feeling. Our
boldness is not simply a belief, but
indeed a certainty, an experience.

ἐάν τι αἰτώμεθα] quodcunque petierimus V., if we ask anything. The

κατὰ τὸ θέλημα αὐτοῦ ἀκούει ἡμῶν. ¹⁵καὶ ἐὰν οἴδαμεν
ὅτι ἀκούει ἡμῶν ὃ ἐὰν αἰτώμεθα, οἴδαμεν ὅτι ἔχομεν
τὰ αἰτήματα ἃ ᾐτήκαμεν ἀπ᾽ αὐτοῦ. ¹⁶Ἐάν τις ἴδη τὸν

θέλημα: ὄνομα Α.   15 καὶ ἐὰν (ἂν Β) οἴδαμεν (ἴδωμεν א° me) ὅτι ἀκ. ἡ. ⸲
(א°) Β syrr (me) the: et scimus vg: om. א*Α.   ἔχομεν: ἔχωμεν א (ἐὰν ἔχ. א*).
ἀπ᾽ αὐτοῦ אΒ: παρ᾽ αὐτοῦ ⸲Α.

distinction between the middle (αἰ-τεῖσθαι) and the active (αἰτεῖν) is not sharply drawn; but generally the personal reference is suggested by the middle while the request is left wholly undefined as to its destination by the active. Compare John xvi. 24, 26; xiv. 13, 14; xv. 16 with xv. 7; James iv. 2, 3. For αἰτεῖσθαι see Matt. xxvii. 20 (and parallels), 58 (and parallels); Acts iii. 14.

κατὰ τὸ θέλημα αὐ.] according to His will. Comp. 1 Pet. iv. 19; Gal. i. 4; Eph. i. 5, 11. This will finds expression in the soul: John xv. 7; and is the continuous manifestation of the divine nature through Christ. Thus asking 'according to the will of God' is equivalent to asking 'in Christ's name': John xiv. 13 note.

'The will of God' regards the spiritual consummation of man (c. ii. 17; Rom. ii. 18), and all external things only so far as they are contributory to this.

ἀκούει ἡμῶν] Compare John ix. 31; xi. 41 f. This sense of 'hearing' is peculiar to St John. The 'hearing' of God, like the 'knowledge' of God, carries with it every perfect consequence. For the thought see c. iii. 22.

15. καὶ ἐὰν οἴδαμεν...] Et scimus V., si scimus F., And if we know... The force of this unusual construction appears to be to throw the uncertainty upon the fact of the presence of the knowledge and not upon the knowledge itself. The sense required is not 'and should we know,' but 'and should it be that we know.'

ὃ ἐὰν αἰτώμεθα] whatsoever we ask. This universal phrase can be substi-

tuted for the limited phrase which was used before (ἐάν τι αἰτ. κ.τ.θ.). The believer would not make his own any prayer which is not according to God's will. And since he has made God's will his own will, he has all he truly seeks in immediate and present possession (Mark xi. 24) though the visible fulfilment may be delayed.

τὰ αἰτήματα] petitiones V., the petitions (Phil. iv. 6; Luke xxiii. 24): the substance of the requests, if not necessarily the actual things asked for (τὰ αἰτηθέντα).

ἀπ᾽ αὐτοῦ] from Him. These words go perhaps more naturally with 'have' (c. ii. 20) than with 'asked.' Yet see Matt. xx. 20 (ἀπ᾽ αὐτοῦ).

16, 17. That boldness of access to God, which finds expression in prayer, finds its most characteristic expression in intercessory prayer. Fellowship with God involves fellowship with man (i. 3). The energy of Christian life is from the first social. Hence St John passes naturally from the general thought of prayer to that of prayer for the brethren. And in doing this he fixes attention on the failures of Christians. These are the sorest trial of faith.

The prevailing power of intercession corresponds with the Christian revelation of the unity of the Body of Christ. When this power is exercised for others it is exercised in a true sense for ourselves, and not, arbitrarily as it were, for those apart from us. Apostolic teaching recognises a mysterious dependence of man upon man in the spiritual order like that which is now being shewn to exist in the physical

ἀδελφὸν αὐτοῦ ἁμαρτάνοντα ἁμαρτίαν μὴ πρὸς θάνατον,
αἰτήσει, καὶ δώσει αὐτῷ ζωήν, τοῖς ἁμαρτάνουσιν μὴ

16 αἰτήσει...δώσει: αἰτήσις (-ήσεις)...δώσεις א*.　　τοῖς ἁμαρτ. μή : τοῖς μὴ
ἁμαρτάν. ἁμαρτίαν μή A.

order; and throughout the Epistle St John assumes the reality of this inner fellowship among those whom he addresses, and he bases his arguments upon it. Compare 1 Pet. iv. 8 τὴν εἰς ἑαυτοὺς ἀγάπην; id. 10 εἰς ἑαυτοὺς αὐτὸ διακονοῦντες; Eph. iv. 32; Col. iii. 13 χαριζόμενοι ἑαυτοῖς; Col. iii. 16 νουθετοῦντες ἑαυτούς.

16. Ἐάν τις ἴδῃ...] *If any one see* ... The duty, the instinct, is universal in the Christian Society. At the same time the character of the sin towards which the duty is exercised is clear even outwardly. It is not a matter simply of suspicion or doubt.

τὸν ἀδελφὸν αὐτοῦ] *his brother*. The end of prayer is the perfection of the whole Christian body. The Christian prays for himself only as a member in the society. The sight of sin in 'a brother'—a fellow Christian (c. ii. 9 note)—and it is only with Christians that St John is dealing—necessarily stirs to intercession. Comp. Clem. *ad Cor.* i. 2 ἐπὶ τοῖς παραπτώμασι τῶν πλήσιον ἐπενθεῖτε· τὰ ὑστερήματα αὐτῶν ἴδια ἐκρίνετε.

ἁμαρτ. ἁμαρτ.] *peccare peccatum* V., *sinning a sin*. The form of expression (ἁμαρτάνοντα, inadequately rendered in the Latin) emphasises the outward present character of the act. There is no exact parallel in N. T. to the phrase. Comp. c. ii. 25. Winer iii. § 32, 2.

μὴ πρὸς θάνατον] *not unto death.* Life is fellowship with Christ (v. 12). Death is separation from Him. All sin tends to make the fellowship less complete. Yet not all equally; nor all in a fixed and unalterable degree. The thought is not of the definite

external characteristics of particular acts, as having an absolute value, but of acts in relation to the man's whole nature and life.

The clause 'not unto death' goes both with the participle and with the noun, as is shewn separately afterwards.

For the conception of 'death' see c. ii. 14 (the only other place in the Epistles where the word occurs), John v. 24 (viii. 51 f.; vi. 50; xi. 26; viii. 24). The thought is evidently not of physical death as James v. 14 ff. Compare, in another connexion, John xi. 4 αὕτη ἡ ἀσθένεια οὐκ ἔστι πρὸς θάνατον. The subjective negative (μὴ πρὸς θ.) naturally follows from the supposition (ἐάν τις). It is otherwise in v. 17.

αἰτήσει] *petit (-at)* V., *postulabit* F., *he shall ask.* This will be his natural and spontaneous action. There is no need of a command.

καὶ δώσει] *and he will give.* The subject has been taken to be (1) the intercessor, or (2) God (*dabit ei vitam Dominus* Tert. *de Pudic.* 19; but *dabitur ei, id.* 2). In favour of the first view the continuity of the construction (αἰτήσει, δώσει) and the parallel James v. 20 have been urged.

The second view is that which is at first suggested by the language of Scripture generally. To 'give life' is elsewhere treated as a divine prerogative; John vi. 33; x. 28; xvii. 2; v. 11. But there is nothing unscriptural in the thought that the believer does that which God does through him; James v. 20. Still on the whole it seems more natural to see here a reference to the direct action of God.

If 'God' be the subject of 'give'

πρὸς θάνατον. ἔστιν ἁμαρτία πρὸς θάνατον· οὐ περὶ
ἐκείνης λέγω ἵνα ἐρωτήσῃ. ¹⁷πᾶσα ἀδικία ἁμαρτία

ἐρωτήσῃ: +τις vg syrvg. ἐρωτήσῃς ℵ°.

then αὐτῷ may be the 'ethical' dative, and τοῖς πιστ. the direct object of δώσει: 'God shall give life to those that sin not unto death for him, in answer to his prayers.' This however seems to be artificial. The αὐτῷ is most naturally the sinning brother in any case.

δ. ζωήν] *give life.* The sinner is not 'dead,' nor yet 'sinning unto death,' but his life is, as it were, suspended in part. Comp. John x. 10.

τοῖς ἁμαρτ.] even *to them that...* The single case (ἁμαρτάνοντα) is now generalised. Comp. *v.* 13.

The apposition of a personal plural to an abstract noun is not strictly parallel; 1 Cor. i. 2.

ἔστιν ἁμ. πρὸς θ.] *Est peccatum ad mortem* V., *There is sin unto death.* The translation 'a sin' (ἁμαρτία τις) is too definite. The thought is not of specific acts as such, but of acts which have a certain character: 'There is that which must be described as sin unto death, there is that which wholly separates from Christ.' The phrase, it must be remembered, comes in a passage which deals with the prayer of Christians for Christians and not for heathen. See Additional Note.

οὐ περὶ ἐκείνης λέγω ἵνα...] *non pro illo dico ut roget quis* V., *not concerning that do I say that...* The sin unto death is isolated and regarded in its terrible distinctness (ἐκείνη). The words περὶ ἐκείνης may be connected either with λέγω or with ἐρωτήσῃ. Perhaps it is best to connect them with ἐρωτήσῃ. Comp. John xvi. 26; xvii. 9, 20.

The construction λέγω ἵνα is not common: Acts xix. 4. Comp. εἰπεῖν ἵνα Matt. iv. 3, &c.; ἐρρήθη ἵνα Apoc. vi. 11, &c.

ἐρωτήσῃ] *make request.* The change of the verb from αἰτεῖν (V. *petere*), (αἰτεῖσθαι), to ἐρωτᾶν (V. *rogare*), cannot but be significant. 'Ερωτᾶν is the word which is used of Christ's prayer to the Father (John xiv. 16; xvi. 26; xvii. 9, 15, 20; comp. 1 Thess. iv. 1; 2 John 5). It seems to mark the request which is based upon fellowship, upon a likeness of position. Here then it would naturally express the prayer of brother for brother as such, to the common Father. Such a prayer is not enjoined by the apostle. At the same time he does not forbid it. It does not lie within his scope[1].

17. πᾶσα ἀδικία...] *omnis iniquitas...* V., *all unrighteousness...* The words are added to shew the wide scope which is given for the exercise of Christian sympathy and intercession. Apart from such sins as are open manifestations of a character alien from God, there are other sins which flow from human imperfection and infirmity, and in regard to these Christian intercession has its work. All unrighteousness (c. i. 9), all failure to fulfil our duty one to another, is sin; and in this ample field there is abundant opportunity for the exercise of prayer. There is a sin not unto death, of which the consequences may be removed by the brother's petition.

The statement that 'all unrighteousness is sin' must be compared

[1] It is interesting to notice that ἐρωτᾶν is used in this sense of Christian prayer for Christians in a very early inscription in the Roman Catacombs: ΖΗϹΗϹ ΕΝ ΚΩ ΚΑΙ ΕΡΩΤΑ ΥΠΕΡ ΗΜΩΝ (Northcote and Brownlow, *Roma Sotterranea,* ii. 159).

ἐστίν, καὶ ἔστιν ἁμαρτία οὐ πρὸς θάνατον.   ¹⁸Οἴ-
δαμεν ὅτι πᾶς ὁ γεγεννημένος ἐκ τοῦ θεοῦ οὐχ ἁμαρ-

17 οὐ πρός: om. οὐ vg syrhl the Tert.

with the comprehensive definition of
sin in c. iii. 4 *lawlessness is sin*, and
conversely *sin is lawlessness*. Sin is
the most general term and is used in
regard to the will of God for man.
By whatever act, internal or external,
man falls short of this will, as it is
spiritually apprehended, he 'sins.' The
will of God may be conceived of as
embodied in 'law,' in respect of the
whole constitution of things, or in
'right,' in respect of the claims made
by others. So it is that all violation
of law and all violation of right is sin
looked at in a special aspect. Unrighteousness is one manifestation of
sin. Comp. Rom. vi. 13 ὅπλα ἀδικίας
τῇ ἁμαρτίᾳ.

3. *The certainty of spiritual knowledge* (18—20).

The thought of sin, of sin among
the brethren, of sin unto death, forces
the Apostle to recal once more the
assurance of faith. In spite of the
sad lessons of daily experience he re-
affirms the truths which the Christian
knows: the privileges of the divine
birth (18); the fact of the divine
kinsmanship (19); the advance in
divine understanding issuing from
divine fellowship (20).

The threefold repetition of οἴδαμεν,
we know (18, 19, 20), gives a rhythmic
form to the paragraph.

¹⁸ *We know that everyone who is
begotten of God sinneth not, but He
that was begotten of God keepeth him
and the evil one toucheth him not.*

¹⁹ *We know that we are in God
and the whole world lieth in the evil
one.*

²⁰ *We know that the Son of God
hath come and hath given to us understanding that we may know Him
that is true; and we are in Him that*

*is true, even in His Son Jesus Christ.
This is the true God and life eternal.*

18. The power of intercession to
overcome the consequences of sin
might seem to encourage a certain
indifference to sin. Therefore St John
re-affirms the elements of Christian
knowledge. From this point of sight
the first truth of which the Christian
is assured is that, in spite of the ab-
normal presence of sin even among
the brethren, the child of God 'sinneth not.' He has a watchful Pro-
tector stronger than his adversary.

Οἴδαμεν] *Scimus* V., *We know.*
St John uses this appeal to absolute
knowledge in two forms : 'we know,'
and 'ye know.' The former occurs :

iii. 2 οἴδαμεν ὅτι ἐὰν φανερωθῇ ὅμοιοι
αὐτῷ ἐσόμεθα, ὅτι ὀψόμεθα αὐτὸν
καθώς ἐστιν.

iii. 14 ἡμεῖς οἴδαμεν ὅτι μεταβεβήκαμεν ἐκ τοῦ θανάτου εἰς τὴν ζωήν, ὅτι
ἀγαπῶμεν τοὺς ἀδελφούς.

v. 18 οἴδαμεν ὅτι πᾶς ὁ γεγεννημένος
ἐκ τοῦ θεοῦ οὐχ ἁμαρτάνει.

v. 19 οἴδαμεν ὅτι ἐκ τοῦ θεοῦ ἐσμέν.

v. 20 οἴδαμεν ὅτι ὁ υἱὸς τοῦ θεοῦ
ἥκει καὶ δέδωκεν ἡμῖν διάνοιαν ἵνα γινώσκομεν τὸν ἀληθινόν.

In contrast with these appeals to
fundamental knowledge, St John elsewhere appeals to the knowledge
brought by actual experience (γινώσκομεν): *v.* 2 note.

St Paul uses the same form (οἴδαμεν) not unfrequently : 1 Cor. viii. 1,
4; 2 Cor. v. 1; Rom. ii. 2; iii. 19;
vii. 14; viii. 22, 28; 1 Tim. i. 8.

Οἴδατε is found :

ii. 20 οἴδατε πάντες...τὴν ἀλήθειαν.

iii. 5 οἴδατε ὅτι ἐκεῖνος ἐφανερώθη ἵνα
τὰς ἁμαρτίας ἄρῃ.

iii. 15 οἴδατε ὅτι πᾶς ἀνθρωποκτόνος
οὐκ ἔχει ζωὴν αἰώνιον ἐν αὐτῷ μένουσαν.

τάνει, ἀλλ᾽ ὁ γεννηθεὶς ἐκ τοῦ θεοῦ τηρεῖ αὐτόν, καὶ
ὁ πονηρὸς οὐχ ἅπτεται αὐτοῦ. ¹⁹οἴδαμεν ὅτι ἐκ τοῦ
θεοῦ ἐσμέν, καὶ ὁ κόσμος ὅλος ἐν τῷ πονηρῷ κεῖται.

18 ὁ γεννηθείς: generatio vg.   αὐτόν A*B vg: ἑαυτόν ϛℵA**.

πᾶς ὁ γεγενν. ἐκ τοῦ θ.] omnis
qui natus est ex Deo V. Comp. c.
iii. 9 note.

οὐχ ἁμαρτάνει] Comp. iii. 9 note
(ἁμαρτίαν οὐ ποιεῖ). While St John
states this without reserve he yet
recognises 'the brother'—brother as
son of the one Father—'sinning a sin
not unto death' (v. 16). The paradox
remains unsolved.

ἀλλ᾽ ὁ γεννηθεὶς...τ. αὐ.] sed generatio (nativitas F.) Dei conservat eum
V., but He that was Begotten of God
keepeth him. He does not depend
on his own strength or vigilance. He
has an active Enemy (ὁ πονηρός), but
he has also a watchful Guardian.

The phrase ὁ γεννηθεὶς ἐκ τοῦ θεοῦ
is unique. Standing as it does in close
juxtaposition with ὁ γεγεννημένος ἐκ
τοῦ θεοῦ it is impossible to regard it
as identical in reference, and the mention of the great adversary naturally
suggests the thought of the Son of
God. The peculiar expression is probably used to emphasise the connexion of the Son with those whom
He 'is not ashamed to call brethren'
(Hebr. ii. 11 ἐξ ἑνὸς πάντες); while
the difference of γεννηθείς from γεγεννημένος suggests that difference in
the sonship of the Son from the sonship of men which is marked in John v.
26 τῷ υἱῷ ἔδωκεν ζωὴν ἔχειν ἐν ἑαυτῷ.

The remarkable Latin reading appears to represent the Greek ἡ γέννησις τοῦ θεοῦ (Matt. i. 18).

τηρεῖ] The verb is used of persons
Matt. xxvii. 36, 54; (xxviii. 4); John
xvii. 11, 15 (note); Apoc. iii. 10;
Jude 21 (ἑαυτοὺς τηρήσατε). It expresses a watchful regard from without rather than safe custody.

ὁ πονηρός] malignus V. See c. ii.
13 note.

ἅπτεται] tangit V. The verb occurs
elsewhere in St John only in John xx.
17. It describes 'a laying hold on,'
more than a mere superficial touch
(θιγγάνειν). Even when it is used of
simple physical contact, a deeper
connexion is indicated, as when the
Lord 'touched' the sick. See Col. ii.
21 μὴ ἅψῃ μηδὲ γεύσῃ μηδὲ θίγῃς.
Compare Ps. cv. 15 μὴ ἅψησθε
τῶν χριστῶν μου. The ground of
safety is revealed in John xiv. 30 ἐν
ἐμοὶ οὐκ ἔχει οὐδέν. As yet the principle of evil is without.

19. From the general statement
of the privilege of Sons of God St
John goes on to the affirmation of
the personal relation in which he and
those whom he addresses stand to
Him (ἐκ τοῦ θεοῦ ἐσμέν).

The structure of the verse is expressive. The absence of the personal pronoun (contrast iv. 6) in the first clause
throws all the emphasis upon the
divine source of life: 'We know that
it is from God we draw our being.' In
the second clause the emphasis is
changed. Over against the Christian
Society, only faintly indicated in the
preceding words, stands 'the whole
world,' and on this attention is fixed.
The relation of the Church to God
is widely different from that of the
world to the Evil One.

This difference is brought out in
the two corresponding phrases ἐκ τοῦ
θεοῦ εἶναι and ἐν τῷ πονηρῷ κεῖσθαι.
The first describes the absolute source
of being: the second the actual (but
not essential) position.

ἐκ τοῦ θ. ἐ.] See Additional Note
on iii. 1.

καὶ ὁ κ. ὅ.] This clause like the
corresponding clauses in vv. 18 (ἀλλὰ
ὁ γενν.), 20 (καί ἐσμεν), is an inde-

²⁰ οἴδαμεν δὲ ὅτι ὁ υἱὸς τοῦ θεοῦ ἥκει, καὶ δέδωκεν ἡμῖν διάνοιαν ἵνα γινώσκομεν τὸν ἀληθινόν· καί ἐσμεν ἐν τῷ

20 οἴδαμεν δέ אB me: καὶ οἴδαμεν A vg syrr the.   ἥκει: +et carnem induit nostri causa et passus est et resurrexit a mortuis; adsumpsit nos et dedit....(Latt.). δέδωκεν: ἔδωκεν A.   γινώσκομεν אAB*: γινώσκωμεν ϛ.   τὸν ἀλ.: τὸ ἀλ. א* the: +θεόν A vg me (Latt.).   ἐσμέν: simus vg.   ἐν τῷ ἀλ.: om. me: in vita the.

pendent statement and not dependent on ὅτι. The Christian is able to look upon the saddest facts of life without being overwhelmed by them.

The order ὁ κόσμος ὅλος suggests a slightly different conception from ὅλος ὁ κόσμος (c. ii. 2): 'the world, the organization of society as alien from and opposed to God, is wholly, in all its parts and elements, placed in the domain of...' The two thoughts of the world, and of the entirety of it, are given separately. The same form occurs Matt. xvi. 26 and parallels; and the same order in Matt. xxvi. 59; Lc. xi. 36; John iv. 53; Acts xxi. 30; 1 Cor. xiv. 23; Apoc. iii. 10; vi. 12; xii. 9; xvi. 14. There is a similar difference of colour given by the corresponding position of πᾶς: John v. 22; xvi. 13; Matt. x. 30; xiii. 56; xxvi. 56; Acts xvi. 33; Rom. xii. 4; xvi. 16; 1 Cor. vii. 17; x. 1; xv. 7; xvi. 20, &c.

ἐν τῷ πον. κ.] in maligno positus est V., lieth in the evil one, is placed in the sphere of his influence. There is no question here of the Evil One 'laying hold on' (ἅπτεσθαι) the world, as from without (v. 8): it has been placed 'in him.' The phrase answers to the εἶναι ἐν τῷ ἀληθινῷ which follows, and to the characteristic Pauline ἐν χριστῷ. Comp. c. iii. 24, iv. 15 note. The connexion shews beyond question that τῷ πονηρῷ is masculine, and the converse of κεῖσθαι ἐν τ. π. is given in John xvii. 15 ἵνα τηρήσῃς ἐκ τοῦ πονηροῦ. Compare Luke xi. 15 ff. ἐν Βεελζεβούλ.

A close parallel to the expression is found in Soph. Œd. Col. 247 ἐν ὑμῖν ὡς θεῷ κείμεθα τλάμονες. Comp. Œd.

R. 314; Alc. 279.

20. The third affirmation of knowledge is introduced by the adversative particle (οἴδ. δέ). There is, this seems to be the line of thought, a startling antithesis in life of good and evil. We have been made to feel it in all its intensity. But at the same time we can face it in faith. That which is as yet dark will be made light. There is given to us the power of ever-advancing knowledge and of present divine fellowship. We can wait even as God waits. The particle δέ is comparatively unfrequent in St John's writings: c. i. 7; ii. 2, 5, 11, 17; iii. 12, 17; iv. 18; 3 John 14.

ἥκει, καὶ δέδωκεν] hath come and hath given. Faith rests on the permanence of the fact and not upon the historic fact only. Comp. John viii. 42 note.

δέδωκεν] c. iii. 1, iv. 13. Contrast iii. 23, 24; v. 11 (ἔδωκεν) note.

διάνοιαν] sensum V., understanding. This is the only place in which the term occurs in St John's writings; and generally nouns which express intellectual powers are rare in them. Thus St John never uses γνῶσις, nor is νοῦς found in his Gospel or Epistles. Διάνοια, as compared with νοῦς, represents the process of rational thought. Comp. Eph. iv. 18 ἐν ματαιότητι τοῦ νοὸς αὐτῶν, ἐσκοτωμένοι τῇ διανοίᾳ ὄντες (the first principles of the Gentiles were unsubstantial, and they had lost the power of right reasoning). Exclusive of quotations from the LXX, διάνοια is found: 1 Pet. i. 13 ἀναζωσάμενοι τὰς ὀσφύας τῆς διανοίας; 2 Pet. iii. 1 διεγείρω τὴν εἰλικρινῆ διάνοιαν; and, in a more concrete sense, Lc. i.

ἀληθινῷ, ἐν τῷ υἱῷ αὐτοῦ Ἰησοῦ Χριστῷ.   οὗτός ἐστιν

'Ι. Χ.: om. A vg.

51 διανοίᾳ καρδίας; Col. i. 21 ἐχθροὺς τῇ διανοίᾳ; Eph. ii. 3 τὰ θελήματα τῆς σαρκὸς καὶ τῶν διανοιῶν.

That with which 'the Son of God' Incarnate has endowed believers is a power of understanding, of interpreting, of following out to their right issues, the complex facts of life; and the end of the gift is that they may know, not by one decisive act (ἵνα γνῶσιν) but by a continuous and progressive apprehension (ἵνα γινώσκωσι), 'Him that is true.' Thus the object of knowledge is not abstract but personal: not the Truth, but Him of Whom all that is true is a partial revelation.

It is evident that the fact of the Incarnation (υἱὸς τοῦ θ. ἥκει) vitally welcomed carries with it the power of believing in and seeing little by little the divine purpose of life under the perplexing riddles of phenomena.

The language in which Ignatius describes this gift is remarkable: διὰ τί οὐ πάντες φρόνιμοι γινόμεθα λαβόντες θεοῦ γνῶσιν, ὅ ἐστιν Ἰησοῦς Χριστός; τί μωρῶς ἀπολλύμεθα ἀγνοοῦντες τὸ χάρισμα ὁ πέπομφεν ἀληθῶς ὁ Κύριος; (ad Eph. xvii.).

ἵνα γινώσκομεν] This clause finds a remarkable commentary in John xvii. 3. Eternal life is the never-ending effort after this knowledge of God. Compare John x. 38, ἵνα γνῶτε καὶ γινώσκητε ὅτι ἐν ἐμοὶ ὁ πατὴρ κἀγὼ ἐν αὐτῷ.

It seems likely that γινώσκομεν is to be regarded as a corrupt pronunciation of γινώσκωμεν. It is remarkable that in John xvii. 3 many authorities read γινώσκουσιν for -ωσιν. Comp. Winer, iii. § 41. 1.

τὸν ἀληθινόν] verum Deum V., quod est verum F. (i.e. τὸ ἀλ.), Him that is true, Who in contrast with all imaginary and imperfect objects of worship completely satisfies the

idea of Godhead in the mind of man, even the Father revealed in and by the Son (John i. 18, xiv. 9). Christ is also called ὁ ἀληθινός, Apoc. iii. 7; compare also Apoc. iii. 14 (vi. 10). For ἀληθινός see John i. 9, iv. 23, xv. 1 notes. Comp. 1 Thess. i. 9 θεὸς ζῶν καὶ ἀληθινός.

καί ἐσμεν...Ἰ. Χρ.] et simus (as depending on ut) in vero filio eius V. St John adds a comment on what he has just said. Christians are not only enabled to gain a knowledge of God: they are already in fellowship with Him, 'in Him.' We are in Him that is true, even in His Son, Jesus Christ. The latter clause defines and confirms the reality of the divine fellowship. So far as Christians are united with Christ, they are united with God. His assumption of humanity (Jesus Christ) explains how the union is possible.

οὗτός ἐστιν...] As far as the grammatical construction of the sentence is concerned the pronoun (οὗτος) may refer either to 'Him that is true' or to 'Jesus Christ.' The most natural reference however is to the subject not locally nearest but dominant in the mind of the apostle (comp. c. ii. 22; 2 John 7; Acts iv. 11; vii. 19). This is obviously 'He that is true' further described by the addition of 'His Son.' Thus the pronoun gathers up the revelation indicated in the words which precede (comp. John i. 2 note): This Being—this One who is true, who is revealed through and in His Son, with whom we are united by His Son—is the true God and life eternal. In other words the revelation of God as Father in Christ (comp. ii. 22 f.) satisfies, and can alone satisfy, the need of man. To know God as Father is eternal life (John xvii. 3) and so Christ has revealed Him (c. i. 2).

ὁ ἀληθινὸς θεὸς καὶ ζωὴ αἰώνιος.   ²¹ Τεκνία, φυλάξατε
ἑαυτὰ ἀπὸ τῶν εἰδώλων.

θεός: om. (Latt.).   ζωὴ αἰ. ℵAB: ἡ ζ. αἰ. 5ʹ: ἡ ζ. ἡ αἰ. all.: +et resurrectio
nostra (Latt.).   21 ἑαυτά ℵ*B: ἑαυτούς ℵcA.   εἰδώλων: +ἀμὴν 5ʹ.

ὁ ἀληθ. θ.] Comp. Is. lxv. 16 (LXX).
Compare the famous words of Ignatius: εἷς θεός ἐστι ὁ φανερώσας ἑαυτὸν
διὰ 'Ιησοῦ Χριστοῦ τοῦ υἱοῦ αὐτοῦ, ὅς
ἐστιν αὐτοῦ λόγος ἀΐδιος, ἀπὸ σιγῆς
προελθών, ὃς κατὰ πάντα εὐηρέστησεν
τῷ πέμψαντι αὐτόν (ad Magn. viii.).
Aristides is said to have maintained
before Hadrian 'quod Christus Jesus
solus (al. verus) esset Deus' (Mart.
Rom. ap. Routh Rell. Sacrr. i. 80).
This statement may be regarded as a
summary paraphrase of the Greek
text: γινώσκουσι τὸν θεὸν κτίστην καὶ
δημιουργὸν τῶν ἀπάντων ἐν υἱῷ μονο-
γενεῖ καὶ πνεύματι ἁγίῳ καὶ ἄλλον θεὸν
πλὴν τούτου οὐ σέβονται (c. xv.). The
Syriac text has no reference to the
Son and the Holy Spirit. Yet see
Harnack, Text. u. Untersuch. i. 114.

οὗτος...ζωὴ αἰών.] The phrase is not
exactly parallel with those which describe (as far as we can apprehend it)
the essential nature of God (John iv.
24, c. i. 5, iv. 8). See Additional Note
on iv. 8. It expresses His relation to
men, and so far is parallel with Hebr.
xii. 29 (Deut. iv. 24).

On 'Eternal life' see Additional
Note.

4. *A final Warning* (21).

From the thought of 'Him that is
true' St John turns almost of necessity
to the thought of the vain shadows
which usurp His place. In them the
world asserted its power. They forced
themselves into notice on every side
in innumerable shapes, and tempted
believers to fall away from the perfect
simplicity of faith. One sharp warning
therefore closes the Epistle of which
the main scope has been to deepen
the fellowship of man with God and
through God with man.

²¹ *Little children, guard yourselves
from idols.*

21. Τεκνία] Once again the anxiety
of the Apostle calls up the title of
affection which has not been used
since iv. 4. See ii. 1 note.

φυλάξατε ἑαυτά] *custodite vos* V.,
guard yourselves. The exact phrase
is not found again in the N. T. Compare τηρεῖν ἑαυτόν Jude 21; and with
an adj. James i. 27; 2 Cor. xi. 9; 1
Tim. v. 22. This 'guarding' of the
Christian answers to the 'keeping' of
Christ (v. 8). The use of the active
with the reflexive pronoun as distinguished from the middle (Lc. xii. 15
φυλάσσεσθε ἀπὸ π. πλεονεξίας) emphasises the duty of personal effort.
The use of the neuter (ἑαυτά) in direct
agreement with τεκνία seems to be
unique. For the use of ἑαυτά with
the second person see c. i. 8 n. The
aorist imp. (φυλάξατε) is remarkable:
compare 1 Pet. ii. 17 for its exact force.
Elsewhere in the Epistle (except iii.
1) St John always uses the present.

ἀπὸ τῶν εἰδ.] *a simulacris* V. The
word εἴδωλον is comparatively in-
frequent in the N. T., and elsewhere
it is always used literally (*e.g.* 1 Thess.
i. 9). But 'idolatry' (Col. iii. 5) and
'idolater' (Eph. v. 5) have a wider
.sense in St Paul; and the context
here seems to require a corresponding
extension of the meaning of the term.
An 'idol' is anything which occupies
the place due to God. The use of the
definite article call up all the familiar
objects which fall under the title.
The command to Christians is not
generally to keep themselves from
such things as idols (ἀπὸ εἰδ.) but
from the well-known objects of a false
devotion. Compare 2 Cor. vi. 16 μετὰ
εἰδώλων with Rom. ii. 22 ὁ βδελυσσ.
τὰ εἴδωλα.

This comprehensive warning is probably the latest voice of Scripture.

Additional Note on v. 1. *The use of the term 'the Christ.'*

The use of the term 'the Christ' in the Apostolic age not from the Old Testament.

The history of the title 'Messiah,' 'Christ' (הַמָּשִׁיחַ, ὁ χριστός, 'the Anointed One') is very remarkable. It is not a characteristic title of the promised Saviour in the O. T. It is not even specifically applied to Him, unless perhaps in Dan. ix. 25 f., a passage-of which the interpretation is very doubtful. And still in the apostolic age it was generally current among the Jews in Judæa, Galilee, Samaria, and in the Dispersion; and it was applied by them to the object of their religious and national hope (Matt. ii. 4, xvi. 16, xxii. 42; John i. 20, 41, iv. 25, xii. 34; Acts ix. 22, xvii. 3, xviii. 28, xxvi. 23). The Hebrew word had been clothed in a Greek dress, and was current side by side with the Greek equivalent (Μεσσίας John i. 42, iv. 25).

The use of the term in (i) the Law,

The word מָשִׁיחַ, 'anointed,' occurs several times in the Book of Leviticus in the phrase הַכֹּהֵן הַמָּשִׁיחַ: Lev. iv. 3 (ὁ ἀρχιερεὺς ὁ κεχρισμένος), v. 16; vi. 15 (ὁ ἀρχ. ὁ χριστός). Comp. 2 Macc. i. 10 (ἀπὸ τοῦ τῶν χριστῶν ἱερέων γένους).

(ii) the Historical Books,

In the Historical Books the word is used of the representative kings of the theocratic nation: Of Saul:

1 Sam. xii. 3, 5 מְשִׁיחוֹ, ὁ χριστὸς αὐτοῦ.

1 Sam. xxiv. 6, 11; xxvi. 16; 2 Sam. i. 14, 16 מְשִׁיחַ יְהֹוָה, LXX. ὁ χριστὸς κυρίου.

1 Sam. xxvi. 9, 11, 23 מְשִׁיחַ יְהֹוָה, LXX. χριστὸς κυρίου.

Comp. 2 Sam. i. 21 בְּלִי מָשִׁיחַ בַּשָּׁמֶן, LXX. οὐκ ἐχρίσθη ἐν ἐλαίῳ.

Of David:

1 Sam. xvi. 6 מְשִׁיחוֹ, LXX. ὁ χριστὸς αὐτοῦ.

2 Sam. xix. 21 מְשִׁיחַ יְהֹוָה, LXX. ὁ χριστὸς κυρίου.

2 Sam. xxiii. 1 מְשִׁיחַ אֱלֹהֵי יַעֲקֹב, LXX. χριστὸς θεοῦ Ἰακώβ.

2 Sam. xxii. 51.

Ps. xviii. 50.

Of Solomon:

2 Chron. vi. 42 מְשִׁיחֶךָ, LXX. ὁ χριστός σου.

Of Jehu:

2 Chron. xxii. 7 LXX. πρὸς Ἰηού...χριστὸν κυρίου, אֲשֶׁר מְשָׁחוֹ יְהֹוָה.

Compare the wider use in:

1 Sam. ii. 10 קֶרֶן מְשִׁיחוֹ...וְיָרֵם...יְהֹוָה, LXX. ὑψώσει κέρας χριστοῦ αὐτοῦ.

„ ii. 35 לִפְנֵי מְשִׁיחִי, LXX. ἐνώπιον χριστῶν (χριστοῦ) μου.

1 Chron. xvi. 22.

Ps. cv. 15.

(iii) the Prophets,

In the Prophets the word is used of Cyrus:

Is. xlv. 1 כֹּה אָמַר יְהֹוָה לִמְשִׁיחוֹ לְכוֹרֶשׁ, LXX. οὕτως λέγει κύριος ὁ θεὸς τῷ χριστῷ μου Κύρῳ.

In the second passage where it occurs it is doubtful whether it is used in a personal or national sense :

Hab. iii. 13 לְיֵשַׁע אֶת־מְשִׁיחֶךָ, LXX. τοῦ σῶσαι τοὺς χριστούς σου.

It occurs twice in a difficult passage of the Book of Daniel :

| Dan. ix. 25 מָשִׁיחַ נָגִיד, | Theod. χριστὸς ἡγούμενος. |
| „ 26 יִכָּרֵת מָשִׁיחַ, | Theod. ἐξολεθρεύσεται χρίσμα. |

Compare also :

Amos iv. 13 LXX. ἀπαγγέλλων τὸν χριστὸν αὐτοῦ.

Hebr. מַגִּיד...מַה־שֵׂחוֹ.

In the Psalms the Divine King who is the type of 'the Christ' is spoken of as 'the anointed of the Lord'; and there can be no doubt that it was from the Psalms, and especially from Ps. ii., that the word passed into common use in the special technical sense. (iv) the Hagiographa.

Ps. ii. 2 עַל יְהֹוָה וְעַל מְשִׁיחוֹ, LXX. κατὰ τοῦ κυρίου καὶ κατὰ τοῦ χριστοῦ αὐτοῦ.

Ps. xviii. 50 לִמְשִׁיחוֹ לְדָוִד, LXX. τῷ χριστῷ αὐτοῦ τῷ Δαυείδ.

Ps. xx. 6 מְשִׁיחוֹ, LXX. (ἔσωσεν κύριος) τὸν χριστὸν αὐτοῦ.

Ps. xxviii. 8 מָעוֹז יְשׁוּעוֹת מְשִׁיחוֹ הוּא, LXX. ὑπερασπιστὴς τῶν σωτηρίων τοῦ χριστοῦ αὐτοῦ ἐστίν.

So Ps. lxxxix. 38, 51, cxxxii. 10, 17.

Compare Ps. lxxxiv. 10 אֱלֹהִים מְשִׁיחֶךָ, LXX. ὁ θεός...τὸν χριστόν σου.

It occurs in the plural :

Ps. cv. 15, 1 Chron. xvi. 22 מְשִׁיחַי, LXX. οἱ χριστοί μου.

The full phrase is found :

Lam. iv. 20 מְשִׁיחַ יְהֹוָה, LXX. χριστὸς κύριος.

Compare Luke ii. 11.

It will be observed that in all these passages, with the exception of those in Leviticus, 2 Sam. i. 21, Dan. ix. 25 f., the Anointed One is always spoken of as the Anointed of the Lord or of God.

The title χριστός occurs in connexion with κύριος Ecclus. xlvi. 19 ἐπεμαρτύρατο ἔναντι κυρίου καὶ χριστοῦ. The use of the term in later books.

It occurs several times also in the *Psalms of Solomon :*

Psalms of Solomon.

xvii. 36 (there shall be no unrighteousness, because) πάντες ἅγιοι καὶ βασιλεὺς αὐτῶν χριστὸς κύριος.

xviii. 8 (happy are they who are) ὑπὸ ῥάβδον παιδείας χριστοῦ κυρίου ἐν φόβῳ θεοῦ αὐτοῦ ἐν σοφίᾳ πνεύματος καὶ δικαιοσύνης καὶ ἰσχύος.

xviii. 6 ...εἰς ἡμέραν ἐκλογῆς ἐν ἀνάξει χριστοῦ αὐτοῦ (τοῦ θεοῦ).

It is found in the Book of Henoch : Henoch.

c. 48, 10...they have denied the Lord of Spirits and His Anointed.

c. 52, 4 All these things which thou hast seen minister to the rule of His Anointed that he may be strong and mighty upon the earth.

But even here the title has not become an absolute title ('the Christ,' 'the Anointed,') but describes one who has the character of 'an anointed one.'

Targums. And it occurs twice in the Targum of Onkelos on the Pentateuch :

Gen. xlix. 10 מלכותא היא דדיליה משיחא דייתי עד, *until Messiah come, whose is the kingdom.*

Num. xxiv. 17 מישראל משיחא ויתרבא מיעקב מלכא כד־יקום, *when a king shall arise from Jacob, and a Christ from Israel shall rule.*

and commonly in the Targum of Jonathan. Comp. Buxtorf *Lex.* s.v.

It may be added that it is found also in 4 Esdras vii. 28 f. *my Son Christ* (comp. xii. 32).

And in the Apocalypse of Baruch: cc. xxiv, xxx, xxxix, xl, lxx, lxxii.

The use of the term in the New Testament a result of the study of Old Testament.

From this general view of the use of the word it appears that the limited application of the title to the Divine King and Saviour of Israel is, with the possible exception of the passage of Daniel, post-Biblical. And it is likely that the combination of the ideas of a coming of the Lord to judgment and of the establishment of a Divine Kingdom in Daniel served to concentrate attention on the scriptural language in regard to 'the Anointed of the Lord' (Luke ii. 26) which was seen to transcend any past application. Thus it could not but be felt that every one anointed to a special function in the divine economy pointed to One greater in whom all that he foreshadowed should find a final accomplishment. The offices of king and priest and prophet were concentrated upon 'the Christ'; and now one office and now the other became predominant according to the tempers of men.

Use of the term by St John.

With regard to the usage of St John it may be observed that ὁ χριστός is without question uniformly an appellative ('the Christ,' 'the Anointed') in the Gospel: i. 20, 25, iii. 28, iv. 29, vii. 26 f., 31, 41 f., x. 24, xi. 27, xii. 34, xx. 31 (compare also the use of χριστός: i. 41, iv. 25, ix. 22). So it is also in the first epistle: ii. 22, v. 1. This large collection of examples seems to decide that the same sense must be adopted in 2 John 9; Apoc. xx. 4, 6, where otherwise the title might have seemed to be a proper name.

Additional Note on v. 6.   References to the facts of the Gospel.

Reference to the fact of the Gospel in the Epistles of St John.

The Epistles of St John are permeated with the thoughts of the Person and work of Christ but direct references to the facts of the Gospel are singularly rare in them. In the third Epistle there is nothing in the language which is distinctively Christian except the pregnant reference to 'the Name' (*v.* 7). The Baptism is not spoken of plainly; nor yet any one of the crucial events of the Life of the Lord which were included in the earliest Confessions of faith, the Birth of the Virgin Mary, the Crucifixion, the Resurrection, the Ascension, the Session at the right hand of the Father, the Coming to Judgment.

But though these facts are not expressly mentioned they are all implied, and interpreted. Without them the arguments and language of St John are unintelligible.

(1) The Birth of the Virgin Mary: iv. 2 *Jesus Christ came in flesh.*

(2) The Baptism: v. 6 *This is He that came by water.*

(3) The Passion: iii. 16 *He laid down His life for us*—v. 6 *This is He that came...by blood.*

(4) The Resurrection, Ascension and Session at the right hand of the Father: ii. 1 *we have an Advocate with the Father, Jesus Christ.* Comp. 2 John 7...*confess that Jesus Christ cometh in flesh;* 1 John i. 3.

(5) The coming to Judgment: ii. 28 *that we may have boldness and not be ashamed before Him at His presence;* iii. 2 *If He should be manifested we shall be like Him, for we shall see Him as He is.* 2 John 7.

In addition to these allusions to articles of the Baptismal Creed the first Epistle assumes a general knowledge of the Life and Teaching of Christ: ii. 6 *He that saith he abideth in Him ought himself also to walk even as He walked;* iii. 1 *The world knoweth us not because it knew Him not;* ii. 25 *the promise which He promised;* iii. 23 *as He gave us commandment.* Compare also i. 1 note.

The revelation of the purpose and issue of Christ's work is made with singular fulness:

iii. 5 *He was manifested to take away sins.*

— 8 *The Son of God was manifested that He might destroy the works of the devil.*

iv. 9 [*God*] *hath sent His Son, His only Son, that we may live through Him.*

— 10 [*God*] *sent His Son, as a propitiation for our sins.* Comp. ii. 2.

— 14 *The Father hath sent the Son as Saviour of the world.*

v. 20 *The Son of God is come and hath given us an understanding that we may know Him that is true.*

Comp. i. 7; v. 18.

Additional Note on the readings in v. 6 f.

The variations of the three chief Greek MSS in the passage οὗτος...μαρτυροῦντες deserve to be studied in detail. Happily in this case the common text follows in the main that of B.

B.	ℵ.	A.
οὗτός ἐστιν ὁ ἐλθὼν	οὗτός ἐστιν ὁ ἐλθὼν	οὗτός ἐστιν ὁ ἐλθὼν
δι᾽ ὕδατος καὶ αἵματος	διὰ ὕδατος καὶ αἵματος	δι᾽ ὕδατος καὶ αἵματος
	καὶ πνεύματος	καὶ πνεύματος
Ἰησοῦς Χριστός·	Ἰησοῦς Χριστός·	Ἰησοῦς Χριστός·
οὐκ ἐν τῷ ὕδατι μόνῳ	οὐκ ἐν τῷ ὕδατι μόνον	οὐκ ἐν τῷ ὕδατι μόνον
ἀλλ᾽ ἐν τῷ ὕδατι	ἀλλ᾽ ἐν τῷ ὕδατι	ἀλλὰ ἐν τῷ ὕδατι
καὶ ἐν τῷ αἵματι	καὶ τῷ αἵματι	καὶ ἐν τῷ πνεύματι
καὶ τὸ πνεῦμα...	καὶ τὸ πνεῦμα...	καὶ τὸ πνεῦμα...
ὅτι τρεῖς εἰσὶν	ὅτι οἱ τρεῖς εἰσὶν	ὅτι τρεῖς εἰσὶν
οἱ μαρτυροῦντες...	οἱ μαρτυροῦντες...	οἱ μαρτυροῦντες...

For τὸ πνεῦμα the Latin Vulgate gives *Christus.*

Additional Note on the readings in v. 7, 8.

The inter-
polated
gloss.

The words which are interpolated in the common Greek text in this
passage (ἐν τῷ οὐρανῷ ὁ πατὴρ ὁ λόγος καὶ τὸ ἅγιον πνεῦμα· καὶ οὗτοι οἱ τρεῖς
ἕν εἰσι. καὶ τρεῖς εἰσιν οἱ μαρτυροῦντες ἐν τῇ γῇ) offer an instructive illustration of the formation and introduction of a gloss into the apostolic text
without any signs of bad faith. Happily the gloss was confined within
narrow limits till the age of printing. If it had been known in the East in
the sixth or seventh century, it is not rash to suppose that it would have
found wide acceptance just as it did in the printed editions of the Greek
text, and the evidence would have been complicated though essentially
unchanged. In this respect the history of the Vulgate reading is of singular importance. The mass of later Latin copies which contain the interpolation obviously add nothing to the evidence in favour of the authenticity of the words, and do not even tend to shew that they formed part of
Jerome's text.

The state of the external evidence can be summed up very briefly.

Summary
of external
evidence.

The words are not found

(1) In any independent Greek MS (more than 180 MSS and 50
lectionaries are quoted). Both the late MSS which contain it have un-
questionably been modified by the Latin Vulgate[1].

(2) In any independent Greek writer. The very few Greek writers
who make use of the words derived their knowledge of them from the
Latin (not in Ir Cl.Al Orig Did Athan Bas Greg.Naz Cyr.Al)[2].

(3) In any Latin Father earlier than Victor Vitensis or Vigilius
Tapsensis (not in Tert Cypr Hil Ambr Hier Aug Leo 1[3]).

(4) In any ancient version except the Latin; and it was not found
(*a*) in the Old Latin in its early form (Tert Cypr Aug), or (*b*) in the Vulgate as issued by Jerome (*Codd. am fuld*) or (*c*) as revised by Alcuin (*Cod.
vallicell* *)[4].

On the other hand the gloss is found from the sixth century in Latin
Fathers; and it is found also in two copies which give an old Latin text, in
some early copies of the Vulgate and in the great mass of the later copies
and in the Clementine text.

It becomes of interest therefore to observe how the words originally

[1] The *Codex Ravianus* which was
formerly quoted as a MS authority
has been shewn to be a copy made
from printed texts, chiefly from the
Complutensian, which it follows in
this passage. Comp. Griesbach, N. T.
I. ii. *App.* 4 f. The clause is also written
on the margin of a Naples MS 173
'manu recenti, unius ut mihi videtur ex bibliothecariis, sæc. fine 17'
(Tischdf.).

[2] The gloss of Claudius Apollinaris,
quoted in the note on the text, shews

that he connected 'the word' and 'the
spirit' with v. 8 in a different sense.

[3] Compare Griesbach *l. c.* 13 ff.

[4] The words are found in the Theo-
dulfian Recension (Paris *Bibl. Nat.*
Lat. 9380) in the following form : quia
tres sunt qui testimonium dant in
terra spiritus aqua et sanguis et tres
unum sunt ; et tres sunt qui testimonium dicunt in cælo pater *et filius*, et
spiritus sanctus et hi tres unum sunt
(Prof. Wordsworth).

found a place in the Latin texts, and were carried from that source into the Greek text, and into the printed editions of other versions.

The words are not, as has been already stated, found in any early Latin Father; but a passage of Cyprian, which shews that he was not acquainted with them as part of the apostolic text, shews at the same time how natural it was to form a distinct gloss on *v.* 7 according to their tenor: Dicit dominus: *Ego et Pater unum sumus;* et iterum *de* Patre et Filio et Spiritu Sancto scriptum est; *et tres unum sunt* (*de Eccles. unit.* c. 6; comp. *auct. de rebapt.* cc. 15, 19). The force of this application of 'the spirit and the water and the blood' with the false reading 'unum sunt' for 'in unum sunt' (εἰς τὸ ἕν εἰσιν) is made clear by a later reference to it in Facundus:...De Patre et Filio et Spiritu Sancto sic dicit: *Tres sunt qui testimonium dant in terra, spiritus, aqua et sanguis, et hi tres unum sunt;* in spiritu significans Patrem, sicut Dominus mulieri Samaritanæ... loquitur...in aqua vero Spiritum Sanctum significans sicut in eodem Evangelio exponit (John vii. 37)...in sanguine vero Filium...Quod... Johannis apostoli testimonium beatus Cyprianus...in epistola sive libro quem de Unitate scripsit de Patre Filio et Spiritu Sancto dictum intelligit (*Pro def. tr. Cap.* i. 3). The same mystical interpretation is found in Augustine (*c. Maxim.* ii. 22), and Eucherius (*Instruc.* i. *ad loc.* Migne, *Patr. Lat.* l. 810); and Augustine supplies the word 'Verbum,' which is required to complete the gloss: Deus itaque summus et verus cum Verbo suo et Spiritu Sancto, quæ tria unum sunt, Deus unus et omnipotens (*de Civ.* v. 11)[1].

The origin of the Latin gloss.

The gloss which had thus become an established interpretation of St John's words is first quoted as part of the Epistle in a tract of Priscillian († 385), who quotes the passage with remarkable variations[2]. Sicut Johannes ait: *tria* sunt *quæ* testimonium dicunt in terra, aqua *caro* et sanguis, et *hæc tria in unum* sint; et *tria* sunt *quæ* testimonium dicunt in caelo, pater uerbum et spiritus, et *hæc tria* unum sunt *in Christo Jesu.*

The gloss inserted in the text.

The use of the neuter (comp. Eucherius *l.c.*) in both clauses is peculiar and in itself proves conclusively that the passage was not taken directly from any Greek text. The substitution of *caro* for *spiritus* (transposed) in the earthly triad is found also in Vict. Vit. *c. Varim.* 5 (p. 204); and so the connexion of *in Christo Jesu* with the heavenly triad is likewise found in one of the quotations from the same group of writings (see below).

---

[1] It is by no means unlikely that the mystical interpretation of *v.* 8 may have taken a definite shape in Africa from a very early time. The language of Tertullian, which shews conclusively that he was not acquainted with the words *tres unum sunt* as a scriptural phrase, indicates the beginning of its growth: *adv. Prax.* 25...connexus patris in filio et filii in paracleto, tres efficit cohærentes, alterum ex altero. Qui tres unum sunt non unus; quomodo dictum est *ego et pater unum sumus* (John x. 30) ad substantiæ unitatem, non ad numeri singularitatem. It is possible that the gloss may have found a place in copies of the Latin Version as soon as it was definitely shaped; but there is no evidence that it was found in the text of St John before the latter part of the 5th century.

[2] *Liber Apol.* § 4.

On the whole this earliest example of the interpolation recedes farthest of all from the original apostolic words; and seems to shew that it took shape among a people ignorant of Greek. Perhaps it indicates yet more, and points to Spain as the country where it was formed (see below *m*, *Codd. Cav.* and *Tol.*).

The interpolation occurs next in a group of writings which come from Africa in the last quarter of the fifth century:

(1) Ut adhuc luce clarius unius divinitatis esse cum Patre et Filio Spiritum Sanctum doceamus, Joannis Evangelistæ testimonio comprobatur. Ait namque *Tres sunt qui testimonium perhibent in cœlo, Pater, Verbum et Spiritus Sanctus, et hi tres unum sunt* (*Prof. Fid.* ap. Vict. Vit. *de Persec. Vand.* iii. 11)[1].

(2) Pater est ingenitus, filius vero sine initio genitus a patre est, spiritus autem sanctus processit (Casp. procedit?) a patre et accipit de filio sicut evangelista testatur, quia scriptum est: *Tres sunt qui dicunt testimonium in cœlo, pater, verbum et spiritus, et hæc tria unum sunt, in Christo Jesu.* Non tamen dixit: unus est in Christo Jesu[2].

It was not unnatural that in the stress of the Arian persecution words which were held to give the plain meaning of St John's words as they were read should find their way from the margin into the text, or if they had already obtained a place in the text of any copies should gain wider currency. But still the form is fluent:

(3) [Johannes Evangelista] ad Parthos: *Tres sunt*, inquit, *qui testimonium perhibent in terra, aqua sanguis et caro, et tres in nobis sunt; et tres sunt qui testimonium perhibent in cœlo, Pater Verbum et Spiritus...et hi* (ii) *tres unum sunt* (c. *Varim.* 5). And again:

(4)...dicente Joanne Evangelista in epistola sua: *Tres sunt qui testimonium dicunt in cœlo, Pater et Verbum et Spiritus; et in Christo Jesu unum sunt*, non tamen unus est, quia non est in his una persona (*de Trin.* i. p. 206; Migne, *Patr. Lat.* lxii. 243).

From this time the words seem to have maintained partially their position in the text. They are quoted by Fulgentius (c. 550) as St John's in the form: *Tres sunt qui testimonium perhibent in cœlo, Pater, Verbum et Spiritus; et tres unum sunt* (*Resp. c. Arian.* p. 68, Migne, *Patr. Lat.* lxv. 224); though the same writer in another place (c. *Fabian. fragm.*) speaks of the application of the clause *et tres unum sunt* to 'the Father, Son and Holy Spirit' as established by argument, a process wholly unnecessary if the gloss had been admitted as part of the text.

On the other hand the language of Cassiodorus (c. 550) seems to me to shew that he did not find the gloss in his text of St John, though he

---

[1] The authorship of this 'Exposition of the Faith' is uncertain. It is perhaps a later addition to the history of Victor (Papencordt, *Gesch. d. Vand. Herrsch.* 369 n.); but in no case does it prove more than that the words were found in the copy of the Epistle used by the writer.

[2] This remarkable form of the gloss has been printed by Caspari in an *Expositio fidei* preserved in the Ambrosian MS which contains also the Muratorian fragment on the Canon (*Kirchenhist. Anecdota*, pp. xxiv. 305 and notes).

accepted it as a true interpretation of the apostle's words. Cui rei [quia Jesus est Christus], he writes, testificantur in terra tria mysteria, aqua sanguis et spiritus, quæ in passione Domini leguntur impleta; in cælo autem Pater et Filius et Spiritus Sanctus; et hi tres unus est Deus (*Complex. in Epp. ad loc.* Migne, *Patr. Lat.* lxx. pp. 1372 f.)[1].

Not long afterwards the addition was expressly defended in 'a Prologue to the seven canonical Epistles' issued under the name of Jerome, which seems to have been written with this express purpose: [In prima Johannis Epistola] ab infidelibus translatoribus multum erratum esse a fidei veritate comperimus, trium tantum vocabula, hoc est, aquæ sanguinis et spiritus, in ipsa sua editione ponentibus et Patris, Verbique ac Spiritus testimonium omittentibus; in quo maxime et fides catholica roboratur et Patris ac Filii ac Spiritus Sancti una divinitatis substantia comprobatur (Migne, *Patrol. Lat.* xxix. 829 f.). *Expressly affirmed to be authentic.*

This Prologue is found in one of the earliest copies of the Vulgate (*Codex Fuldensis*) written in 546, though the gloss itself is not found in the text of the Epistle.

But the gloss is found in early MSS both of the Old Latin and of the Vulgate, and in substantially the same form, so that it must have been introduced into both from the same source. These are (*a*) (of the old Latin) a *Speculum* (a classified series of Scriptural passages) *m* (sæc. viii. or ix.) and a Munich fragment *q* (*cod. Fris.* sæc. vi. or vii.); (*b*) of the Vulgate, the Spanish (Visigothic) MSS *Cod. Cav.* (sæc. ix.) and *Cod. Tol.* (sæc. x.). *The earliest MS authority for it.*

The whole passage appears in these authorities in the following form:

Cod. Fris.[2]	Spec. (m).	Codd. Cav. Tol.
quoniam tr	quoniam tres sunt qui testimonium dicunt	quia tres sunt qui testimonium dant
in terra	in terra	in terra
spiritus et aqua et sa	spiritus aqua et sanguis;	spiritus et aqua et sanguis;
	et hi tres unum sunt in Christo Jesu.	et hi tres unum sunt in Christo Jesu.
	Et tres sunt	et (om Tol) tres sunt
tificantur	qui testimonium dicunt	qui testimonium dicunt
in caelo	in caelo	in caelo
pater e	Pater verbum et spiritus	pater verbum et spiritus
tres unum sunt.	et hi tres unum sunt.	et hi tres unum sunt.

Here, it will be observed, the testimony on earth is placed first, so that

[1] The passage of Cassiodorus is well discussed by Bp Turton in his *Vindication of Porson*, pp. 279 ff.

[2] The MS is unfortunately mutilated. About half of each line is lost. The lines of the MS so far as they are preserved run thus:

quiaspsestueritas qmtr
in terra . spsetaquaetsa

tificanturincaelop tere
tresunumsunt sitestim

There is room in each line for about 21 more letters. It is not possible therefore that the words *et hi tres unum sunt in Christo Jesu* could have formed part of the text. It is further to be noticed that this MS reads *spiritus* in v. 6 for *Christus.*

the heavenly testimony retains its position as an interpretative gloss[1]. And there is also a second similar though shorter gloss *in Christo Jesu* which is even older than that which follows; for it is indicated in the Latin translation of the *Outlines* of Clement of Alexandria: *et hi tres unum sunt*: in salvatore quippe istæ sunt virtutes salutiferæ, et vita ipsa in ipso Filio ejus existit (p. 1011 P.).

Modification of the text. After a time the second gloss *in Christo Jesu* was omitted; and the two clauses were transposed; so that the passage assumed the form which was generally current in the fourteenth and fifteenth centuries, and was finally pronounced authentic in the Sixtine and Clementine editions of the Vulgate. The main forms in which the passage appears in the Latin texts are given in the following table:

Cod. Cav.	*Cod. Vallicell.***	Common Text.
quia tres sunt qui testimonium dant in *terra*, *spiritus et aqua et sanguis*; et *hi* tres unum sunt *in Christo Jesu*	*quoniam* tres sunt qui testimonium dant in *terra*, *spiritus aqua et sanguis*; et tres unum sunt	*quoniam* tres sunt qui testimonium dant in *caelo*, *pater verbum et spiritus sanctus*; et *hi* tres unum sunt.
et tres sunt qui testimonium *dicunt* in *caelo*, *pater verbum et spiritus*; et hi tres unum sunt.	*sicut* tres sunt qui testimonium *dant* in *caelo*, *pater verbum et spiritus sanctus*; et tres unum sunt.	*et* tres sunt qui testimonium *dant* in *terra*, *spiritus et aqua et sanguis*; et *hi* tres unum sunt[2].

The first appearance of the words in Greek. Here the history of the Latin interpolation ends: we have to notice how it passed into the Greek text. It appears first in a Greek version of the Acts of the Council of Lateran held in 1215, coeval with the Council. The Latin text is: Quemadmodum in canonica Johannis epistola legitur: *Quia tres sunt qui testimonium dant in cœlo, Pater, Verbum et Spiritus Sanctus; et hi tres unum sunt.* Statimque subjungitur: *et tres sunt qui testimonium dant in terra, spiritus aqua et sanguis; et tres unum sunt,* sicut in quibusdam codicibus legitur[3]. For this the corresponding Greek, as far as it has been preserved, is: ὃν τρόπον ἐν τῇ κανονικῇ τοῦ

---

[1] Another form of the reading preserved in a St Gall MS: Quia tres sunt qui testimonium dant spiritus et aqua et sanguis, et tres unum sunt. *Sicut* in cælo tres sunt, Pater Verbum et Spiritus, et tres unum sunt (Dobbin, *Codex Montfort.* p. 45), points clearly to the original gloss-form of the addition. This MS is now in the British Museum (Add. 11,852) and was formerly in the possession of Bp Butler. (See Dict. of Bible, *Vulgate*, p. 1713 n. q). A Greek MS has notes in v. 8 τουτέστι τὸ πνεῦμα τὸ ἅγιον καὶ ὁ πατὴρ καὶ αὐτὸς ἑαυτοῦ and on ἕν εἰσι:

τουτέστι μία θεότης, εἷς θεός (Tischdf. *ad loc.*).

[2] This last clause is omitted in many late MSS. Some account of the Latin MSS known up to his time is given by Bp Turton, *l. c.* pp. 141 f. Griesbach *l. c.* 12 calculates that the gloss is omitted by 50—60 MSS of the Vulgate. In collections which he mentions it is omitted by 18 MSS out of an aggregate of 234.

[3] This remark refers to the last words *et tres unum sunt* which were omitted by many late MSS of the Vulgate.

Ἰωάννου ἐπιστολῇ ἀναγινώσκεται ὅτι τρεῖς εἰσιν οἱ μαρτυροῦντες ἐν οὐρανῷ, ὁ
πατὴρ, λόγος καὶ πνεῦμα ἅγιον· καὶ τοῦτοι (sic) οἱ τρεῖς ἕν εἰσιν. εὐθύς τε
προστίθησι *** καθὼς ἕν τισι κώδηξιν εὑρίσκεται.

The clause was quoted afterwards incompletely by Manuel Calecas (saec.
xiv.), and perhaps by Jos. Bryennius (saec. xv.), who both wrote under
Latin influence; and at last it found a place in a Graeco-Latin MS of the
Epistle (*Cod. Vat. Ottob.* 162) of the fifteenth century, and in a Greek MS
of the sixteenth century (*Cod. Montfort. Dubl.* 34, the *Codex Britannicus*
of Erasmus). The Greek text in both these MSS has been adapted in other
places to the Latin Vulgate; and in this passage both follow a late Latin
text in omitting the εἰς τὸ ἕν εἰσι after the earthly witness. The language
of both, especially that of *Cod. Montfort.*, shews decisively that the Greek
is a translation of the Latin[1].

The passage is thus given in the two MSS:

Cod. Montf. (34).	*Cod. Vat. Ottob.* (162).	
ὅτι τρεῖς εἰσὶν	quia tres sunt	ὅτι τρεῖς εἰσὶν
οἱ μαρτυροῦντες	qui testimonium dant	οἱ μαρτυροῦντες
ἐν τῷ οὐρανῷ,	iu caelo,	ἀπὸ τοῦ οὐρανοῦ,
πατὴρ λόγος καὶ πνεῦμα ἅγιον·	pater verbum et spiritus sanctus:	πατὴρ λόγος καὶ πνεῦμα ἅγιον·
καὶ οὗτοι οἱ τρεῖς	et hi tres	καὶ οἱ τρεῖς
ἕν εἰσιν·	unum sunt.	εἰς τὸ ἕν εἰσι·
καὶ τρεῖς εἰσὶν	et tres sunt	καὶ τρεῖς εἰσὶν
οἱ μαρτυροῦντες	qui testimonium dant	οἱ μαρτυροῦντες
ἐν τῇ γῇ,	in terra,	ἐπὶ τῆς γῆς,
πνεῦμα ὕδωρ καὶ αἷμα·	spiritus aqua et sanguis	τὸ πνεῦμα τὸ ὕδωρ καὶ τὸ αἷμα·
εἰ τὴν μαρτυρίαν...	si testimonium.	εἰ τὴν μαρτυρίαν...

The Complutensian editors introduced another translation of the Vulgate similar to that in *Cod.* 162, into their text[2]. Meanwhile Erasmus
had published his first edition giving the whole passage as he found it in
his Greek MS with the note: In Graeco codice tantum hoc reperio de testimonio triplici ὅτι τρεῖς εἰσὶν οἱ μαρτυροῦντες τὸ πνεῦμα καὶ τὸ ὕδωρ καὶ τὸ
αἷμα; and on the clause *et hi tres unum sunt*, which he retained in his
translation, he writes: *Hi* redundat: Neque est *unum* sed *in unum*, εἰς
τὸ αὐτό. i. sive *in idem*. In his third edition, in fulfilment of a promise
which he had made to insert the clause if it could be shewn to exist in a
single Greek MS, he inserted the words on the authority of the *Cod.
Montfort.* retaining however the words καὶ οἱ τρεῖς εἰς τὸ ἕν εἰσιν.

The words were afterwards brought into a more correct shape without
any manuscript authority; and at last the passage assumed the form which

The introduction of the gloss into the printed Greek text.

---

[1] It has been shewn by Dr Dobbin
that *Cod. Montf.* is 'a transcript with
arbitrary and fanciful variations' of
the MS in Lincoln College, Oxford 39,
in which the gloss is not found (*Codex
Montfortianus*, p. 57).

[2] The ἀπὸ τοῦ οὐρανοῦ in the Greek

text of *Cod.* 162 is very peculiar. Is it
possible that ἐπί has been misread
ἀπό, as was done in the corresponding
clause, and that the translator intended ἐπὶ τοῦ οὐρανοῦ to answer exactly to ἐπὶ τῆς γῆς?

is given in the texts of Stephanus in 1550 and Elzevir of 1633 ('text. rec.'), and from them has assumed general currency.

The chief forms in which the whole passage appears in early printed texts are given in the following table:

Erasm. Ed. 1, 1516.	Erasm. Ed. 3, 1522.	Erasm. Ed. 4, 1527.
ὅτι τρεῖς εἰσὶν	ὅτι τρεῖς εἰσὶν	ὅτι τρεῖς εἰσὶν
οἱ μαρτυροῦντες	οἱ μαρτυροῦντες	οἱ μαρτυροῦντες
* *	ἐν τῷ οὐρανῷ,	ἐν τῷ οὐρανῷ,
* *	πατὴρ λόγος καὶ	ὁ πατήρ, ὁ λόγος, καὶ
	πνεῦμα ἅγιον·	τὸ πνεῦμα ἅγιον·
* *	καὶ οὗτοι οἱ τρεῖς	καὶ οὗτοι οἱ τρεῖς
* *	ἕν εἰσι.	ἕν εἰσι.
* *	καὶ τρεῖς εἰσὶν	καὶ τρεῖς εἰσὶν
* *	οἱ μαρτυροῦντες	οἱ μαρτυροῦντες
τὸ πνεῦμα καὶ τὸ ὕδωρ	ἐν τῇ γῇ	ἐν τῇ γῇ,
καὶ τὸ αἷμα·	πνεῦμα καὶ ὕδωρ καὶ	πνεῦμα καὶ ὕδωρ καὶ
καὶ οἱ τρεῖς	αἷμα·	αἷμα·
εἰς τὸ ἕν εἰσιν.	καὶ οἱ τρεῖς	καὶ οἱ τρεῖς
εἰ τὴν μαρτυρίαν...	εἰς τὸ ἕν εἰσιν.	εἰς τὸ ἕν εἰσιν.
	εἰ τὴν μαρτυρίαν...	εἰ τὴν μαρτυρίαν...

Ed. Compl. 1514 (Cod. Rav.).	Erasm. Ed. 3, 1522.	Ed. Steph. 1550; Elz. 1633 (text. rec.).
ὅτι τρεῖς εἰσὶν	ὅτι τρεῖς εἰσὶν	ὅτι τρεῖς εἰσὶν
οἱ μαρτυροῦντες	οἱ μαρτυροῦντες	οἱ μαρτυροῦντες
ἐν τῷ οὐρανῷ	ἐν τῷ οὐρανῷ	ἐν τῷ οὐρανῷ
ὁ πατὴρ καὶ ὁ λόγος καὶ	πατὴρ λόγος καὶ πνεῦ-	ὁ πατὴρ ὁ λόγος καὶ τὸ
τὸ ἅγιον πνεῦμα	μα ἅγιον	ἅγιον πνεῦμα
καὶ οἱ τρεῖς	καὶ οὗτοι οἱ τρεῖς	καὶ οὗτοι οἱ τρεῖς
εἰς τὸ ἕν εἰσι.	ἕν εἰσι.	ἕν εἰσι.
καὶ τρεῖς εἰσὶν.	καὶ τρεῖς εἰσὶν	καὶ τρεῖς εἰσὶν
οἱ μαρτυροῦντες	οἱ μαρτυροῦντες	οἱ μαρτυροῦντες
ἐπὶ τῆς γῆς	ἐν τῇ γῇ	ἐν τῇ γῇ
τὸ πνεῦμα καὶ τὸ ὕδωρ	πνεῦμα καὶ ὕδωρ καὶ	τὸ πνεῦμα καὶ τὸ ὕδωρ
καὶ τὸ αἷμα[1].	αἷμα.	καὶ τὸ αἷμα.
* *	καὶ οἱ τρεῖς	καὶ οἱ τρεῖς
* *	εἰς τὸ ἕν εἰσιν.	εἰς τὸ ἕν εἰσι.
εἰ τὴν μαρτυρίαν...	εἰ τὴν μαρτυρίαν...	εἰ τὴν μαρτυρίαν...

[1] A note is added which seems to shew that the editors found the following clause καὶ—εἰσίν in their Greek mss: Sanctus Thomas in expositione secundæ decretalis de sermone Trinitate et Fide Catholica tractans istum passum contra Abbatem Joachim viz. *Tres sunt qui testimonium dant in cælo, pater verbum et spiritus sanctus*, dicit ad litteram verba sequentia. Et ad insinuandam unitatem trium personarum subditur, *et hii tres unum sunt*. Quod quidem dicitur propter essentiæ unitatem. Sed hoc Joachim perverse trahere volens ad unitatem charitatis et consensus inducebat consequentem auctoritatem. Nam subditur ibidem: *et tres sunt qui testimonium dant in terra S. spiritus aqua et sanguis*. Et in quibusdam libris additur: *et hii tres unum sunt*. Sed hoc in veris exemplaribus non habetur: sed dicitur esse appositum ab hæreticis Arrianis ad pervertendum intellectum sanum auctoritatis præmissæ de unitate essentiæ trium personarum. Hæc beatus Thomas ubi supra.

This is, as far as I have observed, the only note of the kind in the New

When the gloss had gained a place in the Greek text it naturally influenced the texts of other versions. Gutbir and Schaaf introduced with very slight modifications a translation which had been made by Tremellius into their printed texts of the Peshito[1]. It was introduced into editions of the Armenian and Slavonic Versions; and into the modern European versions.

The supposed dogmatic importance of the gloss has given a value to the evidence in its favour out of all proportion to its critical weight. The MS authority, for example, for the spurious *Epistle to the Laodicenes* is essentially the same. This also is supported by *m*, and by the *La Cava* and *Toledo* MSS and by a multitude of later MSS of the Vulgate. In the preceding verse (*v.* 6) of the Epistle almost all Latin authorities read *Christus* for *Spiritus* (τὸ πνεῦμα). A remarkable group of ancient authorities of the same type including *Cod. Tol.* add to c. ii. 17 *quomodo Deus manet in æternum.* In c. v. 20, *m* and *Cod. Tol.*, with Hilary substantially, add a clause very similar in character to the gloss on *v.* 8; and in the same verse *m. Cod. Montf.* with the Lat vg (Hil Ambr Vigil Fulg Leo) read *simus* (ὦμεν).

It will also have been observed that the gloss itself sprang from a false reading *unum* for *in unum*, a change due to an omission which was equally easy in Greek (τρεῖς εἰς) and in Latin.

Additional Note on v. 16. Sin unto death.

The phrase 'sin unto death' is introduced as one which was familiar to the readers of the Epistle and is evidently borrowed from current language. And so in fact the distinction of 'sins unto death' and 'sins not unto death' is common among Rabbinic writers (Schoettgen *ad loc.*) and represents, it cannot be doubted, an old traditional view. Comp. Is. ii. 9; xxii. 14.

The phrase 'sin unto death' in use among Jews.

1. In the first and simplest sense a 'sin unto death' would be a sin requiring the punishment of natural death: comp. Num. xviii. 22 ἁμαρτία θανατηφόρος[2]. Death in such a case was final exclusion from the Divine Society.

A sin punishable by death.

Testament. The treatment of the passage is wholly exceptional; for elsewhere the Edition marks prominently in the Greek text the absence of Latin additions: *e.g.* Acts viii. 37, ix. 5, 6, x. 6, xiv. 7, xv. 41; 1 John ii. 23; 2 John 11; and conversely the absence of words found in the Greek text from the Latin: *e.g.* Acts x. 21, 32, xv. 24; 1 Pet. iii. 12, iv. 14; 1 John v. 13.

[1] Gutbir's note is worth quoting: Cum notum sit Arrianos nec ipsi Græco Textui nec Versionibus Orientalibus hic pepercisse, ex Notis Tremellii hunc versum in aliis E. E. desideratum adscripsimus. Schaaf's note is to the same effect.

[2] Origen identifies the two phrases: ἐπὶ ἁμαρτήμασι τοῖς μὴ πρὸς θάνατον ἢ ὡς ὠνόμασεν ἐν 'Αριθμοῖς ὁ νόμος τοῖς μὴ θανατηφόροις (*in Matt.* T. XIII. § 30). In another passage he treats the infliction of death as the complete expiation of the crime for which it is inflicted: Absolvitur peccatum per pœnam mortis, nec superest aliquid quod pro hoc crimine judicii dies et pœna æterni ignis inveniat (*Hom. in Lev.* xiv. § 4).

A sin of the same class.

2.   It was a natural extension of this meaning when the phrase was used for an offence which was reckoned by moral judgment to belong to the same class.   Words very closely resembling those of St John are used *Test. xii. Patr.* Issach. 7 οὐκ ἔγνων ἐν ἐμοὶ (al. ἐπ᾽ ἐμέ) ἁμαρτίαν εἰς (for πρὸς) θάνατον.   Comp. 1 Cor. v. 11.

A sin carrying exclusion from the Christian society if persisted in.

3.   If now the same line of thought is extended to the Christian Society, it will appear that a sin which in its very nature excludes from fellowship with Christians would be rightly spoken of as a 'sin unto death.'   Such a sin may be seen in hatred of the brethren (c. iii. 15), or in the selfishness which excludes repentance, the condition of forgiveness (i. 7), or in the faithlessness which denies Christ, the One Advocate (v. 21; iv. 2).   But in each case the character of the sin is determined by the effect which it has on the relation of the doer to God through Christ in the Divine Society. We are not to think of specific acts, defined absolutely, but of acts as the revelation of moral life.

Death the tendency not the necessary issue.

4.   It must be noticed further that St John speaks of the sin as 'tending to death' (πρὸς θάνατον) and not as necessarily involving death.   Death is, so to speak, its natural consequence, if it continue, and not its inevitable issue as a matter of fact.   Its character is assumed to be unquestionable, and its presence open and notorious.

The mode of dealing with such a sin.

5.   The question then could not but arise, How is such flagrant sin in a brother—a fellow Christian—to be dealt with?   For it must be remembered that the words of the apostle are directed to those who are members of the Christian Church, sharing in the privileges of the common life.   The answer follows naturally from a view of the normal efficacy of Christian intercession.   The power of prayer avails for those who belong to the Body (comp. John xiii. 10).   But for those who are separated from the Body for a time or not yet included in it the ordinary exercise of the energy of spiritual sympathy has, so far as we are taught directly, no promise of salutary influence.   The use of common prayer in such cases is not enjoined; though it must be observed that it is not forbidden.   St John does not command intercession when the sin is seen, recognised by the brother, in its fatal intensity; but on the other hand he does not expressly exclude it.   Even if the tenour of his words may seem to dissuade such prayer, it is because the offender lies without the Christian Body, excluded from its life but yet not beyond the creative, vivifying power of God.

In some cases uttermost

6.   We can understand in some degree how such sins, either in men or in nations, must be left to God.   Chastisement and not forgiveness is the one way to restoration[1].   The book of the prophet Jeremiah is a divine lesson

---

[1] The truth finds a noble expression in Browning's *The Ring and the Book: The Pope*, 2116 ff.

For the main criminal I see no hope
Except in such a suddenness of fate.
I stood at Naples once, a night so dark
I could have scarce conjectured there
    was earth

Anywhere, sky or sea or world at all:
But the night's black was burst through
    by a blaze—
Thunder struck blow on blow, earth
    groaned and bore,
Through her whole length of mountains
    visible:
There lay the city thick and plain with
    spires,

of the necessity of purification through death for a faithless people. And chastise-ment necessary.
the fortunes of Israel seem to illustrate the character of God's dealings
with men.

7. The patristic comments upon the passage offer an instructive Patristic comments.
subject for study.

CLEMENT of Alexandria in discussing the different kinds of voluntary Clement of Alex-andria.
and wrong action (*Strom.* ii. 15, § 66) refers to the language of St John as
shewing that he recognised differences in sin (φαίνεται...τὰς διαφορὰς τῶν
ἁμαρτιῶν ἐκδιδάσκων), and quotes as illustrating the kind of distinction to
which he refers Ps. i. 1, but he gives no classification of specific offences.

TERTULLIAN naturally lays down a clear and definite interpretation : Tertul-lian.
'Who, he asks, can escape from the sin of rash anger...of breaking engage-
'ments, of speaking falsely through shame or necessity...so that if there
'were no pardon for such acts, no one could be saved. Of these then there
'will be pardon through Christ, our Advocate with the Father. There are
'however offences of a different character, heavier and deadly, such as admit
'no pardon, murder, idolatry, fraud, denial [of Christ], blasphemy, and
'assuredly also adultery and fornication, and every other violation of the
'temple of God. For these Christ will no longer plead: these he who has
'been born of God will absolutely not commit, as he will not be a son of
'God, if he has committed them [1].'

ORIGEN speaks with wise reserve; after referring to 1 Cor. iii. 15, Matt. Origen.
xvi. 26, he continues, 'There are some sins which are to loss (ad damnum)...
'some to destruction (ad interitum)...What kind of sins however are sins
'to death, what not to death but to loss, cannot, I think, easily be deter-
'mined by any man' (*Hom. in Ex.* x. § 3[2]).

And, like a ghost disshrouded, white
the sea.
So may the truth be flashed out by
one blow,
And Guido see, one instant, and be
saved.

With this compare Guido's last words,
    Abate—Cardinal—Christ—Maria—
        God—
    Pompilia, will you let them murder
    me?

[1] *De pudic.* 19, Cui enim non ac-
cidit aut irasci inique et ultra solis
occasum, aut et manum immittere,
aut facile maledicere, aut temere ju-
rare, aut fidem pacti destruere, aut
verecundia aut necessitate mentiri;
in negotiis, in officiis, in quæstu, in
victu, in visu, in auditu, quanta
tentamur; ut si nulla sit venia isto-
rum nemini salus competeret. Horum

.ergo erit venia per exoratorem patris
Christum. Sunt autem et contraria
istis, ut graviora et exitiosa, quæ veniam non capiant, homicidium, idolo-
latria, fraus, negatio, blasphemia, utique et mœchia et fornicatio...Horum
ultra exorator non erit Christus. Hæc
non admittet omnino qui natus ex
Deo fuerit, non futurus Dei filius si
admiserit. The classification is instructive. In an earlier chapter (c. 2)
he divides sins into 'remissible' and
'irremissible': the former are fit subjects of intercession, the latter not,
and he concludes: Secundum hanc
differentiam delictorum pœnitentiæ
quoque conditio discriminatur. Alia
erit quæ veniam consequi possit, in
delicto scilicet remissibili; alia quæ
consequi nullo modo possit, in delicto
scilicet irremissibili.

[2] Comp. *in Joh.* Tom. II. (IV. p. 62

HILARY.

HILARY brings out an important aspect of the truth. 'There is,' he says, 'a limit to mercy (*misericordiæ*), and justice must be used in shewing 'pity. We can feel sorrow for those whose crimes are great, but there is 'no room for mercy. For mercy turns to ask pardon of God for that which 'is done; but to give pardon to wrong deeds is not to shew mercy but not 'to observe justice in mercy. This consideration the apostle John observed 'most carefully saying: *Si quis scit fratrem suum delinquere sed non ad* '*mortem, petat et dabit illi Deus vitam. Est enim peccatum ad mortem* '*sed non pro eo dico*' (*in cxl. Psalm.* § 8).

AMBROSE.

AMBROSE regards the direction of St John as applying to the general action of the Church but not as excluding absolutely all intercession. 'He 'did not speak to a Moses (Ex. xxxii. 31 f.) or a Jeremiah (Jer. xiv. 11; vii. '16; Baruch iii. 1 f.; v. 1), but to the people, who required to employ 'another to pray for their own sins; for whom it is enough if they pray 'God for lighter faults, and think that the pardon of graver must be re-'served for the prayers of the just' (*de pœnit.* i. 10).

JEROME.

JEROME combines the language of 1 Sam. ii. 25 with that of St John, when he is insisting on the different degrees of the heinousness of sins. '*Qui scit fratrem suum peccare peccatum non ad mortem, petat, et dabit* '*ei vitam peccanti non ad mortem. Qui vero peccaverit ad mortem quis* '*orabit pro eo?*' 'You see,' he continues, 'that if we pray for smaller sins we 'obtain pardon; if for greater, the obtaining pardon is difficult; and that 'there is a great interval between some sins and others' (*adv. Jovin.* ii. § 30).

AUGUS-
TINE.

The interpretation of AUGUSTINE is of great interest. His commentary on the verse of St John's Epistle is not preserved, but in his treatise on the *Sermon on the Mount* (c. A. D. 393) he treats of the passage, and says: Aperte ostendit esse quosdam fratres pro quibus orare non nobis præcipitur, cum Dominus etiam pro peccatoribus nostris orare jubeat...Peccatum ergo fratris ad mortem puto esse cum post agnitionem Dei per gratiam Domini nostri Jesu Christi quisque oppugnat fraternitatem et adversus ipsam gratiam qua reconciliatus est Deo invidentiæ facibus agitatur (*de Serm. Dom.* i. 22, 73)[1]. In reviewing this passage afterwards in his *Retractationes* (c. A. D. 426—7) he writes: Quod quidem non confirmavi, quoniam hoc putare me dixi: sed tamen addendum fuit, si in hac tam scelerata mentis perversitate finierit hanc vitam; quoniam de quocunque pessimo in hac vita constituto non est utique desperandum, nec pro illo imprudenter oratur de quo non desperatur (*Retract.* i. 19, 7).

He developes this idea of deliberate persistence in evil in treating of the sin against the Holy Spirit:

R.). In *Hom. in Lev.* IV. § 5 Origen compares with 1 John v. 16 the words in 1 Sam. ii. 25; and in the treatise *On Prayer* (§ 28) he follows out the comparison, implying that sins of idolatry, adultery and fornication are not to be remitted by the prayer and offerings of the Church.

[1] Bede silently quotes this interpretation in his Commentary; and afterwards a singular alternative: Potest etiam peccatum *usque* ad mortem accipi, pro quo rogare quempiam vetat, quia scilicet peccatum quod in hac vita non corrigitur ejus venia frustra post mortem postulatur. But he prefers Augustine's view.

Hoc [peccatum in Spiritum Sanctum] est duritia cordis usque ad finem huius vitæ qua homo recusat in unitate corporis Christi, quod vivificat Spiritus Sanctus, remissionem accipere peccatorum...Huic ergo dono gratiæ Dei quicunque restiterit et repugnaverit vel quoquo modo fuerit ab eo alienus usque in finem vitæ non remittetur ei neque in hoc sæculo neque in futuro ; hoc scilicet tam grande peccatum ut eo teneantur cuncta peccata quod non probatur ab aliquo esse commissum nisi cum de corpore exierit (*Epist.* clxxx. v (l), xi. § 49). No one can be pronounced guilty of it while life still continues : Hæc blasphemia Spiritus, cui nunquam est ulla remissio,... non potest in quoquam, ut diximus, dum in hac adhuc vita est deprehendi (*Serm.* lxxi. 3, 21).

The fatal consequences of the sin are, he points out, involved in its essential character :

Ille peccat in Spiritum Sanctum qui, desperans vel irridens atque contemnens prædicationem gratiæ per quam peccata diluuntur et pacis per quam reconciliamur Deo, detrectat agere pœnitentiam de peccatis suis et in eorum impia atque mortifera quadam suavitate perdurandum sibi esse decernit et in finem usque perdurat (*in Ep. ad Rom.* § 14; comp. § 22).

Quisquis igitur reus fuerit impœnitentiæ contra Spiritum in quo unitas et societas communionis congregatur Ecclesiæ nunquam illi remittetur; quia hoc sibi clausit ubi remittitur...(*Sermo* lxxi. 21, 34).

For chastisement is the way to restoration : Plane si in tantas ieris iniquitates ut repellas a te virgam verberantis, si repellas manum flagellantis et de disciplina Dei indigneris et fugias a Patre cædente et nolis eum Patrem pati quia non parcit peccanti, tu te alienasti ab hæreditate, ipse te non abjecit ; nam si maneres flagellatus non remaneres exhæreditatus (*in Psalm.* lxxxviii. *Serm.* ii. § 3).

CHRYSOSTOM, like several earlier writers, connects the passage in St John with the words of Eli (1 Sam. ii. 25), and finds the description of the sin in Ps. xlix. 18 ff. The fatal consequences which it brings are due to the accompanying wilful impenitence. ' How,' he adds, ' can (God) forgive ' one who does not allow that he has sinned, and does not repent ? For ' when we ask medicine from the physician we shew him the wound' (*in Ps.* xlix. § 7). CHRYSO- STOM.

In a letter attributed to GELASIUS the issue of the sin in death is made to lie wholly in impenitence. He has spoken of the sin of heretics against the Holy Spirit which was incapable of forgiveness as long as they persisted in it; and then he goes on : ' As the passage of the apostle ' John runs in like sense : *Est peccatum ad mortem, non dico ut oretur* ' *pro eo; et est peccatum non ad mortem, dico ut oretur pro eo.* There is ' a sin unto death when men abide in the same sin : there is a sin not ' unto death when men abandon the same sin. There is no sin for the ' remission of which the Church does not pray, or which it cannot absolve ' when men cease from it in virtue of the power given to it from God'... (*Cod. Can. Eccles.* xlvii. § 5; Migne, *Patrol. Lat.* lvi. p. 622). GELASIUS.

ŒCUMENIUS, in the same spirit, when commenting upon the passage sees the ground of the apostle's instruction in the absence of all signs of ŒCUME- NIUS.

repentance in him 'who sins a sin unto death.' The brother is not to pray for such an one, he says, 'for he will not be heard, because he asks amiss, 'speaking for one who shews no intention of return (περὶ τοῦ μηδεμίαν 'ἐπιδεικνυμένου ἐπιστροφήν). For this sin is alone unto death that has no 'regard to repentance (ἡ μὴ πρὸς μετάνοιαν ἀφορῶσα), from which Judas 'suffered and was brought under the eternal death' (ad loc.)[1].

Distinction of 'venial' and 'mortal' sins.

8. The language of St John gave occasion to the current distinction of sins as 'mortal' and 'venial.' In Augustine this distinction occurs frequently under the contrast of 'crimina' (in Joh. xli. 9 crimen est peccatum gravi accusatione et damnatione dignissimum) and 'peccata': c. duas Epp. Pel. i. § 28; in Ps. cxviii. 3, 2; de perfec. Just. Hom. ix. 20; Enchirid. c. lxiv. So he writes: Non peccata sola sunt illa quæ crimina nominantur, adulteria, fornicationes, sacrilegia, furta, rapinæ, falsa testimonia: non ipsa sola peccata sunt. Attendere aliquid quod non debebas peccatum est; audire aliquid libenter quod audiendum non fuit peccatum est; cogitare aliquid quod non fuit cogitandum peccatum est (Serm. cclxxi. 9, 9).

The later technical distinction is well summed up by RICHARD of St Victor who discussed the difference in a brief tract: Mortale peccatum, quantum mihi videtur, triplici recte ratione distinguitur. Mortale est quod a quovis non potest committi sine grandi corruptione sui. Item mortale est quod non potest committi sine gravi læsione proximi. Mortale nihilominus quod non potest committi sine magno contemptu Dei. Cetera vero omnia videntur mihi venialia (Migne, Patrol. Lat. 196, p. 1193).

Additional Note (1) on v. 20.   The idea of Life.

The idea of 'Life' in St John has been already touched upon in the note on i. 1; but it requires to be discussed somewhat more in detail. For the characteristic message which St John gives is of a life through which fellowship with man and God—the end of human existence—is perfectly realised.

i. The Source of Life.

The Father the source of life.

Of the Father alone it is said that He 'hath life in Himself' as the absolute final source of all life. This is the last limit of thought: John v. 26 ὁ πατὴρ ἔχει ζωὴν ἐν ἑαυτῷ, the Father hath life in Himself (comp. 1 Tim. vi. 16).

At the same time it is made known that the Father communicated to the Son the absolute possession of life: in this is expressed the idea of Sonship. The Son 'hath life in Himself,' but not as the final source of life. John v. 26 ὥσπερ ὁ πατὴρ ἔχει ζωὴν ἐν ἑαυτῷ, οὕτως καὶ τῷ υἱῷ ἔδωκεν

---

[1] In the Council of Troyes A.D. 879 it was forbidden to mention the names of those who had died under excommunication on the ground of this passage. Peccatum enim ad mortem, it is said, est perseverantia in peccato usque ad mortem (Conc. Tric. II. § 3). This widespread interpretation came from the ambiguity of the Latin preposition. See Bede above.

ζωὴν ἔχειν ἐν ἑαυτῷ, as *the Father hath life in Himself, even so gave He to the Son also to have life in Himself.* Compare John vi. 57 ζῶ διὰ τὸν πατέρα, and Apoc. i. 17. But men have not 'life in themselves,' either originally or by divine gift. Their life is a life of necessary, continuous, essential dependence (ἐν Χριστῷ 'in Christ,' according to St Paul's phrase). This must remain so to the end. Even when they participate in the virtue of Christ's humanity, they have life through Him and not in themselves: John vi. 57 (ὁ τρώγων), xiv. 19.

ii. *The Nature of Life.*

Three terms are used by St John to describe 'life' under different aspects :

(1) ἡ ζωή (the life), 'life which is truly life': c. iii. 14 note.

(2) ζωὴ αἰώνιος, 'eternal life' (not in Apoc.): c. i. 2 note.

Terms for 'life' and 'living' in St John.

For the shade of difference between ζωή and ζωὴ αἰώνιος see John iii. 36 (1 John iii. 14 f.; John v. 24).

(3) ἡ αἰώνιος ζωή (John xvii. 3; comp. Acts xiii. 46; 1 Tim. vi. 12); ἡ ζωὴ ἡ αἰώνιος (1 John i. 2, ii. 25), 'the eternal life': c. i. 2 note.

In connexion with those terms the following verbal phrases must also be noticed :

(1) ζῆν to live: John v. 25, vi. 57, xi. 25, xiv. 19; 1 John iv. 9 (Apoc. xx. 5). Comp. 1 Pet. iv. 6; 1 Thess. v. 10; 2 Cor. xiii. 4; Rom. viii. 13; Hebr. xii. 9.

(2) ζῆν εἰς τὸν αἰῶνα, 'to live for ever': John vi. 51, 58. Comp. Apoc. iv. 9, 10, xv. 7 ὁ ζῶν εἰς τοὺς αἰῶνας τῶν αἰώνων (peculiar to St John in N. T.).

(3) ἔχειν ζωήν, 'to have life': John x. 10, xx. 31; 1 John v. 12 (τὴν ζ.) (peculiar to St John in N. T.).

(4) ἔχειν ζωὴν αἰώνιον, 'to have eternal life': John iii. 15 f., 36, v. 24, vi. 40, 47, 54; 1 John v. 13 (iii. 15). Comp. Matt. xix. 16.

In considering these phrases it is necessary to premise that in spiritual things we must guard against all conclusions which rest upon the notions of succession and duration. 'Eternal life' is that which St Paul speaks of as ἡ ὄντως ζωή, 'the life which is life indeed' (1 Tim. vi. 19), and ἡ ζωὴ τοῦ θεοῦ, 'the life of God' (Eph. iv. 18). It is not an endless duration of being in time, but being of which time is not a measure. We have indeed no powers to grasp the idea except through forms and images of sense. These must be used; but we must not transfer them as realities to another order.

Eternal life essentially excludes time.

Life for a finite creature is union with God (comp. Col. i. 16, 17 ἐν αὐτῷ ἐκτίσθη τὰ πάντα...τὰ πάντα ἐν αὐτῷ συνέστηκεν; Acts xvii. 28 ἐν αὐτῷ ζῶμεν). Such union is for a rational being involved in a real and progressive knowledge of God in Christ. For spiritual knowledge is not external but sympathetic; and necessarily carries with it growing conformity to God. Hence 'the eternal life,' which Christ is and gave, is described as lying in the continuous effort to gain a fuller knowledge of God and Christ (John xvii. 3 ἵνα γινώσκωσιν); or, as the apostle writes out the Lord's words more fully: '*the Son of God hath come and hath given us understanding that we may*

Life lies in knowledge of, that is fellowship with, God.

'know (ἵνα γινώσκωμεν) Him that is true; and we are in Him that is true, 'in His Son Jesus Christ' (1 John v. 20). So it is that Christ's words are 'words of life' (John vi. 68; comp. vi. 63; viii. 51; xii. 50; James i. 18; Acts v. 20 is different). Real knowledge rests on fellowship and issues in fellowship.

Universal life.

Under this aspect all being is a revelation of life to man (John i. 4), which may become intelligible to him. The thought is one which is especially needed in an age of scientific analysis. We are tempted on all sides to substitute the mechanism, or the part, for the whole : the physical conditions or accompaniments for the vital force. The life is not in us only but in the world.

Individual life.

Under another aspect it can be said that the Gospel is 'the revelation of life,' and that in the Incarnation 'the life was made manifest.' By the personal coming of the Word in flesh the worth of individual life is shewn. He who 'lives' is conscious of power and office, and so far as he lives uses his power and fulfils his office.

The two lives one.

This view of life corresponds with and completes the former. All power is finally the gift of God: all office is for the accomplishment of His will. Life therefore is the use of the gifts of God according to the will of God. Or, to combine both notions, we are brought back to the original idea : life is fellowship with God, which includes fellowship with man, and this fellowship is realised in Christ.

iii.　Christ the Life.

Christ is the Life in Creation and in the New Creation.

Christ is 'the life' and that both in regard to the individual (John xi. 25 ἐγώ εἰμι ἡ ἀνάστασις καὶ ἡ ζωή I am the Resurrection and the Life) and in regard to the whole sum of being (John xiv. 6 ἐγώ εἰμι ἡ ὁδὸς καὶ ἡ ἀλήθεια καὶ ἡ ζωή, I am the Way and the Truth and the Life). Even before His Coming in flesh, the Creation which He sustained by His presence was a divine revelation (John i. 4); and by His Coming 'the life was manifested' and men recognised it (1 John i. 2).

He came that men may have life and the fulness of all that life needs (John x. 10 ζωὴν περισσὸν ἔχειν). The life which He gives is not and cannot be separated from Himself. Therefore, as things are, His Coming was crowned by His Passion and Exaltation (John iii. 15), whereby His Life was made available for others through Death (John xii. 32 (24)).

His offer of Life is universal (John vi. 51 ὁ ἄρτος ὃν ἐγὼ δώσω ἡ σάρξ μου ἐστὶν ὑπὲρ τῆς τοῦ κόσμου ζωῆς, the bread which I will give is my flesh for the life of the world). And the offer is made of the pure love of God (John iii. 16; 1 John iv. 10). The new creation is a work of spontaneous divine love even as the first creation, while it answered, necessarily answered, to the fulfilment of the divine idea (John i. 17 ἐγένετο.

In one sense the gift of life is made and complete (1 John v. 11 ζ. αἰ. ἔδωκεν ἡμῖν) ; but under another aspect it is still offered, promised, given (John x. 28 δίδωμι αὐτοῖς ζ. αἰ.; xvii. 2 ἵνα...δώσει ζ. αἰ.; 1 John ii. 25 ἐπαγγελία). The spiritually sick, if living in one sense, require 'life' (1 John v. 16 δώσει αὐτῷ ζωήν, τοῖς ἁμαρτάνουσιν μὴ πρὸς θάνατον : comp. John iv. 50). Comp. § v.

iv. *The Life of the Believer.*

The universal gift of life offered by Christ has to be personally appropri- The life ated (John vi. 35, 50 f., 58). In this process it comes through Christ, as the of the agent (1 John iv. 9 ἵνα ζήσωμεν δι᾿ αὐτοῦ, V. *per eum*: comp. John v. 40); is the and it comes for the sake of Christ, as the ground of quickening (John vi. 57 possession ζήσει δι᾿ ἐμέ, V. *propter me*), because He is what He is (1 John ii. 12). of the Liv- In other words the life of the believer follows from the life of Christ ing Son. (John xiv. 19 ὅτι ἐγὼ ζῶ καὶ ὑμεῖς ζήσεσθε, where the future is used in regard to the completer fulness of Christ's working ; comp. 2 Cor. iv. 10 f.; Col. iii. 4; Eph. ii. 5), and is realised in (that is, by union with) Him (John iii. 15; 1 John v. 11: comp. Rom. vi. 23; 2 Tim. i. 1), as He has been made known (John xx. 31 ζ. ἐχ. ἐν τῷ ὀνόματι αὐτοῦ). For the life is in the Living Son (1 John v. 11) and not in the letter of the Law (John v. 39); so that the possession of the Son is the possession of life (1 John v. 12, comp. Rom. v. 10 κατηλλάγημεν...διὰ τοῦ θανάτου...σωθησόμεθα ἐν τῇ ζωῇ αὐτοῦ). And he who is one with Christ is one with God (John xvii. 21 ἵνα ἐν ἡμῖν ὦσιν: comp. 1 John ii. 24 f.; John vi. 56 f.).

For the believer the transition from death to life has been made In the (John v. 24; 1 John iii. 14 μεταβεβήκαμεν ἐκ τοῦ θανάτου εἰς τὴν ζωήν: realisation comp. 1 John v. 12). But the consequences of the transition are realised, man as the transition itself is conditioned, by the activity of faith (John iii. 16, 36, unites . vi. 47, xx. 31; 1 John v. 13 [ὁ πιστεύων, οἱ πιστεύοντες]; John vi. 40 ὁ with God θεωρῶν καὶ πιστεύων)[1]. So man in a true sense works with God; and in by faith. John i. 12 the human and divine elements in the beginning, the growth and the issue of life are set side by side in a striking parallelism (ἐγεν- νήθησαν, ἐξουσίαν, τέκνα—ἔλαβον, πιστεύουσιν, γενέσθαι). By this energy of faith the believer finds union with Christ's humanity (John vi. 51, 54, 58: comp. vi. 35, 56, 58, x. 10).

v. *Life present and future.*

The life which lies in fellowship with God in Christ is, as has been Eternal seen already, spoken of as 'eternal' life in order to distinguish it from the life, life of sense and time under which true human existence is veiled at present. Such a life of phenomena may be 'death' (1 John iii. 14: comp. v. 16). But 'eternal life' is beyond the limitations of time: it belongs to the being of God (1 John i. 2 ἦν πρὸς τὸν πατέρα), and finds its con- summation in the transforming vision of the Son seen as He is (1 John iii. 2; John xiv. 23, 2 f.). For us now therefore it is spoken of as both present and future.

1. The 'life eternal' is essentially present, so far as it is the potential present fulfilment of the idea of humanity (John iii. 36, v. 24, vi. 47, 54, xx. 31; and

---

[1] In all these places the force of the present participle is conspicuous. St John uses the aor. partic. once only: John xx. 29. The force of the present can be seen by contrast with the aorist: [Mark] xvi. 16 f.; Luke i. 45, viii. 12; Acts iv. 32, xi. 21, xix. 2; 2 Thess. i. 10, ii. 12; Eph. i. 13; Hebr. iv. 3; Jude 5; and again with the perfect: Acts xv. 5, xvi. 34; [xviii. 27, xix. 18;] xxi. 20, 25; Tit. iii. 8.

1 John v. 12); and the possession of life may become a matter of actual knowledge (1 John v. 13: comp. 1 John iii. 15).

This thought of the present reality of 'eternal life' is characteristic of St John, and in its full development is peculiar to him (but comp. Gal. ii. 20).

future.   2. At the same time the life is regarded as future in its complete realisation, so far as it is the fulfilment of Messianic promises (John iv. 14, 36, vi. 27, xii. 25, v. 25, vi. 57, xi. 25, xiv. 19, vi. 54: compare 1 John ii. 25, iii. 2; and also Mark x. 30; Gal. vi. 8).

Hence it is intelligible how 'eternal life' is spoken of as 'the commandment' of the Father (John xii. 50); and again as the progressive knowledge of the Father in the Son (1 John v. 20). For the commandment of God is represented to us in the work of Christ; and to embrace this in faithful obedience is to 'have life in His name' (John xx. 31), on which we believe (1 John v. 13) with growing intelligence.

If now we endeavour to bring together the different traits of 'the eternal life' we see that it is a life which with all its fulness and all its potencies is *now*: a life which extends beyond the limits of the individual, and preserves, completes, crowns individuality by placing the part in connexion with the whole: a life which satisfies while it quickens aspiration: a life which is seen, as we regard it patiently, to be capable of conquering, reconciling, uniting the rebellious, discordant, broken elements of being on which we look and which we bear about with us: a life which gives unity to the constituent parts and to the complex whole, which brings together heaven and earth, which offers the sum of existence in one thought. As we reach forth to grasp it, the revelation of God is seen to have been unfolded in its parts in Creation; and the parts are seen to have been brought together again by the Incarnation.

Additional Note (2) on v. 20. ‘The true God.’

'The true God' answers to the words 'God is love.'

When St John speaks of God as 'He that is true' (ὁ ἀληθινός), He who alone (John xvii. 3 ὁ μόνος ἀληθινὸς θεός) and absolutely fulfils the idea of God which man is constituted to form, and then in significant and mysterious words identifies union with 'Him that is true,' with union 'with His Son Jesus Christ,' he explains in the terms of historical revelation that which is involved in the statement 'God is love.' He indicates in what way the 'personality' of God is to be held and guarded from false conclusions. St John, as all the biblical writers, everywhere uses language of God which assigns to Him 'action' and 'will.' But, as far as our human observation reaches, 'will' implies resistance, and 'action' implies succession. Such limitations can find no place in the idea of God. The conception of 'personality' which we can form therefore expresses only a fragment of the truth, that side of it which assures us of the possibility of approach to God on our part as to One Who loves and may be loved.

'Personality' as applied to God.

Love involves a 'tri-personality.'

But we cannot rest here. When we endeavour to think of God Himself we are necessarily led to inquire whether Scripture does not help us to rise to a thought in which we can see represented from the divine side that which is in the Divine Being the analogue of sole-personality in a finite being. This thought we find in the words 'God is love.' The phrase, as we have seen, describes the essence and not an attribute of God. It presents to us, as far as we can apprehend the truth, something of God in Himself. It must hold good of God in His innermost Being, if we may so speak, apart from creation. Now love involves a subject and an object, and that which unites both. We are taught then to conceive of God as having in Himself the perfect object of love and the perfect response of love, completely self-sufficing and self-complete. We thus gain, however imperfect language may be, the idea of a tri-personality in an Infinite Being as correlative to a sole-personality in a finite being. In the Unity of Him Who is One we acknowledge the Father, the Son and the Holy Spirit, in the interaction of Whom we can see love fulfilled.

The language in John i. 1, where we have opened a unique view of the Divine Being without any regard to a revelation to man, indicates the same thought. The relation of 'the Word' to 'God' is described as a relation of active love: ὁ λόγος ἦν πρὸς τὸν θεόν, the personal energy of the Word was directed towards, and (so to speak) regulated by 'God,' while the Word Himself 'was God.' In the Epistle the thought is presented differently. There it is 'the Life' and not 'the Word' which is spoken of. The conception of 'the Life' is wider in its range than that of 'the Word,' though it is through 'the Word' that 'the Life' is revealed. This life is 'the life eternal.' It is not of this temporal order though it is made known in it, under its limitations. It is a life which essentially finds its original in the Godhead: ἦν πρὸς τὸν πατέρα, it was realised in the intercommunion of the Divine Persons, when time was not. Thus we have in this twofold revelation of an activity of 'the Word' towards 'God,' of a fulfilment of 'Life' towards 'the Father,' beyond time, such a vision as we can look upon of the fulness of the Being of God in Himself. And when 'the Word' and 'the Life' are brought within the sphere of human existence, this action is characteristically described: 'the Life was manifested': 'the Word became flesh.' *This fact indicated in the opening words of the Gospel, and of the Epistle.*

Nothing is said in either passage directly of the Holy Spirit. But His action is involved in the phrase ἦν πρός in such a connexion. He is, so to seek a definite expression for the idea, the Mediating Power through Whom the love that goes forth is perfectly united with the love that answers. He gives unity to the Life, which we can only conceive of in fragments.

It will be evident that this view of the nature of God prepares the way for revelation. The Word, Who is God (θεός and not ὁ θεός as in Sabellian teaching), has a personal Being and can make the Father known (1 John ii. 22 ff.). The Spirit, Who is God, has a personal Being, and can make the Son known (John xiv. 26, xvi. 14). At the same time, while this fulness of life fulfilled in God Himself is disclosed to us, the divine unity is maintained as essential and not numerical. The Word and the Spirit are both spoken of in personal relations to 'God' (John i. 1; 32 f.). That is when the Persons in the Godhead are recognised, the unity of God is simultaneously affirmed. *This tri-personality opens the way for revelation.*

Such glimpses are opened to us of the absolute tri-personality of God as *Elsewhere*

St John speaks of 'the Economic Trinity.' preparatory to the account of the historical Gospel by St John, but elsewhere, like the other apostolic writers, he deals with the Trinity revealed in the work of Redemption ('the Economic Trinity'). The Father is spoken of in His relation to the Incarnate Son, and through Him to men. The Son is spoken of as manifested to men through the Incarnation in the union of the two natures (yet comp. John v. 26). The Holy Spirit is spoken of as 'proceeding' on His Mission to the Church (John xv. 26 note), sent by the Father and by the Son; and taking of that which is the Son's to declare to men (John xiv. 26, xv. 26, xvi. 14; 1 John ii. 20 f., 27). The truths are stated side by side in connexion with our creation, redemption, sanctification; and we are enabled to see that they answer in some way, which we have no power to determine adequately, to the very Being of God as He is in Himself.

Two errors to be avoided: Arian, and Sabellian. The maintenance of the supreme Sovereignty of One God (μοναρχία) in this tri-personality has to be guarded against a twofold tendency to error : (1) towards a distinction in essence between God and Christ (the Father and the Son); and (2) towards a confusion of the Persons of the Father and the Son and the Spirit. The first error found its typical expression in Arianism : the second in Sabellianism. The first has affinities with Polytheism by introducing the idea of a subordinate Divinity. The second has affinities with Pantheism, as seeing in things transitory manifestations of the Person of God. Both rest upon a false Neo-Judaic conception of Monotheism.

The dualism of the subordination of the Son in Person not in essence. The authority of St John has been brought forward in support of each of these views : for the first John xiv. 28 (see note, and Compare Athanas. de Syn. § 28); and for the second John x. 30 (see note, and compare Tertull. adv. Prax. cc. xx. xxii.). It must however be noticed that the great Greek Fathers understood the first passage of the Personal Subordination of the Son as Son to the Father in the one equal and absolute Godhead. And this view, which has been obscured in the West by the teaching of Augustine, is of the highest importance ; for it leads to the apprehension of the fitness of the mediatorial and consummative work of the Son. The assumption of humanity and the laying aside of the divine conditions of existence by the Son are everywhere spoken of by St John as voluntary acts. They correspond therefore to the Being of the Son as Son, for we cannot conceive of the Father or of the Spirit as Incarnate. In other words the unchanged and unchangeable ' I ' of the Word, the Son, includes either the potentiality or the fact of the Incarnation, the union with the finite.

ΙΩΑΝΟΥ Β

ΙΩΑΝΟΥ Β

Ο ΠΡΕΣΒΥΤΕΡΟΣ ἐκλεκτῇ κυρίᾳ καὶ τοῖς τέκ-

The structure of the letter is simple and natural. It consists of (1) the salutation (1—3); (2) the counsel and warning (4—11); (3) the conclusion (12, 13). Whatever may be the interpretation of the individual address in *vv.* 5, 13, the main part of the letter is addressed to more readers than one (*v.* 6 ἠκούσατε, περιπατῆτε, *v.* 8 βλέπετε ἑαυτούς, *v.* 10 πρὸς ὑμᾶς, *v.* 12 ὑμῖν, πρὸς ὑμᾶς, ἡ χαρὰ ὑμῶν).

1. *The Salutation* (1—3).

The salutation is framed on the usual type : ὁ πρεσβύτερος ἐκλεκτῇ κυρίᾳ... ...χάρις ἔλεος εἰρήνη παρὰ θεοῦ πατρός, καὶ παρὰ Ἰησοῦ Χριστοῦ...But this outline is filled up by successive amplifications as the apostle dwells on each word which he writes in relation to the circumstances of the case. In this respect the Salutation may be compared with that in the Epistle to the Galatians, where in like manner St Paul expands his usual formula in view of the peculiar condition of the Churches which he is addressing.

¹ *The Elder to one who is an elect lady and her children, whom I love in truth ; and not I only but also all they that know the truth ;* ²*for the truth's sake which abideth in us—and it shall be with us for ever :* ³*grace, mercy, peace, shall be with us from God the Father, and from Jesus*

Christ the Son of the Father, in truth and love.

1. ὁ πρεσβύτερος] *Senior* V. *The elder.* The definite form of the title marks the writer as completely identified by it. In this connexion there can be little doubt that it describes not age simply but official position. The writer was recognised by the receiver of the Epistle as 'the Elder.'

The title 'elder' appears to have had special currency in the Asiatic Churches, where it was used of a particular class (Papias ap. Euseb. *H. E.* iii. f.; Iren. v. 33. 3; 36. 2); yet not without a recognition of the Apostles as 'the elders' in point of time (Papias, *l. c.*). It is easy to see why St John would choose such a title, which, while it described official position, suggested also a fatherly relation, and perhaps even pointed to intercourse with Christ (1 Pet. v. 1). For the history of the word πρεσβύτερος see Lightfoot, *Philippians,* pp. 228 f.

ἐκλεκτῇ κυρίᾳ] *electæ dominæ* V. The rendering of the phrase is beset by the greatest difficulties. No interpretation can be accepted as satisfactory.

The difficulty seems to have been felt from a very early time. Two distinct views have found support, that the title describes a person, and that it describes a society.

νοις αὐτῆς, οὓς ἐγὼ ἀγαπῶ ἐν ἀληθείᾳ, καὶ οὐκ ἐγὼ

1 καὶ οὐκ ἐγώ **NB** vg me the syrhl: οὐκ ἐγὼ δέ A.

The first view has been held in several different forms. The Latin fragments of the *Hypotyposes* of Clement of Alexandria represent the letter as written 'to a certain Babylonian (comp. 1 Pet. v. 13) Electa by name' (ad quandam Babyloniam Electam nomine); 'it signifies however' (that is, this proper name, *Electa*), Clement adds, 'the election of the holy Church.'

Others again (so the [late] Syrian version) have regarded Κυρία as a proper name ('to the elect Kyria'). Such a name is found (see Lücke, 444 n.); but if Κυρία were so used here it is in the highest degree unlikely that St John would have written ἐκλεκτῇ Κυρίᾳ, and not Κυρίᾳ τῇ ἐκλεκτῇ as *v.* 13; 3 John 1; Rom. xvi. 13.

It has also been supposed that the two words form a compound proper name ('to Electa Kyria'). This view removes the difficulty of the construction; but the combination is at least very strange.

On the other hand it is not easy to suppose that the letter was addressed to an unnamed person, a single Christian 'lady' ('To an elect lady,' so Vulg.); though this is the most natural rendering of the text (comp. 1 Pet. i. 1).

All these notions of a personal address moreover are unsupported by such allusions in the letter as might be expected to mark an individual relationship.

Feeling these difficulties many from the time of Jerome (*Ep.* cxxiii. (xi.) § 12 *ad Ageruchiam*) have taken the title, the 'elect lady,' to be applied to some particular Christian society (Schol. ap. Matt. ἐκλεκτὴν Κυρίαν λέγει τὴν ἐν τινὶ τόπῳ ἐκκλησίαν ὡς τὴν τοῦ Κυρίου διδασκαλίαν ἀκριβῆ φυλάττουσαν...), or even to the whole Church: 'to her who is a chosen Lady, a

Bride of Him who is the Lord.' But of such a use of Κυρία no example is quoted.

On the whole it is best to recognise that the problem of the address is insoluble with our present knowledge. It is not unlikely that it contains some allusion, intelligible under the original circumstances, to which we have lost the key. But the general tenour of the letter favours the opinion that it was sent to a community and not to one believer.

τοῖς τέκνοις αὐ.] *natis eius* V., *her children*. The phrase can be understood either literally, 1 Tim. iii. 4; or spiritually, 1 Tim. i. 2; Gal. iv. 25. Comp. Apoc. ii. 23. The context here and the use of the term in *vv.* 4, 13 (comp. 3 John 4) favour the spiritual sense. It has been suggested that the 'children' may have been orphans or the like committed to the 'lady's' care, some of whom had gone out into the world while others were still with her.

οὓς ἐγὼ ἀγ.] *whom*, mother alike and children, *I love*. It seems better to take this comprehensive sense than to refer the relative to the children only.

The emphasis which is laid upon the apostle's feeling (ἐγὼ ἀγ.) points to some unknown facts (compare 3 John 5). Both the shorter letters imply the existence of divisions in the societies to which they were directed; and St John brings his authority to bear against those from whom the persons addressed may have suffered.

ἐν ἀληθείᾳ] *in truth*, that is with a feeling which rightly deserves the name; see John xvii. 19 note; Col. i. 6.

καὶ οὐκ ἐγὼ μόνος...] *and not I alone* (*solus* V.), a single person, *but also all that have come to know the truth*. The love is directed to a character.

μόνος ἀλλὰ καὶ πάντες οἱ ἐγνωκότες τὴν ἀλήθειαν, ²διὰ
τὴν ἀλήθειαν τ:ὴν μένουσαν ἐν ἡμῖν, καὶ μεθ᾽ ἡμῶν ἔσται
εἰς τὸν αἰῶνα· ³ἔσται μεθ᾽ ἡμῶν χάρις ἔλεος εἰρήνη παρὰ

2 μένουσαν : ἐνοικοῦσαν Α.   3 ἔσ. μεθ᾽ ἡμῶν (ὑμῶν me) : om. A.   παρὰ
θ.: ἀπὸ θ. ℵ*.

Wherever the character exists, the love exists. This is made clear by the words which follow. The love felt by St John and by those whom he describes is felt 'for the truth's sake...'

μόνος] Luke xxiv. 18; Hebr. ix. 7. Contrast 2 Tim. iv. 8 οὐ μόνον ἐμοί (1 John ii. 2); Rom. iii. 29.

ἐγνωκότες] 1 John ii. 3 note. John viii. 32. Contrast 1 John ii. 21 οὐκ οἴδατε τὴν ἀλ.

τὴν ἀλ.] the truth, which is identical with Christ's message (John i. 17), and with Christ's Person (John xiv. 7). Comp. 1 John i. 6, 8, notes.

2. The common acknowledgment of the eternal Truth is the certain foundation of love.

διὰ τὴν ἀλ.] The words recal ἐν ἀλ. The Truth makes true love possible. This Truth is not said to abide 'in you' or 'in them,' but 'in us.' The apostle at once identifies himself with the whole society of the faithful. Compare v. 5 ἵνα ἀγαπῶμεν. 1 John i. 4 (ἡμῶν).

τὴν μένουσαν ἐν ἡ.] See 1 John iii. 15 note.

καὶ μεθ᾽ ἡ. ἔσται] and with us it shall be. The position of μεθ᾽ ἡ. emphasises the peculiar privileges of those whom St John identifies with himself. The change of construction from the participle to the finite verb (μένουσαν...ἔσται) answers to a pause during which the writer contemplates the fact which he has affirmed, and then solemnly confirms the fulness of his faith in it. Compare 1 John iii. 1 καὶ ἐσμέν, i. 2 note.

μεθ᾽ ἡμῶν] with us and not only in us. The Truth itself has through Christ a personal power. Comp. 1 John iv. 17. The different relations

of the Paraclete to believers are described in John xiv. 16 f. by μετά, παρά, ἐν.

εἰς τὸν αἰῶνα] See 1 John ii. 17 note.

3. ἔσται μεθ᾽ ἡμῶν...] There shall be with us... This unique form of salutation seems to have been determined by the preceding clause (μεθ᾽ ἡμῶν ἔσται): 'with us truth shall be ...yes, there shall be with us...' The wish passes into assurance. In the Epistles of St Paul no verb is expressed in the salutation (e.g. 1 Thess. i. 1, χάρις ὑμῖν καὶ εἰρήνη). In 1, 2 Peter, Jude πληθυνθείη is added (1 Pet. i. 1 χάρις ὑμῖν καὶ εἰρήνη πληθ.).

μεθ᾽ ἡμῶν] v. 2. The readers are identified with the writer.

, χάρ. ἔλ. εἰρ.] The succession 'grace, mercy, peace' marks the order from the first motion of God to the final satisfaction of man. 'Mercy' defines as it were the manifestation of the divine 'grace' and prepares for the restoration of 'peace' to man's disordered life.

The same combination occurs in salutations in 1 Tim. i. 2; 2 Tim. i. 2 (Ign. ad Smyrn. 12). Χάρις καὶ εἰρήνη is found in Apoc. i. 4; 1 Pet. i. 2; 2 Pet. i. 2, and in all the other Epistles of St Paul. In St Jude 2 the salutation is ἔλεος καὶ εἰρήνη καὶ ἀγάπη. (Comp. Mart. Pol. Inscr.)

χάρις ἔλεος...] The word χάρις occurs elsewhere in St John only in 3 John 4; John i. 14, 16, 17; Apoc. i. 4; xxii. 21; and the absence of the cognate forms (χαρίζομαι, χάρισμα) from his writings is worthy of notice. Ἔλεος is not found elsewhere in his writings nor yet ἐλεεῖν.

In regard to the divine action 'grace' points to the absolute free-

θεοῦ πατρός, καὶ παρὰ Ἰησοῦ Χριστοῦ τοῦ υἱοῦ τοῦ
πατρός, ἐν ἀληθείᾳ καὶ ἀγάπη.

om. παρά (2°) ℵ*.   Ἰησοῦ AB vg the: +κυρίου Ἰ. 5ℵ me syr hl.   τοῦ
π.: +αὐτοῦ τοῦ π. ℵ*.

dom of God's love in relation to man's
helplessness to win it; and 'mercy' to
His tenderness towards man's misery.
εἰρήνη] John xiv. 27; xvi. 33; xx.
19, 21, 26. The peace which is the
gift of 'the God of peace' (1 Thess. v.
23; Rom. xv. 33; xvi. 20; Phil. iv. 9;
Heb. xiii. 20) answers to all the dis-
harmonies of being in man himself, in
his relation to his fellow-men and to
God, and in creation generally. Compare especially Rom. viii. 6; Eph. ii.
14 ff.

παρά...παρά...] The repetition of
the preposition in such a form is
unique. It serves to bring out distinctly the twofold personal relation
of man to the Father and to the Son.
Elsewhere in parallel cases the preposition used is always ἀπό: e.g. Rom.
i. 7; 1 Cor. i. 3, &c. Comp. 2 Tim.
i. 18.

θεοῦ πατρός] God the Father: more
commonly God our Father (θ. π.
ἡμῶν), e.g. Rom. i. 7; 1 Cor. i. 3 &c.
Comp. 1 Tim. i. 2; 2 Tim. i. 2; Tit. i.
4; Eph. vi. 23; Col. iii. 17. Special
stress is laid upon the revelation of
God in this absolute character. Comp.
v. 9.

Ἰ. Χρ. τοῦ υἱοῦ τοῦ π.] The phrase
is unique. It seems to have been
chosen to connect the revelation of
the Father as definitely as possible
with the Son. Comp. 1 John ii. 22 f.;
and 1 John i. 3; Col. i. 13.

It may be noticed that the title
'Lord' (κυρίου Ἰ.), which is added by
some early authorities, is not found
in the Epistles of St John, though it
occurs in every other book of the N.T.
except the Epistle to Titus.

ἐν ἀλ. καὶ ἀγ.] The threefold divine
gift is realised perfectly both in regard
to thought and in regard to action.
Truth and love describe an intellec-

tual harmony and a moral harmony;
and the two correspond with each
other according to their subject-
matter. Love is truth in human action;
and truth is love in regard to the
order of things.

The combination is not found elsewhere.

2. Counsel and warning (4—11).

The rise of false teachers, who seem
to have affected superior knowledge
(v. 9 προάγων), and neglected moral
duties (comp. 1 John ii. 4), leads St
John to emphasise the duty of active
love, which is the sum of the divine
commandments (4—7); and then to
insist upon the necessity of guarding
inviolate 'the teaching of Christ,' the
historic Gospel which conveys the revelation of 'the Father and the Son'
(8—11).

4—7. Past faithfulness is made the
foundation for the apostle's counsel
(v. 4). He enjoins practical love because deceivers have arisen who by
denying the coming of Jesus Christ
in flesh deprive earthly life of its
divine significance (5—7).

4 I rejoice greatly that I have
found of thy children walking in
truth, even as we received commandment from the Father. 5 And now
I pray thee, Lady, not as writing
a new commandment to thee, but
that which we had from the beginning, that we love one another. 6 And
this is love, that we should walk according to His commandments. This
is the commandment even as ye heard
from the beginning, that ye should
walk in it (love). 7 Because many
deceivers are gone out (went out) into
the world, even they that confess not
Jesus Christ coming in flesh: this is
the deceiver and the antichrist.

⁴Ἐχάρην λίαν ὅτι εὕρηκα ἐκ τῶν τέκνων σου περιπατοῦντας ἐν ἀληθείᾳ, καθὼς ἐντολὴν ἐλάβομεν παρὰ τοῦ πατρός. ⁵καὶ νῦν ἐρωτῶ σε, κυρία, οὐχ ὡς ἐντολὴν γράφων σοι καινὴν ἀλλὰ ἣν εἴχαμεν ἀπ᾽ ἀρχῆς, ἵνα

4 ἐλάβομεν: ἔλαβον ℵ.　　παρά: ἀπό A.　　τοῦ π.: om. τοῦ B.
5 γράφων σοι καινήν B the: καινὴν γρ. σοι ℵA vg me.　　ἀλλά: +ἐντολήν ℵ
(+ an old commandment syr hl).

4. Ἐχάρην...ὅτι εὕρηκα] *I rejoiced ...that I have found*... The joy is referred to its initial moment: the ground of it still continues.

For the precedence given to the expression of joy compare St Paul's thanksgivings: 1 Thess. i. 2; 2 Thess. i. 3; 1 Cor. i. 4; Rom. i. 8; Phil. i. 3 f.; Eph. i. 16; Col. i. 3; Philem. 4.

εὕρηκα] Comp. 3 John 3; and John i. 44, note.

ἐκ τῶν τ. σ.] V. *de filiis tuis. Some of thy children.* For ἐκ see John xvi. 17.

The words appear to refer to an experience of the writer in some other place than that to which the 'Lady' belonged.

περιπ. ἐν ἀλ., καθώς...] *walking in truth even as*... The phrase (περιπ. ἐν ἀλ. 3 John 3) is not identical with *walking in the truth* (περιπ. ἐν τῇ ἀλ. 3 John 4). Comp. John xvii. 17, 19. It describes the general character of the life as conducted 'in truth,' really and in very deed in a certain fashion, even after the commandment of God.

ἐντ. ἐλάβ.] John x. 18; Acts xvii. 15; Col. iv. 10.

παρὰ τοῦ π.] *from the Father* in the Person of Christ. The preposition (*v.* 3) marks the directness of the divine injunction: Apoc. ii. 27.

5. καὶ νῦν] *and now*, looking back upon that former feeling (*v.* 4) of joy... The words may mark simply a logical connexion: 1 John ii. 28.

ἐρωτῶ] *I pray thee*, in the exercise of the full privilege of Christian fellowship. Comp. 1 John v. 16, note.

The request is directly personal and not a general exhortation (παρακαλῶ). It is remarkable that the words παρακαλεῖν, παράκλησις, do not occur in the writings of St John. The singular address (σέ) occurs again in *v.* 13. In the intermediate verses the plural is used.

οὐχ ὡς ἐντ....] *not as writing a new commandment*... The order is significant (ἐντ. γράφων σ. κ.). The prayer is first distinguished from a command generally: 'I pray thee, not as writing a command to thee'; and then the command is more exactly described, which is indeed the substance of the prayer. Comp. 1 John ii. 7.

εἴχαμεν] *we had.* Contrast 1 John ii. 7 *ye had.* Throughout the apostle identifies himself with those to whom he is writing, Christian with Christians.

ἵνα ἀγαπῶμεν...] *that we love*... The words seem to depend upon *I pray thee* (John xvii. 15), the intervening clause being parenthetical. The apostle includes himself in the object of his prayer (*that we*, not *that ye*). It is possible that the form in which the request is thus shaped is occasioned by the reference to 'the command which we had.'

ἐρωτῶ σε...ἵνα...] *I pray thee...that...* The infinitive and a final particle are both used by St John after ἐρωτᾶν: (1) *infin.* John iv. 40 ‖ Luke v. 3; viii. 37; Acts iii. 3; x. 48; xvi. 39; xviii. 20; xxiii. 18; 1 Th. v. 12. (2) ἵνα John iv. 47; xix. 31, 38 ‖ Mk. vii. 26; Luke vii. 36 (vii. 3; xi. 37 ὅπως); xvi. 27 (Acts xxiii. 20 ὅπως).

ἀγαπῶμεν ἀλλήλους. ⁶καὶ αὕτη ἐστὶν ἡ ἀγάπη, ἵνα
περιπατῶμεν κατὰ τὰς ἐντολὰς αὐτοῦ· αὕτη ἡ ἐντολή
ἐστιν, καθὼς ἠκούσατε ἀπ᾽ ἀρχῆς, ἵνα ἐν αὐτῇ περιπατῆτε. ⁷ὅτι πολλοὶ πλάνοι ἐξῆλθαν εἰς τὸν κόσμον, οἱ

6 αὐτοῦ: +'ἵνα καθώς' ℵ* (by the omission of a line of the archetype in
copying).   ἡ ἐντ. ἐ. AB (vg) syr hl: ἐ. ἡ ἐντ. ϛℵ me the.   ἡ ἐντ.: +αὐτοῦ ℵ.
καθώς...ἵνα ἐν αὐτῇ... B syr hl: ἵνα καθώς...ἵνα ἐν αὐτῇ... ℵA: ἵνα καθώς...ἐν αὐτῇ
(vg) (me) (the).   περιπατῆτε: περιπατήσητε ℵ.   7 ἐξῆλθαν: εἰσῆλθον ϛ.

6. The two thoughts of 'commandment' and 'love' are taken up in the
inverse order: 'this is love,' 'this is
the commandment.' In treating them
St John appears to reason in a circle.
'Love,' he says, 'is the effort to walk
according to the divine commandments'; and again, 'The divine commandment is that we endeavour to
walk in love.' The key to this difficulty lies in the difference between
'commandments' and 'commandment.'
Love strives to realise in detail every
separate expression of the will of
God. The summary expression of the
will of God is that men should walk
in love, the spirit of sons (1 John
iii. 1).

καὶ αὕτη ἐ. ἡ ἀγ.] And this is love...
The description of love is simply
joined to the request to realise it:
1 John v. 4, 11. 'Love' is left completely undefined. Love to God and
love to man are not finally distinguished. Comp. 1 John iii. 16; iv.
10, 16—18.

αὕτη...ἵνα...] See 1 John v. 3, note.
περιπ. κατὰ τὰς ἐ. αὐ.] walk according to... Compare Mk. vii. 5 περιπ.
κατὰ τὴν παράδοσιν...; 2 Cor. x. 2;
Rom. viii. 4 κατὰ σάρκα (πνεῦμα) περιπ.;
Rom. xiv. 15 κατὰ ἀγάπην περιπ.; 1
Cor. iii. 3 κατὰ ἄνθρωπον περιπ. Elsewhere the construction is περιπ. ἐν (1
John i. 6, note). The two constructions stand side by side 2 Cor. x. 2 f.

αὕτη ἡ ἐντ. ἐ....] this is the commandment which gathers up in one the
many commandments. Compare 1
John iii. 22, 23. The change of order

from the first clause is significant
(αὕτη ἐστ. ἡ ἀγ., αὕτη ἡ ἐντ. ἐ.).

ἠκούσατε...περιπατῆτε...] ye heard
...ye walk... The second person is required by the definite reference to the
first teaching of the Church: 1 John
ii. 7, note.

ἵνα ἐν αὐτῇ περιπ.] that ye walk in
it, that is in love, which is the main
subject of the sentence (comp. Eph.
v. 2). No adequate sense is gained by
supplying in the commandment (in
eo V., sc. mandato). The complete
identification of the life of love with
the fulfilment of all the commandments of God is characteristic of St
John: 1 John v. 2, 3.

7. The peril which arises from
false teachers moves St John to stir
believers to the active exercise of love
one with the other. Love so realised
is a safeguard against error. On the
other hand the failure to realise the
Lord's true humanity in the present
imperils the love of man for man.
There is a passage here from 'love' to
'truth' (v. 3 ἐν ἀλ. καὶ ἀγ.).

πλάνοι] seductores V., seducers, deceivers, who lead to wrong action,
and not only to wrong opinion. Comp.
1 John ii. 26 οἱ πλανῶντες. 1 Tim.
iv. 1 πνεύμασι πλάνοις. 2 Cor. vi. 8 ὡς
πλάνοι; Matt. xxvii. 63.

ἐξῆλθαν] went out. The tense (1
John ii. 19) appears to mark a particular crisis. They went out from the
bosom of the Christian society to fulfil
their work.

πολλοί...οἱ μὴ ὁμολ.] The participial clause does not only assert a

μὴ ὁμολογοῦντες Ἰησοῦν Χριστὸν ἐρχόμενον ἐν σαρκί·
οὗτός ἐστιν ὁ πλάνος καὶ ὁ ἀντίχριστος.   ⁸Βλέπετε
ἑαυτούς, ἵνα μὴ ἀπολέσητε ἃ ἠργασάμεθα, ἀλλὰ μισθὸν

ὁ ἀντίχρ.: om. ὁ ℵ.   8 ἀπολέσητε ἃ ἠργασάμεθα...ἀπολάβητε B the (syr hl):
ἀπολέσητε ἃ εἰργάσασθε ...ἀπολάβητε (ℵ) A vg me (syr hl): ἀπολέσαμεν ἃ εἰργα-
σάμεθα...ἀπολάβωμεν ς.   ἀπόλησθε ℵ*.

definite fact as to these deceivers (οὐχ ὁμολογοῦντες), but marks the character of the class (comp. 1 John iv. 3): 'even they that confess not.' See Mk. xv. 41 ἄλλαι πολλαὶ αἱ συναναβᾶσαι.

οἱ μὴ ὁμ.] they who confess not... The frank and open confession of the truth is required. Not to make confession, even when this does not take the form of denial, becomes practically identical with it. Comp. John i. 20; 1 John iv. 2, 3.

Ἰ. Χρ. ἐρχ. ἐν σ.] Jesus Christ coming in flesh. The thought centres upon the present perfection of the Lord's Manhood which is still, and is to be manifested, and not upon the past fact of His coming, 1 John iv. 2 (ἐληλυθότα): 1 John v. 6 (ὁ ἐλθών). Comp. John xiv. 3, note; i. 9 ἦν— ἐρχόμενον. Apoc. xxii. 20. Cf. ἡ ὀργὴ ἡ ἐρχ. 1 Thess. i. 10; Col. iii. 6.

οὗτός ἐστιν...] this is... The general description is individualised. He that offers this character is the deceiver— the typical deceiver—and the antichrist. We might perhaps look for other marks: these are decisive. Comp. v. 9; 1 John ii. 22; v. 6, 20.

ὁ ἀντίχρ.] the antichrist, of whom the readers had already heard. 1 John ii. 18, note.

The idea of the 'deceiver' is mainly relative to men: that of 'antichrist' to the Lord.

8, 9. The action of false teachers imposes upon believers the duty of self-examination. The danger which they embody is internal as well as external. There must be a careful watch within; and this necessity is shewn to be more urgent by the consideration

that what seems and claims to be progress may be fatal error.

⁸Look to yourselves, that ye may not lose (destroy) the things which we wrought, but may receive a full reward.   ⁹Every one that goeth forward and abideth not in the teaching of Christ hath not God: he that abideth in the teaching, the same hath both the Father and the Son.   ¹⁰If any one cometh unto you, and beareth not this teaching, receive him not into your house, and give him no greeting;   ¹¹for he that giveth him greeting hath fellowship with his evil works.

8.   Βλέπετε ἑαυτ.] Videte vosmet ipsos V., Look to yourselves that... Mark xiii. 9; 1 Cor. xvi. 10.

ἵνα μὴ ἀπολ....] ne perdatis...V., that ye may not lose (or destroy) what we wrought, the manifold results of our labours among you, which were as talents entrusted to your charge for use.

For the confidence of the apostle see 1 John iv. 6; but the word ἠργασάμεθα appears to refer to the apostolic teachers generally.

ἀλλά...ἀπολ.] accipiamusV.,but may receive, receive back, from the Great Judge... Comp. Luke vi. 34; xv. 27; xvi. 25; xxiii. 41; Rom. i. 27; Gal. iv. 5 (non accipiamus sed recipiamus, Aug.).

μισθ. πλ.] mercedem plenam V., a full reward, in which no one element is wanting (Ruth ii. 12, LXX, &c.). Comp. Mk. iv. 28 πλ. σῖτος; 2 Chron. xv. 17 καρδία πλ. (בְלֵשָׁי). For the idea of μισθός see Apoc. xi. 18; xxii. 12;

20*

πλήρη ἀπολάβητε. ⁹πᾶς ὁ προάγων καὶ μὴ μένων ἐν
τῇ διδαχῇ τοῦ χριστοῦ θεὸν οὐκ ἔχει. ὁ μένων ἐν τῇ
διδαχῇ, οὗτος καὶ τὸν πατέρα καὶ τὸν υἱὸν ἔχει. ¹⁰εἴ
τις ἔρχεται πρὸς ὑμᾶς καὶ ταύτην τὴν διδαχὴν οὐ φέρει,
μὴ λαμβάνετε αὐτὸν εἰς οἰκίαν καὶ χαίρειν αὐτῷ μὴ

9 προάγων אAB vg me the: παραβαίνων ϛ.   μένων (2°): +'καὶ μή' א* (as the
copyist looked back three lines in the archetype to προάγων).   διδαχῇ:
+τοῦ χριστοῦ ϛ me.   10 τὸν π. καὶ τὸν υἱ. אB me the syr hl: τὸν υἱ. καὶ
τὸν π. A vg.

John iv. 36; Matt. v. 12 and parallels;
1 Cor. iii. 8.

9. πᾶς ὁ προάγων καὶ μ. μ.] omnis
qui præcedit et non m. V., Every one
that goeth forward and abideth not...
every one that advances in bold confidence beyond the limits set to the
Christian Faith. True progress includes the past. These false teachers
proposed to enter on new regions of
truth leaving the old. The two characteristics are taken together (ὁ πρ.
καὶ μὴ μ.).

μένων ἐν] abideth in...John viii. 31;
2 Tim. iii. 14.

ἐν τῇ διδ. τοῦ χρ.] in the doctrine of
Christ, the doctrine which Christ
brought, and which He brought first
in His own person, and then through
His followers (Hebr. ii. 3). This sense
seems better than the doctrine of
(concerning) the Christ, and the usage
of the N.T. is uniformly in favour of
it: Apoc. ii. 14, 15; John xviii. 19;
Acts ii. 42. Ἡ διδ. is used absolutely
(as below) in Tit. i. 9 (Rom. xvi. 17).

θ. οὐκ ἔχει] hath not God, Whom he
claims to know more perfectly. Comp.
1 John ii. 23 (οὐδέ) note.

ὁ μένων...οὗτος...] The pronoun emphasises the definition given. Comp.
John vi. 46; vii. 18; xv. 5. Faithful
continuance in 'the doctrine' brings a
living possession of God as He is revealed in the fulness of His Fatherly
relation in 'the Father and the Son.'
The change from the abstract title

'God' in the former clause is significant. Comp. 1 John ii. 22 f.

10, 11. Not only is there danger
within, but false teaching may come
from without under a friendly guise.
The confession of the revelation in 'the
Father and the Son' is the indispensable test of fellowship.

10. εἴ τις ἔρχεται...] If any one
cometh... The form of expression is
not found elsewhere in the Epistles
or Gospel of St John. It assumes the
case, and does not simply regard it as
possible (ἐάν τις). By 'cometh' is to
be understood an official · coming.'
St John is not dealing with the casual
visit of a stranger but with that of a
teacher who claims authority.

The picture of the itinerating 'prophet' in the Διδαχή is a vivid illustration of the scene present to St John's
mind (§§ 11 f.).

πρὸς ὑμᾶς] 'the lady and her children' vv. 1, 12.

ταύτ. τ. δ. οὐ φ.] and beareth not
as his message, this doctrine of Christ
which declares the Father and the
Son, the decisive revelation of the
Gospel. For φέρειν compare John
xviii. 29; Acts xxv. 18; 2 Pet. ii. 11.
See also 2 Pet. i. 17, 18, 21; 1 Pet. i.
13. The negative is not affected by
εἰ, because it goes closely with the
verb: εἴ τις [ἔρχ....καὶ οὐ φέρει].

μὴ λαμβ....] nolite recipere...nec ave
ei dixeritis V., receive him not...and
give him no greeting.... These words

λέγετε· ¹¹ὁ λέγων γὰρ αὐτῷ χαίρειν κοινωνεῖ τοῖς
ἔργοις αὐτοῦ τοῖς πονηροῖς.

¹²Πολλὰ ἔχων ὑμῖν γράφειν οὐκ ἐβουλήθην διὰ
χάρτου καὶ μέλανος, ἀλλὰ ἐλπίζω γενέσθαι πρὸς ὑμᾶς
καὶ στόμα πρὸς στόμα λαλῆσαι, ἵνα ἡ χαρὰ ὑμῶν

11 ὁ λέγων γάρ: ὁ γὰρ λ. ς.   12 ἔχων : ἔχω א*Α*.   γράφειν : γράψαι Α.
ἀλλὰ ἐλπίζω אΒ the syr hl : ἐλπ. γάρ Α vg me.   γενέσθαι : ἐλθεῖν ς the.
στόμα (1°): +τι א*.   ὑμῶν ΑΒ vg me : ἡμῶν א syr hl (my the).

are to be interpreted with the limitation suggested by the character of the
'coming': 'Do not receive such a
teacher as one who can justly claim
the privilege of Christian hospitality
as a brother; and do not even welcome
him with a greeting of sympathy.' In
the N. T. χαίρειν is always used of the
greeting of first address (Acts xv. 23;
xxiii. 26; James i. 1); otherwise the
context would perhaps suggest that
the thought here is of the greeting of
farewell : 'Do not entertain such a
one : do not send him on his way with
good wishes.' Clement adds: arbi-
tror autem quia et orare cum talibus
non oportet, quoniam in oratione quæ
fit in domo postquam ab orando sur-
gitur salutatio gaudii est et pacis in-
dicium (Fragm. *Hypotyp.* p. 1011 P.).
Whatever may be thought of the application the picture of family devotion is of singular interest.

11. κοινωνεῖ τ. ἔ....] *communicat
operibus illius malignis* V. Comp.
1 Tim. v. 22. The word κοινωνεῖν
implies more than participation in the
definite acts. It suggests fellowship
with the character of which they are
the outcome.

τοῖς ἔ....τοῖς πον.] Comp. 1 John ii.
7 note. John iii. 19; 1 John iii. 12;
Col. i. 21; 2 Tim. iv. 18.

3. *The conclusion* (12, 13).

The main request and the main
warning have been spoken. Other
subjects St John reserves for a per-

sonal interview. A general salutation closes the letter. Comp. 3 John
13—15.

¹²*Though I have many things
to write to you, I would not write
them with paper and ink; but I
hope to be present with you, and to
speak face to face, that your joy may
be fulfilled.*
¹³*The children of thine elect sister
salute thee.*

12. Π. ἔ. ὑμῖν γρ.] The pronoun (v.
10) stands in a position of emphasis
(contrast 3 John 13): the special circumstances of those addressed suggested topics to the apostle.

οὐκ ἐβουλ.] *nolui* V., *I would not*
communicate them.... The aorist regards the letter as complete: the decision is made. Comp. 1 John ii. 14
note. Some general word such as
'communicate' must be supplied from
'write.'

διὰ χ. καὶ μέλ.] *per chartam et atra-
mentum* V. Jer. xxxvi. 18.

ἀλλὰ ἐλπ. γ. πρ. ὑ.] *spero enim me
futurum apud vos* V., *but I hope to
be present with you*. The delay in
the communication was to be but
brief. For γεν. πρ. ὑ. see 1 Cor. ii. 3;
xvi. 10.

στόμα πρὸς στόμα] *face to face,*

פֶּה אֶל־פֶּה (Num. xii. 8, LXX. στόμα
κατὰ στόμα). Comp. 1 Cor. xiii. 12.

ἵνα ἡ χ. ὑ. πεπλ. ᾖ] *that your joy
may be fulfilled*. Comp. 1 John i. 4
note.

πεπληρωμένη ἦ. ¹³'Ἀσπάζεταί σε τὰ τέκνα τῆς ἀδελφῆς σου τῆς ἐκλεκτῆς.

πεπλ. ᾖ (ℵ) B : ᾖ πεπλ. A.   ἦν ℵ*.   13 ἐκλεκτῆς : +ἀμήν ϛ syr hl.

13. 'Ασπ. σε] v. 5. The singular
pronoun answers to τῆς ἀδελφῆς.
τῆς ἀδ....τῆς ἐκλ.] 1 John ii. 7 note.
The adj. ἐκλεκτός is found in St John's
writings elsewhere only in v. 1 and
Apoc. xvii. 14. The verb ἐκλέγεσθαι
occurs in the Gospel: vi. 70; xiii. 18;
xv. 16, 19.

No sure argument as to the individual or corporate interpretation of
κυρία (v. 1) can be drawn from the occurrence of τὰ τέκνα τῆς ἀδ. without ἡ
ἀδελφή.   On the whole however the
general tenour of v. 13 seems to favour
the corporate view.

ΙΩΑΝΟΥ Γ

ΙΩΑΝΟΥ Γ

Ο ΠΡΕCΒΥΤΕΡΟC Γαίῳ τῷ ἀγαπητῷ, ὃν ἐγὼ ἀγαπῶ ἐν ἀληθείᾳ.

The letter is marked throughout by personal circumstances, and is broken up into short paragraphs which are severally suggested by these. After the salutation (*v.* 1) St John (1) expresses in general terms his joy at the tidings of Gaius which he hears (2—4); and (2) specially approves his hospitality towards missionary brethren (5—8). In contrast with this generosity (3) he condemns the ambitious self-assertion of Diotrephes (9, 10); and then (4) gives his witness in favour of Demetrius (11, 12); and so (5) concludes (13—15).

1. *The salutation.*

The salutation stands in contrast by its brevity with the salutations in the other personal letters of the New Testament. The wish of blessing is transposed in another form to the following verse.

¹*The Elder to Gaius the beloved, whom I love in truth.*

1. 'Ο πρεσβύτερος] 2 John 1 note. Γαίῳ τῷ ἀγ.] The name 'Gaius' (Caius) occurs Acts xix. 29 (a 'Macedonian'); xx. 4 ('of Derbe'); 1 Cor. i. 14 (a Corinthian); Rom. xvi. 23 (a Corinthian). There is nothing to identify this Gaius with any one of these. Another is mentioned as having been made bishop of Pergamum by St John (*Const. Ap.* vii.

46). The position which Gaius occupied in the church to which he belonged is not shown by the letter. The epithet 'beloved' is afterwards used as a title of address (*vv.* 2, 5, 11). It occurs several times in salutations of St Paul: Rom. xvi. 12; Philem. 1 ('the beloved'); Rom. xvi. 5, 8, 9 ('my beloved'); 2 Tim. i. 2 ('my beloved child').

ὃν ἐγὼ ἀγ.] The emphatic personal pronoun (2 John 1) seems to point to some gainsayers with whom the apostle contrasts himself. Compare 'thou' (σύ) in *v.* 3.

ἐν ἀληθ.] Comp. 2 John 1 note. ἐν ἀληθείᾳ ἀγαπᾷ ὁ κατὰ Κύριον ἀγαπῶν (Œcumen.).

2. *The teacher's joy* (2—4).

St John, having much ground for sorrow and disappointment, begins with the expression of joy (comp. 2 John 4). Some of his own children (comp. 2 John *l.c.*), Gaius among them, were loyal to the Truth. He could wish him nothing better than that all his circumstances should correspond to his spiritual progress.

The salutation is completed, after the common model, in *v.* 1. The second verse adds what corresponds to the fuller Christian greeting (2 John 3).

²*Beloved, I pray that in all things*

²᾽Αγαπητέ, περὶ πάντων εὔχομαί σε εὐοδοῦσθαι καὶ
ὑγιαίνειν, καθὼς εὐοδοῦταί σου ἡ ψυχή. ³ἐχάρην γὰρ
λίαν ἐρχομένων ἀδελφῶν καὶ μαρτυρούντων σου τῇ ἀληθείᾳ, καθὼς σὺ ἐν ἀληθείᾳ περιπατεῖς. ⁴μειζοτέραν

3 ἐχάρην γάρ ABC me syr: om. γάρ א vg the.   μαρτυρούντων : μαρτυρουν B
(at the end of a line).   καθὼς σύ : om. σύ A.

thou mayest prosper and be in good
health even as thy soul prospereth.
³For I rejoiced (rejoice) greatly when
brethren came (come) and bore (bear)
witness to thy truth, even as thou
walkest in truth. ⁴I have no greater
grace than these tidings, that I may
hear of mine own children walking
in the truth.

2. ᾽Αγαπητέ] carissime V. (vv. 5, 11).
For the use of the plural see 1 John
ii. 7 note.

περὶ π. εὔχ. σε εὐοδ....] de omnibus
orationem facio prospere te ingredi
V. In all things I pray that thou
mayest be prosperous... The phrase
περὶ πάντων is remarkable. It may
go with εὐοδοῦσθαι or with the sentence generally (comp. 1 Cor. xvi.
1). The sense 'above all things' is
not justified by any parallel in the
N. T. or LXX.; and the context points
to a contrast between 'the soul' and
other things. The thought appears
to be of the public and social work of
Gaius as distinguished from his personal progress, though ὑγιαίνειν may
point to some illness.

εὔχομαι] The word is rare in N.T.:
2 Cor. xiii. 7, 9; Acts xxvi. 29; xxvii.
29.

εὐοδ. καὶ ὑγιαίνειν] The elements of
progress and vigour are combined.
For εὐοδοῦσθαι see 1 Cor. xvi. 2;
Rom. i. 10. In St Paul ὑγιαίνειν is
always used metaphorically of sound
doctrine; but it occurs in the literal
sense of sound health in St Luke: v.
31, vii. 10, xv. 27.

καθὼς...ψυχή] sicut prospere agit
anima tua V. Ψυχή expresses here
the principle of the higher life ('soul')

(Hebr. vi. 19, x. 39, xiii. 17; 1 Pet. ii.
11, iv. 19). The nearest approach to
this sense elsewhere in St John's
writings is John xii. 27 (x. 24). In
other places he uses it only of the
principle of the 'natural' life.

3. ἐχάρην γάρ...] Comp. 2 John 4.
The joy which the apostle felt at the
tidings of the action of Gaius is given
in explanation of his far-reaching wish
for his welfare, and not only as an
assurance of his spiritual well-being.
The words evidently point to some
difficulties from false teaching which
Gaius had boldly met, though as yet
the issue of his work was uncertain.

ἐρχομ. ἀδ.] when brethren came not
on one occasion only (ἐλθόντων) but
from time to time, though all these
visits belonged definitely to the past
(ἐχάρην) when the apostle wrote. The
words give a vivid picture of continued troubles even in the apostolic
church.

ἀδελφῶν] vv. 5, 10. Comp. 1 John
iii. 14 addit. note.

μαρτ. σ. τῇ ἀλ.] testimonium per-
hibentibus veritati tuæ V., bore witness to thy truth, attested the perfect
and sincere loyalty with which you
maintain the fulness of the Christian
faith in life. Christian thought and
Christian action are inseparable.

καθὼς σύ...] even as thou walkest
in truth, truly. Comp. 2 John 4.
The emphatic pronoun (σύ) suggests
a contrast with others as (for example) Diotrephes. Gaius walked not
only in word but really (ἐν ἀληθ. 1
John iii. 18) according to the standard
of the Christian revelation (ἐν τῇ ἀλ.
'in the Truth'). The clause seems to

τούτων οὐκ ἔχω χάριν, ἵνα ἀκούω τὰ ἐμὰ τέκνα ἐν
τῇ ἀληθείᾳ περιπατοῦντα.　　　⁵Ἀγαπητέ, πιστὸν

4 τούτων οὐκ ἔ. χ. ℵAB : τούτων χ. οὐκ ἔ. C.　　　ἔχω : ἔχων B*.　　　χάριν
B vg me : χαράν ﭏℵAC the.　　　τῇ ἀλ. ABC* : om τῇ ﭏℵ.

be one of those personal comments
in which St John pausing on what is
written, as it were, thinks aloud :
'They witnessed to thy truth ; yes,
and when the vision of vain profes-
sions rises before me I know that
thou at least livest indeed as thou
teachest.'

4. μειζοτέραν...χάριν, ἵνα...] majorem horum non habeo gratiam quam
ut...V.　I have no greater grace
—favour from God—than these tidings, that I may hear... The plural
τούτων 'these things' does not refer
to what follows ('that I may hear')
but to what precedes, the manifold
testimonies which St John received of
the courageous resolution with which
Gaius maintained the Truth in the
face of difficulties. The end assured
by such tidings was the open acknowledgment of the fidelity of disciples
('that so I may hear'). Even if St
John had himself no doubt of the
fact, it would be a joy to know that it
was also observed by others. For the
construction see John xv. 13 note.

For the form μειζότερος compare
ἐλαχιστότερος Eph. iii. 8.

ἔχω χάριν] The use of χάρις is remarkable ; but χάρις makes the 'joy'
(χαρά) of the common text itself a
divine gift. The word is very rare
in St John (2 John 3 note). Here
it expresses the divine favour in a
concrete form, So it is used of the
gracious gift of men : 1 Cor. xvi. 3.
' To have grace' (or 'a grace') here
corresponds with 'giving' (Rom. xii.
6, &c.) and 'receiving' grace (Rom. i.
5). Ἔχειν χάριν is used elsewhere in
different constructions and senses :
ἔχειν χάριν τινί Luke xvii. 9 ; 1 Tim. i.
12 ; ἔ. χ. πρός τινα Acts ii. 47.

τὰ ἐμὰ τ.] mine own children

(Philem. 10), not simply τὰ τέκνα μου.
Those Christians to whom the apostle
had been the human author of spiritual life : 1 Cor. iv. 14, 17 ; 1 Tim. i.
2, &c. ; 2 John 1, 13. Τεκνία, the title
of affection, would be used of all to
whom he at present stood in the position of father : 1 John ii. 1, note.

ἐν τῇ ἀλ. περιπ.] The phrase is not
found elsewhere in N. T. Comp. ἐν τῷ
σκ. (ἐν τῇ σκ.) π. 1 John i. 6 ; ii. 11 ;
ἐν τῷ φωτὶ π. 1 John i. 7 ; ἐν αὐτῇ (τῇ
ἀγάπῃ) π. 2 John 6. For the image
see 1 John i. 6, note.

3.　The duty of generosity to the
brethren (5—8).

Gaius appears to have incurred the
displeasure of some in his Church
by entertaining strange brethren. St
John emphatically approves what he
had done, and enforces such hospitality as a Christian duty.

In this brief notice we have a vivid
sketch of the work and of the difficulties of the first 'Evangelists' : Eph.
iv. 11. Compare Doctr. of App. 11 ff.

⁵Beloved, thou makest sure whatsoever thou doest unto the brethren and
strangers withal, ⁶who bore witness
to thy love before the church ; whom
thou wilt do well to help forward
on their journey worthily of God ;
⁷for they went out for the Name's
sake, taking nothing from the Gentiles.
⁸We therefore ought to welcome such
that we may be fellow workers with
the truth.

5.　πιστὸν π.] fideliter facis V. The
phrase is commonly interpreted : 'thou
doest a faithful work,' a work which
answers to thy faith : so Œcum. ἄξιον
πιστοῦ ἀνδρός. No parallel is quoted
in support of such a sense of πιστός.
The more natural rendering is rather

ποιεῖς ὃ ἐὰν ἐργάσῃ εἰς τοὺς ἀδελφοὺς καὶ τοῦτο ξένους,
⁶οἳ ἐμαρτύρησάν σου τῇ ἀγάπῃ ἐνώπιον ἐκκλησίας, οὓς
καλῶς ποιήσεις προπέμψας ἀξίως τοῦ θεοῦ· ⁷ὑπὲρ γὰρ

5 ἐργάσῃ: ἐργάζῃ A.   καὶ τοῦτο ℵABC vg me the syrr: καὶ εἰς τούς ϛ.
6 οὕς: ου B*.   ποιήσεις προπέμψας: ποιήσας προπέμψεις C (lat).

'thou makest sure'; that is, such an
act will not be lost, will not fail of its
due issue and reward (Apoc. xxi. 5).
This sense falls in well with the context
(comp. Apoc. xiv. 13), and explains
the use of the two verbs, ποιεῖν, ἐργάζεσθαι, which are combined also in
Col. iii. 23.

ὃ ἐὰν ἐργ.] The indefinite form (ὃ
ἐάν as contrasted with ὅ) marks the
variety of service. For ἐργάζομαι see
John vi. 28, ix. 4; and for ἐργ. εἰς,
Matt. xxvi. 10.

καὶ τοῦτο ξ.] et hoc in...V., and
strangers withal. The fact that this
detail is emphasised in the commenda-
tion of the hospitality of Gaius seems
to imply that it had been made the
occasion of unjust blame. For καὶ
τοῦτο compare 1 Cor. vi. 6; Phil. i.
28; Eph. ii. 8. Viewed rightly the
fact that these brethren were strangers gave them a more pressing claim
upon the common ties of brotherhood.
Comp. Hebr. xiii. 2 note.

6. οἳ ἐμαρτ....] Those who in one particular case experienced the habitual
hospitality of Gaius bore open testimony to his character in a public assembly of the church where the writer
was, gathered together, as it may seem,
to receive their report: comp. Acts
xiv. 26 ff. For ἐνώπιον ἐκκλ. (not τῆς
ἐκκλ.) compare ἐν ἐκκλ. 1 Cor. xiv. 19,
35: ἐν συναγωγῇ John vi. 59, xviii.
20; 2 Macc. xiv. 5 προσκληθεὶς εἰς
συνέδριον i.e. a meeting of the Council.
Doctr. Ap. iv. 14 ἐν ἐκκλησίᾳ ἐξομολο-
γήσῃ τὰ παραπτώματά σου.

οὓς κ. π. προπέμψας] quos benefa-
ciens deduces (benefacies ducens)_V.
Those who had before found help
from Gaius now again required it for
a special work. The future implies a

wish which, it is assumed, will at once
be fulfilled. Comp. Rom. vi. 14. For
προπέμψας see Acts xv. 3; Tit. iii. 13.
The latter passage suggests that the
word includes some provision for the
journey as well as sympathetic attend-
ance: Acts xxi. 3. St John regards
the act in its completeness (προπέμψας) and not in process (προπέμπων).
This makes the combination of the
aor. and fut. natural. For προπ.
compare Polyc. Phil. 1 συνεχάρην
ὑμῖν...προπέμψασιν ὡς ἐπέβαλεν ὑμῖν
τοὺς ἐνειλημμένους τοῖς ἁγιοπρέπεσι
δεσμοῖς.

καλῶς ποι.] Acts x. 33; James ii. 8
(19); 2 Pet. i. 19; 1 Cor. vii. 37 f.;
Phil. iv. 14.

Compare Ign. Smyrn. 10 Φίλωνα
καὶ Ῥέον Ἀγαθόπουν, οἱ ἐπηκολούθησάν
μοι εἰς λόγον θεοῦ, καλῶς ἐποιήσατε
ὑποδεξάμενοι ὡς διακόνους Χριστοῦ θεοῦ.

ἀξ. τ. θ.] worthily of their dedication to the service of God: John xiii.
20. Comp. 1 Thess. ii. 12; Col. i. 10
ἀξ. τοῦ κυρίου.

7. ὑπὲρ γὰρ τ. ὀν.] pro nomine
enim V., for the Name's sake, that is,
to make the Name better known:
Rom. i. 5.

'The name' is used absolutely Acts
v. 41 (comp. v. 40 ἐπὶ τῷ ὀν. Ἰησοῦ).
Comp. James ii. 7. It is also found
in the letters of Ignatius: ad Eph. 7 τὸ
ὄνομα περιφέρειν: ad Philad. 10 δοξάσαι
τὸ ὄνομα. Comp. ad Eph. 1 δέδεμαι
ὑπὲρ τοῦ κοινοῦ ὀνόματος καὶ ἐλπίδος:
id. 3 εἰ...δέδεμαι ἐν τῷ ὀνόματι οὔπω
ἀπήρτισμαι ἐν Ἰησοῦ Χριστῷ. From
the contexts it is evident that 'the
Name' is 'Jesus Christ' ('the Lord
Jesus'), or, as it is written at length,
'Jesus Christ, the Son of God' (John
xx. 31; 1 John iv. 15). This 'Name'

τοῦ ὀνόματος ἐξῆλθαν μηδὲν λαμβάνοντες ἀπὸ τῶν
ἐθνικῶν. ⁸ἡμεῖς οὖν ὀφείλομεν ὑπολαμβάνειν τοὺς τοι-
ούτους, ἵνα συνεργοὶ γινώμεθα τῇ ἀληθείᾳ.

7 ὀνόματος: +αὐτοῦ Elz.   ἀπὸ τῶν: om. τῶν C.   ἐθνικῶν: ἐθνῶν ⲋ.   8
ὑπολαμβάνειν: ἀπολαμβάνειν ⲋ.   γινώμεθα: γινόμεθα C.   ἀληθείᾳ ℵBC vg:
ἐκκλησίᾳ ℵ*A.

is in essence the sum of the Christian
Creed (comp. 1 Cor. xii. 3; Rom. x. 9).

When analysed it reveals the triune
'Name' into which the Christian is
baptized, Matt. xxviii. 19. Compare
also 1 Pet. iv. 16 ἐν τῷ ὀνόματι τούτῳ,
i.e. *Christian.*

With the absolute use of 'the
Name' may be compared the absolute use of 'the Way'; Acts ix. 2, xix.
9, 23, xxiv. 22.

See Additional Note.

ἐξῆλθαν] *profecti sunt* V., *they went
forth* from some Church, well known
to the apostle and Gaius, on a mission
of Truth, as others went forth on a
mission of error (2 John 7; 1 John ii.
19). Comp. Acts xv. 40.

μηδὲν λαμβ....] *taking nothing* as
their habitual rule. This trait is given
not as a simple fact (οὐδὲν λαμβ.), but
as a mark of character. These teachers
refused to receive hospitality from
Gentiles who were unconverted. Many
reasons may have recommended such
a rule. St Paul alludes frequently to
difficulties which arose even from that
reasonable provision by the Church
which St John here claims: 1 Thess.
ii. 6 ff.; 1 Cor. ix. 14 f.; 2 Cor. xii. 16 ff.
For λαμβ. ἀπὸ see Matt. xvii. 25.

ἀπὸ τῶν ἐθνικ.] *a gentilibus (genti-
bus)* V., *from the Gentiles* to whom
they carried the Gospel. The form
used (ἐθνικός) describes character rather than mere position: Matt. v. 47,
vi. 7, xviii. 17. It does not seem to
be found in the LXX.

8. ἡμεῖς οὖν...] *We therefore*, as
fellow Christians, *ought* (are bound,
1 John ii. 6 note) *to receive* (support)
such. The word ὑπολαμβάνειν (*sus-
cipere* V.) gives the notion of wel-

coming with hospitable support.

ἵνα συν. γιν. τῇ ἀλ.] *ut cooperato-
res simus veritatis* V. The phrase is
ambiguous. The fellowship may be
either with the teachers: 'that we
may be fellow-workers with them in
support of the truth'; or (better) with
the truth, the substance of their teaching: 'that we may help the truth which
is effective through them'; comp.
Phil. i. 27 συναθλοῦντες τῇ πίστει τοῦ
εὐαγγελίου and Bp Lightfoot's note.
The word συνεργός is not used elsewhere in the N. T. or LXX with the
dat. It is used with the gen. of the
person with whom the worker coope-
rates (*e.g.* Rom. xvi. 21 ὁ συν. μου, 1
Cor. iii. 9 θεοῦ συνεργοί), and with the
gen. of the object, 1 Cor. iii. 9 συνεργοὶ
τῆς χαρᾶς, 1 Macc. xiv. 5. It is also
used with εἰς (Col. iv. 11 συν. εἰς τὴν
βασιλείαν) and πρός (2 Macc. viii. 7
πρὸς τὰς...ἐπιβουλὰς συν.) of the object. The verb is used with the dat.
of that which is helped, James ii. 22
συνήργει τοῖς ἔργοις, 1 Macc. xii. 1; and
this construction is sufficient to support the connexion of συν. with τῇ ἀλ.

4.   *The temporary triumph of
ambition* (9, 10).

As yet St John had not succeeded in
removing the opposition from which
Gaius suffered; but he makes it clear
that the issue cannot be doubtful.

⁹*I wrote a few words to the
Church; but he that loveth to have
the preeminence among them, Diotrephes, doth not receive us.* ¹⁰*For
this cause, if I come I will call to
remembrance his works which he
doeth, prating of us with evil words;
and, since he is not content therewith*

⁹"Εγραψά τι τῇ ἐκκλησίᾳ· ἀλλ' ὁ φιλοπρωτεύων
αὐτῶν Διοτρέφης οὐκ ἐπιδέχεται ἡμᾶς. ¹⁰διὰ τοῦτο,
ἐὰν ἔλθω, ὑπομνήσω αὐτοῦ τὰ ἔργα ἃ ποιεῖ, λόγοις
πονηροῖς φλυαρῶν ἡμᾶς, καὶ μὴ ἀρκούμενος ἐπὶ τούτοις

9 ἔγραψα ℵ*AC: ἔγραψα ἄν ℵᶜ vg syrr: ἔγραψας B.   ἔγρ. τι: om. τι ⟨ℵᶜ vg
syrr.   10 ἡμᾶς: εἰς ἡμᾶς C.

neither doth he receive the brethren
himself and them that would he
hindereth and casteth out of the
Church.

9. *Εγραψά τι] scripsissem forsitan
V., I wrote a few words. The use of
τι to express 'something of importance' is foreign to the N. T. and un-
suitable to the context. St John
treats his letter lightly. The letter,
which may be regarded as the type of
a class, has not been preserved. To
escape from the difficulty supposed to
be involved in the loss of an apostolic
letter several early authorities introduced ἄν (as V.).

τῇ ἐκκλησίᾳ] to the Church to which
Gaius belonged, as well as now to
Gaius himself. St John had by this
time heard that his letter had for the
present failed. This is the only passage in his Epistles (v. 6 is different)
in which St John speaks of 'a Church.'
The word ἐκκλησία does not occur
in his Gospel. In the Apocalypse (as
here) 'the Church' is always used of
the special society in a particular
place (comp. Apoc. xxii. 16 ἐπὶ ταῖς
ἐκκλησίαις); so that St John nowhere
gives a distinct expression to the
thought worked out in Eph. i. 22, v.
23 ff.; though he records the gift of
its new life, John xx. 21 ff.

ὁ φιλοπρ....Δ.] is qui amat prima-
tum gerere in iis D. V., he that loveth
to have the preeminence among (or
over) them.... The word φιλόπρωτος
occurs in late Greek (Polyb. Plut.), but
φιλοπρωτεύειν is not quoted from any
other passage. The idea of πρωτεύειν
governs the gen. αὐτῶν, which answers

to ἡ ἐκκλησία (comp. 1 Cor. i. 2 τῇ
ἐκκλ., ἡγιασμένοις). It is of interest
to compare the two sources of failure
noticed in the two Epistles, προάγειν
(2 John 9) and φιλοπρωτεύειν, the undue claims to intellectual progress
and to personal authority. There is
nothing to indicate that Diotrephes
held false opinions: his ambition only
is blamed. Comp. Herm. Tim. viii.
7, 4 ἔχοντες ζῆλόν τινα ἐν ἀλλήλοις περὶ
πρωτείων καὶ περὶ δόξης τινός: id. 7.

οὐκ ἐπιδέχ. ἡ.] In v. 10 the word is
used of the literal welcome of visitors:
here it is naturally understood of the
recognition of the apostle's wish as
authoritative. Comp. 1 Macc. x. 1
ἐπεδέξαντο αὐτόν (as sovereign); xii.
8, 43; x. 46 ἐπεδ. λόγους; Ecclus. vi.
26 ἐπεδ. παιδείαν. By the use of ἡμᾶς
(contrast ἔγραψα v. 1 ἐγώ) St John
removes the question from a personal
issue. He identifies himself with the
society (vv. 8, 12 ἡμεῖς, 1 John iv. 6; v.
14 f.).

10. διὰ τοῦτο...] St John implies
that his personal presence will be decisive. By using the form ἐὰν ἔλθω
there is no doubt thrown on the main
fact of his coming (v. 14). Comp. 1
John ii. 28.

ὑπομν. αὐτ. τ.·ἔ.] commoneam ejus
opera V., I will call to remembrance
his works, I will bring them to his
notice and to the notice of others.
Ὑπομιμνήσκειν is used with the acc.
of the person (2 Pet. i. 12) and of the
thing (2 Tim. ii. 14), and of both
(John xiv. 26).

λ. πον. φλ. ἡ.] verbis malignis gar-
riens in nos V., prating of us with

οὔτε αὐτὸς ἐπιδέχεται τοὺς ἀδελφοὺς καὶ τοὺς βουλομένους κωλύει καὶ ἐκ τῆς ἐκκλησίας ἐκβάλλει.

¹¹Ἀγαπητέ, μὴ μιμοῦ τὸ κακὸν ἀλλὰ τὸ ἀγαθόν.
ὁ ἀγαθοποιῶν ἐκ τοῦ θεοῦ ἐστίν· ὁ κακοποιῶν οὐχ
ἑώρακεν τὸν θεόν.　¹²Δημητρίῳ μεμαρτύρηται ὑπὸ πάν-

βουλομένους: ἐπιδεχομένους C the.
ὁ δὲ κακοπ. ϛ me.

ἐκ τῆς ἐκκλ.: om. ἐκ א.　11 ὁ κακοπ.:

evil words (Matt. v. 11; Acts xxviii.
21). The adj. φλύαρος occurs 1 Tim.
v. 13.

μὴ ἀρκ. ἐπὶ τ.] quasi non ei ista
sufficiant V., and since he does not
rest content therewith... Ἀρκεῖσθαι is
used with the simple dat. Luke iii.
14; Hebr. xiii. 5; 1 Tim. vi. 8.

οὔτε...καί...] nec...et... V. John iv.
11.

κωλύει...ἐκβάλλει] The verbs do not
necessarily express more than the
purpose and effort: comp. John x.
32 (Matt. iii. 14). It is difficult to
realise the circumstances of the case.
It may perhaps be reasonably conjectured from ὁ φιλοπρωτεύων that
Diotrephes regarded the reception of
the brethren as an invasion of his
authority.

ἐκβάλλει] Luke vi. 22; John ix. 34 f.

5.　The witness to the faithful disciple (11, 12).

Self-seeking may have its tempting
successes, but they rest on no secure
foundation. The faithful are supported
by many converging testimonies.

¹¹Beloved, imitate not that which
is evil but that which is good. He
that doeth good is of God; he that
doeth evil hath not seen God. ¹²De-
metrius hath witness borne to him
by all and by the truth itself: yea
we also bear witness; and thou
knowest that our witness is true.

11.　Ἀγαπητέ...] The transition lies
in the thought of the power which
Diotrephes had won by wrong means.

μὴ μιμοῦ] noli imitari V. Comp.
2 Thess. iii. 7, 9; Hebr. xiii. 7. The

noun μιμητής occurs several times: e.g.
1 Cor. iv. 16; Eph. v. 1.

τὸ κ....τὸ ἀγ....] malum...quod bo-
num est V. Rom. xii. 21.

ἀγαθ....κακοπ....] Mk. iii. 4; Luke
vi. 9; 1 Pet. iii. 17.

ἐκ τοῦ θ. ἐ....οὐχ ἑώρ. τ. θ. ...] The
two stages of divine relationship correspond with the two characters. He
who does good proves by his action
that his life springs from God as its
source (εἶναι ἐκ τ. θ. Addit. Note on
1 John iii. 1): he who does evil has not
made the first step towards participation in the Divine Nature (1 John
iii. 6 note). In one sense the vision of
God (the Father) in Christ (John xiv.
9) is the condition of fellowship with
Him: in another sense the vision of
God as God lies beyond the power of
man (John i. 18).

It is likely that here, as elsewhere,
St John points to men who professed
to have deeper insight into truth and
disparaged the importance of virtuous
action.

12.　Δημητρίῳ μεμαρτ.] From the
unfaithful St John turns to the faithful: from the 'evil' to the 'good.' It is
likely from the context that Demetrius
was the bearer of the letter. For μαρτ.
τινί see John iii. 26; Luke iv. 22;
Acts xv. 8; and in pass. Acts vi. 3; x.
22; xvi. 2; xxii. 12; 1 Tim. v. 10, &c.

St John appeals to a threefold witness given in favour of Demetrius (1)
ὑπὸ π. by all, that is the general witness of men arising out of the experience of life; (2) ὑπ' αὐτ. τ. ἀλ. by
the Truth itself, so far as the ideal of
Christianity was seen to be realised by

242 THE THIRD EPISTLE OF ST JOHN. [13—15

των καὶ ὑπὸ αὐτῆς τῆς ἀληθείας· καὶ ἡμεῖς δὲ μαρτυροῦμεν, καὶ οἶδας ὅτι ἡ μαρτυρία ἡμῶν ἀληθής ἐστιν.
¹³Πολλὰ εἶχον γράψαι σοι, ἀλλ᾽ οὐ θέλω διὰ μέλανος καὶ καλάμου σοι γράφειν· ¹⁴ἐλπίζω δὲ εὐθέως σε
ἰδεῖν, καὶ στόμα πρὸς στόμα λαλήσομεν. ¹⁵Εἰρήνη σοι.
ἀσπάζονταί σε οἱ φίλοι. ἀσπάζου τοὺς φίλους κατ᾽
ὄνομα.

12 τῆς ἀληθείας: τῆς ἐκκλησίας καὶ τῆς ἀλ. C: τῆς ἐκκλησίας A* (?).   οἶδας: οἴδατε
ς΄.   ἡ μαρτ. ἡ. ἀλ. ἐστ.: ἀλ. ἡ. ἐστ. ἡ μαρτ. C.   13 γράψαι σοι: γράφειν ς΄.
οὐ θέλω: οὐκ ἐβουλήθην A (2 John 12).   σοι γρ. ℵBC: γρ. σοι A vg me the syrr.
γράφειν: γράψαι ς΄.   14 σε ἰδεῖν ABC vg: ἰδεῖν σε ςℵ me.   πρός: πρό B*.
15 οἱ φίλοι: οἱ ἀδελφοί A.   ἀσπάζου: ἄσπασαι ℵ.

him; (3) καὶ ἡμ. δὲ μαρτ. *yea and we
also bear witness:* St John and those
with him spoke with the authority of
the Church.

For the combination μεμαρτ., μαρτυροῦμεν see John v. 33, 36. The
witness given in the past was still
effective while it was also complete:
the witness of St John came with
present fresh force.

ὑπὸ π.] *by all.* It is possible that
these words are to be taken quite
generally: 1 Tim. iii. 7; though it is
not necessary to extend them beyond
the circle of Christians.

καί...δέ...] See 1 John i. 3.
καὶ οἶδας] The words in John xxi.
24 sound like an echo of this sentence.

This verse serves the purpose of 'a
commendatory letter' (συστατικὴ ἐπι-
στολή 2 Cor. iii. 1).

6. The conclusion (13—15).

¹³*I had many things to write to
thee, howbeit I will not write to thee
with ink and pen;* ¹⁴*but I hope to
see thee shortly, and we will speak
face to face.*
¹⁵*Peace be to thee: the friends*

salute thee: salute the friends by
name.

13. εἶχον] The writer goes back to
the time when the letter was begun.
See 2 John 12. The variations in
form are worth notice: ἔχων οὐκ
ἐβουλήθην, εἶχον ἀλλ᾽ οὐ θέλω—ὑμῖν
γράφειν, γράψαι σοι—διὰ χάρτου καὶ μέλανος, διὰ μέλανος καὶ καλάμου—γενέσθαι πρὸς ὑ., εὐθ. σε ἰδεῖν—λαλῆσαι,
λαλήσομεν. If the second Epistle was
addressed to a Church it would not
be difficult to shew that there is a
fitness in the subtle differences in
tone.

15. Εἰρήνη σοι] *Peace be to thee:*
1 Pet. v. 14. As a formula of greeting:
Luke x. 5; xxiv. 36; John xx. 19, 21,
26. And so (in combination with
other words) in epistolary salutations:
2 John 3 note.

οἱ φίλοι] *our friends.* The word
does not occur again in the Epistles in
this connexion. Comp. Acts xxvii. 3.
It gives a faint glimpse of personal
relationships. Comp. John xv. 13 ff.

κατ᾽ ὄνομα] *per nomen* V. Comp.
John x. 3 (xx. 16). Polyc. *Phil.* 13
ἀσπάζομαι...πάντας κατ᾽ ὄνομα.

Additional Note on v. 7. The Divine Name.

The idea of the 'Name' (שֵׁם, ὄνομα) has a far deeper significance in The Biblical language than in our own. As applied to God it expresses that Divine which has been made known of Him; or, more exactly to distinguish the Name in two factors in the revelation, that which he has made known of Himself, the O. T. and which man can apprehend as addressed to him. Thus the Name of God does not represent His Essence as He is in Himself but the manifestation of Himself which He has been pleased to give: that view of His Being and Character by which it is His will to be known, and under which He authorises man to address Him (comp. Gen. xvi. 13, xxxii. 29; Ex. vi. 3). And as applied to men the new name symbolises a new state, a new work and new powers for its fulfilment (Apoc. ii. 17, iii. 12, xxii. 4).

Under this aspect the name of God is used in two ways. It may express some particular revelation, expressed by one definite title (El-Shaddai, Jehovah, Father), or the whole sum of these manifold revelations taken together as one supreme revelation (ὁ θεός, God).

Hence it comes to pass that the 'Name' often stands for God Himself so far as it brings Him before man: Ex. xxiii. 21 (my Name is in Him, i.e. the Angel of the Covenant); I K. viii. 29 (the place of which Thou hast said: My Name shall be there); Is. xxx. 27 (Behold the Name of the Lord cometh from far).

'To blaspheme the Name' was the same as 'blaspheming the Name of the Lord' (Lev. xxiv. 11, 16), that is blaspheming God as He had revealed Himself through Moses to His people (comp. Ex. vi. 3). And in the Acts (iii. 13, 16) it is said that the Name of 'Jesus, the Servant of the God of Abraham and Isaac and Jacob' gave strength to the lame man (comp. Acts iv. 30, 12).

It follows as a natural consequence that the Divine Names in the Bible give in a broad outline the course of revelation.

There is first the general name El, Elohim, which expresses man's feeling after God, apart from any special revelation.

Then follows the patriarchal title El-Shaddai, which indicates the exercise of the sovereign might of God for the fulfilment of His counsel.

Then the covenant name Jehovah, which is developed in the titles 'the Holy One,' 'the Lord of Hosts.'

Then follows a silence, when the Divine Name is unspoken.

At last the revelation of the Father is given: ὁ πατήρ μου καὶ πατὴρ ὑμῶν καὶ θεός μου καὶ θεὸς ὑμῶν' (John xx. 17).

Two names present the two main views of God in the O. T., Elohim and Jehovah. The former, the generic name, gathers up what St Paul speaks of as τὸ γνωστὸν τοῦ θεοῦ...ἡ ἀΐδιος αὐτοῦ δύναμις καὶ θειότης (Rom. i. 19 f.), all that man is made to recognise little by little from the study of his own constitution and the world without. The latter, the proper name, gathers up all that God made known of Himself in His dealings with His people during the discipline of the first Covenant. Speaking generally

Elohim describes the God of Nature, *Jehovah* the God of revelation. The former includes the ideas of the creation, preservation, and general fixed government of finite things : the latter, the idea of living, progressive intercourse with men, of whom Israel were for the time the representatives. The great confession of the chosen people was to declare that the God of revelation is the God for Whom man's soul craves, One in His infinite perfections: Deut. vi. 4 ' *Jehovah* our *Elohim* (or is our *Elohim*), *Jehovah* is One' (comp. 1 John v. 20). For the use of ' the Name' absolutely see 2 Sam. vi. 2 (R. V.).

The Divine Name in the N. T.

Not to dwell in detail here upon the Divine Names in the O. T. it must be noticed that the idea of 'the Name' is no less prominent in the N. T. Thus the Lord characterises His own Mission as a ' Coming in the Name of His Father' (John v. 43); and the Mission of the Holy Spirit as a Mission in His Name (John xiv. 26 ὃ πέμψει ὁ πατὴρ ἐν τῷ ὀνόματί μου). He glorified His Father and manifested His Father's Name to men (John xvii. 4, 6) ; and it is the work of the Holy Spirit to glorify Him, and to take of His and declare it to His disciples (John xvi. 14). In the one case, if we may so speak, the Name of the Father was completely shewn : God was made known perfectly in this relation by the fact of the Incarnation. In the other case the Church is learning little by little the Name of the Son.

The most complete expression of the Divine Name is that given in Matt. xxviii. 19 τὸ ὄνομα τοῦ πατρὸς καὶ τοῦ υἱοῦ καὶ τοῦ ἁγίου πνεύματος, but the essence of this Name so written at length is the simple Name ' Jesus Christ' or 'the Lord Jesus,' or even ' Jesus' alone, when the context determines the office attached to it : ὄν. Ἰ. Χρ. (Acts ii. 38, iii. 6, iv. 10, viii. 12, x. 48, xvi. 18; ὄν. τοῦ κυρίου Ἰ. Acts viii. 16 (ix. 14) (xv. 26), xix. 5, 13, 17, xxi. 13; ὄν. Ἰ. Acts iv. 18 (30), v. 40, ix. 27, xxvi. 9).

In the Epistles the Name of revelation, the Lord's Name, occurs in several forms: 'the Name of Christ': 1 Pet. iv. 14(16); 'the Name of the Lord': James v. 14 (? contrast *v.* 10); 'the Name of our Lord Jesus': 2 Thess. i. 12; 'the Name of our Lord Jesus Christ': 1 Cor. i. 2, 10; (v. 4, vi. 11;) Rom. i. 5; Eph. v. 20; (Col. iii. 17;) 'the Name of Jesus': Phil. ii. 10. Compare Additional Note on 1 John iii. 23.

The phrase 'the Name of God' is found in the Epistles only in 1 Tim. vi. 1, besides quotations from the LXX. (Hebr. vi. 10, xiii. 15), and the context explains its use. In the Apocalypse it occurs xvi. 9 (comp. iii. 12).

The characteristic Name of God in the N. T. is 'the Father' (Matt. vi. 9; John xii. 28; comp. Additional Note on i. 2).

From what has been said the full force of the phrases 'to believe in the name' (πιστεύειν εἰς τὸ ὄν. 1 John v. 13 note), 'to ask in the name' (John xiv. 13 note), 'to be gathered in (into εἰς) the name' (Matt. xviii. 20), 'to have life in the name' (John xx. 31) becomes evident. In every case the Name brings before the mind that aspect of the Divine Person which is realised by faith in each action of the spiritual life.

In close connexion with the idea of the Divine Name is that of the Divine Glory (Introd. to Gosp. of St John pp. xlvii. ff.). The Name expresses the revelation as it is apprehended and used by man. Man is called by the Name and employs it. The Glory expresses rather the manifestation of the

Divine as Divine, as a partial disclosure of the Divine Majesty not directly intelligible by man (comp. Ex. xxxiii. 18 ff.). In this relation it is of interest to notice that while St John's Gospel is, in one aspect, a record of the unfolding of the Divine Glory in Christ, there is no mention of Glory in his Epistles. This is the more remarkable since the idea of Glory is found in the Apocalypse and in all the other Epistles except that to Philemon.